Letters of H. P. Lovecraft

VOLUME XIII

LETTERS TO WILFRED B. TALMAN AND HELEN V. AND GENEVIEVE SULLY

Wilfred Blanch Talman

H. P. Lovecraft

LETTERS TO WILFRED B. TALMAN AND HELEN V. AND GENEVIEVE SULLY

EDITED BY DAVID E. SCHULTZ AND S. T. JOSHI

Hippocampus Press

New York

Published by Hippocampus Press
P.O. Box 641, New York, NY 10156.
http://www.hippocampuspress.com

Cover design and Hippocampus Press logo by Anastasia Damianakos.
Cover production by Barbara Briggs Silbert.

First Edition
1 3 5 7 9 8 6 4 2

ISBN 978-1-61498-256-2

Contents

Introduction

The informal Kalem Club of New York City consisted of a small group of writers, of varying degrees of accomplishment and profession. They were men (and *only* men) whose last names started with the letters K, L, or M— more a matter of coincidence than a membership requirement—who gathered, roughly weekly, for fellowship and also to hold forth on all manner of literary subjects, rarely practical topics (and never women or sex). They were broad-minded enough to welcome kindred spirits, even if they did not align with the supposed unifying principle of the group, and accepted the likes of Vrest Orton and Donald and Howard Wandrei into the group. And also Wilfred Blanch Talman. Curiously, Talman may have become the most successful writer of the bunch, at least while living. According to Talman, Frank Belknap Long's mother declared him "the most normal of the Kalems,"[1] including her son. Elsewhere he reported her saying he "was the most practical"[2] of the group, and he may well have been that, too, for most of the Kalems were misfits of one kind or another. Talman described them as square pegs in round holes. Mrs. Long's evaluation of Talman is quite telling. Considering that the Kalems often convened at the spacious home of Frank Belknap Long's parents, she had plenty of opportunity to encounter the various members, each exhibiting his personal quirks and idiosyncrasies.

Talman was born in 1904 and raised in Spring Valley, New York. His ancestor, Douwe Harmansen Talma (1624–bef. 1687), a Dutch fur trader, in 1675 became the first white settler in what is now Nyack in Rockland County. Talman graduated from Spring Valley High School, attended Brown University (1924–26) as a special student, and obtained a Bachelor of Literature in Journalism from Columbia University's Pulitzer School of Journalism in 1928. He began writing as a junior in high school, his stories appearing in *Leslie's Weekly* and his first articles on local history in the *Nyack Evening Journal.* As with most aspiring writers, his early writings included verse. In the early 1920s, Talman belonged to both the National and the United Amateur Press Association. His credential, the poem "Home-coming," appeared in *New Member* in May 1922. H. P. Lovecraft also was an active amateur journalist at the time. When Lovecraft first heard from Talman, Lovecraft, oddly enough, was living in Brooklyn, whereas Talman had spent most of his college tenure in Lovecraft's hometown of Providence. For a time Talman lived at 256 Benefit Street, a third of a mile from 135 Benefit Street, the location of the "Shunned

---

1. "The Normal Lovecraft," *Ave* 109.
2. "Lovecraft Revisited" (1960). See Appendix.

House" of Lovecraft's story, written while Lovecraft lived in Brooklyn and Talman attended Brown University. Had Lovecraft not left to live in New York with his wife, he might well have met Talman face-to-face in Providence.

Lovecraft wrote home to his aunt: "I lately received a thin brochure of very fair verse from an amateur in Spring Valley, N.Y.—Wilfred B. Talman— & after acknowledging it learned that the poet is a Brown University student whose first lines appeared in the college paper, *The Brown Jug!* Naturally, my latest epistle to him has been full of the local colour of College Hill!"[3] That "brochure" was Talman's first book, a slim collection of poetry titled *Cloisonné and Other Verses.*

The reason Talman had first written Lovecraft was to see if Lovecraft could recommend to him where he might gain part-time employment— preferably writing, although he also had some skills in lettering and illustration. "He fancies that I must, from long residence, know something about Providence industries; but as an herrmit I had little chance to acquire data in such fields. All I can do is to express my profound regrets."[4] Lovecraft soon learned that Talman was descended from ancient Dutch families of his native area and that he had done considerable genealogical work, just as Lovecraft had. Talman's knowledge of genealogy and heraldry impressed Lovecraft, and in later years Talman would help Lovecraft with his own genealogical research at the Providence Public Library.

Lovecraft met Talman when the latter visited him in Brooklyn on 27 August 1925 for a small Kalem meeting, with only Long and Everett McNeil in attendance. Talman returned to Brown that fall, but he was not so immersed in studies that he could not find time to send Lovecraft his stories and artwork. Lovecraft shared Talman's stories with his aunts. He described Talman's crayon sketches of the house at Angell and Benefit Streets as amateurish, although one was displayed in an exhibit at the Rhode Island School of Design. While in New York, Lovecraft mentioned several times to his aunts that Talman would call on them. It does not appear that Talman ever paid such a visit, though he did meet them at a later time.

Talman was a lifelong writer and editor. His pursuit of a publishing career in business reflects the practicality that Mrs. Long saw, whereas his friend Howard pursued (or rather dabbled in) the impractical career of writing weird fiction with little economic reward. Following graduation, his professional career began in 1928 as a reporter for the *Brooklyn Standard Union* and then the *New York Times,* which he left in 1930 to become an editor of Texaco Corporation's publications until his early retirement in 1959. He also did much of the research and writing on the history of the company, published on the its

---

3. HPL to Lillian D. Clark, [20 July 1925]; *LFF* 315.
4. HPL to Lillian D. Clark, 7 August 1925; *LFF* 337.

fifty-year anniversary.[5]

Talman married Charlotte A. Hinrichs (1902–2000) in 1929 and remained with her for the rest of his life. Lovecraft remarked that she had a cat phobia, and so her husband, who liked cats, could not keep any. They had a daughter (for whom fellow Kalem Rheinhart Kleiner wrote a poem in honor of her birth) and two sons. Although Talman was employed in New York City, on the eighteenth floor of the Chrysler Building, he despised the city and for a time commuted from Spring Valley to New York every day, a two-hour trip. He made a home for himself, wife, and infant son in a disused stable on his father's estate, where he and all his direct paternal forbears since the seventeenth century were born.

That arrangement did not last long. In June 1930, Lovecraft informed a correspondent that Talman and his family were living on the top floor of 277 Henry Street in Brooklyn, where Talman had once formerly boarded, about two blocks from 169 Clinton where Lovecraft had lived during his Brooklyn years. (Arthur Leeds, another Kalem, lived at 228 Henry Street around January 1936.) In October 1936, Lovecraft was notifying correspondents that Talman resided at 135 East 42nd Street in New York City, where he still lived when Lovecraft died in 1937.

Lovecraft's letters indicate that Talman wrote more than the four stories he published in *Weird Tales,* but the unpublished stories apparently are lost. In assessing his fiction-writing ability, Lovecraft observed: "As a weird writer Talman will never be in a class with Smith and Howard and Wandrei and Long and Price. He is too much of an intellectual as opposed to a dreamer to shine in bizarre and fantastic conceptions. Yet his ideas are often tremendously clever, and occasionally tales of his are really splendid."[6] This is reflected in Lovecraft's mock transcription of a discussion among Kalems who had been inspecting the work of Clark Ashton Smith: "*Wilfred B. Talman:* I don't see anything weird in these drawings, Belknap. Gosh! who cares about the coasts of Saturn?"[7] Of the surviving stories, Lovecraft revised somewhat "Two Black Bottles" (1926). A lengthy synopsis (1930) with suggestions for revision of Talman's story "The Pool" survives, but it appears that Talman never acted on Lovecraft's suggestions.

Talman was unable to persuade Lovecraft to write an article for the *Texaco Star,* but he did elicit pieces from Lovecraft's writer friends Paul J. Campbell and Robert E. Howard, and he himself wrote an article about Providence for the magazine. He did obtain from Lovecraft a brief article for the journal

5. The book *The Texaco Story: The 1st 50 Years: 1902–1952* by James Marquis was based on WBT's manuscript at the Dolph Briscoe Center of the University of Texas at Austin.
6. HPL to Duane W. Rimel, 29 March 1934, *Letters to F. Lee Baldwin . . .* 158.
7. HPL to Donald Wandrei, 19 December 1927, *Letters with Donald and Howard Wandrei . . .* 189.

of the Holland Society of New York, *De Halve Maen*.[8] Talman was one of the Society's members who established *De Halve Maen* as a Society publication. He became editor of the journal beginning with the issue for 1 January 1933 and served in that capacity for eight years. When Lovecraft's "Some Dutch Footprints in New England" appeared in October, Talman gave the following as Lovecraft's credentials: "Mr. Lovecraft is descended from some of New England's oldest families, and is not only an amateur student of the history of Providence and Rhode Island, but [also] a writer of fiction." Talman admits that he deliberately engaged Lovecraft in nit-picking over the details of this essay as a payback for what he felt were Lovecraft's unwarranted revisions in "Two Black Bottles." Talman contributed historical and genealogical articles to *De Halve Maen* during his membership in the Society. In 1936 he served as secretary of a special Society committee headed by Franklin D. Roosevelt, a trustee at the time, that published *Pre-Revolutionary Dutch Homes and Families in Northern New Jersey and Southern New York*.

Several of Talman's photographs of Lovecraft are well known, particularly one in which Lovecraft appeared

> somber and hollow-eyed, full face to the camera with a brick wall in the background. Lovecraft in these pictures wore an old suit of mine he had unabashedly accepted as a gift. In this suit, with a 10-cent necktie he bought to go with it, he was caught in a rainstorm soon afterward and tried with ludicrous success (the idea was new to him!) to press both pants and coat beneath a mattress.[9]

A less flattering image, as described here by Lovecraft, was published after his death: "The young rascal caught me as I was looking upward & saying something which put my mouth in an utterly comic position . . . as if I were going to whistle or expectorate!"[10] Talman also was an accomplished graphic artist. He designed not only Lovecraft's bookplate—a simple yet evocative design of a typical colonial doorway with fanlight, a far less busy affair than what Lovecraft had first conceived—but also one for fellow Kalem James F. Morton.

Talman stated that he received about one hundred fifty letters from Lovecraft. Presumably he refers to actual letters and does not include postcards. Only ninety-five letters (some only as Arkham House transcripts) and eleven postcards are known to exist. Letters from Talman to August Derleth

---

8. I.e., the *Half Moon*, a vlieboot of the Dutch East India Company that sailed into what is now New York Harbor in September 1609. It was captained by Henry Hudson, an Englishman in the service of the Dutch Republic, hoping to find a western passage to China.

9. "The Normal Lovecraft," *Ave* 115.

10. HPL to R. H. Barlow, 15 January 1935, *O Fortunate Floridian* 202. The photograph was first published as "H.P.L. Addressing The Kalem Club" in *The Normal Lovecraft*.

might have shed light on his transmission of letters to Arkham House for transcription, but none survive.

Not only did Lovecraft not address Talman by a coined name such as those he devised for other correspondents, he apparently never referred to Talman by such a name in his letters to others (perhaps because the polysyllabic initial of Talman's first name). He did, however, employ various Dutch epithets in salutations in his letters to Talman, chiefly "Jonkheer" (an honorific denoting the lowest rank of the nobility), although he frequently misspelled it as "Jonckheer" or other variants.

In 1958, Talman published *The Eternal Spring: An Anniversary History of the American Association of Industrial Editors*. The following year he retired from Texaco to work once again in the newspaper, first with the Sherwood Newspapers in Spring Valley, N.Y., later as an associate editor of the weekly *Rockland Independent* in Suffern, N.Y., and as an editor with the *Orangetown Telegram*. He concluded his fifty-year career with the Ridgewood Newspapers in Bergen County, N.J. Specializing in colonial history, he wrote the "Liberty Pole" column for the *Rockland County Leader* and over the years numerous other historical columns, which became the main body of his writing. Many of these articles were adapted into his book, *How Things Began—in Rockland County and Places Nearby*.

In 1936, Talman was contemplating leaving Texaco to become an author's agent. He thought he might gain as clients former associates from the *Times,* and Lovecraft as a key client. The others showed interest, but Lovecraft balked, because he felt he was unable to deliver manuscripts on demand and on schedule. Lovecraft's letters to Talman on the matter express a certain agitation, because at the time Lovecraft was quite ill and not up to such a challenge, though it must be said that such an arrangement was completely antithetical to Lovecraft's writing habits.

When Lovecraft died in March 1937, there was a great outpouring of written sentiment from friends and fans, but Talman himself was silent. He broke that silence in 1960, when he published "Lovecraft Revisited" in *Fresco,* but that was something of a parlor game—no memoir or reminiscence. But in 1973, just ahead of a veritable tsunami of books *about* Lovecraft—Kenneth W. Faig's monograph *Lovecraftian Voyages* (1972; unpublished until recently, though parts appeared over the years), L. Sprague de Camp's *Lovecraft: A Biography* (1975), Willis Conover's unusual collaboration *Lovecraft at Last* (1975), Frank Belknap Long's *Howard Phillips Lovecraft: Dreamer on the Nightside* (1975)—Talman published *The Normal Lovecraft* in an attempt to present Lovecraft as something other than the grotesque caricature of him that was emerging. Talman, after all, knew Lovecraft personally, unlike many writing about him who did not, and he was one of few people who knew Lovecraft still living. The book was a small but heartfelt memoir, but it had very limited distribution and readership.

Helen V.[11] Sully (1904–1997) and her mother, Genevieve Knoll Sully (1880–1970), became late correspondents of Lovecraft following Helen's visit to him in July 1933. Genevieve was a friend of Lovecraft's California correspondent Clark Ashton Smith. Smith and the Sullys (including Genevieve's other daughter, Marion [1911–1994]), all lived in Auburn. According to Lovecraft, the Sullys were the only people in Auburn with whom Smith associated, since he, like Lovecraft, had no like-minded associates in his hometown.

Helen Sully was, unlike virtually all Lovecraft's other correspondents, not a writer. When they first met, she was twenty-nine and Lovecraft described her as "a young gentlewoman, a teacher of music & drawing." Her reason for traveling east was to inspect the historic and antiquarian sights of New England and Quebec. Smith, not Sully, informed Lovecraft of her intentions. Lovecraft conveyed instructions to her not directly, but through Smith:

> I think a day will enable Miss Sully to see most of the historic high spots of urban Providence, & I shall be glad to exhibit them when she arrives. Tell her to let me know exact place & date of arrival, & I will be on hand—trusting to ingenuity in establishing identification. When she is in New York she ought without fail to look up the *Longs*—*230 West 97th St.* They are in a better position to entertain her than any other "gang" family.[12]

Smith kept Lovecraft apprised of Sully's movements.

> I trust Miss Sully's trip is proving pleasant; & shall, unless contrarily instructed, be on the lookout July 19 at 6 a.m. at the Colonial Line pier . . . . which lies right in the lee of the ancient hill's southerly extremity, on a waterfront having considerable picturesqueness. The yellow poppy ought to facilitate identification—though it's too bad you couldn't have furnished some of your typical nameless vegetation from Saturn & Antares! A second day in Prov. would enable many picturesque suburbs, (& perhaps ancient Newport) as well as the city proper to be covered; thus affording an extremely [good] picture of R.I. I hope that young Melmoth & Sonny Belknap [take] part in displaying seething Manhattan to the visitor—[& if she is] not already provided with Bostonian guidance, I think that [W. Paul] Cook would be delighted to shew off the Athens of America [i.e., Boston]. I [envy] Miss Sully her coming sight of Quebec—to which I fear I can't get this year [. . .][13]

Sully duly arrived, and during her brief stay Lovecraft squired her around Providence and also took her to Newport, where the two composed a joint postcard to Smith on July 20 (nonextant). Sully was no writer, and in general

---

11. The V. apparently does not stand for anything.
12. HPL to Clark Ashton Smith, 29 June 1933; *DS* 423.
13. Clark Ashton Smith to HPL, 12 July 1933; *DS* 425–26.

is something of an unknown figure in Lovecraft circles. She is, however, well remembered for her very brief reminiscence of the night Lovecraft took her to the churchyard of St. John's Episcopal Church—a favorite pastime with which Lovecraft regaled any visitors to Providence—where he told her

> strange, weird stories in a sepulchral tone [. . .] something about his manner, the darkness, and a sort of eerie light that seemed to hover over the gravestone got me so wrought up that I began to run out of the cemetery with him close at my heels, with the one thought that I must get up to the street before he, or whatever it was, grabbed me. I reached street lamp, trembling, panting, and almost in tears, and he had the strangest look on his face, almost of triumph.[14]

Sully also observed that, although Lovecraft was "very poor at the time," he paid all her expenses in Providence: trips, meals, souveniers, and also her stay at the boarding house just behind 66 College, where Lovecraft and his aunt took meals. Sully wrote favorably to Smith about her meeting with Lovecraft—that is, except for the churchyard episode and a meal taken at Jake's, Lovecraft favorite eatery in Providence (primarily because of it inexpensiveness, not its cuisine).

In the course of her trip, Sully met, on her own, many of Lovecraft's friends and associates. As Lovecraft told August Derleth:

> She looked up Wandrei & Belknap in N.Y., & the Longs brought her here in their car when bound for Onset last Wednesday [i.e., 19 July]. After seeing Prov. & Newport she has gone on to Gloucester & Quebec. On the return trip she will pass through Chicago & look up Wright—& if you can get down there (about Aug. 8 or 9—I'll let you know when she decides & notifies me), she would like very much to meet you.[15]

Those who met Sully in the course of her journey all wrote glowing accounts of their meetings with her. Lovecraft observed: "She seems to have created a devastating havock amongst Manhattan's susceptible gallants—I am trying to keep this young rascal Belknap from fighting a duel with Wandrei!"[16] She was unable to meet Derleth in Sauk City or thereabouts, but she did meet Farnsworth Wright in Chicago, where she also attended the 1933 World's Fair. Lovecraft himself was pleased to meet her, for she gave him personal accounts about Clark Ashton Smith, her fellow denizen of Auburn, though he was sorry to learn at firsthand of Smith's struggles, which he of course did not mention in his letters to Lovecraft.

Despite the offputting churchyard incident, Sully wrote Lovecraft when she arrived back home and a surprisingly robust correspondence between the

---

14. "Memories of H.P.L." (1969), *Ave* 365–66.
15. HPL to August Derleth, 23 July 1933; *Essential Solitude* 595.
16. HPL to Clark Ashton Smith, 25 July 1933; *DS* 428.

two ensued. The two must have made very favorable impressions on each other. It does not appear that she stayed in touch with any of the other individuals she encountered on her trip, and the meeting between her and Donald Wandrei in Auburn was more of a visit to see Clark Ashton Smith than romantically motivated. Lovecraft, ever the gentleman, addressed his correspondent as "Miss Sully," just as he always addressed C. L. Moore as "Miss Moore," Elizabeth Toldridge as "Miss Toldridge," Jonquil Leiber as "Mrs. Leiber," and Anne Tillery Renshaw as "Mrs. Renshaw" (or finally "A T R" in an echo of the playful nature of Renshaw's letters to him). Sully finally objected to such stiff formality between friends, accusing him of being a "surname-addict," and so he finally relented and in subsequent letters addressed her as "Helen." (It is unknown how Sully addressed Lovecraft, for none of her letters to him survive, and he doesn't mention the matter to anyone, but we can be assured it was not as "Mr. Lovecraft.") That, however, was the extent of Lovecraft's letting his hair down with her. He never addressed her by her initials or by the phonetic or other coined names that he used with other correspondents, although in letters to others he referred to her as H V S, E'ch-Vi-Es, Hlensu-Li, Soo-Lhi, and the Priestess of Hyperborea or Tsathoggua.

Sully married Nelson Best in 19__. At age fifty-two she married again, this time to George M. Trimble, age fifty-seven. As in the case of Talman, there is no surviving correspondence of Helen Sully with Arkham House regarding the transcription of her letters from Lovecraft.

Little is known about Genevieve Knoll Sully (1880–1970), whose grave marker probably provides the only information about her that we are likely to know: besides dates, she is characterized as a "Lover of Beauty." She lived in Auburn with her daughters Helen and Marion, and they first met Clark Ashton Smith in the fall of 1919. Smith referred to her as his "girlfriend," but the extent of their romance is not known. Genevieve is best remembered for threatening to break up with Smith if he did not find a means of income, and this challenge sparked his brief career as a fiction writer. Even less is known about her correspondence with Lovecraft. Only four of his letters to her survive for the period September 1934–February 1937. Lovecraft reported to Clark Ashton Smith, "I have heard several times from Mrs. Sully, who is—most emphatically—as brilliant & appreciative a person as one could well encounter."[17] Besides hearing all about Lovecraft from her daughter Helen, Genevieve undoubtedly had heard much about Lovecraft from Smith, who may have lent her Lovecraft's letters or read them to her. On one occasion, Smith read "'[The] Picture in the House' aloud one evening by the light of our campfire in the mountains; and it was received with great enthusiasm by [. . .] Mrs. Sully and her daughters."[18] Lovecraft

---

17. HPL to Clark Ashton Smith, 30 January 1935; *DS* 592.
18. Clark Ashton Smith to HPL, 22 August 1930; *DS* 227.

maintained great formality with Genevieve—addressing her always as "Mrs. Sully" and signing his letters "H. P. Lovecraft."

A Note on the Text
Virtually all the letters to Wilfred B. Talman and Helen V. Sully derive from original manuscripts held at the John Hay Library of Brown University. Talman had sold some items (pertaining mostly to Lovecraft's essay published in *De Halve Maen*) before his letters arrived at the library. None of Lovecraft's postcards were deposited at the library. A few letters derive only from the Arkham House transcripts. It is unknown if the entirety of Lovecraft's letters to Helen Sully are at the library, but it is likely. The letters to Genevieve Sully are held privately.

Acknowledgments
The editors would like to thank the following for their assistance in preparation of this volume: Bobby Derie, Kenneth W. Faig, Jr., Patrice Louinet, Donovan K. Loucks, Jordan Douglas Smith, and John H. Stanley and Christopher Geissler of the John Hay Library, Brown University, Providence, RI.

Abbreviations

AT	*The Ancient Track* (2nd ed. 2013)
Ave	Joshi & Schultz, *Ave atque Vale* (2018)
CE	*Collected Essays* (2004–06; 5 vols.)
CF	*Collected Fiction* (2015–17; 4 vols.)
DS	*Dawnward Spire, Lonely Hill* (2017)
LFF	*Letters to Family and Family Friends* (2019)
LL	Joshi, *Lovecraft's Library* (2017 edition)
LR	Cannon, *Lovecraft Remembered* (1998)
SHL	*The Annotated Supernatural Horror in Literature* (2nd ed. 2012)
SL	*Selected Letters* (1965–76; 5 vols.)
WW	Joshi, *A Weird Writer in Our Midst* (2010)

FBL	Frank Belknap Long, Jr.
HPL	H. P. Lovecraft
HVS	Helen V. Sully
MWM	Maurice W. Moe
WBT	Wilfred Blanch Talman

AHT	Arkham House Transcripts
ALS	autograph letter, signed
ANS	autograph note, signed
JHL	John Hay Library, Brown University
TLS	typed letter, signed

Wilfred Blanch Talman

Letters to Wilfred B. Talman

[1]   [AHT]

169 Clinton Street
Brooklyn, N.Y.
September 7, 1925

My dear Talman:—

I digested the contents of your recent envelope with a great deal of interest; and have been reflecting as maturely as possible on the short story,[1] in order that any comment may be not altogether unintelligent.

The tale seems to me exceedingly well told—simply, with uninterrupted action and unflagging interest and with a true sense of atmosphere, geographical fitness, and dramatic setting and situation. The general cast of the language shows command and assurance, and whatever trite or hazy spots there are (as marked once or twice in pencil on the MS.) can very easily be ironed out. Of course, language is a delicate instrument on which one may play to perfection only after years of practice; but your style shows that you are headed exactly right, and advanced very substantially toward the ultimate goal. Several passages struck me as particularly notable in point of linguistic felicity—a quality which your poetical work no doubt helps you to achieve. You may have seen the proverb that nothing helps one to write good prose so much as the writing of verse.

Now as to plot—the only trouble is that it is not altogether novel. The broad theme of cosmic punishment for evil-doing is as old as literature, and even this particular type of fatality is fairly familiar to the omnivorous fiction-reader. Of course, when we analyse, we find that the exact events are more or less original; but the casual and unanalytical reader is apt to pass over details and merely recognise the sketchy outlines of things he has met before—the drunken villain lured to his proper end by cupidity, and the scheming murderer overcome and annihilated by the final struggles of his victim. It is this element of the fictionally usual which might cause an editor to think twice before accepting it. I would not call the ending *anticlimactic* so much as *predictable*—and believe you are an acute critic when you suggest the introduction of extra plot to lead up to a more unique and unexpected denouement. This matter of denouement is, beyond doubt, the single definite thing which merits attention; and I really think that with a little judicious emendation you might achieve something readily salable to such a magazine as *Adventure*. I wish you had met our member Leeds, who is a very thorough technician, and experienced in the art of practical suggestion.

Looking over the pencil-marks I have made on your MS., I see that the pleasant subject of mortality and decomposition puzzled me a bit. Firstly—it is my impression that among the South Sea isles a body has to be buried within a very few hours of death, thus preventing the next-day burial mentioned in the story. Secondly—and from an apparently opposite point of view—is it possible, even in view of this rapid rate of tropical dissolution, for a corpse to become a heap of 'whitening bones' *only two or three days* after death? Possibly the buzzards and other carrion feeders of the region would effect this—and if so please criticise my criticism to the fullest extent. But anyhow, think it over. Oh, yes—one thing more. Don't you think the *title* is the least bit melodramatic? I can't for the life of me suggest a better one, and yet the impression persists that the existing caption is just a trifle over-theatrical. Not but what I've done much worse myself a dozen times! I'll return the tale for whatever further ministrations you may choose to give it, meanwhile congratulating you on the ingenuity, sureness of touch, and rapidly maturing style which it displays.

"Izrim" is a delightfully fashioned allegory, and I should certainly send it to Bacon[2] for the U.A. if I were you. You can use your own judgment about condensing—it really doesn't need it, and would probably not be too long for publication. The style is very appropriate and graceful, the only really weak spot being, curiously enough, the opening sentence—for which I have added a possible alternative version. The original text was here a little too prosy for the poetic style of the whole. One thing to guard against is the overworking of the same word in a simple passage, unless done purposely, at certain points for rhetorical effect. Thus where you had 'lived . . . . lived . . . lived' I have taken the liberty to substitute 'lived . . . . dwelt . . . . bode'. Yes, I like "Izrim" very much, and shall eagerly welcome it in print.[3]

As to that list of appreciative members—enclosed is a National list, with the moderately intelligent characters checked off. Since I haven't an extra United list to mark up, I'll herewith append a catalogue of active brains in that association; the two forming a basis for the mailing of literary matter.

> *California*
> Clark Ashton Smith, Box 388, Auburn
>
> *Colorado*
> Rev. Eugene B. Kuntz, Minturn
>
> *District of Columbia*
> Anne T. Renshaw, 1603 Connecticut Ave., N.W., Washington
> Edward L. Sechrist, 423 Dorset Ave., Chevy Chase, Washington
>
> *Massachusetts*
> Edgar J. Davis, % Herman F. Davis, 16 Main St., Merrimac, Mass.
>
> *New Hampshire*
> Mrs. Myrta L. Davies, Westville

New York
Jonathan E. Hoag, 17 Prospect St., Greenwich

Pennsylvania
Washington Van Dusen, N.W. Cor. Broad and Arch Sts., Philadelphia

Canada
John Ravenor Bullen, Warren Ave., Petrolea, Ontario.

England
Ernest Lionel McKeag, "Glautefi", Kew Gardens, Surrey.[4]

As other names suggest themselves I'll jot them down for you, and will let you know of any changed addresses. Why not send that notice to Bacon for publication as soon as possible—about requests for "Cloisonné"?[5] As to the critique—depend upon it, amateurdom will be only too glad to supply that article, and you may expect in the course of the ensuing weeks a suitable review based on "Cloisonné". I shall try to get Long to write it, since he is undoubtedly our best and most discerning critic of poetry.

Good luck with the novel you are planning! I have thought of such things at times, and may yet attempt one. What I would like to do is something extremely fantastic—the picaresque progress of a wandering spirit through the marvellous and undiscovered voids and worlds of the remotest universe.[6] In more local vein is another pet theme of mine—the witchcraft of Salem, viewed in retrospect, and with shivery suggestions of an aftermath.[7]

[. . .]
Most cordially and sincerely yours—
H P L

Notes

1. Unidentified.
2. Victor E. Bacon (1905–1997), amateur journalist and editor of *Bacon's Essays*, which published work by HPL and Clark Ashton Smith; Official Editor of the UAPA (1925–26).
3. HPL described the story to his aunt Lillian as "mediocre, but I trust I've found a tactful way to tell him so whilst suggesting improvements" (*LFF* 384).
4. Eugene B. Kuntz (1865–1944); Anne Tillery Renshaw (1890–1947?); Edward L. Sechrist (1873–1953); Edgar J. Davis (1908–1949); Myrta Alice (Little) Davies (1888–1967); Washington Van Dusen (1857–32); Jonathan E. Hoag (1831–1927); Ernest Lionel McKeag (1896–1974). For Bullen, see the Glossary.
5. A book of poetry by WBT. See Appendix.
6. HPL wrote such a novel in late 1926 when he wrote *The Dream-Quest of Unknown Kadath*. See also WBT 15.
7. HPL did not write a novel of witchcraft per se, but in 1927 he wrote *The Case of Charles Dexter Ward*, which was originally planned to be set in Salem and seems to have fulfilled his desire to write about strange doings centuries past.

[2] [ALS, JHL]

[GEORGE KIRK
Dealer in Rare Books and Modern First Editions
1894 Charles Road / Cleveland, O.]
169 Clinton St.,
Brooklyn, N.Y.,
Jany. 20, 1926

My dear Talman:—

I wish I were able to tell you more, in a really authoritative way, about that Dutch clock face; but it has been my ill fortune never to live with an antique timepiece of the sort. The one in my family which I've heard most about, descended to a branch now settled in Illinois—damn the luck! That had the traditional moon disk & all accessories, & I'd give nearly anything I possess if I could get hold of it. You see, to get the real hang of such a device, one needs to know something of the clockmaking tradition as well as of astronomy—that is, unless one has a supremely acute & deductive mind, which I can scarcely boast. However—let's see what unaided astronomy *can* do!

For one thing, we can dispose of the *outer revolving disc* at once. It's division into 29½ parts shews clearly that what it represents is the *moon's age*—that is, the number of days after the moment of lunar conjunction, (the phase called "new moon" in the almanacks) when the moon is invisible (except in the rare case of a solar eclipse) & on a line between the earth & the sun. This is clear, because the mean synodic revolution of the moon—the time occupied between any two successive occurrences of the same phase—is approximately 29½ days. The *sidereal* revolution of the moon—i.e., the actual time it takes to revolve around the earth—is only 27⅓ days; but the annual motion of the earth itself around the sun causes the time to be spun out to 29½ days before the same relative position of sun, earth, & moon (on which the phases depend) can be repeated. This, then, is plain—that the outer revolving disc, as measured by the stationary pointer at the top, refers to the moon's age. When the pointer is at 2, the moon is a slender "shoestring" crescent glimpsed just above the western horizon at sunset. When it is at 7 or 8, we have the first quarter, or half moon seen in the evening. Then at 14 or 15 we have full moon. 21 or 22 means last quarter—half moon in the morning. 26 or 27, verging toward 28, means the thin, pale, wan old moon—the tenuous silver thread seen just above the eastern horizon before sunrise; after which the moon disappears into the "new moon" phase, to reappear in the evening when the pointer is at 2 again.

But the matter of inner discs—although I imagine that it may mean the moon's place in the zodiac*—gives me pause so far as the actual working is concerned. I'm thinking this out as I write—just as though we were in oral conversation—so don't mind if I say something stupid or incorrect & then re-

---

*Later—I've changed my mind—but will let this stand.

vise it afterward—eating my own words with proper humility. As you probably know, the apparent revolution of the moon around the earth in a 29½ day period causes it to be seen against a different background of stars every night; since the stars themselves make their apparent revolution around the earth only once in a year, as the earth's real motion takes it around the sun. [Don't get *any* of this mixed up with the *diurnal* motion of the sky—rising & setting—caused by the earth's axial rotation. You realise that what we mean by an *apparent revolution* has reference only to the changing position of a celestial object *as viewed at the same hour & minute on successive days, weeks, & months.*] Now the particular belt of stars against which the moon, & planets* seem to move, (they all move within a zone 16° wide—8° on each side of the ecliptic, or plane of the earth's orbit, since their own orbits are nearly in the same plane) is called the *zodiac*, & divided into 12 equal spaces or "signs" of 30° each—each representing the amount of space apparently traversed by the sun in a month's time. Beginning with the place of the sun at the opening of spring, (the "vernal equinox"—March 21st—which formed the start of the ancient year) these "signs" are identified with the constellations, or apparent groupings of stars, which marked their places in the ancient Babylonian & Egyptian times when the system was devised. [Now, however, the precessional movement of the earth's axis in space has caused the "signs" to move backward out of their respective constellations, so that the vernal sign Aries (No. 1) now occupies the constellation Pisces (No. 12), & so on] You have, of course, heard all these signs listed many a time & oft—& know how closely they are associated with the months in which the sun enters them. Likewise you probably know the respective parts of the human body which each one is supposed to govern—a superstitious astrological association extending back to prehistoric times & first crystallised in its present form by the famous astronomical poet Marcus Manilius—a Latin Augustan whose "Astronomicon"[1] is an invaluable source-book for students of the history of science.

1. ARIES (Ram) = March—head
2. TAURUS (Bull) = April—neck
3. GEMINI (Twins—Castor & Pollus) = May—arms
4. CANCER (Crab) = June—breast
5. LEO (Lion) = July—heart
6. VIRGO (Reaping Virgin) = August—belly
7. LIBRA (Scales) September—reins[2]
8. SCORPIO (Scorpion) = October—secrets
9. SAGITTARIUS (Centaur archer) = November—thighs
10. CAPRICORNUS (goat) = December—knees
11. AQUARIUS (water man) = January—legs
12. PISCES (fishes) = February—feet.

Incidentally—if I may put a "footnote" topic in the text—the twelve Zodiacal constellations themselves were probably named from the attributes of the

---

*and of course, the sun also shares this motion on account of the earth's rotation—seeming to circle the stars once in a year.

months (as experienced in the Nile & Tigris-Euphrates valleys) in which the sun occupies them. Thus Aries—the Ram—signifies March, when the shepherds lead their flocks out to the hills. The Bull comes at the cattle-breeding season*. The Twins—two young men—represent the planters of the summer crops. The Crab—which crawls backward—represents the summer solstice, when the sun, having moved to its northernmost point, begins to recede southward. The Lion symbolises July's raging heat—as well as the literal lions which come down to the Nile from the Nubian desert. The sickle-bearing Virgin represents the late summer reaper. The Scales signify the equal days and nights of the autumnal equinox. Scorpio illustrates the diseases of the fruit-eating season, & Sagittarius is the archer who shoots the leaves from the trees. Capricornus, the climbing goat, represents the beginning of the sun's *ascent* at the winter solstice. The last two signs apply only to the warm regions where they originated—Aquarius, the *water-bearer* of the January *rainy* season, & Pisces, the fishes of the brooks where melting ice permits February fishing. But hell—let's get back to the moon! Of course the moon moves through all these twelve signs once in its apparent revolution of 29½ days, & in the old days its place among them was thought to have some occult medical significance—based on the table given above. Thus when the moon was in Aries, herbs for *head* ache were to be gathered—or something of the sort. I'm not enough of a folklore student to say just what the details were. But anyway, the moon's place in the zodiac was carefully noted; as you may deduce from the fact that most of the old Almanacks (like the Farmer's) had a column especially devoted to this matter—using the names of the governed bodily parts rather than those of the signs themselves. Thus you'll see still in the Old Farmer's Almanack a column headed "☽ 's place", & reading down most anatomically—"arm, arm, arm, br., br., h'rt, h'rt, h'rt, bel., bel., rei., rei., rei.," &c. The moon, of course, takes 2 or 3 days to pass through each sign of 30° in its full circuit of 360° in 29½ days. Now—to arrive at brass tacks (or brass clock dials) at last—since that inner disc has 12 figures & is mixt up with stars, may we not imagine that it has to do with zodiacal signs—1 meaning Aries, 2 meaning Taurus, & so on? NO, DAMN IT! I arrived at this sudden conclusion upon again examining the diagram, & noting that the 12 seems to be *repeated*—making 24 in all, & in such a manner as to suggest A.M. & P.M. *hours* instead of zodiacal signs. You see, I'm not an expert interpreter of diagrams, & didn't realize at first what I now think is true—viz., that you intend to imply that the figures on these discs are really spread around the circumferences instead of occupying only the visible halves. Thus:

---

*footnote to a footnote—April 30—Walpurgis-Night—is dreaded as a witch festival because of the hideous phallic orgies of primitive pre-agricultural herding peoples, celebrated at this season to ensure the fertility of their cattle. Vestiges of these rites survived late.

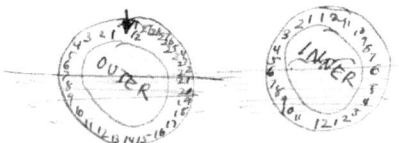

Now, as the plebeians say, "*listen*"! (1) Does the **moon's image** revolve *separately from either disc*? (And what do you mean by "#12 at the top of the moon?") (2) Does the *inner disc* revolve with or separately from the *outer disk*—& with or from the moon's image? (3) In other words, tell me exactly the relation or lack of relation, & motion or lack of motion affecting each & all of the three elements—(a) outer disk, (b) inner disc, & (c) moon's image. Also—does the *starry sky* move or not—& *with what* (moon image or inner disc) if it *does* move?

I might as well tell you that my **new** theory—adopted when I was ¼ down this page—is that the moon image & inner disc are meant to tell the time of the **moon's rising & setting.** You know that in average European & American latitudes, except in the season of Harvest & Hunter's moon, (when the shrewd clock owner can reasonably be expected to use tolerance & help out with his own judgment a situation too complex for simple mechanism) the *moon rises and sets just about 51 minutes* (or say an hour) *later* every night. (or day) Thus at "NEW MOON" it rises, souths, (i.e. crosses the celestial meridian, or line running due north & south through the zenith, so as to be just midway betwixt rising & setting) & sets with the sun. At first quarter it rises at noon, souths at sunset, & sets at midnight, & sets at sunrise. At last quarter it rises at midnight, souths at sunrise, & sets at noon. You can figure out for yourself about what the "between-times" hours would be. Now if that inner disc revolved with the outer one in 29½ days, & were properly graduated, it might *very roughly* hint at the hour of moonrise by the figure just appearing at the eastern or left-hand horizon, & at the hour of the moon's setting by the figure just disappearing at the western or right-hand horizon. Of course all this is very rough indeed. In the latitude of Spring Valley the daily retardation of the moon's rising & setting is sometimes as little as 23 minutes & sometimes as great as 1 hour & 17 minutes. But 50 or 51 minutes is a fair average, & would do for a 17th century New-Netherland country squire whose object was not to make astronomical calculations, but to have his slaves plant corn under the proper lunar auspices! And by the way—if that moon-image revolves independently of either graduated circle, it could, by being timed to make a complete revolution in 24 hours & 51 minutes, follow with some rough suggestiveness the motions of the real moon; being above the mimic horizon when the real moon is above the real horizon, & vice versa. ¶ As to setting the mechanism—well, I can tell you one thing, & that is to set the *outer disc* by the *moon's age* as you'll find it in any good almanack. That is, bring the desired figure to the pointer at the top. As for the *inner disc*—if it is, as I think, attached to the outer, you'll have nothing else to do. If not, be copious with details & let me shew my dulness by giving another blundering guess. And about the moon image—*if it is* separate from the rest & timed to revolve in 24h 51m., just *see that it is set in fullest view, with its top exactly under the pointer at the top of the dial, at the time given in the almanack under the heading "moon souths".* This, you see, will put it definitely in place as being half way betwixt rising & setting when the real moon is. This pointer permits of greater definiteness than one could get by setting the disc at the horizon with reference to the moon's rising or setting time.

Well! Is the foregoing an incoherent mess, or has it helped a bit in the solution of the enigma? Pardon my slowness & bungling—I may be an ass, but at least I'm interested! Especially must you excuse all that detail about the *zodiac*, which I ought to have discarded when I abandoned my foolish zodiacal theory. I retain it merely to avoid the bother of beginning another letter— otherwise I'd be like the yokel who complained in a long letter that the handlebars were missing from his newly arrived mail-order bicycle, & then added a careful P.S. as he faithfully sealed & mailed the missive—"N.B. I have found the handlebars after all. Excuse my complaining!" Don't fail to let me know all you can about the clock matter; for I'm very anxious to learn about those moon dials which I've stupidly seen, without questioning or studying, all my life. Meanwhile, if possible, I shall look up such things at local museums; & may have something authentic to tell you next time.

My aunt mentioned your call, & told me how keenly she enjoyed it— adding that she hoped she had not bored you as the elderly often bore the young. You would feel quite flattered if you could read her allusions to you! By the way—have you heard from a new friend of mine—Vrest Teachout Orton, who has recently come to N.Y. to work on the *American Mercury*? He is a descendant of Annetje Jans,[3] & is keenly interested in your iconoclastic work concerning her origin—in fact, he is inclined toward controversy with you on the subject of her royal origin. He took your name & Providence address the other day, & says he may write you. He, too, has attended Brown University—though most of his academic erudition was imbibed at Harvard. If you want to get in touch with him, address him in care of the *Mercury*, 730 Fifth Ave., N.Y.C. He is 30 years of age (looks about 23!) & seems to me delightfully brilliant.

Hope you won't wear yourself out with multiplex activities, & shall be glad to hear from you when you have the time. Has your September *United Amateur* come? Mine did—but I fancy Marlowe[4] may be as irregular about mailing as about printing. I suppose you know we have a new printer now— Chester O. Hoisington of Idaho.

With all good wishes, & trusting that we may meet again when you are in N.Y., I remain

Most sincerely & astronomically yours—

H P L

Notes

1. Marcus Manilius (fl. 1st century C.E.), Roman poet, astrologer, and author of a poem in five books about celestial phenomena called *Astronomica* or *Astronomicon.*
2. An archaic term for the kidneys.
3. Annetje Jans (1605?–1663), American Dutch settler remembered because of a 200-year dispute over her valuable holdings in Manhattan.
4. Harry R. Marlowe, Official Publisher of the UAPA for the 1925–26 term.

[3]   [ALS, JHL]
[GEORGE KIRK
Dealer in Rare Books and Modern First Editions
1894 Charles Road / Cleveland, O.]
Thursday, March 4[, 1926]

My dear Talman:—

Congrats on the clue! Well—I guess you've solved it. Since high tide comes, at any given place, at about the same time—morning & evening—at any given point in the moon's course; that is, since (let us say) it always occurs at 12 noon & midnight at Boston at new & full moon; it follows that the inner circle figures are probably meant to express, in conjunction with the outer ones, the hours of high tide at the spot where the instrument was meant to be used. Since I see there is no double pointer system for the inner circle, I fancy there is no intention to bother with separate morning & evening high tide hours—for as you know, the morning high tide comes at *about* the same time A.M. that the evening tide comes P.M.; (An hour or less of difference hardly counts) so that one figure (to be read off at the top by the same pointer which indicates the moon's age) will answer for both. But anyhow, if there's only *one* movable disc, you *can't* go wrong on the mere *setting.* Anyone can see that the 29½ graduations of the outer circle indicate the moon's age, so that the setting of this circle by the "☽ 's age" column of an almanack becomes a primary & imperative step. Well—if there aren't any more discs, there isn't any more *setting*—& it merely becomes your task to *interpret* the thing as you have set it! According to present indications, the best way to do this is to see whether the same approximate hour on the inner circle comes under new moon (age 29½ or 1) & full moon (age 15 or 16) on the outer circle. If this is so, I think the tidal solution is highly probable. Next I would look up tides at leading Dutch seaports (local differences are often very great) & see whether any table corresponds significantly to the readings of the dial. If so, the chances are that you have solved the problem. Unless the inner circle can somehow be moved in relation to the outer one, I see no way of setting the clock to serve for any locality other than that for which it was made. The only way would be to re-letter the inner disc. Variations in high tide hours are not alone due to latitude & longitude, but to local topographical considerations which cause the most surprising variations within relatively slight areas. For example—there is three hours & fourteen minutes' difference betwixt Providence & Boston, 2^h 6^m between Governor's Island & Hell Gate, & almost 10 hours' difference between N.Y. harbour & Albany—as the tidal flow is transmitted up the Hudson.

Anyhow, I wish you luck. If the foregoing harangue seems mixed up, never mind it—but *simply set the outer disc by the moon's age as given in an almanack.* I'm just now in a whirl of desperate haste & labour which prevents any coherent thought or expression—on account of my low financial state I'm about to try some supplementary work for the bookshop with which Loveman is connected; a job that may keep me utterly inundated for several weeks,[1] so that a sort of temporary farewell to the bright world of flowers & sunshine will be in order!

So your genealogical data has taken a new & inspiriting turn, & the flow of royal blood is again turned on! Orton will be interested, & you'll probably hear from him sooner or later. He's a great chap, & you'll like him when you return to these parts & get to know him. We take all-night exploring tours—walking through colonial sections when they are utterly deserted, & indulging in appropriate historical reflections.

And so it goes. I trust that all is well back in civilisation, & send my sincerest regards to the 1st Baptist steeple & the Arcade.[2] Let me know what comes of your horological adjustments, too.

With every good wish, I have ye honour to subscribe myself your most obt., most h'ble Servt,

H P L

P.S. Do you ever see *The Netopian,* published by The R.I. Hospital Trust Co.? The new issue has some fine illustrations of R.I. colonial fireplaces.[3]

Notes

1. The task consisted of addressing envelopes for three weeks at Dauber & Pine for $17.50 per week.
2. The First Baptist Meeting House (1775), designed by Joseph Brown, 75 North Main Street, and Arcade Providence at 65 Weybosset Street, the nation's oldest indoor shopping mall.
3. "The Fireplace: An Architectural Tradition in America," *Netopian* No. 11 (February 1926): 7–10.

[4]   [ALS, JHL]

April 23[, 1926]

Dear W B T:—

Well, you certainly have plumbed the depths this time! God! What is that sound .... that subtle, damnable, insidious fumbling at the door? Keep it off! Take it away! .... nnggrrh ... Help! The window, the window![1] I agree with Belknap that it's a very effective yarn, & hope that *Weird Tales* will share the opinion. I see no reason for your being dissatisfied with the tale on second reading—for while it is not of course an elaborately subtle or minutely atmospheric study, it is surely a first-rate thriller in its succinct way, & presents some pictures which are not soon eradicated from the memory. I return it herewith with many thanks for the opportunity of perusal.

I duly note the pertinently relevant epistle which you ascribe to a fair fellow-student, & can only say in regretful reply that I have *not* bought my new spring coat—or indeed any coat, waistcoat, or small-clothes since the wholesale purchasing campaign which followed that memorable Red Hook robbery of May 24, 1925. (GAWD DAMN those thieves—clothing is still a ticklish subject with me, & I don't mean red flannel underwear, at that!) No—my spring coat (spring of '25) isn't in baize or in "kasha";[2] (whatever that is) but thank heaven it isn't in hock! As yet, anyway!

Concerning a word to supplant *excubicularian*[3]—I must have time to brush up on etymological usages. Off-hand, I'd advise you to cut down on syllables by using *lectus* rather than *cubile* as a root. The classical adjective from *lectus* is *lectualis*, & a late post-classical variant is *lectuarius*—which perhaps lends itself more smartly to Anglicisation. Since you wish an adjective conveying the idea of "from bed" or "out of bed", I fancy that *electual* or *electuary* would be about as good as you could devise. It seems, at least, to fall into the main stream of philological usage, & in phonetic quality has subtle associational overtones suggesting on the one hand statesmanship & on the other hand scholarship; both very appropriate for a landed patroon of liberal cultural & political influence under the States-General. Incidentally—I think *excubicularian* conveys a wrong idea. *Cubicularius* alludes not to a *bed* but to a *bed-room*, & you surely did not emerge from your entire quarters to compose that Auroral triumph. However—if you speak of writing *from* your bedchamber in the sense of sending out your words from that point, I suppose your form is warranted. At any rate, this is all the erudition on Indo-European roots which I can air without looking the matter up in a manner most distressful to my constitutional indolence. Ask me something easy, like the lunar configurations on an Amsterdam clock-dial!

I trust the Kalem outfit[4] still functions harmoniously, & that you still get around to most of the meetings. I have begun to emerge from hibernation, & took a long scenic ramble (both urban & agrestic) night before last, during the course of which I discovered one of the most hellish slums ever imagined by mankind. It was in a place whose existence I had not before realised—the end of Chalkstone Ave. near Randall Sq. & the railway—& its dark hilly courts approach the very ultimates of blasphemous horror.

Yrs. for ghouls, afreets, & undertakers—HPL

Notes

1. The WBT story is unidentified; evidently it was not published. HPL's comment is reminiscent of the conclusion of his story "Dagon" (1917): "God, *that hand!* The window! The window!" (*CF* 1.58).
2. Baize is a coarse woollen (or, in cheaper variants, cotton) cloth. Kasha satin is used to line a winter coat.
3. A neologism (adjective) evidently coined by WBT, evidently intended to mean "pertaining to one who has performed a task from his bed."
4. The so-called Kalem Club consisted of friends of HPL in New York whose last names primarily started primarily with the letters K, L, or M. HPL had returned to Providence six days before writing this letter.

[5]   [ALS, JHL]

10 Barnes St.,
Providence, R.I.,
June 25, 1926

My dear Talman:—

Your plot is decidedly interesting, & I have been making notes of possible amendments ever since I received it.[1] It was my intention to send these notes along, just as jotted down in spare seconds during the rush of getting my aunt moved over here despite a slight setback in her recovery; but now that I come to look them over, I find them of doubtful legibility—so will transfer the main ideas to this *slightly* more decipherable document.

To my mind the chief troubles with the tale were *complexity,* uneven *motivation,* & a slight tendency toward melodramatic tableaux. I'd suggest simplification both in characters & incidents, with one staggering climax to overshadow everything else. *Concentration* is the watchword—& with this put fully into effect, you'll find less of the novelette atmosphere about what ought distinctly to be a short story. Let there be *few characters,* & tense, creeping, suspenseful situations. Cut out the visit of Haines, Pryor & Hodge to the old man altogether, & let everything develop through Hoffman—who ought perhaps to tell the story. Force is gained by giving the reader such a special point of narrative contact. If you don't want to sacrifice the incident of trying the formula on Pryor, (p. 3) let it be tried on Hoffman during the old man's explanation of his forbidden delvings. But first, let's get the *motivation* tightened up, so that there won't be any suspicion of fumbling or pinchbeck devices— or yet of that *extravagance* which one finds in the fantastic tales of that Gothic celebrity who shares your hero's name—Ernst Theodor Wilhelm Hoffmann, whose influence on some of Poe's lighter work was so marked.[2]

As a central fact, let it be brought out in any way you wish that Abel Foster was a magician & wizard of the worst sort. It would give added force & continuity to have him *not* a mere newcomer influenced by old Dominie Slott's papers, but *an actual colleague of the old wizard-pastor,* whose soul had been bottled by Slott himself in such a way as to keep the body alive indefinitely. Let him come back after two centuries to get access to certain of Slott's books & documents, which he needs in order to pursue advanced ramifications of his hellish studies; & let him covet the soul of Dominie Vanderhoof *to add to his own in some occult way*—to strengthen his unnatural dominion over the forces of nature.

Now to the story. Your beginning is good—& (unless you prefer to defer this bit to the end) you might add that old wives say that in the full of the moon there walks about the churchyard a gigantic & bewildered figure clutching a bottle & seeking some goal which it cannot remember. Follow this with your description of the scene & of the strange doings which led to the successive desertion of the church & the village—& have Parson Vanderhoof buried as you describe.

Then have young Hoffman sent for in the natural course of events, & duly warned against the church & the old sexton. Have him laugh aside the warnings & go up to the church one late afternoon—noting in the sunset the adjacent graves of Dominie Slott with its ancient cross, & that of Dominie Vanderhoof with its new cross.

Hoffman finds Foster locked in the belfry, drinking heavily. He is in deadly fear of something. "The cross over Dominie Vanderhoof's grave keeps falling down in the night. I can't make it stay set in the earth—something in the dark hours is pushing it up from beneath!" Hoffman inquires the reason, & drops out a long and hideous story of black magic. Have it appear here that Foster came to study Guilliam Slott's diabolic papers—but save for another tense moment the revelation that he was actually Slott's colleague, surviving by unhallowed arts. At this point let the incident of the trial of the formula occur if you wish. Foster has stolen Vanderhoof's soul & bottled it, having hastily buried the body which appeared lifeless. But now the cross won't stay put over his grave at night, & each successive morning the loosened sod is harder & harder to put down. The bottle idea is no encroachment on my tale— heaven knows it's common property enough! As I told you, I got it from that old hermit of 30 years ago in Phillipsdale.[3] Hoffman demands that they dig up the Dominie & restore his soul, but Foster is afraid. He says the consequences would be fearful, and that a very abstruse & daemoniac formula would be required to join the spirit to the giant body again. H. then demands to know where the bottled soul is, but F. will not tell. H. then sees the queer black bottles [the title—3 Blk. Bottles—must be changed] on the table, & takes up one which has a small label—"V". Foster furiously interposes, so that H. is obliged to struggle with him. In the struggle the table is knocked over, & the other bottle breaks with a sulphurous puff. Instantly the old sexton goes limp & begins to turn a greenish-black—croaking with noxious malevolence—"Curse ye, ye whelp, I'm done for—that one was mine—Dominie Slott took it out two hundred years ago!" [This is the deferred revelation of F.'s age & affiliations.] As Foster dissolves or crumbles to a heap of grey dust [make it that instead of liquescence, to avoid paralleling Poe's "Valdemar"] on the floor, Hoffman looks at the other bottle; which he had wrested from his collapsing adversary. It glows with a faint phosphorescence.

But now from outside there comes a crash as of falling wood. A pause—then the trickling of gravel, as if someone were disturbing a mound of earth. H. looks out—*and in the light of the rising moon sees that the fresh cross, which he had noticed upright when nearing the church before dark, has fallen.* The sound of sliding earth comes again distinctly as he looks—so in terror, leaving the bottle on the table as a fearsome thing, he flees for the village. [He had demanded the exhumation of the corpse when talking to F., but feels very differently now that the grave is opening of itself, & now that he is alone after the hideous disintegration he has witnessed.]

As he descends the hill he hears a groan, scream, or roar behind; & turning, sees that part of the churchyard where Slott & Vanderhoof were buried silhouetted against the moon—[CLIMAX] with a gigantic & grotesque black shadow climbing out of V's grave & plunging & floundering loathsomely toward the church.

Hoffman tells his story, but only one old antiquarian—familiar with certain bizarre colonial legends—believes him. That old man & he proceed to the church by daylight & find the grave of Vanderhoof open & deserted. Grave-robbers? Perhaps—but . . . . They search the church belfry—the "V" bottle is gone, the fragments of the other broken bottles are found on the floor. And—if you wish another weird touch—in some strange grey dust are certain immense footprints which the boots of the late Dominie Vanderhoof exactly fit. After looking at some of the hellish books & papers surviving from Guilliam Slott's time, they burn them with many a shudder, *& take down the cross from Dominie Slott's ancient grave.*

Vanderhoof is never heard from again—*but old wives say—&c*—here you can add the touch about the wandering bottle-holding figure at night, unless you've used it at the start of the story.

Such, then, is the tale as I'd advise simplifying it. Of course, you may feel that I've taken all the "meat" out—in which case pray remember that you're by no means bound to swallow all the advice you get! Certainly, in any possible shape, it's a rousing good plot, & very strong in potent "creeps" of the most convincing sort. I should think it ought to go in 3500 or 4000 words as amended,[4] & believe that *Weird Tales* would be very glad to accept it for publication. By the way—I've just received advance sheets of my "He", to appear in the issue after "The Terrible Old Man". The "artist" has perpetrated a discouragingly stiff & wooden-looking pictorial heading.

Thanks exceedingly for the cutting anent the Albany historical exhibits. Wish I could have seen the documentary treasures. Morton, by the way, would *not* be likely to prove a fruitful source of information concerning old chests & such—for his curatorial labours have principally to do with *minerals*. The Paterson museum will have to get a damn sight richer—or the colonial proprietors of the Jersey hinterland a damn sight more recklessly generous— before he can begin to specialise in domestic antiquities.[5] But drop in on him just the same—he's a delightfully genial character, & will be cordially glad to see you. I've told him you may be around his way.

Glad you liked the postcards—here are some more recent finds. I can get you a whole set of splendid *Pawtuxet* cards if you want them—for Chase's Drug Store at the bridge handles all the best & quaintest scenes. My pedestrian explorations have been quite extensive lately; involving not only many scenes previously unvisited by me, but several long stretches of familiar ground. Last Saturday I "did" Mount Pleasant, Davis Park, & Federal Hill— & was astonished by the great Italian churches. Sunday I hiked to Warren & rode back on the 'bus. Monday I visited Ft. Independence at Field's Point, & followed Narragansett Boulevard to Pawtuxet. And last night I ascended to the State House to see the colonial Duncan Mansion across Smith St.[6]—but lo! found only the gaping cellar where it had been. Confound this criminal vandalism in the name of progress!! Something ought to be done about it!

Abundant thanks for that tip about the Dyer St. stationer. Neilan in Weybosset St.[7] always charges me fiendish rates for my paper, despite the fact that I bought my machine of him back in 1906 when he was a young clerk in the Remington Co. I'll need some new 8½ × 11 sheets soon, & you can wager that I won't be backward in inspecting Friend Hammond's stock! The kind you got at $1.25 per 1000 will do finely for the MSS. I send away—light & postage-saving, & perfectly adequate when one only types on one side. Of course, for letters, I need a coated stock able to take pen script on both sides. This long paper is some which our fellow-amateur George Kirk—whom you'll meet soon—insisted on giving me when he ceased to have a commercial use for it. If my correspondence weren't so devastatingly immense, I'd say that my present stock was enough to last an ordinary lifetime!

Well—I must desist. Hope you can forgive me for my narrowing-down & pruning of your plot—but I fancy you'll appreciate my temptation to unify the incidents & limit the characters for the sake of a more closely concentrated impression. Now I'm anxious to see the finished story, & hope you'll send me a copy whether or not you adopt the suggestions. Meanwhile I trust you're duly enjoying the home atmosphere, & revelling in the piquant antiquities of the New-Netherland province.

With every good wish,
Yr most obt hble Servt
HPL

Notes

1. HPL is discussing the revision of "Two Black Bottles."

2. Ernst Theodor Amadeus Hoffmann (1776–1822), a German Romantic author of fantasy and horror, composer, and music critic. HPL felt that his work was more grotesque than weird.

3. HPL refers to "The Terrible Old Man" (1920). It is unclear whether HPL is stating that he derived the plot as early as 1896.

4. The final draft of the story came in at 4870 words.

5. HPL's friend James F. Morton had become curator of the Paterson, NJ, museum in July 1925.

6. The Alexandar Duncan (1805–1889) mansion (1800) was razed to make way for the State Office Building.

7. Providence Paper Co., 42–48 Weybosset Street; Neilan Typewriter Exchange was at 43 Weybosset Street.

[6]   [AHT]

> 10 Barnes St.,
> Providence, R. I.,
> July 21, 1926

My dear Talman:—

[. . .]

"Two Black Bottles" begins very promisingly, & I still think it will be all right to let Hoffman tell the story. The amount of matter which he has to transmit rather than tell is of course considerable; but no more, I think, than occurs in many tales of similar kind by the best authors. However—you can use your own judgment about choosing between first & third persons. The really important part of my suggestion was merely that the central scene & climax develop through Hoffman alone rather than through the three later visitors as outlined in your rough synopsis. This simplification & concentration of events upon one central figure in whose place the reader can put himself would seem to me the most essential step in the strengthening of the plot.

As for what I've done to the MS.—I am sure you'll find nothing to interfere with your sense of creation. My changes are in virtually every case merely verbal, & all in the interest of finish & fluency of style. I have not been very lavish with elaborately sinister words, because my maturer judgment tells me that these things must be used sparingly in order to retain their potency. Only in a definitely prose-poetic composition can they be scattered about at all freely—& your style is straightforward narration rather than atmospheric impressionism. Save your extreme words for the climax—you'll need them, unvitiated by previous employment. Begin to lay on the colour when Hoffman approaches the church at sunset & sees the graves of Slott & Vanderhoof—

making this approach something like the beginning of Poe's "Usher" in repressed menace. Work in a sort of subsidiary climax—or rather, an exceptionally tense moment, when Foster—fuddled with drink & terror—begins his confession by saying in a terrible whisper that the cross over Vanderhoof's grave keeps falling down in the night. That confession calls for adroit work—homely diction—semi-dialect—but necessarily chilling to the core. Use great care when Slott's connexion with the deviltry begins to appear, & let the collapse & pulverisation of Foster have a very marked "punch". From that point on, you can safely increase the "colour" content of your style. The crash outside—the fallen cross in the moonlight—the sliding earth—the terrified flight—& then, *Oh, Boy!* The *big* sight! The gigantic corpse clambering out of its grave, silhouetted against the moon, & floundering toward the church! After this the sense of a pause must occur, & the aftermath should be told in a lowered key—& as briefly as possible. Again economise on the colour words, & rely on dark & skilful *suggestion* to convey the requisite impression of lurking terror. Make all final explanations as brief as possible—& as inconspicuous. Begrudge every word you have to use after the climax. I'll be glad to see the finished story, & hope that my suggestions may prove a help—at least so far as details of diction are concerned—rather than a hindrance.

  I am ever

    Yr. most obt Servt

    H P L

List of Weird Fiction[1]

  I. Early "Gothic" Novels.

The Castle of Otranto by Horace Walpole. Daddy of 'em all, but itself very mediocre and unconvincing

The Mysteries of Udolpho by Ann Radcliffe. Interminably long and a bit naive, but with some good horror moments. Mrs. Radcliffe explains things naturally in the end—a mistake, I think.

The Monk by Matthew Gregory Lewis. Blood and thunder—crude but intense. Rambling plot, but no rational explaining away of the horrors. Rather long.

*Melmoth the Wanderer by Charles Robert Maturin. Greatest of all early horror novels, but devilish hard to get nowadays. I've never seen the full text. Prodigiously long. Theme—sale of a man's soul to the devil.

History of the Caliph Vathek

Episodes of Vathek by William Beckford. Oriental tales of great power, with grotesque fantasy and strong horror element.

Frankenstein; or, the Modern Prometheus by Mary Godwin Shelley. Short but very powerful. Artificial semi-human being.

Zanoni

The House and the Brain   by Edward Bulwer-Lytton. Diffuse in a Victorian way, but very good—especially the last, which is long yet continuously interesting.

A Strange Story

Wuthering Heights by Emily Brontë. Not strictly in old Gothic tradition, but an immensely powerful masterpiece with a strong weird element.

Minor Gothic horror-tales by Sheridan Le Fanu, Wilkie Collins, Harrison Ainsworth, and George W. M. Reynolds.

II. Continental Horror Tales in Translation

(German)

The Serapion Brethren by E. T. A. Hoffmann. Famous, but a disappointment. More grotesque than horrible.

Peter Schlemihl by Adelbert von Chamisso—Fairly good.

Undine by Baron de la Motte Fouque. A masterpiece of beauty with moving tones of terror.

The Amber Witch by Wilhelm Meinhold. A classic of weird realism in the form of a clergyman's diary. Witchcraft during the 17th century.

(French)

The Wild Ass's Skin   ) by Honore de Balzac. Great, though the
Seraphita   ) greatness is not always in the direction of
Louis Lambert   ) the weird element.
Clairmond (Vampire)   ) short tales by
The Mummy's Foot (light—not very good)) Theophile Gautier
Avatar (fair)   )
One of Cleopatra's Nights (atmospheric—)
    spirit of antique Egypt)   )

Temptation of St. Anthony by Gustave Flaubert. Colour and imagery

*The Venus of Ille by Prosper Merimee. Short story—very good. Based on ancient legend.

*The Horla   )
Who Knows?   )
The Spectre   ) excellent short stories by Guy de Maupassant
He   )
The Diary of a Madman   )
The White Wolf   )

The Man-Wolf   )
The Invisible Eye) Erckmann-Chatrian (available in "Lock and Key Library")
The Waters of Death)

III. American Horror Tales

Wieland; or, the Transformation by Charles Brockden Brown. Imitation of Mrs. Radcliffe. Laid among Germans of Pennsylvania. Rational explanation.

Tales of a Traveller by Washington Irving. Mostly too light to be thrilling, though "The German Student" is good.

*The Complete Works of Edgar Allan Poe

The House of the Seven Gables	)
Dr. Grimshawe's Secret	)
The Minister's Black Veil (short)	) by Nathaniel Hawthorne.
The Ambitious Guest (short)	) delicate rather than intense
Ethan Brand (short)	)

*Can Such Things Be?) by Ambrose Bierce. *Intensely* powerful collections of short tales. Critics have called one story, "The Death of Halpin Frayser", the most hideous thing in the literature of the Anglo-Saxon race.

*In the Midst of Life)	
The Diamond Lens)	
What Was It?) by Fitz-James O'Brien. Short tales.	

Elsie Venner by Oliver Wendell Holmes. Novel of New England Life with sinister undercurrent.

The Turn of the Screw by Henry James. Very subtle. Two children possessed by ghosts of evil servants.

*The Upper Berth by F. Marion Crawford. A *great* short story.

The Wind in the Rosebush by Mary E. Wilkins. Fine collection of New England weird tales.

*The Yellow Wall-Paper by Charlotte Perkins Gilman. A short story masterpiece. Madness in a terrible pattern.

IV. Modern British Horror

The Phantom Rickshaw	)
The Finest Story in the World	) by Rudyard Kipling.
The Recrudescence of Imray	)
*The Mark of the Beast	)

Fantastics) by Lafcadio Hearn. Latter book consists of Japanese weird tales.
Kwaidan)

The Picture of Dorian Gray by Oscar Wilde. A classic

*The Pale Ape and Other Stories by M. P. Shiel. Contains "The House of Sounds"—a true masterpiece.

Markheim) Robert Louis Stevenson	
Dr. Jekyll and Mr. Hyde)	

*Dracula (classic vampire novel)	)
The Jewel of Seven Stars (Egyptian aftermath)	) Bram Stoker
The Lair of the White Worm (great *idea*, miserably written)	)

The Beetle by Richard Marsh. Pretty creepy. A curse.

The Door of the Unreal by Gerald Biss. Good werewolf novel.

*Cold Harbour by Francis Brett Young. Accursed house.

The Smoking Leg and Other Tales by John Metcalfe. Very good

The Man Who Went too Far   ) by E. F. Benson.

*Visible and Invisible (contains splendid tales)   ) Short. Fine colour and sug-
gestion. Great God Pan.

The Return   )

The Riddle and Other Tales   )   by Walter de la Mare. Contains

The Connoisseur and Other Stories   )   gems of real horror—"Seaton's Aunt,
"The Tree", "Out of the Deep", "Mr. Kempe", "All-Hallows.

The Celestial Omnibus by E. M. Forster. Has one or two good weird tales
among a whimsical majority.

V. The Modern Masters

Arthur Machen

*The House of Souls—contains the magnificently subtle study "The White
People", and the famous "Great God Pan."

*The Three Impostors—connected episodes, including "The Black Seal" and
"The White Powder"—horror at its wildest! In the new American Edition is also included "The Red Hand" a hideous thing.

The Terror—wartime tale—rather short, but with potent horror.

The Great Return—small brochure—very delicate tale of the Holly Grail.

Algernon Blackwood

*Incredible Adventures—fine longish stories, especially "The Regeneration of
Lord Ernie" and "The Damned".

The Wolves of God—fair short tales

Ten Minute Stories—not so good

Day and Night Stories—one or two fair

*The Listener and Other Stories—splendid! Contains "The Willows", which
is perhaps the finest weird tale in literature.

*The Lost Valley and Other Stories—contains the magnificently breathless
North Woods yarn "The Wendigo".

*John Silence—Physician Extraordinary—fine series of related tales.

Lord Dunsany

Five Plays (contains "The Gods of the Mountain")

Plays of Gods and Men (contains "A Night at an Inn" and "The Laughter of
the Gods")

The Book of Wonder—many fine bits

A Dreamer's Tales—contains "Poor Old Bill" and "Idle Days on the Yann."

Montague Rhodes James
*Ghost Stories of an Antiquary—fine and distinctive
More Ghost Stories of an Antiquary
A Thin Ghost, and Others
A Warning to the Curious
(All potent and unusual tales of stark horror by a noted scholar and antiquarian.
    James is the Provost of Eton College.)

Also much good weird material in early H. G. Wells books. Get his "Thirty Strange Stories". A. Conan Doyle has some fair stuff, too. "Mystery of Sasassa Valley", "Captain of the Pole Star", "Round the Fire Stories". H. Rider Haggard has weird touches.[2]

    Exceptionally fine items, recommended for immediate perusal, marked with an asterisk.

Notes

1. At the time HPL was writing "Supernatural Horror in Literature." "The Modern Masters" is in fact the name of the final chapter of the essay, dealing with Machen, Dunsany, Blackwood, and M. R. James.
2. HPL briefly discusses Haggard's *She: A History of Adventure* (1887) in "Supernatural Horror in Literature."

[7]   [ALS, JHL]
10 Barnes St.,
Providence, R.I.,
August 24, 1926
My dear Talman:—
            I must thank you most profusely for the piquant & varied treats comprised within your communication of the 22nd! Truly, I feel quite aesthetically & historically enriched after a thorough survey & assimilation. I'm glad you managed to see Kirk on the 11th, even if there was no formal meeting; & hope you will get to one of the latter before long. Too bad you didn't make Belknap's gathering last Wednesday—nearly everyone was present, & I am told that the discussion attained the maximum degree of intensity short of a free fight! If you attend Columbia this coming term—as I believe you had an idea of doing—you must certainly become a regular member.
    As to my list of allegedly weird books—don't be discouraged; *some* of 'em are gruesome enough even for you. The exact effect of a given type of impression undoubtedly varies with the psychology of the recipient, but a certain proportion of horror-writing is sufficiently direct to be fairly sure of a predictable response from all readers. As to what is meant by "weird"—& of course weirdness is by no means confined to horror—I should say that the real criterion is *a*

strong impression of the suspension of natural laws or the presence of unseen worlds or forces close at hand. Minds of differing perspective or degrees of sensitivity react differently to a given tale. To me, "The Pit & the Pendulum" contains nothing at all of true weirdness except the introductory atmospheric touches. The horrors are too patently *physical,* & of merely human origin. Poe's supreme tale— & perhaps the supreme weird tale of all the ages—is to me "The Fall of the House of Usher". Second comes "Ligeia", & of course "Facts in the Case of M. Valdemar" is full of breathless anticipation up to the last hideous cataclysm. "Ms. Found in a Bottle" & the later parts of "Arthur Gordon Pym" have a strange & potent aura of mystery & expectancy, & there are touches in "Metzengerstein" which few besides Poe could achieve. In the realm of sheer, sombre prose-poetry, uniting horror & beauty, nothing could excel "The Masque of the Red Death", "Silence, a Fable", & "Shadow, a Parable".

Of the recent horror-authors I think the most potent is Arthur Machen, though one more responsive to physical than to spiritual torture might prefer the Frenchman Maurice Level—who I may or may not have mentioned on my list. I have one of his books, which I'd be glad to lend you at any time if you haven't read it before.[1] Incidentally—the magazine extracts you enclosed proved highly entertaining. That Watertown business certainly is *thorough*—although it would want considerable moulding & remodelling before it could become a really artistic tale with a single potent climax. The item on "Hours with the Dead" reminds me of a two-volume collection of mortuary anecdotes which W. Paul Cook once lent me—a very quaint set of essays called "Dealings with the Dead".[2]

I am profoundly & vociferously grateful for the historical matter—both epistolary & pictorial—of which you send such a wealth, & shall file everything in the choicest part of my archives. That Washington's headquarters must be an extremely fascinating place, & I am doubly grateful for your sketch of the front to supplement the rear view given. As to the roof—I presume you are aware that the "regulation Dutch" type which one commonly finds in the 18th century N.Y. & N. J. cottages did *not* occur in the first Dutch houses of the region, & that it never reached the more inland & architecturally conservative sections. The earliest Dutch colonial houses had straight, steep roofs reaching quite near the ground, & were most often without dormers—end windows lighting the enormous garrets. Only with later development do we see the projecting eaves, the graceful gambrel, the curved lower pitch, & the pillared porch appearing. The best large-scale example of the earliest Dutch colonial architecture one can find is the village of Hurley, N.Y.—near Kingston. I have never been there, but have seen pictures—& a highly interesting set of *models* of the houses. You really ought to see this latter, which can be found in the basement of the N.Y. Historical Society at Central Park West & 77th St. Your De Windt–Washington house seems to be a transitional type with backward leanings. It has the steep roof of the primitive species, but possesses dormers & a slight curve upward at the eaves—on the rear side at least. Oh, yes—& on second inspection I see that the eaves project, as indeed you mention in your letter! This curved, projecting eave is clearly the immediate predecessor of the familiar porch of the typical 18th century Dutch house. Carried out a little further from the wall, & provided with a row of columns & a platform, it becomes that ultimate American institution, the front piazza! In very late Dutch specimens, we see a dormer wall of low "lie-on-your-stomach" windows in the attic above the place where roof becomes piazza-top, & in its final evolution the porch became wholly dissociated from the sweeping roof-line. It appears that by 1800 or 1810 the type had virtually ceased to be built—at least, in the more settled parts—English hybridisation having become complete. Poe's cottage is a good specimen of a late or hybrid type. In the later Dutch houses Georgian ornament & detail were often worked in with a surprising degree of originality, & without sacrifice of the purely Dutch atmosphere. If you haven't seen it already, you owe it to yourself to visit the Lefferts homestead in Prospect Park, Brooklyn, just across the road from the Botanic Garden. Take a Flatbush Ave. car at Brooklyn Bridge—or take the B.M.T. subway & alight at the Prospect Park Station. This house fuses Dutch outline with Georgian detail in a magnificent way. And whilst you are in Flatbush, don't forget to see the old churchyard with the stones in the Dutch language. The church is of Georgian design, built in 1796. Also—remember the Dyckman homestead (1783) in New York at Broadway & 204th St. The connexion of your family with those Tappan antiquities, & your knowledge of the bits of legend & history surrounding them, must increase your interest & appreciation threefold. It is dramatic to think of the events surrounding the death of Andre,[3] & I am glad Genl. Washington was ashamed enough to shut the blinds. I can't forgive him for what seems to me an act of needless reprisal for the equally censurable execution of Nathan Hale. The church at Tappan has a modest tower of a type often built in the early 19th century—you've probably seen the same on the old white church (1810) at Rumford. Ecclesiastical architecture in America has to some extent been gratifyingly conservative—so that churches built in the '30s, '40s, or even '50s, show in many cases strong reminders of the Georgian influence. Among such are the Arlington St. church in Boston, the Brick Church in 5th Ave., N.Y., & the reformed Dutch church in Bushwick, Brooklyn, which the family of our fellow-amateur Kleiner attends. As to the windows of the Providence 1st Baptist Church—you are wrong for once! They are arched—*not* square—at the top, as indeed were the majority of church windows at the time. They are also arched in Newport's Trinity (1726)—a Peter Harrison[4] specimen of which I am particularly fond. I wish you could have seen the archaic vault beneath the Tappan church—but anyhow, you can write a story about it. The old man of the churchyard sounds delightful—find him some midnight, cut his beard free, & let him pursue his haunting ways again! Glad you got some good sepulchral paper-weights—I wish the slate of New England churchyards would break up as conveniently as the sandstone of N.Y. & N.J.! My Elizabethtown fragment reads thus: You were lucky to get a curved top & star. What I've always wanted is one of the winged cherub faces or skulls so common on the earlier slabs. The '76 house must be decidedly interesting, though it would be improved by a removal of the modern cluttering in front. What shades & memories of poor Maj. Andre must linger there! As to the start of the Revolution in that edifice—I suppose one may say it started there as much as anywhere else, since the whole sad affair came from a wide dissatisfaction which numerous colonists & assemblages of colonists had expressed at numerous places ever since the enactment of the Stamp Act in 1765. You will recall that a lawless gang from Providence—led, I blush to say, by [my] own revered forefather Capt. Abraham Whipple—attacked & burned His Majesty's armed Schooner *Gaspee* on June 9, 1772, as she lay aground on Nanquit Point after chasing one of the revenue-evaders with which this seditious bay was infested. Your Mr. Ryerson, I think, is eminently correct in saying that the Stamp Act was indeed a torch which did much to set off the dangerous magazine of ill feeling underlying the political life of the colonies. It was not, however, against this act in particular that your meeting of 1774 was aimed—for the Stamp Act was repealed a year after its passage—in 1766—& the colonists were so grateful that they set up on Bowling Green that leaden equestrian statue of the King which they afterward tore down. The big excitement in 1774 was occasioned by the passage of the Boston Port Bill—closing Boston to sea trade in reprisal for the "tea party" of December 1773, which in turn was in reprisal for the remaining tax on tea, to which had been reduced the new set of taxes (designed mostly for the technical assertion of authority) enacted in 1767 after the repeal of the Stamp Act. In any event, your part of the colonies was certainly a seat of the most important happenings; & I wish I had had an opportunity to explore it when I was within a reasonable distance.

But I have done *some* exploring, as you may have deduced from my postcards. *Newport* is my latest hobby; & truly, it is remarkable that I was not awake to its colonial spendours before. The whole place is a living survival of what it was before the Revolution—due to a decline in commercial prosperity which prevented the replacement of the quaint old buildings by the garish intrusions of later times. My latest trip was on my birthday—last Friday—when I went by boat. The waterfront is incredibly ancient—venerable gambrel roofs appearing on every side, colonial wharves & warehouses stretching into the harbour, & the delicate white steeple of Trinity Church (1726) crowning the entire landscape. One lands on the same old Long Wharf used by British & French fleets, & sees at once, up a long vista, the great brick Colony House designed in 1737 by Richard Munday.[5] Threading along the narrow hill streets, one may find any number of old houses built betwixt 1690 & 1800— together with notable public buildings like the Old City Hall, (1763) the Redwood Library, (1750) & the Old Jewish Synagogue, (1763) designed for the most part by the celebrated Peter Harrison—who is the presiding architectural genius of Old Newport as Charles Bulfinch is of Old Boston, Samuel McIntire of Old Salem, Russell Warren of Old Bristol, or Andrew Hamilton of Old Philadelphia—yes, & John Holden Greene of Old Providence. On this occasion I did what Morton & I lacked time to do earlier in the month, & visited "Whitehall", (1729) the country-seat of the eminent Bishop (then Dean) Berkeley[6] during his sojourn in America. It is a very modest house of plain design, about four miles from the town, & pleasantly embowered by a murmurous grove of sturdy trees, & explored it inside & out—is owned & exhibited by the Colonial Dames—& completed my Berkeleian pilgrimage by visiting the Hanging Rocks not far distant, where the Dean was wont to sit by the hour & meditate, or write upon his "Alciphron; or, The Minute Philosopher". I mean to visit Newport much more frequently than formerly; for truly it is a treasury of those memories & reliquiae which now interest me more than anything else in the universe. I'll enclose a card of that house occupied as headquarters by Genl. Prescott & his successor during the occupation of Newport by His Majesty's forces from Dec. 1776 to Octr. 1779. It is the old Bannister house.

　　With all good wishes, & renewed thanks for many favours, I remain
Yr most oblig'd & obt Servt
H P L

P. S. (1) Good luck with your Black Bottles! (2) I've just bought some thin paper like yours at Hammond's. Some dump! But the paper is a great bargain! (3) That Waite black magic book[7] is still at the Old Corner Book Shop—& *I'm* getting tempted now—although stone-brokeness saves me from myself.

Notes

1. At this time, HPL owned a copy of Level's *Tales of Mystery and Horror* (1920; *LL* 565), but in 1927 he obtained Level's novel *Those Who Return* (1923; *LL* 566).

2. By Lucius M. Sargent.

3. John André (1750–1780), a British Army officer hanged as a spy by the Continental Army during the Revolutionary War for assisting Benedict Arnold's attempted surrender of the fort at West Point, NY, to the British.

4. Peter Harrison (1716–1775), colonial American architect born in York, England, who emigrated to Rhode Island in 1740. Considered to be the first professionally trained architect in America.

5. Richard Munday (c.1685–1739), prominent colonial American architect and builder in Newport, RI.

6. George Berkeley (1685–1753), Irish philosopher, spent the years 1728–32 in and around Newport.

7. Probably *The Book of Black Magic and of Pacts: Including the Rites and Mysteries of Goëtic Theury, Sorcery, and Infernal Necromancy*. A[rthur] E[dward] Waite (1857–1942) was an American-born British poet and scholarly mystic who wrote extensively on occult and esoteric matters.

[8]   [ALS, JHL]

10 Barnes St.,
Providence, R.I.,
Septr. 8 1926

My dear Talman:—

I have just digested with the keenest pleasure your communication of the 5th, & am properly envious of the artistic talent shewn in the bookplate & bungalow. If I ever adopt either, I shall certainly have no other designer prepare the sketches & diagrams! I am sure you could adapt your decorative skill, just for once, to the more angular lines of the New England Georgian mode.

But really, that Dutch cottage of yours is a genuine triumph! Besides the aesthetic, you have managed to work in the practical—which is always a sealed mystery to me. I have not seen any Dutch dormers pedimented like yours; but the use of the cyma curve suggested by the roof line is certainly congruous enough, & in my lowly opinion forms quite a stroke of genius. I have, by the way, a very strong notion that the use of the cyma curve in bold architectural features is originally a Dutch conception. It appears in British architecture toward the end of the seventeenth century & culminates in Queen Anne's time, & may very possibly be among the Dutch ideas brought across by William the Third. A highly interesting example of its belated use in Providence will be found in the Joseph Brown house (1774) in South Main St.—the house of the old Providence Bank until a few months ago. This, as you possibly recall, has been copied in the new building of the Gas Co. in Weybosset St.[1] Brown was an amateur architect of great ability, & is responsible for the choice of our 1st Baptist Steeple from among three designs by Gibbs. As to those quadrant windows in the attic beside the chimney—I would not be in the least surprised if they *were* Dutch. They are almost never found outside the New Netherland area, yet abound in the colonial houses of that region. Whilst those I have actually seen have been in English houses—both town houses in New York and country houses in various suburbs—it is only natural to assume that an English feature flourishing *only* where Dutch influence is strong, must owe something to the Holland tradition. It is so with the gambrel roofs of English New York—they all have the short upper & long lower pitch characteristic of Dutch design, (though they never adopt the *curve*) whereas the gambrel roofs of New England have nearly equal pitches. Oh, yes—& about that drawing of Washington's headquarters. The relative position of that peep-hole—or what I took to be the peep-hole—was what made me think you had sketched the front instead of the rear; but I can easily see how my untrained eye might have misinterpreted the perspective. Thanks for the correction—I don't want anything misleading in my archives! Incidentally—let me express the hope that your designs may fare well at the fair. If the judges have any taste at all—& unless your region is a positive incubator of general genius—I am sure your bookplate & cottage ought to be in the line for all the Grand Prixes floating about! And anent furniture—that book of mine which interests you is *The Furniture of Our Forefathers*, by Esther Singleton. If you can't find it at the local bibliothecae—including Morton's joint in Paterson—I'll lend you my copy.

That old desk must constitute a notable addition to your array of immediate & tangible background, & I trust that it may prove the birthplace of many an inspired verse & tale. You are fortunate to have awaked so early to the charm & values of family antiquities. When I was little less than your age I let a delightful old table desk slip through my fingers in the course of a domestic reapportionment—& now I would give much to have it again. Mine was not a folding one, but had a slanting surface which raised as a lid. It was not made by any kinsmen, but was used very steadily by one three generations behind me. How little I appreciated things when I was young!

I guess that black magic book will be yours in the end! It is still on its accustomed shelf in Market Square, & my cash situation shews no signs of amending. But beware of further meddling with the law in your ceaseless quest for romance, or your library will grow very slowly indeed! My own immediate cash—if there is any such thing—is going for one or two more antiquarian trips in the near future. Since writing a hellish story about ancient Boston horrors the other day,[2] I have had a longing to visit the actual scenes I described—& there are several Rhodinsular villages (notably Wickford) to which I desire to give a further architectural examination.

I wish I could get around your way this autumn, but doubt if I can make it quite so soon. Dutch houses—aside from the few specimens in & near N. Y. City—will be very new to me; & I am sure your local collection will be hard to beat. Some day, too, I'd like to see the up-river villages of Hurley & New Paltz, about which I have heard much.[3] Your graveyards, too, would prove a rich pasturage for a confirmed old ghoul—& when I do get around you had better watch the Major's father's cherub pretty closely!

As autumn approaches, I presume your studies will loom more & more in the foreground. Do you intend to commute to Columbia on that gorgeous new omnibus (which I saw for the first time on my last day in N.Y.) or will you take a room somewhere on Morningside Heights? In any event you will no doubt see something of our "gang"—& I fancy you will be interested in that member who can claim, through half his ancestry, those selfsame old Dutch ghosts which populate your native churchyards. Look him up some time—Vrest Orton, 1 Grove Court, N. Y. City. He lives in a real Colonial house (somewhat remodelled, however) in a picturesque Greenwich Village backwater which still strongly suggests the Georgian age.

I had a call Monday from the super-amateur W. Paul Cook, whom I hadn't seen for five years. He looks just the same as ever, & says he may get around again in the course of his petrol peregrinations. Don't forget that you, too, need a decided brushing-up in Providence antiquities, & that enthusiastic—if somewhat less than expert—guidance may be found not far from Barnes Street!

And so it goes. Just now I am groaning & sighing in the midst of the devil's own job of typing. That thin Hammond paper is excellent—but the drudgery of key-tapping is a bane to which I shall never become reconciled!

With the customarily collective good wishes of the household, I am ever

Yr most oblig'd & obt Servt

HPL

P.S. Those plans & the bookplate design are safe—so speak up if they were to be returned!

Notes

1. The Providence Gas Company is at 100 Weybosset Street.
2. "Pickman's Model," written in early September.
3. HPL did not visit these villages until 1929.

[9]   [ALS, JHL]

10 Barnes St.,

Providence, R.I.,

Septr. 28, 1926

My dear W B T:—

Vae mihi![1] Sensible of the slowness with which the Old Corner[2] turns over its stock, (they still have a 2-volume Gay's Poems which they had years ago up on Empire St.!) I cashed your money order & sailed confidently in—but lo! The daemon-book had performed an incantation on itself, & evaporated like a puff of smoke into the sinister & tenebrous aether! In other words, it wasn't there—& just as I was looking forward to a free reading of it before mailing it on to you! Damn sorry—but fate is fate. And to think that it still remained on the shelves till only a little while ago! Well—one may only shrug one's shoulders philosophically & make the best of it. Here's the $3.25. I had my aunt make out a cheque, since I've nothing in a chequing account just now. Oh, yes—& the Weird Tales safely came. There was really no need to return them, but thanks just the same. Hope you'll land something there before long.

Too bad we didn't meet in N Y last week or the week before—I was there both before & after an unexpected trip to Philadelphia, & attended two meetings of the gang. Kirk says you called on him during my Philadelphian sojourn. All told, I had a great time; & was delighted with the reproduction of ancient High St. at the centennial—which latter is otherwise a frost. But the main pleasure was Old Philadelphia itself—my explorations extending through the town proper, Germantown, Fairmount Park, & the marvellously beautiful Wissahickon Valley. The country houses around Philadelphia are generally of stone, & represent the second phase of Middle-Colonies Georgian at its best. I ask for no finer colonial houses than Cliveden, the Chew seat at Germantown, (still in the Chew family) or Mt. Pleasant, in Fairmount Park above the Schuylkill. The latter was once inhabited by Benedict Arnold & his bride, & is now the property of the city. It has just been furnished & opened as a public museum, & I succeeded in getting in for the first time.

On my trip home I took the 'bus from N Y to Providence, & had a most glorious ride through rural Connecticut—undulant rock-ribbed meadows, vistas of hills beyond hills, & white ancient villages dreaming under their elms. I advise you to choose this way when you come—take a 'bus at 9 a.m. at the Hotel Woodstock—43d St. just east of Times Square. There was a stop of 40 minutes for lunch at New London, but I passed up the meal & spent the time exploring & card-buying. It's a great old town—quaint & colonial—& I must visit it some time when I can have leisure there. The enclosed cards give some idea of the local colour.

I suppose you're now getting settled in N.Y. Kirk says you mean to have a room in Greenwich Village—but I fear you'll find it devilish squalid after the novelty wears off. I'd advise you to settle around Morningside Heights, where things are a bit cleaner & more respectably American.

With regrets about the book, & good wishes generally,
        Yr obt Servt
            H P L

Notes

1. Latin for "Woe is me."
2. I.e., the Old Corner Bookshop of Herbert Douglass Dana (1888–1969) at 44 Weybosset Street, the bookstore that acquired HPL's books after his death. The bookstore had formerly been at 77 Empire Street.

[10]   [ALS, JHL]

                    10 Barnes St.,
                    Providence, R.I.,
                    Octr. 11, 1926.

Dear W B T:—
            Well—here is the desiderate title:

Nieuw Nederlandsch Biografisch Woordenboek
oner redactie van
DR. P. C. MOLHUYSEN EN PROF. DR. P. J. BLOK.

A. W. Sijthoff's Vitgevers—Maatschappij
LEIDEN
1911

It is a very delightful looking thing, though I fancy you will have to draw pretty hard on hereditary memory to puzzle out the contents. Evidently the modern Dutch take a proper pride in their old colonial venture—perhaps stimulated by the American Knickerbocker families who no doubt spend much research in Holland when perfecting genealogical data.

Thanks enormously for the cards—your high school is what I call a pronounced success, & I certainly hope it will outlast the decade you so modestly—or cynically—allot to it. It is truly an exceedingly good example of the third Georgian manner modified to suit current needs, & I trust that a reasonable proportion of its occupants may absorb some echo of its taste along with their formal curricula.

Glad you met the gang, & hope you'll manage to get around to most of the weekly assemblages now that you're in New York. Yes—I guess your catalogue about exhausts them, with the exception of Orton. They tell me that Orton doesn't get to many meetings nowadays, so that perhaps he can't be reckoned as a "regular" any more—but that's merely a question of nomenclature.

This present season I'm as busy as hell with some special revisory work which I've been doing for the well-known conjuror Houdini. I've done stuff for him before;[1] but last week he performed in Providence, & took the opportunity to have me go over a lot of stuff which required constant consultation. It was the raw material for a campaign against *astrology;* & being somewhat in my line, (I had a campaign of my own on this subject in 1914)[2] I rather enjoyed the digging up of data—though it was beastly laborious, & forced me to work continuously till night before last with very little sleep. If it doesn't knock out all the star-gazing charlatans in the country, I shall feel deeply disappointed! My next job for the sprightly wizard is an article on *witchcraft*—which makes me lament with redoubled intensity the lack of a peek at that Waite book in the Old Corner!

Had a letter in the Sunday Journal yesterday—on the ancient buildings of Providence.[3] Usually I think it's rather common to spread oneself promiscuously over the "Letters-to-the-Editor" page, but this time I had to get a great deal of accumulated matter off my chest. I didn't sign my full name—just initials—so that no one can accuse me of publicity-seeking under the guise of civic concern. I'll let you have a carbon of the thing—see how many of the old buildings you know! You might return this sometime—no hurry—since there are two or three more persons to whom I'd like to show it in the future. You must admit that Prov. is quite a town, when sophisticated Nieuw-Nederlanders have to apply to its learned institutions for source-material in their genealogical & archaeological researches!

Yr ob^t Servt

H P L

Notes

1. HPL had ghostwritten "Under the Pyramids" for Harry Houdini (born Ehrich Weiss, 1874–1926) at the request of *WT;* it was published as "Imprisoned with the Pharaohs." J. C. Henneberger, owner of *WT,* assumed HPL would write the story as if he were a collaborator; but because HPL wrote it in the first person, it was published as by Houdini alone. In the fall of 1926 HPL wrote an article attacking astrology (a partial ms. survives in private hands) and, with C. M. Eddy, Jr., began work on a treatise called *The Cancer of Superstition,* but the project came to a halt when Houdini died on 31 October.

2. HPL had written articles and satires (the latter under the pseudonym "Isaac Bickerstaffe, Jun.") attacking articles on astrology written by J. F. Hartmann and published in the [Providence] *Evening News* in late 1914.

3. "Asks Preservation of Old Buildings."

[11]   [ALS]

THE MOORLAND

BASS ROCKS GLOUCESTER / MASSACHUSETTS

10 Barnes St.,

Providence, R.I.,

Octr. 15, 1926

Dear W B T:—

Thanks for the junk shop suggestion—which I am strongly tempted to pursue despite the undeniable fact that I hardly know what I'd really do with a table desk in these congested quarters! If I found one as low as 2 bucks—at a time when I had that much in my pocket—I'm afraid I'd invest on the strength of undefined & improbable hopes of future expansion.

Your Steuben house is a mystery to me. With a date in the 1750's it can't very well be connected with the Revolutionary Baron Steuben—but yes! Of course, the date may refer to its erection rather than to the time of historic events associated with it. Steuben was not with the rebel army at the time of the fighting around New-York in 1776, but he may very possibly have occupied it toward the end of hostilities, when Genl. Washington's forces were marching north to their final headquarters at Newburgh. However, there's a large chance that another Steuben—one of the early German settlers—(for there were many in New-Jersey toward the end of the XVIIth century) is the one in question. Could the name possibly be *Dutch?* I trust that you may be able to shed more light on the matter as months pass.

As to Dutch doorways—the early houses had absolutely no artistic embellishment, though there was often a stoop with settles on each side, & a transom with small, square panes. The transom, by the way, is by some held to be originally a Dutch invention; English examples (& New England as well) having been derived from Holland sources. There were no side lights in the early New Netherland doorways, & the doors themselves were usually divided—though many plain ones were used. Of the panelling of the earliest divided doors I cannot speak with certainty, but I can say that their hinges were often of *leather* instead of metal, & that the upper half frequently contained (near the top) two round bull's-eyes of Greenwich glass (not transparent) to admit light to the hall within. One may assume that this bullseye arrangement occurred most frequently where transoms were wanting. You can find excellent examples of *later* divided doors—even more appropriate for your neo-Dutch cottage—at the Philipse Manor House in Yonkers, the Lefferts cottage in Flatbush, the Van Cortlandt house at the end of the west side subway, & the Dyckman cottage in upper Broadway. Each of these houses deserves a long & careful visit from any Dutch antiquary—especially the Van Cortlandt, which has a "Dutch Room" upstairs containing many

highly pertinent & interesting relics of New Amsterdam's early days. As for undivided doors—some were panelled like the English—with two small panels at the top & some latitude regarding lower panels—whilst some of the very earliest ones were unpanelled, with two full-length vertical braces, as shown in the accompanying design. This type corresponds in date with the earliest *nail-studded* doors of New England, though I have seen no evidence of the existence of the latter in New Netherlands.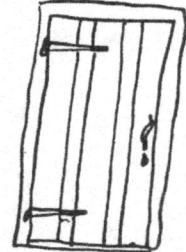

After the introduction of classic Georgian architecture into the New York region—early in the XVIIIth century—we find elaborate colonial doorways in most of the better Dutch houses, though the Dutch were very ingenious in devising appropriate modifications which brought the new designs into harmony with the old general architectural lines, & often removed them very far from the English originals. On the whole, the typical Dutch cottage of the New York neighbourhood, (as distinguished from more remote & usually simpler specimens in New Jersey & the Hudson River region) favoured by modern architects as a model for residences, is one of this adapted Georgian type; so that I would advise your use of it in your plan, rather than any of the earlier designs I have cited. The finest Georgian-Dutch doorway I have ever seen is that of the Lefferts cottage in Flatbush, now moved to a very advantageous site at the so-called "Willink" entrance to Prospect Park. You really *must* see this! Take the B.M.T. subway to the Prospect Park Station, or a Flatbush Ave. surface car at Brooklyn Bridge. One good first-hand study will give you more workable ideas than twenty pages of amateurish description. This house will also give you useful hints on the *panelling* of the later divided doors. I certainly advise you to go the rounds of the various Dutch houses. To reach the Dyckman, taken the West Side Subway to 207th St., walk west to Broadway, & then go south three blocks. The house & grounds surmount a high bank wall on the N W corner of B'way & 204th. The *Poe Cottage,* (East Side subway to Kingsbridge Rd. & walk east to Grand Concourse) though associated with a non-Dutch character, is really an excellent example of a very humble *late* Dutch colonial cottage. It is amply worth your inspection.

As for *lamps*—I really don't know of any well-defined type, though such were often hung beside doorways in colonial times. I doubt if they can be really considered part of the architectural design. As for *canopies*—as you know, the porch evolved from projecting eaves generally precludes any such device; though I fancy many individual cases can be found. These were common in English houses of the Middle Colonies, & mutual adaptations constantly went on. But I'd advise projecting eaves or porch, & no canopy. The curved eave line is certainly the more characteristic, & the more purely Dutch. As for types of English canopy which *might* be used—here are a couple—if you can make 'em out. You'll see many of these canopies in the Penn. region— *never* in New England.

To sum up: for a modern Dutch colonial cottage I'd advise a somewhat late type; with projecting eaves evolved into a full porch, but not so late as to have the porch roof detached from the gracefully curving eave line. I'd recommend a middle or later 18th century doorway with Georgian design modified to Dutch lines, & a divided door whose panelling can easily be determined by existing examples. (The Phillipse, Lefferts, Van Cortlandt &c houses are all carefully restored to their proper original state) For doorway in general, the Lefferts house absolutely can't be beat; & there's no excuse for your not going to see it!

I'm glad to hear that you have a convenient room in the general Columbia neighbourhood rather than squalid Greenwich. Kirk used to have a room in 106th St at the corner of Manhattan Ave. But you'll go a long way before getting anything as attractive in outlook as 256 Benefit![1] Where you are now, you can get over to see Belknap quite easily; & I trust you have made the Wednesday meetings a regular feature of your schedule. Let us hope that your work is not too arduous at the start. I, for my part, have been rushed to death lately with special revisory & research orders; & am only just now taking a breathing spell before tackling some new junk. Nevertheless, I may add to my burdens a Thursday night attendance at the astronomical lectures of Prof. Currier of your erstwhile alma mater, since I see he is offering a fine course in the Univ. Extension series, covering just the ground (ultra-modern discoveries in the stellar universe) I am most anxious to explore.[2] Well—so much for the present.

Yr obt hble Servt

H P L

P.S. I'm enclosing a Dutch colonial picture which may be of interest to you.

Notes

1. When attending Brown University, WBT boarded at 256 Benefit Street, the former residence of Lewis Howe Kalloch, HPL's dentist.

2. Clinton Harvey Currier (1876–1943), professor of mathematics and astronomy at Brown (1899–1936). He was director of Ladd Observatory (1921–31) and wrote a column on astronomy for the *Providence Journal.*

[12]   [ALS, JHL]

Sunday [23 October 1926]

Dear W B T:—

          I was very glad to see the completed "Black Bottles", & believe that you have made truly an excellent story out of it. The changes necessary in the latter half are, as you will see, very few; & need cause you no sense of deficient originality. The main point of alteration was the climax, where I couldn't quite visualise the scene as given. I had suggested silhouetting Vanderhoof against the moon at the top of a hill, but you (perhaps thinking this tritely melodramatic) chose the moonlit wall of the church. Now in reading this scene—the church & the corpse beheld in proximity by an observer at a distance—I cannot readily envisage a set of conditions allowing Vanderhoof to appear as a *black shadow.* Of course this is a quick impression at first glance, for the laws of optics could allow several arrangements making this possible. But what was my first impression may be that of others—that the moon in bathing the church wall ought to bathe Vanderhoof too—so I have altered the text in conformity with the idea. If I am wrong in so doing—if my impression is too obviously the result of my having formed an arbitrary imaginative picture in advance—pray eliminate the change & restore your text to its pristine form. Another thing I've done is to fuse together sentences which seemed excessively short. Probably you have developed this staccato tendency as a reaction against a former inclination toward long periodic sentences; but to my mind it is [a] weakening feature when carried to excess. Belknap follows it to far greater extremes than I wish he would.

          As to your hesitancy about following revisory suggestions—I can appreciate fully how you must feel in the case of anything intended purely as a piece of original & personal artistic expression, & will be careful not to make disconcerting alterations in later MSS. of yours. This one tale, however, as I said upon first seeing the synopsis last summer; [*sic*] may well be taken as a wholly academic proposition—a typical exercise & object lesson illustrating certain principles of composition which could not be conveniently demonstrated in any other way than this actual, visible, & concrete alteration of the outline & text as prepared. But even in this instance I don't think my share is enough to gain me notice as co-author, hence urge you to publish the tale under your name only. If accepted by *Weird Tales,* it will prove a good entering wedge for other work of yours.

So you didn't recognise many of the old buildings in my letter to the Journal? Bless me, but I'll have to show you Providence some time! The Arcade ought to be fairly plain to you, whilst you would have a great deal of trouble avoiding the Market House & the warehouses stretching south of it on the east or hill side of South Water St.—the only side at that particular point. The 1761 colony house is the 6th District Court in North Main St.— the brick building set back in a long yard—whilst the 1770 College Edifice is what you youngsters call "University Hall." I'll excuse you so far as the buildings in Gaol Lane (Meeting St.) are concerned, but must reprove you if you've overlooked the Golden Ball Inn (Benefit & S. Court Sts.—now called the Mansion House) which has housed Genl. Washington, Marquis de Lafayette, & other notables of the 18th century.

Since writing you last, I have been emulating your ancestral trips of last summer around the New-Netherland countryside, & have made what promises to be the first of many antiquarian tours to my own ancestral region of Moosup Valley, in the township of Foster, R.I. I had previously been there but twice in my life; in 1896, when I spent two weeks at the colonial farmhouse of my great-uncle James Phillips, & in 1908, when I took a very casual single day's jaunt with my mother; this infrequent visiting being due to difficulties of transportation only just solved by means of one o' them newfangled autymobile stage coach lines.

On this occasion—last Wednesday—I accompanied my younger aunt Mrs. Gamwell on quite a tour of hereditary soil; & picked up much family lore hitherto unknown to me. We started at 9 a.m. from the Eddy Street 'bus terminal over the ancient Plainfield Pike, noting in due time the historic Fenner farmhouse (1677)—homestead of one of Rhode-Island's greatest old families—& later on the region devastated to create the new Scituate reservoir. In less than an hour we reached the general section identified with our lineage, & were delighted with some of the Georgian doorways around Clayville. At length we disembarked at the quaint hilltop village oddly known as "Rice City",[1] & struck northward along a back road for Moosup Valley.

Here I was destined to be surprised by the beauty of the countryside. Having seen it only twice before—once thirty years ago & again eighteen years ago—I had never properly appreciated it; but now in my old age I was forcibly struck with its incomparably graceful lines of rolling hill & stone-walled meadow, distant vale & hanging woodland, curving roadway & nestling farmstead, & all along the route the crystal convolutions of the upper Moosup River, crossed here & there by some pleasing rustic bridge. At one bend in the stream I paused with proper pensiveness; for there in 1848 my great-grandfather Capt. Jeremiah Phillips met an untimely end in his own mill, (now demolished) being dragged into the machinery by the skirts of his voluminous frock coat as a malign wind blew them against some wheel or belt. Whenever we enquired the way we found that our names were well known to the inhabitants, & I doubt if any person we saw was not related to us in some more or less distant fashion—such being the universal consanguinity of an ancient pastoral community. Finally we beheld across the meadows at our left the distant roofs & white church belfry of Moosup Valley, & were soon descending to it past the idyllic farmhouse of Aunt Jerusha Foster—now used as the country-seat of a Providence man—one of the Nicholsons of the Nicholson File Co.

Crossing the rushing Moosup by another of those delicious bridges, we were soon in the pine-shaded village cemetery, where for some time the colonial slate slabs (none of 'em *crumbling*, damn the luck!) kept us busy. There were scores of our kindred there—Tylers, Howards, Fryes, Hopkinses, Rathbones, & Places—although our closest relatives all rest in private burying grounds near their respective homesteads. We now walked through the "civick centre" of the village, noting the church, schoolhouse, grange, & publick library—all of which are family 'property' through association. A distant relative—the Rev. George Kennedy—built the church & was its first pastor, whilst my grandmother's cousin, Casey B. Tyler,* (a local writer & historian) left his private library to the village to form the present Tyler Free Library—which has some 5000 volumes & is annually aided by the state. The village formerly contain'd a smithy, two stores, a slaughter-house, & a tannery; but commerce has declined with the years, & the omnipresent Ford has driven out all that could support a blacksmith. Beyond the "civick centre" we climbed the hill to the old Tyler house where my aunt Mrs. Clark was born, & here we were literally enchanted with the beauty of the landscape. Across the road a wooded valley dips magnificently to the lower meadows, while to the east & north are incredibly lovely vistas of stone-walled rolling pastures, clumps of forest, bits of stream, & purple ranges of hills beyond hills. The house itself, a large three-story structure, is of early 19th century origin; but beside it is the still intact colonial homestead of a story & a half which housed the Tylers before they built it. I told my aunt[2] when I got home that she had certainly chosen an ideal spot to be born in. From there we retraced our steps to the village, this time stopping to see our cousin Mrs. Nabby [Abigail] Tyler Kennedy,[3] whom Mrs. Clark asked us to look up, & who lives in the oldest homestead of all—the antient Judge Tyler† Tavern whose oldest parts date back to 1729, (according to some, 1728) when William Tyler made the region his family seat, & took up most of the land in sight. That land, called the "Tyler Purchase", was later divided amongst other colonial proprietors; & a surprisingly large part of it still remains in the hands of blood descendants. The region is the most truly American & colonial I have ever seen; for there seems to be no break or al-

---

*Town Clerk, Notary Public, & State Senator 1850–51
†The 'Squire Tyler of Revolutionary times was a magistrate, & in his day a business-like whipping-post stood in front of the house!

teration in the steady stream of hereditary habits & traditions which dates back to the times when Col. Thomas Parker married William Tyler's daughter & whipped the local raw recruits for the French & Indian Wars into shape on the training-field back of the old Tyler Tavern. Much of the Tavern, by the way, was blown down in the great gale of 1815; so that the house at which we stopped is really a composite, with its final form dating from 1816. The room in which we sat, however, was part of the original house; & had the immense floor-boards, exposed corner-posts, & panelled overmantel which told authentically of the early Georgian period. Our cousin, though only 72 years of age, is now the oldest inhabitant; & I was astonished at the amount of family lore she has preserved. She has much better genealogical records than ours, & will be a mine of information if ever I follow your example in establishing an extensive research. Her mother was my grandmother's closest confidante & associate, so that she knows as much about my particular branch as about her own. Among the pleasant things I learned from her was that we are connected with the great Newport house of Wanton—which gave Rhode Island three colonial governors & some spectacular privateersmen. The main branch—like me personally—was loyal to His Majesty's government, so emigrated to Halifax after the evacuation of Newport by the regulars in 1779. Joseph Wanton was at that time Governor of the Province, but the rebels deposed him & set up Nicholas Cooke in his stead. All in all, I was very glad to run across this rural family Sibyl, with whom my immediate kindred had been wholly out of touch since the 'seventies, when she attended a seminary with my elder aunt. She was, indeed, able to unlock the present as well as the past; being custodian by right of seniority & ancestral position of all the keys in the village. Kindly enough, she took us through the old church—where her husband's father had preach'd—the grange in which she is an active worker, & the Tyler Free Library, which her kinsman founded & of which her daughter (who now lives in my grand-uncle James Phillips' homestead where I visited in 1896) is the present librarian. The latter building is simple, but the collection is astonishingly good. I have a new respect for the taste of my bygone cousin, whose old desk occupies a place of honour at the end of the main room. The recent accessions are as well chosen as Casey Tyler's original private stock, & if the natives read many of them, they will be in no danger of retrograding to the yokel state.

Now leaving Moosup Valley, we climbed another hill past "Aunt 'Rushy's" [Jerusha Foster's] homestead & enter'd the especial territory of the Places—encountering on our right the well-beloved homestead whose picture you may have noticed on my wall. I had seen this twice before—in 1896 & 1908—but had really never given it the appreciation it deserves. Now, in my latter years, I can accord greater credit to the bygone Stephen Place who built it; for truly, I never saw a house so intelligently adjusted to make the most of all the aesthetic features of the landscape. In front, across the road, one sees on the right the ascent of rocky meadow extending to the James Phillips house & later to the Job Place estate atop the hill; this slope balanced by a breathlessly lovely valley panorama on the left, in which the stone-walled meadows descend in terraces to the gleaming bends of the river, whilst the white village belfry peeps alluringly through embowering verdure (now turned to the riotous red & gold of autumn) & sets off the endless undulations of purple hills beyond. Behind the house & its attendant orchard a sparsely wooded ravine winds gently down to lower pastures, & forms a background worthy of any artist's brush. Altogether, I was prodigiously imprest with the beauty of the whole picture; & wished ardently that I might buy back the place, which pass'd from the family some half-century ago. The house, in which my own mother & her mother before her were born, is of the prettiest New England farm type; & dates from a late colonial period when the larger homestead on the same site was burned down. It is now tenanted by the parvenu newcomers who took it fifty years ago, (anyone around Moosup Valley is a stranger & newcomer unless his family has a good two centuries of settlement there!) & has quite sadly deteriorated since our forbears had it. I can even see a marked falling off since 1908, when I was last there. We paused at length in the family burying-ground, separated by a bank wall & iron gate from the roadside, & admir'd several comely skulls & cheerful cherubs—to say nothing of urns, fountains, & weeping willows—on the many slabs of slate & marble. Nothing, unfortunately, was chipped or crumbled; though I was strongly tempted by an entire slab of the 1840 period, remov'd from the grave of Stephen Place Jr. in 1903, when a Western relative erected a finer stone, & now lying against the wall at the rear of the enclosure. Epitaphs were abundant, but I found nothing really quaint or grotesque. The rural academies trained the taste of the local 'squires all too well in those days, so that they did not blossom forth with the engaging illiteracy found in other parts of New England. Time has not been kind to the ancient slate, & moss has played its obscuring part; so that the earliest epitaph I could read was that of my great-great-grandfather, Stephen Place, (there were endless Stephens!) who died in 1817. His stone (willow weeping over an urn at top) reads thus:

> "The dust must to the dust return,
> And dearest friends must part & mourn;
> The gospel faith alone can give
> A cheering hope, the dead shall live."

Inane, but hardly *quaint* in the truest sense. His wife Martha, who died in 1822, revels in equal inanity:

> "Hail, sweet repose, now shall I rest,
> No more with sickness be distress'd;
> Here from all sorrows find release—
> My soul shall dwell in endless peace."

We now proceeded to the old James Phillips place, scene of my 1896 visit, & here again I was astonisht by the beauty of the landscape. The ancient house nestles against a side hill whose picturesque rocks & greenery almost overhang the north gable end, while across the road is a delicious combination of hill & vale—hill to the left, with the Job Place estate & its burying ground at the top, & to the right the exquisite "lower meadow" with its musical winding brook. The only flaw in the picture is an ethnic one—for FINNS, God damn them, have bought the old Job Place house! This Finnish plague has afflicted Northern Foster for a decade, but has hardly secured a real foothold in Moosup Valley, only two families marring the otherwise solid colonialism. But it does make me crawl to see these accursed peasants in the house where my great-uncle's wife was born—and tramping about an ancient Place graveyard! Well—after this I fancy people will be careful about how they dispose of their real estate! Entering the James Phillips house—which has not altered since 1896—we were welcomed by its present inhabitants—a distant kinsman named Bennis, & his wife, daughter of Nabby Tyler Kennedy & librarian of the Tyler Free Library. News of our presence in the region had travelled ahead of us; & I was greeted with two bygone letters of my mother's, which Mrs. Bennis had found among Uncle James' old papers in the attic! This rustic "grapevine telegraph" (or rather, Bell Telephone) is really quite amusing—for we were heralded in advance wherever we went. Even our first chance inquiry at Moosup Valley caused us to be overtaken at the Tyler Tavern by an honest housewife bearing a newspaper cutting of my grandfather's obituary, which the village thought might be of interest! At Uncle James' place I continued some observations on the feline part of the population which I had begun in Moosup Valley, & decided that the prevalence of tailless Manx cats was mark'd enough to constitute a distinct local feature. Evidently the breed secured a strong foothold at an early date, diffusing its blood throughout the continuously settled region adjacent, but stopping when the distances became extreme. These uncaudal creatures are lively & graceful, & one soon forgets the handicap imposed upon them by Nature—a handicap, indeed, which we poor bipeds are not ashamed to share! The house pleased me as much as it did in 1896, & I envied afresh the wealth of colonial furniture. I was allowed to revisit the corner room where I slept thirty years ago, & where I used to see the green side-hill through the archaic small-paned windows as I awoke in the dewy dawn. Certainly, I was drawn back to ancestral sources more vividly than at any other time I can recall; & have since thought about little else!

Later in the afternoon Mr. Bennis took us in his car to another scene of our family history—the village of Greene, across the taown line in Coventry; where my grandfather established himself & his enterprises in early manhood, & where his last two children (including Mrs. Gamwell) were born. He found the place a tiny crossroads hamlet called Coffin's Corner, but at once proceeded to build a mill, a house, an assembly hall, & several cottages for employees—

finally renaming the village after Rhode Island's foremost Revolutionary character. All his edifices are still standing, though some of them are diverted from their original uses. The house—a capacious Victorian affair of 16 rooms—remains in the hands of those distant kinsfolk (the Tillinghasts, descendants of old Pardon Tillinghast, who founded the Providence sea-trade in 1681 & whose old private burying ground is at Benefit & Transit Sts.) to whom it passed when my grandfather came to Providence for good in the 'seventies, whilst the mill is broken up into shops & tenements. The hall retains its pristine impressiveness; its lofty rooms forming the present home of Ionic Lodge, the Masonic branch founded by my grandfather, & of which he was the first Grand Master. It did me good to see his picture there, enshrined in proper state. All the population speak of him with affection, & I was especially pleased to talk with those who knew him in person—the old folks like 'Squire Wood & Col. Brown, & the ancient cracker-box senate in the general store, many of whose bearded or stubbly patriarchs worked for him some sixty years gone. One old boy named George Scott shed actual tears of sentimental reminiscence at being confronted with Whipple Phillips' darter & gran'son!

Well, by that time it was night, and we had to take the 6:12 stagecoach home. We had had a great day, but even so had hardly scratched the surface of what we wanted to see. The territory covered was more Place & Tyler than Phillips country, & a first sight of the ancient Phillips homestead (the Asaph Phillips place—1750) & burying ground at Mt. Vernon (near the Plainfield Pike) still lies ahead of me. I hope to take it in before winter—but if I don't, I shall have something to live till next summer for. Anyway, I've caught your mania about the personal as distinguished from the general atmospheric or historic past; & there's no telling into what labyrinths of research or rhapsodies of sentimental anecdotage it may lead me. Already I am acquiring a distinctly rural accent!

Yr obt Servt
HPL

Notes

1. The Rice City Historic District in Coventry, RI, encompasses the 19th-century village of Rice City, extending several miles along Plainfield Pike between Sisson Road and Gibson Hill Road in the northwestern part of Coventry.
2. I.e., Lillian D. Clark (b. 1866). She and her brother Edwin E. (b. 1864) were both born in Greene, RI.
3. Note the character Nabby (Abigail) Gardner in "The Colour out of Space," written about five months after this letter.

[13]   [ALS, JHL]

10 Barnes St.

Providence, R.I.

Octr. 31, 1926

Dear W B T:—

    I see that I must appropriately take my pen in hand on a double Sabbath—the regulation hebdomadal article, & that *Witches' Sabbath* which survives in commonplace folklore as "Hallowe'en". Hellish things were done this night—if you don't believe it, read "The Witch Cult in Western Europe", by Margaret Alice Murray, which you can find at the N.Y. Public Library.

    I was greatly interested to hear different reactions to your Black Bottles. As for sentences—yours *used* to be too long, as I think I mentioned last spring; but have recently become what I call too short—doubtless through reaction. It is possible that a few remained in 2 B.B. which some carping moderns might criticise on the ground of length, but I'm sure I didn't notice any. The only things which tripped up my ear were the short ones, whose effect was to me a somewhat noticeable intellectual staccato. I still think unreservedly that these tabloid affairs ought to be joined up as in my version.

    The Columbia dame's remarks on motivation are very good. I think I suggested in my original outline that Foster returned to Daalbergen because of his desire to study certain forbidden works which he recalled seeing there two centuries before—& the need for which had doubtless become apparent as his slow peasant mind advanced little by little through the boundless fields old Dominie Slott had opened up to him. No doubt those works suggested the augmenting of his soul by the absorption of another's—& when seeking a soul, whose could be more convenient than that of the pastor Vanderhoof with whom his presence at the church threw him into closest contact? That was the way I looked at it; & if that is strongly emphasised, I don't fancy many readers will bother to analyse further. As for Foster's mean & servile spirit— well, blood is thicker than magic, & a born peasant is a born peasant. The narrator's need for seeing the thing through, as suggested in my preliminary synopsis, was his relationship to Vanderhoof & his natural insistence that his uncle's soul be set at liberty. Perhaps you could emphasise this more—if the narrator is at all naive or pious, the matter of this spiritual restoration will be of utmost importance to him, & justifying the most extreme hazards . . . until the actual events of the night, the disintegration of Foster & the impending emergence of the corpse itself from the grave, set up a supreme fright which effaces everything else from his tried & wrenched consciousness. I thought I made this change in attitude especially prominent in the outline.

    As for Loveman's criticism—I don't know how you could work much local colour in without transforming it to a genre study & losing the concentrated essence of fright, but you might add a few characteristic landscape & character touches. As to the matter of "punch"—that will all come with *at-*

mospheric development. At present you're laying more stress on *plot* than on those intangible subtleties of mood and colouring which come from studied choice (really, a *poetic* choice) of cadenced words & phrases, & from a minute selective attention to the thousand-&-one almost invisible details which add up collectively into a living background. This primary attention to plot is probably a wise choice on your part, because to the weird writer plot is so much more difficult to achieve than atmosphere. I, for instance, have an absolute minimum of plot in the formal, academic sense, & depend almost entirely upon atmosphere. But in the end, atmosphere repays cultivation; because it is the final criterion of convincingness or unconvincingness in any tale whose major appeal is to the imagination.

Yes, if I were you I'd try 2 B B on *Ghost Stories* first, though they specialise in tales of much lower grade—psychologically infantile spectre yarns without the least subtlety or intellectual content, & coloured with the cheapest contemporary sensationalism. The whole atmosphere of the Macfadden enterprises is ineffably tawdry & plebeian. But there's no harm in trying, & their rate of 2¢ per word certainly doubles the best pay *Weird Tales* has ever offered. They've rejected three things of mine, & I'm in doubt about sending them my latest.[1] Better get a copy—or let Belknap lend you his—& see what the damn thing's like.

I read over the synopsis of "Teeth" with the keenest interest, & note what you say of it in your letter. As to the alleged improbability of a murder suspicion on the strength of the charred teeth—I don't quite see it. Foul play would certainly be the first & most natural thought; for ordinary people—especially if poor & unable to get new teeth—don't carelessly toss their false teeth into the fire, or cough so violently & appositely that their plates jes' nachelly hit the flames accidental-like! All these things *might be*, indeed, but they wouldn't be the first explanations to occur to a speculative group around the stove of a country store. Suspicion of murder would easily be the first thought—& if you don't want to precipitate an arrest, let the trip to the shanty be one purely of *investigation*. The arrest could quickly follow when the disappearance of Red becomes known, (he could fail to show up for a job which some prison welfare worker had provided for him) & when the authorities recall that they had quarrelled—or that Langdon feared Red. The fact that Red was obviously last seen by Langdon would possibly be enough to warrant arrest & (in connexion with the teeth as evidence & the fear or enmity as motive) indictment. But as a matter of fact, I don't believe many readers would question an immediate arrest on the strength of the teeth.

I'd be more inclined to marvel about the coincidence of the dentist's presence in that out-of-the-way village store at exactly the time the teeth are produced. Could you devise some sort of possible linkage to explain this? It would be hard, unless the thread of connexion (through Sing-Sing) of *Langdon* & the dentist could somehow be twisted into plausibility. What else could bring a distant prison dentist to the Ramapaugh [that's the way Genl. Washington spell'd it in a letter of 1780 to Gov. Greene of R.I., & I stick by it!] region at just the right time? And if he were a native of that place, *that* would be a coincidence! I'm too old to rack my tired brain about sech-like things—but anyhow, you could dodge the issue by boldly introducing the tale with a sententious paragraph on the power of coincidence. As a whole, the tale sounds great—& the climax is marvellously effective!

I am glad you found the biographical dictionary title of value, & that it has added to the antiquity of an already ancient name. You surely must go to Holland some time; for you would not only revel in the vital statistics, but be regaled with the sight of many quaint towns (such as Vollendam) which preserve their archaic appearance & recall with perfect fidelity the old New-Amsterdam of 1660 with its canal & windmills & stepped gables. I am sure that your genealogical cessation will be more of a recess than a permanent abandonment—for after qualifying yourself so thoroughly as an expert, it would be a pity to let your accomplishment slide. You will never have any rivalry from me, no matter how enthusiastic I become through occasional rural trips. When I read of your two-page bibliography, & compare it with my constitutional indolence, I heave a sigh of resignation & admiration only! What I shall ever add to my data will be in large slices dug up & correlated by more diligent workers than I!

Speaking of work—I see that Houdini still survives, though with a very slim chance of recovery.[2] It would really be a pity for him to be cut off at this time; for he is an enormously good-hearted chap, & has that keen enjoyment of life which only the naive & crude can retain. Just before his seizure he was trying to get me to confer with him in Detroit—though I was declining except in case of urgent necessity. It would be a good arrangement if I could see to all his writings on a regular basis, though I'd hate to be on the jump from town to town—or in N.Y. much—as he might require. He was recently urging me to arrange for a month of intensive revision of scattered data in N.Y. next summer. Whatever I do regularly, by god, will be done in Providence, R.I.!

That Steuben house sounds interesting—certainly, a 2-story house of the curved-roof Dutch variety is very extraordinary. In giving my files a very exhaustive classification lately I came across an account of the oldest house in N.Y.—the Schenck house in or near Jamaica Bay, built in 1656 by a Dutch privateer from the timbers of his ship. I had vainly tried to find this cutting throughout my sojourn in N.Y., & was unable to find the place through lack of directions—no one in the metropolis being able to tell me anything definite about it. Now that I have it classified I shall consult it if ever I take another N.Y. trip, & shall certainly visit it in that event. If you are sufficiently interested to make the pilgrimage yourself, I'll copy the printed directions for you; though I suppose there is danger that the house is no longer standing. The article is from a N.Y. Times of 1923. Don't miss the American Wing—that's the first thing I made for during my visit of last month—& don't fail to look over the Lefferts, Dyckman, & Van Cortlandt houses before embarking on your genealogical vacation. You deserve that amount of illustrative colour to enliven your laborious statistical excavations! I hadn't heard of that exhibition of old N.Y. life, but am hang'd if it doesn't sound interesting!

Your Masefield[3] session must have been interesting, & I hope John comes across with an autographed copy of his complete works—reciprocity, & all that. At least he'll probably write you—he did Belknap when the kid sent him a copy of "The Man from Genoa". I trust he will profit by the genealogical information you furnished. The papers spoke of his presence in N.Y., & of his visit to the site of the old saloon in Greenwich Village where he once worked. I had had a bookshop in Christopher St. near 6th Ave. pointed out to me as this place, but according to the recent item, it was in 6th Ave. itself. Possibly he worked in more than one during his days of adversity. Anyhow, the region is as geographically interesting as any in N Y—with quaint Milligan & Patchin Places & Gay St. within a stone's throw.

Glad you're enjoying the gang. Have you met your fellow-Dutchman Orton yet? He writes that he'll probably be attending meetings during the winter. When you see him he'll no doubt explain the precise affiliations of his middle name *Teachout,* which you say you can't identify as Dutch, though I'll swear I saw it in some book or record of ancient Harlem. He has just moved, & tells me that he has fitted up his apartment in colonial style.

Yes—I did take vast satisfaction in my ancestral trip last week, & hope to work in another soon. I may use the region in some tale, & will see how diabolical an interpretation I can put upon the mishap of my worthy frock-coated progenitor. The trouble is, that Capt. Jeremiah wasn't at all an old man when it happened. He was cut off in the prime—or even before—of life; & the swiftly ensuing death of his wife[4] from the shock & grief left my grandfather & his brother & sisters orphans at an early age, to be brought up by their Aunt Nabby Howard—from whom, by the way, (so close is the consanguinity of all Foster gentry) was named that still living Nabby Tyler Kennedy whose closest cousinship to my line comes on an entirely *different* side—the Place side. But enough of agrestic reminiscence! Your breakfast musn't get cold again.

Too bad you can't get to Providence this fall, for the Georgian steeples & colonial doorways are exquisite against an autumn background. Good luck in the re-collection of your baubles. Did I mention that honest old Smith of the Tryout has moved back to his old home in Haverhill?[5] He's so happy he hardly knows what to do, & he's going to resume his quaint little publication again. All these homecomings are of interest to me after my own of last April!

Well—I won't pile up your epistolary obligations any more heavily. There isn't much of interest in what a mild, prosaic old man has to say, anyhow. I'll duly convey your regards to their several destinations, & meanwhile forward you the standing regards always proceeding from the same sources. Which done, I'll leave you for the nonce to the subtleties & complexities of fictional composition. Don't fail to shew me what you make of "Teeth"!

Yr obt hble Servt

HPL

Notes

1. *Ghost Stories* was published by Constructive Publishing Co. (Bernarr MacFadden) from July 1926 to March 1930; by Good Story Magazine Co. from April 1930 to December 1931/January 1932. It was a companion magazine to *True Story* and *True Detective Stories,* and its stories followed a confessional format. HPL submitted "In the Vault," "Cool Air," and probably "The Nameless City" to the magazine. "Pickman's Model," written c. September 1926, had a "somewhat colloquial" tone not previously found in HPL's fiction, and may have been written with *Ghost Stories* in mind. It does not appear that HPL ever submitted the story there.

2. Houdini in fact died the day this letter was written.

3. John Masefield (1878–1967), British poet and writer, Poet Laureate of England from 1930 until his death. Long had also sent a copy of his book to Thomas Hardy.

4. Actually Roby (Rathbun) Phillips died in July 1848; her husband was killed in his mill in November 1848.

5. In 1922, Charles W. Smith had suffered an attack of nervous prostration and under doctor's orders was convalescing in Plaistow, NH. He remained in Plaistow until 1926, when he returned to Haverhill, MA.

[14] [ALS JHL]

Wednesday

[26 November 1926]

Dear W B T:—

Well, well! The dear old neighbourhood at Red Hook is certainly winning fame! I am certain that my story must have started this investigation. Someone else sent me a cutting from the Tribune on this theme, but it was not nearly so ample as the extracts you so kindly enclosed. The old Hook is surely a picturesque & colourful backwater, &I feel a faintly reflected glory in having once sojourned within its bounds. 'Tis distance &c.[1] One paragraph caught my eye—"The region nearest Borough Hall is a centre of burglaries". I'll tell the flat-roofed world it is![2] Witness—3 suits, 1 overcoat, 1 blanket, 1 suit case, 1 stored radio set! I think I told you of that classic break from the next room in May 1925.

Anent the Peter Randall[3] house—I am happy to have later news to offer. Sure, whilst I was a-talkin' & a-moanin' & a-keenin' over the coming loss, wasn't Mayor Jimmy Dunne[4] a-doin' something on the quiet—writin' to the White Motor Co. of Cleveland, whose garage was to displace the storied gambrel-roofer, & suggesting that they sell the house to the city for removal & preservation. Well, Sir, I takes off me hat to Cleveland—for what does

Walt White of the motor people do, but go Jimmy one better and **give** the old house to our progressive municipality! It will be moved to city land near the North Burial Ground, standing eternally as a memorial to the manners of our fathers. It nearly broke my aged heart before I learned of this salvation, but time & relief are now healing the wound. Incidentally, some changes are occurring in your old neighbourhood. The wooden colonial house half way up Hopkins St. has vanished, [tears] but behind the brick Joseph Brown house (old Prov. Natl. Bank—with ornate roof) has been built an extension reaching up the hill in fine Georgian style.[5] And the old Stephen Hopkins house is to be moved up to the S W corner of Hopkins & Benefit, displacing (alas) the colonial house on the corner, & the small store adjacent thereto.[6] The section will still remain colonial, but there will be a net loss of two ancient houses. And of course the court house will displace the old Brown and Ives counting-house at South Main & Hopkins St. Speaking of S. Main—if you want a fine coloured art view of the most picturesque part of the street, send for the 1927 calendar of the Title Guarantee Co. of Rhode Island, 66 S. Main St. I am greatly interested in the exploits & affiliations of the Mr. McDonough mentioned in your cutting. It is always a pleasure to see new fame and honours overtake a former fellow-citizen!

Shall be glad to hear from you amidst the new leisure which is to be yours. Don't venture into Red Hook & get murdered!

Yr obt Servt

H P L

P.S. My aunt Mrs. Gamwell is catching my Colonialism. She is taking a room at the Handicraft Club—in the old brick Truman Beckwith house with its terraced yard & colourful courtyard at College & Benefit Sts.[7]

Notes

1. HPL alludes to the line "'Tis distance lends enchantment to the view." Thomas Campbell (1777–1844), *The Pleasures of Hope* (1799), Part 1, l. 7.

2. A variation on the phrase "I'll tell the cockeyed world," going back to wartime slang of 1917–18.

3. Years later, HPL named one of the cats in the "Kappa Alpha Tau fraternity" in the neighborhood of 66 College Street for this historic figure.

4. James Edward Dunne (1882–1942) was mayor of Providence for twelve years (six two-year terms), from January 1927 to January 1939.

5. The Joseph Brown House (1774; Joseph Brown architect), 50 South Main Street. John and Moses Brown founded the Providence Bank at this location in 1791, which remained the bank's headquarters until construction of a new bank at 100 Westminster Street (1929).

6. The Stephen Hopkins House (1743; original cottage built 1707 by John Field), 15 Hopkins Street, Providence. In the late 1920s the house was carefully restored by

Norman M. Isham. It formerly stood at the foot of Hopkins Street on South Main Street and was moved halfway up the hill in 1804.

7. The Handicraft Club at 42 College Street was founded in 1904 by Julia Lippitt Mauran, Mary Parsons, and eight other women. They promoted interest in all kinds of handicrafts and provided a place where such work could be done.

[15]   [AHT]

> 10 Barnes St.,
> Providence, R.I.
> Dec. 19, 1926

Dear W B T:—

[. . .]

As for my novel—you'll be disappointed to hear that weirdness is the thing of which it ain't got nothin' else but! It is a picaresque chronicle of impossible adventures in dreamland, & is composed under no illusion of professional acceptance.[1] There is certainly nothing of popular or best-seller psychology in it—although, in consonance with the mood in which it was conceived, it contains more of the naive fairy-tale wonder-spirit than of actual Baudelairian decadence. Actually, it isn't much good; but forms useful practice for later & more authentic attempts in the novel form.

About the American Wing[2]—the absence of a Dutch department is certainly a serious defect, & one which I am sure will be remedied eventually. As a whole, it impressed me less on my visit last September than it did two years ago when it was first opened—for in those early days, of course, I was living away from home & desperately homesick for anything even remotely suggesting ancestral New England. However—it is really very good in spite of its obvious deficiencies; & shows better than any other exhibit I know the gradual transition from mediaeval to Renaissance decoration, & the later transition to the purely classic ornament & design of the Adam period. The room from Woodbury, L.I. is *not supposed* to be Dutch—but represents an English colonial house with Dutch influence, such as you can find anywhere in the regions east of Hempstead.[3] The only really Dutch article in the room is the painted *kas.* I also enjoyed the 17th century floor with its Hingham trusswork. Hingham, with its "Old Ordinary" & "Old Ship Church" is a place I have long meant to visit. So far I've never seen it, but I expect to get there next summer.

[. . .]

With cordial regards from my wife[4] & myself, I remain

> Most sincerely yrs.
> H P L

Notes

1. *The Dream-Quest of Unknown Kadath* (completed 22 January 1927).

2. Of the Metropolitan Museum in New York.

3. The Hewlett room (1740–60) from Woodbury, Long Island at the American Wing of the Metropolitan Museum of Art.

4. Sonia Lovecraft was visiting at the time. She and HPL never lived together after April 1926 (aside from a few weeks in the spring of 1928). Although they filed for divorce in 1929, HPL did not sign the final decree and so technically they were married until his death.

[16]   [ALS, JHL]

Friday [7? January 1927]

Mynheer:[1]—

    Your story is very good, & really ought to take very well with some contemporary magazine. I can't think of a specific thing to say in criticism, unless to suggest that the effect of a climax be secured with a little more decidedness. Just how to do this I'm sure I don't know—though I suppose one might devise circuitous means. You could have the book at the library (how well I know that room—good old 328[2]—where you have to sign the register! That's where I spent all my N.Y. evenings reading about Old Providence!) not only confirm your hero's worst fears, but indicate also that he is himself a descendant of this Antony Van Salee—unspeakable & murderous corsair, & natural son of an elder Antony by some Arab's or Turk's daughter. *Then,* after his shock, you could have a stranger also looking in the Vans—a noted genealogist—observe his perturbation & ask him if he is a Van Salee. It could then develop that the stranger is the author of the genealogical book, & that he had made a mistake in his data; the real ancestor of the Van Salees being another Antony born in Holland before the original wander[er] ran off on his Barbary buccaneerings.[3] At the same time—if you wish to get your hero reconciled to non-Nordics—the stranger could inform Van Horn of some noble French or Italian ancestor—but quickly, so that the climax need not be weakened by subsequent long paragraphs. Of course, this is only random conjecture—the tale is undoubtedly all right as it is. You have a splendid air of naturalness all through it, with a quite professional handling of dialogue & situation.

    This was quite a story day for me—for in the selfsame mail came a 32-page horror from Belknap; a magnificent orgy of damp, tentacled, nameless monstrosity! Has he read it to you? I hope Weird Tales will take it.[4]

    Trust you aren't overworking—or overplaying—these days, & that you get around to the gang meetings occasionally. How is the kitten at Kirk's growing up?

    Good wishes from Prov. & all the family—

      Yr obt Servt

        H P L

Notes

1. A male Netherlander—used as a title equivalent to Mister.
2. Room 328 at the New York Public Library at the time was the genealogical reading room.
3. Anthony Janszoon van Salee (1607–1676) was an original settler of and prominent landholder, merchant, and creditor in New Netherlands, believed to be the son of Jan Janszoon (Jansen), a Dutch pirate who after 1619 served a Moorish state on the Barbary Coast.
4. "The Man with a Thousand Legs" (*WT*, August 1927).

[17] [ALS, JHL]

Saturday [29 January 1927]

Mynheer:—

Glad to hear of the success of the Black Bottles, & wish the same to its successor. Some day we'll have to have all the gang represented in Weird Tales—those so far on the list being Belknap, Leeds, (whom we still ought to call a member) yourself, & yr ob^t hble Servt. Mortonius almost qualifies, though, for verses of his have been printed in the Eyrie. Honest old Mac has written weird stuff—& by no means bad, either—but none of it has graced our Chicago contemporary as yet.

No—I hadn't given up hope on the Schenck homestead cutting. Hope you find the place—I shall surely look it up the next time I am in the N Y region. I tried to find that article at odd times throughout my metropolitan sojourn, but did not succeed till after my return home—although it was with me, tucked away in a chaos of other papers, all the time! Let me know what the old place looks like—if it still remains—when you visit it.

Your "wake" sounds very interesting, & reminds me of almost parallel phenomena during my own days within the gang's tangible radius. Have you & Kirk taken any of those all-night sightseeing walks which used to be such a standby of his & mine? It was pretty interesting to explore obscure corners in the small hours, & watch the dawn come up pale over the East River toward the end. And then I'll never forget the sight of the newly-risen sun streaming in a glorious flood of molten gold up the length of Wall St. into still darkened Broadway one morning. It was as if all the past—the brilliant past of Dutch settlers & glamorous shipping & gay coffee-houses—were shining from a land outside time, & welling up from the sea into the dismal & shadowy present.

I note that you've now met Orton, & hope that you've settled the question of just how his middle name—Teachout—fits into the scheme of Nieuw-Nederland nomenclature. Yes—I've seen Spriggs—but I've also seen some gems which are worthy of competitive mention. Ask Morton to show you "The Bride of Gettysburg",[1] "Selected Gems" (& believe me, they *are!*)

by P. J. Pendergast, & whatever he has of the poetical works of the Reverend David V. Bush—especially "Suppose" and "Duelling".[2] Also ask Belknap to let you see the immortal achievements of J: Howard Flower of Vermont, author of "With Shelley in My Soul".[3]

I've just finished a 110-page thing which I guess is more of a novelette than a novel, & am working on what might be called a *genealogical* horror-tale.[4] But it won't interest you, because it isn't Dutch. It is, on the other hand, highly Rhodinsular; & gives its venerable author many excuses for introducing passages of Old Providence local colour. This reminds me that I heard a great lecture last week by the architectural authority Norman M. Isham—"Early Rhode-Island Houses".[5] He dwelt mostly on Newport specimens, but fortunately my intensive explorations of last summer made me able to appreciate his remarks in full.

Well—good luck, & don't let the banquets "get" you. The quantities they used to serve at "Jake's" ought to have hardened your digestive processes enough to rob the purely physiological part of these feasts of their terrors![6]

With greetings for all the gang, & hoping you'll get around for a visit to Gawd's Country before long, I have the honour to subscribe myself

Yr most obt hble Servt

H P L

Notes

1. By J. Dunbar Hylton (1937–1893).

2. See David Van Bush's *Peace Poems and Sausages:* "Suppose" (141–42) and "War and Dueliing—Mr. Muling" (42). Bush was prolific author of inspirational verse and popular psychology books, many of which HPL revised.

3. J[ames] Howard Flower (1883–1967), a Vermont poet, author of *Flower of the Road* (1919) and *Bobolinks at Dawn and Whippoorwills at Dusk* (1923). His poem (or book) has not been found. All persons cited here were HPL's revision clients.

4. *The Dream-Quest of Unknown Kadath* and *The Case of Charles Dexter Ward.*

5. Norman M[orrison] Isham (1864–1943), prominent architectural historian, author, and professor at Brown University and the Rhode Island School of Design, an ardent preservationist and a pioneer in the study of early American architecture. HPL owned his *The Meeting House of the First Baptist Church in Providence: A History of the Fabric* (1925).

6. See HPL to Maurice W. Moe [24 March 1935], in which he describes Jakes as "the famous stevedore restaurant at the foot of the hill which Wilfred B. Talman (then a Brown student) discover'd in 1926 and introduced to the gang. Here have gorg'd such dignitaries as W. Paul Cook, James Ferdinand Morton, Donald Wandrei . . . and now Robert Ellis Moe. This is the joint where good food is serv'd in such fabulous quantities." *Letters to Maurice W. Moe and Others* 379.

[18]   [ANS][1]

[Postmarked Providence, R.I.,
9 February 1927]

Congratulations! I thought that Alabad & Co.[2] would land! Pay is very decent, too, as such things go. Keep it up! And the more trouble you make for that " "—(the quotes are the *only* important part of his title!) the better I'll like it! If you can possibly induce him to resign, you will deserve well of the weird reading public. ¶ Went up to Ladd Observatory[3] last night for the first time in 20 years. It certainly brought back the old days! I saw the telescope used by Joseph Brown of Providence in 1769.
Yr obt H P L

Belknap tells me that you & he have taken to attending seances!

Notes

1. *Front:* Roger Williams. Copies of Engraving, Engraved by F. Halpin, from an Original Painting, for "Benedict's History of the Baptists."
2. WBT's "The Curse of Alabad and Ghinu and Aratza."
3. Brown University's observatory, on Doyle Avenue in Providence. HPL was allowed access to it as early as 1903.

[19]   [ALS, JHL]

April 29[, 1927]

Dear W B T:—

I trust that by this time your fit of ennui has passed off, & that you now have no difficulty in disposing of your leisure. Boredom is a terrible thing—but why didn't you start hunting for some of the antiquities which I've described to you from time to time? The Dyckman, Lefferts, & Van Cortlandt houses still await your critical gaze, whilst there is yet before you the alluring adventure of discovering the old Schenck house—built from privateer timbers—which that Times cutting described. I didn't begin to get bored with New York till I had exhausted all its historic reliques. Glad you are not neglecting nice old Mac—he complained last month that nobody but Belknap had been to see him in his new quarters.

"Chetwode Arms" has not yet arrived, but I am alertly on the lookout for it. You have my sympathy regarding the typing. Gawd! My vertebrae still throb from the 32-page job of last month which gave "The Colour Out of Space" to a trembling world. And I still have two novelettes of respectively 110 & 147 pages, long-hand—which will probably never earn the distinction of Remingtonian minuscules.[1]

Glad you had a good meeting last Wednesday, & that you have finally decided on a means of saving our declining civilisation. I agree thoroughly—

& fancy Belknap would have done so had he been present—& would now suggest a ways & means committee for inaugurating the counter-revolution & establishing the reign of an American Fascism. I'm surprised that young Lazare[2] agreed—for in the old times he took the stand of a fils du peuple, & shouted for socialism in his boyish, ingenuous way. We live & learn—if we are able. I'd certainly like to meet this Munn, & hope he'll drop around Providence way some time. I respect his exotic erudition very highly, & have thought his work in *Weird Tales* very promising. Yes—our gang surely has been well represented among those present, although Wright's increasing disinclination to accept my stuff may prevent us from actually acquiring a corner. I don't recall having read anything by Manley [*sic*] Wellman[3] in W.T.—a circumstance which might or might not irritate his egotism were he aware of it. Incidentally, I shall welcome the printing of those pieces of yours—both prose & verse—which Wright has accepted. Your verse for Kirk's shop starts out well—but is Kirk still in Chelsea? Belknap told me he had moved to 8th St. near 6th Ave., which is certainly in Greenwich rather than in Chelsea. I believe that 14th St. is now considered the dividing line—although it used to be even north of that. But perhaps Kirk has kept the name despite quitting the territory—as the Washington Square bookshop did.

I note the Eddy cutting—& assume you are aware that this fortune-hungry lady is the mother of the *Weird Tales* contributor C. M. Eddy Jr., whom I have mentioned to you.[4] He shewed me a whole scrapbook full of this material a couple of months ago—but hasn't many illusions about getting the limitless opulence in question. There's hardly anyone without a vague tradition of withheld money in the family—like the Maine lands of the Pyncheons in "The House of the Seven Gables"—but few ever get hold of the resources whereof they dream.

About the little Benefit St. grocery—it hasn't gone yet, but it's going soon. The proprietor has vainly looked for neighbouring sites, & is still undecided as to the future. I didn't know it was a focus of so many tender memories for you—it assumes a new & heightened dramatic significance in the light of your reminiscences. But Gawd! don't ever let my correct & churchgoing aunt Mrs. Gamwell hear of those dark-red vinous suspicions, for that selfsame store was sacred to her in an elder day, & in a vastly milder & primmer fashion! Back in the 1880's, when she attended Miss Abbott's select & sedate institution for the completion of accomplished young females, (which occupied a house still standing somewhat to the south on the same side of the street)[5] that modest emporium was in the full bloom of existence, & a favoured dêpot [*sic*] of supply for more or less studious misses in quest of candy, pickles, crackers, apples, & other delicacies dear to the nymphs of that day & generation. She & her classmates still regard the venerable place with retrospective affection, & it would break their hearts to learn that it has fallen into unconventional & Bohemian ways! Within the past month, by the way, my aunt has *again* become a patron—having taken quarters at the Handicraft Club in the big brick colonial house at the N E corner of College & Benefit Sts. Only last Tuesday night I called on her & was regaled with crackers & cheese & milk—all purchased at that dear, doomed establishment whose place in history is so secure. Your block, by the way, is getting frightfully tough. Only a week or so ago I noticed in the paper the trial of one William Beebe (*not* the celebrated naturalist, I hope!) whose bootlegging headquarters at #260 were recently the subject of investigation. The case came before Judge Hahn, but he passed it on to a brother jurist because his membership in the new court house committee controlling the doomed block made him in a legal sense an interested party. I'm glad my dentist (with whom, by the way, I have an appalling siege in prospect!) moved safely away from #258 to the corner of Angell & Hope Sts. some fifteen years ago! As I may have said, I recall that stately row of brick with many a dreamy twinge of eye-tooth & molar!

And so you are in touch with someone who knows that slum I just discovered! Hell! It didn't look to me like that kind of a slum—it struck me as too stupefied & choked with N Y N H & H smoke to have any rough stuff left in it. But if it does have dances, I'm sure they must be Dances of Death in Holbein's best manner. I had always noted the grim squalor of Ashburton St. as seen from the in-bound Woonsocket cars, so thought I'd explore the region on foot for the first time. Fancy my surprise, upon doing so, to find an utterly unknown street (Chalkstone Av.—which I thought ended at Smith St.) stretching west across a railway bridge & down into a hideous valley of grey horror! Truly, the place is accursed beyond anything I ever saw before! Shapeless & unpaved courts & alleys of tottering & diseased wooden houses crawl loathesomely [*sic*] up precipitous cinder-banks, & there is a bulging & worm-eaten Jew synagogue where I am certain the Black Mass must be celebrated by cloven-hoofed rabbins. The denizens are half Jew & half nigger, & their bloated, distorted faces are an atavistic reflection of the primal amoeba. Ugh! I shall certainly use the shocking realm in fiction! Well—more when I get your story.

Yr obt Servt

H P L

Notes

1. HPL's fanciful way of describing typing his two stories (minuscule being lowercase letters, as distinct from capitals or uncials). He never typed either of them.

2. Edward Lazare (1904–1991), a member of Hart Crane's literary circle whom HPL met in Cleveland and New York in the 1920s. He was later a longtime editor of *American Book-Prices Current*.

3. Manly Wade Wellman (1903–1986), American writer of fantasy, science, and detective fiction. Wellman's first story in *WT* was "Back to the Beast" (November 1927). As WBT

was acquainted with Wellman (see letter 27), he may have notified HPL about the forth-coming story, and HPL misunderstood him in thinking the story had already appeared.

4. Muriel E. Eddy (1896–1978), C. M. Eddy's wife, claimed that Grace Eddy (1873/4–1932) met HPL's mother at a woman suffrage meeting in 1918, at which they learned both their sons were enthusiasts of weird fiction. This assertion has not been verified.

5. J[osephine] L. Abbott's (1840–1928) school for the education of young ladies was formerly known as Miss Shaw's School, by whom it was established in 1860. The school occupied the building at 280 Benefit Street.

[20]   [ALS, JHL]

Wednesday [early May 1927]

Dear W B T:—

"Chetwode Arms'" is splendid—far and away your best yet! The scene is finally laid out, & the touches of detail all contribute effectively to the central situation. The complexity of plot & development is well overcome by the perfect joining of parts, so that an outward effect of clear movement & uninterrupted straightforwardness is secured. The thing convinces—it has vital-ity—& the changes in the escutcheon are so handled as to be cleverly symbol-ic rather than extravagantly grotesque or intrusively trivial. If Wright doesn't accept this on the spot he's an even greater ass than I have always thought!

I really can't find any flaws to pick! If any suggestions or recommenda-tions are in order, I suppose the thing to urge would be a more bizarre, cos-mically external, & utterly non-human set of motives & phenomena—in order to achieve that effect of *the unknown outside clawing at the rim of the known* which forms spectral horror in its acutest form. But heaven knows the tale has enough dark necromancy as it is—the suggestion is merely a general one, that there are things more terrible to the imagination than any phenomena connected with the nature, passions, & aspirations of mankind.

If this note is incoherent, lay it to the truly cacodaemoniacal *toothache* which is at this moment convulsing me! I have a triad of dental appointments just ahead—beginning next Monday—but now is now—& if that damned molar doesn't stop soon I shall telephone the former occupant of 258 Benefit St. for an emergency sitting this afternoon!

Had a great walk yesterday—Rhode Island rusticity at its best, around Lime Rock, just north of the Quinsnicket reservation. Now that I'm shaking off hibernation, I'm shaking it thoroughly!

By the way—Edwin Baird, the former editor of *Weird Tales,* announces the founding of a new magazine to handle all sorts of stories—the unusual sorts which others reject. You might try some material on him—I forget the address, but his present magazine is *Real Detective Tales,* (Chicago) which you can see on any news stand.

Had a letter from honest old Mac yesterday—the poor old boy feels very lonely & neglected, & complains that the gang meetings are so late at night nowadays that he'll have to cut 'em out entirely, since they disrupt his hide-bound working programme beyond repair! Better pay him a call & try to cheer him up—he's a rare character in this decadent age!

Yr obt servt

HPL

[21]   [ALS, JHL]

10 Barnes St.,

Providence, R.I.,

July 25, 1927

Dear W B T:—

"The Wyvern of St. Morteuil" duly arrived, & I will send it on to Belknap as soon as I receive a forwarding address from him. As you know, he is constantly on the move, & has all his mail come in my care to be re-despatched each week according to temporary directions.

We've been having festive times around here, as you've no doubt deduced from occasional postcards. Wandrei—a splendid young chap whose work you will notice in the next W.T.—arrived July 12, & on the 19th I had the pleasure of welcoming both James Ferdinand Morton & the entire Long family. The Longs left on the 22nd, but on the 23d another contingent arrived—this one composed of W. Paul Cook & H. Warner Munn, both of Athol, Mass. All have now gone except Wandrei, & he will not leave till Friday next. You ought to meet him some time—he is certainly an authentic genius, & will go far in the literary world unless I am much mistaken. His age is 19—& next fall he will begin his senior year at the Univ. of Minnesota. He lives in St. Paul.

Naturally all this company has involved a lot of interesting sightseeing. I've taken Wandrei to Boston, Salem, Marblehead, & Newport, to say nothing of numerous rural scenes north of Providence. On a second Newport trip Morton & the Longs went along, whilst another day Wandrei & I accompanied Morton on a geological expedition. Wandrei is about to move on to Athol to spend the next week-end with Cook, & after that he will stop in West Shokan, N.Y., to see our gang's newest corresponding member Bernard Dwyer. The Longs have been around Cape Cod & are now north of Boston—expecting later to strike Portland, Me., & Quebec. Speaking of the gang—we had a regular meeting here Wednesday night, with honest C. M. Eddy of Providence to add the necessary touch of the grotesque in lieu of naive old Mac. I think I have said how enthusiastically Wandrei & Morton have taken to "Jake's". They have almost made a regular patron of me, although I shall probably be less diligent in attendance when the visiting season is over.

Now as to the "Wyvern"—it certainly has the popular "action" atmosphere in abundant degree, & ought to appeal strongly to editors of the Wright type. The central idea of a gargoyle coming malignly to life is a splendid one—

indeed, my commonplace-book has long contained two notes of possible plots involving this element.[1] At the same time I think that some additional going-over might help the "Wyvern" aesthetically. In the first place I question the potency of the *atmosphere*—the light, whimsical tone of brisk cheerfulness which subtracts so much from the sum total of the weird impression. Seabury Quinn affects this tone in his "De Grandin" series, but the result is not to be commended. This idea of providing a grotesque, homely, light-comedy setting for a weird tale is an artificial convention very popular among certain authors, but for which I have never been able to discover any artistic justification. I'd advise that a *tenser, darker* atmosphere be provided. And in sketching the character of Herschal himself I wouldn't have his souvenir-collecting quite so *trivial* in the main. Of course this change of atmosphere would demand an alteration of style & conversation as well as of incident. Pare down the commonplace details & introduce something more ominous & foreboding. Also—this introductory setting matter is infinitely too *long*. That would be the main objection from a *popular* point of view. Another thing—as the story stands, it is very easy to see what is about to happen far in advance. Could the matter of the gargoyles & the legend be kept under cover till a relatively late date in the tale? When the legend is told, it might be well to tell it in a darker manner than is possible with artificial & conventional "clubroom" conversation. Then there is the matter of causation & motivation. If *light* brings the gargoyles to life, then they would be animated every day. You ought to change the legend so as to have the wyverns in a particularly *dark* angle of the castle, & have their destructive appearances coincide with rare appearances of illumination—torches, or unusual beams of the sun. (Say, that they come to life only at the time of the summer solstice, when the sun is so far north as to cast rays into unaccustomed corners at its setting.) Another point is the weeding out of *coincidence*. Why does the opening conversation about Hershal occur so close to the actual disaster? And why does the outward leap of the wyvern come so opportunely in respect to the search for the fingers? A tremendous amount of added *tenseness* & *concentration*, together with an improved *motivation* & *sequence*, would make an exceedingly powerful yarn. Let the thing *begin on a high key*—Hershal's call for help. The antecedent details & legend can come as a "flashback", as such things are termed in the cinema. And some of the amiable village details really ought to be eliminated. When the action really does begin, I think it might be well to condense & strengthen. Eliminate unnecessary details & comment, & speed up the doomward rush of incidents with a fatalistic relentlessness. Above all things, don't introduce the idea of the animated wyvern without *adequate preparation*. Remember that the *fact of this animation* is the climax & focus of the whole tale, & that it must not be lightly treated, as if the coming to life of stone gargoyles were an every-day & easily explainable matter. You must surround this phase of the tale with a certain hush of horror—a breathless awe—marked by a distinct change in the tempo. But the main thing is *length* & *general tone*. The story ought to be about half as long as it is, & the light, trivial style ought to be replaced by a tense, sinister air of impending horror. Toward the last a great deal of change is needed—the policeman's pursuit & the others' reaction to it verging on the extremes of incongruity & anticlimax. Things as abnormal as the living wyvern must be treated in a tone which fully recognises their abnormality. And keep in mind the elements of causation & motivation. Don't have the gargoyle come to life & turn to stone again without an adequate causative force in each case. It will take extreme adroitness & subtlety to handle this—as well as the whole idea of animated stone. This matter of pursuit & capture is a ticklish proposition, & requires extreme care. I must, by the way, congratulate you sincerely on the idea of the *cement block* as a means of disposing of the wyverns. That is a master-stroke—clever & original—& it might be enough to sell the story to an alert editor. Eliminate the *comic* from this pursuit and capture—forget Seabury Quinn & re-read Poe & Arthur Machen. The policeman's dialect grates annoyingly on any reader seriously attuned to the major mood. Now as to the *explanation*—for God's sake eliminate that if you can, since that type of finale is an artificial convention as stale as . . . . . but all metaphors fail! It was new in the early Sherlock Holmes days, but now it has been run into the ground by every detective & mystery writer unhung! Arrange to have the tale end (as well as begin) on a definite high spot—preferably some dramatic phenomenon incident to the encasing of the thing in the cement block. There is room for great ingenuity here—make use of the effect of light & darkness on the Beast. The comic ending is altogether out of place. It may be (though I doubt it) that weird comedy has its place in literature; but the general plot of this tale is not one which lends itself to the purposes of weird comedy. It is essentially the nucleus of a horror-tale—hence must be developed strictly as such.

Now I hope you can pardon the crudity & sketchiness of this hasty criticism! If I had more time just now, I would offer more constructive suggestions; but the fact is that I am in the midst of a desperate mess of accumulated mail, owing to the unaccustomed social whirl of the past week. In view of this, I am sure you will view my shortcomings with a lenient eye.

As to Carolyn Wells'[2] stuff—the only thing to do with it is to ignore it. She is absolutely trivial, artificial, & mechanical to the last degree—as you can see not only in her stories, but in her famous text-book for cheap hacks—on the technique of the mystery novel. Don't follow her as a model if you develop the series you project.

Of late I've had rather good luck with fiction—I think Wandrei's visit to *Weird Tales* office en route east stirred up Wright in a salutary way. He has now accepted my "Cthulhu" after having once rejected it, & has probably accepted "The Strange High House in the Mist". Moreover—my "Red Hook" has just been reprinted in the third number of the British anthology which used two of Belknap's tales.[3]

I was very glad to meet Munn (for the first time) & discuss weird plots with him. You have doubtless noticed his werewolf stories in W. T. He has an idea for a future story of submarine horror which sounds absolutely magnificent to me.

Well—I shall have to knock off for the nonce & tackle some other epistles. I'll send the "Wyvern" on to Belknap as soon as I get a forwarding address. He'll probably be less harsh than I, since he is inclined toward the same lightness & whimsicality of which I so violently complain. But all the same, I'd advise your giving the tale a thorough overhauling. The central idea & cement-block are too darned good not to have the very best possible setting.

With all good wishes, & trusting that your summer is proving a highly enjoyable one, I have the honour to subscribe myself, Sir,

> Yr most hble,
>> most obt Servt.
>> H P L

Notes

1. See entries 76 and 77 of the commonplace book. George T. Wetzel believed that the entries were inspired by George Macdonald's *Phantastes* (1868).

2. Carolyn Wells (1862–1942), American writer and poet, author of more than 170 books, most of them detective stories. The work referred to later in the paragraph is *The Technique of the Mystery Story* (Springfield, MA: Home Correspondence School, 1913; rev. ed. 1929).

3. I.e., *You'll Need a Nightlight* in the "Not at Night" series. Long's "Death-Waters" was included in *Not at Night* (1925) and his "The Sea Thing" in *More Not at Night* (1926).

[22]   [ALS]

> 10 Barnes St.,
>> Providence, R.I.,
>>> August 9, 1927

Dear W B T:—

I was very glad to hear from you, & am much interested in the brilliant friend you describe. His erudition, I fear, is infinitely beyond any of the shallow phases of smatterings which I can boast; but his love of the weird is a link which levels the most formidable inequalities! In accordance with your suggestion, I have sent him a few of my hell-raisers for perusal—not the ones you mentioned, unfortunately, since these seem to be lent to others just now; but some which are at least comparable with them in quality. They are as follows:

The Statement of Randolph Carter (1919)	The Terrible Old Man (1920)
The Temple (1920)	The Doom that Came to Sarnath (1919)
The White Ship (1919)	Dagon (1917)
The Strange High House in the Mist (1926)	The Picture in the House (1920)

I have suggested to Prof. Wheeler[1] that he return them through you—& if you care to repeat & authorise the suggestion you may do so. I fear he will be somewhat disappointed if you have led him to expect anything notable, but trust he will have the sense to stop reading as soon as he is bored. If, on the other hand, he cares to see more; there will of course be plenty to shew him. Your description paints a very attractive figure, & I surely hope that after September he will have the leisure for some epistolary exchanges of ideas. He certainly comes honestly by his literary inclinations—I've just looked his father up in an encyclopaedia & found him at the first shot! Let us hope that his W.T. story will "land"—though Wright's standards are far from being based on merit.[2] If it doesn't, I'd like to read it anyway. Incidentally—if you want to see my own latest attempt, "The Colour Out of Space", you can find it in the September *Amazing Stories,* now on the news stands. "Pickman's Model" comes out in the next *Weird Tales.*

About the "Wyvern"—don't get discouraged, for the idea's good, & the cement block is a master stroke. It's only the details which need touching up. Belknap will give you his report soon, for he expects to be back in N.Y. Aug. 15. He missed the MS. at Belgrade Lakes, & it came back to me; but I re-mailed it & it caught him at Lake George, N.Y. To my mind, the weird-humorous tone represents a fundamental fallacy; & I'd never recommend Quinn's wooden & hackneyed De Grandin as a model. You can perhaps enhance the grotesque humour of a comic tale by adding a touch of the mock-weird, but it won't be a *weird tale.* If you want a weird tale, you must carefully exclude all atmospheric qualities antagonistic to the mood you're trying to establish; & the lightly comic certainly kills all receptivity to mystic images about as quickly & effectively as anything yet devised by man! If you don't believe it, read all the pitifully floundering attempts which eminent authors have made in this direction—like the late Frank R. Stockton's "Transferred Ghost" & Brander Matthews' "Rival Ghosts." These things may be fun in their way, but there's no such thing as a weird thrill either in or anywhere near them. The light comedy mood is utterly destructive of all illusion of reality in any field, hence can be profitably employed only in such literary bric-a-brac as is essentially decorative & frivolous in purpose. Where any attempt at a tense moment is designed, there must be a total absence of shallow & artificial jauntiness, & a sober adoption of objective, plausibly realistic narration—tempered only with emotions (& these more in the characters than in the author) rationally suited to the action. I am speaking, of course, from the artistic point of view. I realise that the middle-class herd has artificial moods & atmospheres of its own, which it expects in its best-sellers, & enjoys according to conventions & traditions beyond philosophic fathoming; but in giving literary recommendations I hardly take this sort of thing into account. And of course there is such a thing as power in light irony, in the manner of Cabell or Anatole France—but that is something else altogether. Returning to the Wyvern—you certainly can make something good out of it, so don't throw it away even if Wright returns it. You can, indeed, adopt either one of two courses—light revision to make a well-proportioned & smoothly-working comic, mock-weird story, or extensive revision to eliminate the comic & create a genuine record of darkness & mystery & mounting terror & hideous realisation. This latter course, however, will need extreme adroitness, & a very carefully devised handling of the final incidents. As to my mistake—it's odd how I got the impression, but I don't see that my error removes the need of better motivation. If it's the dark & not the light that wakes the wyvern, why didn't he give certain chained manifestations of life *every night* whilst on the castle? And how are the various vivifications after the detachment motivated? I was so rushed with company when I read the tale that I don't wonder at blunders of some sort. As I recall the plot, I can hardly believe I made the one I did, since the petrifying power of the light was so salient a feature of the pursuit. But wait for Belknap's verdict. He doesn't share my basic conviction that weird-humorous tales are impossible, hence can give you a verdict from your own angle.

That Jersey Devil article is very clever—I read a cutting about the monster only the other day, & concluded that IT is an overgrown mosquito.[3] No doubt you're prepared to follow up this initial sally with other reports on the beast—both its present movements & its cryptic & terrible history. The plot you outline is surely unique & original, & I strongly hope you will develop it at leisure—whether or not as a "Van Kampen" tale. But don't let the anti-Dutch devil carry *you* off, now that your genealogical activities have made you such a shining mark amongst the patroons of Nieuw Nederland!

"The Strange High House in the MIST" (not *Moat*) was written last November, & is a "Kingsport" (Marblehead, Mass.) fantasy. I thought Wright was going to take it, but he backed out at the last moment, saying the story was not plain & simple & obvious enough for his discriminating clientele of half-wits.

Munn has immense possibilities as a writer, & I was highly pleased to make his acquaintance last month. He may be down again next Saturday & Sunday with Cook—& I may accompany them on their return trip to Athol, staying there a day or two & then coming home circuitously, so as to include some Colonial exploration in the very distinctive Connecticut Valley region, whose archaic towns—such as Deerfield—I have never yet beheld. Munn mentioned his double-walled city plot, but the one which impressed me most was a submarine idea which allows for more bizarre atmosphere & involves less conventional human motivation. Did he mention it to you—the undersea plateau, toward which hordes of *things* are climbing? Like you, I found the later "Master" material disappointing—especially the MS. just accepted by Wright,[4] which Munn doubtless showed you when in N.Y. But all the germs of power are there, & only time is needed to bring out the slowly maturing talent. It may be, however, that he will turn out to be a romancer or adventure-writer rather than a sheer fantaisiste. One of his best things was "The City of

Spiders",[5] though Wright provokingly removed one of the choicest points—about the extra-terrestrial origin of the spiders. (of *all* spiders, in fact.)

Your offer of a book-plate is indeed most generous & welcome, & I scarcely know how to thank you for such a spontaneous favour! I had not thought of affording any such thing for aeons to come, but the turn of Fate which brings down the cost to the neighbourhood of $2.50 is indeed too vast a temptation to resist. A thousand times, thanks! And now comes the question of whether to adopt an heraldic or pictorial design. The heraldic is the more traditional & conservative, beyond a doubt; & for that reason naturally suggests itself first; but your alluring description of a colonial village scene (of course with the 1st Baptist steeple!) colonially mirrored through a colonial doorway so grips my imagination that I find myself hopelessly wavering. I suppose you would be careful to make the scene the New England Colonial rather than Dutch—remembering our characteristic doorways & steeples & roofs as distinguished from your own. But again I waver toward heraldry, since that has such a quiet & tasteful dignity all its own, & since so many of my inherited books already bear plates of that order. The Lovecraft coat-of-arms is described as follows—& I will add a crude pictorial representation as best my inept pen can give one.

Description	
Arms:	Vert, a Chevron engrailed, Or, between three Foxes' Heads, erased, Or.
Crest:	On a wreath, a Tower, Or.
Motto:	QUAE AMAMUS TUEMUR[6] (or—better render it QVÆ.AMAMVS. TVEMVR)

according to some renderings, this wreath is a straight line. Take your choice, from the art standpoint, & add whatever decorative scroll work you wish

In making a cut I presume you would—as in most of the plates I have or have seen—observe the heraldic conventions of shading—i.e.,

 for vert,   for or,   for gules,   for azure,   for sable, &c.

Well—so far, so good. But what of old New England in this? Unfortunately the Lovecrafts came from Devonshire to northern N.Y. State without stopping in Providence-Plantations or The Province of Massachusetts-Bay. Obviously, something must be done about this, since I don't mean to lose the credit for that psychologically dominant half of my ancestry which is absolutely & utterly New-England back to 1630, when the Rev. George Phillips alighted in Salem (before taking a pastorate in Watertown, begetting 11 sons, & sending 3 of them to R.I. in due course of time) from the stout ship *Lion!* (a darned appropriate ship, heraldically speaking—vide infra) Apparently the thing to do is to adopt *quarterings*—taking the arms of the Rev. George & letting you assign them to whatever is their proper place as maternal blazonings. These Phillips arms are as follows:

Description

Arms: Azure, a Lion rampant, Sable, ducally gorged & chained, Or.

Crest: On a wreath, a Lion, sable,* as in the arms.

Motto: DUCIT AMOR. PATRIAE

PHILLIPS–LOVECRAFT

Now I suppose the correct thing to do in quartering would be to keep the Lovecraft crest & motto, & Lovecraft arms in 1st and 4th quarters of the shield; giving 2nd & 3d quarters to Phillips, & reluctantly sacrificing the extra lion & patriotic sentiment—thus:

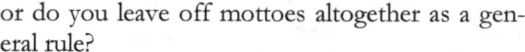

or do you leave off mottoes altogether as a general rule?

As for the book-plate wording—*plainness* is the prime desideratum, hence I would have only EX.LIBRIS at the top & H. P. LOVECRAFT at the bottom or wherever else such things properly go. You might, though, add PROVIDENCE, RHODE-ISLAND (the abbreviation R.I. seems out of place here) below the name. Yes—if I decided on heraldry, I'd surely want the New England Phillips quartering . . . . but damn it all! I can't be sure I don't want that New-England village skyline instead of a bally menagerie of crafty foxes & rampant lions out of Æsop's Fables! Your heraldic specimen is delectably prepossessing—yet who knows what greater charm your Novanglian reflection might not possess? I can almost see it now! In the long run I guess you'd better do your own choosing. As an artist you must have preferences as to subject-matter; i.e., pictorial versus heraldically conventional; & I urge you to follow those preferences without external suggestion. If you do the picture, don't forget to make the N.E. architecture ring true. Remember that our gambrel roofs tend to break *evenly*, & are *never curved*. See il-

---

*(They tell me this colour-on-colour arrangement is rotten heraldry, but somebody started it too far back for me to help now. The *same scheme* of sable on azure is mentioned in Scott's Marmion)

lustration at right. You never find the short upper pitches so universal around N.Y.—for those are all derived from the Dutch plan, even when occurring on English colonial houses & not concaved. The New England houses, almost all, were untouched by Dutch influence; & if any of the two gambrel pitches is inclined to be shorter it is the bottom rather than the top. But equality is the best  rule. Remember, too, the style of our doorways*—*rayed FANLIGHT* instead of transom[†] as in N.Y. Don't fail to put in a steeple—it's the life & focus of every N.E. village green! You might have a typical Providence double flight of steps with iron railing on the one house—but don't give this a gambrel roof, for such things go with the later (1750–1800) type of plain slant-roof house. Anyhow—use your judgment & do your own choosing—& here's hoping you win 1st prize at all the county fairs! Yr obt Grandsire H P L

P.S. As to *number* of bookplates—well, there are only about 500 books in my library in decent condition enough to need or merit plates, so I guess that'll do for a starter. But you needn't bother with even that many if I have the cut.

Notes

1. Paul Mowbray Wheeler (1892–?) of Englewood, NJ, professor of English at Columbia and later Johns Hopkins University. His father, A[ndrew] C[arpenter] Wheeler (1835–1903), a once famous newspaperman and writer, wrote under a string of pseudonyms. He was the author of *A Journal to Nature* (1902).

---

*and don't forget that our old *doors* are 6-panelled, the small panels at the top—thus:

†except of course the simple rows of lights above the doors of the small gambrel-roofed cottages or farm houses. But the door through which the view comes would not be of that kind.

2. Wheeler had no stories published in *WT*.

3. The Jersey Devil is a legendary creature said to inhabit the Pine Barrens of Southern NJ, often described as a flying biped with hooves, but there are many variations. During the week of 16–23 January 1909, newspapers of the time published hundreds of claimed encounters with the creature. Leah Bodine Drake's poem "The Ballad of the Jabberwock: A True Tale of Squankom Town" was about the Jersey Devil.

4. "The Werewolf's Daughter," a three-part serial (*WT*, October–December 1928).

5. *WT*, November 1926.

6. "We defend the things we love."

[23]   [ALS, Leaf II at JHL]

Home Again
Sunday [4 September 1927]

Dear W B T:—

I arrived late Friday night,[1] looked at the mail stacked mountain-high on my table, & soulfully murmured "My Gawd!" I am still murmuring the same pious invocation—though the pile has not yet appreciably diminished its altitude. Never in my life have I been so hopelessly paralysed—epistolarily & industrially. A whole book to proofread,[2] at least three long prose MSS. to revise, & letters, letters, letters, ad infinitum, infernum, et nauseam!!! I am certainly reaping the whirlwind[3] after my glorious two weeks of diversified scenic & colonial absorption! But it sure was a titanic fortnight, as you may have gathered from the pictorial echoes reaching you from time to time; & I trust I have stored up enough impressions to last me through the winter. I saw the White Mountains for the first time, but as a matter of fact they didn't impress me nearly so much as the old seaports. I'll back up any favourable reports Belknap may have given you concerning Gloucester. I did all my stopping at Y M C A's, finding them sometimes as reasonable as 75¢ a night.

Now as to bookplates—I could have traced you the foxes' heads as they appear in an apparently well-engraved plate of the arms; but on the whole (& especially after this trip!) fancy that the colonial scene would be just about as appropriate for a plate expressing my individual personality. Don't take too much trouble—& where there is any choice of methods always choose the simpler. I like the scroll top of the middle Georgian period, & will be satisfied with any version of it which you may deem easy & suitable. That shewn in your sketch is admirable, it seems to me. And as to the mechanical medium—my purse tells me that a line drawing would be infinitely preferable to a half-tone!

As for the scene—I do not think it is necessary to reproduce any one landscape with literal fidelity. I have noticed that many purely decorative designs, prepared to symbolise certain regions, include certain outstanding or typical features in a grouping which is purely conventional, & not at all true to topographical fact. This is, of course, for the sake of inclusiveness—to crowd in as many symbolic or characteristic objects as possible, & in a manner more psychologically related to your art of heraldry than to the ordinary field of pictorial delineation. It seems to me that an ideal view would be very closely related to your original conception—that of a colonial house, (either gambrel, peaked, square, or with cyma-curve pediment like the Joseph Brown house in S. Main St.) a colonial steeple, & the distant spars of a square-rigged ship to typify the maritime interests of old Providence. The Joseph Brown facade is so characteristic of this town (you are aware, I presume, that it is reproduced in the new Providence Gas Co. Building in Weybosset St.) that I am almost tempted to recommend its inclusion if possible—indeed, I think I'll enclose a newspaper view for

[Verso of Leaf I unavailable]

In drawing the Joseph Brown house, give it its original appearance with high double flight of steps as in folder. As for the doorway—a plain frame or moulding is all you need if the house is to be one of the middle (circa 1750–1770) Providence type, with semicircular (or slightly elliptical, though not great-ly flattened) fanlight & no side-lights. Here is a view of such a door, open:

[Cornice of hall I think this arrange-ment of fanlight tracery is about as good as any.]

Of course, all this is only sugges-tion—not to be copied or followed as a real model, but merely to be kept in mind as you make your own artistic decisions & exer-cise your own selective faculty. It may be that in the main landscape you will not wish to crowd the composition with so many de-tails—in which case you can select any typical symbols you choose, such as the distant ship rig-ging, the steeple, & any one building you like. Your own judgment will tell you how to handle the tangle of ancient roofs & bel-fries on the hillside—& as for the main buildings in the foreground, (if you can only use one) I will otherwise leave it to you whether to choose the Mar-ket House or Joseph Brown house. It occurs to me that the Jos. B. house may be a trifle ornate or fussy for a simple & conventionalised design, but that on the other hand the Market House is very austere & appropriate to a classically decorative motif. I'm no artist—I pass it up—& do just as you prefer about the wharves & water & warehouses & ship in the foreground. It may be that they're all out of place—obvious & obtrusive—& that a glimpse of *distant* yard-arms & masts would be infinitely more effective in suggesting the sea-ward leanings of the young town. The *shape* of your panel will have much to do with the composition of your design. The doorway & mirror effect will render it essentially tall & narrow, hence too much lateral panorama must be avoided. I'll send you pictures of any especial building which you may desire to include. The *lettering* must be ordinary Roman capitals to go well with the style & period—& I wish you could give them an 18th century cast (the Caslon Old Style of the printer) in order to sustain the mood. You can find lettering of the required style, size, & shading on the title page of almost any book printed before 1800.

I'm sorry I couldn't get all this to you sooner—but you can easily see how my trip interfered. I hope you're not too late for the county fairs you were aiming at—it would be a shame to cheat you out of your merited laurels! Don't hurry on my account—if you're too late for the fairs, take your own sweet time. Again let me express my unaffected gratitude for the whole idea!

My trip was certainly the premier event of recent years. First I visited W. Paul Cook in Athol, & was taken by him on some magnificent side-trips—including colonial Deerfield, primitive Vermont, & picturesque New Hampshire as far north as Lake Sunapee. In West Brattleboro we called on the amateur poet Arthur Goodenough,[4] I being the second amateur to meet him personally. He lives in a 200-year-old peaked farmhouse in some of the most glamorously fascinating hill country I have ever seen, & is himself the most delightful conceivable relic of simpler & gentler days. He has never seen a large city, & seldom visits even the small neighbouring town of Brattleboro. To see him in his natural setting, with quaintly courtly hospitality & rusty black "Sunday best" frock coat, is to realise that the last of the ancient New England rural gentry is not yet dead. I'll send you a picture later on, which W. Paul Cook snapped with a new camera bought especially for the purpose. Athol is a very attractive town, & my stay there was enjoyable in the highest degree. Upon leaving there I went by stage-coach to Boston, stopped at the Y, & the next day took the coach for Portland; to which I accorded two days of exploration. It is a marvellously attractive town, with many fine old houses & a series of incredibly fascinating harbour views from various lofty points of vantage. It was from there that I took the White Mountain excursion—a very imagination-whetting experience. From Portland I retraced my steps to Portsmouth, which is far richer in colonial antiquities. I had seen this place before, but gave it a closer survey & made the trip to Little Harbour to see the (very disappointing) Benning Wentworth "mansion" mentioned in Longfellow's famous poem.[5] From Portsmouth I proceeded to Newburyport, in which I found new antiquarian riches. Thence I entrained for Ipswich, where I explored the old Whipple house (circa 1640—& ancestrally connected with me)[6] & embarked for Gloucester. Here I was hampered by rain on the second day, but managed to do the sights very thoroughly—including Rockport & the Magnolia cliffs. Thereafter I set sail for Manchester, Beverly, & Salem—familiar ground at last—& finally wound up with an afternoon of superbly sunshiny antiquarianism at incomparable Marblehead. Thence to Lynn, Boston, & Providence, reaching home Friday midnight. And now—migawd, the piled-up work! I shall never pull clear of it—only heaven knows what will come of the avalanche of mail & tasks! First of all I must read proofs of a book I'm editing—& then—oh, hell! But anyhow, receive a doomed man's blessing!

I trust that your summer has been pleasant, & hope your autumn will be equally so. Are you returning to Columbia this year? Don't let the bookplate matter bother you, & don't attempt any difficult design where a simpler one is possible. My suggestions are only the vaguest ideas for general guidance—not specific instructions in any sense of the word. And remember that I'll lend you a picture of any Providence building for which you may lack a pictorial model.

With renew'd expressions of appreciation & gratitude, I am, Sir,

Ever yr most oblig'd, obt Servt & grandparent,

H P L

Notes

1. HPL had just returned from a trip (19 August–2 September) to sites in Massachusetts, New Hampshire, and Vermont (described later in the letter).
2. At the time HPL was working on John Ravenor Bullen's posthumous book, *White Fire*.
3. Hosea 8:7: "For they have sown the wind, and they shall reap the whirlwind."
4. Arthur H. Goodenough (1871–1936), amateur journalist and poet.
5. Built in 1750 for Benning Wentworth (1696–1770), now known as the Wenworth–Coolidge Mansion, at 375 Little Harbor Road, Portsmouth, NH. Longfellow's "Lady Wentworth" is about the scandalous marriage of Wentworth (age 64) to Martha Hilton (age 23 or 33).
6. The John Whipple house at 53 South Main Street in Ipswich, originally built c. 1638 and then sold to John Whipple (1596–1669), who expanded it. His son, Capt. John Whipple, is not identical to John Whipple (1641–1700), an ancestor of HPL.

[24] [ALS, JHL]

10 Barnes St.,
Providence, R.I.,
Octr. 19, 1927

Dear W B T:—

Both instalments of returned matter arrived safely, & I note your critical opinions with interest. Wheeler also favoured me with some remarks & recommendations, whose general trend struck me as quite sound, though I did not agree entirely regarding details. All critical estimates depend largely on the critic—both his natural cast of mind & the standard of criticism which he consciously adopts—hence one is likely to receive the most amusingly opposite opinions from different judges of equal culture, intellect,

& erudition. I myself work on altogether different lines—with altogether different ideals & objects—from your own, hence in many cases my own judgments of my stuff will seem to you quite extraordinary & inexplicable. Primarily I write for atmospheric effect rather than plot. My tales are not meant to be "short-stories" in the conventional sense, but belong technically in what one might call the borderland of prose-poetry. I agree with you about the "Horror at Red Hook", which was so rotten that I hesitated about sending it to Wright in the first place, & about "Beyond the Wall of Sleep", which belongs to a peculiarly experimental & uncertain period. I differ concerning "The Rats in the Walls" & "The Terrible Old Man", which to me seem barren & obtrusively mechanical in a cheap popular way. On "The Outsider" I'm neutral, though my grounds of neutrality might not coincide with your own; but I'm with you again on "The Cats of Ulthar", which is a favourite of mine. "Dagon", you may be amazed to know, I consider my best story. It realises the intangible thing I am trying to realise, & has almost always been placed on top by imaginative critics like Belknap, Vincent Starrett, the late George Sterling, & so on . . . . not to omit our good friend Mortonius.[1] "Sarnath" also is a favourite of mine—as a descriptive phantasy. "The Strange High House" is almost my best attempt if imaginative critics (Wandrei, Belknap, Clark Ashton Smith, Bernard Dwyer &c) speak truly, & I am not disposed to dissent extensively from them. After all, it's very much a matter of individual taste, & you'll get my point of view more fully after reading my article in Cook's new *Recluse*,[2] which has probably gone to your Spring Valley address.

Cook, by the way, was here Saturday & Sunday, & will be again in about two weeks. He didn't feel like counter nourishment, hence passed up Jak . . . . er, *Jacques;* but we did some very Jake-obean gorging in a literary way, damn near buying up the entire stock of Eddy's bookshop in Weybosset Street.[3] He's about to invest in *70* old bound volumes of *Harper's Magazine.*

Thanks for the genealogical tip—but I don't recall seeing that tercentenary book on the library shelves when we were there. I uncovered floods of old jottings (some of which I had to copy, like that Allgood dope, in order to save 'em from crumbling to powder) when I opened the papers my aunt brought down, including enough coats-of-arms in verbal description to keep you busy for a year drawing. Some were qualified with question-marks, including the Whipple & Hazard arms, which leads me to ask you (pending my own discovery of the terc. book) whether the following two blazonings coincide with what you saw:

> *Whipple* — sable, on a chevron between 3 swans' heads erased argent, as many crescents of the field. (no crest given)
>
> *Hazard* — *Arms:* Azure, 2 bars argent; on a chief or, three escallops gules. *Crest:* An escallop gules.

The Perkins coat given was not the same complicated one which we saw at the library, but the Field one differed only in crest. Ellis, Mathewson, (or Mathison) & Brownell coats were given with a question-mark, & I could find no Malavery coat at all. On the *paternal* side the data was much fuller, requiring translation from words to designs rather than research. Three lines connect up very anciently—back to the Conquest, & including all sorts of luminaries—& one has a pleasantly dogmatic though not detailedly given assurance of descent from one Owen Gwynedd, Prince of North Wales.[4] Heigho! The Caseys come from the 137th King of Ould Erin, & the Parrys from the Prince of North Wales! To hell with your Dutch monarchs! Us Celtic royalty represent the pre-Teutonic original rulers of the Isles—compared to whom youse guys are all parvenus & usurpers! Seriously, I was astonished to see the amount of Celt in me, for I hadn't been over those records in twenty years. My father's grandmother— William Allgood's wife, was a Morris of Clasemont—Welsh in residence, & with four known strains of Welsh Celtic blood—Rees, (Rhys) Purcell, Parry, & Jenkins of Machynlleth. (Get that last. It's the name of his seat, buy do you fancy that *Machynlleth* is allied to the *Machen* of Arthur Machen?) And my paternal grandfather George Lovecraft was the son of first cousins, Joseph Lovecraft & Mary Fulford, whose respective mothers were both Edgecombes & daughters of Margaret Carew *of Cornwall,* whose mother in turn was a Cornish-Celtic *Trefusis.*[5] All this, with the maternal Casey strain, ought to give me a Celtic imaginativeness far removed from the stolid Teutonism of the average Yankee or Dutchman! Gad, Sir, I shall cultivate mysticism!

Glad 24 Willow is turning out well. I knew it was a great place for quiet & spotlessness, though about the size of a modest cupboard. Look up the gang when you can—you know Belknap's new address.

Yr obt Grandsire
H P L

P.S. I learned just yesterday venerable fellow-amateur Mr. Hoag is no more.[6] A fall in his room on the 9th fractured his hip, & he died Monday morning. But for the accident, I feel sure he would have rounded out a century & more. I have prepared an obituary & a metrical elegy for *Tryout.* ¶ Thanks for the Casey coat. I knew it was easy, but wasn't quite sure about that term effronteé. [*sic*]

Notes

1. Only the comments by George Sterling on "Dagon" are extant. Sterling had written (in a letter to Clark Ashton Smith, 13 February 1923): "The story you enclose is very well written, and I enjoyed it decidedly. Its main fault is that it's an echo of former tales, *without* surpassing them." *The Shadow of the Unattained: The Letters of George Sterling and Clark Ashton Smith,* ed. David E. Schultz and S. T. Joshi (New York: Hippocampus Press, 2005), 227. Smith relayed Sterling's comments to HPL, who wrote (letter to Clark Ashton Smith, 11 June 1923): "I was interested to hear what Sterling said of

'Dagon', & am glad he found something to praise" (*DS* 52). HPL was in correspondence with Vincent Starrett at this time, but no discussions of "Dagon" appear in HPL's surviving letters to Starrett; Starrett's letters to HPL do not survive.

2. I.e., "Supernatural Horror in Literature."

3. Arthur E. Eddy was the proprietor of the Eddy's Book Store at 260 Weybosset.

4. Owain ap Gruffudd (c. 1100–1170), was King of Gwynedd, North Wales; called "Owain the Great" and the first to be styled "Prince of Wales."

5. The family genealogical records on which HPL was relying were in error. The spouse of Joseph Lovecraft the immigrant was Mary Full. (The name of their firstborn child was John Full Lovecraft.) Francis Fulford (d. 1774), whom the records claimed as father of Mary (Fulford) Lovecraft, died unmarried. There is no marriage for a Thomas Lovecraft and an Edgecombe. See Faig and Docherty.

6. The amateur Jonathan E. Hoag (b. 1831) died on 17 October at the age of 96. HPL, who had been writing annual birthday poems for Hoag, named his final poem in recognition of Hoag "Ave atque Vale" (hail and farewell).

[25]   [ALS, JHL]

10 Barnes St.,
Providence, R.I.,
Decr. 28, 1927.

Sir Wilfred Blank-Blank Taelman Talema,
    Brenckelen, Nieuw-Nederland.

Dear W B T:—

Glad to get a line from the late-Georgian home of Ethical Culture, even tho' its date bear no excessively close relation to the 19th of last October! I haven't heard from your academic friend for quite some time, but am secure in the virtuous confidence that the last epistle was a south-bound one. Maybe that bad taste which my stories gave him shed a faint unsavouriness over my letter as well—or more probably, my critical opinions impressed him as representing a standard so absurdly intangible & generally flighty that serious discussion would be quite hors-de-la-literature! [*sic*]

As to your entry for the "andWHERE" contest—well, I'll admit it, but I won't guarantee a prize.[1] Providence's andwhereness is of a natural, vestigial, & spontaneous sort—genuine reliques of a primal rurality which the march of the city has been powerless to efface. These Brooklyn sheep, on the other hand, are a bit of conscious scenery, as artificial & sophisticated in their way as the sheep & shepherd-folk of Watteau.[2] They are not a survival but a restoration—not a true, lingering bit of the past, but a deliberate museum-device of jaded modernity. And so, although I will not indeed rule them wholly out, I cannot concede that they are in the same class with the lane back of the Athenaeum, or the bits of uncorrupted farmyard glimpsed here & there around Congdon St. There is, after all, only one Providentium!

You gain, alas, an erroneous impression of my genealogical industry from my recent bulletins on ancestral matters to you & Belknap. My researches have so far been confined wholly to predigested data dug up & formulated by earlier & better family archivists than myself, & have not indeed included any outside delvings whatsoever. All I have done is to collate certain maternal papers possessed by my aunt, & to exhume from storage some paternal charts & notes not seen by me for twenty years. These two sources are the only reservoirs I have tapped—but they were enough to yield monotonous reams of heraldic blazonings—so many that I would never have the nerve to ask you to translate even an eighth of them into visual form—& a pedigree containing the Celtic revelations of which I have already made mention. Such, in fine, is the modest extent of my recent investigations—though I do deserve credit for recopying a vast amount of data which I had copied in 1905 on that rotten yellow paper, & which was fast assuming the state of pulverisation which we noted in connexion with the separate Allgood notes! Oh, yes—but I did buy the Casey book[3] spoken of in that *Journal* editorial I showed you, & fancy I got a fair money's worth. These East Greenwich Caseys are descendants of Thomas Casey's second son Adam, whereas I come from his third & youngest son Samuel. Others of Samuel's descendants were Tories in the revolution—GOD SAVE THE KING!—& their posterity is now settled in Ontario, Canada, whither they migrated in 1781. I have not seen the Tercentenary book as yet—& don't know whether it's available at any local institution—but shall surely keep my eyes open for it when I get a spare moment to devote to outside delving. I fear my enthusiasm flags when real work is demanded of me. It's all right to look over what other genealogists have prepared—but when it comes to duplicating their industry & extending their results, I am of less than Talmanic persistence! My researches since Oct. 19 have been nil—for what I wrote Belknap was only a résumé of what I had found before.

As to my attitude toward ancestral Celts—well, I fancy it's still a bit ambiguous. I like 'em when they're kings, yet after all mere Druid-hounds can't compare in solidity & majesty with golden-bearded Vikings & conquerors. I'm for the Teuton in the last analysis—although of course a Celt or two on the loftier branches doesn't poison a whole family tree! My *Machen* query wasn't *quite* as far-fetched as you think, for you didn't get the spelling right from my scrawl. The name of the seat of this David Jenkins was MACHYNLLETH—*Machenlleth*, as it were—unless I myself made a mistake in originally copying the name from my great-aunt's data in '05. However—I shan't be addressing Arthur M. as "Cousin Arthur" quite yet! Another pleasant suggestion of literary relationship came from the Fulford (my father's paternal grandmother) coat-of-arms, which is nothing but a veritable checkerboard of quarterings. (Some of these Fulfords must have been as keen on genealogy as you!) One of the tiny compartments represents the *Moreton* shield—which of course implies descent, though the actual connexion is not given on any paper I have—thus giving me an actual though infinitesimal link with Edward John *Moreton* Drax Plunkett, 18th Baron Dunsany! Another still farther-fetched literary link only just occurred to me. As I think I said, one of my Celtic streams—Parry—claims descent from Owen GWYNEDD, Prince of North Wales. Now GWYNEDD is obviously the source of the modern name *Gwinnett*—you know that Button Gwinnett[4] was a Georgia signer of the Dec. of Ind.—& thus I am very clearly a second or third or three-thousandth cousin of my fellow-fantaisiste *Ambrose* **Gwinnett** Bierce! Yeah—we're all one great family, me & Art Machen & Dunsany & Amby Bierce! Well—shew me proof to the contrary ef ya don't believe it! No use talking—all us Machyns & Moretons & Gwynetts jes' nacherlly take to imaginative writing. It's in the blood—ya can't stop us!

Yes indeed, I properly noticed the honours paid to "Haunted Island", & trust that you may repeat this success with many a spectral stanza! Glad that Alabad & Ghinu & Aratza are to appear next month, because my Cthulhu slithers around in the same number, & these synthetic monsters do love company! I hope to see "Dragon-Fly" when it's done—& likewise hope that Brother Wright can "see" it, too! Meanwhile I have made my fictional debut betwixt cloth covers—though only by being represented in that "Not at Night" anthology which has previously used two of Belknap's yarns. The included piece is "The Horror at Red Hook"—one of my dullest—but it surely looks a bit encouraging to see oneself at the tail end of a nice red cloth book with cheap paper, a gaudy jacket, & a price of two shillings nett. As a Tory, I am properly gratified to have my cloth-cover debut take place in London. God save &c. Wright still talks of that volume of my selected tales, but I think he values vocal exercise for its own widely acknowledged therapeutic qualities. Oh—but the main item comes from one of my fellow-Celts—a true lodge-brother of the K. of C. & A. O. H.[5] Pipe the following note which blew in a week or so ago—addressed care of *Amazing Stories* & forwarded—with a Swiss stamp & postmark. Some Killarney yodel—eh, what?

> Hôtel Fleur-de-Lys,
> Gruyéres, Switzerland,
> Nov. 29, 1927
>
> Dear Sir:—
>
> I should be grateful if you would send me a short biographical note for inclusion in "The Best Short Stories."
>
> Faithfully yours,
> Edward J. O'Brien
>
> H. P. Lovecraft, Esq.

Sure, now, an' how iver did Idward come to know as Oi was wan av the ould Cǎseys from Country Tyrone? But we Oirish hov a way a foindin' out these matthers, & wance we foinds it out, we're the grǎǎte bh'ys for shtickin' togither! Begorra, but 'tis glǎǎd Oi om this Cǎsey business come to loight in toime fer the 1928 Bist Shōārt Shthories—at laste, I'm thinkin' 'tis the '28 me name will be in, sinct Oi'm seein' the '27 one advertoised as bein alriddy out.[6] I sent O'Brien a short paragraph, & will be interested to see—a year hence—how much of it he uses in his concise directory of the year's fictionists. The story which won his approval was obviously (in view of the address he used) "The Colour Out of Space". I'm really pleased at this incident, since O'Brien is quite a recognised authority & not altogether indiscriminate in his praise. I hope the importance of this majestic accolade will properly impress Wright!

Don't hurry in the least about the bookplate—indeed, I had no idea that you could attend to such a matter except in vacation time. I'll look up what I can about bookplates—in fact, I saw one or two last October whilst rummaging about the storage place—but am not very diligent about library research, as you know. I'm hibernating now—haven't been out but three or four times in the last month—but in the spring I'm likely to be a little spryer. It may be that the best dope of all will come from something right in this house, but just now hopelessly packed away—a bookseller's catalogue with a lot of reproductions of bookplates, which I'm sure I had once, & which there's not at least a possibility of my having still. If I find it I'll send it along for your inspection & possible emulation.

Got a queer revisory client recently—an old guy once associated with Cousin Ambrose Gwinnett Bierce, & now trying to capitalise the publicity obtained through the circulation of a new Bierce death report. This bird appears to be a German savant originally known as Dr. Gustav Adolf Danziger, but now sporting the Latinised appellation of "Adolphe de Castro". He had a hand in the preparation of "The Monk & the Hangman's Daughter", but later fell out with Bierce, so that (according to George Sterling) his final interview with that austere worthy was signalised by Cousin Gwinett's breaking a cane over his head.[7] That's the way us Princes of North Wales does when any guy gits fresh wit' us! But the head was thick, & it is still with us—& just now it wants Grandpa Theobald to fix up some old tales for re-publication in book form. The specimen whereon I'm now toiling is pretty bad—in fact, I'm consoled by the realisation that the rest can't be worse—& in the end I guess total re-writing will be more effective than revision.[8] If this business goes through, the old boy may have me help on a volume of Bierce reminiscences—indeed, he speaks of bringing his MS. to Providence for consultation.[9] Financially, I shall be on my guard—for I think (judging by Sterling's comment & by Bierce's own preface to the 1906 reprint of "Monk & Hangman's Daughter") the old geezer is a bit slippery; but with advance pay I don't need to be too close in my ethical analysis.

And W. Paul Cook & I have got that damn Bullen book done at last! It proved a frightful nuisance, & the premature printing of much of the text caused vast delay & reprinting; but I've seen a copy at last & am pretty well satisfied. I suppose I told you about it—the posthumous poems of the late amateur John Ravenor Bullen, which a wealthy friend of his in Chicago wished edited by me at his own expense.[10] It's a pretty choice item mechanically—text 100% perfect, & very well arranged by Cook—& ought to sell well among those who knew the author.

Speaking of Cook—I hope he did not fail to send both you & Wheeler his recent *Recluse* containing my article on weird literature. I gave him both your names & told him to be sure to remember. The venture has been very favourably received by the humble & the eminent alike—Vincent Starrett expressing particular enthusiasm. If you haven't received it, be sure to let Cook—or me—know. The cover design is by your fellow-artist & fellow-Dutchman Vrest Teachout Orton. Cook was here again early this month, & we made the usual raid on Eddy's bookstall. I think I told you that we're both collecting Old Farmer's Almanacks in an effort to expand our respective hereditary files to something like completeness. Mine now goes back solidly to 1839, & scatteringly to 1805. I've still a lot more to get!

Well—write when you can, & may Cthulhu & Ghinu jointly bless thee!

Yr obt
O'Howard McPhillips ap Lovecraft

Notes

1. See W. Paul Cook, *In Memoriam: Howard Phillips Lovecraft* (1941), who notes that "and where" was "one of Howard's favorite phrases when showing visitors around the city. He would stop at a spot where the view would be comparable to that of a country village. 'Where, except in Providence,' he would ask, 'in the midst of a large city, will you find a view like that?' The next view would be a sylvan scene. 'Where save in Providence, in the midst of a large city . . .' he would say. The next step it would be, 'Where, save in Providence. . . .' And after that the single word 'Where . . .,' with an expressive gesture embracing the scene before him" (*Ave* 67).

2. Jean-Antoine Watteau (1684–1721), French painter credited with inventing the genre of fêtes galantes, scenes of bucolic and idyllic charm, suffused with a theatrical air.

3. See bibliography under Charles A. Meader. The small book was "Reprinted from the East Greenwich News of September 5, 1927, and published by subscription." Rev. Meader was rector of St. Luke's Episcopal Church, East Greenwich, R.I. from 1925 to 1942.

4. Button Gwinnett (1735–1777), representative of Georgia to the Continental Congress and one of the signatories (first signature on the left) of the Declaration of Independence; also provisional president of Georgia in 1777.

5. HPL refers to the Knights of Columbus and the Ancient Order of Hibernians, both Catholic fraternal organizations. (HPL jokingly assumes that Edward J. O'Brien, as a man of Irish ancestry, is a member of these organizations.)

6. See "[Biographical Notice]" in Bibliography.

7. "Danziger was the person over whose head Bierce broke his cane to fragments . . ." George Sterling, "Introduction" to Bierce's *In the Midst of Life* (New York: Modern

Library, 1927), x. HPL owned the volume (*LL* 99).

8. The story that HPL was revising for de Castro at this time was "The Last Test" (originally titled "A Sacrifice to Science" by de Castro), one of three stories in *In the Confessional and the Following* (1893) that HPL revised. The other two are "The Electric Executioner" (orig. "The Automatic Executioner") and "In the Confessional" (HPL's revised version is nonextant).

9. The reminiscences were published as *Portrait of Ambrose Bierce* (1929). HPL did not in fact revise them, but Frank Belknap Long did (and wrote a preface).

10. The friend was Archibald Freer (1862–1943).

[26]   [ALS, JHL]

Friday the 13th
[13 January 1928]

Sir Clarencieux King-at-Arms:—[1]

The address of *Tales of Magic & Mystery* is 931 Drexel Bldg., Philadelphia, Pa. I certainly think they'd at least consider "The Charnel Den", & I'd advise you to try it on 'em. Enclosed is a bit of information on one of the disagreeable slips which accompanied on the return trip 7 out of the 8 MSS. I submitted.[2] Congrats, incidentally, on the appearance of Alabad, Ghinu, & Aratza in the current W.T. Young Derleth tells me that a reader gives my "Colour Out of Space" a delightful puff this month in the correspondence columns of *Amazing Stories*—so that I'll have to buy the magazine out of vanity, although I dropped it a couple of months ago!

And here is your design, minus the retainable corners. Let me apologise for my greedy gobbling—I wouldn't have done it had not the heraldry worn so personal a look. It certainly is a *superb* piece of "mantling"—if that's what you call it,—& I take off my hat to your skill in shading & vivifying it even though the transparency of the paper suggests a tracing process. Such work as that indeed tempts me to veer to the heraldick side in the bookplate question, though I dare say my next walk past the old Baptist steeple will shift me to the other side again. Hell! I guess I'll have to sport *two* plates, one for the inside front cover & t'other for the inside back cover!!

That's a clever EX LIBRIS [/] H P Lovecraft [overprinted] device of yours for saving space, & I'll leave to you & to precedent—provided I don't decide on the Old Providence design before summer—whether to follow that way & put the motto in the ribbon, or whether to print "Ex Libris" straight, & put the name in the ribbon. By the time we get to the decision—if we do decide on *an* heraldick pattern—I may possibly have seen some precedent-affording samples. It all depends on my time & energy—neither of which is anything to brag about this month.

I shall be all ears & courtesy when your business proposition comes along—& acceptance will doubtless depend on (a) how much cash is demanded, (b) how much effort is demanded, & (c) how much profit is promised. I'm a hard business guy—no aesthetic nonsense about me—that's what laid the foundations for my enormous fortune!

Well—back to the grind. I'm on the damnedest job in years—all the more exasperating because I let myself get beaten down to a cut rate before I saw how hellish a task it would be to make anything out of the sloppy drivel in question![3] May Alabad, Ghinu, & Aratza take the whole Cthulhu-cursed business!

Yours for snappier shields & bigger & better crests,

Owen Gwynedd O'Casey Ui Niall.

Notes

1. An officer of arms at the College of Arms in London. Gordon Ambrose de Lisle Lee (1862–1927) held the office, but his death in September left the post vacant. It was next held by Sir Arthur William Steuart Cochrane (1872–1954).
2. HPL had submitted 8 stories ("The Strange High House in the Mist," "The Nameless City," "From Beyond," "Beyond the Wall of Sleep," "In the Vault," and others) to *Tales of Magic and Mystery,* a short-lived pulp magazine (December 1927–April 1928; 5 issues) edited by Walter B. Gibson. All were rejected except "Cool Air," which appeared in the March 1928 issue.
3. Presumably "The Last Test."

[27]　[ALS, JHL]

Friday
[20 or 27 January 1928]

H. R. H. Wilfred I, Dec de Blauvelt & Prince of Orange,
Excellency:—

Yours pleasantly at hand, & "Dragon-Fly" perused with appropriate emotions. Ygghhrrhr!!! Take it away . . . that Thing at the window . . . .!!! Upon my word, Sir, you have turned out a great little story, & Brother Wright is an absolute candidate for the cerebral infirmary if he doesn't snap it up! The only changes I can suggest are the merest details. On page 2, toward the bottom, I think the wording might be clarified a trifle. What is meant is the following, is't not?

$$\left\{ \begin{array}{l} \text{as a foil} \\ \text{as a contrast} \end{array} \right\}$$

. . . . but she felt that even they would be welcome *in contrast* to} Johnson's taciturnity, or *to* the boisterousness of the young people who ignored her *so* completely.

Of course this is only a suggestion—do as you like about it. You prepare the plot splendidly—throwing out just the right ideas for ultimate development. You also suggest the coming of IT with admirable atmospheric skill. Good work, son! Keep it up! The Visitor is finely drawn—& if there's anything in that scene I'd suggest changing, it's the Voice from Below. Literal statements somehow make one pause. Why not suggest, indirectly, the substance of the message, & have the Voice utter something in the unknown & wholly extra-terrestrial language? The second climax is good, & I don't know whether or not I ought to suggest a subtler treatment—or a more *surprising* treatment. I was wondering if a vivid study in *degrees* of fear couldn't be made by having only Blackmoor discovered first, & by having him give his story before the searchers know where his wife's body is. He shews fear as he tells of the dragon-fly, but when they ask him where the woman is he displays a *fresh* fear so great that the other fright—at the Visitor—is dwarfed. The men search—fancying perhaps that he has killed his wife—& then, in another room, they find . . . . . The Thing That May Once have been Paula Blackmoor. Here somebody ought to faint, or something—& the more *indefinite* the description can be made, the greater the potentiality of utter, ultimate panic fright. To me it's a tossup whether this oughtn't to be the end. Of course, the vacant grave is a big asset—perhaps it had better be retained—with the whirring, & with a faint voice from below, speaking *unknown* words in an unknown tongue. *Vagueness* is the chief asset of horror, & the plot elements are really definite enough without the spirit voice in careful English-language Explanation. But don't let my remarks give you the idea that I don't think it's a splendid tale. It is—& I'm sure it'll land big with Wright. If not, try it on the new *Tales of Magic & Mystery*—they've just accepted my "Cool Air". I'm sending the story on to Belknap as you request, with instructions for its final return to you.

Speaking of stories—after a look at the older O'Brien annual I can say pretty positively that my fellow-Celt is only going to give me an also-ran's consolation prize. The "Biographical Roll of Honour" is so long as to form no real distinction, whilst very few tales are reprinted. And the letter—or note—made no mention of anything save wishing a short biographical paragraph. So that's that—nothing to get excited about. What *is* of greater import is Wright's determination—despite my warning about technical consequences—to reprint "The Lurking Fear" from Houtain's defunct *Home Brew* & give me 78 iron men therefor! Thus at last I'm really cashing in on your Nieuw-Nederland atmosphere—& the frightful House of Martense. Wright, by the way, just sent me the firm's new book—"The Moon Terror" &c. Well edited[1] & tastefully printed, I think, despite the cheap paper. Wheeler is right in praising "Haunted Island", though one mustn't forget some other fine work in "Cloisonné". I think your Standard–Onion[2] associate is right, too, about the merits of "Dragon Fly". Speaking of associates—I saw a story by your friend Wellman in W.T.,[3] & although it wasn't altogether distinctive, it was nevertheless amazingly far from rotten.

As for Hibernian fortunes—our whole family had a Thanksgiving dinner with the Brennans this year,[4] & I wish we'd then known of their coming luck. Sure, 'tis on the right side av thim I must be after gettin', & many's the foine dinner they'll shlip me in ther Campus Shop or Ristyraunt—or maybe fix up me plumbin' chape the nixt toime it lakes! That is, unless the McGranes win. I'll match that offer of a million rakeoff if you'll shift the legacy to the Caseys of the County Tyrone—you're afther knowin' us—us widh the rid hand—the sinishther rid hand[5]—fer our thrade-marrk! Speaking of elusive fortunes—did you know our fellow W.T. contrib Eddy of Providence is a descendant of Dukes of Marlborough & heir to untold millions of the try-&-get-it sort? I had a press cutting all about that, but can't find it now. My grandfather once looked up a Rathbone fortune—when in London for other reasons—just long enough to see how impossible it is to land any of these vaguely floating hereditaments, & I have seen the name Lovecraft in lists of missing heirs-at-law without having any unsophisticated impulses to take the next boat over & besiege Chancery with a dramatic "I-am-the Man!" act. But I'll tell you what. I'm a sport—& when you can shew legal proof of having raked in your An-netje Jans legacy & turned them Trinity rascals out, I'll start a campaign for both Rathbone & Lovecraft fortunes! I'll let you be my genealogical adviser—& I'll get you honest Eddy as a client, too.

Thanks for the cuttings. Here's Socony again—& I've just dropped John D. a card asking for his mag regularly.[6] I wish I could get a back file—why didn't somebody tell me about this before, damn it all? Of the churches shewn in the cutting, I've seen all except the Lyme reproduction & the Old Ship in Hingham. I mean to visit the latter next summer, when I plan a Cape-Cod-&-South-of-Boston orgy as extensive as my North-of-Boston orgy of last August. Thanks also for Bierce. I suppose I told you that I'm going revision for the old bird "de Castro" (whose real name is Dr. Gustav Adolf Dan-ziger) responsible for this latest death rumour. He may come to Prov. for a discussion when he recovers from his present grippe attack—but meanwhile I'm having untold trouble with his alleged fiction. It is even more unbelievably rotten than I thought at first, & is taking so much of my time & energy that I can't do a damn thing else. I'll have to call a halt unless he'll pay more.

Yes—a Christmas card surely is a bit cramped for a full pedigree! Gord knows I can't copy all my charts just now—but here's a rough sketch which at least beats the Yuletide offering.[7]

———

DAMN! I started to do something brief, but look what a mess I've dished up! Fear it isn't much more legible than the Christmas card! The Phillips side needs more research, for the chart fails to show half a dozen hookups orally & indeterminately known. I think I know of one book (which I haven't seen) & one old lady in Foster R.I. (whose set of charts is very ample, & who is related to us on the Tyler side, wherever that may happen to join up with Place & Phillips) whence good results may some day come, but hell only knows when I'll ever get the time or patience to do the work. I must buy the book I spoke of—the Rathbone genealogy, by John C. Cooley. It isn't in the library, & I begrudge the 6 bucks it costs. I'll look up the Tercentenary book—but I certainly didn't notice it the day we were at the libe. Also—you contract for more hard work than you dream when you offer to do these coats! The specimen of mantling you enclosed is magnificent—I've drawn in the fox heads & called it the official archive copy of the Lovecraft coat. The Allgood crest & Place lion are also finely done! As for others—I'll give 'em to you gradually, in order of closeness to myself. We can consider Lovecraft, Phillips, (newspaper copy) Place, Rathbone, Allgood, & Casey as done—& therefore turn to the next generations earlier. This brings Whipple, Perkins, Wilcox, & Hazard in the maternal line, but you needn't attempt these till you've checked up with the plates in the Tercentenary book. On the paternal side the next tier of new names gives Fulford & Morris—but oh, boy, what a mouthful is the former!! This checkerboard seems to be what the family now regularly sport, but I won't make you duplicate it. As you see, one quartering is for FULFORD proper, & I'll let that go for the whole. It's commendably simple. In the next tier I get Edgecombe, Wood, & Purcell; but in order not to overload you I'll give at present only the one present in a double dose. As you'll see by the chart—if you can read it—I'm full of consanguineous ancestry on both sides; a cause which Belknap thinks is responsible for my decadence. Maternally, I'm simply a tangle of Phillpses, Rathbones, Caseys, Hazards, & Mathewsons—they get monstrously mixed toward the top of the chart. In all truth, the old R.I. stock is perhaps more thoroughly intermarried than that of any other region outside the decadent Tennessee hills. R.I. was more a *family* than a *colony*. I don't think *any* old Rhode Islander can claim to be absolutely free from a strain of common blood with *any other* old Rhode Islander. For example—your ghostly neighbour of the 256 district, Steven Hopkins, was the great-grandson of that same Capt. John Whipple who is my 6-times-great grandfather. (His house, by the way, is now safely on its new foundations at Hopkins & Benefit. O Shades of Adams' store!)

I know all about the Montague "branch" [try & find the main dump that it's a branch of!] of the Bklyn. publibe. It was my nearest haven in 1925—though I actually spent more time at the NY one in 42nd St & 5th Ave. I have both cards still—but I'd give a damn sight more for the little red Prov. one now in active use! Glad you have the *Recluse,* & hope Wheeler got his. Cook may reprint my article some time—Vincent Starrett wants him to—but if [/] when he does I want to make some revisions—both deletions & insertion. Note the misprint of "Clarence" for *Clemence* Housman. There is only the one number of *The Recluse*—it was bound in a variety of colours, of which I have two. Orton did pretty well with the cover, I think. Now you & Bernard Dwyer & Clark Ashton Smith ought to submit designs. I'd vote for you any day where decorative elements are concerned. You really have remarkable gifts in that direction. Yes—I'd try the "Charnel Den" for the next *Recluse.* That's a darned good story, & I'm sure Cook would be glad of it. What sort of a magazine is this *Thrills* anyway? That *National Amateur* is for you to keep. It is the most notable issue ever published,[8] but Cook never gave it wide distribution. When I was in Athol last August I persuaded him to send out some more, (his cellar is full of them) & addressed a few envelopes to give him a start. He is only just getting around to it. I suppose I've told you that the posthumous Bullen book is done at last. Boy, what a job! But I'm really proud of the result as a piece of bookmaking. Could you get it reviewed in the Standard Onion if Cook or I slip you a free copy? Well—back to my de Castro work. G'dam!!!!!

Ancestrally & heraldistically thine, Theobald O'Casey.

Notes

1. By Farnsworth Wright, though not credited. See Bibliography under A. G. Birch.
2. HPL mocks the name of the *Brooklyn Standard Union*, a newspaper.
3. Probably "Back to the Beast" (November 1927).
4. Not neighbors or friends but a local restaurant/caterer at 214 Thayer Street/104 Waterman Avenue (HPL called it a "hash joint").
5. The Latin word for left is *sinister*, and so HPL jokes about the right hand being "sinister."
6. The *Socony Standard* was published by the Standard Oil Company of New York.
7. There is no such "sketch" in the letter. If it was done on a separate page, it has been lost.
8. *National Amateur* (41, No. 6), dated July 1919, but Cook did not publish it until roughly two years later, apparently shortly after the NAPA election in the summer of 1921. It contains HPL's "The Picture in the House," written in December 1920, and "Idealism and Materialism—A Reflection."

[28]   [ALS, JHL]

Candlemas [2 February 1928]

Arch-Herald!—

Thanks & congrats! Again my impotent envy of your artistic skill must take itself out in grateful panegyric! As one might expect of modern postal menials, your underscored "do not bend" was blithely disregarded— but the design was by no means ruined. It could even be framed without visible impropriety. The motto, as I have it, begins with QVAE or QVÆ— plural—instead of "QVA", though you may have found some authority of the latter in your varied delvings. However, I'll stand by the written record in preference to any printed version; since even my slight acquaintance with heraldic & genealogical works has shewn me how capriciously variable & generally unreliable they are. That QVAE comes from what amounts to two separate sources, & I'll stand by it—even if merely on the strength of three generations' continuous usage, which is absolutely indisputable. In your design I have *very* carefully made the A into an Æ by means of penknife & pen.

Though I am no skilled craftsman, the result doesn't look at all bad; & will look still better when the blue-black ink turns jet black, as it will eventually. I didn't want to bother you to change it yourself in this instance—but remember I stand by the QVAE if you decide to do the heraldic bookplate. I'll leave wholly to you & to custom the question as to whether the diphthong ought to be joined—Æ—or separate—AE.

Just finished the worst revision job of the season, & am trying to take a much-needed breath despite the task of coping with piled-up correspondence. Going to read a new weird book that the reviews have mentioned favourably—"Witch Wood", by John Buchan. I try to keep up on the weird stuff nowadays, in case Cook ever asks me to prepare a revised edition of my Recluse article for publication as a separate brochure, as he says he may do some day. Two other new ones I want to read are "The Dark Chamber" by Leonard Cline, & "The Place called Dagon" by Herbert Gorman.

Got a cheque from Tales of Magic & Mystery—only $18.50 for a story which must contain at least 3000 words. Poor pay—but since W.T. had rejected the item, it's better than nothing. The issue containing it will be on the stands presently.

I have a copy of the Bullen book all wrapped in case you can get a review in the Bklyn Times. We've only sent out 10 review copies so far, preferring not to waste 'em where they won't bring results.

By the way—Ackerman Co. & the Title Guarantee Co. both have fine Providence antiquarian calendars this year. The Ackerman one is splendid—& I got the *last one!*

    Yr obt Servt
      H P L

P.S. New court house starts next week. Enclosed are pictures—which please return.* The handling of mass effects—clustering of many gables—suggests at once the roof line of an old colonial town, & the newer type of American commercial architecture.

[29] [ALS, JHL]

                Thursday
              [7? June 1928]

Dear W B T:—

    Well, I'll be . . . . say, what is "gorddamned" in good old Nieuw Nederlandt Dutch? So that ass Wright returned "Dragon Fly", did he? He *would* do a thing like that! Well—here's hoping Tales of Magick & Mystery has better sense. If it doesn't land there, try tinkering with it a bit as to atmosphere & detail. There's great stuff in it, & if you only handle it right, somebody

---

*unless you can use it on account of Adam's store!

ought to see it sooner or later. Glad you found "Cthulhu" less than a total bore. Did you notice the nawsty crack I worked in about the Fleur-de-Lys building in Thomas St. near my favourite steeple? I wish somebody would send a marked copy to Sydney R. Burleigh, the goof responsible for that monstrosity[1] . . . . . though on the other hand I don't, since I have reason to think the old duffer may have repented. He draws historical & traditional maps in the Ortelian manner[2] nowadays—I have his Providence one & am about to get his South County one. And he lives in a real Colonial house on College Hill. As for the overworked word in Cthulhu—tell me when you think of it, & I'll tell you whether the repetition was intentional or not. Overwork of certain words is an old fault of mine, but I fancy you'll find it somewhat less in my newer work.

Thanks for the heraldry—I do feel damn guilty making you look up so much stuff when I can't afford to come across with the 0.75 to 1.00 per horam! As for that Fulford checkerboard—I suppose different bearers varied it to suit their taste, as was probably more or less permissible so long as they didn't tamper with their own quartering—i.e., *Fulford*. Glad you hear the Fulfords go back to Coeur de Lion's time. But say—you have that *Moreton* quartering spelled *Morton!* However, I've lately heard that the two are identical in origin; so that instead of giving up Dunsany as a cousin I'll merely annex our friend James Ferdinand! What you get for *Carew* is not quite so ambitious as the arrangement recorded in the data I have. As I told you, this outfit has *supporters* 'n' everything—though I know not on how good authority. Do you suppose the supporters are in error due to the fact that some lone member of the family once gained them through a now-extinct peerage or baronetcy, & that other branches informally but unauthorisedly swiped the critters? Gawd, if that's so I could tack 'em onto *Phillips*, since as you'll recall from a book we saw at the pub, there is now a baronet of the collateral line. Here's what I had for *Carew:*

Arms:	Or, 3 lioncels[3] (not *lions*) passant in pale sable armed & langued gules.
Crest:	A mainmast, the round top set off with palisadoes, or, a lion issuing thereout sable.
Supporters:	Dexter, a lion sable; sinister, an antelope gules.
Motto:	J'espere bien.

These damn things seem to *vary* so much that a guy can never be sure of what's right. Suppose one had one's coach-panels & silver plate all fixed up one way, & then along came some evidence that it ought to be t'other way! It's a tense & exacting game, kid! My sainted grandsire's notes on this line gave the Saxon ancestor as *Otho*, not *Otheus*, and *didn't say a bally word about that Celtick marriage.* My gawd, how them Celtic princes pursue me! Princes of North Wales—Princes of South Wales—Hell! I ought to own all of Wales! I shall certainly fall off the very next horse I mount! Well, well . . . . if one must have Celts it's a good thing to have 'em royal & knightly ones. And Otho was a good Teuton anyway, I'm sure! As for that *Morris*—it is of Clasemont, Glamorganshire, Wales, if that means anything. Come to think of it, I sent you the blazoning as I found it. So *Gorton*[4] had a goat . . . if you've read anything of R.I. history you'll see how often some of the other colonists got it! Glad my records were O K on *Whipple. Hazard,* if you ask me, is anybody's guess; since according to the book we saw at the libe nobody has ever succeeded in conclusively placing the old Tom from whom all the R.I. Hazards—a really eminent line, in the direct descent—are sprung. The only standard of choice is whatever the main branch choose through caprice to sport. There has been dispute as to whether the first ancestor was really a *Hazard* or *Hassard,* though the two are nearly related, as extreme similarity of arms proves. Both are in our notes—the one you cite being *Hazard,* whilst *Hassard* is gules, two bars argent; on a chief, or, 3 escallops of the first—crest, an escallop or. Glad to know which is considered most O K. I note your Perkins correction. Your version is about like mine, though the chart I have doesn't connect conclusively with other lines. I have a Wood coat in the papers I dug up, & guess it's the right one. It's supposed to be of Tawton, Devon. Hope it's the ancient one you mention. The blazoning I've got is *Argent, a tree vert; on a chief azure 3 trefoils slipped or.* No crest given. I don't know from what Morrises William sprang, but I guess I'll claim him even if he was a socialist.[5] I enjoy sitting in his chairs, though they're damn ugly. Glad to claim Mark Twain—all I know about my Clemences is that the first in R.I. was Thomas (d. 1688) son of Richard & Sarah. He was also known as *Clement.* (not *Clemons*) Arms as given in my notes—*gules, 3 garles, argent,* no crest. As for "wheel charts"—bless me, that's *just what I want!*[6] I saw some of 'em in the possession of that old Foster lady—Nabby Tyler Kennedy—whom I told you I must consult for Place–Phillips data, when I called on her in 1926; & admired them almost as much as I admired her 3 naturally tailless cats. I didn't know their technical name, but they were circular-looking affairs, & must surely have been the sort of thing you mention. I'll be glad to get some from your friend—let me know the price & I'll fork over. I'd better have an extra if you want a copy of my dark past— I'm damned if I feel like drawing another home-made affair, which would probably turn out as bad as the existing specimen toward the top! I'll be delighted with the drawing of the Lovecraft arms you tentatively promise—& as for the bookplate—well, if you follow your high-handed design you'll at least have saved me the agonies of decision! I guess heraldick design is easier to do than Georgian steeples of cyma-curve pediments, at that!

Speaking of bookplates—after all, I found one in an old (1767) volume (Derham's Astro-Theology) right on my shelves, despite the fact that I thought they were all in that batch still down at the storage stable. I don't know what it is, for there's no name, & it isn't anything mentioned in the ancestral notes I found, so it may be an ancestor & may not. The book is of paternal inheritance, though its remoter past history is to me unknown. Here it is—not that I can do the mantling really Talmanick justice:

If the shadings mean anything, the base is vert, the wee beastie Or, & the tree trunk azure.

(exact size) I guess the leaves are oak leaves. The tree is growing out of a stag's back, or else (on second thought) the stag is seated in the front of the tree.

I'll look up others when spring releases some dormant energy & I get the present damn revision job out of the way. And I'll try to hunt up that catalogue with so many sample bookplates in it.

If you think you can get a review, I'll do more than send full details about the Bullen book. I'll send de tail & body & head all together & compleat—alteris verbis, the damn book itself! I'm authorised by the financial sponsor to distribute review copies at my discretion. Bullen was a Canadian amateur of such fine old family that you'd have loved to get at his heraldick wake. He was a royal good fellow & a poet of the mild, cheerful Victorian sort—to say nothing of being a lifelong invalid who bore his affliction with more than ordinary fortitude & cheerfulness. He died last February, & a wealthy friend in Chicago—one Archibald Freer, who speaks of Bullen as "the most ideal man I ever knew"—decided to launch a tribute to his memory in the form of a posthumous book of his poetry, to be financed by him as a gift to the Bullen family. Looking about for an editor, Bullen's mother decided that I knew about as much as anybody what he had been doing in the poetic line, hence asked me to prepare the book. It was no easy job, for all the revision & classifying had to be done by me; but I tackled it out of regard for Bullen's memory—for he was really a delightfully appealing & profoundly admirable chap. He had meant to have me help in preparing a book of his poems, & had chosen an essay of mine in the U.A. about his work[7] as a preface for the future volume—which he wished to call "White Fire". So, seeing that I was really the logical editor, I pitched in last August & reduced the bulk of rough, unclassified poems to standard book form, technique, & arrangement. Mrs. Bullen insisted on having the volume dedicated to me—saying that that had been her son's intention had he lived to issue a book. In seeking a publisher I of course turned to our good old friend W. Paul Cook of the Recluse Press—& boy! how he did back me up! In the face of all sorts of troubles & delays & blunders on the part of his office force he turned out what is undoubtedly the finest piece of bookmaking ever produced in amateur journalism; so that he really ought to have had an equal share in the dedication. Above all, he was ineffably patient with my hyper-critical proofreading, so that we have produced that rarest of literary marvels—a volume absolutely without typographical errors. The sale edition is bound in cloth, soft grey in colour, with grey paper labels, & will sell for $2.00 retail & $1.50 wholesale. Besides this, however, there was a special presentation edition of 24 copies in dark green leather stamped with gold—one of the richest & most austerely sumptuous bibliophilic items I have ever seen in my life. So exquisitely impressive is this edition that I am going to send one in Belknap's care for the gang's inspection. The book is of 86 pages, 6 × 9, on finest quality art paper, with genuine photographic frontispiece in sepia on an impressed panel. Cook, at Freer's urgent request, is handling the marketing & distribution; & I am helping by sending out complimentary & review copies, trying to place it in one or two bookstalls. I shall also ask Kirk & Loveman to list it in the next catalogues they issue. Yes—if you think you can get it a good review, I'll feel amply empowered to shoot you a free copy. It's really quite intoxicating to have this power of flinging about two-berry items with lavish hand, just as judgment or caprice may dictate.

Now as to your business proposition—I'd like to help, but must admit that my habits of seclusion & hermitage make me a dolefully bad candidate for the Providence agency! I am such a congenital recluse, & so poor a persuader in matters of commercial solicitation, that I fear my aid would be at best very meagre; although I shall be glad to bring up the subject of genealogy whenever I do find myself in conversation, & shall naturally not be slow to recommend the very best researcher in that field with whom I am acquainted. I'll keep your prices in mind—to me they seem surprisingly reasonable—& can surely be properly eloquent both concerning your powers of decorative draughtsmanship & your keen & conscientious ability in matters of ancestral research. If I ever landed you a prospect, I'd have to let you decide what a local agent's commission ought to be! Poor business-man that I am, I have not the remotest notion of what the custom is in such cases—10%? 20? Search me! Anyhow—alas—it doesn't look as if I could dig up any patients before your coming free days, since I'm just now absolutely ground into the dust beneath a load of the most discouragingly prostrating revision I've ever struck. I haven't been out since Jany. 2nd, & don't know when I can ever get out again. Only in a spirit of rare reaction & desperation do I take the time to write a necessary letter or two. I don't know when the peak will be past—but gord speed the day!

[balance missing?]

Yr obt Servt

H P L

Notes

1. Sydney Richmond Burleigh (1853–1931), American artist, known primarily for wa-

tercolors but also for oil paintings, drawings, illustrations, and building and furniture designs. He designed the Fleur-de-Lys Studios (1885) in Providence in collaboration with the architect Edmund Russell Willson of Stone, Carpenter, and Willson. In "The Call of Cthulhu," HPL had written that the building "flaunts its stuccoed front amidst the lovely colonial houses on the ancient hill, and under the very shadow of the finest Georgian steeple in America" (*CF* 2.42).

2. Referring to Abraham Ortelius (1527–1598), Flemish cartographer and geographer, recognized as the creator of the first modern atlas, the *Theatrum Orbis Terrarum*.

3. A lion: so called when three or more are displayed on an escutcheon.

4. Samuel Gorton (1593–1677), early settler and civic leader of the Colony of Rhode Island and Providence Plantations and President of the towns of Providence and Warwick.

5. William Morris (1834–1896), English textile designer, poet, novelist, translator, and socialist activist.

6. A fan, or wheel, chart is a half circle chart with concentric rings. The person of interest is represented by the inner circle; the second circle is divided in two (each side for one parent), the third circle is divided in four, and so forth.

7. "The Poetry of John Ravenor Bullen."

[30]   [ALS, JHL]

Tuesday [October? 1928]

Dear W B T:—

Alas! Eheu! Saline ocular effusions! An hour's search through my files has failed to disclose the lunch-wagon data you wish, & I can only conclude that the article is either lost or discarded as insufficiently colonial during one of my biennial overhaulings & elimination sessions. Again I exude decorous tears.

I hate to think of such a golden chance to make your journalistic reputation as lost—but what the hell can one do? If you weren't in a hurry, I'd advise you to write the Providence Journal & ask the date of the Sunday article (some time in 1925, I think) in question—in fact, I'd gladly do so, & look it up in the files for you. But since it's rush stuff—good night!

All that my senile memory holds is that the lunch wagon as an institution was invented about 50 or 60 years ago by a Providence Journal employe (still living, I think) named Scott—George Scott, if I recall rightly—who began by serving lunches to his fellow night-workers, & finally made a main business of the all-night belly-stuffing; adopting an abandoned horse-car on wagon-wheels as his migratory cafe.[1] Later he enlarged his fleet of gastronomic filling-stations with other obsolete rolling-stock, & finally built new wagons along the same general traditional lines. In time, of course, he had competitors—& I think he finally sold out his interests. Meanwhile the idea spread, & the all-night lunch wagon is now a standard institution in the economical life of an industrial republic. That's all my aged brain holds of the matter—for what has a gentleman to do with trade?—but I fancy all the sources of further information are accessible if you want to look up the matter at leisure. In such a case pray count on me for all possible coöperation. And once more let me repeat that I'm damn sorry I didn't save the Sunday Journal article whence my own fugitive scraps of half-information proceeded.

Hope the "White Fire" review isn't killed—slip me a copy, if convenient, if it does appear ultimately. Don't expend any extra effort with the *Citizen*—simply drop a good word for the Recluse Press if a chance handily develops in the ordinary course of Nature. The Boston Transcript & N Y Times did no more than list the book in 6-point type, & the Prov. Journal hasn't done as much as that! Damn those snobs!

I've been absolutely crushed—pulverised—triturated—annihilated—by a goddam mess of hellcusst revision which won't yield any impressive profits even when (or if ever) it is done. The result on my temperament has been deplorable—I'm as snarling & snappish as a fretful tortoise!

With appropriate lamentations—

Yr obt

H P L

Notes

1. Food vendor Walter Scott (1841–1924) conceived of the lunch wagon in 1872. He cut windows in a small covered wagon, parked it in front of a newspaper office in Providence, RI, and sold sandwiches, pies, and coffee to pressmen and journalists.

[31] [ALS, JHL]

Jany. 15, 1929

Mynheer:—

Welcome back to the land of the living! I wasn't quite sure whether your body would be found floating in a hidden Red Hook canal, or whether there would be tales of your footprints leading up to some ancient Dutch tomb, *and not leading away again.* Glad you still find the old Hook habitable—you must have a mercifully selective vision . . . . . & audition! I think the Tahoma was there during my exile, though I never paid much attention to any of the beastly slum mess beyond 169—except the tailor in the same block, the grocer on the corner of Atlantic, & the laundryman around the corner. As for the Tiffany—the rose-garlands & chandeliers may be new, but the mirrors were there in the old days. Indeed, the reason I chose the damn place as main eatery was that—while offering the low rates of a one-arm—it was free from the cursed white tiling that rubbed the idea of cheapness into the patron of most such joints. Dark woodwork, with mirror panels arranged like arched Georgian windows—that's what won me the Tiffany! And the food was decent & ample, too. But soon enough did this tasteful haven begin to sicken me, for the clientele was past enduring. Young toughs & gangsters, cheap sports, foul-mouthed gutter-scum . . . . ugh! Picturesque enough at first—but no place for a quiet old gentleman to dine regularly. Once a party of plain-clothes men dropped in & went though the pockets of one of the characteristic groups of young noisy bums. Fine home atmosphere! Well—I got all my stomach could stand in three or four months, & thereafter switched to Bickford's—near Borough Hall. White tiles were better than Red Hook decadence! Of course, when I felt able to afford something better than a one-arm, I had a greater choice of acceptable filling-stations. I know McCann's, though I ate more often at Joe's, at Peter's in Joralemon St., & at John's—the Italian joint around the corner in Willoughby St. For quality & variety, you can't beat Joe's—or at least, you couldn't in 1925. Once Kirk & I tried Johnson's Coffee Pot in Court St., & overheard a bunch of gaolbirds discussing the food & cells of Blackwell's Island. Believe me, the social & moral tone of Red Hook's modestly priced bean-bureaus is pretty nifty!

Glad your lunch-cart tale landed profitably, though sorry you couldn't get a copy. Absorption is in the Brooklyn air now—I read the other day that even the good old *Eagle* is now a link of a chain. Thanks for the Schenck–Crooke article—whose picture is really delightful. I knew the pirate dope in most of the accounts of this place was really pure fiction—indeed, I've heard that many Schenck descendants are rather furious about it; so much so that one or two have written to the papers and demanded that the libellous misinformation cease. Since you're emotionally Poe-proof, I suppose I ought not to wonder at the failure of the Schenck–Crooke house to impress you—but I must say it didn't disappoint me. I am infinitely glad to hear that the Flatbush C of C[1] is taking measures to safeguard it, for it is really an architectural specimen of the highest importance. Incidentally—have you heard that the city may take over & restore the old tide mill on Gerritses Creek beyond Ave. U—where the future Marine Park will be? As for the Nicholas Schenck house at Canarsie—I don't think it's as interesting as the S-C; though its perilous state of roofless ruin lends it a certain spectacular quality. Did I tell you that I virtually covered all the sights in that City History Club book before leaving the NY region last spring? There were some splendid specimens, & I wish to Gawd I'd had the book during my period of residence. Have you followed up all of its leads? Don't miss Gravesend Village—or the regions south of Flatbush in general. You will find that local differences in Dutch architecture occur—all-wood & shingle cottages predominating in the southern Long Island region where stone was scarce.

About Saints' Days—great Scott! don't you Dutchmen have any almanacks that give 'em? We New England rusticks get all that sort of dope from Robert B. Thomas's Old Farmer's Almanack, now in its 137th year.[2] But I can give you even more than the Old Farmer's gives, since I have a British annual for 1814 which specialises in such matter.[3] Here's a list—& you can ask me about any of the saints & festivals which you can't elucidate readily at the public library. I like to refer to these old institutions—it gives one a sense of tradition & continuity.

Jany 1—Circumcision
Jany 6—Epiphany
Jany 13—St. Hilary
   1st Sun. after Epiph.
Jany 18—St. Prisca
Jany 20—St. Fabian
   (1929) 2nd Sun. after Epiph.
Jany 21—St. Agnes
Jany 22—St. Vincent
Jany 25—Conversion of St Paul
Jany 27 (1929) Septuagesima Sun.
Jany 30—King Charles I, Martyr
Feby. 2—Candlemas, or Purifica-
   tion of B. V. M.
Feby 3—St Blase—
   (1929) Sexagesima Sun.
Feb. 5—St. Agatha
Feby 10—Quinquagesima (1929)
Feby 12—(1929) Shrove Tues.
Feby 13 (1929) Ash Weds.
Feby 14—St Valentine
Feby 17—(1929) Quadragesima
Feby 24—St. Matthias
   (1929) 2nd Sun. in Lent
Mar 1—St David
Mar 2—St Chad
Mar 3—(1929) 3d Sun in Lent
Mar 7—St Perpetua
Mar 10—1929) 4th Sun in Lent
Mar 12—St Gregory
Mar 17—St Patrick
   (1929) 5th Sun. in Lent
Mar 21—St Benedict
Mar 24—(1929) Palm Sun
Mar 25—Annunc. B. V. M. or Lady
   Day
Mar 28—(1929) Maundy Thurs.
Mar 29—(1929) Good Fri
Mar 31—Easter
Apr 1—All Fools'
Apr 3—St Richard
Apr 4—St Ambrose
Apr 7—Low Sunday (1929)

Apr 14—2nd Sun after Easter (1929)
Apr 19—St Alphage
Apr 21—1929 3d Sun after Easter
Apr 23—St George
Apr 25—St Mark
Apr 28 (1929) 4th Sun. after Easter
Apr 30—Black Sabbath[4]
May 1—May Day—SS. Philip & James
May 3—Invention of Cross
May 5—(1929) Rogation Sun.
May 6—St. John Evangelist Deliver'd
May 9—Ascension (1929)
May 12—Sun. after Asc. (1929)
May 19—St. Dunstan
   (1929) Whitsuntide
May 26—St Austin
   (1929) Trinity Sun.)
May 27—Venerable Bede
May 29—Charles II Restored
May 30—(1929) Corpus Christi
Jun 1—Nicomede
Jun 2—(1929) 1st Sun after Trin.
Jun 5—St Boniface
Jun 9—(1929) 2nd Sun After Trin.
Jun 11—St Barnabas
Jun 16—(1929) 3d Sun After Trin.
Jun 17—St Alban
Jun 20—Translation of Edward,
   King of West Saxons.
Jun 23—(1929) 4th Sun. After Trin.
Jun 24—St John Baptist—
   Midsummer Day
Jun 29—SS. Peter & Paul
Jun 30—(1929) 5th Sun. after Trinity
July 2—Visitation B. V. M.
Jul 3—Dog Days begin
Jul 4—Translation St Martin
Jul 7—Thomas-a-Becket
   (1929) 6 Sun after Trin
Jul 14 (1929)7 Sun aft Trin
Jul 15—St Swithin
Jul 20—St Margaret
Jul 21—(1929) 8 Sun aft Trin

Jul 22—S. Mary Magdalen
Jul 25—St James
Jul 26—St Anne
Jul 28—(1929) 9 Sun aft Trin
Aug 1—Lammas
Aug 4—(1929) 10 S. a. T.
Aug—Transfiguration B. V. M.
Aug 7—Name of Jesus
Aug 10—St Lawrence
Aug 11—(1929) 11 S. a. T.
Aug 15—Assumption B. V. M.
Aug 18—12 S. a. T.
Aug 24—St. Bartholomew
Aug 25 (1929) 13 S. a. T.
Aug 28—St Augustine
Aug 29 St John Baptist beheaded
Septr 1—St Giles
    (1929) 14 S. a. T.
Septr 2—London burnt 1666
Septr 7—St Eunrclus
Septr 8—Nativity B. V. M.
    (1929) 15 S. a. T.
Septr 14—Holy Cross
Septr 15—(1929) 16 S. a. T.
Septr 17—St Lambert
Sep 21—St Matthew
Sep 22 (1929) 17 S a T
Sep 26—Sy Cyprian—Old Holyrood
Sep 29—Michaelmas—St Michael
    & All Angels
    (1929) 18 S a T
Sep 30—St Jerome
Oct 1—St Remigius
Oct 6—St. Faith
    (1929) 19 S a T
Oct 9—St Denis
Oct 13—Trans. Edward Confessor—
    (1929) 20 S a T
Oct 17—St Ethelrede
Oct 18—St Luke

Oct 20—(1929) 21 S a T
Oct 25—St Crispin
Oct 27—(1929) 22 S a T
Oct 28—SS. Simon & Jude
Ocr 31—All Hallows
Novr 1—All Saints
Novr 2—All Souls'
Novr 3—(1929) 23 S a T
Novr 4—Landing of Wiliam III
Novr 5—Guy Faukes' Day
Novr 6—St Leonard
Novr 9 Lord Mayor's Day, London
Nov 10—(1929) 24 Sun. aft Trin
Nov 11—St Martin—Martinmas
Novr 13—St Britins
Novr 15—St Malo
Novr 17—St Hugh
    (1929) 25 S a T
Novr 20—Edmund King & Martyr
Novr 22—St Cecilia
Novr 23—St Clement (old Mar-
    tinmas)
Novr 24 (1929) 26 S a T
Novr 25—St Catharine
Novr 30—St Andrew
Decr 1—Advent Sun. (1929)
Decr 6—ST. NICHOLAS
Dec 8—Conception B. V. M.
    (1929) 2nd S. in Advent
Dec 13—St Lucy
Dec 15—(1929) 3d S. in Adv.
Dec 16—O Sapientia
Dec 21—St. Thomas
Dec 22—(1929) 4th Sun. in Advent
Dec 25—Christmas
Dec 26—St Stephen
Dec 27—St John Evangelist
Dec 28—Holy Innocents
Dec 29—(1929) 1st Sun aft. Chr.
Dec 31—St. Sylvester

For Pete's sake, I didn't realise myself there were so many of 'em! You have a
course of study ahead of you!

No haste about the bookplate business—& the simple door minus the scene will be perfectly all right for me. There surely is art, mystery, & dignity about an austere, half-closed door! The design you furnish is quite suitable to follow in the main—but erase the old lady & have the panelling of the door as here shewn—with the *small* panels at the *top*. That was the most usual mode of panelling for a New England door. You are surely most considerate in proffering your artistic skill for this enterprise, & I shall certainly prove a highly appreciative beneficiary.

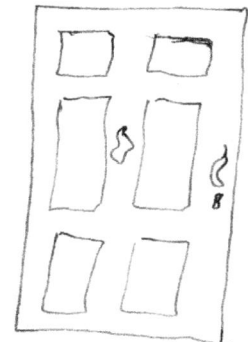

Sorry to hear the gang's so dispersed—why don't you call Riverside 3465 & arrange for a conference with Belknap? Bring your new discovery around, too. Loveman made a business trip to New England a couple of weeks ago, so I had a chance to shew him a few of my favourite antiquities. He couldn't stop long in Providence, but I accompanied him to Boston (I had been planning to go anyway & see the new decorative art & colonial wing at the Museum of Fine Arts) & took him over the historic rounds there. We also worked in a trip to Salem & Marblehead—the latter of which is absolutely the best preserved colonial town in America. At the Museum Loveman was so enraptured by the Greek stuff that we couldn't see the colonial wing—but I stayed over another day after the early departure which commercial necessity forced upon him. Then I did see the new wing—*& how!* Believe me, it's the most important thing of its kind in the country—far outclassing the American Wing at the Metropolitan! Not only American rooms, but rooms from France & England illustrating sources—away back to a genuine Tudor room of 1490 & a stained glass chapel window older than that. You must make a New England trip in the real antiquarian spirit some day!

Glad to hear you are doing so well on the *Times*—& wish I could get hold of something as remunerative as that. Youth, ability, & enterprise must be great things to have! I'm enclosing some things which I've had saved up for you for some time. That article on R.I. town arms ought to reawaken all your heraldic interest! Well—behave yourself reasonably, & don't let the Syrian assassins get you![5]

Yours for more & better Saints' Days—H P L

P.S. O'Brien gave me an 18-line biography in "Best Short Stories of 1928", & I am listed among third-raters in "O. Henry Memorial Prize Stories". The "Not at Night" anthology (Macy-Masius) edited by Herbert Asbury contains my "Red Hook" & two tales of Belknap's. A new weird anthology to be published by the Macaulay Co. will have my "Cthulhu", as well as tales by Munn & Belknap, & possibly Wandrei.[6]

Notes

1. I.e., Chamber of Commerce.

2. Robert B. Thomas (1766–1846), founder of *Old Farmer's Almanac* (1792), a reference book containing weather forecasts, tide tables, planting charts, astronomical data, recipes, and articles on such topics as gardening, sports, astronomy, and farming.

3. The item is probably *Merlinus Liberatus* (1814). See Bibliography under John Partridge [pseud.]. But HPL's list of saints' days is clearly taken from a 1929 almanac.

4. No saint's feast day. HPL refers to Walpurgis Night (Central and Northern Europe).

5. When HPL lived in Brooklyn, he said he had a Syrian neighbor, one Alexander Messayeh, in the apartment below his.

6. The book was *Beware After Dark!* It did not contain stories by the others named.

[32]   [AHT]

Somewhere in County Tyrone
2nd day after St. Patrick's
[19 March 1929]

Jonckheer O'Talman:—

Sure, now, an' 'twas rale kind of yez to be afther sendin' an ould man that chaart av ancesthral sates & hiraldries so prompt-like! Arrah, but it did make me homesick for a soight av the good ould sod, & the shamrock blossoms (if shamrocks have blossoms) Oi used to pluck by the soides of Lough Neah phwin a bye! I did not foind anny mintion of a *Casey* sate; but sure is it not possible that the *O'Neill* dominions cover all av that? 'Tis in O'Hart, ye'll be moindin', that the *Caseys* arre in rayallity *O'Neills;* their especial name comin' from one Cathasach (mainin' "the brave") who was an O'Neill. If iver Oi foind anny av thim othe graat houses in me lineage, Oi'll be askin' yez fer a copy av the arrums & such other information as ye kin give. Sure Oi'm half-moinded now to copy the O'Dwyer coat for the benefit av me frind & correspondent Bernar Dwyer av Kingston—in the New World county av Ulster—who was me host last year in the toime we came so nigh to meetin'. But incidentally—my Celtic blood got almost jolted out of me the other day when (after reading the fairly new book about my great-great-granduncle, the silversmith & counterfeiter Samuel Casey of Kingston, R.I.) I looked up the R.I. Casey line in J. O. Austin's Genealogical Dictionary of R.I. at the R.I. Historical Society. I hadn't done any looking since over a year ago, & had never tackled this book before—but bless me, what a point Austin raises! He *disputes* O'Hart on the origin of the R.I. Caseys, & says that they are **English Caseys of Gloucestershire** who had settled in Tyrone not more than a generation or two behind the 1641 massacre! I suppose he argues that the abundance of really Celtic Caseys in Ulster caused O'Hart to follow a false lead . . . . but then again, who ought to know best, a real Mick on the spot, like O'Hart, or a mere Yankee provincial like Austin? Who shall decide, when heraldiscists disagree!? What a bunch of deludherin' fellers ye all arre, annyways. Sure, betwixt the lot av yez, a mon can't tell phwither his grandfather's raley his grandfaather or ownly his grandson in disgoise! Now Oi don't know phwither a brogue comes nacheral-loike to me or not! Shall the Casey side av me sing "The Wearin' av the Grane" or "God Save the King"? Ochone! Ochone! Phy didn't Oi have the since to lit that felly Austhin alone? However—the book I spoke of—"The Silversmiths of Little Rest", by William David Miller—surely did re-interest me in the Caseys; for it cleared up my exact relationship to the artist-counterfeiter whose tankard masterpiece adorns the silver cases of your Metropolitan Museum. (I think I told you about the curious career of Sam the Silversmith—how his house burned down in 1764, & how in his subsequent poverty he turned to counterfeiting & was sentenced to be hanged. How, thereafter, his neighbours blacked their faces & stormed the gaol in a body to liberate him, & how he finally vanished toward the west on horseback, nevermore to be seen by his old friends.) Here is the way the thing goes:

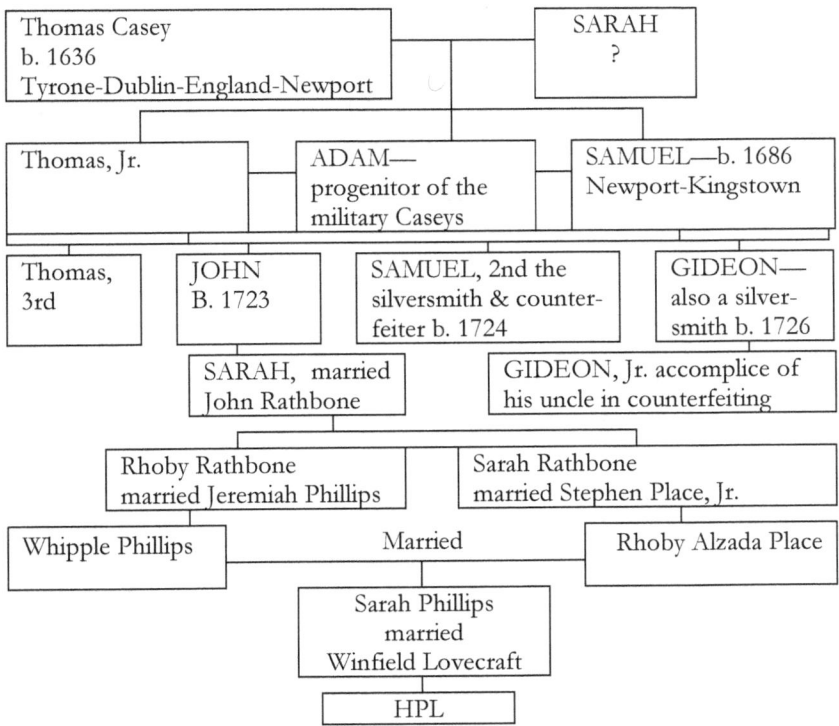

Well—the whole story is told in detail in this Miller book. We behold extracts from the papers recounting the burning of the house, & later on read reports of the arrest, trial, conviction, & liberation of the hapless hero. The coining plot was a piece of the same lawlessness which made the best Rhode Islanders natural-born smugglers, harbourers of pirates, and rebels against their lawful sovereign. Half the planters of South County were in it or winked at it—bringing all sorts of silver to Casey for purposes he took no special pains to explain! No wonder they felt it their duty to liberate him. The judges who condemned him in 1774 included Stephen Hopkins, Metcalf Bowler, (a room from whose Portsmouth country-seat is in the Met. American Wing) & James Helme—the latter the father of Casey's own pupil Nathaniel Helme! Great old times! And now whom shall we credit for Sam Casey's art & law-lessness . . . . . the English Caseys of Gloucestershire, or the Celtic Caseys of Tyrone? Austin or O'Hart? Well, I guess we'll split the difference. Give the art to the English Caseys, & trace the crime to the wild Micks! If this Miller book would interest you, you might find it in the N Y libe—either Room 328 or the art department. By the way—it's a good idea of yours to square us criminal Caseys with society by making an Howard Phillips a reg'lar detecka-tiff—an austere upholder of that legal majesty which Sam the Silversmith so rudely affronted! No—if the verbally prolific Mr. Oppenheim is one of our Phillipses,[1] he has neglected to prove his place on the line! Which reminds me that as soon as the weather gets decent, or as soon as I get back from a southerly tour I plan, I must look up that chap in Foster about whom I told you last fall—Frank Phillips of Clayville,[1] who can possibly tell me where to find the graves of two lineal forbears!

. . . . .   Yrs for the Ould Sod—
                  Pathrick O'Casey of Tyrone.

Notes

1. E[dward] Phillips Oppenheim (1866–1946), British novelist who wrote more than 100 novels between 1887 and 1943.
2. Frank Darius Phillips (1872–1958). See Kenneth W. Faig, Jr. "Lovecraft's Trave-logues of Foster, Rhode Island" 75n.133.

[33]   [ALS, JHL]

[Van Ross Hotel / Kingston, N.Y.]

Three Days before
St. Barnabas'
[8 June 1929]

Jonckheer:—

For the love of St. Nicholas![1] So *you* were up around old Wilt-wyck too when I was writing you them cards! Well, at 3 a.m. after the evening of Saturday May 11 I was finishing an aesthetick-historical discourse with my genial host Bernaardt Van Duier (or however you Nedelandise a straight Irish

Bernard Dwyer) & preparing to hit the hay in view of the fact that we were scheduled to meet Mynheer Franz Belnaap Van Long at 9 a.m. sharp. Knowing how you Dutchmen all cluster together, I ought to have known enough to ask some of the pipe-smoking burghers on their steps whether you were around the place—for of course all the villagers are posted on the whereabouts of the young patroon. But I jest nachelly forgot—hence was not present at the Liberty Inn when your riotous crew swaggered in & drank up all the toddy!

But at that I soaked up quite a bit of authentick Nieuw Nederland colour, for Wiltwyck hasn't changed much at heart since the ousted settlers of Rensslaerwyck came down to the Esopus in 1652, or since they built the palisado & got their charter from old Piet Stuyvesant in 1661. Did I not go into the old Ten Broeck house built in 1676? And did I not sleep four nights just around the corner from the still older Hoffmann house? But even Wiltwyck was not purely Dutch enough for me, so I paid a visit to that still unspoil'd village of Hurley, which a modern Dutch diplomat has called "more purely Dutch than anything left in Holland."

> "Wat zullen wij met die pannekoeken doen?
> Doop het met die stroop van Horley!"[2]

Here I went into the ancient Van Deusen house & the old Elmendorf store, & loafed along the broad village street in true Dutch fashion; noting the trim stone-built cottages, the graceful orchards & cultivated fields, & the purple heights of distant mountains in the background. Story'd Nieuw Dorp—with its Indian burning of 1663 & its harbourage of the rebels & senate from Wiltwyck in 1777! And still it dreams on untouch'd by the present—long may it do so!

I took in New Paltz also, tho' for reasons vastly less contemporaneous than those inspiring your visit. There, though, you & I are both outsiders—for what right have a Dutchman & an Englishman in a *French Huguenot* village? You probably know that New Paltz was founded in 1677 by Huguenots who wished to preserve their language & customs untouched by the Dutch influences of the neighbouring region. The founders had lived both in Wiltwyck & Hurley, but finally decided to strike out for themselves. There they settled in the backwater valley under the shadow of the Shawangunks—DuBoises, LeFevres, Freres, Hasbroucks, Tebenius, Deyos, Beviers, & so on—& there they built the line of ancient stone houses still standing along old Huguenot St.—down across the railway tracks from the modern village you haunt. Poor Frenchies! They couldn't keep you Dutchmen out in the end, & about 1730 their own children began talking Dutch—there's an anecdote about a child sent to borrow something from a neighbour, & refused it because he couldn't ask for it in French. And in 1752 they had to change their church service to Dutch! But even youse guys had to give way in turn—for English got the upper hand about 1800. God Save the King! Now let's hope

& pray that English will hold out against any northward spread of Brook-a-lynese & Yiddish! Yes—after Wiltwyck, Hurley, & New Paltz, I think I ought to have a diploma for erudition in Knickerbockery. This session ably rounds off those Hollandish studies which I began at the Dyckman, Van Cortlandt, & Lefferts houses, & which my ably piloted cruise around Rockland County brought to meridian height. God Save St. Nicholas & the States-General!

But I wasn't sorry to get home to my own New England! I went up to Albany hoping to get a coach over the Mohawk Trail, but found the damn line didn't begin running till May 30. So I had to put up with an Hoosack Tunnel train, & burrow under what I wanted to see most! Still—it was great to get on home soil again. As the train left New York state the air grew clearer & the hills grew greener—& suddenly I realised that I was again in gawd's country—North-Pownal, in the New-Hampshire grants latterly call'd Vermont, & nam'd from Tho: Pownall, Gent., Governor of His Majesty's Province of yᵉ Maſsachusetts-Bay! Hurrah! Home again! Once more New England's gently rolling meadows, winding roads, stone walls, white farmhouse gables, & steeples embower'd in distant vales! Then across another boundary into the good old Maſsachusetts-Bay—which is the next thing to my own Rhode-Island, & by chance the scene of my first infant memories. (1892) I think I appris'd you by card what a good time I had in & around Athol with Cook. He lodged me on as typical & primitive a New England hill farm as I ever saw in my life, & took me up to Brattleboro to see the poet Goodenough on one of the most glorious days of the season. Pleasing & varied tho' the realms I had been visiting, this real Yankee countryside gave me a kick that nothing else could. Finally we came down here, & Cook stocked up with books at Eddy's whilst I renew'd my acquaintance with hearth & home. Here have I tarried ever since, trying to catch up with back numbers of papers & magazines & get my correspondence in working order again. On Sunday the 16th I shall welcome as a distinguish'd guest the amiable James Ferdinand Morton, who in the next few days will probably do to our local mineral quarries what Cook did to Eddy's bookshop & what you did to Jake's. Why not beg off from news-gleaning & come along with him? Make it an old home week!

I accept all your corrections regarding the Bogardi et al. But anyway, Kingston had the famed Bogardus Tavern, where Aaron Burr saw the little stable-boy John Vanderlyn chalking pictures on a barn door—saw & admired, & sent the kid to Paris to blossom into an eminent painter![3] You Dutch all have an artistick streak to you, I guess.

Well, I'm glad to know where good old Mac is, & that he's well enough to write letters. Hope the rumour about his return to the bouweries of Hurl Gate[4] is true—long may the van Nyl stoep face the gardens of the Polhemi & Rapelyes who preceded him in the region! Belknap wrote me that he had left Sinjin's Hospital, but said he couldn't ascertain over the telephone whither the transfer had been. I imagined it was to some government infirmary. I'm dropping him a line at the Naval Hospital—they'll forward it, even if he's flew the coop.[5] I've addressed it "Henry"—he probably thinks he ought to make all the records tally with his legal name as it appears on the veterans' record through which his present placement comes.

Now as for that bookplate design . . . . lud, Sir, but I must hand it to you!! You've got it this time!!! Hold it!!!! Migosh, but this thing is *art!* If it doesn't take a prize at your county fair, then all the judges are dumb! I vow, Sir, when or if I get the completed product I'll send a specimen to that Australian bookplate collector[6] who has appealed in the columns of *Time* for one from every plate-possessor among the readers. This thing conveys the whole message of Providence colonialism in a minimum of lines. All complete & adequate, yet no cumbering detail. I haven't a single suggestion to make. Never mind about the *number* of panes in the fanlight—Providence has all varieties. Merely be careful to have them *equal* in size. In drawing the fanlight as a whole, remember that this middle-&-early-18th-century type tends toward the semicircular rather than flattened form—the latter being the late-Georgian design associated with side-lights. The theory of the *old* fanlight aperture is a cutting-off of the top of a round arch. But of course use your artist's discretion to the full. If a too close approach to a semicircle offers less potentialities of grace than a slightly more elliptical form, go ahead & flatten! What you now have will do admirably if you can hit it again with ink & cardboard. Good luck & congratulations—not to forget abundant thanks as well!

About "aëroplane"—that cutting, if you'll pardon my saying so, is mostly applesauce. The one original form of the word, in English as well as French, is *just that—aëroplane,* pronounced in English a'-e-ro-plane. It comes honestly enough from the Latin words *aër,* meaning *air,* & *planus,* meaning a *flat* thing; & is analogous to the words *aëronautics* or *aërostat.* Who ever heard of *"air-nautics"* or *"air-stat"*? Up to & including the middle of the recent war period nobody ever heard of such a word as "air-plane"; but then, impelled by that occasional freakishness which once went so far as a flyer in "simplified spelling", the U.S. government hit upon the corrupted form & adopted it legally for military & naval purposes. Of course the press followed like a herd of sheep—so today all the rabble of the U.S. is mouthing a gross neologism which is hardly more than a decade old & would excite nothing but a pitying smile in England. *"Air-plane"*, indeed! Bah! As a matter of fact, the word *aëroplane* has an honourable history of over half a century; it having been used at least as early as 1867 to describe the theoretical machine then so far from objective & workable reality. In the '80s & '90s—the period of Langley's[7] experiments—the word was even common among aëronautical technicians; so that there was never any question about what to call the new invention when it finally came. And now a government tries to disturb good etymological usage by edict! Conservative folk shun the new word. I myself have never used it but *once*—& that was when I needed it as a dissyllable for a line of satirical verse. I was spoofing this craze for "modernistic" furniture patterned upon the machine-age forms of daily life—chairs designed from skyscrapers, lamp shades from dynamos, &c—& perpetrated the following:

> Gods of the Waste-Land! say what monster new
> Should grace a shelf by *Benda* or *Leleu?*
> What best befits a bookcase carv'd to ape
> An *air-plane's* angles, or a subway's shape?[8]

The temptation to use the corruption, because its disyllabic value fitted it for the available space, was too great to resist! But this piece wasn't for publication. I certainly wouldn't use "air-plane" in publick! All this I shall make plain to Belknap when I forward the somewhat misleading cutting.

The Crowley[9] cutting is interesting. What has the poor devil-worshipper been up to now? When I was in Leominster (near Athol) with Cook & Munn last month, calling on a bookseller, I saw a copy of a book by Crowley—"The Diary of a Drug-Fiend." The merchant informed me that it has been suppressed by some branch of the powers that be—though he agreed to part with his copy for three thalers. I did not take him up—but I told Belknap about the offer.

Speaking about exotic cultists—I have indeed heard from our sacerdotal friend "* Harold," & received a copy of the Beebe High Catechism of All the Mayas, or something to that effect.[10] I duly acknowledged the honour, & have heard from the dignitary again. He shines to saner advantage in epistles than in his rituals, & professes to base his theology on sound physico-chemical fact. No doubt the Mayan prehistorick lore is just decorative colour—I haven't dared to discuss archaeological matters with His Holiness as yet. But really, he seems a remarkably pleasant chap—perhaps destined to become an interesting correspondent.

By the way—have you heard of the riots between your fellow Brunonians & the police?[11] The ancient hill hasn't seen so much liveliness since the French troops & their horses were stabled in the college edifice during the revolution! Even now echoes persist, as prosy investigations drag their course along. I'll send you some cuttings herewith if I haven't discarded the papers containing the accounts . . . . . . Yes—I have 'em safely. Here they are—under separate cover. Needn't return 'em—you'll find the long article in the Memorial Day morning Journal the spiciest. Talk about Red Hook for lawlessness . . . . . !

And so it goes. Trust all goes serenely in the decadent metropolis, & that you can haul together a gang meeting once in a while. Thanks again for the bookplate design—it certainly is a winner, & ought not to be changed a jot. Shall be grateful for the sheet of proofreading marks as applied to specimen text whenever you happen to find such a thing conveniently lying about. Heard from old 'Dolph De Castro the other day—he says he's been ill. I should think he would be, after the reviews his Bierce book has received! Well—Lahun be with you! Yr obt Servt HPL [stylized]

Notes

1. HPL alludes to St. Nicholas often in his letters to WBT. Santa Claus evolved from Dutch traditions regarding Saint Nicholas (Sinterklaas). When the Dutch established the colony of New Amsterdam, they brought the legend and traditions of Sinterklaas with them. Thus, HPL renders the saint's name in all caps in letter 31.

2. "What shall we with the pancakes do? / Dip them in the syrup of Hurley!" (Eberlein, *Architecture of Colonial America* 18).

3. John Vanderlyn (1775–1852), an American neoclassicist painter, who in 1796 was sent by Aaron Burr to study art in Paris.

4. Hell Gate is a narrow tidal strait in the East River in New York City, separating Astoria, Queens from Randall's and Wards Islands. The name is a corruption of the Dutch phrase *Hellegat*, which could mean either "bright strait" or "clear opening," and originally applied to the entirety of the East River. Everett McNeil had moved to Queens from Brooklyn.

5. I.e., St. John's Episcopal Hospital of Brooklyn and the Brooklyn Naval Hospital.

6. George FitzPatrick of Sydney. See David Haden, "Additions and Corrections for 'Lovecraft's 1937 Diary,'" *Lovecraft Annual* No. 7 (2013): 180–81.

7. Samuel Pierpont Langley (1834–1906), American astronomer, physicist, and aviation pioneer.

8. "To a Sophisticated Young Gentleman, Presented by His Grandfather with a Volume of Contemporary Literature" (15 December 1928; *AT* 187), ll. 19–22. The poem was written for Frank Belknap Long to accompany a copy of Proust's *Swann's Way* as a Christmas present.

9. Aleister Crowley (1875–1947), British occultist, ceremonial magician, poet, and mountaineer, known in the press as "the wickedest man in the world."

10. Harold Davis Emerson (1891–?) founded the Mayan Temple and Alliance of American Aborigines of Brooklyn, New York, in 1928. He was also associated with the Order of the White Friars and the Liberal Catholic Church. He wrote HPL on 11 May 1929 at WBT's suggestion and sent him a pamphlet. He signed his letter "❈ Harold," and his stationary identifies him as "Rev. Dr. Harold Davis Emerson, Ph. I. D. / High Pontiff" of the "Mayan Temple" in Brooklyn.

11. HPL refers to the "tunnel riot" of 1929, when the freshmen of the Class of 1932 intended to burn the black ties they had been made to wear that year. The event was to take place at Thayer Field after a march downtown, followed by an illegal return through the East Side Tunnel. After a skirmish with police at the Arcadia ballroom, the men proceeded to the tunnel. They were blocked from entering it by policemen at both ends. The arrival of Dean Kenneth O. Mason precluded the tie-burning.

[34]   [ALS, JHL]

6th Sunday after Trinity
[7 July 1929]

Jonckheer:—

      Lud, Sir, but you are grown marvellous swift! I have the highest anticipation regarding your work of art, & can already see the finished product in my imagination. With three bookplates & a Christmas card, your vacation will not hang heavy on your hands. I surely wish I had at least a small fraction of your artistic ability! Thanks for the first draught of the plate, which I shall eye with admiration from time to time.

      Glad to hear that Mac is getting along well. Belknap—who leaves for a Canadian outing on the 13th—called on him recently, & said he still seemed rather weak & depressed. A session of comfortable rest at home will do him good—I hear that he does not intend to begin on his new book till autumn.

      Thanks exceedingly for the style book, which is highly interesting despite the lack of applied proofreading marks. One does not readily realise how fixed the usage is on a large paper, & how minutely the practice of uniformity is carried into the smaller details of typography. For the most part, *Times* usage seems commendably conservative; though there are instances where I prefer a still more conservative choice of mode.

      Sorry I didn't save the rest of the Brunonian epic—I meant to, but papers were mislaid amidst the anxiety of household illness; my aunt being down again with that painful spinal neuritis of hers, so that I am again busy in the capacity of semi-nurse. Anyway, 25 students were expelled from Brown for participation in the riot, & one policeman will be disciplined for striking a student prisoner under provocation of obscene & abusive language. Apparently the incident is closed without the establishment of a permanent feud betwixt gownsmen & watch—& the university authorities declare their intention of keeping student processions off the public highways in future, if it can be managed.

      Haven't heard from Chicken-Itza lately, & hope my second epistle didn't impress "* Harold" as stridently argumentative. From his point of view, I am undoubtedly a hard case! He would be interested by some claims lately made by certain Mexican savants that the oldest pyramids of Mexico (as estimated by their astronomical orientation) date back to 11,300 B.C., thus being older than any other authentically dated historic remains in the world. Archaeology is an alluring pursuit, even if its results are more gradual & fragmentary than those obtained through "* Harold's" dashing psychic method of exploring the primal past.

      Aleister Crowley still keeps in the news! Don't take any especial trouble to send the clipping unless you find it lying around, for my interest in the gent is perhaps less intense than Belknap's.

      Yes—Samuelus spoke of his move, & avers that he now possesses a harbour & skyline vista again, as he did in his first metropolitan period. With Mac fled to Queens,[1] you & S L form our sole remaining Brooklyn outposts

. . . . . . yet the Tiffany, no doubt, still lives to enjoy its glorification! Did you attend Mortonius' amateur convention in Paterson? I hope so, for he was pathetically eager to make it a success. Victor E. Bacon came all the way from St. Louis—& incidentally, he intends to revisit the New England scenes he once inhabited, dropping in here some time next week. An East Greenwich postcard no doubt told you of the get-together Morton & I had three weeks ago. We made some mineral excursions, of course, but also indulged in a bit of colonial exploration. East Greenwich is a fine old town of Georgian hill streets, at whose famous academy many of my kinsfolk of three generations have received instruction. The court house was built in 1750. But quainter still is Wickford, some distance below it down the bay, & off the main trunk lines of rail & motor travel. *There* is a *real* colonial backwater, utterly & profoundly unchanged since the 18th century. Elm-shaded, sidewalkless streets, white Georgian houses, a church built in 1707, sleepy deserted wharves, & a 100% ancestrally-seated population to match. One of the leading families, by the way, is *Updike*—a branch of your Dutch stock whose original name-form was *Op Dyck*. Wickford is comparable to New-Netherland's Hurley as a perfect survival of bygone days & ways. I had not seen it in 21 years, & my renewed glimpse transcended all my memories.

A couple of weeks ago Cook & Munn were down from Athol, & made one of their customary raids on the local bookstalls. They expect to repeat the process before the summer is over.

Just now I may about to plunge into an abyss of labour, old Adolphe de Castro—the Bierce biographer—having shoved an inexcusably exasperating but non-dodgeable (because paid in advance) pass of fictional revision upon me.[2] The old bird himself is going to London, & expects me to slave on his damned work whilst he sails the bounding deep & refreshes his mind at the centre of civilisation!

Well—be tolerably good, as Red Hook standards go.

Yr most oblig'd, most ob[t] Servt H P L

Notes

1. McNeil had previously lived at 457 Fifth Street, Brooklyn.
2. I.e., "The Electric Executioner." The original version was published in de Castro's *In the Confessional* as "The Automatic Executioner."

[35] [ALS, JHL]

3rd Day after St. Ann's
[29 July 1929]

Jonckheer:—

Well, I'll be damned! Fancy such cosmick genius in old Flatbush, where the 1796 church lifts its Georgian spire above the sandstone slabs of honest Dutch graves! Maybe it's spreading north from the temple of Kulkulkan or Quetzalcoatl at Sheepshead Bay—for surely this dame has a more exaggerated, even if less formalised, case than "* Harold." I shall hardly dare look at the clouds again—although these phenomena may be peculiar to Flatbush clouds. And to think I dwelt a year in dear old Midmont without seeing anything of the sort! Too bad the conservative *Times* wouldn't handle the tale—but I'll pass the drawings along to Belknap in order to ensure some sort of appreciative audience. I'll tell him to pass 'em back to you. He's on loyal British-Empire soil just now, & expects to pass through Providence next month when he motors southward through New England.

Thanks for the *Times* cutting about the *Journal's* centenary. I was wondering how the outside press reacted toward the event & its literary monument. Have you seen the Journal supplement in question? I think I'll send you one if I can land a duplicate, on the chance that you haven't. It beats that Bklyn. *Standard-Union* supplement all hollow—on fine book paper, & with a magnificent array of data & pictures illustrating the Providence of 1829. 24 pages— but wait till you see it!

Your filing activities are beyond me—I couldn't keep it up! But even as things are, I have an appalling heap of unclassified antiquarian matter awaiting such simple sorting as I customarily give it. I shall have to investigate that "Pathfinder"—I've heard of it all my lifetime, but never realised that it amounted to much until you mentioned it. Also the Studebaker "Wheel"[1]—though if I send for a copy it'll probably expire promptly as the "Socony Standard" did!

Bacon will be glad to hear from you. He's trying manfully to aid in a rehabilitation of the National, & would welcome any literary copy you could give him. I had a very pleasant session with him here—we went to Newport & Pawtuxet, & he seemed to appreciate all the various antiquities exceedingly. Oh—by the way—I went inside the restored & removed Steve Hopkins house the other day for the first time . . . . . the house whose exquisitely landscaped grounds include the site of Adams' store of golden Brunovian memory. Norman M. Isham has done a splendid restoration job, & I was surprised at the amount of fine original panelling which still remains. I'll send you a view of the restored place as soon as any are published.

Don't hurry about the bookplates—but I am naturally all eagerness! I'll send you that cutting about the man in Australia who is collecting such things. When you get his address you ought to send him specimens of all that you've printed for yourself & others. He offers to send his—a fine view of Sydney

Harbour & waterfront skyline—in return. By the way—that Special Delivery stamp picture surely does look like a possible grandparent of your design! I have noticed it repeatedly ever since it first appeared. But you've put enough distinctiveness into your version to ward off all suspicion of commonplaceness!

Good work on the smoking campaign—& welcome to the ranks of Georgian snuff-users! My grandfather dropped tobacco at sixty—on physician's orders—without a quiver or palpitation, shewing that there are more than one who can "take it or let it alone" at will.

Am busy as hell on revision—which includes some advisory work on Moe's forthcoming textbook on poetic appreciation.[2] That's going to be a great volume—you must see a copy. I'll hand it to Moe as a top-notch pedagogical genius!

Best wishes & all that—

  Yr obt grandsire H P L

P.S. Here's a sidelight on the outcome of the Brown riots. Mortonius will appreciate the Paterson sub cutting[.][3]

Notes

1. *The Studebaker Wheel: A Monthly Magazine for the Motorist* (1926–33, 1937–40).

2. *Doorways to Poetry.* The volume, when completed, was apparently accepted by a publisher, but it never appeared and is now nonextant.

3. The Paterson Museum, of which James F. Morton was the curator, had in its collection the *Fenian Ram* (launched in 1881), the first practical submarine, built by John Philip Holland (1840–1914).

[36] [Postcard; *Normal Lovecraft*]

[18 August 1929]

Just back AND have found the bookplate proofs awaiting me!!! Mynheer, I am knock'd out . . . I grow absolutely maudlin & lyrical ... the thing is as *splendid,* beyond even those high expectations which I form'd from a survey of your pencil design! You have caught perfectly the spirit that I wished to see reproduced, & I can't find anything to criticise in any detail of the workmanship. Your drawing skill is honestly impressive.

[37] [ANS; privately held][1]

[postmarked Providence, RI
3? September 1929]

Ave, Jonckheer! Just heard from Belknap, & he says that poor old Mac is in a frightfully failing state—can hardly talk out loud, has stopped shaving, & probably can't take half the pains with food-preparation that he ought. Hope you'll be calling on him before long, & that you can persuade him to visit some hospital for observation. I know he's a hard person to drag to a doctor, but this time he's had a severe object-lesson anent the consequences of neglect! If his organic state is as generally un-alarming as that medico at St. John's led us to believe it's plainly a shame to let it get run down again through neglect or bad diet. But you'll know how to talk to him when you see him. Make him think he's suggesting the consultation business himself, if you can! Belknap is going to see him again this week. Regards—& good luck with the bookplates this time! Yr obt *HPL

Notes

1. *Front:* University Hall and Manning Hall, Brown University.

[38]   [ALS, JHL]

> Day after the Nativity of
> Blefsed Virgin Mary
> MDCCCCXXIX
> [9 September 1929]

Jonckheer:—
    Trust you duly recd. the card of yesterday, telling of the pleasing & unexpected—tho' all too brief—pafsage of the Kirk party through antient Providentium. On that brief document I properly exprefs'd my sympathy concerning your—or our—late calamity, & suggested what seems to me the simplest course out of our difficulty. You'll probably be having the other plates professionally printed now, hence will be right in touch with the most suitable & reasonable artisans—so that I fancy it wouldn't be any trouble for you to get my order sandwiched in with the others. Tell me the price, & I'll have it right on the spot. Being damn near broke, I'd hate to go over five bucks if I could help it; so I'll give you discretionary powers on a downward revision of the quantity order'd, if 500 plates comes to over a Lincoln portrait. I don't want to waste such a masterpiece on my tatter'd odds & ends, anyhow; so I shan't need a very staggering quota at first. I shall begin inserting the plate in my favourites, & accomplish the totality of the pasting very gradually. But bless me, what a triumph that design is! I haven't been equally maudlin with admiration for anything in years! It *just* hits the nail on the head, & expresses everything that a Theobaldian bookplate ought to express! So that is that. If it isn't just as easy for you to attend to the thing as not to, forget all about my suggestion & mail the cut along—for heaven knows that Providence is fairly lousy with printers! Otherwise, get me the figures, stand ready for instant reimbursement, & tell the printer to send me the edition plus cut by express. I don't want any misfortune to befall that cut—for believe me, it represents my *permanent* bookplate! If it ever gives out, I'll get a photo-engraving from one of the printed plates in my books.
    Thanks for Ma Lydia's guide to gawd's country—but damn the old hag

for leaving Providence out! Oh, well—a real town prefers to keep its name out of cheap quack nostrum literature! A couple of weeks ago I made an all-day pilgrimage with my aunt—Mrs. Gamwell—to the western Rhode Island countryside where my maternal ancestors came from; a region I hadn't visited since I browsed around Place homesteads and burying-grounds in 1926. This time we chose a predominantly Phillips terrain, and found an equally interesting array of scenic, architectural, and necropolitan material—the expedition reminding me very much of that delightfully memorable pilgrimage which you and I took around the Talman–Blanch–Blauvelt country a year ago last May. I wish you could have been along—though you would have found the New England slate slabs, (which don't chip well for paperweights!) harsh Yankee names, and severely straight farmhouse roofs rather bleak as compared with the red sandstone, mellow Netherland nomenclature, and gracefully curving gable-silhouettes of drowsy and sightly Rockland County. But for scenery you certainly can't beat Rhode Island's town of Foster! Gently rolling hills, picturesque woods, narrow, winding roads, stone-walled pastures, gnarled sloping orchards, white farmhouse gables embower'd in fresh verdure, alder-fringed streams with ancient water-mills, hilltop vistas of far plains, purple horizons, & distant village belfries—& best of all, a still untainted native population of 200 years' settlement; as gracefully & naturally adjusted to the scene & soil as any Blauvelt or Bogardus west of the Hudson! Here is one corner of the world, by St Paul, into which the curse of the machine age hath not yet intruded! God Save the King! On this occasion I copied all the epitaphs in the *later* Phillips burying-ground, which contains my gt-gt-grandfather Asaph (1764–1829) & his progeny, & interviewed several collateral kinsfolk in the farmsteads of neighbouring Howard Hill. They helped to correct many minor matters on my long-neglected ancestral charts, & gave me certain directions for reaching the scene of my next-plann'd trip— to the *older* Phillips country south of the Plainfield Pike, where Asaph's father James Jr. (d. 1807) is planted, & where I may possibly find James Sr. (d. 1746) unless (as some assert) his mortal reliquiae were shipp'd back to Smithfield, whence he had but recently come when he resign'd his spirit. On this trip I shall also try to see Mrs. Nabby Tyler Kennedy, the old lady with the loads of data & the circular or "wheel" charts on whom I count to fill up blank spaces & rectify errors in Tyler, Perkins, Howard, Foster, & other directions. Hope I can get a good day—today the earth & sky are one indistinguishable aqueous blur!

Have been working like hell lately, helping our fellow-amateur Maurice W. Moe prepare his manual of poetick appreciation—"Doorways to Poetry"—for publication. It's going to be a great book—the best & most explicit guide to the art of knowing good verse from bad that I've ever seen in the course of a long & not unobservant life. Moe knows how to put his finger on the difference betwixt poesy & hokum, knows how to test the reader's knowledge in a truly illuminative way. The book ought to be a tremendously useful & popular high-school text, besides having some vogue as a guide for private readers. This is the first truly enjoyable revision job I have ever tackled! ¶ Well—be good, bear your typographick bereavement nobly, & use your own judgment about the plates. Lahun love you!

Yr obt *Theobald

P.S. I enclose the art sketches, which I ought to have sent back long ago. Belknap found them highly interesting. Hope you can manage to scrape together a crowd for an old-time Wednesday meeting. How is good old Mac? Haven't had a line from his direction for nearly a month.

[39]　[ALS, JHL]

Wednesday before
St Matthew's Day
[18 September 1929]

Jonckheer:—

Congratulations, Sir! What consequences accrue from a typographical breakdown! But it would have been a pity to run off a large edition of a plate which you probably have made obsolete anyhow, sooner or later. Trust you can change the surname on the original drawing & get a new cut made at no vast expense—for it is a damn fine design, & I'm sure you'll be magnanimous enough to allow your new helpmeet a few shelves of her own as a personal library in addition to the main Talman collection!

As for non-publicity—Sir, the lips of old age are hermetically sealed! Not even an aunt shall dream of the coming peal of Dutch Reform'd Church bells—& as for the gang; if they want any dope they'll have to apply the rack & thumbscrew to Mac & Belknap, for the Inquisition hath not yet invented the device that cou'd break the iron silence of grim & hoary Theobaldus. Indeed—I shall proceed to delete the tidings from mine own head as soon as this note is writ; so that your October announcement will find me as naively surprised as any other recipient. Send Tryout Smithy a report when you're ready, & expect a gorgeous misspelling of all the names, fanes, & places concern'd![1]

All told, it looks as though your step were a predominantly wise one, & with the odds heavily on the side of success & permanence. From your account, the party of the second part seems eminently well qualified to reign by the side of a gifted erudite young patroon; & I am sure the haughty Talmans, Blanchs, Blauvelts, & Bogardi will be glad to accord her a cordial rectangle on the family charts, & a prominent & favourable place amidst the innumerable quarterings of the family shield! Perhaps you can learn new & valuable financial & œconomic measures from your illustrious statesman relative-in-law if you approach him in the right way—but don't forget to spell his name *Hjalmar*, & not as you record it in your epistle!

Yes, young man, you have the best wishes of an aged cynic; & I think that with your sober good judgment & analytical knowledge of human nature you are probably laying the foundations of a solid domesticity whose attractions & advantages will far outweigh the prosaicism inevitable to settled life. Your new quarters, I presume, are to be somewhat more commodious than the present outfit—but how you do stick to dear old Red Hook!

I'm sure good old Mac will excuse you for apparent negligence during this exciting period, & will extend you his heartiest congratulations. He has a soft spot toward domesticity, & once confided rather pathetically to Belknap & me that he wished there were more *homes* he could visit now & then—places with the conventional loving couple & innocent prattlers, all of which his naive, 19th century view of life has taught him to regard with idolatrous glamour. Have the old boy over as often as you can after the Grand Fall Opening—that is, if he can make the trip, poor old duffer! I wish to Hades he could be taken in hand & rested & dieted up properly.

No hurry about the bookplates—& am glad you find it easy to take the responsibility off my hands. Quote me the figure when the time comes, & you won't have to dun me for the vulgar but necessary material in order. Whatever it is, it's worth it! I'm still maudlin & lyrical about the utter perfection & appropriateness of that design! Hope the poor old press will turn out better than you think—but even if it doesn't, you can get a new one without going broke. I fancy that the mere press isn't always the most costly part of a printing outfit involving type, designs, &c. &c.

And so it goes. Again accept my congratulations & assurances of profound & cryptical silence. One—two—three—the matter is relegated to oblivion already! Yr moſt oblig'd, moſt Obt Servt
* Theobald

Notes

1. "Tryouts," *Tryout* 13, No. 4 (November 1929): 23, contains a brief notice of WBT's wedding.

[40] [ALS, JHL]
Tuesday [5 or 12 November 1929]
Jonckheer:—

Well, for Gawd's sake! Who was idly rambling—Mac or Belknap—when the latter said the leaving-time of the former was the 20th?[1] Of all confounded, deodamnate slip-ups! ...... Mortonius missed him, too—& so must my final bon voyage letter have done—timed to get to Astoria on the 19th. Hell! But if it's Little Belknap's fault, I'll spank the child within an inch of his young life!

Mac's present address—transmitted through Belknap—is

% *Collins,*
6227 Warner St., South Tacoma, Wash.

I've written him at that address, though of course assuring him he needn't try to reply until he feels fully recovered from the strain of the voyage. Morton writes (with information evidently relayed from Belknap) that the genial Dr. Magill of St. John's was indeed right, & that Mac's malady is a straight diabetes case[2]—his future welfare depending on his faithfulness to a special diet. Here's hoping his sister will see that he sticks to orders! The rest, & the Pacific Coast climate, ought to do him good. He'll be delighted to hear from you, I'm sure.

Have you seen any of the gang lately? Orton wrote the other day & said he wanted to get in touch with you, so I gave him your address. He has moved from his Yonkers farm to a flat in the terra incognita north of Woodlawn Cemetery, & is to be found at *530 East 236th St., N.Y.C.* His bibliographic study of Theodore Dreiser is coming out soon—a real book, between cloth covers. I read the proofs of the preface for him. Wish you all could get together in an old-time meeting some evening.

Enclosed is something Nederlandsch which may interest you—what a chance to pick up some books in your mother-tongue! I also send some circulars I received from a bookplate firm—recalling your wish of some time ago to see as many samples as possible. Of course this is mere ready-made stuff, but the designs might give you a stray idea or two. Mortonius wants a bookplate, but says he can't afford it because he'd probably be soaked a hundred bucks for it. Hades! I'll bet you could quote him a better figure than that! He has his own distinctive ideas & tastes—for he wants *an elephant holding high a torch, with the motto LUX ET FORTITUDO.* He knows his own weight class, all right enough! By the way—I'll send you that bookplate collector's letter & address (from *Time*) in a few days, when I can get off a letter to the guy myself. I've only just pulled clear of a hellish mess of revision, & am scrambling to get my piled-up correspondence attended to.

Chapin of the R.I. Hist. Soc. has just published some sort of a work on R.I. Heraldry—which I must see soon. I'll let you know if there's anything of interest in it, or perhaps Room 328 of your local 42nd St publibe will have a copy.

Well—behave yourself—& when you find a copy of that book or booklet you told me about—with old N Y views—send it along, & I'll come across financially at once. I've just bought Hervey Allen's life of Poe, & am revelling in descriptions of all the places Poe inhabited. It seems that I missed several in Richmond, Baltimore, Philadelphia, & N.Y.

Regards to you & the rest of the household—& to the gaudy old Tiffany!
Yr obt grandsire
H P L

Notes

1. McNeil was leaving New York City to stay with his sister in Tacoma, WA. He died on 14 December 1929.

2. HPL to Zealia Bishop, 26 January 1930: "at one time [McNeil] had nothing to eat but the sugar which he could pick up free at lunch rooms and dissolve in water for the sake of its nourishment." *The Spirit of Revision: Lovecraft's Letters to Zealia Brown Reed Bishop,* ed. Sean Branney and Andrew Leman (Glendale, CA: H. P. Lovecraft Historical Society, 2015), 173.

[41]   [ALS, JHL]

Saturday
[30 November 1929]

Jonckheer:—

Hang'd if I know what individual answered my City History Club inquiry—but the way I got the address was the simple & prosaic one of looking in the Manhattan telephone book. The place was somewhere in the forties, I recall. Now if, by any chance, it is not in the latest book, I'd suggest your getting hold of a Spring 1928 book & seeing just what I saw. Even if the address is changed, it's still your best clue—& the P.O. would undoubtedly forward your communication. However—it may be that you haven't looked in the new book—in which case, don't fail to do so!

I thought a hundred fish was pretty steep for a bookplate—but Morton says that just now he's too broke to indulge in anything of the kind. I shall send him the figures you quote, & have no doubt but that you'll get the job whenever he has the cash to spare. I don't think he'll prove a fussy patron—indeed, I'd be willing to wager that he'll accept your first design, right off the reel! Your figures are surely astonishingly reasonable. Oh, yes—that Silver stuff was for your permanent file. Here's hoping you get a useful hint or two from it in the course of time. By the way—here's a Georgian gateway you can keep if it's of any use for your morgue. You know the building—my aunt Mrs. Gamwell roomed there in 1927, & still belongs to the club.[1]

Mac'll be glad to hear from you, though you must not expect a reply—he hasn't dropped a word yet to Morton, Belknap, or myself. I hope he stood the trip well. The date mistake was his own. Belknap was at his place *Oct. 6,* & he told him he was going to start *in 14 days*—which of course meant the *20th* so far as Belknap could see. Actually, I suppose he meant to say he was leaving on the 14, but made a fatigued blunder just as he did when giving his new address as "Dakoma" instead of *Tacoma.* Belknap'll be glad to hear from you, too—he's slaving on a vile revision job. And Orton said that he'd like to get in touch with you—his new address is 530 E. 236th St., N.Y.C.—north of Woodlawn Cemetery.

I saw a review of "Berkeley Square",[2] & was intensely interested in the situation portrayed—since I myself seem to divide my time betwixt 18th & 20th centuries. Certainly I shall take it in if it ever gets to Providence—& shall read it if the printed text is ever bibliothecally available. I've used the same idea myself in "The Silver Key"—which appeared in *Weird Tales* about a year ago—except that my time-juggling was only a matter of a few years, whereby a person's boyhood & late middle age oddly & Einsteinically coalesce.

By the way—I am no longer a prophet without honour in my own country. The literary editor of the Journal—Bertrand K. Hart—has started a daily "colyum" called *The Sideshow*, & quite lately opened a discussion as to what the weirdest tale in all literature is. I couldn't resist sending him my *Recluse* article, plus lists of best weird tales prepared by myself, Belknap, & August W. Derleth; & the result was quite a little flattering publicity for us. I enclose some of the printed results—two cuttings, or three if my aunt calls around with the extras of yesterday's which she promised to bring. This last is a puff of "Cthulhu"—which Hart discovered all himself in the Harré anthology, since I never told him I wrote tales.[3] His column also informs me *for the first time* that I have again "made" E. J. O'Brien's year book—Best Short Stories of 1929—with a three-star item—this time "The Dunwich Horror."[4] You might return these Sideshow cuttings unless you really have a use for them in your files. I also send a tribute to a familiar Providence vista which you needn't return.

Had a great Thanksgiving—dragged my elder aunt Mrs. Clark to Brennan's for a gorgeous feast . . . . her first ride in a trolley & her first meal in a public restaurant in a year & a half. But Gawd, what cold weather! That's what gets me—I about cashed in last night trying to walk home from my other aunt's. Ought to have taken a taxicab.

¶ Well—be good & all that!
  Yr obt Grandsire
    H P L

P.S. Here's a brief but poignant Nederlandsch cutting for your morgue.

Notes

1. I.e., at the Handicraft Club (see letter 14n7). See HPL to Frank Belknap Long, "Saturday" [June 1927] (AHT): "[the] local feminine organisation of some prominence . . .] rents rooms to ladies of suitable background who are engag'd in artistic pursuits. Mrs. Gamwell, it is true, is not an artist; but through friends she succeeded in having that point minimized—and is consequently about to move into that austerely panelled abode of Georgian dignity."

2. HPL refers to the play by John L. Balderston (1889–1954), which premiered at the Lyceum Theatre on Broadway on 4 November 1929. The play, which concerns a man from the 20th century who switches minds with his ancestor from the 18th century. was published in 1932 and was filmed in 1933. HPL saw the film version four times,

and it had some influence on his own tale of personality exchange over time, "The Shadow out of Time" (1934–35).

3. Bertrand Kelton Hart (1892–1941), literary editor of the *Providence Journal* and author of the column, "The Sideshow." The "puff of 'Cthulhu'" appeared in the column of 29 November 1929. For a reprint of all the "Sideshow" columns mentioning HPL, see *Lovecraft Annual* No. 11 (2017): 51–66.

4. "The Dunwich Horror" received a 3-star rating in O'Brien's *The Best Short Stories of 1929* (1929); "The Silver Key" received a 1-star rating.

[42]   [ALS, JHL]

Tin Bărrnes Sthrate,
Province, Rowd-Oiland
Aapril fiftaneth
[15 April 1930]

Jonckheer:—

Sure, 'twas just about to be writin' yez Oi was, phwin yer racent litther was afther' comin'. 'Tis mesilf will be arroivin' in Manhattan (the saints willin' & barrin' changes) wan wake from the day afther tomorry—manin' Thurrsday the 24th—& shtayin' about a wake or a day or two more thin thot. Me quarthers will be thot silfsame cell at the Benedictine Monastery in Wist 97th Sthrate[1] phwere you & Fr. Wandrei helped me to brighten the shmall hours one year gone. Just after Roodmas Fr. Belnapius will head a pilgrimage of holy folk to a priory at Atlantic City, N.Y., where the bones & other reliques of a very potent saint, Marinus of Atlantaea, are held to be of great efficacy in dispelling melancholic humours. With this pious cavalcade I shall set out; accompanying it as far south as it goes, & thereafter continuing southward alone—even unto the Thebaid, where holy hermits are wont to congregate, & where the 2nd upper wisdom tooth of St. Carolinus is preserved in a miraculous shrine. At Charleston I shall pause as long as my holy wafers (with the green of ould Oireland on one side) will hold out—duly allowing, of course, for return fare—& thereafter I shall edge reluctantly northward again, pausing for meditation & prayer at suitable antiquarian shrines & abbeys along the way .... Norfolk, Williamsburg, Richmond, Fredericksburg, Washington, Philadelphia, & so on. If all goes well, it ought to be a great trip—well worth the effort even if the O'Theobald parish stays bankrupt for the balance of the summer! Needless to say, I shall be delighted to participate in the Red Hook meeting which you so thoughtfully plan . . . old home ties, & all that! You and Fr. Belknapius can decide on matters of date. I dare say the old Hook will shew changes, even since last year. What's this about the Tiffany—has the old joint moved, or is this dive in your street a branch of the main works?

An' about me ancesthral sate—sure, now 'tis no Caseys av moine can be down at the bottom of the map nixt the O'Dwyers, for doesn't O'Hart say plain in his book that the Rhowd-Oisland line comes from the *County Tyrone?*

There may be all sorts of Caseys shprinkled over the Ould Sod, (for a name derived from an abstract adjective can be duplicated as independently & unrelatedly as Smith, Jones, or Tall-Man!) but the only ones that consarn me are the shtock in good ould Tyrone—& aiven they *may* not consarn me if Austin instead of O'Hart is right!

By the way—I enclose a couple of items for that incomparable file system . . . . items which may give you a touch of Providential nostalgia. What do you think of old South Main through modernist eyes? And don't you wish there had been *elevator service* to old 256 in your day?[2]

And so it goes. 'Tis glad Oi'll be to seein' yez, come tin days or so, & grateful Oi am for yer thoughtfulness in arrangin' a matein' of the lay bretheren. The Vargin's blessin' on all yer household, & may St. Nicholas trate all yer cares as St. Pathrick trated the shnakes back in Ould Tyrone!

Appreciatively & expectantly—The O'Casey

Notes

1. Frank Belknap Long, Jr., and his family lived at 230 W. 97th Street.
2. To avoid walking up the steep hill, Providentians would "use the elevator of the immense new court-house which clings to the hillside on the south side of College St. The lowest floor of the building—in South Main St.—is at the downtown level, but the fifth floor is flush with Benefit St., half way up the hill. If, therefore, you walk boldly in & say "5th floor, please" to the elevator-boy, you will be deposited on a level more than half way up [. . .]—the stretch escaped being the steepest part of the hill, at that!" HPL to R. H. Barlow, [10? February 1934]; *O Fortunate Floridian: H. P. Lovecraft's Letters to R. H. Barlow*, ed. S. T. Joshi and David E. Schultz (Tampa, FL: University of Tampa Press, 2007), 110. HPL himself did not mind walking up the hill.

[43]   [Postcard][1]

[Postmarked Fredericksburg, Va.,
17 May 1930]

Jonckheer:—Headed north, alas, but antient Fredericksburg is some consolation. Great old place—I've been doing all the available interiors, including this office of James Monroe, Esq. Washington tonight—tomorrow undecided, but probably Annapolis & Baltimore. See you in less than a week.
Yr obt Grandsire, O'Casey

Notes

1. *Front:* Law Office of James Monroe, 5th President of U.S., Fredericksburg, Va.

[44]   [Postcard]¹

[Postmarked Philadelphia, Pa.,
19 May 1930]

Brrrrr . . . . O let me not lie in the frozen waste . . . . rescue my congealed corpse & give it a decent cremation . . . . hellamighty, Jonckheer, but why in St. Nicholas's name did any sensible Dutchman or Englishman ever try to settle in the damn North? And why, alas, did I ever leave Charleston? I'll bet it isn't over 45° this minute! ¶ Yet in spite of the cold this museum gives me a 100% kick. Have you ever seen it? If not, lose no time in so doing, at your first opportunity . . . . which reminds me that I have a PROVIDENCE room to say nothing of several Dutch rooms, to see at your Brooklyn Museum. ¶ If it doesn't get decently warm tomorrow, I shall have to move on to N Y & get the overcoat I parked at Belknap's. No use trying to explore my favourite Wissahickon Valley in cursed weather like this. And to think that only day before yesterday I was in the civilised temperature of Fredericksburg!! No use talking—the North is fit to live in only about 2 months of the year—June & July! Well—I'll see you soon.

Yr obt grandsire, The O'Casey

[*On front:*] P.S. I have a whole catalogue of praise to recite to you concerning that *bookplate*. All the various curators, &c. in the South to whom I shewed it, went wild over it, & many asked for a sample. The old lady in charge of the Poe Shrine in Richmond took an extra sample for her daughter, a discriminating bookplate collector.

Notes

1. *Front:* Untitled photograph of mansion interior.

[45]   [ALS, JHL]

Saturday—
SS. Alabad, Ghinu, &
Aratza.
[12 or 19 July 1930]

Jonckheer:—

I appreciated both your communications, with their piquant enclosures, & would have acknowledged them earlier had I not been in the midst of the worst vortex of piled-up duties on record. I let everything slide for a week & attended the Boston convention of the National Amateur Press Assn.—afterward taking antiquarian side-trips to Salem, Marblehead, & Quincy—& when I got back July 10 I found an utterly unmanageable stack of mail on my desk. Only now am I beginning to see the light . . . . . & not so damn much light, at that!

"Doom Around the Corner" is great stuff! Keep it up, Son! And thank Gawd for the lucid interval which impelled Wright to accept it! You achieve a genuine & elusive atmosphere of the unreal in this thing, & the incidents are admirably graduated & arranged. I can feel the authenticity of the local colour. Did I tell you that I once *almost* secured a room in Garden Place? I had it all picked out, but found that some other guy had beat me to it. Then I fell back on Clinton St. Strange musick around Red Hook seems quite a usual thing. I always noticed gangs of sinister-looking youths marching about with ukeleles & harmonicas, & wondered what dark & furtive gods of the nether world they were hymning in their cryptic rituals! Sorry Wright didn't take "The Charnel Den." His idea of "excessive gruesomeness" is the most irrational & elastic thing I ever heard of—you may recall that he turned down my "In the Vault" (also written in Red Hook) for a similar reason. That was the tale about a strange reprisal inflicted on a rural undertaker who had cut off a corpse's feet to make it fit a short coffin. Good luck with "The Wyvern"—which will certainly be much better as a purely mediaeval thing. You are such a mediaevalist that you ought to correspond with my Kingston friend Bernard Austin Dwyer, (292 Fair St., Kingston, N.Y.) who is also a devotee of the Middle Ages.

The cuttings are all highly interesting, & the one about the Ramapaugh[1] [that's the way Genl. Washington spell'd it, & I refuse to adopt modern versions!] decadents is surely a gem. You ought to get a story out of that. Why not visit the region & collect first-hand dope? It seems rather hard to find these mountain backwaters one reads so often about. Dwyer has never been able to spot any thoroughly decadent communities in the Catskill region, though he was born & bred there.

As for Providence's reading—the 40% which we don't read is made up of tabloids, popular best-sellers, & other undesirable matter which the barbarians of Des Moines eat up by the bushel. The sort of people who make up Des Moines' high quota are not part of our discriminating English-speaking population! And as for plain epistolary conclusions—the Washington rebel government can do as it likes, but real Tories & gentlemen will stick to those forms which their ancestors thought most proper. Glad to see the recognition Orton's book is receiving. The reviewer pulled one bad break, though, if my memory holds good. That book for which Drieser wrote an introduction is *not* French but American—& the work of a *Charles Fort* of Chicago—*not* the eminent French writer Paul Fort.[2]

Another vastly interesting thing is your visit with Wright. He had told me of his disease some time ago, but I had hoped it was better by this time.[3] His new magazine plans sound interesting. I think he accepted two of Belknap's tales for the Oriental one.[4] Glad that W.T. prospers. I did receive 1½¢ per word at one time, but it's so long since I have contributed a story that I can't be sure of what he pays now.[5] He occasionally tries to beat Belknap down in flat rate offers. Despite his expressed wish for more of my stuff, he has rejected so much of mine that I have no real enthusiasm about supplying him. I shall, however, send him "The Whisperer in Darkness" when I get a chance to re-write it. I have decided that it won't do in its present form.[6] The new format of W.T.—type &c—rather pleases me, & I fancy there may be an attempt to live up to it by improving the illustrations. The present Mayan cover-design isn't half bad.[7] Derleth has promised to send me that thesis, & it is possible that Cook may publish it in *The Recluse*.[8] Yes—he included some W.T. material, & asked me to read the items & see how well I agreed with him. I think that both Belknap & I are among those present—& I know Little Augie himself is; for humility forms no part of the psychology of modern youth! Interested to hear that Quinn is editor of an undertaker's journal. Quite a job for a sup-posedly macabre writer! Now I wish he'd begin to write some *weird* stories.

Your vacation must surely have been delightful. I wish I could afford a really decent aëroplane ride.[9] The one I think I'll try is *half* the Boston–N Y route, (either Boston–Springfield or Springfield–N Y) which is reputed to be quite reasonable. The Prov.–N Y line was abandoned for lack of patronage, so that Morton flew to Boston last month & came to Providence by train.

I must see Chicago some time, too—although there are lots of ancient towns in the East (Quebec, St. Augustine, New Orleans) which I want to see first. Illinois scenery, I think, must be rather poor on the whole, though Wis-consin & Michigan do not share this deficiency. No—you won't find Dutch influence in architecture beyond the Hudson Valley. Western New York state was settled after the Revolution, when everything Dutch was on the wane. The general Georgian designs, however, were universal & persistent. I'd like to see that nameless Canadian town some time.

I'll pass that Wright interview on to Belknap when I get his next tempo-rary address—he starts for Canada tomorrow with his family, though I fear the quaint nameless town is not their destination. For the banishment of Felis he pleads two excuses: (a) paternal initiative, & (b) lack of neat household habits on Felis's part. The High Court of Ulthar will decide on the extent of his punishment.

Cook is out of the hospital, though without the appendicitis operation which he really ought to have. He may make a Vermont trip shortly—& I may go with him if my elder aunt's health (she has had another neuritis spell lately) permits of my absence. Munn has been making a motor tour of Pa. & Western N.Y.—scenic spots like Watkins Glen, of which he recently sent me a folder. Morton leaves tomorrow for the south, & will first visit my favourite town of Charleston. He will also see Savannah, St. Augustine, & New Orle-ans—maybe I don't envy him!

The Boston convention was more enjoyable than I had anticipated. Mor-ton, of course, was the focus & central luminary of all the proceedings. I met the young Official Editor Helm C. Spink,[10] (an incredibly brave diabetic suf-ferer—would that Mac had been as careful as he!) who accompanied me to

Salem & M'head, & will stop in Prov. on his return trip. Also, I saw the local Boston amateurs for the first time in many years. Some have changed greatly—E H Cole has grown fat—but Lynch[11] looks about the same despite having been through a nervous breakdown.

Well—I must return to less pleasant tasks! Best wishes, & don't let the daemons of Red Hook ingulph you! Yr obt grandsire

O'Casey

Notes

1. The Ramapough Mountain Indians (also spelled Ramapo), living around the Ramapo Mountains in northern New Jersey and southern New York.

2. Theodore Dreiser, an old friend of Charles Fort (1874–1932), American writer and researcher specializing in anomalous phenomena, was the first president of the Fortean Society. Founding members of included Tiffany Thayer, Booth Tarkington, Ben Hecht, Alexander Woollcott, Dorothy Parker, and H. L. Mencken. But Dreiser wrote no introduction to any book by Fort. Paul Fort (1872–1960) was a French poet associated with the Symbolist movement.

3. Farnsworth Wright had Parkinson's disease.

4. FBL's "The Rajah's Grandmother" (February/March 1931) and "The Pearl Robber" (April/May/June 1931) appeared in *Oriental Stories,* a spinoff of *WT.*

5. For "The Dunwich Horror" (April 1929), HPL was paid $240, or less than 1½¢ a word (c. 17,500 words).

6. HPL revised the story based on comments made on it by Bernard Austin Dwyer.

7. *WT,* August 1930, featured a cover by Hugh Rankin for the story "The Curse of Ximu-tal" by Harry Noyes Pratt.

8. Cook never published more than one issue of the *Recluse.* Instead he published Derleth's "The Weird Tale in English Since 1890" (his honor's thesis at the University of Wisconsin, 1930) in the *Ghost* No. 3 (1945): 5–32.

9. HPL had taken a plane ride the previous year, in Onset, MA, at a cost of $3.50.

10. Helm C. Spink (1909–1970), printer and Official Editor of the NAPA in 1930 and again in 1935, when President Bradofsky removed O. W. Hinrichs from the office and replaced him with Spink. He printed HPL's *Further Criticism of Poetry.*

11. Joseph Bernard Lynch (1879–1952), amateur journalist and member of the Hub Club.

[46]   [ANS postcard][1]

[Postmarked Provincetown, Mass.,
3 September 1930]

Well, Jonckheer, I couldn't bear to go straight home after all! Had a hellish ride from Quebec in a train full of vulgar & non-armigerous beer-swilling swine, & am getting the stink out of my nostrils by taking this long-planned sail from Boston to Provincetown. Ideal day—warm & sunny, but just mist enough to give the impression of being out of sight of land for the bulk of the voyage. At one point a picturesque school of porpoises was sighted. ¶ Quebec is the most beautiful city I have ever seen—bar none—yet for steady habitation I'd prefer something more in the English tradition, where English is the dominant speech. Still—Boston seems detestably flat & ugly & tame as compared with Quebec. ¶ Provincetown itself is quaint & pretty in a mild way but nothing up to Marblehead. Only have 2 hrs. here, but guess I've seen all there is to be seen. Regards & all that—

Your obt servt, O'Casey

Notes

1. *Front:* Provincetown Monument Showing Memorial Bas Relief Tablet and World War Memorial, Provincetown, Mass.

[47]   [ALS, JHL]

Thor's Dæg [4, 11, or 18 September 1930]

Hail, Jonckheer:—

Thanks for the glimpse of the Wyverns, which certainly looks to me like a damn good story. Your fellow-mediaevalist Dwyer will hail it with rapture—& if Wright has the least fraction of sense he will not hesitate about accepting it. It is prodigiously improved since the first draught, & ought to satisfy the most exacting this time.

Glad to hear of Godridge,[1] & hope I can get around there some time. My taste of still-loyal soil makes me eager for more—& especially for a region less Frenchified than the one I visited. I want to see New Brunswick, Nova Scotia, & Newfoundland, where most of the Rhode-Island loyalists went in 1779–80, & where most of the churchyards are said to contain good old Rhode-Island names. And then I'd rather like to see Colborne, Ontario, where the loyal branch of the Caseys is said to flourish even to this day.

But as a scenic imaginative spectacle, Quebec surpasses everything I've ever seen or am likely to see in my few remaining years. What a town! I must go there again at length & drink it up minutely.

Yes—I wouldn't mind another taste of open water. My resurrection of maritime heredity is a gradual process. In 1929 I saw the New Bedford Whaling Museum—with its half-size model of a whaling ship—for the first time. In 1930 I began my acquaintance with the open sea. And too—I have just inspected a full-grown embalmed *whale* exhibited in a great flat car in the freight yards behind the Union Station. Next thing you know, I'll be shipping before the mast for a voyage around Cape Horn!

I'd like to see that Mayan data some time, though at present I'm so badly swamped with accumulated work that I couldn't do it full justice. Thanks for the offer—of which I mean to take advantage in the not remote future.

And speaking of your precious files—have you seen reviews of the new book about that suave diabolist Aleister Crowley? Belknap sent me a cutting from the *Tribune*. The biographer—abetted by the reviewer—(Herbert S. Gorman, who claims to have dined with Crowley) tries to depict this reputed ally of Satan as a much-wronged and basically blameless poet—whose eccentricities are merely the harmless foibles of genius![2]

Mortonius is home at last. Before long the gang ought to hold an autumnal reunion.

Just had an echo of marine adventure in the form of a letter from the New Zealand amateur Robert G. Barr.[3] Stampless, watersoaked, & marked with a rubber stamp

Salvaged from
S.S. Tahiti
Lost at sea.

Well—behave yourself & don't let the wyverns get you!
Yrs for more & better ancestors,
Theobaldus Avus[4]

Notes

1. Goderich is a town in Ontario, the county seat of Huron County.
2. See Bibliography under Percy Reginald Stephensen.
3. Barr published HPL's "Harbour Whistles" in his *Silver Fern*.
4. Latin for "Grandpa Theobald."

[48]　[ALS, JHL]

Septr. 20[, 1930]

Jonckheer Arminius:—

Well, well—upon my soul! Just as you had gotten worked well into the Times staff fabric—to quit 'em cold & plunge into the arena of Big Business & financial expansion & all that! That's the way with modern youth—money, money, money! Well—I hope you get plenty of it to reward your pains. According to your description, you'll surely be earning all you get. Working for four magazines at once, each with a different keynote & tempo! If you don't learn the magazine business, it'll surely be your own fault! Put me on the free list of as many as have such a thing outside Texaco circles. Yes—I'll be glad to diffuse the tidings, & am sure that all the group will pause in awed admiration at the responsibilities you are undertaking.

As for the Wyverns—Wright *would* do a thing like that! Have just been reading a letter about Wright's policies which the W.T. author Henry S. Whitehead (the Ph.D. who writes West Indian "Jumbee" stories) wrote to Bernard Dwyer. It seems that Whitehead's best work has been rejected. By the way—you ought to lend the Wyvern MS. to Dwyer, (292 Fair St., Kingston, N.Y.) since he is just as enthusiastic a mediaeval fan as you are.

Thanks for the proofreading cutting—which I've placed carefully on file beside my transcriptions from the Times style book. Also glad to see the Charleston item—though the initial mention of *shrimps* (you know my reaction concerning sea-food, I believe!) rather diluted the enthusiasm which the old streets, iron grilled porches, & flower-gardens would have created by themselves.

So you had a local suicide the other day? Rather conveniently situated for you to report! Here's hoping the strain of your new job doesn't drive you to emulation!

I haven't seen Oriental Stories, & doubt very much if I shall except through some other channel than paying a perfectly good quarter for it. I seem to sense by instinct that it is no market for me.

Those mysterious initials F O F A sound highly alluring![1] Who knows what nighted secret—so horrible that your healthy consciousness refused to retain it—may not lie buried here? Fiends of Forest Abbey—Fifty Ogres From Acheron—ugh!

Did you notice the Jellyfish story in the latest W.T.? I am in correspondence with the chap who wrote it.[2] A tuberculous resident of Tucson, Arizona—very brilliant, but a *communist* in social & political philosophy. He lately wrote me a 40-page (*closely* typed) letter in defence of his position—which I refuted in 60 pages of script. Both retain the same opinions as before.

Munn is "laid off" from his Athol position, & is doing some temporary work at Putney, Vt. Orton has been yachting down the St. Lawrence, & has visited *Quebec.* Cook is resting up at his sister's home near Lake Sunapee, N.H. And possibly Loveman has told you of his return to Dauber & Pine's—which he ought never to have left in the first place.

And so it goes. Planning any Kalem meetings for the autumn season? Loveman says that good old Leeds was in N Y recently—just passing through on a theatrical tour. Glad the old boy has some sort of an income for the nonce!

Yrs for oil, format, & prosperity
O'Casey

Notes

1. Such initials appear near the closing of letter 45, but their author is uncertain.
2. "The Jelly-Fish" (*WT,* October 1930), as by "Francis Flagg"; see 80n3.

[49]   [ALS JHL]

Castle Theobald
[October 1930]

Jonckheer Arminius:—

I didn't receive the *Star* till after completing my letter

to you, but I *thought* I added a very appreciative comment on the envelope. In case I somehow failed to do so, let me here append the intended expressions of approval. Most certainly, it is not a bit too commercial for its purpose—& indeed, it seems to me a thoroughly admirable exponent of its type. In format, contents, illustrations, & general aspect it stands on a high level; & I must certainly congratulate you sincerely on the enterprise. I read many of its items with keen interest—especially the one on Frio Cañon in Texas, which piece of scenery I certainly hope will escape olefic desecration. The whole magazine group must form a veritably titanic affair, & can hardly wonder at the nonchalant manner in which allowances of just a trifling million or two are discussed. A good thing, so to speak, on the ground floor of which to be in!

I get the idea about "terminals"—of which, for aesthetic reasons, I wish there were a damn sight less hereabouts! Hell, the way both shores of the bay are getting cluttered up! No doubt the local Chamber of Commerce takes pride in such things, & has folders of dry statistical information about them.

Probably that decision on the Star policy is essentially sound—especially if the magazine is for stockholders & not (as I imagine the late lamented So-cony Standard use to be) for potentially road-covering consumers of the finished product. Anyway, I fancy the Standard Co. has so thoroughly developed the tourist angle of gasoline-sales-promotion that the Texacoes would consider it "old stuff." I imagine that I had better hold off until the indicated readjustments in your personnel take place—especially since I am on the one hand a notoriously poor & unappealing self-salesman, & on the other hand the very last person to handle commercial data from an intelligent, sympathetic, & prepossessing angle.

Yes—I spoke of your magazine to Campbell,[1] but hardly expected that he would be the first to talk pure business! Aside from his own propositions, I think he ought to be able to furnish some interesting & pertinent material for you—for he certainly knows all there is to know about oil-drilling at first hand. Howard is the chap who can give you the colour—the sweep of the oil camps across the primal Texas plains, & the pageantry & social developments connected with them.[2] He does not welcome the coming of the derricks & the slimy black ooze, but he is acutely sensitive to their place in the long drama of the Lone Star country. Campbell & Howard are the oiliest guys I know—if I come across any others, I'll pass 'em on. Meanwhile, as you imply, the ultimate 2¢ per would be by no means unwelcome to a fairly deserving case in Providence! I shall have to try to stomach a prowl around the Texaco terminal—wherever it is—& a cramming on Chamber of Commerce sawdust & bran. Also—similar things abroad. But even so, I'd scarcely predict my own evolution into a leading trade-journal contributor. One has to be built a certain way to read a zestful story-element into the anfractuosities of a prosaic industry, & I have graver fears that my basic structural frame is not of that profitable sort! Still—one may experiment . . . . . & shall carefully file your epistle, as well as diligently perusing the November & December *Stars* upon their respective risings.

It was with a genuine emotion, very remote from the usual bored response one gives to Christmas pap & hokum, that I perused the tale based on our good old friend.[3] Honest Mac! How I wish I had made my Quebec trip during his lifetime, for that sight of New-France's ancient capital has set me off on a veritable orgy of reading & reflection connected with the epic of French colonisation in the New World! I've been over half of Parkman[4] again, & am correlating him with all sorts of other scraps in an effort to visualise the titanic pageant of conflicting forces & contrasted cultural streams. In the old days there was nobody in the gang who could discuss these things with Mac with any degree of spontaneous interest—yet now, if he were only around, I could write him page after page without effort or condescension! Good old boy—just a year ago I was addressing a Christmas card to him, which Fate never permitted me to send. I wish your tale could have formed his actual fortunes, & that he were now enjoying some reward commensurate with his merits, & with his real charm as a perpetual boy telling stories to other boys! What an ass the boss editor was to raise that silly objection to the non-stenographer point! That shews how remote from reality these stereotyped commercial robots get in the end. This fellow, used to thinking only in terms of large business enterprises, (shall we have 1 or 2½ millions for postage stamps this morning?) has simply lost the power of envisaging the position of a struggling & uncommercial author, or of realising the character of unworldly craftsmen in general. As if it were *illogical* for a writer not to be able to hire a typist, or not to provide for stenographic preservation every time he opens his mouth in personal conversation, social discussion, or informal storytelling! Hades, think of what our gang has lost in not having its meetings taken down in shorthand, & in not having its personal letters—argumentative & descriptive—copyrighted & sold! Bah! These big-winded office-hounds give me a pain in the neck! I'd have told the fool to go to hell before consenting to adopt his idiotic correction! I'm lending the MS. to Belknap—too bad we can't see the original version in print.

Well—more anon. Don't drop any matches into the petrol!

Yr obt Servt,

Theobaldus O'Casey

Notes

1. The amateur journalist Paul J. Campbell (1884–1945). He provided "The Joke Was on the White Man," *Texaco Star* 18, No. 10 (December 1931): 25–26, 32.

2. Robert E. Howard's article "The Ghost of Camp Colorado" appeared in the *Texaco Star* (April 1931), but his article "Kelly the Conjure-Man" was rejected.

3. WBT's "The Story Teller: A Tale of Christmas."

4. Francis Parkman's *The Conspiracy of Pontiac and the Indian War after the Conquest of Canada.*

[50]   [ALS, JHL]

Octr. 28[, 1930]

Jonckheer Arminius:—

Thanks prodigiously for the tip, & for getting me on your mailing list. I'll study the articles in question carefully, & see what I can do about producing a Providence homologue. Of course the commercial data would have to be swiped uncritically from some Chamber of Commerce folder, & of course any dope about Texaco in Prov. would have to come from Texaco sources. What about a *"terminal"*? Do you mean the proposed— or rather, half-completed & abandoned—railway line to Palmer, Mass. begun by the Grand Trunk system a score of years ago? There have been attempts to arrange for its completion by groups of local men, but nothing seems ever to come of it. Or are you referring to some hypothetical 'bus terminal to help get rid of the thousands of motor-coaches that ball up traffic at Fountain & Eddy Sts? That, so far as I know, is only a dream of the future—though, come to think of it, the N Y N H & H *has* talked of devising a terminal of its own, somewhere around or beyond the Union Station, which would take care of the New England system coaches—perhaps ¼ of the total—or less. Lemme know whatcha mean when the time comes. As for *pictures*—I suppose postcards or newspaper photographs are copyright, hence no good for your purpose. I haven't any camera in working order except a vest-pocket kodak— could these microscopic views be enlarged sufficiently for half-tone use?

By the way—if you're looking for travelogue material, I'm by no means limited to my own town. Belknap can tell you what an inveterate scribbler of descriptive travel-treatises I am! I could fix you up a whole series of articles— "On the Trail of the Past"—dealing with Quebec, Portland, Me., Portsmouth, N.H., Newburyport, Salem, Marblehead, Boston, Concord, Lexington, Quincy, Plymouth, Cape Cod, New Bedford, Newport, Kingston, N.Y., (with Hurley & New Paltz—old-time Dutch & Huguenot stuff) anything in the N Y metropolitan area from Tarrytown & Hempstead on the N. & E. to Elizabethtown, N.J., on the southwest—Philadelphia & Germantown, Baltimore, Annapolis, Washington, Alexandria, Fredericksburg, Va., Richmond, Petersburg, & (above all) *Charleston, S.C.,* of which I prepared an exhaustive study only last July for the guidance of our friend J. Ferdinand Morton, Armiger. Just name your region, & Grandpa can turn on the words. But of course the commercial & special Texaco angles would in each case have to be the product of special research, & I could not furnish pictures except through the loan of postcards in my collection. Possibly you may not want such stuff—but I thought I'd mention it anyway. I'll give the contents of the Nov. issue a careful looking-over—as I have given those of the Oct. issue.

By the way—did I tell you that our friend Wandrei has just got our fellow Weird-Tailor Derleth an editorial job on the Fawcett magazines in Minneapolis?[1]

I see the Times has gone up on its local Sunday price. Desperate situations, like the resignations of young star reporters, must be met by drastic measures!

Have just sold my newest story, "The Whisperer in Darkness", to Wright for 350 bucks—the best price I've yet received for any one tale. It will appear next June & July as a 2-part serial.

Well—here's wishing you success! Enclosed is a rather wicked little dig at your favourite sideline from the Sunday Journal.

Yr oblig'd ob^t Servt

Theobaldus O'Casey

Notes

1. Derleth was a sub-editor at *Mystic Magazine,* a position he held less than a year.

[51]   [ALS, JHL]

Dec. 10, 1730.

Jonckheer Arminius:—

Well—I'll say you done noble with the plates! Thanks a thousand times for this choice addition to my local archives! Glad the Prov. article will come later, so that you won't have to write it in a hurry. Don't cut it down any shorter than you have to—damn the pica ems & all such obstructive nonsense! Crowd in all the test and pictures you can—there's plenty of other matter, oil stuff & the like, that you can cut out! Too bad you missed that exhibition at the Art Club—there were some magnificent Old Providence drawings.

Now about "The Pool"—I am enclosing a long set of comments ending with a synopsis of the plot I prefer.[1] You must excuse the rambling chaoticism of the remarks. Not knowing just what you prefer, I had to throw out miscellaneous parallel suggestions just as I would in conversation—leaving to you the job of choosing & adapting. I did, though, indicate a clear line of preference—which developed spontaneously as I was conducting the discussion. That's the way all good plots grow—gradually & half-accidentally. I strongly advise you to use the narrative framework I have suggested—also the added touch of irony (which didn't occur to me till I got near the end!) involving the identity of the odd stranger who tells you the yarn in the ancient inn with the ominous rear-door lintel. You have a great idea here, but it's one which requires infinitely adroit development in order to escape the superficial unconvincingness characteristic of most W.T. tripe. I've tried to touch on all the points which need elaboration, & to suggest ways of supplying the requisite substance. Any dope you haven't at your finger tips can be secured at the 42nd St. library in the Spence & Murray books mentioned—or I'll supply any passages you like. In fact, I'll be glad to discuss the story at any later stage if you'll send the MS. (plus the comments herewith enclosed) to refresh an old man's memory. Don't feel constrained to follow all my recommendations literally—I simply suggest, & you can build the suggestions into any form you like. I'm anxious to see this tale when you get it done, & it seems to me that Wright would be a fool not to take it. Yes—he told me about the W.T. retrenchment. Too bad—& I hope it isn't merely the prelude to failure. All serials will be cut out in view of the 60-day waits, & my "Whisperer" will appear in one issue as a complete novelette—about as long a thing as they've ever carried at once, I fancy, since it came to 69 pages typed. I don't know when the new policy begins—not at once, probably, since Belknap's 3-part serial his just started. Have you seen this latter?[2] I could disembowel that brainless ass Senf for the hash he made of the illustration. Good god, can't the idiot read? Look at the nice, pretty Jumbo he has drawn on its pedestal, & then note Belknap's description of the loathsome & unutterable hybrid-thing that is dreaded Chaugnar Faugn!!

Concerning the hapless Rombout [*sic*]—I'll be van Dam'd if I can find his direful history anywhere in the immortal works of friend Wash.[3] The place where a lot of this Nieuw-Nederland legendry is, is Mynheer Diedrich Knickerbocker's History of New-York. It is here that we learn of the naming of Antony's Nose, & of the mishap that gave rise to the appellation "Spuyten Duyvil." I cannot, however, seem to unearth anything concerning the mariner of the Tappan Zee. 'Tis many years since I perus'd the work in its entirety; & lacking an index, I cannot say with certainty whether or not the tale be included. However, I can attest that a diligent thumbing & a close study of the table of contents have avail'd me nothing—it being a case of Westminster St.'s clam-shell pavement over again! Now as to what other Irvingana might be likely to yield the story—here once more I must confess myself stumped. Of the well-known works that I have read, only "The Sketch Book" & "Tales of a Traveller" seem to hold much Hudson-Valley legendry—& I can say with some degree of safety that Rombout will not be found therein. What, then, remains? Well, there is always the possibility that the tale is sandwiched in somewhere as a whimsical illustrative allusion—that is, in a work wholly unrelated to the Hudson. Whether I've so seen it & forgotten it, I can't say. There is also a possibility that it is contain'd in Irving's early "Salmagundi" papers, written in conjunction with his brother & other young wits. These I have never seen, yet they may very conceivably hold the missing item—as well as much more quaint & pleasing Dutch legendry. I really think it might be worth your while to look these up. It is also possible that the tale is not in Irving at all. Just how much of the Hudson legendry is really autochthonous, & how much is the invention of Irving, I am too superficial a student to say; but certainly there was no copyright on that kind of tale. The only place where I can recall Rombout van Dam in written form is Skinner's "Myths & Legends of Our Own Land"—& no credit is here given to any source. Altogether, though, I have an idea that the thing might be found in some Irving footnote or glancing allusion—or in some relatively minor piece of Irvingana. You might make inquiries at the public library, or in some other quarter likely to yield results. Let me know if you find anything—I will meanwhile keep my own eyes open for any data which may be floating about.

As for the genealogical matter—local history, as represented in my library, is quite silent concerning any Thomas Welles who settled in Rhode-Island in 1633. That is extraordinary, too; because if such a settlement were well-authenticated, I am sure that much would be made of it. As it is, all books assert with confidence that the only predecessor of Roger Williams on what is now Rhode-Island soil was the Revd William Blackstone, who settled in Cumberland in 1635—it being their part of the Plymouth Colony. Now since your Welles is associated with *Connecticut,* I assume that it is in the western part of R.I. that he is presumed to have settled. This was claimed by Conn. until as late as 1728, on the ground that the original Connecticut grant of 1630 gave that colony "all that part of New-England which lies west from Narragansett River, 120 miles on the seacoast"—assuming "Narragansett River" to mean *Narragansett Bay,* although in 1663 it had been expressly defined by Royal authority as meaning the *Pawcatuck River;* very early nomenclature having been irregular & variable. Now it is conceivable that ambiguity regarding the eastern boundaries of Connecticut existed from the start, & that land grants were made to Connecticut settlers, even as early as 1633, which really fell upon the then unformed territory soon to become Rhode-Island. Certainly, a purchase from the *Narragansetts* argues this, insomuch as their region did not extend to the true Connecticut area, the tribe at the border being the Niantics. But it must be remembered that a land purchase does not by any means imply personal settlement—& I cannot think that history has overlooked any rival of Blackstone as a pre-Williams colonist. The silence of all books is so complete, that one feels a mistake must exist somewhere. Where did you find the allusion in question? In a work on genealogy? Occasionally such books make curious historical errors. The name "Chimney Orchard" is exceedingly familiar to me, though I cannot in any way place it. Probably my recollection has nothing to do with your Wellestown, since names of this type are very frequently duplicated. I will make inquiries concerning this matter, & will let you know anything I discover. Meanwhile my curiosity is most genuinely piqued! As for the other genealogical point—I may be able to give you some results when I can get down to the R.I. Historical Society. Briggs is an old R.I. name—found in that selfsame Western area whence my Phillipses, Places, Rathbones, Caseys, &c. come—& its genealogy has been extensively studied by a scholarly descendant in Cambridge, Mass.—one Anthony Tarbox Briggs, with whose wife my aunt Mrs. Gamwell is very well acquainted.[4] Briggs died a few years ago, bequeathing his vast card-catalogued array of family data to the R.I. Hist. Soc., where it is kept as a separate file or collection. I once glanced through it & found many of my own ancestors as collateral connexions of the Briggs line, though I have no Briggs blood that I know of. As soon as possible I will get around to the Hist. Soc. & see if I can find anything of interest & significance to you. Meanwhile any available *dates* would help—if you have any on record. By the way—when I started to fill out that wheel chart which I owe to your kindness, it occurred to me that I do not know whether there are any accepted customs regarding the disposal of the several quadrants. You told me that it didn't matter which half-circle was paternal & which maternal; but having chosen, I am wondering if the choice of upper quadrants has any effect on the proper use of the lower quadrants. As it is, I put Lovecraft—paterno-paternal—in the upper left, & Allgood (paterno-maternal) in the upper right. Now does this disposal of elements impose any slated allocation on the corresponding maternal elements? That is, which lower quadrant should go to Phillips (materno-paternal) & which to Place (materno-maternal)? I want to do the thing right & proper if at all! Diagramatically speaking—how should the quadrants (a) & (b) be assigned to the Phillips & Place lines, respectively? Perhaps it doesn't matter, but on the other hand perhaps it does. On a rough guess—acting purely from instinct, I incline to give (a) to Phillips. Am I right or wrong or neutral? As I ponder the matter, I'm almost inclined to reverse my opinion; since the inversion of the chart—bringing the maternal half above the line—would place quadrant (b) in a position corresponding to the one used for the paternal line in the paternal half. Let me know the straight dope—if any—some time, for I don't want to expend labour on an incorrect job.

I shall certainly be damn'd grateful sooner or later for a sight of that Holland Society book[5]—& you must let me shoulder the transportation both ways. Whether I eventually shell out 15 fish for a personal copy, will form a complex psychological study. Of late, I've found that of all wild extravagances, *antiquarian travel* gives biggest dividends in the way of permanent imaginative enrichment; hence have become a miser in everything except 'bus fare & Y M C A room rent & guidebooks. Last spring, just as I hopped off for my Charleston jaunt, Loveman offered me a copy of the long-sought "Melmoth" for 10 bucks—but I resolutely passed it up,[6] & really think the sacrifice was worth it in view of my 11 days in Charleston & 8 days in Richmond. But who can say? After seeing those pictures of all the ancient stone houses I have come to love in Old Wiltwyck, Hurley, & New Paltz . . . .

Thanks for the stylographic pen information—on which I may act sooner or later, in such a case carefully heeding your hints. Thanks also for the address of the historic photographer—in writing for whose catalogue I shall not fail to mention your Blauvelt-mediated purchase. Trust I may eventually get a glimpse of the Ridgefield photographs you mention. I recall from occasional cards that the place is a highly attractive & by no means colonially barren one.

Glad that all your household enjoyed the Hudson River travelogue. I have my doubts about the commercial availability of such material, since my style—as well as my basic principles of selection in assembling material—would seem to me to be one to which the modern world of trade is antipodally alien & even actively hostile. I have seen some of the publications of coach companies—which are stacked for distribution in waiting rooms—& have so far found their travel material altogether different in tone, atmosphere, & content from mine. Possibly I might artificially turn out something to suit their needs if I studied those needs more exactly—indeed, I think that on my next trip I will make a more systematic collection of this sort of "literature." Marketing, though, is easier said than done. Various persons have thought my stuff might fit the Christian Science Monitor, which has rather a bias toward travel; but upon examination it appears that Monitor stuff always concerns more exotic & unusual places than I visit. As a beginner in the art of travel, I am woefully bound to beaten tracks. About the use of *het* in the Hurley quotation swiped from Eberlein[7]—blame the other guy, not me! But couldn't there be some special idiom in the Dutch language providing for the use of *het* as a pronoun as well as article? And how about provincial dialects of Dutch? Just how classical, anyway, were the forms of Dutch spoken in the widely separated Dutch settlements of the Hudson Valley? Hurley was a long way up the river & inland, but didn't get books & papers from Holland every day! But of course I know nothing whatever about it—my knowledge of Dutch being confined to the headstones in the Flatbush churchyard. Eberlein probably knows as little as I do—his ancestry, I think, being not Dutch but Pennsylvania High-German. If you ever solve the mystery, pray let me know. Meanwhile no harm is done, since my travelogue is a private affair which will expose my linguistic ignorance to only a limited number.

Well—I must knock off writing, for my left eye is raising hell. Lately the nerves or muscles give a kind of twitching or tugging when I focus it too intently—hope I shan't have to have an old-time oculistical siege & take to constantly-worn specs again! But you never can tell about aged eyes.

Thanks again for the pictures—& don't forget the duplicates when the article appears. If the company objects, tell 'em its good free advertising for Texaco .... maybe I can swing all the car-owners in the gang over to your camp, even though such owners are not numerous. Anyhow, the next time I take a trip I'll recommend your goods to all the 'bus drivers—unless I see them using it already. How about the lines I use going south? P.R.T. Mitten Lines, Greyhound, & Camel City Coach Co.? I think you said the New England (NYNY&H) lines do use Texaco.

Well—good luck with "The Pool"—& I'll try to look up that genealogical material at the earliest possible date. Haven't been to Jake's since your visit, but am thinking of paying a visit at some uncrowded hour, if only to see what that ten-cent pork pie is like!

  Sir, I have yᵉ Honour to Subſcribe myſelf
    Yr moſt obᵗ, moſt hᵇˡᵉ Servt
      Theobaldus

Notes

1. See Appendix.

2. Long's *The Horror from the Hills* was published in two parts in *WT*, January and February/March 1931. The story was illustrated by C. C. Senf (1873–1949).

3. Rambout van Dam (the Flying Dutchman) is mentioned in Washington Irving's "Wolfert's Roost," in *Wolfert's Roost and Other Papers* (New York: G. P. Putnam's Sons, 1855), 21.

4. Anthony Tarbox Briggs (1851–1918) was married to Ella Maria Eddy (1849–1934). HPL used the name "Briggs" in "The Howler" (*Fungi from Yuggoth* XII).

5. Perhaps *Year Book of the Holland Society of New-York* (1928–29). The next yearbook published was that for 1930–37.

6. HPL later received the book as a gift from W. Paul Cook.

7. See WBT 57n9.

[52] [ALS, JHL]

               Saturn's Day
              [December 1930?]

Jonckheer Armicius:—

        Thanks abundantly for the proofreading data. I have copied the whole business—table & corrected text—which wasn't much more bother, & was a half-dollar cheaper, than hunting up a photostatic reproducer. I shall practice this on the next proofs I have to read, & fancy the markings will get fixed in my aged head sooner or later. The article on proofreading is very illuminating. I think I could qualify on all points except the *speed*—& I might on that for all I know. Of course, though, the matter of knowledge of printing technique might trip me up. The headline business reminds me of our night-long rehearsal of 1929 in the upper regions of 230 W. 97ᵗʰ—it would take some time & drill to make me a lightning calculator in such matters! I herewith return everything—safely, unless the P.O. fails it do its part.

  Thanks for the postcards. Ann Arbour must be quite a place, & I wouldn't at all mind touring through that region after covering the high spots of the historic east. Mortonius' last card to me was from Columbia, S.C.— next door to glorious CHARLESTON. I wrote him out a full travelogue of Charleston,[1] so that he won't be likely to miss much there. Columbia is all right enough—I like it exceedingly—but it's pale beside the really incarnated past as exemplified by Charleston. Belknap has just been to *Quebec*—gad, how

I envy the little rascal! He's now headed for Portland. I don't yet know whether he can induce the paterfamilias to trundle the Essex through Providence on the return trip. Hope so, for I'd like to see the kid!

I'll see if I can get hold of that Satevepost with the Southern City dope, but it's probably off the stands by this time. Your own Sunday Times had some pretty good articles on the South a few weeks ago—in the magazine section.

Congrats on the leisure time! That's the kind of journalism I'd enjoy! I'm trying to get caught up on a hellish lot of revision so that I can fix up some fiction of my own.

Trust Newkirk Ave.² wears well as a residential headquarters. May no malign chants from Outside lure you to annihilation!

St. Nicholas be with thee!

Father O'Casey

Notes

1. "An Account of *Charleston*, in His Maj^ty's Province of *South-Carolina*."
2. WBT lived at 2215 Newkirk Avenue in Brooklyn.

[53]   [Postcard]¹

[Postmarked Providence, R.I.,
19 December 1930]

Yup—December ★ came safely, & was perused with interest. Sorry to see your tale mangled, but of course it would seem all right to one who hadn't known good old Mac. Maybe it's my imagination, but it seems to me that illustration looks a bit like him—except for the frock coat, which is a conventionalism that doesn't belong there anyway. Hope you're sending copies to all the gang. I lent your original ms. to Belknap. ¶ This cold spell has about finished me, so that I haven't had a chance to get out to the R.I. Hist. Soc. about your data. But have patience—with a little more moderate weather, & a little less crowded programme, Grandpa will get into action!

Best wishes—O'Casey

EXTRA

It hath just come! And done up by the same master hand that packed Morton's minerals! A thousand thanks for the loan—truly, the book is a marvel!! I'll be very careful in returning it! I can't promise so good a job of packing as yours!

Notes

1. *Front:* First Baptist Church, Providence, R.I.

[54]   [ALS, JHL]

2242

[January 1931]

To Selenkos Nikator, Ptolemaios Philadelphos sends greetings:—

Thanks prodigiously for the illustrated extracts, both of which go instantly into my files. And, let me remark, those files are now restored to the semicoherent state of 1927 by virtue of an exhausting cleaning & sorting campaign from which I have only just emerged. *You* would not call this state coherent at all—for it merely consists of the rough dumping of certain basic classes (such as astronomy, archaeology, Providence, &c., &c.) into some 20 or so boxes or envelopes—but it's all the classification I'll bother with. It's a relief to have the circumambient cluttering a bit abated. My room doesn't show any external change; but many a corner heap is done away with, & I managed to throw away about a ton of accumulated odds & ends.

That article makes me veritably homesick for Charleston, though it's still an open question whether I can get down there this spring. There are some errors in the text—such as the period of Stede Bonnet's hanging—but in the main it succeeds in hinting the actual charm of the place. What wouldn't I give to be walking along Tradd or Legare St., or loitering in ancient Longitude Lane, right now! Warm breezes, luxuriant live-oaks, & the scent of magnolias . . . . oh, boy!

Ere long I shall reluctantly ship back that monumental Hudson Valley volume whose study has virtually doubled my knowledge of the Nieuw Nederland region.[1] It is the most fascinating thing I have seen in aeons, & makes me wish someone would cover New England in the same way. It also makes me wish I could tour indefinitely over the archaic back roads of Renssaelerwyck, Esopus, Vys Kil, & other realms where time has trodden lightly. The differences betwixt various parts of Nieuw Nederland are now manifest to me as never before—& I see that the Ulster region whose surface I have scratched is really the most primitive & unchanged of all. I do not think I have seen *any* houses of the Albany type, & hope I can do so some day. In Albany itself none seem to remain—indeed, I fancy that Albany has suffered a more ruthless destruction of early architecture than any other colonial town in America. It is, apparently, in *Schenectady* that one must look for any possible reliques of old Albany designs. One thing seems to be quite settled by this book; & that is, that aside from Manhattan, stepped gables existed only in Albany. Since all of these have vanished, it remains a melancholy fact that not a single original example of the stepped gable exists in North America. No use, therefore, looking hopefully here & there. The steep-roofed houses of Albany suggest to me the earliest houses of Quebec, & probably illustrate a phase of continental architecture existing both in France & in the Netherlands.

It is rather unfortunate that the volume limits itself so arbitrarily to the upper Hudson Valley—unless, indeed, a companion volume for Nieuw Amsterdam, New Jersey, & Long Island is contemplated. The wooden houses of

Brooklyn, Flatbush, & Flatlands, & the brownstone houses of your own region, surely merit treatment in any representative survey of the colony's architecture. Also, I think it highly arbitrary to close the record with the year 1776. As a matter of fact, one typically & exclusively Dutch feature was *only just beginning* at that period—i.e., the familiar curved gambrel with porch whose angle measurements you are so carefully noting. In all the book, only about 3 of these specimens are included—yet why are they less a pure Dutch form because they happened to be evolved after a certain arbitrary date? The whole *gambrel* question presents great difficulties—especially as to region of origin. Some have thought that you Dutchmen evolved the gambrel roof, & that we Yankees merely copied & adapted—but the evidence of this book is that you didn't take up the style on any considerable scale till long after we were using it in our differently proportioned form. We began to gambrelise about 1710 or 1715, & by 1730 were hardly doing anything else but . . . yet you didn't get to the peak of this style until 1760 or so.

I see that this author, unlike Eberlein, thinks that Hurley has indeed changed since the old days. It was news to me to learn that the south side of the village street had ever been densely built up. I must go all over that region again, & take the entire Kingston–Ellenville 'bus ride.

Well—be good. Hope Texaco matters go well, & that you've found nothing as yet to contradict our researches on Syro-Ægypto-Macedonian matters!

Yr obt
Ptolemaeus

[P.S.] Again—thanks for Charleston & Craik!

Notes

1. Probably Helen Wilkinson Reynolds (1875–1943) and the Holland Society of New York, *Dutch Houses in the Hudson Valley Before 1776* (New York: Payson & Clarke, 1929). HPL took extensive notes on the book; see "Notes on Hudson Valley History" (*CE* 5.195–204).

[55]   [TLS, JHL]

Tenbarnes Manor, Jan. 21. [1931]

Jonckheer Arminius:—

And speaking of changes, how about a little typing from Grandpa? Left eye a bit on the bum, & wrist shaky from overuse, hence this damn machine wears, temporarily, the aspect of a lesser evil. A somewhat unexpected mess of work early this month has queered my whole programme, causing a pile of more than 20 unanswered letters to pile up. Today, in a way, forms my first conscious glimpse of 1931!

Meanwhile abundant thanks for the various pictorial enclosures, which I

1have scanned, and shall continue to scan, with the keenest interest and appreciation. The Hartford Georgian world-beater interests me profoundly—and damn it all, I suppose it technically invalidates the magnitude claim of our new court house! It would probably be quibbling to take advantage of the loophole you hint, and which likewise suggests itself to me upon a study of the picture—that is, a refusal to accept this structure as authentically Georgian. Certainly, in its whole organic symmetries it does little to sustain the traditions of 18th-century design-feeling, so that an especially venous pedant might well place it on the wrong side of the line, along with those Georgianly ornamented skyscrapers and hotels and apartment-houses (like the Hotel Whitehall, formerly Carlton Terrace, up near Belknap's at Broadway & 100th St.) which nobody even tries to call real Georgian edifices. Sustaining this view, they could consult architect's drawings of our new court house as it will look, and see how perfectly the component masses follow truly Providence-colonial lines, and how truly Georgian is the manner in which the various masses are grouped. The central belfry tower will rise above the huddle of gables in a fashion preëminently early-American, yet I defy anyone to say that the belfry of this Hartford building does the same. The whole feel of that central pile of the building is modern—of the terraced school, thinly camouflaged. Assuredly, as a work of art this falls far below the Providence specimen. Yet on the other hand it would be folly to pass it off as utterly non-Georgian. It has the belfry, the decorative details, the balconies and urns, the occasional pilasters and bevelled corners, etc. etc., which surely remove it vastly from the mere pseudo-Georgian office-building type. It would not be fair to rule it out—so I suppose if your article is not already set up, you will have to modify your superlative statement about the Prov. C.H. But again I say I'll be damned if I think this new thing represents old Hartford as well as the court house will represent Old Prov.

Thanks tremendously, too, for the Ridgefield pictures. I well recall the part of this town in Tryon's raid, and Benedict Arnold's connexion therewith. Arnold has always interested me on account of the Rhode Island origin of his line. Ridgefield must be a delightful place today—another reminder of how sadly little of His Majesty's Connecticut Colony I have so far seen. I must assemble a body of guide data, plan out a trip, look up the stagecoach routes, and start on an exploration some day. I've never seen Norwich, have seen New-London only during 40-minute coach stops, and have never been off a wheeled vehicle in New Haven or Guilford. Of Hartford I have had no more than a train-glimpse—the one time I passed through it being in 1928. Cass Gilbert shews good taste in a residence. I note that the pitch of the gambrel roof is here wholly Novanglian—unaffected by the New York type (with upper pitch much shorter) whose characteristics, even in English houses with uncurving lower pitch, are probably of Dutch derivation;. It would be interesting to study houses close to the New-York–Connecticut line, as well as on

Long Island, and see just how far east the New York influence filtered. Ridgefield, at any rate, is safe on our side of the fence! The Bedford scene interested me, for Bedford is one of my favourite villages. I have seen it often on drives with the Longs; and its central green, old burying ground, and occasional archaic structures make me think exceedingly of New England soil.

The January Star came yesterday, and I must hasten to transmit my thanks and congratulations. Truly, it is a splendid number; and a credit alike to you and to the company. The New London article interested me vastly, and almost made me vow to stop off there longer on my next trip. It really wouldn't be a bad idea to do a little Connecticut exploring on either the outward or inward passage. I was also greatly captivated by the whaling article and its well selected illustrations. You clearly appreciate the atmosphere of the old whaling days—and I wish you could explore the New Bedford whaling museum and climb all over the half-size model of the barque Lagoda as Belknap and I did in 1929. Even the child—professedly insensitive as he is to New England antiquities—couldn't help admitting that this old maritime atmosphere had a curiously stirring quality about it. Another alluring thing was the Jamaica article. What wouldn't I give to be on the scene there right now? The Smithfield glimpse, too, was welcome. Smithfield is, I think, the nearest town to the oldest structure of English origin in America—old St. Luke's church, built 1632, in Isle of Wight County, Va. But of course the thing I am most avidly waiting for is the Providence article. Don't forget to slip me as many extra copies as you can! Glad the text got by as written—I'll wager you made a good job of it.[1]

Glad you found my remarks on "The Pool" worth noticing. Any time you feel like more discussion of the theme, just shoot. Too bad W.T. has curtailed, but it's not a bad market even now. Actually, the change will affect very few of us—for we have scarcely ever had things in except at long intervals. Your book idea seems to me excellent—capable, indeed, of development to almost monumental proportions. I don't recall seeing anything exactly of the kind in plan and development, although of course there have been innumerable treatises on popular superstitions. Surely, your "morgue" would be a magnificent foundation for such a thing. I am all in favour—but why not put it up to some of our better read members—such as James Ferdinand?

Any new discoveries about Rombout Van Dam? Too bad I couldn't track him down. As for Welles—there never was a part of R.I. which passed to Connecticut. What there was, was a part of R.I. which is still such, but which Connecticut claimed until a royal edict negatived the claim. What I thought was that Welles might have had a land grant in the disputed section—which would have been on Rhode Island soil after the settlement of the claim adversely to Connecticut. The disputed area, of course, was our whole South County—where most of my own ancestors dwelt before their 18th century drift northward into the Scituate region. Connecticut claimed that the "Narragansett River" allowed as her boundary was Narragansett Bay, whereas we claimed—rightly, without a doubt, for the difference betwixt a river and a broad bay is too obvious for any but pettifogging doubts—that the stream so designated (at a date when all local nomenclature was in a state of flux) was the Pawcatuck River, which flows north from Westerly. King Charles decided in our favour, so that was that. Welles interests me, and as soon as I get more active I shall try to look him up. The same goes for Briggs. I haven't been out of the house—except twice over to my aunt's in Slater Avenue—since I last wrote you. Simply dead to the world! Oh, yes—about the wheel chart—I'll toss up a coin and go ahead—when I get around to it. I don't envy you your labour on the morgue. Nothing yet done toward straightening out my own hopeless cutting-chaos.

Hope Belknap's visit came off without a hitch. I guess it'll be the first time the little imp has been as high as 18 stories since I took him up to the top of the Woolworth Bldg. in 1922. As for other gang-news—the projected Cook–Orton partnership fell through, and each blames the other. Another fight for Grandpa to patch up! Any recent local meetings or prospects of such? Well—thanks again for the pictures, &c. Glad the "Rats" wear well after all these years.[2] And when I've had a chance to go through that Hol. Soc. tome I'll probably write a 200-page volume! Yrobtservt H P L

P.S. The new Netopian has an article on *Olneyville*,[3] in the course of which I am reminded that my own lineal ancestor Thomas Clemence founded the place in 1654.

Notes

1. HPL refers to the following articles in the *Texaco Star*, 18, No. 1 (January 1931): PCH, "Peanuts, Spices and Smoke," 9–11; WBT, "'There She Blows,'" 13–17, 32; [Unsigned], "'Texaco at Home IV—New London,'" 24–26; E. C. Battersby, "Globe-Trotting with Texaco," 27–32.
2. "The Rats in the Walls" was reprinted in the June 1930 *Weird Tales*, and also in *Switch On the Light*, although the latter may not have been in print at the time.
3. "From River Valley Settlement to Metropolitan Sub-Center: The Interesting Growth of Olneyville Square and Vicinity from the Days when the First Settlers Came into Possession," *Netopian* 11, No. 5 (January 1931): 1–2.

[56]   [ALS, JHL]

Thor's Day [19 February 1931]

Jonckheer:—

Well—if I'd waited a bit longer I might have done more answering with the same 2¢ stamp & charity envelope! And to think that postage is threatened with a rise to 2½¢![1] The bum sinistral optick isn't so bum now—

hence the relapse into my equally inimitable & indecipherable cacography. I'm trying to go as easy on the vision as an overstuffed programme will allow—but it'll take summer heat to set the old man up again. At that, though, I'm not half as nearly 'all in' as I was at the close of last winter. My more complete hibernation has had a good effect.

Too bad about Brer Farnsworth, who is a damn good fellow for all his occasional vagaries of editorial taste. I hope the hospital session will bring results. His nerve trouble is a very rare one—a sort of pseudo-palsy, or something like that, called Parkinson's Disease. So *Oriental* is going down to the quarterly class, eh? That's real news to me! Not that I'm personally interested, since nothing of mine would ever be likely to fit it. Belknap speaks of having a story in the latest issue—whether he means the latest out or the one just coming he doesn't make clear.[2] No—I haven't the alleged attack on Sonny's style—in fact, I haven't seen a copy of *The Editor* in years.[3] Have my own criticisms to make in this direction—as to the affectedly short sentences, laboured attempts to maintain a pointlessly ironic tone, & artificial parade of current idioms of popular science & sophistication—but I can't imagine that such objections could coincide with the censures of anybody who would hold up *Arthur Brisbane* as a model![4] *Arthur Brisbane* . . . . . oh, my gawd! I don't wonder Wright, after receiving an opinion like that, has to go to the hospital! Nine chances out of ten, the criticisms is a pure dumbbell affair—for Belknap's *natural* style is one of the finest & most vividly rich that I have ever encountered in a personal acquaintance. He knows how to make words & images fairly radiate music, pictorial value, & associative intensity—his only trouble being a sheltered & quasi-infantile remoteness from life which cuts down his natural fund of things to write about & makes him fall back on aesthetic theories, mannerisms, "smartness," & a sort of professional "rebel" pose in consonance with his cut & dried abstract views on art & life. But set the little rascal going on a theme which really 'gets' him, & there isn't a member of the gang who can even catch up with his dust in the matter of spontaneous, colourful, & really artistic eloquence. Only the other day I gave him a tremendous grandpaternal scolding about his waste of real expressive genius on sterile & frivolous themes—urging him to get anchored to some engrossing *reality* in the objective world, & then proceed to develop its overtones & symbolisms in a solid, serious, & non-extravagant way. His best bet, as I view it, is **the sea**—which (aside from the pageantry connected with ancient art & anthropology) is the one actual external thing that seems to possess an authentic hold on his feelings. What the kid needs is to be shaken out of that empty narcissistic attitude which makes his chief pastime the dramatisation of himself as 'the picturesque but oppressed young rebel artist of the Great Tradition.' But heaven knows these objections aren't vital or permanent ones— but are, on the other hand, things which will probably right themselves as Sonny matures emotionally & looks outside himself into the objective world.

He has a magnificent aesthetic equipment all ready for use—& which has indeed already turned out a very sizeable batch of notable work. I'll wager the criticism is a stupid & low-grade one which merely resents Belknap's departure from ready-made 'human interest' themes & from the tawdry 'action & sentiment' style of the conventional 'pulp' magazines. I don't know how one would get hold of the magazine in question except by sending to the company, but you'd better tip Sonny off & let him get it if he thinks it's worth while. I'm sure I'd be highly interested to see what it's all about!

Too bad no more van Dam data came to light—but I'll wager your article is a good one just the same. Your company is surely doing folklore a distinguished service—my note of yesterday will have let you know how captivated I was by the map. I hope, by the way, that this background-exploitation will eventually include New England. Haven't you service stations around Boston, Lexington, Concord, Salem, Marblehead, & so on?

This *Welles* business surely does pique my curiosity to a rare degree, & I expect I shall have more to say after an afternoon & evening spent jointly at R I Hist & publibe. There is little question but that the emphasis in that phrase *"about* 1633" belongs very emphatically on the qualifying adverb; (or preposition—be your own Priscian!)[5] since the presence of a white man in Rhode Island before Blackstone (or rather, Williams, for Blackstone's region did not become a part of R.I. till 1747) would, if actual, be prominently recorded in all histories of this colony. I feel sure there's a mistake in date somewhere—you know how slipshod & contradictory & ambiguous these books of local or family annals sometimes are. But I can tell you more after I really do make that long-promised round of neighbouring archives. The clues you furnish are very good—or look so to me—hence I feel sure I can pick up the trail somewhere & piece out in a more definite way. The same goes for Briggses as well. Rhode Island teems with them—& there is that special set of Anthony Tarbox Briggs records in the Hist Soc. which ought to help some. Incidentally—my aunt Mrs. Gamwell has just been visiting this Briggs's widow. If I'd thought in time I might have given her your earlier letter to take along & see if she could help. But I don't believe she was very diligent in studying her husband's records—for of course his tree was no especial affair of hers.

No hurry about "The Pool"—I have ideas 14 or 15 years old still kicking around in note form, some of which will probably even profit in point of technical development from the long postponement. You have a first-rate central theme, & it'll make a good story whenever you tackle it. As for that *het*—it ain't "my" way, nor (I suspect) Eberlein's way. I don't know where he got the jingle—but it is really very appealing, with all the rich flavour of the soil which I admire so much in folklore. After seeing the Hurley–New Paltz–Wiltwyck region I am able to appreciate such things with redoubled poignancy. That region is to the old peaked Dutch house what your Rockland County region is to the later curved-gambrel type. And this reminds me what a feast your volume de luxe is proving! I'm digesting it by slow stages, & will see that it gets started back as securely (if not as neatly & artistically) packed as when it started out. I'd be less dilatory with it if my programme were less distractingly packed with current demands. If you have any sudden need to recall & use it before my leisurely survey drags out to its natural extent, pray have no delicacy or hesitancy about so doing.

Your recent reading is certainly ample enough for one as busy as you are—& is all very sensibly in line with your natural interests. I read van Loon's "Story of Mankind" when it was new, & have half a mind to get it now that it is reprinted in the Star Dollar series. Some day I must read "Pieter Stuyvesant & his Times". I either read or skimmed Motley in my youth—a truly monumental work.[6] "The Crusades"[7] ought to be exciting stuff, even though my interest in mediaeval things is nothing to brag about. Virtually all my reading this winter has been concerning Quebec & New France generally—Parkman, Bancroft,[8] & all sorts of minor junk. As I said a little while ago, I could now talk by the hour with good old Mac on his pet themes—just my luck not to get the "bug" till too late! Your Dutch colonists come briefly into the picture now & then—did you know that your States-General once had a momentary foothold on the Maine coast? By the way—I read a review a week or two ago in the Sunday Times which touches a somewhat little-known chapter in colonial history, the New-Sweden enterprise in Delaware. Since, as you know, this was one of the prime adversaries of New-Netherland, it ought to interest you from the Dutch angle. Possibly you've seen the review—if not, I'll try to locate & send it. The book it describes ought to be well worth reading.[9]

Interested to hear that there are brokerage statisticians who read W.T.! I've often wondered if there wouldn't be a limited field for a higher-grade magazine of the same nature—presenting material of the Machen–Dunsany–Blackwood–de la Mare–M R James level—but probably there wouldn't, since if there were, somebody would have discovered & exploited it ere this. Leeds & Morton used to dream about something of the kind.

Well—I'll give your ocular & Champollionic faculties a rest for the moment; again thanking you for those maps, & intimating how welcome a liberal additional supply would be. My aunt Mrs. Gamwell is going to have one on the wall of her room.

¶ Regards to everybody on the wheel charts from Horman Donwenszen Taelman to the present—

Yr ob^t grandsire,
    Ludwig van Theobaldus

P.S. Have just dropt an appreciative line to Mynheer Vos.

Notes

1. Postage rates for a letter increased to 3¢ (first ounce) on 6 July 1932.

2. See WBT 44n4.

3. *Editor and Publisher* (1901f.), a leading magazine for the journalism and publishing fields, still being published. The article in question is by E. Irvine Haines, "The Use of Ambiguous Words," *Editor and Publisher* 92 (17 January 1931): 46–48.

4. Arthur Brisbane (1864–1936), prominent American newspaper editor of the 20th century, and also a speech writer and public relations man who coached many famous business people of his time.

5. Priscianus Caesariensis (fl.□500 C.E.), commonly known as Priscian, Latin grammarian and the author of the *Institutes of Grammar,* the standard textbook for the study of Latin during the Middle Ages.

6. John Lothrop Motley (1814–1877), *The Rise of the Dutch Republic: A History* (1856), a landmark work of history.

7. Probably Harold Lamb (1892–1962), *The Crusades: The Flame of Islam* (1930).

8. Hubert Howe Bancroft (1832–1918), American historian and ethnologist. HPL probably refers to his *History of the Northwest Coast* (1884–90), particularly Chapter 12, "New France and the Fur Trade: 1524–1763."

9. [Unsigned], "When the Dutch and Swedes Colonized the Delaware," *New York Times Book Review* (8 February 1931): 7; a review of Christopher Ward's *Dutch and Swedes on the Delaware, 1609–64* (Philadelphia: University of Pennsylvania Press, 1930).

[57]   [TLS, JHL]

March 24, 1931.

Jonckheer:—

If anybody ought to be making apologies, it is I; since a veritable stream of favours has lately come from you without any response on my part—duplicate maps, Texaco Star with interesting Ridgefield article, Shenandoah booklet, and gawd knows what else. But I have been wrestling with a new antarctic story—which has turned out to be a novelette of 30,000 or 35,000 words,[1] and which I consequently dread to type—and with a spell of bum sight in my left eye which is even now driving me to the machine in spite of my detestation of that barbarous contraption. I may have to take to wearing glasses again full time—which I found myself able to cease doing about the time you first knew me—though I dread to think of it on account of the way the damn things irritate my ears and nose-bridge. My aunts suggest that I try shell rims, which are undeniably less irritant than the more traditional types—but I'll be curst if I want to look like a typical George F. Babbitt or a middle-aged caricature of Harold Lloyd.[2] However, a spell of rest may avert or at least postpone this dilemma.

Trust the Sinn Feiners didn't mob you on St. Patricius' day. Surely orange is the right colour for a true-born subject of the house of William the Silent[3]—and more, was not the original name of idyllic Tappan Orange Town?

Damn this Providentian postponing! As for the Court House—such is my zeal for the spread of Georgian architecture in general, that I'll be quite reconciled even if some newcomer does horn in and push the pride of College Hill down to third place! After all, what is mere size? In New England, it's quality that counts! When I make my next excursion out into the world, I think I'll do the Prov.–N.Y. stretch on a stage-coach that goes through Hartford instead of my usual shore line one, and see if I can get a look at the cyclopean rival of 256 Benefit's successor.

As for the Pilgrim–Puritan matter—hell, can't you make some excuse to slip in the change without anybody's getting too personal about the reason? Never before in my life have I heard the name Pilgrim, in the sense of a new-world colonist, applied to any group save the separatists who settled Plymouth in 1620. These Pilgrims may conceivably be called Puritans, and sometimes are by easy-vocabularied moderns; but you can't put across the converse and call any other Puritans Pilgrims. Get the distinction? The Pilgrims proper were generally a rather humble lot, and held religious notions—or rather, notions of religious government—very remote from those of the Massachusetts bunch. They were, more than anything else, the cultural descendants of the old Lollards—the Wyckliffe outfit. They flouted the whole system of church ritual and church authority upheld by the established faith; and believed that any two devout Christians could form a church as valid as anything set up by St. Pete, the civil state, or any other constituted power. About the last thing those birds ever would have done is to kick out a guy because of some little difference in creed or doctrinal practice. They probably wouldn't have gone the whole way with Roger Williams and welcomed "Papists, Infidells, Turkes, and Iewes"; but they'd have been satisfied to boot the Papists, Infidells, Turkes, and Iewes out and let Roger alone. In other words, they were very mild and unassuming folk. At home they'd tried to set up a church according to their ideas at Scrooby, in Nottingham; but being harassed, they decided to sample the liberties of your own beloved fatherland; hence crossed over to Leyden, when they stayed 12 years. The only reason they left there was that they saw their children would grow up as Dutchmen. Not that they didn't like Dutchmen, but that they naturally wished their own posterity to be the same as they were, and speak the beloved old English tongue. As a result, they looked over a map of the new world to see if there wasn't some vacant corner where they could live by themselves as Englishmen without any mutual toe-treading ...... and finally lit on the region around the Delaware, for det vass befoor your olt enemies der Svedes bane coom dere. They had also thought for a time of going to New Amsterdam, but decided that would be just as overwhelmingly foreign as Leyden. Being dead broke, the poor devils virtually apprenticed themselves to the London

Company of merchant-adventurers, and were packed off in 1620 in a couple of rotten ships with captains who despised them—and one of which, the Speedwell, had to put back from the open sea before it foundered. Thus buffeted, they reached New England half by mistake, and wearily settled down at Plymouth, after a trial landing at Provincetown, as duly recorded in the schoolbooks. They certainly weren't in any shape to pester anybody else—and indeed, but for the fortifying presence of an outsider—the gentleman-adventurer Myles Standish—they probably couldn't have held their own against the cold and the wilderness. Such were the Pilgrims. It may be remarked that their action against Thomas Morton of Merrymount (NOT a forbear of James Ferdinand) was not due really to puritanic bigotry but to genuine fear of the results of his giving rum and muskets to the Indians. Now at this point pause to form a picture of the well-defined and characteristic Pilgrim type—the humble, oppressed total Separatist from the established church; weary and tolerant, poor and unassuming—content to let the rest of the world alone and to tolerate any law-abiding Protestant.

ACT II—enter a new element on the stage of New England. Gentlemen, meet the Puritans proper! A powerful and arrogant faction of the Church of England, strong in numbers, cash, and political influence, and having a high proportion of important landed gentry and rich merchants among them. NOT the spiritual heirs of the Lollards, but a direct evolution of Luther's reformation; and thoroughly in sympathy with the established church's organisation and polity, though not with its ceremonies. Here are some guys who know what they want and aren't going to take any back talk from anybody. No humble, oppressed, broken people here—but grim, fervent, competent citizens in the main line of old-world tradition, and just as ready to persecute outsiders as the Romans were to persecute the Catholics, the Catholics the Anglicans, and the orthodox Anglicans, them! And what do these birds do? Bind themselves out to anybody else? Not by a damn sight! They organise their own merchant-adventuring outfit, the Company of the Massachusetts-Bay, and prepare to make a thorough and well-equipped colonising venture on a large scale—just like your Dutch West India people. Being disgusted with the forms and emotional life (NOT with the authority and organisation) of their home church, they resolve to carry themselves, their ample worldly goods, and their rigid ecclesiastical organisation competently and prosperously across the sea to build another England in which they can lord it unhampered, wax prosperous, and persecute everybody else. These people rather despised the Separatists, and had nothing to do with them in England. In New England they were prepared to live at peace with the Separatists as their southern neighbours, but were quite prepared to put on the screws if these same neighbours didn't do as they liked. Their territory, of course, was the area between the Pilgrims on the south and the Mason–Gorges grant—New Hampshire and Maine—on the north. The first big settlement was made at

Naumkeag, a good harbour where Roger Conant, a Pilgrim who had turned against Separatism and desired a more formal church, had founded a small settlement in 1626. This was in 1628—when the Pilgrims were still a small struggling bunch of less than 300, though they had managed to purchase their independence of the London Co. The new Naumkeag settlement, made by John Endecott, Gentl., of Dorchester, England (whose descendants mis-spell their name Endicott), was re-named SALEM, and the bigoted, arrogant, and fanatical Colony of Massachusetts-Bay was born. You know the rest—or ought to, after reading of last year's Boston Tercentenary. The preponderant large-scale settlement came in 1630, when John Winthrop, Gent., of Groton in Suffolk, was made Governor of the company to succeed Endecott; coming over with Thomas Dudley, Gent. (of the family of the Earls of Leicester) as his Deputy. Winthrop came to Salem on the Arbella, which also bore my lineal ancestor Rev. George Phillips, son of Christopher Phillips, Gent., of Rainham St. Martin's in Norfolk. The whole colonial enterprise comprised 11 vessels carrying over 700 persons with horses, cattle, and all necessaries. Some contrast to the Pilgrims' poor little Mayflower—Mrs. Hemans couldn't say of the Puritans what she said of the Pilgrims—that they came "not as the conqueror comes!"[4] In 1630, too, the ship Lyon bore the Rev. Roger Williams—destined, as paradox would have it, to found a colony more radically un-Puritan than that of the Pilgrims of whom he wasn't one! Also in 1630, as you know, Winthrop moved the main body of colonists successively to Charlestown and the Shawmut peninsula—the latter becoming the larger and celebrated Irish town of Boston. William Blackstone, who had been settled there before, stood the Puritans (of whose doctrines he had quickly repented after seeing a working-out in Salem) just five years, and then packed up for Rhode Island. (an area, however, on Plymouth land at the time)

Now get this Williams business straight. Roger didn't move to Boston with the Winthrop bunch, but stayed with the original Naumkeag folks at Salem as minister of their church. Then the fur began to fly—and in a year Roger and the Bay government (not his own parishioners) grew so cool that he lit out for Plymouth, probably by request. This is why the idea of his fleeing from the "Pilgrim Fathers" grates on one's historic sense so. He was O.K. with the Pilgrim Fathers. They liked him, and had him assist in pastoral duties, and hated so see him go—even though the ruling elder Brewster was a bit anxious about the latitude of his doctrines. The reason he did go—in 1633—was that his old parishioners were wildly anxious to get him back, and had fixed things with the Bay authorities so that he could return. He liked Salem, too—it is easy to see why he, an university bred scholar and gentleman, would find the meek peasantry of Plymouth just a bit tedious after a couple of years. His chief friend whilst there was one of the few gentlefolk among the Pilgrims—Edward Winslow, Esq., of Worcestershire, who became Governor of Plymouth in 1633, and who is a lineal ancestor of my elder aunt's late husband Dr. Clark. You can see how fundamentally erroneous it is to suppose the Pilgrims would even have had trouble with Williams. Their government was not a theocracy at all, but a perfect and absolute democracy, with everyone a freeholder, & having an equal vote in affairs. It was a perpetuation of the famous compact signed in the Mayflower's cabin—the church had nothing to do with the political organisation. On the other hand, the totally different Puritans of the Massachusetts-Bay Colony had a frank and rigid theocracy, with suffrage limited to church members, and all church matters regulated by the civil law. Church and state were never— not even in the Papal States of yesterday or in Vatican City today—so closely connected as in early Massachusetts; a condition utterly and antipodally alien to Pilgrim-Plymouth polity and feeling. And here's another thing that ought to get under your Dutch skin—the Massachusetts Puritans were overwhelmingly Calvinists; whilst the Plymouth Pilgrims were equally emphatic in their devotion to the modified doctrines of ARMINIUS, with which they had of course become impressed during their stay in Leyden. Well—I don't have to tell you about how Williams' second stay at Salem turned out. Of course, his doctrines about the lack of a state's right to interfere with any man's belief, and about the lack of the king's right to grant American lands without lawful purchase from the Indian proprietors, were utterly anathema to the arrogant Bay Puritans—hence his trial, banishment, and all that. You will now ask why, if he was so oke with the Pilgrims, he didn't go back among them—to which I reply, you don't know those goddam Massachusetts high-hats! The fact is, that although there wasn't the slightest political connexion betwixt Plymouth and Massachusetts except the common sovereignty of England, (the union as Province of the Massachusetts-Bay did not come till 1691, under William and Mary—your good old House of Orange) the arrogant Puritans with their ability to wield tacit coercive forces like economic advantage, military support in Indian trouble, etc., constantly exercised a policy of browbeating toward their Pilgrim neighbours; getting away with it all the better because of their superior birth, education, subtlety, and so on. Whenever Plymouth thought of doing anything Massachusetts didn't like, the Salem–Boston bunch had a few Capone-like words to say, and poor Plymouth pulled the Caspar Milquetoast act. All extra-legal, of course, but so is Scarface Al, and so are the Washington-dictated policies of Cuba, Santo Domingo, Nicaragua, etc. Hence Roger harboured no illusions about his being allowed to remain peacefully on Plymouth soil. The Pilgrims would have been glad to have him—but the men higher up said nix! What he did do was to beat it secretly to Mount Hope (Plymouth soil, of course, but safe for a while) and make a land dicker with Big Chief Massasoit for something outside both Massachusetts and Plymouth. He had met and become friends with Indians of several tribes during his Plymouth stay, hence knew he was sure of a welcome. The good old Wampanoag sold him a choice corner lot with a Seekonk water frontage on the east shore, just where Omega Pond and the Ten-Mile empty, and there he went in the spring of 1636—but alack! It turned out the Plymouth soil reached legally all the way to the Blackstone–Seekonk–Narragansett Bay line, so that the new home was on forbidden territory after all. Governor Winslow wrote this to Roger with pretty rueful and apologetic feelings—and I'll wager he felt like a plugged sixpence when he asked R. W. to help him stand in with the Big Works at the Bay by moving on quietly and peaceably! But Roger was a broad-gauge guy, and held no hard feelings. As soon as he had time to reap an early planting he moved on in a canoe with his few companions, received a friendly What Cheer[5] from a bunch of Bravas—I mean Injuns—on the Gano St. Waterfront, rounded George M. Cohan's[6] native Fox Point into the Providence River, and proceeded up that sweet-breezed (in 1636) estuary till he saw a spring and fresh-water rill at the foot of the great bluff on the east shore. There landing where now the Cohens and Ginsburgs haggle, he posed for the rotogravures and announced to the world that the Texaco Town of Providence had at last, after all these years, come into being. Nor did he fail to buy the soil lawfully, according to his own doctrines, from the natural Narragansett proprietors—not the present hotel management, but the sachems Canonicus and Miantonomi.

Well—I could go on indefinitely piling up instances of the diff betwixt Plim and Mass, Pills and Pures, but what's the use? If ya ain't got me by this time, ya never will. It remains to be said merely that Massachusetts always remained a definitely hostile neighbour, though glad enough to secure Roger's good offices with the Injuns in times of trouble. The attempts to lay claim to Warwick, to jazz up our boundaries, to egg on the Puritans of Connecticut in their absurd Narragansett land claims, to provoke the Indians regardless of our peaceful wishes, etc., etc. are all too well known. The Bay tyrants made the poor Plymouth folk expel Quakers and others, and tried to make us do likewise—but Williams soon told them where they got off! What would work on the mild-mannered Pilgrims wouldn't work on the independent and adventurous people who formed Rhode Island and Providence-Plantations—for truth to tell, most of us were of the same haughty temper, being members of the Massachusetts Puritan migration who had become fed up and were getting out in disgust . . . some going back to the regular Church of England (especially in Newport and the Narragansett Country), some becoming Baptists, and some taking up with the new Quaker movement. I think I have pointed out that the original or western Rhode Island stock is absolutely without Pilgrim antecedents, being either a disgusted overflow from Massachusetts, or a wholly later influx direct from Old England. Rhode Island had no really perceptible amount of Mayflower blood until 1747, when His Majesty George the Second favoured us in readjusting our eastern boundary to include the Little-Compton–Tiverton–Bristol–Warren–Barrington–Cumberland strips—(we didn't take in East Providence and the eastern half of Pawtucket till 1862) former Plymouth soil incorporated into Massachusetts in 1691. This, of course, gave us a considerable new population of Pilgrim blood; so that to this day you will find Mayflower names and descendants in the eastern part of the state—though never in the older regions like Newport, Narragansett, Warwick, Providence, etc., except through later moves. I don't know of any drop of Pilgrim blood in me, and doubt if any of the remaining genealogical stub ends could bring it in, since they are all obviously of western-R.I. provenance. Phillips, Place, Whipple, Mathewson, Dyer, Field, Hazard, Brownell, Ellis, Rathbone, etc. etc. are all Massachusetts-Puritan; Casey is Ould Oireland via Britannia; and Dodge (which as you'll recall we found twice in the Rathbone interval unearthed in Room 328 three years ago) has Newfoundland as its only cisatlantic stopping-off place . . . . . . whilst my paternal line is more directly British, with New York State as its intermediate habitat. But for all that, I'll hand it to the Pilgrims for being good neighbours. They're the only ones we ever had who didn't hate us and go out of their way to make trouble for us. And if the damn Puritans hadn't browbeaten them, they would have been in still more cordial sympathy with all our enterprises. I'm for them every time—and that's why I don't like to see them blamed for the raw deals which those stuffed shirts at Salem and Boston pulled! However—I'll admit that certain individuals among the Bay Puritans were very decent in their unofficial relations. Governor Winthrop, for example, really had much personal regard for Roger Williams; and is probably the one who advised him to leave the Bay before the General Court ordered his arrest and confinement. Winthrop's son—the Connecticut governor—met Williams in London when they were back on colonial business; and formed a very close and firm friendship despite the continued bad relations between the two colonies.

Wish I could have seen that antique show—but even if it's still going it'll probably be over before I pass through your decadent cosmopolis. Thanks exceedingly for the fragments thereof—I have similar reprints of several old-time papers, but unfortunately most of them are on such rotten paper that they perish in the course of a very few years. I mourned bitterly for my Evening Bulletin reprint published on the 50th anniversary of the paper in 1913. This Sun affair seems to be on stouter stock, and will perhaps weather the storms of time more valiantly. The silversmith stuff is interesting—but of course the absence of Samuel Casey renders it of only secondary value. I think I told you, did I not, that the Boston art museum now has a tankard of his—said to be as good as the one in the Metropolitan?

I shall try to see the cinema you mention—though I saw the original play "Outward Bound"[7] in Nieuw-Amsterdam in June, 1924, in the company of two individuals no less distinguished than the late Houdini and the late (so far as ownership of Weird Tales is concerned) get-rich-quick Henneberger, who were then collaborating on the details of a column run (or signed) by the celebrated conjuror. I recall that performance especially well because Houdini, conversing before the rise of the curtain, aired what is said to have been a favourite parlour trick of his—apparently pulling off his own left thumb and snapping it back after it had seemed to be away from its stump for as great a distance as an inch—or perhaps two. The wholly impromptu setting, and the fact that the whole thing was in the very next seat nor four feet from my eyes, made the effect highly impressive. I wasn't prying enough to beg an explanation, but logic seems to suggest that the cardinal principle was the snapping of some dark strip of material down and back to create an apparent gap between the base and tip of thumb. But it was damn clever—an absolutely perfect illusion, so far as my aged eyes were concerned. As for the play—it seemed pretty good as a whole, and I hope I'll remember to catch it when it comes in celluloid form. By the way—has Berkeley Square been made into a cinema?[8] If so, I don't want to miss it. But these things come and go so swiftly that an old man can't keep track of them all!

No—I've never seen Bierce's "Write it Right", though I've heard a great deal of it, and of Bierce's almost pedantic punctiliousness in minutiae of composition. I myself don't favour too great a primness in rhetorical niceties; believing that a vivid and vital style is more important than a strainedly correct one; though naturally I recognise certain well-marked limits of latitude beyond which one ought not to go.

I didn't know you were planning a Dutch house on the old sod. Why can't you get hold of a real one and have it moved to the spot you select? However, in case you can't, here are the roof angles you request .... which *were* in the book with the Hurley jingle, despite your contrary opinion. Lower and long pitch—45 degrees. Upper and very much shorter pitch, 25 degrees.[9] A pretty graceful arrangement, all told—though of course to me it isn't so *homelike* as our Yankee curveless roofs with equal pitches.

Here is the bookplate thing I mentioned—forgot to try for another, and it's too late now—so kindly return it unless it fills an utterly burning need in your aesthetic life. Possibly it'll be a disappointment, insomuch as it treats not of drawn designs, but merely of juggled type-ornaments.

Too bad your Headless Horseman tale fell a victim to Semitic economy. Not so smart now Meestah Vos shood t'ink himself, efter he gets it Meddum Vushinkton shood leef by Kenmore, an' Bruton ess ah Briton a'ready! Glad the pub firm got the Bruton point right. There's a job I'd like—29 grand per annum for doing very little! Both salary and duties fit my natural tastes admirably.

Thanks for the glimpse of Father O'Dwyer's startling contributions to heraldic and historical knowledge. Fra Bernardus must hear of this! The bit about the O'Neill red hand interested me vastly, insomuch as O'Hart assigns this device to my especial Casey branch—us bayin' descinded from the O'Neills, incluthin' the hunthred an' thurrty-sivinth King av Oireland. I've been afther seein' "historical" arrticles av Father O'Dwyer's befoor, an' must admit that they appear to best advantage whin uncorrelated wid the findin's av more prosaic scholars.

But speaking of this kind of thing—it takes a certain type of Latin-American antiquary to hate the Oirish! Of such the Senores in that Phoenicio-Venezuelan item are glowing specimens. They remind me of the Brazilian Senhor who also found Punic hieroglyphs a couple of years ago on the upper Amazon, (they were natural rock weatherings) and the Mexican geologists who positively place certain early sub-pedregal artifacts at dates around 10,000 B.C. etc. etc., and accept as a matter of course a 12,000 year antiquity for some of the Nahuan pyramids. As for the dinosaur allusion—I'll do Dr. Requena the honour of believing that some dumb reporter has misquoted him. By this time it's common knowledge enough that the great saurians all died off 30 or 40 millions of years ago—at least twenty million years before anything resembling an human being existed.

By this time I suppose you've actually met that Great Man whose very name makes the readers of W.T. breathe more tensely—the immortal, one and only creator of M. Jules de Grandin![10] What kind of a bird is he? As a guess, I'd say he is probably very attractive and intelligent, since his stuff is obviously the hasty, tongue-in-cheek hokum of a well-read and competent craftsman who knows better. He sees what hauls in the jack, and keeps on grinding it out as long as it will work. And at that, the stuff has a certain glib smoothness and mechanical snap which raises it above the utter, amorphous tripe of Nictzin Dyalhis[11] and other total losses. This bird could write stories, and damn good ones, if he wanted to take the time. Most of the gang, I imagine, will be eager to hear your report. Pull it at the next Kalem gathering and be the life of the party!

As for a critique of your style—let me see if I can think of any especial puffs or digs to hand out! I can't pick out any one thing to jump on, like Belknap's self-conscious pseudo-sophistication, since you don't run to any subjective mannerisms that I've been able to detect. I couldn't say that you have anything to unlearn or guard against. The worst I can say of any prose of yours that I've seen is that it merely isn't *careful* enough. That is, it perhaps goes ahead and says what it has to say too merely literally—without sufficient attention to the details of image-unfolding, and the precise mirroring of the moods and atmospheric values connected with each scene or turning of narration. To make a story effective in the highest degree, the inner rhythms of the prose structure must be carefully fitted to the incidents as they march along; while each word must be chosen with infinite care—a care which considers not only the dictionary meaning, but the subtle aura of associations which it has picked up through folk-usage and previous literary employment. In other words, prose must be created with just the same exactness, delicacy of ear, imaginative fertility, etc. as verse. One must study profoundly the art of *how* to present each new development in a narrative. Often everything depends on the dramatic manner in which some turn of plot is unfolded—so that one must study hours to discover just the right way to lead up to a revelation, bridge over a transition of scene or mood or perspective or time or action, build a foundation for some future event so that it will have an air of half-expectedness when it comes, express the delicate suggestions, associations, and implications which surround some specific act or object or incident, etc. etc. etc. I would say, in a roughly generalised way, that some of your hastier prose skims over these needs rather lightly—giving perhaps an impression of imaginative insensitiveness at times; or at least arousing a vague wonder as to whether you have extracted all the gold you might from the given chunk of ore. But as I have said, this goes only for certain specimens of your prose. It is certainly not true of "Doom around the Corner" and other high spots. Once in a while a hasty piece of yours may have merely mechanical flaws—isolated bits of cumbrous locution, excessively repeated words, etc.—but probably you catch all these points yourself before preparing a final version. Certainly, I don't think your style is retrograding. On the contrary, I think it is much maturer now than it was a few years ago. You will note that of your various tales it is a very recent one that I seem to be the most naturally enthusiastic about. In any case, you're not on any wrong track. If you need any admonitions, they are only such as would have you realise more keenly the vital connexion between the dramatic value of an incident and the precise manner of telling it—the precise way of introducing it, or building it out of earlier incidents, and the precise sentence-rhythms and word-choices to pick as a presentation-medium of maximum effectiveness. Boiling things down still further, one might say that if you tend to lack anything, it is on the atmospheric side. Perhaps you don't always bother to build up with words and rhythms and implications a general framework of vague feeling which will prepare one for what will happen, and make such happenings seem more expected and less improbable than they might otherwise have seemed. That is the fault of hasty composition. You can't write good prose rapidly unless in the throes of a special mood so poignant as almost to dictate vivid phases for you . . . . . and you don't get moods like that every day. At least most of us don't. Still—don't let any advice drive you so far to the opposite extreme that your prose will become affected and mannered and primly lifeless. Don't be self-conscious about your prose style. Get the right principles fixed in your mind through exercises apart from what you mean to be serious work, so that when you come to write seriously you can keep all your thought on your subject and preserve the natural vigour of spontaneous expression. Your ideal of straightforward simplicity is admirable, and I hope you won't lose it no matter how much you may cultivate narrative niceties. Steer clear of the artificially literary involutions which almost spoil Loveman's prose, and the extravagant vocabularial exhumations that clutter up Clark Ashton Smith's. Steer clear, too, of my own plethora of Latin polysyllables and my tendency toward monotonous and repetitive rhythms in periodic sentences. And don't chop your sentences up into half-inch pieces as Little Belknap does, or try to emulate his habit of always wearing a faintly superior smile about nothing in particular. Yea—and avoid the lethal ponderosity and habitually conventional formality of James Ferd's elaborately correct and seldom quite unhackneyed rhetoric. The best prose models you're ever likely to get hold of are Arthur Machen, Dunsany, and Walter de la Mare. Algernon Blackwood would whet and sensitise your fantastic imagination, but his prose is so accursedly bad and journalese that he'd do you more harm than good unless you read him with closed eyes (that comes from the O'Casey strain) and ignored his verbal tricks for the sake of the way he marshals images and impressions.

Oh—and before I forget it—I am told that a new weird magazine is about to be established by Harry Bates, editor of Astounding Stories, (80 Lafayette St., N.Y.C) and that it is already in the market for material.[12] A word to the wise . . . . . Probably it will be, like Astounding, one of the Clayton group; so that it will have an unfortunate bias toward prosaic Philistinism. But Claytonism also means 2 cents per word—which is an admirable thing in case of acceptances!

Thanks especially for the Shenandoah booklet. It makes me wish I could get around Winchester way—all I've seen of the Blue Ridge and Shenandoah Valley is what one trip from Washington to the Endless Caverns gave. That went too far south to catch the Winchester region—Strasburg and New Market. I want to make a whole trip through piedmont Virginia some day— taking in the U of Va, Monticello, etc. Still in doubt about how much of a trip I can make this spring. Florida, an active hope a month ago, looks rather dimmish just now. Some of those packet advts. in the 1833 Sun tantalise me. I'd like to take the elegant coppered ship Orbit for Jamaica (not Long Island), and Capt. *Rathbone's* (did you get that family touch?) fast-sailing coppered ship Nashville for New Orleans. Things were cheap in those days. I see you could get to Albany for one buck, whereas the Day Line soaks you three now.

Well, so it goes. Let me know if I've left anything out. I don't need to be told that I've put a boresome excess of matter in. The undeniable rapidity of this contraption seems to accentuate the old man's garrulousness!

Thanks again for the miscellany—and don't let the Texes postpone Providence till vandals tear all the old buildings down and make the article a back number. Right now the ancient colonial houses on Stamper's or Constitution Hill at the foot of Olney St.—a niggerville—are about to succumb in the course of a widening of North Main's notorious bottleneck.[13]

God Save the King—and the States-General too.

Yr ob^t Servt

Grandpa Theobald

Notes

1. *At the Mountains of Madness,* begun on 24 February and completed on 22 March.

2. George F. Babbitt was the central character in Sinclair Lewis's satire on American bourgeois life, *Babbitt* (1922). Harold Lloyd, Sr. (1893–1971) was a well-known actor and producer who gained celebrity in both silent films and talkies. Some of his films featured him with the nickname "Glasses" because he wore spectacles with round rims.

3. William I, Prince of Orange (1533–1584), known as William the Silent or William the Taciturn or more commonly known as William of Orange, the main leader of the Dutch revolt against the Spanish Habsburgs that set off the Eighty Years' War (1568–1648) and resulted in the formal independence of the United Provinces in 1581.

4. Felicia Dorothea Hemans (1793–1835), "The Landing of the Pilgrim Fathers in New England" (1820), l. 9.

5. "What Cheer, Netop" [friend]. What the Narragansett Indians said to R. Williams when they met him—thus name for *Netopian.*

6. George M. Cohan (1878–1942), an American entertainer, composer, actor, singer, and dancer, was born in Providence.

7. A play by the British playwright Sutton Vane (1888–1963). It opened in London in 1923 and premiered at the Ritz Theatre (219 W. 48th Street) on 7 January 1924. HPL must be in error as to when he saw the play, for it closed in May 1924.

8. *Outward Bound* (Warner Bros., 1930), directed by Robert Milton; starring Leslie Howard, Douglas Fairbanks, Jr., and Beryl Mercer. Based on the play by Sutton Vane. *Berkeley Square* (Fox Film Corp., 1933), directed by Frank Lloyd; starring Leslie Howard, Heather Angel, and Valerie Taylor. Based on Balderston's play.

9. See Eberlein, *Architecture of Colonial America:* "In the Dutch gambrel roof, on the other hand, the steeper slope usually makes an angle of forty-five degrees, or less, and is by far the longer, while the top slope is quite short and has an angle of about 25 degrees" (26–27). The "jingle" HPL refers to ("What shall we with the wheat bread do? / Eat it with the cheese from Hurley," etc.) is on p. 18.

10. I.e., Seabury Quinn. HPL himself met him on 6 July 1931, at a meeting of the Kalem Club at WBT's apartment.

11. Nictzin Dyalhis (1879?–1942) was a popular writer of horror and science fiction tales for *WT* and other pulps.

12. *Strange Tales of Mystery and Terror,* a Clayton magazine (7 issues, September 1931–January 1933). HPL submitted several tales to it, but all were rejected.

13. These include the house at 6 Olney Street, Jonathan Curwen's town residence in *The Case of Charles Dexter Ward* (there called "Olney Court").

[58]   [TLS, JHL]

Freyr's-Daeg
[27 March or 3 April 1931]

Jonckheer:—

　　　　Before I get to confession of ignorance, let me strut around with what I *do* know. Imprimis—I can tell you right offhand that there isn't any "Greek Year" or ["]Egyptian Year" 28 corresponding to the reign of Ptolemaeus Philadelphus. The Greeks reckoned by Olympiads, and about 123 of them had elapsed before Philadelphus came to the throne. And in the Egyptian dynastic reckoning 30 had long since been passed. Indeed, I don't think the Egyptians kept up the dynastic reckoning after the final Persian conquest—though that would be the subject for another bit of special research. The only conceivable explanation of the "28" is that it means in the 28th year of Philadelphus' reign. If it isn't that, you can count me out. He reigned 37 or 38 years, beginning with B.C. 285; so that the 28th year of the reign would be B.C. 257 or so. That, of course, is some 2188 years ago. I'm rather betting that this is the answer. I don't know just where you found this oddment, but if it was in a cutting in the morgue I may remind you that all reporters are not as accurate as Taelman of the Times used to be. Perhaps, of course, you have read the papyrus in the original Greek—in which case I'll lay the puzzle to some obscurity of translation. There's no question about the Ptolemy—gawd knows there was only one Philadelphus, the greatest Macedonian sovereign Egypt ever had. He's the bird who so extensively developed the Museum and Library at Alexandria which his father (old Ptolemaeus Soter, Alexander's general) had founded, and who tried to check the rival scholarly pretensions of Pergamum (Loveman's favourite Hellenistic burg) by declaring an embargo on papyrus . . . . . which, however, only stimulated the Pergamenes to invent parchment as a substitute! Also—it was under him that the celebrated Septuagint version of the Old Testament was prepared, and that the great scholars of Alexandria— Aristarchus, Aratus, etc. etc. began to flourish. It was in his time, too, the the [*sic*] Sicilian-Alexandrian bard Theocritus sounded his immortal pastoral reed, thus founding a school destined to bring fame to Virgil and to excite emulation all the way down through history to Alexander Pope and L. Theobald Jun. I didn't know that Ptolly was a Texaco customer, but am glad to find out.

Well—now for the ignorance. I haven't the slightest idea what happened to the cadaver of P. Philadelphus after the court physician announced in B.C. 247 (or 246, acc. to some) that it was all over with the poor devil. It probably was mummified, since the Macedonian Greeks took up with many Egyptian customs (this bird Ptolly married his own full sister for one thing) and had pretty well abandoned the traditional Aryan-Greek custom of burning on the pyre—Alexander himself had a sumptuous entombment, and there's no reason to think differently of his successors. Research might disclose more on this subject—but if I'm to get this to you quickly, I must confine myself to what's stored in the old bean. As it is, I must admit that I don't know where or how Ptolly was planted, or whether he's ever been excavated. If so, his body would not be as well mummified as those of the ancient Egyptians, since by Ptolemaic times the art had declined throughout Egypt, and the Greeks were but indifferent imitators of it. Probably he was buried somewhere in the Necropolis outside the city wall—where now, I believe, an expedition is looking for the tomb of Alexander the Great himself. The difficulty of this search leads me to suspect that none of the Macedonian-Greek royal bodies have been unearthed—though I may be all wrong on this.

But just use the agile Taelmanic imagination a bit, and you can have Ptolly all finely pickled in guaranteed Texaco products—bitumen and all that. Incidentally, I suppose you know that it was this guy who built the celebrated Pharos of Alexandria—or had the architect Sostratus do it for him—one of the 7 wonders of the world. There's a topic of special research for one of your staff—did they use Texaco in the Pharos to guide the sea-borne commerce of the ancient world?

Oh—I guess I've got just about time to speak of my first quest for Briggs–Welles data. I have pretty well exhausted the publibe without finding anything helpful to you except in a negative way; but I'll tackle the Histsoc soon. And now for debunking.

It looks as though your pre-Blackstone Rhodinsularian would have to recede into the domain of family mythology, since all accounts say that the Welles or Wells families did not arrive in these colonies till 1635 at the earliest. There were *two* immigrant Thomas Welles's, which no doubt has play'd hell with many an amateur genealogist's calculations. Both sent branches into Rhode Island, but no "Chimney Orchard" appears in the visible accounts. One Thomas Welles (1605–1666) came to Boston in 1635 in the ship Susan and Ellen—but he is not your Connecticut one. He settled in Ipswich and some of his children emigrated to western Mass. Your Tom (1596–1660) came to Boston in 1635 or 1636 (uncertain), soon (1636) transferring to Saybrook and in 1637 settling at Hartford. It is he who was successively Deputy-Governor and Governor of Connecticut—a fact which contradicts your account in which the Governor is said to be the son of the immigrant. This Thomas may have been a Junior for all I know, but he was the first Tom of his line to come to these colonies. Yankily speaking, there ain't no Seniorer! His descendants, filtering into Rhode Island after 1679 (a long way from 1633!) by way of Westerly and the South County, are the principal Rhode Island Welles's today. And that's all I know about Welles's for the moment.

Poor luck on Briggses, too. All R.I. Briggses so far found stem from South Kingstown, and no Walter is among them. None found in Providence. First, so far as is known, was John Briggs, (1609–1690) who came to Newport from England, held important Rhode Island offices, and later in life moved across the bay to Kingstown where he founded the family. In the Hist. Soc. is that special Briggs genealogy I told you about, hence I may have more to say in my next. This Anthony Tarbox Briggs who comes from my own ancestral region is undoubtedly an offshoot of the Kingstown stock, for as I have pointed out, our Scituate-Foster region was peopled almost wholly by a Narragansett-Country overflow—younger sons of the planters of that patriarchal and Virginia-like region.

This is a race against time, for I am due over to my aunt's in Slater Ave. right now, but I can't resist adding one more item of late news. I'm quite on edge with vanity through a series of letters from G. P. Putnam's Sons, who saw my junk in W.T., got my address from them, and want to look over as many of my MSS. as possible with a view to possible book publication.[1] Probably nothing'll come of it, but after two rounds of flattering correspondence I bit to the extent of sending the 30 loose MSS. kicking around here— with a promise to copy others from my file if the acceptance-chances prove really strong. It costs no more than the 39¢ express to give the firm a look . . . . . and if a miracle did happen, I would feel distinctly complacent as a real author with a book bearing the solid old Putnam imprint. However, I'll wait a bit and make sure before studying up an arrogant pose. And by the way—did you meet Quinn?

Sorry I can't dish up more Ptolly dope—but you see what you get when you ask an ignoramus. Oh yes—I mustn't forget to mention that I took dinner at Jake's after getting your library data. Beefsteak Pie (I managed to down it all, but not the accompanying bread) and Strawberry Shortcake!

Well—stick to your Arminian principles and don't go over to the Calvinists!
　　　Yr Obt
　　　　　Grandpa Theobald

Notes

1. Winfield Shiras (1900–1985) of Putman's had written HPL requesting to see his work.

[59]　[TLS, JHL]

　　　　　　　　　　　　　　　　　Tiw's-Daeg
　　　　　　　　　　　　　　　　7th of Xanthicus,
　　　　　　　　　　　　Anno 2242 of the Syrian Realm.
　　　　　　　　　　　　　　　　　[7 April 1931]
Jonckheer:—
　　　　　EXTRA—SPECIAL—RECANTATION—HUMBLE PIE!!
Humiliation . . . . Senile Decline . . . . .
Gawd, an old man's memory! . . . .

You win . . . . Grandpa is getting past the age of usefulness! Here I was telling you that no era existed which could give a "Year 28" around the time of Ptolemy Philadelphus, when all the time . . . . . but what's the use? Old age is old age!

Gawd, but it does give me a jolt to get caught napping like that, after having known a thing perfectly well. And I'd still be wallowing in the same sea of forgetfulness this minute if your just-received note and MS. hadn't happened to contain one key-word that has set the old memory back on the job at last. . . . . Apellaeus. . . . . . . Απελλαιος . . . . . . Hell's Bells! It's all as plain as the nose on your face . . . . or even that on my face, which is something else again. And to think that a whole major calendar had completely dropped out of my brain, just as though it had never existed, though I knew all about it when I first read up on the Hellenistic period back in '04 and '05.

This way out! My only defence is that the calendar in question is neither old-Greek nor locally Egyptian, and that when I had to reel off that hasty note to you my non-agile head was sort of stalled betwixt those two landmarks. I never stopped to cogitate around for a tertium quid, but began to strut pompously on a basis of fragmentary information. Eheu . . . . pride antedates a banana-peel descent! And I'm the guy that was razzing you for mixing Pils and Pures! Yeah—a helluva sharp on history! Yet now just that one little word—Apellaeus—starts up the whole mnemonic works and enables me to say what I'd orta of said last Friday. Just my luck to miss the chance of posing as an encyclopaedic authority!

Well, after this grovelling, I'll get down to brass tacks. The era in question, which (as I ought to have recalled in the first place) was indeed used by the Macedonians in Egypt as well as in many Levantine countries of the same period, is the *Era of the Seleucidae,* or Syro-Macedonian Era, reckoned from the foundation of the Graeco-Syrian kingdom as represented by the capture of Babylon by Seleucus from Antigonus in B.C. 312. There you are, all set—and in 1905 or so I knew all this just as well as I know my own name. Of course this was the official era in Syria itself from the very first, and I now realise that the other Hellenistic regions—beginning with Egypt, which was closely allied with Syria—soon adopted the system; although peninsular Hellas itself (also, probably, Sicily and Magna Graecia in Italy) did not, but stuck to the ancient custom of measuring years by the terms of magistrates and using the old months Hecatombaeon, Metageitnion, etc. (The Olympiads, invented about this time, were used more in historical chronology than in daily or legal computations). My old head, thinking of only Greece and Egypt, left Syria out altogether—yet the mere mention of the Syrian month Apellaeus sets it all straight. The invention of the Syro-Macedonian Era by Seleucus Nicator probably represents his carrying on of Alexander's policy of merging East and West. The Seleucian year was partly a lunar year, but its management and divisions did not correspond to those of the old Greek lunar year. Instead, they followed the prevailing arrangements in Syria, which were a corrupted form of the Jewish calendar—somewhat altered by slow decay from the form you'll find in Bible dictionaries. This has what might be called a luni-solar year—a lunar year with certain rough attempts to square it with the solar year. Instead of beginning around the summer solstice, as in Old Greece, the year followed the Judaeo-Syrian custom of beginning around the autumnal equinox; and all the months had brand new names—unlike any of the older Greek month-names, and equally different from the Semitic names of the Judaeo-Syrian months (luni-solar) which were adopted. Thus your month Appellaeus (roughly, December) was simply a renaming of the Judaeo-Syrian Canun I (old Hebrew Kislev).—and calculated on a rather different basis from the nearest corresponding old Hellenic month—Poseideon. These new month-names were so characteristically unique* that they naturally had a sort of sub-conscious hold on my memory—hence the flood of recollection brought up by the word Apellaeus. After the invention of this new calendar, the Seleucid monarchs forced it on the native Syrians in preference to their own system—which had different names and dates, though of course an identical astronomical divisional basis. The Jews called it the "Era of Contracts" or "Era of Kings", and it finds mention in the books of Maccabees in the Apocrypha. Nearly all Jews used it until the 15th century A.D., and in some parts of Arabia it is still in use locally. It is also the official system of reckoning in the Eastern or Nestorian Christian Church. As I now realise, it was the accepted chronology of Ptolemaic Egypt—and why I didn't remember that fact is something for psychologists to figure out!

Well—since the Seleucid Era begins on Septr. 1, B.C. 312; the year 28, month of Apellaeus, would naturally be December of B.C. 284 according to our reckoning—the very first year of the young Philadelphus' reign. You can't go wrong on this—December, B.C. 284 . . . . . . exactly *2215* (get that significant number, O Jonckheer van Nieuwkirck!)[1] years ago next December, Old Ptolemaeus Soter was then still living and had about a year to go—for he had handed over the power to his famous son Philadelphus two years before his death in B.C. 283.

There's your date, then—December, B.C. 284—2215 years ago. The backward-reckoning idea must be some mistake, for you can see that a plain cycle dated forward from a specific event like the taking of Babylon from Antigonus in B.C. 312 admits of no such thing. The only place where backward reckoning occurred in the ancient world was in giving days of the month in certain calendars such as the Roman. As you know, Roman dates were calculated as being so many days *before* the kalends, nones, or ides of a month. Just how extensively a corresponding practice existed outside the Roman world, I confess I am uncertain—though it did prevail in certain non-Roman cases. The old Hellenic months were alternately of 30 and 29 days, with occasional extra months to even up years; and they were divided into equal thirds called decades. Dates were given as related to decades within the months, not numbered throughout the whole month, and I think there were some cases where the reckoning was backward—especially in the last decade, where a date would be estimated as so many days *before* a new lunation or month. But this whole thing requires particular study, and is too complicated for any layman to know more than casually and imperfectly. What was true for one Grecian state was not true for another, and so on. And more–as I have said, the Seleucid month was not the old Hellenic month at all, nor any local modifica-

---

*Possibly they are derived from older month-names used in Macedonia proper, but none occurring in any classical reference I have ever seen. There's a good subject of research—the old calendar of semi-Hellenic Macedonia in the years before Alexander.

tion of it; but an entirely different thing taken from the Judaeo-Syrian calendar. It is my general impression that in all these Eastern calendars the days of the month were reckoned straight through as in our modern calendar, though I cannot take any oaths on the subject. I haven't a wide array of books on hand that would shed light, but what Smith's Bible Dictionary and Nevins's Biblical Antiquities have to say about the old Hebrew calendar would seem to point to a straight-through 1-to-30 monthly reckoning.[*] And as we have seen, the Judaeo-Syrian calendar was a corruption of this ancient Hebrew system, and the Syro-Macedonian a further adaptation.

HEY! HEY! ANOTHER EXTRA!

My self-respect takes a moderate rise as a result of some book-scouring started by the Smith and Nevins quests. Have just gone over some cross references in the Britannica and find that the universal use of the Seleucid Era in Ptolemaic Egypt is by no means certain! Of course, it undoubtedly *did* exit, and your reference proves that its use was common—for the month-names Apellaeus and Audyaeus occur in no other system, and positively fix this system as that employed in your papyrus. But according to 19th century scholarship, at least, the general chronology of Ptolemaic Egypt was held to be ambiguous and indeterminate; with the old method of reckoning according to sovereigns' reigns being perhaps more common than any other. (My Britannica is the old 9th edition, circa 1880) Just as I always thought, the dates on coins of the first three Ptolemies—Soter, Philadelphus, and Euergetes—ARE THOSE OF THE YEAR OF THEIR RESPECTIVE REIGNS—this being of course the most usual year-reckoning system of the ancient world—that which both the Egyptians on the one hand, and the Greeks on the other, had been used to. (It survives even now in statute law—for you'll still notice how law-books refer to acts of "18 George III", "42 Victoria", or "3 Edward VII".) Privately, I'll bet you half the Greeks[†] in Alexandria still used the old Hellenic system and spoke of Poseideon instead of Apellaeus—but this is just personal guesswork. The native Egyptians, of course, didn't adopt the Greek or Macedonian systems at all, but kept right on with their old Egyptian year beginning with the month of Thoth—which persisted even into Roman times, when the year was locally reckoned from the time of the Battle of Actium (B.C. 31) and establishment of the Roman power in Egypt. It is not known how the native Egyptians numbered their years during the Ptolemaic period, but it is guessed that they used the year of the current sovereign's reign. Another thing—in the later and more scholarly years of pre-Roman Alexandria, people came more and more to use the astronomical Era of

---

[*]Later—have just confirmed this from a table of Hebrew dates in the Britannica under art. "Calendar."

[†]unless it turns out that the Macedonians (as distinct from Hellenic Greeks) had a system with the apparently new manner

Nabonassar, which dates from certain Babylonian celestial observations of B.C. 747. This, I think, was first made popular by the great astronomer Hipparchus, who lived from 160 to 120 B.C. Boy, you sure have brought up a big subject!

However—don't get confused by these scattering observations. No matter what majority usage was in Ptolemaic Egypt, the key-name Apellaeus makes it absolutely certain that your particular document uses the Seleucid system. And anyway, as I have said, I now recall that this system was indeed widely used throughout the Levantine Hellenistic world. It would be worth studying to see whether the Seleucid month-organisation ever became engrafted on any other system of year-dating[*]—but the student will have to be somebody less rushed than Grandpa Theobald at this precise date.

As for mummies—I'm all humility here. I am driven to the painful realisation that I don't know what became of any of the inhumed Ptolemaei. Maybe they've been dug up, maybe robbers queered them long ago, and maybe they're still planted undiscovered. Now that you've brought the matter up, I may try to do some research when I get the time—there must be special works on Alexandreian archaeology which have something to say on the subject—but I couldn't dig up anything in time for your present essay. What you say will probably get across okay . . . . . unless somebody happens to have some uncomfortably contradictory information, which I haven't.

Your article in general is splendid—nothing to correct except perhaps the slightly awkward use of "Ptolemy" as an adjective—"Ptolemy rulers". Better say "Ptolemaean". (NOT "Ptolemaic", since that adjectival form relates specifically to the astronomical theory of the later Claudius Ptolemaeus—no relation—150 A.D.) Or you might say "Greek rulers" or "Macedonian rulers". Also, you have left the letter "y" out of the name of the Syrian month Audynaeus.

Hope the Pil–Pure[2] correction gets into the Provart. And pardon this rambling, chaotic epistle—and the ignorance which forces me to correct something I told you before. Muddled old men are poor critters to deal with—but thank gawd you cited the key-word Apellaeus! Yrs.

Grandpa

Notes

1. Referring to WBT's address.
2. I.e., Pilgrim–Puritan.

---

[*]Wouldn't it be a rich joke on us both if, after all, the papyrus used the Seleucid month system in connexion with Phil's reign-year! But I don't think this is so.

[60]   [TLS, JHL]

Saturn's Day. [11 or 18 April 1931]

Jonckheer:—

First—as to Audynaeus. I had that form merely from accustomedness, and upon looking it up now in the Britannica find my usage confirmed. I must admit, however, than any authority as substantial as Westermann[1] has a right to a very respectful hearing. But so, for that matter, has the Britannica! Much to my dismay I can't find the name in Liddell and Scott's monumental lexicon—for of course, such tomes aim first of all to help the classical scholar, and the Macedonian-Hellenistic era is rather outside the chief stamping ground of pure classicism. So I guess you can leave it neutral so far as I am concern'd. I'm right and you're right—merely according to what authority we choose. Maybe the Graeco-Macedonian usage itself was variable.

Secondly—confound the exaggeratory tendencies of that little Belknap rascal! All Putnam acceptance dope originated right within that bushy young head, for his old Grandpa told him exactly what you were told and nothing more! It must be delightful to be blest with such an imagination . . . . it ought to be a great help in literature! Actually, I haven't heard an additional word from Put's, and have no real expectation of any favourable action on their part. All they probably want to do is look the ground over and see just what the available manuscript supply is and what it isn't.

I'm sure I'd greatly enjoy co-operating on the Old Wives' Book some day, though just how helpful an unsystematick old man wou'd be in such an enterprise yet remains to be seen. As you can see from my tales, I'm not much for recognised folklore; but have a tendency to weave my own myths as I go along. The master mind of any such book ought to be an arch-collector and classifier like the patroon of Springvaliwyck. However, any help Grandpa can give is at your unreserv'd disposal, and if I ever earn the right to appear on the title-page I shall surely be proud to do so.

Those historic cover designs surely are magnificent material, and I can assure you that they have gone sacredly into that recently tho' clumsily rectify'd filing system. Needless to say, I shall appreciate any further instalments— and I hope they keep up till I have a fat and notable portfolio. Yes—I realise fully all the shortcomings of my morgue and can say no more in defence than that I was just naturally built weak on the classifying side. If you want to see me in an advantageous rather than disadvantageous contrast, ask Sonny Belknap to shew you where and how he keeps the few papers and pamphlets which he has by chance succeeded in not losing!

I thought a second Holland Society volume was very much in order, and I hope that the bowls of the deliberative patroons' and burghers' pipes are not too capacious! Gad, but I wish some society would cover New England in that way. The Am. Architects are doing some of the distinctive towns in a pretty fair way in the Octagon Series, but this enterprise hasn't reached Providence yet. I profited vastly by their Charleston volume last year.[2] As for whether the Rock-land–Bergen roof is really a gambrel—well, just use your eyes on the text and pictures of the present Holland Soc. book where it touches on certain roofs, and draw your own conclusions! A whole specialised study could be made of the gambrel roof in the American colonies—its obscure origin, its variant flow-erings in the New England and Dutch areas, its creeping (in its Dutch pitch and proportions) down the coast through New-Jersey to Pennsylvania in the Eng-lish regions but its apparent absence from Pennsylvania-German houses, its ra-re steep manifestations in Swedish Delaware, its sporadic reappearance in more of the New England form in tidewater Virginia—Williamsburg, Yorktown—& the lone, absolutely unique example in Chalmers St., Charleston. Really, all spoofing aside, this would be a splendid field for a specialist. I won't pretend to know where the gambrel started, but think the earliest specimens in New Eng-land and Nieuw Nederland are about contemporaneous—circa 1700. From present evidence, I feel sure that the first profuse landslide of them was in New England around 1720–30. Certainly, we were building little else then, whereas the Dutch do not seem to have adopted them so fully or universally till the dec-ade of the 1760's. Perhaps the southern Hudson Valley book will have more to tell about the matter—at any rate, it must be regarded as still open to investiga-tion. As for nomenclature—I never heard any one word except gambrel ap-plied to this type of roof. If it sounds too Yankee, just call the things "roofs of double pitch" and let it go at that.

Another study worth making would be just how far east on Long Island the Dutch architectural influence penetrated. Although belonging to Nieuw Nederland, the bulk of the island was simply a Connecticut overflow; and to-ward its eastern tip ought to shew New England architecture without much admixture. In the border villages of Hempstead and Flushing, where both populations mixed despite an ultimate English majority, we find a quite dis-tinctive type of English house with Dutch-proportioned (though uncurved) gambrel roof. The curve seems to be distinctively and indisputably Dutch—which is all to your credit, since the grace of this form is extreme. So far as I can see, no Dutch traces filtered into the Connecticut colony itself, since pic-tures of houses even in the extreme western zone—Ridgefield, etc.—appear to record an uniform Novanglian usage.

As for specs—my primary requirements are (a) nose and ear comfort, and (b) conservative inconspicuousness. I'm still hoping that the eye-resting of my coming trip will obviate the need of full-time readoption—for even the semi-rest already effected has ameliorated the trouble considerably. If I do have to return to the goddam things, I'll probably wind up by keeping my old rimless outfit with the ear curves made of spiral wire. That was some help.

As for Tappan versus Orange Town—it was from some history of the Revolution, treating of the execution of Maj. Andre, that I formed my impres-sion. I can easily see where room for ambiguity in usage could exist, and shall be cautious in dogmatising till additional data be at hand. Nomenclature is a tricky thing, and was very flexible in old times. Look at Fr. Orange–Beverwyck–Albany, Esopus–Wiltwyck–Kingston, and so on. I hope to get up around Wiltwyck in June, and shall study the antient stone houses with redoubled interest.

Your trip fills me with the utmost envy, punctuated by the gratitude evoked by the photographs. Thanks, and an old man's blessing! Another item for my Rockland County morgue shelf. I ought to mention, that my postcard collection is classified with somewhat less lumpish crudity than my cuttings . . . . . . as perhaps you have noticed from your occasional glimpses into that antient nail-studded trunk. The collection hath now overflow'd the trunk, and includes two cardboard boxes as an annex. Congrats, by the way, on your co-authorship of a tome in Room 328.[3] Belknap and Loveman are also, I think, represented in the catalogues of the Nypublibe. I let my imagination follow your itinerary with close attention, and am sorry that the grasping tavern-keepers at your namesake-village are so disrespectful as to favour meer alien horsemen at the expense of the Young Patroon himself. Sorry, likewise, that so many of the antient houses are falling into a decrepitude which wou'd be disintegration but for the stout masonry. Your terrain is a region of marvellous beauty, as I vividly recall from my 1928 glimpse; and I hope I may have a chance to go over it again some day. I am sure your kinsman and co-author will appreciate the piquant way in which you summarise your peregrinations.

Needless to say, I pursued with interest your account of the Grand Panjandrum of the Proletariat, and can form something of a picture of him at his cheerfully funereal work. Non-use of the machine would be no hardship to me except in an eye-spell like the present—but I suppose young moderns like you and Quinn feel quite desolate without your standardised keyboard! So his middle name is Grandin, eh! Bless my soul, I'll have to cook up some adventures of Ward Phillips, the occult deteckatiff![4] And so he has temperament—voila, name of a little blue pig, thees canaille Baird he shall not turn down ze work of ze great de Grendin! Pouf! Friend Trowbridge, there are plenty to write for who have the soupcon more of—how you call it? ze flavour! Anyhow, he must feel complimented to the skies by Brer Farnie's reluctance to let Jules be put out of his misery. That tendency of his stories to write themselves reminds me of our good old Mac—though my latest and still untyped opus involved just a bit of the same phenomenon.[5] Too bad the publishers let him down on the book proposition. It was really foolish of them, too, because his stuff has all the essentials of sales value and popularity. He ought to make a go with Hersey's Ghost Stories[6] and the coming new magazine of the Clayton group—but perhaps even his energies have a limit, so that besides his editing he could not profitably increase his markets. With his skill, he ought to be able to do "scientifiction", though I don't recall seeing anything of his in the magazines devoted to that form. His opinion of my stuff is about what I'd imagine it would be. How you unthrilled and horrorless birds manage to get a kick out of the process of writing weird tales is beyond me! I'll bet Poe evokes no response from him, either!

Well, spring is about half-arrived hereabouts, and I've begun a limited amount of hibernation-breaking. Out to the primal woods and fields twice with my work—but the evening temperatures are such as to freeze up my handwriting about 5 p.m. as a usual thing. Shall be glad of daylight time to-morrow—though on my trip I shall be out of the zone of that new-fangled interferin' with gawd's time. Things look fairly favourable for the jaunt, and some of these days I shall be hopping unannouncedly off for southern parts. Shan't stop in Nieuw Nederland on the down trip, but hope to see you as I trickle back in my more leisurely fashion a month hence. You will not be without postcard bulletins outlining my itinerary. I shall hop off here some morn about 10 or 11, and shall next see the dawn around Wilmington, Del. or Havre de Grace, Md. Richmond that early afternoon, Winston-Salem at mid-night, and CHARLESTON at 2 o'clock on the next day. If I can keep right on without stopping there, I shall have exhibited an unparalleled degree of will-power. Savannah next—shall do some exploring there—and shall pass through modern and undistinctive Jacksonville without a pause. Then for St. Augustine, which according to present plans will be my southward limit. Shall make quite a pause here, amidst the reliquiae of the antient Hispanick civilisa-tion. Really, I've cover'd a tremendous amount of foreign soil in my day . . . . Dutch Nieuw Nederland in 1922, French Quebeck in 1930, and now (I hope) Spanish Florida in 1931. I might, on a pinch, speak of Swedish Delaware—though I've never been off the stage coach there. And though I've explored High-German Germantown, Pa. with minute and admiring attention, this was never under any colonial flag but His Britannick Majesty's.

Orton's recent hint of a brief but well-paying book-editing job in Brattle-boro gave me a cold chill for a while, for I couldn't have afforded to pass that up, yet hated to switch my thoughts from Florida to the arctic. As it turns out, though, this thing will keep till summer—when I shall be glad enough to visit the mystical green hills of that remote polar twilight zone.[7]

And so it goes. Thanks again for the pitchers—and I don't believe I've ever adequately noted that Ditmas Ave. dump. I must get a look at it soon—as well as clearing up that question of doubt concerning the house in Amers-fort Place or somewhere. Best wishes and so on—Yr Obt Grandsire,

Baltus Harmense von Theobaldus

Notes

1. William Linn Westermann (1873–1954), author of *Upon Slavery in Ptolemaic Egypt* (1929) and other works on ancient history.
2. HPL refers to Albert Simons and Samuel Lapham, *Charleston, South Carolina* (New York: Press of the American Institute of Architects, 1927 [part of the Octagon Li-brary of Early American Architecture]).

3. Presumably *Burials in an Old Grave Yard* . . . (1927), co-written with Louis L. Blauvelt. A copy of this hectographed pamphlet is available at the New York Public Library.

4. HPL did so in "Through the Gates of the Silver Key."

5. *At the Mountains of Madness.* HPL He did eventually type the text, completing the 115-page TMS on 1 May.

6. Harold Hersey took over editorship of the pulp magazine *Ghost Stories* (1926–32) in mid-1930.

7. HPL was doing some revision work for the Stephen Daye Press in Brattleboro, VT.

[61]   [ALS, JHL]

> Thursday–Friday Midnight—
> Witches' Sabbat
> [30 April –1 May 1931]

Johckheer:—

Pardon haste & possible sketchiness, but I'm in the midst of a feverish last-moment cleanup of things prior to the trip. Trying to get my new novelette typed double-spaced, so that I can have it out of the way & perhaps get started Saturday. God, what a job! Am nearly all in!

Thanks for Florida article! It puts me on edge with anticipation!

Your tale promises finely, & I hardly know what to say about the title. "The Curse Wheel" fits the central theme most perfectly, but "The Valley of Dark Ghosts" has infinitely more of weird suggestion. What do you think about it?

As for the text—my first suggestion would be to tighten up the atmospheric shadows a bit. Don't let the style be so brisk & cheerful—select words of sombre associative appeal & disturbing cadence & resonance. Manage the rhythms in a more menacing, brooding fashion. Cut out the Belknapian lightness & good-humour, & borrow a bit of Poe's haunting, apprehensive suggestion—in sentence-structure, vocabulary, & tone-colour as well as in substance. Choose words with an eye to vague added overtones of sinister meaning—let them furtively imply the bare possibility of hidden terrors in the universe which cannot be hinted directly. Throw everything into a haze of doubtful nightmare by the use of words implying hideous dream-substance, ambiguity, & fever-clouded perspective—words like *vague, seemed, apparently, cloudy, nebulous, doubtful, implied, suggested, half-glimpsed, suspected, sensed, shadowy, ethereal, hinted, misty, vaporous, subtle,* &c. &c.* Increase the force of your most hideous implications by *denying* them with *unnecessary vehemence* as Poe does. "Of course, such a thing is not to be thought of for a moment! Such things do not exist. It would not be safe for the world's sanity if they existed." &c. &c. &c. *Poe* is the one model you need to study day & night in order to

---

*also use plenty of words conveying *vague uneasiness*—such as *disturbing, disquieting, uncomfortable, suggestive, provocative,* &c.

achieve *convincingness* of weird style. Next come Arthur Machen ("The House of Souls", "The Three Impostors") & Algernon Blackwood ("John Silence", "Incredible Adventures", "The Willows") You need subtilisation & etherealisation. *Suggest* & *imply* instead of *stating* whenever you can manage to do so.

Now as to structure—I think you might make this introduction less rambling. Begin with more punch. I don't know just how—but in some way designed to put the impression of the whole horror across at once; thereafter unfolding its history in the least indirect way possible. You might begin—

"It is hardly necessary to tell anyone the externals of what the Jersey Devil was. For 75 years & more the nameless death that lurked in deserted marshes & stalked across the flat red clay barrens by night has been a subject of recurrent notice, & has been described with every grotesque embellishment which human fancy, credulity, & journalistic enterprise could invent. Its vague, monstrous, & conflictingly described form, or lack of form, its frightful sobbing noises, its noxiously sinister footprints—or suspicions of footprints, & its probable lair near Westborough, or at least in the valley of Acquinatche Creek are all too familiar to every reader of the newspapers & every student of the whispered folklore of an ancient, shadowy, & legend-haunted countryside.

"What is now ripe for revelation is the indisputable fact that the Jersey Devil was in truth a reality, & that it is now definitely no more. It did indeed exist, but has not existed since the steps taken by Detective Sergeant James J. McCarthy of Westborough twenty years ago. All reports of more recent date are sheer vestigial myth & nothing more. McCarthy himself does not know just what he accomplished, & does not tell the little he does know for fear of being thought a madman. It was this dread of being thought mad which made him keep silent when explanation might have saved him dismissal from the force. As it was, he had to turn in his shield on charges of incompetence & under suspicion of having himself committed the killings which excited the investigation.

"The final clearing up has now come from a totally different angle—that of local history—& for this terrible & disquieting solution the credit must go to John Paterson Rutledge, Associate Justice of the Bergen County Court of Common Pleas & author of "The Antiquities of Westborough," recently published by private subscription. Judge Rutledge would not have believed Sergt. McCarthy's inside story had he heard it in 1911; but certain historic facts unearthed in assembling material for the "Antiquities" have put a new & startling complexion on the matter, disclosing malign & incredible roots that twist back into time for more than two centuries & a half. ¶ "And now that he does know, the judge hesitates to tell the basic truth to McCarthy, who is doing well today as a filling-station proprietor in Westborough. McCarthy has suffered much, and definite facts in certain directions would be an aggravation rather than a relief. The truth forms the seed of dangerous speculations regarding the laws of nature & the reality of the visible world around us—& such seed is highly productive when it falls upon soil that has lain fallow for years. A mind as delicately balanced as McCarthy's has been since his hideous experience is better left in peace.

"Even at present it is not really known *what* the Jersey Devil was. There are only the strongly conflicting reports of more than a century to guide one in that. All that Sergt. McCarthy learned was *how* the spectre was brought to life from time to time, & all that Judge Rutledge's accidental discovery has done is to suggest—in a monstrous & uncomfortable way—*why* the nameless thing brought death for more than 250 years to a region scarcely out of sight of Manhattan's crowded towers."

Now begin history of J. Devil as commencing at foot of p 5, specialising in the series of hideous incidents involving Sergt. McCarthy.

Next speak of Rutledge's innocent researches for his book. His stumbling on an uncomfortably significant anecdote in the files of the Newark Historical Society. His unaccountable horror at something which looks, externally, very simple & harmless. His feverish search for added data & his final decision to suppress certain facts in his forthcoming book. Handle this *realistically—not Kiplingistically—& with brooding tensity.* Get as scared, yourself, as a hard-boiled nature will let you!

THEN—hark back 250 or so years, & begin tale of De Maris. Say

"The data which had so disturbed Judge Rutledge carried him back to the earliest days of the Nieuw Nederland Colony, & concerned a certain Huguenot pioneer, by name Jacques De Maris—&c." Don't establish connexion of DeM. with Jersey Devil till late & in tale, & try to save waterwheel revelation as final climax with a punch. ¶ The idea is splendid, & ought to suit Wright to a T. Don't hurry on it—careful background & subtle atmosphere are all-important. ¶ Now I'm off! More anon—postcards from the Old South—& see you in June. Hope these remarks are a help rather than hindrance.

———O'Casey.

P.S. Give added realism to your stories by giving full names & prosaic details about your characters the first time you mention them. "James J. McCarthy", "John Paterson Rutledge", &c. Forget the superficially unctuous Kipling–O. Henry tradition of trashy popular writers.

[62]   [ANS postcard][1]

[Postmarked Dunedin, Fla.,
25 May 1931]

Tropical greetings of Jumbee & Cthulhu to Alabad, Ghinu & Aratza! Great place & a great host here—you don't know what you're missing, Jonckheer, up in the subarctic tundras of bleak Nieuw Nederland! ¶ Watch *Adventure* for the record-busting hell-raiser of modern times—"The Black Beast," by Henry S. Whitehead. Ugh! Nggrrrrh . . . . .

Yrs—Jan Evertse van Theobaldus

Notes

1. *Front:* Recreation Park, Dunedin, Fla.

[63]   [ALS JHL]

Small Hours of Sabbath Morn
[19 July 1931]

Greetings, Jonckheer!

Imposing on you to the last! Last night Samuelus gave me a couple of bulky books; & since the P.O. is closed on the Lord's Day, I'll have to ask you to attend to the mailing for me at the drug store around the corner. I think I have postage enough affix'd. If not, send me a bill for the balance. There is *not the least hurry* about this business—so let the mailing slide till it comes in conveniently. The local sub-station does not open till 9 a.m., hence you can't take it along as you hasten Texacoward in the cold grey dawn. I hate like the devil to bother you—but my satchel is full & the P.O. closed, so I naturally fell into the line of least resistance.

Had a deuce of a drenching in Prospect Park yesterday—no shelter near, & the heavens let down a veritable flood all of a sudden. I returned to 2215, dried my clothes on the new patent thingumajig in your kitchen, & started out afresh in the evening. My 10¢ tie was spoilt by soaking, & my new charity suit surely looks its part! Wish I could get a pressing somewhere today—I hate to blow in on my aunts in such bedraggled finery.

Still undecided about my stage-coach, but I certainly shan't kill myself trying to get the 9:00 one. It would take retroactivity to do that after the Rip van Winkle coma from which I've just emerged—or am just emerging!

Again let me thank you & the good vrouw for your phenomenal hospitality—an hospitality which has been a great factor in making my present metropolitan sojourn a pleasing & memorable event. Hope I haven't caused too much bother. Get around to Providence when you can—& meanwhile pray consider me

Yr most obliged', most ob^dt Servt
Ptolemaeus Philadelphus

P.S. Am trying to press my trousers by putting them under the mattress & sleeping on them! Wonder how they'll look in the morning! I got this idea from a comic picture—hence have no assurances of success!

Later—waking time—11 a.m.

Not so bad at that!! The damn things actually have quite a crease in the right place! Think I'll try this at home right along & save tailor's fees! Wish there were a way of informally pressing a coat!

Still later—have found a way to ameliorate coat creases by local smoothing & stretching. Every man his own tailor!

> Mynheer Wilfredus Talmanus
> Rustenburgh, Midmond,
> Nieuw Nederland.

[64]   [ALS, JHL]

> Tenbarnes—
> July 30, 1931

Jonckheer:—

Damn that efficiency upstart! I don't wonder they canned your Director of Publications for tolerating such a ruthless boor! What are we charity bums going to do if the world gets as coldly businesslike as all that? Thanks for rectifying the omission—I shall be watching the mails.

Also damn the impertinence of that P.O. Yid! Of all technical quibbling! Sorry I unwittingly got you in any Dutcher than your ancestry! And thanks for attending to the job.

About those negatives—why, bless your heart, I thought you knew I had three in safekeeping to get more prints from. The large portrait, the best duo, & the flattering ¾ length of myself. I'll have the prints made as soon as time & cash permit, & will thereafter forward the negatives either to you or to Little Sonny. The child is now at Onset with papa & momma on his vacation.

Thanks for the topics pages. I saw a picture of that pyre in the Evening Bulletin. Very picturesque & traditional, though I do not sympathise with the rebel cause. "Hoodoo" isn't at all bad for its genre.

Hope your advance to Asst. Ed. will mean an advance in remuneration. With all your responsibilities you certainly ought to get a good fat cheque each Saturday evening!

Here's a good newspaper picture of our local bookseller Eddy, whom you probably know through many transactions. It was in the News-Tribune, & I would have missed it if Morton & I hadn't happened to visit the shop—by sheer coincidence—the day after it appeared. I got a dozen copies, since the old boy is a great favourite with all Kalemites who visit Providence.

Just had the charity suit professionally pressed—so that at the moment it really looks too good to wear!

Pardon this writing—which represents an attempt at fountain pen rebuilding. Had a bum point with a good feed, & am experimenting with a re-pointing process involving the use of a small whetstone designed for sharpening microscope accessories. So far, not so good—& yet it's a net gain, for this damn thing wouldn't write at all before. I am out on the Seekonk river-bank, & my main pen has gone dry—hence the secondary affair.

Still swamped by accumulated tasks. Bulletins, Sunday Journals, & Times's now read up, but owe 17 letters, some of them requiring length & detail. It's a great life—but the trip was worth it.

Yrs for the abolition of inefficiency & red tape in P.O.'s & trade papers alike—

————Harmanus Filipse van Tiebout

[65] [ALS, JHL]

Septr. 10, 1931

Jonckheer:—

Oddly enough, I haven't a blessed thing either written or printed anent Cape Cod—but here is antient QUEBECK outspread before you . . . . . if you can read it.[1] Sorry it isn't in better form, but you know how I stand on typing! You won't have to wade through it all, since the table of contents indicates where & what the purely guiding material is. Sorry there isn't much material about routes & rural byways—but if you want to find your way around urban Quebec, there's considerable which you can puzzle out if you have the patience. Gad, Sir, but I both envy & pity you . . . . . envy you because you are to see Quebeck; pity you because that sight must needs be in *October* . . . . brrrr . . . . . My aunt Mrs. Gamwell is now—voluntarily—in Ogunquit, Maine. That's bad enough in September—but Quebec in *October* . . . . . ! ! ! !

By the way, I have eliminated the danger of having to go to Vermont by persuading Orton to transact that proposed book revision job by mail. Cook now has a job in Boston, & is to be addressed at 17 Chambers St. in that antient town. I hope to see more of him now.

Steamfitting goes on at #10—gawd, what a chaos! I take my work to the woods & fields each day when the weather is decent—& when it isn't, I stop in the vacant Gamwell flat at 61 Slater Ave. Typing has to be done in instalments in the evening.

Well—I hope you'll find the enclosed (a) at least partly legible, & (b) of some use to you if you can decipher it. The information is all there—whether or not intelligently presented. Hope your trip will bring you to antient Providence at some stage or other. It'll be a year in November since you have beheld these venerable shoars, & Jake's is fairly pining for patronage!

And so it goes. Hope you found Arturo[2] flourishing. Has Belknap shown you his new story, "The Brain-Eaters"?[3]

With an old man's blessing—

Yr obt hble Servt

Myndaert Pieterse O'Casey

Notes

1. HPL apparently sent WBT the entire handwritten ms. (136 pp.) of his *Description of the Town of Quebeck* . . .
2. I.e., Arthur Leeds.
3. "The Brain-Eaters" (*WT,* June 1932).

[66]   [ANS postcard][1]

[Postmarked Hartford, Conn.,
7 October 1931]

Well Jonckheer—you behold the old gentleman searching out that largest Georgian building in the world! Can't compare with our new Court House in design. ¶ Am in Hartford in response to a telegram I found waiting when I got home from Boston. Orton & his partner Crane had got that book job ready at last, & telegraphed to arrange a preliminary personal discussion at a point midway between Providence & Brattleboro. All hands showed up—& I have agreed to edit & proofread the text of a long & definitive history of Dartmouth College—by a professor therein. Am getting only 50 bucks, but this may prove an interesting wedge for more work of the same kind for the Stephen Daye.[2] ¶ I can see where I'm dead to the world for a solid week—& in the end I may have to go to Brattleboro for a day or so at least. That card you gave me—with the proof symbols is going to prove invaluable. ¶ Great weather. Made the trip through fine scenery—via Willimantic—& shall return via Norwich & Plainfield for variety's sake. Hartford is by no means ugly—but nothing wonderful. This is my very first sight of central Connecticut.
Regards—O'Casey

[*On front:*] Where I am sitting

Notes

1. *Front:* Bird's-Eye View from Traveller's Tower, Hartford, Conn.
2. HPL refers to Leon Burr Richardson's *History of Dartmouth College.*

[67]   [ALS, JHL]

Octr. 25, 1931

Jonckheer Arminius:—

Abundant thanks for the generous envelope of varied enclosures! I am adding the Williamsburg article to my files with the utmost gratitude, am placing "Shadow" in a Solomon Kane[1] envelope for transmission the first moment I get to write that worthy, & am herewith returning the extremely clever Wollcott *conte cruel*[2] & the agonisingly tantalising Doorway prospectus. Would that I had a spare $22.50 to shell out! The "Shadow" has considerable punch, but it is a trifle strained, melodramatic, & artificial—hardly a supreme item among recent Arminiana. Too bad Brother Farnsworth returned "Gyrwy"—but I've long ago given up trying to fathom his caprices. Hope he & Quinn & the local gang enjoyed themselves at the Assembly!

I'll enjoy seeing this *Argosy* specimen—"Voodoo Express"[3]—if you come across a conveniently transmissible copy, though I have no idea that the A. could ever become a market for me.[4] You are of course correct in believing that the "action" story commands the largest low-grade audience, & that it is therefore the most financially profitable type for the non-literary fiction manufacturer to cultivate; correct, too, in recognising that it is extremely difficult to manufacture, as attested by the vast horde of business-minded quantity-producers who strive in vain to make the market with this kind of ware. I do not, however, agree with you in thinking that "action" tales have any genuine *art* in them—except in the very few cases where the subject-matter may inherently call for a swift succession of events.[5] One must not suppose that *difficulty of manufacture* is equivalent to actual *aesthetic expression*. It is very *difficult* to make a watch or calculate the stresses in bridge-building, but the result is not *art*. It is, instead, *applied science*. Just so with cheap fiction. It is devilish *hard* to study the cheap herd emotions (*mind* is too charitable a word) & devise a sort of artificial image-concoction which shall titillate it in precisely a given fashion—but no one could say that such a spurious, cold-blooded concoction has any resemblance to the sincere expression which is *art*. It is applied science—& damn clever applied science—but it has nothing to do with aesthetics. The reason an "action" story can only rarely be real art is that life is seldom made up of massed action. Within the brief time-compass of a short story, life never affords even an approximation of the physical incidents demanded by the cheap fiction market. When, therefore, a mentally adult reader sees a "hero" in danger too many times, he at once loses the feeling of reality as connected with the story. The words become just words & nothing more—since the thing has grown too unconvincing to build up imaginative pictures. Then again, "action" is really only the smallest part of our total impression from the external word. What "happens" is quite microscopic as compared with what simply "is." Any tale which attempts to re-create a section of experience in maturely effective proportions must devote fully as much attention to the static as to the kinetic factors involved. This is even truer of weird fiction than of any other form; since phantasy is not, directly, a picture of objective events at all, but merely the delineation of a certain type of human mood. What a weird story tells is something that never happens; the real portraiture being wholly of the feeling which often gives rise to the illusion of such happenings. The overt incidents are only subsidiary outcroppings of the dominant mood-portraiture. *Atmosphere* is the one essential in this field, because atmosphere is the only medium whereby anything as elusive & intangible as a *mood* can be even approximately re-created. To have the *reader* in mind is absolutely fatal to sincere artistic expression. Art demands that one write what is within one, & nothing more or less. That is why popular fiction is almost totally devoid of art, & why, conversely, only a small part of the material produced artistically happens to fall within the circle of commercial acceptability.

Now I have no quarrel with non-artistic fiction manufacture. It is a profession just as difficult & dignified as steamfitting—& I would gladly follow either if it were practicable & profitable. The only thing is, that I *can't* do it. The process of tinkering cold-bloodedly & inartistically with words & phrases & cadences for purposes other than that of self-expression develops within me certain repugnances which prevent me from duplicating the required patterns in quasi-original fiction. I can *revise,* but I can't concoct new things in the domain of the cheap & spurious. And I don't say that with any pride, because it merely implies a lack of sharp & versatile intellect. Young Derleth, for example, can reel off atrocious & profitable hokum (cf. any issue of W.T.) with his left hand, while with his right he creates delicate things like "People"[6] & "Evening in Spring", which one could scarcely imagine were written by the same person. But I'm no Derleth—& am too old now to develop into one. One can't succeed in a field for which one has only contempt & loathing, so beginning about five years ago I stopped trying to suit shoddy markets & decided to work sincerely. I have no ambition to work in any but the genuine field—that of Machen, Blackwood, or Poe—even though I realise keenly that I shall never be more than a microscopic figure (if even that) in that honourable & fiercely contested area. I had rather fail like an inferior Blackwood than succeed like a glorified Quinn or Kline—although, as I said before, I'd be perfectly willing to grind out the Quinn–Kline brand of pap if I *could* do it without impairing my ability to write sincerely. But I *can't*—so that's that. It must be from fields mainly revisory that whatever dependable remuneration I am to get must come—from those, or from fields totally dissociated from writing.

Just now all my writing is in abeyance, for a succession of small revisory snatches has culminated in the large book job which I went to Hartford to see Orton about. I think I mentioned that this was the superficial revision & proofreading (aided by your chart of symbols) of a long history of Dartmouth College—& I may add that it has kept me tied down for a fortnight with a concentration which may or may not have been responsible for the sick-headache-&-bum-digestion spell out of which I am only just now pulling. I finished the damn thing last Tuesday, & got if off by parcel post Friday. It is possible that I may have to visit Brattleboro briefly before the thing goes to press, though I rather hope not in view of the time of year. If this job suits, I may get quite a stream of work from Orton's "Stephen Daye Press."

By the way—I returned from Hartford by an indirect route for variety's sake; passing through Glastonbury, Colchester, Norwich, & Plainfield, & finding the landscapes even more impressive than along the direct (Willimantic) route. There are bold hills, picturesque sweeps of valley, occasional lakes, & many virtually breath-taking vistas of widespread rolling countryside & distant mystical horizons. Norwich—where I paused several hours for exploration—is an ineffably fascinating old town built on the steep terraces that rise above a bend in the river Thames. Streets spiral upward from a central square, & in certain places are connected by flights of steps reminiscent of Meeting St. & of Quebec. This was the birthplace of the ill-starred Benedict Arnold—as Hartford (or rather, West Hartford) was of Noah Webster.

Your own recent itinerary sounds attractive enough, & must have done much to offset the postponement of Quebec & Cape Cod. Trust the photographs will come out well. I must see Tappan again before I die—it has a pervasive charm that lingers in the memory. Hope you find the stable habitation practicable until you can swing the Dutch cottage. I dare say your motto is "better a barn in Spring Valley than a flat in Flatbush!" That was rather a picturesque—though not wholly unconventional—tale about the fire phantoms of hapless Mount Gulian,[7] & I trust you can employ it to advantage in your Van Kampen story. I am still seething with rage at the incendiary who destroyed that noble & venerable seat.

As for postcards—I didn't know large city post offices balked at overrun space, although James Ferdinand has reported something of the kind in connexion with Paterson. I believe he said the ruling is that not more than ⅔ of the face of a card must be covered with non-addressive writing—or something like that. I consider it very pusillanimous of the authorities to discourage thrift in this fashion, & would certainly start something if I had any sort of a pull with any congressman! Hope my subsequent cards won't be such a bother for the multilingual Christopher—whose acquirements surely are unusual for one in his present profession. Evidently now, as never before, the way of the translator is hard.

What did you find out about G K's presumable histrionic debut? I'm sure I knew nothing of it—yet the part of a book vendor seems almost too appropriate not to be significant. Here's hoping he receives plaudits rather than vegetables, (despite his fondness for vegetable dinners) & that he may speedily work up to the Hamlet & Richard III level![8]

Cook has moved a square or two—to a warmer & less seedy room. Address him now at *7 Hancock St., Boston, Mass.* Whitehead also has a new address—*Box 414, Dunedin Isles, Dunedin, Fla.* He is badly under the weather, & will have to have an operation soon.

Well—Tsathoggua[9] be merciful unto us all.

Olla huula huula hei!—Grandpa Theobald

Notes

1. I.e., Robert E. Howard (1906–1936), prolific pulp writer and pioneer in the subgen-

re of sword and sorcery. He wrote a series of tales about Solomon Kane, a Puritan in 17th-century England who roamed the world in quest of adventure.

2. Probably the celebrated horror tale "Moonlight Sonata" (*New Yorker,* 3 October 1931) by Alexander Woollcott (1887–1943), American writer best known for his theatre criticism.

3. Theodore Roscoe (1906–1992), "The Voodoo Express" (*Argosy,* 10 October 1931).

4. HPL had submitted "The Rats in the Walls" to the *Argosy* in 1923, but the editor, Robert H. Davis, rejected it. In 1935, Donald Wandrei surreptitiously submitted HPL's "The Shadow out of Time" to the magazine, but it too was rejected. See David E. Schultz, "Lovecraft and the *Argosy,*" *Lovecraft Annual* No. 11 (2017): 67–72.

5. Within a few weeks after writing this letter, HPL did undertake a story—"The Shadow over Innsmouth" (Nov.–3 December 1931)—that contained an action scene in the latter portions of the text.

6. "People" was a story (first read by HPL in August 1931) later rewritten as "A Town Is Built." The ms. of the latter is at the Wisconsin Historical Society (Madison, WI).

7. Mount Gulian is an 18th-century Dutch manor house on the Hudson River in the town of Fishkill, NY. The original house served as the headquarters of Major General Friedrich Wilhelm von Steuben during the American Revolutionary War and was the place where the Society of the Cincinnati was founded. It was destroyed by arson in 1931 but has since been restored.

8. It appears that HPL's and WBT's friend George Kirk, the bookseller, had begun to participate in some sort of dramatic presentations.

9. An entity Clark Ashton Smith introduced in his story "The Tale of Satampra Zeiros" (1929) and cited by HPL in "The Mound" (1929–30), "The Whisperer in Darkness" (1930), and other stories.

[68]   [ALS, JHL]

Novr. 12[, 1931]

Jonckheer:—

Thanks immensely for the generous batch of miscellany. Wain surely has seen my favourite species from every angle![1] Hope he makes a full recovery in time to enjoy life a bit toward the sunset. I'm glad of that Creeps review—Belknap had lent it to me but wanted it back. Hope Mr. Cuppy won't be disappointed when he reads my tale.[2]

As for that "oldest house" item—all I can say is "Good Gawd!" Keep it—as a premier curiosity of journalism!! Billop . . . . *1555*!!!! Well, the readers of a Hearst paper will doubtless stand for anything, since they never know the difference. But if by any chance anybody wants facts—well, that's a different matter!

In 1555 the only white men who had ever seen Staten Island—or any part of New York—were the occupants of Verrazzano's ship (1524)—the same Dagoes & Frogs who first saw His Majesty's Colony of Rhode-Island & Providence-Plantations. The only 'houses' of that period in the region were

Algonquin wigwams. Nor—if anybody is curious to know—was there any 'John Billop' around the place in 1624.

Here is the straight goods—as nearly as I can give it without wading through the N Y section of my potter's field, which I ain't got time to do to-day . . . . although I will later if occasion develops. I know I have stuff there about the case.

Some time in the early *1670's*—get this date clearly—(just before the second occupation of Nieuw Ned. by your countrymen) under Govr Francis Lovelace—a dispute arose concerning the title of Staten Island; whether it should belong to your colony or to James Ferdinand Morton's. H.R.H. the Duke of York (afterward H. M. James II) decided that all islands in the harbour which could be circumnavigated in 24 hours should go to N Y. Staten was just about on the borderline in this respect, but Captain *Christopher* (not John) Billopp actually turned the trick & proved it—hence gave the title to N Y. As a reward he was granted a manor of 1163 acres in the south of Staten Island, which remained with his descendants till the late unfortunate uprising against His Maj$^{ty's}$ lawful authority—when it was confiscated by the rebels, the Bil-lopps being opposed to treason. The old Billopp House—which I have seen—was built in all probability in *1688*; certainly not much earlier. It is the oldest house *on Staten Island,* but of course out of all competition as the earliest in the U.S. There are literally *hundreds* earlier, when all the colonies are counted in.

The rest of the article is just as lousy as this part. Your own H. V. book will dispose of the Staats claim, while all the New England cases were spiked long ago—Cradock house in Medford, &c. Tradition had back-dated these things, but good scholarship in the late 19th & 20th centuries set things right. Organisations like the Society for the Preservation of New England Antiqui-ties & the Essex Institute (Salem) are ruthless in brushing aside flimsy folk-lore & getting the straight dope. Without a doubt the Fairbanks house in Dedham (1636) is the oldest building of any kind in the Northern United States,[3] & the oldest frame dwelling of non-Spanish construction in the West-ern Hemisphere. The only older building of non-Spanish construction in America is St. Luke's Church in Isle of Wight Co., Virginia, which dates from *1632.* The church ruins at Jamestown, popularly thought to be of 1617, are really of later date—the 1640's. The same is true of the ruined walls of the Ambler house. The oldest house in the New Netherland area is probably our old friend the Schenck joint (1656) in Flatlands. Santa Fé has some really pre-historic structures, but they are not the work of white men. These edifices were left from the Pueblo Indian culture, & the fact of their later adaptation to Spanish white use does not make them the work of white men. The only authentic white *sixteenth-century* houses this side of Mexico are in St Augustine; the popularly recognised 'oldest house' being *certainly* one of them, though *exact* priority is doubtful. Only the ignorant have ever claimed that this house dates back to 1565. But it certainly is not more than six years later than that, for it is unmistakably described in records of 1571. St Augustine moved from its original site (the Indian village of Seloy—now within the city limits) to its present site within a year of its settlement by Menendez. The old house was an hospital of the Franciscans, whose main monastery (still standing & now a State Arsenal) was built soon afterward just across the street. Coquina stone—the material of the house—was certainly in use by 1570, the deposits on Anastasia Island across the bay having been very soon discovered. There are at least a dozen 16th century houses in St. Augustine, including the present P.O. & former Governor's Palace, which was certainly built between 1591 & 1597. All these houses, however, have seen extensive alterations—especially in the roofs. During the British period (1763–1783) most of the flat Spanish roofs were altered into peaked roofs of the type predominating in Charleston & the West Indies.

I may add that houses just subsequent to 1636 are by no means uncommon both in New England & in Virginia. The Deane Winthrop house in Winthrop, Mass. dates from 1637, while houses of 1640 or thereabouts are relatively common. There is a good one in Haverhill, & there used to be one in Newport till its burning a few years ago. Portsmouth's oldest house really dates from 1664—though in this & in other houses there is possibly lumber taken from older dwellings. Thus the Royall House in Medford (1737) probably incorporates material from an earlier building of 1631.

Oh—by the way—I meant to tell you that I found a fine *Nova Belgica* map in the Boston Museum of Fine Arts last month. That is undoubtedly the correct one of the many discoverable variants. Did I also say that I saw the other Casey tankard there?

Hope the Kalem meeting comes off well. Poor oversystematised Mortonius is having hard work to find a day he can attend! Last Monday night I attended a lecture by one of your eminent fellow-countrymen—Mijnheer Prof. Willem de Sitter,[4] van der University van Leiden, in the old country. He is one of the greatest living astronomers & mathematicians—comparable to Einstein—& he spoke ably & in good English on the Size of the Universe.

Thanks for the cheerful card. There are two cholera cemeteries in ancient Quebec (as you may or may not be able to dig out of my MS.)—grim reminders of the plague which ravaged all parts of the continent. By the way—that phantom cycle must have stirred up staid old Breackelen a bit. Wonder if that Fred Sitter was any distant Nieuw Nederland relative of Prof. Willem de?

> Gratitude & blessings—
> Grandpa

Notes

1. Louis Wain (1860–1939), English artist best known for his drawings of anthropomorphised large-eyed cats and kittens

2. HPL refers to Will Cuppy's review of *Creeps by Night* in the "Mystery and Adventure" column of *New York Herald Tribune Books* (1 November 1931): 14. HPL's name (and FBL's) is cited when Cuppy mentions "a variety of promising items by such professors as . . ." Cuppy went on to write reviews in the *New York Herald Tribune* of HPL's *The Outsider and Others* (17 December 1939), *Beyond the Wall of Sleep* (2 January 1944), and *Marginalia* (11 February 1945).

3. See HPL's "An Account of a Trip to the Antient Fairbanks House . . ." In *CE* 4.

4. HPL heard Willem de Sitter (1872–1934), Dutch mathematician and physicist who, in 1932, collaborated with Einstein in devising the theory of "dark matter," speak on 9 November.

[69]   [ALS, JHL]

Friday [4 or 11 December 1931]

Jonckheer Arminius:—

Recent material received & perused with much pleasure—& that "Fruit" article certainly goes into my files until I get a *Casket* cutting to displace it! By the way, though—you speak of André's tree first as a *pear* & then as a *peach*. How come? Was it a grafted hybrid, or has there been a slip somewhere? But you utterly shock me by saying that Joel Dorman Steele's "Fourteen Weeks" series is now forgotten & unobtainable. O tempora! O mores![1] Eheu fugaces! Such is fame, & all that! Why, Sir, back in the 'seventies & 'eighties J. Dorman virtually ruled the textbook roost, turning out volumes on varied subjects with a fecundity & versatility truly astonishing when one considers their clearness & general excellence. Alone, he covered half the major sciences with his "Fourteen Weeks in Astronomy", ditto Geology, Chemistry, Physics, Botany, Physiology, Zoölogy . . . . & more, for all I know (these being the ones I have) . . . . & in conjunction with his wife, Esther Baker Steele, he prepared for A. S. Barnes & Co. the series of histories (Ancient, Mediaeval-Modern, Greek, Roman, French, American, &c. &c.) known as Barnes' Brief Histories. When my younger aunt was in school she had about all of these books, & I seized on them myself—as they reposed on attic shelves—when I was very young, later picking up a few which she had not preserved. In my own day they were considered just a bit elementary & passé by urban schools, so that I did not encounter them officially; but they were still in print—having been taken over by the American Book Co. At least—the Barnes' Histories were still in print. My elder aunt's husband Dr. Clark knew Steele, & gave him some of the data for his Zoölogy book— being mentioned in the preface on that connexion.[2] And now you tell me poor J. Dorman is forgotten! O cruel world—that I should live to see this day when the idols of my youth are crumbled to dust! Next thing you'll be telling me is that people no longer recall John Howard Appleton's textbooks on Chemistry—the earliest of which, "The Young Chemist", is absolutely the best juvenile introduction to the science that I have ever seen!

Monuments to Roger Williams—in one spot or another—had been proposed off & on for about three-quarters of a century before the existing one in the park was erected. By the way—my younger aunt (the Steele textbook alumna) was one of the chorus of schoolchildren to sing at the dedication of that monument in 1879 . . . a small & piping voice on a memorable occasion! Whether your picture represents that monument or not I can tell when I see the negative or copy. I'm sure I don't know the details of the adoption of the design. The sculptor was Franklin Simmons.[3]

By the way—B K H's *Journal* column—"The Sideshow"—brought up the "Who Ate Roger Williams"[4] question the other day, quoting a passage which looks to me like a verbatim transcript of the note in Steele's Chemistry,[5] but attributing it to another source—a question-book popular in the middle 'eighties. I'll lend you the cutting as soon as I can get it—it being now in the piled-up papers at 61 Slater awaiting my younger aunt's return from Washington (which may take place today). I don't think we need take any credit, however, away from poor forgotten J. Dorman—for he didn't put his footnote in quotes, & it's dollars to Dutch fried cakes that the quiz-editor swiped it from him. But without doubt there were other common sources—for the whimsical question "Who ate Roger Williams?" seems to have been a popular catch phrase in these plantations around 1880. By the way—would you like a copy of Steele's Chemistry for your library? I happen to have a duplicate, & if it would be of any acute enjoyment to you, I'm sure I couldn't find a worthier heir to bestow it on. Your article is great, & if Quinn doesn't use it, he ought to be planted deeper than old Roger in one of his own coffins!

Oh, say,—a thought!! Rare stranger in the Theobald bean! I know a book—2 volumes—that would be *a gold mine* for you in concocting cadaverous features for M. de Grandin! It is a series of essays by one Sargent (I forget his other handles) called "Dealings With the Dead", & probably containing more funereal, ghoulish, & mortuary lore culled from all history, ancient, mediaeval, & modern, than any other collection betwixt four cloth covers. The essays, purporting to be by the sexton of *old* Trinity Church in Boston, (not the present Richardson Romanesque pile in Copley Sq.) originally appeared in the *Boston Transcript* in the 'forties, when that austere journal was young; but were issued in book form about 1850. Why the hell haven't I thought to mention this to you before? But here is the joker—the thing is damn rare, & I'm not at all sure what has become of the copy I read—which belonged to our friend W. Paul Cook. As you know, Cook's library has been largely disintegrated since his financial collapse. Where this item has gone I really can't say; though it may be in the residue stored at Cook's sister's in Sunapee, N.H., or it may be in the batch given to H. Warner Munn. If you're a wise youth you'll lose no time in writing to Cook about this matter—asking him where the volumes are. If they are in his possession, or in Munn's, there is no question about a cheerful loan. You ought not to miss this rare treasury of necronomical lore, & which is exactly in line with what Bre'r Seabury seems to want. Cook's present address is *7 Hancock St., Boston, Mass.* Now go to it, & good luck to you! Of course, there's a remote possibility that Quinn knows about this book & has used it—but it isn't likely, for the thing is extremely obscure . . . . as forgotten as poor Joel Dorman Steele.

Thanks for the cuttings—all the returnable items of which I trust will safely reach you. (Anent covered bridges—I was astonished lately to learn that southern *Ohio,* & not Vermont, has the greatest surviving number. "They Walk Again" has been discussed in B K H's "Sideshow",[6] as the enclosed slips (please return) will apprise you. I gave my judgment of Le Fanu without having read "Green Tea". If I'm really wrong, I'll eat crow & publicly apologise to the memory of one of my Casey ancestor's fellow-countrymen—though that won't alter the fact of the lethal dulness & tameness of all the Le Fanu junk I *have* read. That Long Valley item filled me with melancholy. Damn the way these polyglot cities drain the countryside & wipe out decent white folks's villages in order to get water to mix with their bootleg whiskey! It happened in Dwyer's region in New York State—it happened in Scituate, R.I.—it is now happening in the Swift River valley south of Athol, Mass.—& now another case in James Ferdinand's august commonwealth! I enjoyed the Queens historical item, & have seen most of the old houses therein mentioned—although I did miss, by some malign dispensation, the Foster house whose destruction is now reported. I seriously doubt if it was as old as 1637, however. Most antiquaries, I think, have long regarded the (Flatlands) Schenk house as the dean of Novebaracense edifices. (1656) I saw the old Moore house, I think, in 1928. Damn its partial destruction! I note the picture of the Billopp house, but believe that the assigned date of 1667 is too early—though I have seen this given before. Still, that's better than the sixteenth century date in the canard you previously sent! Glad your Washn. Hdqtrs. is saved from indignity—as indeed the Sunday *Times* apprised me pictorially last week. I hope I can get inside after its transformation to a museum. It is honoured by the presence of the heroic Sir Guy Carleton—afterward Ld Dorchester—Commandant of His Maj^{ty's} arm'd forces in North-America, & governor of the Province of Quebec. God Save the King! You ought to be very proud of your maternal link with this sightly & noble edifice. And so your local banking industries are dignified by the participation of no less an entity than the Omnipotent Oom![7] What a company you would have if you could only get our Mayan friend "* Harold" to immigrate to good old Rockland!

I'm interested in this doughnut controversy, & wonder just how reliable my standards of comparison are. What they call a doughnut in the farther South is lighter & fluffier than the old Novanglian article, but in New York I have seen on sale doughnuts of essentially the classic Yankee pattern. Yes—& come to think of it, many *chain stores* down south *do* sell Yankee doughnuts; such having been bought by Whitehead at the Clearwater Fla. Piggly-Wiggly.

Is it possible that the original Dutch-Yankee differences were so slight that the modern machine-made product is a sort of debased hybrid about as much like the one as like the other? It is probably thirty years since I have eaten a home-made doughnut—& even then they were Celtic or Scandinavian (though Yankee supervised) kitchen products perhaps varying from the oldest Rhodinsular standard. At present there is no discernible physico-chemical difference betwixt the A & P products labelled "doughnuts" & those labelled "fried cakes"—the entire distinction being architectural. As for times for doughnut eating—all I can say is that my breakfast each morning consists of doughnuts & cheese . . . . 365 days per year except when I'm where I can't get such homely fare. I'd like to see that Howey volume on ailurolatry[8]—& wish that domestic arrangements permitted my harbouring a black, playful, & yellow-orbed son of Bast! Dwyer is just now tantalising me with descriptions of a black kitten at his Shokan homestead—a dynamic sprite who chews at his papers & tries to slap his moving pen with a sportive velvet paw. If ever the Temple at Bubastis is exhumed & reopened, I shall at once apply for a high-priest's job! The *Argosy* tale is really excellent of its kind, though not without marks of a certain machine-made glibness & formula-following. If it didn't try to speed along so, it could achieve a more convincing atmospheric quality—though it's by no means bad as it is. For voodoo descriptions it is obviously much indebted to Seabrook's "Magic Island", (Papa Gobo = WBS's Papa Nebo) & of course the device of a train lost in quicksand or swamp is not new. But at that, it does pack a punch at intervals. That *train* alone is worth anybody's dime! Thanks again for the loan.[9]

About an old house article—I'd be delighted to attempt one if anything I could write would be acceptable to the *Star*. Just what is wanted? Bare descriptions, or directions how to reach them by Texaco petrol over Texaco-surfaced roads, or what? Not much can be said in 800–1000 words; but if only a few houses are to be described, one might try. I don't know anything in detail about Santa Fé, N.M., but could do some bibliothecal boning. Also, you could send any morgue dope you may have handy. Let me know particulars.

Best wishes. The old hearth at Spring Valley will doubtless assure you a festive & domestic Yuletide despite temporary celibacy.

     Yr obt grandsire
      O'Casey

Notes

1. "Oh, the times! Oh, the customs!" A sentence by Cicero in the fourth book of his second oration against Verres (chapter 25) and first oration against Catiline.
2. "F. C. Clark, M. D., Providence, R. I." is one of several authorities whose assistance Steele acknowledges in *Fourteen Weeks in Zoölogy* (New York: A. S. Barnes, 1872), 6.
3. Franklin Bachelder Simmons (1839–1913), prominent American sculptor of the

19th century. His statue of Ulysses S. Grant is in the U.S. Capitol Rotunda.

4. An essay by this title, by WBT, had for a time wrongly been attributed to HPL.

5. The note appears on p. 239 of the A. S. Barnes edition of 1873. When Roger Williams was exhumed, it was found that the root of an apple tree had traced his skeleton, leading some to speculate that his remains were taken up by the tree and its fruit.

6. An anthology edited by Colin de la Mare. Hart mentioned the book in "The Sideshow," *Providence Journal* (10 November 1931): 14.

7. Pierre Arnold Bernard (1875–1955), a.k.a. "The Omnipotent Oom," was a pioneering American yogi, scholar, occultist, philosopher, and mystic. In 1931 he became president of the State Bank of Pearl River, NY.

8. *The Cat in the Mysteries of Religion and Magic.*

9. Apparently a reference to Theodore Roscoe's "The Voodoo Express"; see WBT 67n3.

[70]   [ALS, JHL]

Tiw's-Daeg
[15 December 1931]

Jonckheer:—

Cook says "Dealings with the Dead" has gone to Munn, who would undoubtedly be glad to lend it on application. His address, as best I recall it, is Route 1, Athol, Mass.

But the specific purpose of this note is to perpetrate a piece of panhandling for a cause I think you'll agree is worthy. Whether you'll feel like digging up a buck & shooting it along to Grandpa Theobald or to Cook, depends on how closely affiliated with amateur journalism you still consider yourself.

What W P C & I are trying to do is to raise 25 fish to buy a new font of type for good old Tryout. The old boy needs it badly & can't afford it, & we argue that it's a helluva shame if amateurdom can't erase this obstacle in the path of a 79-year-old veteran who's done so much for the hobby in the last 42 years. We got the idea of raising a fund just after our visit to Smithy last October, but hoped to get the old time amateur Leonard E. Tilden[1] to attend to the soliciting, since he knows all the moneyed old Fossils. Tilden, however, couldn't spare the time—so passed the buck to me. He's giving $5.00, the old-timer Wylie the same, & Cook & I are chipping in one bone apiece—the same sum we[']re asking from the majority. If we can't raise the full 25, we'll try to dig something more out of our own jeans—& if we go over the top, we'll send the whole works on to Tryout, since he can very well use any excess on his type-purchasing operations. Of course, all contributions will be acknowledged, so that Smithy will know whom to thank. Cook thinks we can get him to accept the fund without embarrassment or reluctance if we go about it tactfully. But don't let him get an inkling of it in advance. We want it to be a surprise, even though our late start will probably prevent it from being a genuine Yuletide affair.

Thus it stands. Of the immediate gang in N.Y., the only ones I'm approaching are you, James Ferdinand, Loveman, & Little Belknap—since

Kleiner probably isn't any too flush, whilst Leeds & Kirk aren't sufficiently connected with amateurdom to make the request fair. And that last qualification goes for you also, if amateurdom seems a remote & nebulous thing. In case you do incline toward chipping in, you can shoot the one-spot either to Cook or to me.

And so it goes. Best wishes, & thanks in advance for any aid the fund may get from Rustenburgh.

Yr obt Servt
Tiebout van Casey

[P.S.] Heard a good lecture t'other night at your ex-college. Prof. A. E. Murphy (another of us Celtae) on the philosophy of Prof. (not our H. S.) Whitehead.[2]

Notes

1. Leonard E. Tilden (1861–1937) was veteran amateur journalist of New Hampshire and later Washington, DC.
2. The lecture by Arthur Edward Murphy (1901–1962), American philosopher, on 9 December on the British mathematician and philosopher Alfred North Whitehead (1861–1947) was unfavorable.

[71]   [ALS JHL]

Dec. 21, 1931

Jonckheer:—

Thanks for the *Star* with your interesting Wilmington article as well as the article by P J C.[1] You certainly do put out a nifty sheet!

Also recd. & perused with interest the Rockland antiquarian material, which bids fair to make a permanent local oracle of you. Glad you're getting such active results, & hope you won't have to do much conspicuous reversing once the campaign is well under way. In time—when you get that stable converted or that Dutch cottage built—I hope to address you at *King's Road, North-Scotland, Province of New-York*. God Save the King! I am assuming that the carbon of your communication is for retention & addition to the previously filed article. If not, pray apprise me, & prompt return shall be made.

Enclosed are a couple of articles from my favourite "Sideshow" which you can add to your morgue if you like. The one on "who ate Roger Williams" is the one I spoke of before. As I now see upon a full reading, (I only had a glance before) the anecdotal text is indeed properly traced to Joel Dorman Steele as an original source—so that your Sequin article remains as veracious in fact as it always was in intent. And to think poor Joel is forgotten by all you young fellows! This is the full text of what occurs in Steele, so that now you know as much about the matter as I do. Or wait—did you say you had or hadn't seen the root? I have seen it several times in the museum of the R.I. Hist Soc.

The foregoing set me off on a quest for an old catalogue of the Hist. Soc. which reposes in one of the backwaters of my morgue, & in it I found considerable information about old Roger's final disposition—or rather, his dispersal. It seems that most of the nails, hair, carbonaceous matter, &c. found in the graves of Mr. & Mrs. W. was finally placed in the Stephen Randall tomb in the North Burial Ground instead of in Roger Williams Park as originally intended. Other bits are in the Hist. Soc. Lucky that part of Roger was indigestible, so that he didn't get all et!

Thanks for the piquant card. I'm transferring last year's to my morgue— & trying to decide whether it belongs under the heading of art, or that of Manhattan antiquities. Have verified Munn's address. It *is* Route 1—so you have only to write him in order to get a crack at "Dealings with the Dead."

Well—joyous Saturnalia, & all that!

Yr obt. Servt

Theobaldus Senex

Notes

1. Paul J. Campbell, "The Joke Was on the White Man," *Texaco Star* 18, No. 10 (December 1931): 25–26, 32.

[72] [ALS, JHL]

Jany. 22, 1932
(too unimportant to
number for file!)

Jonckheer:—

Well—I'm dedicating this official paper with a mere note too trivial to be included in your archives—but practice is always useful. By the time I have something worth preserving I'll have learned how to avoid the binding holes.[1]

Glad you survived a partial perusal of Quebec. It makes me homesick to glance over the description of those silver belfries & winding, precipitous ways! I'll have to see Quebec next summer if it breaks me.

Thanks profusely for the R. W. statue view. It *is* the design used in the actual park monument. In the monument, Roger stands on a tall pedestal before which kneels the Muse of History, extending him a scroll or laurel wreath or something—urbane 1870 stuff.

Glad to hear the Spring Valley quarters are so near completion. When you get back there you'll have re-achieved your true traditional character of a country squire, so that your communications to the local press will achieve a doubled authoritativeness.

That list of photographs is surely tantalising enough, & makes me wish I had the cash to pick up a couple of dozen or more items. I've copied down the photographer's name, so that if I ever feel reckless or inherit a fortune I can have an added place to waste my resources.

I wish, too, that I had the jack to indulge in Prof Delabarre's opus. He has really made a monumental contribution to American archaeology, for his Cartereal theory of the main Dighton inscription is now fully accepted in most quarters.[2] Have you ever seen the Dighton Rock? I have, though it's rather tedious getting there. The only way is to take the trolley from Taunton toward Fall River, alighting at Dighton Rock Park (if that old resort is still going) & hiring a boat. The rock is on the farther side of the Taunton river; considerably up stream, & so low on the water's edge that the high tide almost completely covers it. One could easily miss it if not told just where to look, & the inscriptions are disappointingly faint.

Did I tell you that a new weird magazine of easy entrance requirements but low remuneration had been started by one Carl Swanson of Washburn, N. D.? He has just accepted my "Nameless City" & "Beyond the Wall of Sleep"—both old & oft-rejected specimens.[3]

Well—behave.

———Grandpa

Notes

1. The paper, provided by WBT, had holes punched along the binding edge. HPL customarily filled the entire page of his letters, leaving very little margin.

2. The Dighton Rock is a 40-ton boulder, originally located in the riverbed of the Taunton River at Berkley, MA. It is noted for its petroglyphs and ancient carved designs of ancient and uncertain origin. In 1963, the rock was moved from the river for preservation in in a museum in a nearby park, Dighton Rock State Park.

3. Swanson's magazine, titled *Galaxy*, never appeared.

[73]   [ALS, JHL]

Woden's-Daeg
[27 January 1932]

Jonckheer:—

Gad's blood, Sir, I swoon! Such generosity toward one who hath done so little to deserve it, & such sumptuousness to irradiate unheard-of splendours amidst the tatter'd volumes of an antient hermit! It hath come . . . . & I stand spellbound with mixt gratitude & admiration![1]

That—& may Alabad, Ghinu, & Aratza smite me if I speak falsely—is what I call a *book!* Bless my soul, but ought one to handle & actually read such an ultimate flowering of craftsmanship? I'll say nothing else could have been done to make it more exquisite! Who but an ultimate connoisseur of connoisseurs would ever have thought of "river"[2] elimination, weighted jacket, & all the rest of the refinements? Or have planned that fabulous binding? Even

Orton, with all his near-pedantic notions of what's what in books, would have to take off his hat to this summit of bibliophilic evolution. Something to hitch a bookplate to!!

And the contents could scarcely be more appropriate for an antient Novanglian dwelling amidst maritime memories. Lud, Sir, but it half makes up what the wanton destruction of our old waterfront took away! Not even the awesome delicacy of the format can keep me from giving the text an early & avid perusal—for here, in full strength, is that peculiar kind of New England glamour whereby the most familiar home people & places are linked with the most exotic & immemorial worlds of alien pageantry & antiquity. Salem & China—Providence & Java—Boston & the Guinea Coast . . . . . . & here we have the neighbour colony of Connecticut (whose venerable capital & archaic central scenery I so opportunely visited for the first time last October) linked with the brooding Sahara region which has known the footstep of the Moor, the Vandal, the Roman, the Carthaginian, & the still more primal Tuareg whose traditions are linked with the mystery of forgotten Atlantis! Creaking Yankee windlasses, groaning yard-arms, flapping canvas . . . . & the sound of Moorish lutes & desert camel-bells! Ah, me, that such piquant days should have passed away.

But let me not, in my ecstasy over the thing itself, forget to record the profusion of my thanks—or my profound appreciation of the thoughtfulness which inspired so sumptuous & appropriate a gift. It's a pity I haven't a birthday handy to afford a suitable setting—but anyhow, this is ex-Kaiser Wilhelm's birthday! And I'll bet he can't shew anything as tasteful amongst all the packages he's undoing at Doorn![3] Oh, for Pete's sake . . . . it's just occurred to me that I've forgotten to use your patent paper! That's the way old men are when flustered by pleasing & unusual events. But anyway, this hasty scrawl is hardly of preservational calibre.

This makes the second—& by far the more resplendent—modern bookmaking triumph to be owned by members of my family. My aunt Mrs. Gamwell has a small privately printed book—a sketch of the late Arnold Green of Providence written by his sister & published by his daughter—from the Merrymount Press of Boston, whose guiding spirit is a descendant of our R.I. Updikes & thus originally of your Nieuw Nederland Op Dycks. This took a prize a few years ago as an outstanding example of typography.[4]

And so it goes. Renewed thanks—& added apologies for the non-regulation paper. Cook expects to get here next Saturday & Sunday, & as a typographical enthusiast he'll probably wax eloquent over Friend Robbins.

   Yr most oblig'd ob[dt] Servt—

      Grandpa

Notes

1. See Bibliography under Archibald Robbins.

2. In typography, gaps that appear to run through a paragraph as a result of a coincidental alignment of spaces.

3. Wilhelm II (1859–1941), Emperor of Germany (1888–1918), was born on 27 January 1859. After World War I, he abdicated the throne and went into exile, eventually settling in a house in Doorn, Netherlands.

4. See Bibliography under Frances M. G. Wayland.

[74]   [ALS]

March 3, 1932[1]

Jonckheer:—

Homage, honourable Trustee! If I only knew the Dutch for congratulations, rejoicing, & general superlatives, I'd unload a whole double paragraph here & now!! As it is, the best tribute I can render is to remember to use your patent paper & steer clear of its perforated margin. Youth is certainly having its innings these days! Or rather, sheer ability & fitness are conquering the usual order of things. Phenomenal as is the choice of so tender-year'd a dignitary, it is certainly a fact that they couldn't have picked a better man. You certainly ought to feel pretty damn good about the matter—for think of the added standing it gives you in all phases of antiquarian pronouncement & debate! Now your articles on local nomenclature will have such weight that Spring Valley might as well order a new set of street signs & be done with it! I assume that your nomination—like a democratic one in South-Carolina—is tantamount to an election; & can only add that the patroons of Nieuw Nederland have again displayed that sound sense & good judgment which gave their colony so high a standing in the good old days.

Now as to contributions—bless my soul, Son, but what business has a rank British outsider in our sacred circle? However, if you do welcome foreign perspectives on things, & if there's anything I can say which will be of genuine interest, I'm sure I shall be glad to effuse. But first I want to see copies of the paper & get an idea of the kind of thing expected. It is very possible that the whole thing is out of my depth, since at bottom my acquaintance with Holland antiquities is damnably casual and laymanlike. As late as 1922 Sonny Belknap & I got fooled by the stepped gable of the fire station near Hanover Square and thought we'd discovered a real Dutch House—until we drew near and saw what it really was! As for Dutch architectural influence in Quebec & Charleston—I don't think I could have mentioned any in the former town, although I may have remarked the superficial & partial *resemblance* (parallelism, not cause & effect) of the curved Dutch roof & the curved eaves of Quebec cottage roofs. As for Charleston—there is a *question* of Dutch influence, (direct from Leyden & not concerned with Nieuw Nederland) but unfortunately for the purposes of your periodical, my own frank opinion attributes a French source to the characteristics (a roof-curve at the eaves like that in Quebec) which some trace to the Netherlands. However—it is a fact of presumable interest to Nieuw Nederlanders that many settlers from the colony did emigrate to Charleston, & that one of the most prominent names in Charleston life is *Vanderhorst*—which soon acquired the local pronunciation *Vandrorst* (2 syllables). There was once a Vanderhorst Creek (now filled in) & there is still a Vanderhorst Street. Moreover, there is a fine multiple house (of English Georgian design) built about 1800 & new in desertion & decay which owes its origin to a Vanderhorst & is to this day known as Vanderhorst Row. This is today pointed out as the first apartment house in America, & I wish to Pegāna that some of your Dutchmen would raise a fund to save it from the ultimate collapse or destruction toward it seems at present to be headed. When I was in Charleston I wrote you of a stepped gable in Queen St., but I think I added that its probable date—say 1820—would classify it as a conscious archaism & exoticism rather than as any natural result of the Dutch element in Charleston. Just what would be acceptable—or what would be trite old stuff—to your clientele, you can judge better than I. One might speak of the pitch of gambrel roofs in English homes—following the Dutch proportions in New York, New Jersey, & Pennsylvania, but having a long upper pitch in New England and in the relatively sparse Virginia examples.

New-England & Nieuw Nederland relations would fill a book, and would demand a far better historian than I. The Plymouth colony had several touches of Dutch influence, but these came primarily from Holland itself & not from Nieuw Nederland—although relations with Nieuw Amsterdam were maintained, & the Dutch man, Isaac de Raiseres, welcomed as a sort of commercial agent. Would accounts of very early Dutch penetrations of New England be of interest? I suppose you know that Adrian Block mapped and named the features of our coast, & that attempts at founding forts & trading posts were made on the coast of Maine & in Rhode-Island. Incidentally—are you Dutchmen paying much attention to the archaeological work at Fort Ninigret in Rhode Island's South County, where evidence of Dutch origin & occupancy are steadily appearing? Up to last year this ruined stronghold was held to be the work of the Niantic Indians. If proved to be Dutch, as now seems almost certain, it will undoubtedly rank as the oldest structure in New England—any date subsequent to 1627 being inconceivable. However, the fact that it is in a ruin & not a true edifice keeps the oldest-house record safe for the ancient Fairbanks homestead in Dedham.

But I can tell better when I see the publication just what sort of material it demands, & whether or not I am too rank a layman & superficialist to supply the right stuff. I wouldn't for the world let you print anything likely to lower your status as a Trustee-Editor amongst a select & highly exacting clientele. Incidentally—thanks enormously for compliment of suggesting that I contribute to this august enterprise. Oh, yes—& I hereby promise to return faithfully & intact any *Halve Maens* which may deign to cast their beams in my direction.

Well—as you saw from my external P.S. of yesterday, I've got some new ancestors! But the richest joke on me came last evening, when I dug out the main chaos of family notes in order to look up a possible Peter Place whom the old lady who sent me the data is trying to discover. I thought I ought to do her a favour in exchange for the information she had given me, so went through the tangled & long-neglected papers with some degree of thoroughness. Well—I couldn't find the Peter she wanted, but I *did* find a whole envelope of papers *which I had never seen before,* & which contained matter of the utmost interest to me. Ædepol! I don't know who's the champion nitwit—myself for never coming across this envelope before, or my aunts (or rather my elder aunt, for I don't think Mrs. Gamwell knew anything about it or paid any attention to genealogy) for forgetting it & letting me flounder about in ignorance of the Rathbone & Perkins lines. But some kind of a joke is certainly on somebody! The point is, that my grandmother had a whole lot of data which for some reason or other was never copied on the charts from which I in turn made my charts when you started me off in 1927—& that many things which were mysteries *to me* were not family mysteries at all! For instance—gawd forgive me for bothering you to help me unravel the Cooley book in Room 328 . . . for my grandmother had the Rathbone line straight back to the first John of Block Island (1661)! Still, I'm not sorry to have seen the book, for there was stuff in it which we didn't have, & it carried the line two steps behind old John to Richard of England. But more—there was a whale of a lot of very clear Perkins data which—although not solving the primary mystery of Jonn Rathbone's wife Olive—completely covered the other Perkins gap & made unnecessary most of the material just supplied so carefully by the old lady & so excitedly announced to you in yesterday's P.S. The Godfrey, Safford, & West lines, it appears, were well known to my grandmother. However—the *Newman* line (which accounts for the repeated use of Newman as a Christian name by Perkinses & Places) was not mentioned in the notes; so I am after all not sorry I made my recent inquiries. There were one or two things in the notes which were not in the data supplied by my recent informant—among them a full tracing of the Perkins lineage to Old England. It seems that one John Perkins, of Nerwent, Gloucestershire, (c. 1590) came to Boston in 1630 on the *Lion* as a shipmate of Roger Williams. In 1633 he settled in Ipswich & became a military captain & deputy to the General Court. He had a John—born in England in 1614—& John had a son Samuel, born in Ipswich 1655. Sam served in King Philip's War & was granted lands in Voluntown, Conn. His son (b. 1681) by Hannah West—was Ebenezer Perkins, who filtered across the line into Coventry, R.I., married Hannah Safford, & in 1711 became the father of Newman Perkins, whose daughter Martha by Mehitable Godfrey became the wife of Stephen Place Sr. Meanwhile this same Newman Perkins in 1752 witnessed the will of the John Rathbone whose son John had married an Olive Perkins . . . . but

Olive is still unaccounted for. My new informant also helps out in another quarter by giving two generations of the ancestry of Patience Fish, who married the John Rathbone born in 1693. She will charge a fee for looking up the Mercy Dyer and Olive Perkins mysteries, but if it isn't great I may let her go ahead. Hope I don't pay good money & then find full data amongst the chaos hereabouts.

Well—congrats once more, O grave Trustee!

Yr obt Grandpa

Notes

1. Written on WBT's "patent paper."

[75]   [ALS, JHL]

March, thank Pegāna!

[Envelope postmarked 5 March 1932]

Jonckheer:—

Thanks abundantly for the timely tip, which is duly assimilated & definitively relegated to utter oblivion. Quinn is surely a fine chap to speak well of Grandpa's efforts—pray give him my most cordial regards when next you cross his path! I haven't sent the 115-pager[1] to Swanson, but if Little Farny is inclined to be touchy about anything, he's already had his chance. When I asked, on Swanson's behalf, about my reprinting rights, (certain tales of mine—prior to 1926—were sold without the later reservation) Wright replied that it was nix on the ones he owned, & that—since Swanson was likely to prove a rival of his—he did not favour the second sale of those tales in which I hold later rights. In other words, this bozo who has exploited his authors for his own profit—cabbaging all their rights until they learned to reserve them, rejecting their best tales, reprinting others without added remuneration, & backing out of book-publishing promises while he pushes the work of his pal Kline—this hard egg who actually boasted to a friend of Belknap's that he has his authors at his mercy financially because for the most part there's nowhere else they can place their work—expects his lamblike contributors to forfeit their legitimate rights as a personal favour to him in exchange for all his unnumbered kindnesses! Gents, I like that! Well—what I did was to give him the civilised Rhodinsular equivalent of that curt injunction so popular in his own tempest-swept cosmopolis—"go jump in the lake"! I'm god-damn'd if I'll be blackmailed, through any implied withdrawal of favour, into passing up legitimate chances for publication! I told Sonny Belknap about the situation, since he is more disposed to compromise with raw tradesmen's ideals than I am; & indeed, he shews some inclination to scuttle out of the Swansonian reprinting proposition. But I myself stand pat—as indeed honour would impel me to do in any case, since I had told Swanson he could have his pick of any reprints of which I owned residual rights. I certainly don't intend to be harassed any further by damn'd hagglers—& I have virtually abandoned the idea of attempting professional fiction contributions. The repeated rebuffs I receive from capricious asses like Wright, Babbittesque dolts like that drivelling Clayton, & conventional namby-pambys like Shiras of Putnam's have about paralysed me into a help-less & disgusted inarticulateness; so that I resolved some time ago to chuck the whole loathsome mess & return to the purely non-professional basis of pre-1923 days, when I wrote spontaneously & without the expectation of marketing, and allowed my junk to pile up for whatever disposal or lack of it the future might provide. I told Wright as much in my letter—but added that of course I'd give him a first look at any extra short or conventional specimen I might happen to evolve. That isn't 'bad business'—because I had reached the point where, except after a stimulating repudiation of degrading commer-cialism, I was absolutely unable to write any fiction at all, despite the most serious efforts. It was a case of either repudiating cheap standards & re-strictions, or of remaining wholly tongue (or pen) tied fictionally. Most unfor-tunately, I haven't the cleverness to concoct ingenious conventionalities according to the commercial specifications of unimaginative editors. I have either to write the stories that are in me, or else keep quiet. And I'll be shot if I'll let any pox-rotted sensation-pander gag me! Since spewing out my alle-giance to current markets I have written two new tales—"The Shadow Over Innsmouth", which comes to 72 pages (2 pp longer than the "Whisperer") & "The Dreams in the Witch-House", [*sic*] which reached 34 pages of pencil script.[2] Having abandoned all hope of getting a fountain pen to suit my aging claw & crabbed cacography, I have returned to the pencils of my infancy. Just bought a mechanical pencil (first I've owned since 1904) at Woolworth's for a dime to obviate interruptive sharpenings.

I have no hope that Swanson's *Galaxy* will prosper, for Klarkash-Ton gives the most pessimistic forecasts. It was merely for the principle of the thing that I told Wright where he got off. As for its possible rivalry—I added to F. W. that if it did nose out its older contemporaries it would be less on account of reprints than on account of the lesser conventionality of con-tents—for new, struggling magazines with starvation rates always carry, be-sides some very poor tales, certain really unique & original items which the vested interests reject. I furthermore added that the logical way for an editor to avoid any rivalry over reprints was to buy up second rights & run them himself—a perfectly sensible proposition if they are of such a nature as to be in demand & form a source of competition. Probably this proved a bit unpal-atable to Brother Farny—who has shewn such a predilection for reprinting my stuff without additional payments—but he must learn that his arrogant czardom cannot be expected to last indefinitely under shifting conditions. Once he did indeed have the upper hand, as he boasted to Belknap's ac-quaintance; (a fat, successful magazine hack named Armitage Traill)[3] [*sic*] but he must learn to take his medicine when time turns the tables! Well—I'm out of it. The fellow can do what he goddam pleases—both as to acceptance of my recent MSS. & as to future publication (if Swanson doesn't issue them first in a paper-bound book as vaguely proposed) of the book of tales promised in 1927. The stuff is his to take or leave, & if he decides to leave it he won't hear any complaints from the old gentleman. I know the kind of hardheaded haggling in which it's of no use for me to mix! But meanwhile pray thank Quinn most warmly & sincerely for the interest & consideration he has exhibited in my behalf. A regular guy, I'll say . . . . & I must express my gratitude before dutifully forgetting the entire incident!

The tales which Swanson has taken are "The Nameless City" & "Beyond the Wall of Sleep"—both Wright & Bates–Clayton rejects. If he's willing to print things without the application of capricious & arbitrary (as well as all other!) standards, I'll be glad to load him up with much of my rejected early stuff—"Sarnath", "Other Gods", "Celephaïs", "From Beyond", &c &c., although there are one or two items which I have myself repudiated. I don't give a damn what his rates are or aren't—or at least, I don't give enough of a damn to influence my policy toward the enterprise. It was young Derleth who told me that Swanson's rates would probably average about ¼¢ per word.

Sorry to hear *Oriental* is such a flop—though it serves Wright right for almost wrecking W.T. in his attempt to float it. Hope the new experiment will do better.[4] That ought to be a rich field for our friend Bob Howard, with his invincible tendency toward what Klarkash-Ton calls "monotonous manslaughter."[5]

Glad "The Curse Wheel" is done, & hope you can dispose of it to the greatest possible advantage. Try Clayton first, for 2¢ per word is ahead of Farny's best. I don't think your rejection percentage is so bad—at least, compared with mine. Let's see how the old man stands with respect to such tales as have been professionally submitted at all. Since you set the example, I'll include *Home Brew* statistics . . . . well, I *did* get paid, anyhow . . . . . even if Klarkash-Ton didn't for his illustrations to the L. F. I'll also follow your example & include Swanson.

Accepted somewhere or other		Rejected
*Tomb	Red Hook	Psychopompos (rhyme)
Dagon	He	Polaris
*Wall of Sleep	*In the Vault	Sarnath
*White Ship	*Cool Air	The Tree (now repudiated)
Randolph Carter	*Cthulhu	Celephaïs
Terr. Old Man	Pickman's Mod.	From Beyond
Cats of Ulthar	*Silver Key	Iranon
Temple	*Str. High House	Other Gods
Arthur Jermyn	Colour out of Sp.	Shunned House

Pict. in House	Dunwich Horror	Mts. of Madness
*Nameless City	Whisperer	
Moon-Bog	————	————
Herbert West	Total 32	Total 10
Outsider		
Erich Zann	*rejected one	I thought there were
Hypnos	or more times	rather more rejects.
Hound	before acceptance.	Some of these aren't
Lurking Fear		so hot, but I'd like
Rats in Walls		to get Psycho, Polaris,
Unnamable		Other Gods, Shunned
Festival		Ho., & Mts. into print
		somewhere.

Oh—by the way—it turns out that Cook's unbound book edition of Shunned House (with Belknap's introduction) is not lost after all. He has recovered it & had the loose sheets transferred to his sister's place in Sunapee N.H. When he gets up there he'll send me about a dozen sets, which I'll gradually have bound & present to various members of the gang as a symbol of picturesque failure.[6]

Thanks for the obituary matter on good old Chace.[7] I knew he'd draw nation-wide notice, for he was really an eminent figure in world scholarship—the kind of boy of whom Old Prov is proud. I used to see him often, with his green eye shade, at the Marshall Woods lectures[8]—especially when their subjects were scientific or philosophical. Requiescat in Pace! My destined sepulchre is in Swan Point, too. As for Cousin Wendell Phillips[9]—that guy's relationship to me is hardly more than technical, the latest common forbear being old Rev. George himself. Cousin Wendell (if memory plays no tricks) comes from the oldest son Samuel, whereas I come from the very youngest—little Mike, who went to Newport & begat a James who begat another James who begat an Asaph who begat a Jeremiah who begat a Whipple who begat a Sarah who begat a Grandpa Theobald. But I'm willing to let the consobrinity stay as it is, at a suitable distance; for that bimbo was an abolitionist of the most rabid stamp, whereas I am a pro-slavery conservative. In R.I. the Narragansett planters owned many slaves, & of the above-listed Phillipses Mike & James I had several niggers, whilst (data on Jas II being uncertain) Asaph had two—who stayed on just the same after R.I. abolished slaveholding in 1784. Or come to think of it—I guess slavery wasn't really abolished, but that the law made the children of slaves legally free if born after March 1, 1784. At any rate, the niggers are buried near the old Phillips burying ground (beside the burned ruins of Asaph's house) on Howard Hill in Foster. Another Mike Phillips—Mike I's son, who built "Mowbra Castle" (still standing) near Wickford—had a full score of blacks. Down in the South County the slaves were very well treated, & used to have a kind of Saturnalian merrymaking in the summer, at which a King of the Blacks was elected. This also occurred in Mass. & the South—& possibly in your Nieuw Nederland as well. By the way, I think the Wendell stock came from your Dutch region; getting absorbed very early into the Mass. Yankee stock just as the Op Dycks—as Updikes— became absorbed into our South County stock. Maybe you & I are related through Cousin Wendell.

Oh—by the way! Speaking of genealogy—I may have a clue to the *Perkins* mystery of which I think I told you. You'll recall that the late XVIII century John Rathbone was married to an Olive Perkins whose origin I couldn't determine, but that this John's father, according to the Cooley book which you helped me unravel in Room 328 four years ago, had his will witnessed in 1752 by one "Norman" (sic) Perkins, whose name must have really been *Newman*, since *Norman* is unknown as a colonial R.I. name, whereas *Newman* was quite common. We argued that the Perkins who witnessed the father's will was probably some relative—perhaps the father—of the son's wife Olive—although we had nothing but guesswork to go by. Well—last week I was shewing the new young Providentian Harry Brobst through the Steve Hopkins house near your old homestead, & the ancient gentlewoman (a Mrs. Marvel) in charge for that day—one of the Colonial Dames—got talking about genealogy. She was, she averred, a professional genealogist. In the course of conversation & mentioned my Perkins dead end, & she replied that she was sure she had come across a *Newman Perkins* in her researches, & that she could probably tell who his forbears were & whether he had a daughter Olive. I gave her my name & address, & later sent such dates as I had not remembered—that of the witnessed will & of Olive's marriage to John Rathbone—& she said she would drop me a line about anything she found. I haven't yet heard from her, but am still expecting to. Hope she turns me up a good new batch of ancestors—though, being a profesh, she may charge a fee despite the volunteer tone of her discourse. It seems she had met & compared notes with the other ancient gentlewoman in Foster—Mrs. Nabby Kennedy—whom I have been on the point of going to see about data ever since you awaked my temporary interest in forefathers in '27. And speaking of forgetfulness—another person I have been meaning to consult by letter (an old & distant cousin named Edgar Balcom) on these topics lives in *Norwich, Conn.*—which fact slipped my mind entirely when I was *there myself* last October!! I was in the town almost a full day, & never recalled that this was the place to which I had been (& still am) intending to address a letter of inquiry! Grandpa's surely getting old!

By the way—young Brobst is proving very congenial. *He appreciates the poetry & drawings of Klarkash-Ton* (which is more than some folks do), & has also interested another fellow at the hospital—a nurse from Pittsburgh—in them. Both youths are going to call here tonight—quite a pseudo-Kalem meeting!

Hope you got the Ulster Co. Gazette safely, & that it will be of real value in your files. Or are other reproductions common this year? Real old Dutch stuff! And from the number of Sheriff's Sales Pete Ten Broeck was conducting, I judge that the close of my favourite century had a depression all its own! Well—be good—Grandpa O'Casey

P.S. Did I say on my card that Whitehead seems to be really recovering at last?

[P.]P.S. Oh, my gawd! I forgot again to use your patent pages! Pardon!! Pardon!!! I'll do better next time!!!!!

Notes

1. *At the Mountains of Madness* (the TMS came to 115 pp.).

2. HPL wrote "The Dreams in the Witch House" (January–February) almost immediately upon completion of "The Shadow over Innsmouth" (November–December).

3. Armitage Trail, pseudonym of Maurice Coons (1902–1930), author of *Scarface* (1930).

4. *Oriental Stories* (later titled *Magic Carpet Magazine*) lasted for 14 issues (October/November 1930–January 1934). It is not clear what the "new experiment" refers to: *WT* published no other companion magazine.

5. It is not clear that Smith ever said these words in regard to Howard's work. In a letter to HPL ([11 September 1931]), he wrote: "Robert E. Howard's omnipresent gore-spattering is surely getting monotonous, but I fear it will prove a hard fault to eradicate" (*DS* 324). Later (20 June 1936), HPL wrote to Smith: "Two-Gun's serial is really splendid despite the 'monotonous manslaughter' & confusing nomenclature" (*DS* 644).

6. The book was printed in 1928 but never bound. Walter J. Coates offered to do the job, but ultimately did not. R. H. Barlow obtained the sheets and bound a few sets, but the print run remained unbound until 1959–61, when the sheets (50 copies unbound, 100 copies bound) were sold by Arkham House.

7. Arnold Buffum Chace (1849–1932), textile businessman, mathematics scholar, and eleventh chancellor of Brown University. He died on 28 February.

8. Marshall Woods (1824-1899), treasurer of Brown University (1866–82); he was succeeded by A. B. Chace. The Marshall Woods Lecture Series was devoted to "the Fine Arts, and on their Application to the Mechanic Arts, or Industrial Pursuits," and was usually held at Sayles Hall on the Brown campus.

9. Wendell Phillips (1811–1884), American abolitionist and advocate for rights for women and Native Americans.

[76]   [ALS, JHL]

March 22[, 1932]

Jonckheer:—

Well, Son, here you are! It's really a fine yarn, & have no doubt but that it will be favourably received by one editor or another.[1] Better try it on Bates–Clayton first, on account of the higher rates. I've corrected in pencil the remarkably few stenographic slips occurring in this carbon.

As for any critical suggestions—as I read along, I jotted down anything which came to my mind; & will enclose the slip with these random observations. Not many of these have to do with anything a popular editor would care about—although conceivably Clayton might ask for a soft pedal on the didacticism in the early part. My own chief objection would be the brisk, cheerful, conversational element supplied by my fellow-Celt McCarthy. It detracts from the tensity of the mood required to float the main point artistically. However—the rabble eat up this kind of thing & grunt for more, so you don't need to worry in a tale frankly motivated by commercial compromise! Another objection would have to do with the overworking of coincidence— these *three* distinct elements being juxtaposed without any evident thread of common synchronising causation:

1. Van K's discovery of the paper
2. One of the J. D.'s flood-aroused rampages
3. Van K's scheduled speech on the old will

But again—no editor of the Batesclaytonesque stamp would balk at a trifle like that. However—look the notes over for yourself & draw your own conclusions. I repeat, in general, that it's a damn good story.

By the way—I had a piece of baddish news in yesterday's mail, which you may have had simultaneously. Swanson's *Galaxy* isn't going to *fail*, because it isn't going to *start!* Eheu! He can't swing the financial end, hence must postpone his hopes of a printed magazine "for a while". However, he's getting a mimeograph, & will investigate the possibilities of publishing either a mag or a series of booklets on that contraption. He gives his contributors leave either to withdraw MSS. or let him keep 'em tentatively with a possible view to mimeograph publication. Lacking any other market for my two, I'm letting him hang on to them for a while. Well—among the mourners the smugly smiling face of Brother Farnsworth may be seen!

By the way—Leeds mentioned my stuff to the editor or sub-editor or something or other of the Vanguard Press the other day, & they inquired whether I had any novel to submit. I told 'em I didn't, but said they could look at some shorts if they wished. They aren't so keen about those, but have asked to see a few. My best are all lent, but I'm sending 'em Dunwich, Cthulhu, Rats, & Pickman. I haven't the slightest notion that they'll be even lukewarmly interested, but there's no harm in going through the automatic motions of shooting a few things along when there's a chance.

I hear you had a good meeting on the 11th, & trust the gathering at Loveman's on All-Fools' will likewise prove a success. Have you subscribed to *Trend?* I haven't plunked down the full two berries, but have sent 50¢ for the opening number. If it survives, I'll buy the rest as they come.[2]

Well—congrats again on a good story. You really break pioneer ground in fictionising the colour-filled countryside of the antient Ramapaugh region!

Regards—

Grandpa McCasey

Notes

1. HPL is presumably discussing "The Curse Wheel" (nonextant).
2. *Trend*, a literary quarterly published in Brooklyn (1932–35). Loveman is listed on the editorial board only for Vol. 1, No. 1 (March/April/May 1932).

[77]   [ALS, JHL]

April 2[, 1932]

Jonckheer:—

De profundis clamo[1]—in the midst of a dental siege!

Damn King Pharnaces for his monotonous rejections! Even with the diluting element I mentioned, the Curse Wheel was better than most of the junk he foists on the public! But I've just recd. my 55 bucks for In the V. Say—do you know of a magazine called *Weird Whispers,* published by W. J. Thompson Co., 615 W. 43^d St., New York City? Its name has just been called to my attention, but I don't see it on the stands. It sounds like a potential market. A crude client tipped me off.[2]

Got a new ancestral name yesterday to add to the wheel chart. Happened to look at a rather new genealogical book in the library, & see that in the Perkins genealogy the blank for the surname of the first John P's wife has been filled in. Instead of merely |Judith ———| she is now |Judith Gater|. How the list grows . . . Godfrey, Safford, Newman, Wist, & now Gater . . . . what next?

That Charleston book must be great. Hope I can get hold of it sooner or later, though I have an excellent guide now.

Was last night's meeting any good?

Best wishes—

O'Casey

[P.S.] Just got May W.T. & noticed your letter.

[P.P.S.] Did I thank you for the recent Star? If not, I do, if so, I do again.

Notes

1. Properly, *De profundis clamavi ad te, Domine* ("Out of the depths I have cried to you, O Lord"): Ps. 130:1 (Vulgate). HPL has used the present tense of the verb ("I cry").
2. No such magazine was ever published.

[78]   [ALS, JHL]

May 12 1932.

Jonckheer:—

Glad to hear that you're settled at last upon your own hereditary soil! It must seem wholesome & refreshing to you to have a daily ride full of Dutch steeples & gables—a soul-saving antidote to the metropolitan mongrelism amidst which your labours are pursued! Hope you settle the nomenclatural question harmoniously & appropriately. "Scotland Back Yard" has an undeniable charm, local significance, & allusive richness—yet *De Halve Maen* has its points as well. I'll be neutral, since only initiates in Rockland County geography ought to cast votes on so subtle a question.

Thanks tremendously for your offer of space in the deserted halls of Castle Newkirk! I don't know whether a camp cot, lamp, & kerosene supply would vastly underbid a week or so's room rent or not—but I'm appreciatively remembering the matter none the less. I might borrow a blanket of Belknap & merely roll myself up on the floor for a night or two if my cash ran short! By the way—coach fares from Providence to the metropolis are down to a comic minimum just now on account of a rate war. Only *$2.00* from the corner of Fountain and Mathewson to the corner of 8th Ave. & 51st St.! At that rate I might some time pay an odd visit to the gang out of season!

Spring plans have been held up through financial uncertainty, but I now have a ray of hope for the long-desired descent on *New Orleans.* There's something to make one's mouth water . . . . it cheers me up to talk about it even before I'm sure I can make it! Winchester, Nashville, Memphis, Vicksburg, Natchez, Baton Rouge, & *New Orleans!* If I can swing it, I shall try to hang on a week at the Y, seeing all I can of the old town & the surrounding plantation country. On my way back, I'll stop at any places which look good on the way down. I'll probably be in the metropolitan region late this month & early next, & hope a Kalem gathering may happen to coincide with that period. Afterward—assuming (perhaps too optimistically) that I'm not flat broke—I hope to get up to antient Ulster County & visit Bernard Dwyer— that sterling Dutchman whose forefathers wielded shillalahs in ould Killarney—amidst his native wild domed hills & hanging woods. There is a new Providence-Albany coach line whereby I can return directly & not unpicturesquely to these Plantations via Pittsfield & Springfield.

The Boston triangular gathering proved very congenial. Munn hadn't seen much of the Hub before, so Cook & I acted as his guides to local antiquities & museums. We climbed to the top of Bunker Hill Monument—my first ascent since the age of seven—& drank in a disappointing view of outspread urban industrialism, & also enjoyed the new Georgian vistas created by Harvard along the banks of the Charles. A side-trip to old Medford also yielded pleasing glimpses. Here are some potential morgue items of possible interest. You'd probably enjoy the Romanesque interior of the Germanic Museum.

Belknap saddens me with the news that poor exiled Felis is now in declining health & not expected to survive the summer. In fond memory of the past, the Kalem Club as a whole ought to pay the patient a last melancholy visit in a body! Best wishes—& hope to see you ere the month is out.—Grandpa

[79]   [ALS, JHL]

[THE CAWTHORN
MOBILE, ALABAMA]

Saturn's Day [30 July 1932]

Jonckheer:—

I appreciate most profoundly—as will Mrs. Gamwell—your expressions of sympathy regarding our recent loss.[1] The melancholy change is certainly hard to get used to.

One good antidote to the current nervous strain has been a series of trips to Newport made possible by the spectacular reduction of round-trip steamboat rates. In the rivalry between the Mount Hope & the all-year-round mail ship Sagamore, the latter has come down to *50¢* for the trip to Newport & back—also allowing a half hour more time in Newport (6¼ hrs) than does its competitor. Accordingly I have been three times & intend to repeat the process. I take my work along, writing both on the boat & on the seaward cliffs at Newport where Dean Berkeley sat & composed his "Alciphron" two centuries ago. Of the ancient town—with its houses dating back to 1673 & its public buildings of 1698, 1726, 1739, 1749, 1760, 1763, &c—I suppose I must have told you many times, though I believe you said you had never been thither. It is one of my favourite havens—easily in the same class with Portsmouth, Salem, Kingston, Charleston, & Natchez—& I am infinitely grateful for this opportunity of visiting it with greater frequency than usual. The disadvantages of the Sagamore are cramped space & freight (sometimes cattle) on the lower deck, but these are minor evils well worth suffering for the sake of the concomitant advantages. I am picking up a tan almost equal to the Florida article of last year.

On Tuesday next—& until the evening of the ensuing Saturday—I shall be honoured by the company of our august friend James Ferdinand Morton, who has lately been exciting my envy with his travels around Cape Cod & Nantucket. During his stay I may propose a further use of the Sagamore's bargain rates—a trip to Block Island, which I have never seen despite my four decades of Rhodinsular habitation. Wish you could get around to Providence & make a real convention of the affair!

Your tour among Netherlandish antiquities with the author of Volume II.[2] must have been a rare treat. I surely envy you—& also the writer, since your guidance & transportation must have been very valuable indeed. Enclosed is something from the Boston Post which both Cook & Tryout Smith sent me—hence the sparable duplicate for your morgue. The erroneous statement about surviving stepped gables is certainly tantalising—& in my naiver days might have sent me off on many a wild-goose chase. I always recall how—in lower Manhattan in 1922—Sonny Belknap & I thought we had discovered an authentic survival of the stepped gable . . . . only to have it turn out to be a modern fire station!

Glad you enjoyed "The Three Impostors", & hope you aren't missing Machen's other weird items—"The House of Souls", "The Terror", "The Shining Pyramid", & (less downrightly weird, but by all odds the most truly artistic of all M's works) "The Hill of Dreams".

Did I tell you that I have lately come into correspondence with the local weird author Hugh B. Cave?[3] He lives in Pawtucket, but is now in Boston for the summer. Not exactly an artist, but slowly improving (& very successful) as a commercial writer. I shall be interested in meeting him when he gets back—or before, if I spend a week-end with Cook during the coming month.

Went over to see C. M. Eddy, Jr. the other night—first time in ages. He has a glorious tiger kitten; but the tenacious quality of its coat, plus the smooth & non-acquisitive texture of your charity summer suit, prevented a repetition of the Carbie episode. ¶ Best wishes—Grandpa

Notes

1. HPL's aunt and Annie Gamwell's sister, Lilian D. Clark (b. 1856), died on 3 July.

2. Rosalie Fellows Bailey (1908–1991), *Pre-Revolutionary Dutch Houses and Families in Northern New Jersey* (New York: William Morrow, 1936). As noted in WBT 99, Franklin D. Roosevelt wrote the book's preface.

3. Hugh B[arnett] Cave (1910–2004), prolific author of stories for the pulp magazines. He lived for a time near HPL in Pawtucket, RI. They corresponded briefly but never met.

[80]   [ALS, JHL]

September 24, 1932

Jonckheer:—

Well—I've dug up the patent paper, even tho' it doesn't take ink quite as uniformly as the F. W. Woolworth product I've been using. Incidentally, I'm giving an allegedly black ink a bit of a tryout. Wandrei left Sunday morning, & since then I've been desperately floundering about in a hopeless pile of work & correspondence. Only yesterday was I able to prepare the sketch of faery lore which you requested, & which you will find enclosed. Hope it's what you want—& that you can read the cacography. One can't be encyclopaedic in small compass, but I fancy you'll find all the points we ever discussed at Kalem meetings. The facts & theories, I think, are all straight—tho' I hadn't time to consult authorities. That AP item appeared in the Evening Bulletin also. It rather amused me to see the old & widely known data brought forward as new—but that's what a smart-aleck reporter would be likely to single out in reporting a meeting whose other business no doubt impressed him as dry.

Glad you could decipher some of the travel cards. It was a great trip—even tho' it did leave me busted. The eclipse was magnificent, & I feel quite distinguished as being a veteran of *two* successful total eclipses. I nearly froze to death during the first one—Jany. 1925. Here are two or three more cards from the scenes of my wanderings. I like Montreal very much, though it lacks the antiquarian perfection of old Quebec. I think I told you that I explored the quaint & unspoiled Isle d'Orleans, which remains much as it was when His Majesty's troops under Gen[1] Wolfe[1] landed in 1759. I certainly hope to get to Quebec again next year.

Let me repeat my congratulations to Carbie! I'll bet the kittens are a delightful lot, despite their *stubbletje*[2] season* of appearance; & I surely hope their careers have not been arbitrarily abbreviated. The next time I'm in Rockland County I hope to add specimens of their fur to my blue Athol store clothes!

Glad you've found a good Dutch bookshop, & hope the linguistic research will prosper. The "Dialect Notes" ought to help—& I hope to be able to avail myself of your tip regarding the Novanglian phases of this publication. As for classical Dutch versus Jersey Dutch—if you take my advice you'll tie to the classical. You don't want to take as a model the corrupt & time-weakened patois of any backwoods modern group—as against the pristine speech of Petrus Stuyvesant & the vigorous founders of Nieuw Nederland. Without question, the common speech of the Nieuw-Amsterdam streets in their heyday was essentially the normal language of Old Amsterdam; & the later outland dialects were probably unknown in the prosperous parts along the Hudson. It is well, of course, to have a glancing familiarity with the backwoods dialects, just as a New-Englander ought to be familiar with the "Haow be ye?" speech of the remoter countryside; but the thing to tie to is the standard language. Wish I could see that series of Dutch house articles in the Bergen Evening Record.

Glad your writing programme goes on satisfactorily—but sorry the postal expense is so great. An agent is, I think, a very good thing for one in the commercial field—that is, if one has the right agent. Whitehead did not like that Ohio agent—Cox—of whom Francis Flagg[3] thinks so highly. E. Hoffmann Price is enthusiastic about an agent in N.Y.—one Lenniger.[4] I'll get you his address if you're interested. Hope the articles go over well. Many seem to find such things a valuable source of revenue. No—I never saw your treatise on the Ghost-Proofing of the Home.

As for hack fiction—it is all right, & an admirable source of revenue, if one can grind it out without spoiling one's ability to create genuine material. The trouble is that not many can preserve the requisite duality. I can't—&

---

*I must be a stubbletje Tom myself—born Aug. 20

that's why I'm cutting out magazine attempts. Belknap can't either—although he still thinks he can. The only person I know who really gets away with it is young Derleth—whose W.T. junk bears absolutely no resemblance to his serious work. He is one in a million in that respect. By the way—he has just secured an O'Brien three-starring for one of his serious stories, & a two-starring for another.[5] The boy's coming on.

My objection to your thesis that hack work gives valuable practice, is that the sort of glib technique developed by popular writing is of *the absolutely wrong sort*—so that it forms a *grave handicap* rather than an asset when one tries to write something really worth reading. Virtually all the adroit tricks of the flashy Satevepost & Cosmopolitan school of writers are mere artificial affectations contrary to the spirit of sincere literature.* The seriously aspiring writer's first lesson is to *forget*, not to *cultivate*, these puerile & flimsy smoothnesses—for there is no bond in common between real writing & the unctuous hokum of the bourgeoisie's favourite picture-books. Between popular junk & actual literature there is only war to the death. The genuine aspirant must forget all about commercial standards & start in with high-grade unremunerative magazines like *Pagany, Contempo, The Midland,*[6] &c. Eventually—if he has it in him†—he will make *Harper's, Scribner's,* &c. But he must think of **literature, not money,** & be careful to have enough other activities to keep him clothed, lodged, & fed. He must never think of writing as a source of revenue. If the revenue comes, well & good—but that must never be an object or matter of chief interest. There is no reason for a writer to think of authorship as a source of money if he has another job sufficient to keep him decently clothed, fed, & lodged. Art is not a business—it is life itself, the thing in order to enjoy which people work at other & more legitimately commercial business. It is like travel, sports, or the other recreational things which we enjoy apart from gainful work. Of course, in addition to literature there is also the fairly honest trade of writing cheap fiction to order to suit cheap people. But usually the people who follow that skilled & admittedly difficult industry are not the same sort of people who create literature. One kind of man writes artificial hokum for pay & plays golf as recreation. Another & more sensitive sort does any old thing for pay & writes or attempts literature as a recreation or justification for being alive. This latter sort really writes primarily to relieve his emotions—because he can't help writing. And there isn't much of a bridge between the two types. Commercialism gets you nowhere in literature. It is certain that the cheap tricks I have unconsciously picked up from W.T. writing were instrumental in causing Putnam's to reject my MSS. last year. Best-sellerism & literature won't mix!

---

*Read Edward J. O'Brien's exposé of commercial fiction—"The Dance of the Machine". I've just picked up a copy for a quarter—as a remainder.
†as I *haven't!*

Enclosed is an echo of amateurdom which may arouse mild interest.[7] Don't bother to return it. Have you seen Wandrei yet? I wish he could have stayed in Prov. longer. ¶ Best wishes—Yr Ob^t Grandpa O'Casey

[P.S.] By the way—do you want to pick up some book bargains? Sonny Belknap—the young idiot!—is selling his library for a mess of pottage, & offers some really surprising items. Look him up if you're interested.

[Enclosure: "Some Backgrounds of Fairyland"; see Appendix.]

Notes

1. James Wolfe (1727–1759), British army officer who led the British forces in their conquest of Quebec in 1759.
2. See HPL to Alfred Galpin (27 October 1932): "In the Dutch Nieuw Nederland this latter group wou'd have been call'd *stubbletje* cats because of their late summer birth at a time when the mown fields bristle with stubble. Such a brood was traditionally held to be of inferior quality, tho' I doubt if many kittens were banish'd because of birthdate alone." *Letters to Alfred Galpin* (New York: Hippocampus Press, 2003), 164.
3. Pseudonym of George Henry Weiss (1898–1946), American poet, writer, and novelist.
4. August Lenniger (1906–1989), literary agent.
5. The stories were "Old Ladies" and "Nella."
6. HPL's correspondent August Derleth appeared in all these little magazines.
7. HPL's booklet *Further Criticism of Poetry*.

[81]   [ALS, JHL]

Octr. 12, 1932

Jonckheer:—

Thanks a thousand times for the painstaking transcript of the Prince[1] article notes—for which I am fabulously & effusively grateful. What an exact science dialect study is getting to be—& I infer from what you say of D. N. that the whole country is covered in just the same minute way. These notes go at once into my most important files; & if you ever wish to consult them again, they are yours to command. What a curious combination "Jersey Dutch" seems to have been! It surely ought to be preserved before it is lost to memory—& yet I wouldn't advise its cultivation in preference to the classical Holland Dutch which was undoubtedly the authentic language of New Amsterdam in its prime. The diacritical marks argue a close observation & minute scholarship vastly beyond the common level, & it would take a lot of time even to apply them to the phoneticising of a good-sized passage. It all goes to shew how infinite are the varieties of sound capable of utterance by the human vocal organs, & how little any one alphabet is fitted to express the phonetic nuances of more than one language. I have come across the trip-a-trop lullaby before, & imagine it is something of a classic in the lore of Nieuw Nederland. As you point out, the Prince version does not seem to be the most favoured. He says *troutses,* whereas I have always seen it *troutjes,* as you have it. Also—the line "zoo groot &c" appears to be the standard. The standard version is probably the nearest to what was brought from Holland—surviving in places where the speech remained purest, as on Long Island & along the banks of the Hudson. The inland regions, where communication with Dutch-speaking centres was relatively slight, & where the influence of English settlers on speech was correspondingly great, may perhaps be regarded as the chief stamping-ground of the more corrupted dialects. It is, I suppose, barely possible that certain local dialects of old Holland predominated in certain parts of Nieuw Nederland, just as the special speech of the German Palatinate predominated in the Pennsylvania-German region. Incidentally, I understand that the speech of the South African Boers is not good classic Dutch. Some of the anti-Imperial die-hards have lately tried to have the language of the Boers recognised officially as a joint language with English in South-Africa—just as French is in Quebec—but many (if I recall a recent article aright) Dutch South-Africans oppose such a step on the ground that the common speech is only a patois. They would prefer not to have a definitely corrupt language given the stamp of officialdom.

The "Indian counting" business stumps me! I fancy there is some connexion with Dutch; for the identical *een* is too much to be a coincidence, as you originally noted. But I can't think of a thing more. *Ding* of course is allied to the *tien* of the Dutch or *ten* of the English. According to Grimm's law, *consonants* shift very easily when words are transferred from one speech to another. *Fimp* is certainly nearer the German *fünf* than either the Dutch *vijf* or English *five*—which may or may not argue a Pennsylvania influence. Whether *feather* & *vier* (or *four*) are connected, remains open for speculation. One feature absolutely unique so far as I know is the use of a *15-unit* & the subsequent compound counting beginning afresh & extending to 20. I give it up! It would take a student of the Algonquin dialects to venture any intelligent opinion. Possibly there was a sort of local pidgin-Dutch as you assume. Possibly, too, this system is not really of Indian origin but a mere folklore relique originating in schoolboy caprice like "Dog-Latin", "Hog-Latin", & things of that sort. Let me know if you ever find anything more on the subject.

As to the Anglo-Manhattanese *erl-woild* dialect—it is possible that the Germanic immigrants had some share in shaping it, yet that would imply an unaccountably sudden change; for I understand that the great German colonialism of the region did not occur till the middle 19th century. Could a speech absolutely universal around New York not much later than that date have been caused by so recent an admixture? Three subjects for research present themselves. (a) When was the special accent of New York first noted? (b) Did any considerable Germanic influence exist in N.Y. prior to the influx of 1848? &c (c) Could the influence of the Dutch language—or any dialect of the Dutch language—have tended to create the special accent? These points would really be worth looking up.

Some good warm weather lately. Last Sunday I made a round of ancient north-of-Boston places on one of the dollar ride-all-day tickets of the E. Mass. St. Ry. Co.—seeing Danvers, Beverly, Salem, Marblehead, & Nahant. Great trip—with foliage just touched with autumnal change. My longest stop, naturally, was in Marblehead.

And so it goes. Trust all is well around Old Scotland, & that the stubblet-je kittens are belying their traditional handicap. I have a new feline neighbour—at the house on the corner near the letter-box. The other day he introduced himself by rubbing around Grandpa's ankles while the Old Gentleman was posting some letters, & since then he has greeted me frequently from the fence-top around his demesne. He is small & grey & youthful—not so unlike Carbie except that his coat is not so readily detachable. I think I'll borrow him some afternoon—I doubt if his masters would miss him for a few hours.

Best wishes—Yr most oblig'd & obt
Grandpa O'Casey.

Well, well—we have a P.S.! Looks as if you were going to have a darned interesting dialect article!

I don't think you make clear the facts regarding the standard English suppression of *r* after vowels. This dropping of the rolled *rrr*.... is by no means peculiar to New England, but seems to have occurred independently in three parts of the Anglo-Saxon world—Southern England, Southern New England, & the Southern American colonies—at some time during the 18th century. Prior to the 18th century it is probable that *r* was more or less rolled thought the Anglo-Saxon world, as it still is in Northern England, Northwestern New England, Northern N.Y. State, Pennsylvania, & the Am. west. The soften or elided *r* is accepted as standard English because the areas using it include those in which scholarship or taste is most highly & traditionally developed—London, Oxford, New England, Virginia, Charleston, &c.

In your rendering of a rustic Yankee's pronunciation of the Bar Harbour sentence it is possible that you exaggerate certain characteristics—though I'm no authority. Generally, rustic Yankees don't flatten their long *a*'s so extremely; though they do flatten their short *a*'s (grăss, hălf, &c) as badly as Westerners.

New York City English is very peculiar. Those who speak it (cf. Little Belknap, a bad case!) do not notice that New Englanders talk differently from them, although those same New Englanders are always able to spot the differences in the New Yorker's speech. New Yorkers pronounce *hard, car, farm*, &c. like the New Englander, without rolling—but in words like *world, furled*, &c. they have a twisting sound peculiar to themselves, which is *not* adequately represented by the familiar comic-dialect spelling *woild*, &c. The real sound is more like *weh-eeld,* uttered as a monosyllable. Then of course they flatten *oil* to *erl,* &c.—& also say *momunt* for *moment, documunt* for *document,* &c. Theodore Roosevelt had this latter dialectic peculiarity despite his Harvard education.

The suppressed *r* in *hard, car* &c. was officially recognised by the beginning of the 19th century. I have a Walker's Rhetorical Grammar of 1814 (London) in which it is expressly stated that *bar, bard, card,* & *regard* are correctly uttered virtually as if spelt *baa, baad, caad* & *regaad.*

I personally prefer the elided *r* because I am accustomed to the suppression as part of my lifelong environment. A rolled Westerrrn rrrr.... always grates a bit on me. Academically, there is probably no justification for ironclad edicts one way or the other[.]

As for the dialect of Nieuw Nederland—why not copy the Sinn Fein Gaelic-hounds & start a campaign for the restoration of the Dutch language? Don't be satisfied with mere Dutchified English or Jersey Dutch—go in for the real classical Amsterdam–Leyden–Hague article!

¶ And thanks prodigiously for the Natchez cutting. Ah wish ah was go'a' dawn thaiah rāght naow! (note the Mississippi dialect)

Notes

1. John Dyneley Prince (1868–1945), American linguist, diplomat, and politician. WBT had copied for HPL material from Prince's "The Jersey Dutch Dialect," *Dialect Notes* No. 3 (1910): 459–84. *De Halve Maen* (which WBT edited) 8, No. 11 (1 January 1933): [4], under "On Our Bookshelf" (unsigned), mentions having a photostat copy of the article on hand. For more, see the following letter.

[82]   [ALS, JHL]

Octr 25, 1932

Jonckheer:—

Well—I'm so grateful for that New-Amsterdam information that I've gone to the length of dragging out your patent paper! I had no idea of the complexity of the linguistic situation in your pleasing & prosperous colony. Of course, I assumed that the humbler orders of the population had sundry jargons reflecting rural & provincial dialects of the homeland, but I thought that the solid people—Governor, officials, patroons, substantial traders, &c—spoke in the normal cultivated speech of the Netherlands & kept up fairly close relationships with the mother country. Standard Dutch, I had fancied, was the language of official documents & law-courts, & of such other written material as was produced in the colony. I understand that there were even poets among the colonists, one of them being named Nicasius de Sille,[1] or something like that. Am I then to understand that Stuyvesant & Kieft, van Rensselaer & van Cortlandt, Steenwyck & Allerton, & others of their quality, spoke a mixed and barbarous jargon? Certainly, no form of speech less pure than that actually spoken & written by the leading man of the colony ought to be taken as the prevailing language. Would you, for example, accept the prevailing *eloquium vulgare* of the United States (do like he done, kew-pon for coupon, add´-ress for add-ress´, cār´-mel for că´r-a-mel, &c. &c. &c.) as the authentic speech of its inhabitants? As for regional variations—I certainly attempted no more than guesswork, even though I did perhaps fall unconsciously into the dogmatic terminology of our little friend the uptown bookseller. (I suppose the young imp has told you how he's trying to sell his library!) Having formed the idea that such places as Flatbush & Albany possessed a social life of considerable cultivation & literacy, & reckoning the influence of Dutch Bibles & the preaching of pastors from Holland a not insubstantial factor, I took it as a matter of course that these regions would speak good Dutch. When I said *Long Island* I really meant the western end, for of course the English zone commenced at Jamaica & Flushing (to say nothing of the isolated group at Gravesend), soon giving to those towns a decidedly English cast. When I spoke of English penetration in the hinterland, I had reference both to the early settlements in New-Jersey, & the somewhat later filtration of English stock across the Connecticut & Massachusetts River, & into your own Rockland county. This filtration, I understood, considerably affected the architecture of Dutchess County; & it seemed only natural that it might have a correspondingly hybridising effect upon the language. On the other hand, I assumed that places like Albany, Poughkeepsie, Tarrytown, &c., where the Dutch had more opportunities of communicating with one another & keeping alive their joint heritage, would adhere more closely to the ancestral idioms. Ulster, I knew, was settled rather humbly & heterogeneously; but I fancied that the importance of Wiltwyck (Kingston) would tend to favour the dominant language at the expense of variant forms. French, of course, was the original language of New Paltz & the Shawangunk valley, but after 1730 that was steadily replaced by whatever language the inhabitants of Dutch Ulster spoke. But of course I very freely concede that I'm no linguist or philologist. I bow respectfully to anyone who can untangle the enfractuosities of the various Dutch, French, German, Spanish, Swedish, Portugese, Danish (Virgin Islands), & Russian (Alaska) dialects spoken by colonists in North & South America. French variants, I know, are highly complex. Louisiana spoke virtually pure French (that is, New Orleans did), while Quebec had a Norman provincial tendency. Today I believe Quebec schools & periodicals & urban speech represent a fairly grammatical French, though there are outlandish *words* used now & then. English loan-words are frequent today—as witness the French half of a common bilingual sign in Quebec City

ARRÊTE DE TRAMWAYS
CAR STOP.

Good French scholars in New-England say that radio speakers from French Canada tend to adhere to a very good French. A pro-Gallic friend of my aunt's habitually tunes in on Montreal. In the American Southwest the prevailing Spanish is archaic, but still understandable by natives of Spain. The German of Pennsylvania, however, never was the classical language of Germany. In the Virgin Islands Danish became thoroughly permeated with English, so that the latter eventually became the dominant language. The niggers speak a distinctly archaic English with Danish, African, Spanish, & French idioms, & there is a decadent French element (the Cha-chas, so often described by Whitehead) whose French has taken on accretions from all the environing languages. An entire library could certainly be written about the varying speeches of the settlers in America. Your analysis of the situation in Nieuw Amsterdam is the best I have seen so far, & I shall enter your epistle in that part of my files which pertains to the history of the Province of New-York. The study of Nieuw-Nederland speech certainly offers a vast field to the scholar, & I trust that you may in the course of time be able to make valuable contributions to knowledge in this direction. It was certainly a splendid idea to have that Prince article photostated for the Holland Society. I shall, by the way, be eager to see the new *Halve Maen*, & will look it over to see if anything in its policy will call for contributions of the sort I could advantageously write. Thanks for the set of proofreading symbols—which I am filing in my professional department beside the other card you so kindly sent. Wish I could get a chance to turn proofreading to financial advantage! I note with vast interest the data on the Jersey Dutch UI & UY—this may explain modern Anglo-Manhattanese, although a vast field for further study yet remains.

Concerning matters of stationery—bless my soul, but what extremes precision is getting to! Of this patent paper I have 8 sheets in addition to the two already full of pen-tracks. If you don't mind punching the holes yourself, I could (when I think of it) save you the trouble of sending stuff by halving ordinary sheets of Woolworth's $8\frac{1}{2} \times 11$ & (also when I think of it) keeping a clear margin. But use your judgment. I could punch the holes, but might not be geometrically accurate. The envelope idea certainly represents efficiency raised to the nth power. Hades—but suppose I tried that with all of my 50 to 75 correspondents! Go ahead with my blessing—the envelopes would come in very handily now that my Kirk charity letterheads are all gone. I thought I had a lifetime supply, but 7 yrs. finished them! My address will stay #10 as long as I have the cash to let it—& I surely hope I can postpone the crash & cyanide another year or two! Oh—about our friend Hammond—I tried to look him up a few months ago & found his shop gone. Later I'll look in the telephone book & directory to see if he's still in business somewhere else—& if he is, I'll buy up a supply of that thin paper for both of us. It cost $1.25 for 1000 sheets—& its great advantage is its light weight coupled with a commendable degree of strength & durability. My supply is almost gone—one more story of average length would finish it.

I read "Ghost Proofing the House" with acute interest, & shall file it amongst valued folklore items. You certainly are a young encyclopaedia of superstitions—& you catch the Sunday-supplement prose style to perfection! This article reminds me of what my poetical correspondent Carl F. Strauch[2] of Allentown, Pa. (who visited here last month) says of the charms painted on Pennsylvania-German barns to keep the "hexes" away. These designs are placed on the gable ends, & are usually in a variety of brilliant colours. Sometimes they are pictures of horses or cattle, but more commonly they are circles containing geometrical patterns. The purpose of these circles is to entice & trap the hex—who can enter, but who becomes lost in the complex labyrinth within. Strauch copied two typical designs for my benefit, which I will reproduce:

Some day I must visit the Lehigh Valley & behold these picturesque reliquiae at first hand. I do not imagine that they will survive many more generations.

Thanks for the cuttings. Yes—I knew that the Brown fortunes were founded on the triangular trade in rum, niggers, & molasses. Emmeline Poujola surely had a striking set of adventures, & I am glad to observe a case wherein a feline was treated with proper consideration. By the way—glad to know that all the stubbletjes are safely installed in pious & respectable homes.

As for Tryout—he got his type safely,[3] so I can afford to be charitable with those hard-pressed youths (including both collaborators on the Jackson White[4] & other articles) who did not respond to the cry for aid a year agone. I'll consider management of the Knollwood type case collection in the near future. Good luck, by the way, with your collaborated articles.

Here is something more on the mortal remains of R. W. which you need not return. The august fragments now repose in a vault at the old Prov. Institution for Savings. The Dr. Brown mentioned was my late aunt's final physician.

Well—be good, & I shall advise classic rather than Joisey Dutch!—Yr obt Grandpa

P.S. I suppose you know Strange Tales has failed.

P.P.S. Loveman may pay me a visit shortly.

Notes

1. Nicasius (de Sille) de Silla (1610–1674). His poems survive in his *Description of the Founding or Beginning of Nieuw Utrecht.*

2. Carl Ferdinand Strauch (1908–1989), friend of Harry Brobst and brief correspondent of HPL (1931–33). He published a slim book of poetry, *Twenty-nine Poems* (1932). He later taught at Lehigh University (1934–74) and became a leading scholar on Ralph Waldo Emerson. HPL's letters to him are included in *Letters to J. Vernon Shea, Carl F. Strauch, and Lee McBride White* (Hippocampus Press, 2016).

3. HPL and others had gathered contributions to purchase a new set of type for Charles W. "Tryout" Smith. See letter 70.

4. "Jackson Whites" was a derogatory and racist term for the Ramapough Mountain Indians, or Lenape Nation. See 45n1. Th name is thought to be short for "Jacks and whites," Jacks purportedly being slang for runaway slaves. Many of the people have albinism that gives them notable facial and skin characteristics.

[83]   [ALS, JHL]

Dec. 21, 1932

Jonckheer:—

This paper is just for discipline's sake—not that anything in this epistle is likely to possess a file-worthy immortality! The date of your blizzard-mentioning communication found me closely immured within #10—it being the third and last day of an utterly savage spell whose temperatures went all the way down to zero. I'm like your 1927 Chev when it comes to arctic temperatures.

I shall surely be glad to see the next *Halve Maen* if you continue to be generous with rank outsiders. Yes—I'm sure the "Jackson Whites" are an authentic part of the Nieuw Nederland milieu . . . . . for what would the South be without its niggers & poor whites, or the Virgin Islands without the retrogressive French "cha-chas"? Too bad Little Dauberpine hasn't proved a more faithful collaborator. He'd have lent an angle of sophistication & metropolitan *savoir faire*. In the course of time I hope to see your R. W. article in print—get me a copy of Deacon Quinn's sprightly journal when the occasion arrives.

It surely is a compliment when linguistic inquiries begin pouring into the *Halve Maen* office! I noted with pleasure the artistically Nederlandish cast of the Yuletide message from Scotland Post Road—for which appropriate thanks. And here—alas—is the data on Nieuw Amsterdam speech whose return you so justly request. Any piece of research as exhaustive as that surely ought to be in the archives of the scholar himself!

You surely have found an ideal compatriot in Brother Hendrik Willem.[1] Nothing like a common interest to give one a foothold with the great! His mode of launching the biographer Joannis van Loon is certainly ingenuity itself—I wonder how many of the reviewing fraternity caught on? I wish I could recall what the *Times* & other critical media said of this aspect of the work. You'd better accept his invitation to call. By the way—I've just had quite a glimpse of Dutch life through reading the recent & highly esteemed novel by Charles Morgan—"The Fountain". Its central figure is an officer interned in Holland during the World War, & the quest of a typical old landed aristocrat Baron van Leyden, at a picturesque castle called Eukendaal.

As for James Truslow[2]—well, well, you certainly have humbled us English! But keep up the good work & we'll give you the credit you deserve—for no one wants to rob Nieuw Nederland of its share in the colonies' culture & development. I am informed, by the way, that the Brooklyn Museum has a fine new pair of Dutch rooms—which I presume you've visited with the same celerity that marked your visits to the Dyckman & van Cortlandt houses. Thanks effusively & abundantly for the Kakiat booklet,[3] which duly goes into my files. That place surely must be delightful for sojourning—although to my eye the house is not very typically Dutch. Actually, I suppose this type of house—with the so-called "lie-on-your-stomach" windows in the attic—is really Dutch in many of its details; although it lacks the curved roof-line, & seems to have been employed by all types of dwellers in the N.Y. & N.J. region in the early 19th century. Which reminds me, that in a series of articles on Rhode Island houses now running in the *Sunday Journal,* the local architect John W. Hawkins expressly gives credit to the Dutch for the invention of the gambrel roof. Who says we Yankees aren't generous in our concessions?

Yes—& just to expand the Netherland link—I heard a fine lecture on Spinoza (Dutch by milieu if less Nordic by descent) last week at your alma mater—by Prof. Emer. Walter G. Everett.[4] Do you know the side-whiskered little gink? My aunt knows his wife. It was the first of a monthly series of philosophic lectures like those I attended last year—Schopenhauer (by Prof. Baylis)[5] being next on the programme. A society called the R. I. Philos. Soc. has just been organised around these lectures, & I may join if I think its activities would be worth the dollar per year dues.

Many thanks for the loan of the dialect cutting. Ædepol! Is it possible that Manhattanese is spreading as far out as Noo Choisey & remote Queens? But the puzzle that sticks in my crop is how the damn thing came into being. There are fatal objections against both the Bushwick German & old Dutch theories—since on the one hand the Germans did not reach New York soon enough to account for the full-blown existence of the dialect in the 1860's & '70s (which is absolutely proved), whilst on the other hand the absence of such a dialect in the other Dutch-speaking parts of Nieuw Nederland—Kingston, Albany, Poughkeepsie, &c.—is extremely significant. The *dose* & *dese* & *youse,* of course—& possibly the *w'ich, w'en, momunt,* &c—are probably Irish ('go 'long wid yez', &c)—but the *oi–er* interchange is a tough nut to be cracked by the Grimms & Max Müllers[6] of the future. Another interesting idea of Greet's is that the Southern accent is not negoid. The mass of opinion is against him there, for other regions settled from the same parts of the Motherland as the South most certainly do not shew the same vocal peculiarities. Incidentally—a pretty good thesis would be on the speech of *northern niggers* who never had any link with the South, such as the slaves in Rhode

Island's Narragansett country. Alas—if any evidence exists—how the niggers in Nieuw Nederland spoke any or all of its 18 linguistic variants. By the way—did you know that the savant who started the present continent-wide survey of American dialects—Prof. Hans Kurath—has recently come from Yale to Brown? He lives in Blackstone Blvd. in an apartment house whose back yard abuts on that of my aunt's apartment house in Slater Ave.

And so it goes. Season's best wishes to you & to the family & the stubbletje cats!

Yr obt servt

Grandpa

Notes

1. HPL refers to the historian Hendrik Willem van Loon (1882–1944). See further letter 105.
2. James Truslow Adams (1878–1949), American historian. HPL may be referring to his landmark volume *The Epic of America* (1931).
3. Apparently a booklet about Kakiat, a settlement in the town of Clarkstown, in Rockland County. The name derives from the Kakiat Indians.
4. Walter Goodnow Everett (1860–1937), professor of Latin, philosophy, and natural theology from 1890 to 1930 at Brown University. His wife was Harriet M. (Cleveland) Everett (1860–?).
5. Charles Augustus Baylis (1902–1975), professor of philosophy at Brown (1927–49).
6. Friedrich Max Müller (1823–1900), German-born philologist and Orientalist who lived in Britain for most of his life. One of the founders of the discipline of comparative religion.

[84]   [AHT]

Woden's Day
[January 27, 1933]

Jonckheer:—

"The Heads at Gyrwy" is great—real Dunsanian stuff! It has atmosphere & suggestion—& I didn't notice any typographical breaks. If it has any fault, it is that of diffuseness—yet even that is a typical element of folklore, of which this tale is presumably an imitation. An editor might suggest that you pare down the prologue slightly, in order to throw all the emphasis on the fate of Gyrwy itself—& (perhaps) that you somewhat simplify the manifestations of the horror in order to promote that *directness* which makes for maximum tensity. Some might claim that the shudders are laid on a bit thickly—& that not all of their aspects are sufficiently coördinated & interdependent—but I would hardly make such a point myself, especially in view of the folklore setting. Many features of this tale are magnificently weird in their suggestion—especially the mounds remaining from some *utterly* unhuman race, & the *slight* unhumanness of the people of Gyrwy. It was a great idea having the decayed huts of the Gyrwians still remaining in the time of Dwerga—through this point might possibly have been enhanced by having them *less numerous*. You could speak of certain huts in Dwerga—ruined & shunned—whose details & proportions are oddly disquieting, & which are awesomely whispered to have survived from the immemorial & half-fabulous Gyrwy. The atmosphere of menace hanging over Dwerga is finely evoked—so convincingly, in fact, that I shall entertain no hope of finding Dwerga when I explore the upper reaches of the River Skai, above Ulthar & just out of sight of Hatheg-Kla.[1] But I shall pause long before that rock & the tale writ thereon in a tongue to which no key exists outside certain hints in the dreaded Necronomicon of the mad Arab Abdul Alhazred. The tale now goes forward to Solomon Kane—who I am sure will echo my own pleasure & appreciation.

I think you'll find I'm right on old Pete's surname.[2] He was born at Wesel, in the Prussian Rhineland, of Huguenot or Walloon parentage; & the only alternative form of his name I have ever seen is the Germanic Minnewit—whose final vowel confirms the probability that the original French form (perhaps retained & perhaps readopted by the bearer) was *Minuit*. The terpsichorean variant[3] is a new one to me, & in my opinion can be no more than an accidentally repeated error. *Nova Belgica* seems much more logical & consistent than the other forms I recall seeing. It is of course adjectival—doubtless implying an accompanying *Terra*. Incidentally—it seems to me the Belgians themselves have a sort of adjectival name for their country . . . . *Belgique*, is it not? All this undoubtedly springs from the Roman usage, whereby the low countries were known as *Gallia Belgica*—or Gaul of the Belgae. As for *Novum Eboracum* (locative = Novi Eboraci)—for Gawd's sake *don't* use it for the *Dutch* period or you'll be pulling a frightful boner!!! *Eboracum*—as you ought to know from Britanno-Roman history—is *YORK;* hence is applicable only after His Britannick Majesty's arm'd forces took over the province from your revered forefathers. God Save the King! This name is undoubtedly a Romanised form of the Celtick *Eburac*, signifying a town on a river-bank or confluence of waters. I thought damn near everyone recalled Eboracum as the leading town of Britannia Romana—seat of the Sixth & Ninth Legions, & residence of the Imperator when in the province. It was at Eboracum that L. Septimius Severus & Constantius Chlorus died; & here in all probability that Constantinus, who fastened the Christian superstition upon the Empire, was born.

As for Secy. Adams's heraldick generalisation—as a matter of fact it *isn't* 100% correct, although it may be 98% so. One complete refutation exists in the *Cranston* family of Rhode Island—descended from the ancient Scottish house of *Cranstoun*. In 1723, four years before his death, Gov. Samuel Cranston (he with whom Lord Ballamont once corresponded concerning the harbourage of pirates in Narragansett Bay) became dissatisfied with the loose way in which arms were displayed by sundry gentlemen of this colony; & made application to the Lyon King at Arms in Edinburgh for a verification of the device borne by himself, father, & grandfather. The Scottish dignitary found that the arms were amply justified in the main; & in 1724 issued a certificate of verification—in which, however, there was some slight modification to signify the American branch of the family. Any direct descendant of Samuel Cranston in the male line would, I assume, be as perfectly entitled to use these arms as any Cranston who ever lived—though some descendants would be technically expected to employ variations signifying cadet branches of the house. Cranstons are still numerous in Rhode Island—one of them having two years ago married a gentlewoman resident in this house. The arms of the Tyler family of Rhode Island (which we copied in 1927 at the library) were issued by the Herald's College *after* the migration to America; hence (tho' more *recent*) are fully as *authentic* as those of any Cranston, Winthrop, or Saltonstall. This is not, however, the case with most—for as I mentioned at the time, the Rhode Island house of Hazard really has no *proved* link with the Hazard or Hassard stock whose arms (with the scallops) they have used continuously for nearly 300 years. However—that continuous unjustified usage is something all in itself. But below the M & D line the story is altogether different. Descent is there kept very clear—so much so that in the 1880's one of the Fairfaxes of Virginia actually succeeded to a Baronage & went to England to become Lord Fairfax.

W. Paul Cook was here last Saturday & Sunday—looking splendidly. He has certainly made a great physical comeback. Next Sat. & Sun. I am going to Boston to see him—& we may go up to Haverhill to see Tryout Smith.

Best wishes—& hoping Quebeck won't freeze you!

—Grandpa

P.S. "The Shadowy Thing"[4] was not so hot—although it did have a monstrously ghoulish passage toward the end. I'd hardly advise you or Belknap to re-borrow it unless you have some idle hours to kill. It is now back with Arturo unless the P.O. done us doit.

Later Wednesday

Jonckheer:—

Just recd. Wilmington article, which is of the greatest interest to me. Some day I must stop off there when on the road betwixt north & south. I've noticed several old houses from the stagecoach. Can't find any mistakes in the article—except a "minu*et*" for "Minuit", & a "with" on the last page where "at" ought to be. If you have GW expressing pleasure *with* a seedling pear, you obviously imply that he gave his host a pear to express pleasure—which does not seem to me the real intent of the sentence in the light of the context.

As for the Nov. Belg. matter—I can't for the life of me be certain what the correct form is; for although I've seen it on old maps & documents, I can't find any example in my files. Your version is clearly wrong as a nominative, though. What we ordinarily see—with *Belgii*—is in the *locative* case; meaning *at or in* New Netherland. Now this implies *Belgium* as the nominative—which would superficially suggest *Novum* as the corresponding adjective; but since the names of countries are generally feminine, I have a vague idea that the form *Nova-Belgium* was generally current, giving rise to the locative form *Novae-Belgii*. But "Nova Belgii" is an impossible contradiction. If I had more time I would look this up at the library—in fact, I will the first moment I can. Or you might find some clue somewhere. Any old Dutch map of the region ought to help. Damnably sorry I haven't the data at my finger-tips!

And don't forget to let me have the *Star* with the printed article!

Yr obt Servt
Theobaldus

Notes

1. These imaginary locales are cited in various of HPL's "Dunsanian" tales of 1920f.
2. Peter Minuit (1580?–1638), director of the Dutch colony of New Netherland (1626–31).
3. I.e., minuet.
4. By H. B. Drake.

[85] [ALS, JHL]

Feby. 18[, 1933]

Jonckheer:—

Effusive gratitude! Sure—send all the maps you can swipe, for I'm a great hand at spreading the gospel of antiquarianism. Really, it's a tremendously attractive layout, & I think I'll write to the creator as suggested. Do you think it would offend him if I mentioned that what he calls Old "Briton" Church is really BRUTON, & that Madam Washington did *not* live at Kenmore (which wasn't called that then, anyhow) with her daughter, but had a cottage in Charles St. near by (now open as museum) brought her by son George? There used to be a shaded path betwixt the houses, but it is now gone—intervening streets having been cut through. I wish your Texaco outfit would cover New England in the same way—a map with Boston near the middle of the right-hand edge could show, on the same scale, a surprising amount of historic material. Nor would a similar map of the New-York & Philadelphia zone—from about Kingston on the north to Chester or Wilmington on the south—be at all bad.

Congrats on the genealogical discovery! You must feel as much exultation as I did when we completed the Rathbone line in Room 328 three years ago. I vow I'll look up that Briggs–Welles dope, as promised, just as soon as I'm really active again in the spring. I haven't been out of the house since dropping you the card, & was out only twice in the month before that!

Thanks prodigiously for the cuttings. Ancient Quebec is certainly Gallior Gallis ipsis[1]—it is really a surviving cultural fragment of old pre-revolutionary Bourbon France. I blush to admit that I never heard tell on Asy Wood afore, despite my mountainous admiration for unspoiled & Georgian Wickford. I am proud that our Rhode Island breed (we were *all* like that once!) has continued to produce such virile specimens down to a relatively recent date!

Yes—I noticed Goderich on the key map, & hope I can get around there some time. So damn much to see, & so damn little cash to see it on! That's life!

Thanks for *Texaco Topics*—a highly prepossessing sheet which ought to prove very congenial to members of the corporate family. That Tappan picture of your mother's birthplace brought up many a pleasant memory of 1928—I can see the graceful tower of the "Reform Church" (as the postcards will have it) in the background. Haven't been to Tappan since that day, but hope to get around there again some time. There must be bus service through it from various west-shore points reachable by ferry.

Hear the gang had a meeting up at Sonny's lately, & that good old Leeds is back—& as a Coney Island barker! This was, I believe, your first sight of him. I'd like to get another glimpse of him myself—haven't set eyes on him for five solid years. Guess I'd know him, though Belknap says he's aged very noticeably.

Well—thanks & best wishes. Hope you had time to correct that Pilgrim-Puritan error in the proofs, for New England readers would pounce on that. I still wait [*sic*] the finished article with eagerness.

Article in Sunday's Journal on post-revolutionary printed bookplates. If I can't get you a duplicate for keeps, I'll lend you my one file copy.

Regards & all that—Grandpa Theobaldus

Notes

1. "More French than the French themselves."

[86]   [ALS][1]

[c. early May 1933]
after May 15
66 COLLEGE ST.

Jonckheer:—

Do you know the little yellow Georgian house with a fan-carved Colonial doorway & railed flight of steps at the back of a court off College St. behind the marble John Hay Library? Well, you'd better, because your Grandpa O'Casey is going to live there! In a real Georgian home at last! My aunt decided that we'd better double up, & on May 1 the place was vacant for inspection. Did the Old Gentleman vote for it? Don't be absurd! Boy, what a place! You certainly ought to remember it considering your one-time connexion with College Hill. In the read is a village-like garden—at a higher level than the front of the house. The doorway is like my bookplate come to life, though of a slightly later period (circa 1800) with side-lights & with fan-carving instead of a fanlight. The upper flat we have taken contains 5 rooms besides bath & kitchenette nook on the main (2nd) floor, plus 2 attic storerooms—one of which is so quaint that I wish I could have it for an extra den! I shall have a large study & a small bedroom on the south side, with my working table under a west window affording a splendid view of the outspread roofs of the lower town. The interior is as fascinating as the exterior—with colonial fireplaces, mantels, and chimney cupboards, curving Georgian staircase, wide floor boards, old-fashion'd latches, small-paned windows, six-panel doors, rear wing with floor at a different level (3 steps down), quaint attic stairs, &c.—a perfect Novanglian counterpart of places like the Dyckman house, or of places familiar to you in Old Rockland Co. After admiring such throughout a long lifetime, it will surely be magical and dreamlike to be *living in one.* You surely must get around this way and see Grandpa in his new & appropriate quarters! But moving will be hell. I shall begin transferring my goods soon, & expect to have the major shift on the 15th. Then will come my aunt's moving. I doubt if the cursed siege will be over till the middle of June. I am now bidding the world farewell preparatory to entering upon the ordeal. Have purchased 3 new bookcases & a cabinet for filing papers.

Regards—

Grandpa van Casey

P.S. This place has steam heat & hot water piped from the John Hay. It is owned by the college. Rent only $40 per month—just what I've paid for my room alone.

Notes

1. The floor plan shown is from AHT, and drawn by in-house staff. The image of the front door in AHT was not used, and instead is from the Grill catalogue.

[87]   [ALS, JHL]

Prospect Terrace
—July 7, 1933

Jonckheer:—

Thanks for *De Halve Maen*—which looks to me like a particularly fine issue. Thanks also for the contribution-invitation—though I fear I am too tied up this summer to set my mind to anything except necessities. Indeed, I'll be damn lucky if I avoid a nervous breakdown!

Yes—we're moved—& the colonial atmosphere of the new abode is fascinating & inspiring—but list to the ensuing tale of disaster!

On June 14 my aunt broke her ankle while descending the stairs in answer to the doorbell during my absence. Doctor . . . . specialist . . . . ambulance to R.I. Hospital . . . x-ray . . . . ether . . . . setting in plaster cast . . . . room in Ward K for 3 weeks . . . . . & now (day before yesterday) a transfer home again in the ambulance with a prospect of 3 more weeks flat in bed with a nurse in constant attendance, after which will come an indefinite period on crutches. It's a great life!

Naturally, all this has kept me desperately busy—& I am especially tied down just now, having to be on duty every afternoon while the nurse goes out. I can't concentrate on any task when interruption may come at any moment—hence must remain virtually at a standstill till the routine relaxes. Add to this the terrific financial outgo—which raises the gravest apprehensions regarding the future of the household unless I can find some dependable source of revenue—& you have all the materials for a first-class breakdown! But at that, my aunt has the worst of it by so wide a margin that groans from others are scarcely in order!

Your non-mention of the N.A.P.A. convention leads me to believe you did not attend—which is rather deplorable in view of Sonny Belknap's report of a general good time. I had hoped to attend until almost the last moment, but couldn't manage it in the end. W. Paul Cook stopped briefly on his way there; seeing #66 & its colonial atmosphere for the first time, & promising to come again later in the summer.

But after all, I had a sort of convention of my own, for during the same period my Georgian hearth was honoured by no less a guest than Malik Taus, the Peacock Sultan—otherwise E. Hoffmann Price of Weird Tales fame, who is visiting in Irvington, N.Y., & rattled hither in his new bargain Juggernaut . . . a 1928 Ford of uncertain condition. We had a delightful time. On two occasions young Brobst came over, & one night the three of us sat up till 7 a.m. discussing literature & philosophy.

Best of all, Price brought his Juggernaut into the service of antiquarian exploration, enabling me to see *for the first time in my life* Rhode Island's "South County"—from which (though a third of my ancestry comes from there) lack of public transportation facilities had hitherto debarred me. This region—

which before the Revolution had large plantations with many blacks in the southern manner—has always been famed from its scenery, though none of this scenery is accessible from the main highways traversed by coaches.

On this occasion we visited the ancient snuff-mill where Gilbert Stuart was born, the famous old Rowland Robinson manor-house amidst its gigantic willows, the deserted, vine-embowered "Glebe" of the Rev. James MacSparran (1727), the "Hannah Robinson Rock"[1] with its peerless vista of winding river, lush green fields, mystical woodlands, white headland church, & shimmering seacoast, & the marvellously unspoiled colonial village of Kingston, called "Little Rest" in the good old days. This is the country where all my Hazards, Caseys, Wilcoxes, Places, &c. come from. As an "heraldicist" you would have been interested in the carved escallop (from the Hazard arms) over the door of the old Robinson house—Hazard being one of the important contributing lines in the Robinson blood. The lecturer at the Stuart mill was a delightfully intelligent old yeoman who explained everything & started the vast water-wheel & restored mill for our benefit.

I trust that all flourishes in Rockland Co. Today is one after my own heart—94°—but I have lately been opprest by the cold. Had my old Clinton St. oil heater fixed the other day. Regards & blessings—Grandpa O'Casey.

P.S. Here's the circular of a brochure which ought to increase your appreciation of Klarkash-Ton. Hope you'll send for it—it's really great stuff.

Notes

1. Hannah Robinson (1746–1773) liked to gaze out at Narragansett Bay from a large boulder at Tower Hill Road in South Kingston, RI. She had eloped with her teacher, Peter Simon, whom her father had forbidden her to see, and they reconciled over the matter only after Hannah had become deathly ill.

[88]   [ALS]

July 17, 1933

Jonckheer:—

Apropos of your suggestion for a *Halve Maen* article, & my fear that strain & congestion might prevent me from preparing such, I enclose a recent extract which you may appraise for yourself. It probably violates all your space & style demands, leaves out half of what it ought to include, & otherwise departs from what is wanted—but at the moment it is about the best I can produce. The question is whether it is better or worse than nothing—or precisely equivalent to that modest quantity. You can do with it exactly what you like—even unto chucking it half-unread into the waste-basket (assuming that the hieroglyphics permit as much as a half reading). If you want to abridge it, go ahead. Better still—you might simply use the data (if it isn't too stale for critical-minded Hollanders) as the basis for an article of your own. But in any case I don't want to fall down utterly on the proposition, even though I lately feared I might have to. Good luck to the H. M., with or without the article!

My aunt has now begun sitting in a chair each day—being lifted thither & back—though the plaster cast can't be off for at least 10 days or so. This sure is a hell of a summer.

Yrs for Niew Nederland & New England
———Hermanus Pietersen van Casey

[Enclosure: "Some Dutch Footprints in New England."]

[89]   [ALS]

Colonial Shades of #66
July 22, 1933

Jonckheer:—

Well, well, well son—Grandpa sure is glad to hear that the Dutch-Yankee article suited your requirements so aptly! Hope your secretary-censor will have an equally kind opinion. As I said before—change as much or as little as you like. Never mind my spelling—I believe all magazines & papers have their "style sheet" of individual usage, to which all contributions must conform. "Connexion" is a very old and common usage, and remains the dominant form throughout the Mother Land and a good part of the Dominions . . . God Save the King! But as for Adriaen Block's Dutch—if I were you, I'd let it alone. Remember what you told me about diverse dialects. Of course, Adriaen wasn't a Nieuw Nederlander—but presumably there must have been some flexibility of usage back home. The form *een rodtlich Eylandken* (get this straight—een rodtlich Eylandken) is quoted precisely as given (spelling, capitalisation, and all) in at least two Rhode-Island histories—Field's and Richman's, and I never heard any other version. It may have been bum Dutch—Jersey Dutch, or what the hell—but the chances are that it's what honest Adriaen, bluff old sea-dog that he was, put down on paper, take it or leave it. It is my impression that modern historians quote verbatim et literatim from some account of Block's, printed contemporaneously with himself. There has long been a *popular folklore impression* 'that Block named the island of Aquidneck *Roodt Eylandt*'—a thing perpetuated in a work as semi-authoritative as Munro's "Picturesque Rhode-Island"—but modern serious works ignore this since it errs in two points. Actually, the island Block called *rodtlich* (or what have you) was *not Aquidneck* but (by Block's own account) one to the west of Aquidneck—the name being transferred later through confusion; and also, the name given came not through a direct proper-noun christening, but merely through a common adjectival description . . . "a reddish islet". If I were you, I'd quote as given unless some definite contrary evidence comes up. If you can dig up any explanatory data, so much the better—nothing boosts an article like a learned editorial footnote. If the given phrase is *too* bad, according to *any* valid dialectic standard, you can justify it and yourself by means of a bracketed [sic] after the quotation. But this is really a minor and pedantic point. The important thing is that, almost undoubtedly one of the foremost of the New-England colonies received a permanent name of Dutch origin.

Do as you like about the derived words and culinary products—I know that many are subject to dispute. But I think you're wrong in attributing *boss* to African Boer influence. In the first place, Bartlett's "Dictionary of Americanisms" (Ed. of 1877, p. 59) says of *boss,* "The word probably originated in New York, and is now used in many parts of the U.S." In the second place, *boss* was undoubtedly known in New England during the first half of the 19th century—a date apparently precluding any substantial South African influence. What contact had Americans with the Boers in 1840 or before? Even if England had picked up the word from its settlers in South Africa, it would not have been very likely to spread here unless of great popularity on British soil—and the fact is, that America seems to have had the word long before England. Bartlett records *boss* as an Americanism, and even today it has not the wide usage in England that it has here. How could America get a South-Africanism *ahead* of England? It is true that the Dutch settled Cape Colony as early as 1652, but what trade had Americans with these Afrikanders? I may be wrong, but I believe that the bulk of the American sea-trade had to do with the gold, ivory, and slave coasts of West Africa, far north of any region which could know Boer influence. When we reflect on the *very slight* connexion [sic] of Americans with the African Dutch prior to 1840, and on their *very close* connexion [sic] with the New-Netherland Dutch, we cannot but draw conclusions favourable to Bartlett's opinion. If, however, any *new evidence* pointing to the African derivation of *boss* has been unearthed since Bartlett's day, I will cheerfully accept correction—for I admit that my statement was a very laymanlike one, unverified by the fruits of recent scholarship. All I know is that, a generation ago, *boss* was usually considered by New Englanders as a Nieuw-Nederland importation.

[. . .]

    Yr obt hble Servt
        Petrus O'Casey

[90]   [ANS postcard][1]

[Postmarked Onset, Mass.,
25 July 1933]

Well, here we are on a *meerstead*[2] in the old Plymouth Colony, checking up on Ike de Raisieres & planning the Bolshevik revolution. You ought to be in on this Kalem meeting! Shall return Wednesday—with young Lenin & party continuing to the bouweries of Mannehattoes. ¶ By the way—it popped into my head yesterday whilst on the stage-coach that Dr. John Clarke[3] of Newport, obtainer of the 1663 King Charles Charter for R.I. & great statesman & physician in general, *was educated in Holland*. Ought that to go into the *Halve Maen* article? If so, leave space in your copy & I'll work it in. ¶ Aunt duly progresses—may be up on crutches by end of present week.

Pax vobiscum—Grandpa O'Casey

[*On front:*] The Curse Wheel!

Notes

1. *Front:* The Old Discarded Mill, Cape Cod, Mass. [HPL's note refers to the water-wheel shown in the photo, alluding to WBT's story of that name.]

2. The land within the boundaries of a farm; a farmstead or farm.

3. John Clarke (1609–1676), co-founder of the Colony of Rhode Island and Providence-Plantations.

[91]   [ALS]

Thor's Dæg
[3? August 1933]

Jonkheer:—

Yrs. duly arrived—just after my adieu to my distinguish'd & mountainous guest[1] . . . whose joint postcard with me doubtless reached you. We had a great time—Jake's, Maxfield's, rural exploration, & a boat trip to Newport.

As for Mynheer van Twiller's[2] dimensions—I never met the genial soul, but merely repeat hearsay. This is what C. B. Todd says in his "Brief History of N.Y. City" (Am. Book Co. 1899), p. 23.

> "But, burlesque aside [he had been quoting Knickerbocker] Van Twiller was a grotesque figure, a mountain of flesh, slow & narrow of mind, with a petty spirit, & a burgomaster's fondness for good dinners & sound wine."

Is Mr. Todd too much of an Anglo-Saxon outsider to be an authority? All I know is what I *read* in the papers &c! Glad John Clarke is good material.

For Dutch tenure in Maine, my *immediate* source is one of the really important historical works issued by the State St. Trust Co. of Boston—"France & New England" Vol. III—by Allan Forbes & Paul F. Cadman (1929). See pp. 70–80. The site of Fort Pentagoët, Castine, Maine, is covered with tablets which refer to the Dutch such as the following:

> FROM THIS BASE OF ATTACK
> Extending to the West
> FORT PENTAGOËT
> Defended by Captain de Chambly, Baron de Saint-Castin his Lieutenant & 38 soldiers & fur traders was carried by assault August 10, 1674 by Captain JURRIAN AERNOUTS & 110 Seamen from the Dutch frigate *Flying Horse* after one of the most desperately contested of the many engagements fought upon this peninsula.

[. . .]

Notes

1. HPL refers to Helen V. Sully, who had visited Providence the previous month.
2. Wouter van Twiller (1606–1654), who succeeded Peter Minuit as director of New Netherland (1633–38).

[92]   [ALS, in private hands]

August 18[, 1933]

Jonckheer:—

Glad that some more illustrious Dutchmen liked the article. I've made the note about the author (if such must appear) a little less exaggerative of the mediocre facts, but I haven't a single idea to add to the fund of Doughnut lore. Thanks for the glimpse of the interesting cutting. Sorry—as I said before—that his High Mightiness Mijnheer op Dyck has left the terrestrial scene.

As for space considerations—I'm damned if *I* can see any excision which can be made; but as I said at the outset, if *you* can think of any cutting down just go ahead & leave my name off the thing. As you see, a proper inclusion of the Pentagoët point even *increases* the length—but I don't know any remedy for the trouble. In adding to the R.I.-section you'll notice that I mentioned Sam Gorton's sailing from N.A. This entire sentence (within pencil brackets) can be omitted if desired[1]—& for that matter, the Clark item doesn't absolutely need to be included. Why not list your additional Dutch-NE contacts in an editorial note?

About Pentagoët—if it is such a high spot, possibly it ought to have a fuller account—hence the enclosed. As you'll see, the duration of Dutch tenure (Aug. '74–Nov. '76) was *more* than two exact years. I guess the Dutch evacuation date is watertight enough, insomuch as it is so given on a tablet erected in Castine. (vide text) The reason it doesn't really conflict with popular histories is that 1674 was indeed the last date that the Dutch laid claim to *English* soil in America; the Penobscot region being then settled as much by the French as by the English, with its outposts constantly changing hands. It was the *French*, not the *English*, that Aernauts conquered at Pentagoët—

indeed, he was aided by John Rhoads of Boston, an English pilot. Pentagoët had once (1629) been held by the Plymouth-colony English, but the French dispossessed them in 1635. In 1654 the English held the Maine coast again, not giving it up till 1670. But in 1670 the Maine treaty of Breda recognised Pentagoët as part of French Acadia—hence the French returned, planting a colony under M. deGrande Fontaine and eventually placing Sieur de Chambly in charge of the garrison. At this period Pentagoët was the capital of Acadia—so that it naturally tends to be reckoned with French Canada rather than with the Anglo-American colonies. In looking up the Aernauts incident in various books around here, I find that *some* of the older accounts *do* speak of a Dutch possession of the mouth of the Penobscot around 1674–6. I don't know what Charlevoix says of the degree of the Dutch claim, for I haven't his full text—what I quoted from being itself in a quoted extract. Later we might look up Charlevoix, if the matter is worth a search. However, the tablet at Castine called Pentagoët the seat of government "of the Province of New Holland, the capture of which by Dawn de St. Austin—Nov. 1676—ended Dutch authority in America." Take it or leave it! Another tablet—also in Perkins St.—marks the site of the Grander–Fontaine settlement, & speaks of St. Castin's expulsion of the settlers "for maintaining allegiance given to the Dutch after the capture of Ft. Pentagoët". So all in all it looks as if you Hollanders had a genuine—even tho' brief—sway at Castine. Incidentally, we took it from the Frogs in 1693, & it had one or two more shuttlings back & forth betwixt France & England, when it finally became ours. Pentagoët is the French way of rendering an Indian name meaning "Entrance of the (Penobscot) river". This is a very fascinating region for research—coinciding with the site of the fabulous city of Norumbega, of which the earliest explorers heard so much. Well, anyhow, here's the amplified text—do what you like with it!

Yes—*Fantasy Fan* would be glad of "Gyrwy", I'm sure.[2] It's going to specialize in the weird now, for Editor Hornig has just been hired as managing editor of *Wonder Stories* & doesn't want to duplicate his scientifiction activities. Also note three new *paying* markets for weird stuff. *Astounding Stories* has been revived by Street & Smith 79-89—7thj Ave., NYC. as a weird magazine paying 1¢ per word *on acceptance*. Wandrei has sold them a story.[3] It seems likely to have a literary quality higher than anything else of the kind yet out. editor Orlin Tremaine; Asso. Ed., Desmond Hall. Shorts up to 7500 words, novelettes to 15,000—no serials. This is the best bet. Another allegedly reliable editor out for weird stuff is Rogers Terrill, Popular Publications, 205 E. 42nd St, N.Y.C. he pays 1¢ per word promptly on publication. Third & not so hot— Jay Pub. Co., 125 W. 45th St. ½¢ per wd—tardily, after publication. Congrats on "Creature Abroad"—I shall be looking for it. Wright asked me for a list of friends when the "Witch House" appeared, but I doubt if it argues decline. He did the same thing back in 1925. Knopf has asked to see more of my stuff—but I doubt if anything comes of the matter.

No news hereabouts; my aunt's cast came off some time ago, but she is not yet up on crutches except for brief practice periods. Nurse still here, & my own imprisonment (except when the nurse can be persuaded to stay in afternoons) likely to continue. Damn tough on the nerves for all hands!

Morton has been doing some extensive genealogical work in Boston—you & he are surely rivals in ancestor-exhumation!

Blessings—& do what you like with the enclosed.

        Yr obt servt
         Grandpa

P.S. Why not write Castine Chamber of Commerce for dope about Dutch towns of Main coast?

[P.P.S.] Have noticed your recent golf controversies in the press. Good luck!

Notes

1. It was.
2. The *Fantasy Fan* was edited by Charles D. Hornig (1916–1999) and ran for 18 issues (September 1933–February 1935). It contained much work by HPL but nothing by WBT.
3. Probably "The Man Who Never Lived," *Astounding Stories* (March 1934).

[93]   [ALS]

                                    Sept. 25, 1933

Jonckheer:—

     Ædepol! You people had better have a staff research bureau, & not contaminate yourselves with unknown articles from the ignorant outside laity!

As to the latest point, I don't like to seem unduly critical, but that change as suggested is so completely *redundant* that I would recommend something else if possible. What needs doing, of course, is simply to remove the perplexity of those who can't believe the Dutch had any hold on North America after the Treaty of Westminster (Oct. 31, 1674). Therefore, the logical thing is not to repeat the just-asserted fact that the French took the fort, but simply to rub in the fact that the Dutch were on hand over time.

Accordingly, what I'd advise—& what I am writing into the carbon—is the following new version of the whole passage in question: (beginning immediately after the words ". . . . submitted to the invaders.")

In November, 1676, two years after the second and peaceable transfer of New Netherland to the English by the Treaty of Westminster (Oct. 31, 1674), a French force under Baron de St. Castin recaptured the stronghold, expelling the settlers because of their readily granted allegiance to the Dutch. Thus for over 24 months after the treaty with England by which the Netherlands nominally resigned all claim to North American soil in exchange for a recognition of their rights in the West Indies and in Surinam, an actual Dutch hold on this continent existed.

You can't get round that. *Any* damn fool can see what that means. Hope it's all right, but let me know when you or somebody else wants more changes. Quite a game! Use your own judgment about *Het Vliegende Parde*.[1] I wish some of your wise guys would take the time to nose the whole episode out of the obscure records in which its details seem to be buried. I wouldn't mind the reading the real close-up dope on the affair! Incidentally—by [. . .]

    Yrs for accuracy & clearness—Grandpa.

P.S. I learn from Klarkash-Ton that a new low-paying weird (scientifiction) magazine is about to appear—UNUSUAL STORIES.[2]

Notes

1. The frigate *The Flying Horse*. It is not mentioned in "Some Dutch Footprints in New England."
2. *Unusual Stories* was one of several semi-professional magazines edited and published by William L. Crawford (1911–1984). It ran for 3 issues (March 1934, May/June 1935, Winter 1935). It contained no work by HPL or WBT.

[94]   [ANS postcard][1]

[Postmarked Providence, R.I.,
17 October 1933]

Well—it looks good to me! Since it's too late for correction, I haven't had the heart to read it through for errors! As for the matter of copies—you know what a hog I am! The more the better. A dozen if you could slip across that many without incurring the restraining hands of the Schents & Schapens! ¶ Have dragged out my 1907 #2 Brownie & taken some shots of 66 College. Will show you results before long. ¶ Good autumn weather—have taken hikes nearly every afternoon, & had 2 good motor rides with kindly disposed persons acting as host to my aunt. ¶ Aunt much better. We got down to the School of Design Museum the other day—they've opened a splendid new formal garden in the interior courtyard. ¶ Good luck on your voyage!
Yr obt grandpa

Sorry for that *the* before *Flying Horse*.[2]

Notes

1. *Front:* Old Powder House, Somerville, Mass.
2. See *CE* 4.254.

[95]   [ALS]

[Hotel Lexington . . .
New York, N.Y.]

Oct. 28[, 1933]

Greetings, Jonkheer:—

Haven't seen my *Halve Maens* yet, but they'll doubtless show up presently. Looking over the proof I noticed some misprints. West *India* instead of Ind*ies,* & only one *c* in *buccaneers.* Tough & ironic luck the text shouldn't receive the same fine-tooth-combing that the substance did. But maybe some of these things were caught at the 11th hour.

Thanks for the glimpse of the Niles article, herewith returned. I don't think the general ignorance of N Y's second Dutch period is as great as he assumes. By the way—he ought not to put an "s" on New-Netherland. Hope he'll enjoy the *Halve Maen* article.

Here's a shot of my colonial doorway with my aunt in it. If you want it for your morgue, it's yours—otherwise, return rather than dump. As you see, I'm trying to live up to my bookplate! Will let you see some other snaps of the house when I get duplicates—but you probably remember it through its proximity to the John Hay.

Have taken some long rural walks this autumn—many to places I never saw before. Discovered an ancient 17th century house (with great pilastered stone chimney & well with perfectly working sweep) which *may* be an ancestral home-stead of mine. Its occupant believes it is the Thomas Clemence (my ancestor) house, built in 1654, though others think it is the Edward Manton house (1680).

Saw a demonstration of *Television* at the Outlet[1] last Saturday. Vague & flickering, like the cinema in 1898 or thereabouts.

I may see you next month, if you are in your accustomed haunts. Sonny has invited me down to 230 if his mother's present illness improves—& my aunt is now entirely self-sufficient at 66.

Patriarchal blessings—
Grandpa

Notes

1. The Outlet Company (formed in 1891) was a corporation based in Providence that owned holdings in both retail and broadcasting, including WJAR radio and television.

[96]   [ALS, JHL]

All-Hallows [31 October 1933]

Jonckeer:—

I mourn at the news of Stubbletje! Has all the countryside been scoured? 2½ weeks is a long time, yet think of the arctic explorers who have turned up months after hope was lost. Sympathetic greetings are forwarded from the Kappa Alpha Tau (Κομπσῶν Ἀιλούρων Τάξις),[1] the fraternity which meets on the roof of a shed across the garden below my west windows. This is a highly important organisation of at least 6 or 7 members, whose President (huge black & white) has come to know me so well that he rolls over & purrs like a kitten whenever I approach him, & whose Vice-President (equally huge tiger) occasionally calls on me.

Tough luck about the misprints—especially in view of the microscopic treatment of the article's pre-typographical stages—but it seems to take a lot of separate readings to get a long galley of text into really accurate shape. Last summer I was exasperated by the blunders in my W.T. story[2]—where in one place "magical LORE" was rendered "magical LOVE", whilst in another place "KNOWN element" appeared as "HUMAN element." This sort of slip, where the misprinted version makes a false & misleading reading instead of appearing frankly as a mistake, is of course the worst of all. Hope the wrong meeting-date won't cause any hapless patroons to congregate about the tavern stoep on Thanksgiving in the hope of encountering the jovial assemblage held two days before! With your rush of work you certainly are amply alibi'd for all such details. Nothing but repeated readings by different persons will really clear up a text.

No—*Unusual Stories* is a wholly separate magazine from *The Fantasy Fan* . . . . & will probably prove a far less amateurish-looking one. The editor spoke very enthusiastically about your contribution, & if he is ever able to pay authors, you will undoubtedly reap the reward of having coöperated in the lean early days. Smith, Derleth, & I have sent in several things—as also to *The Fantasy Fan*.

Keep the picture of the doorway—& here's one of the whole house which you can likewise keep if your morgue would really find it a permanent asset. You must remember the place—though I think it had blinds on the windows (which gave it a slightly different look) when you last saw it. That 1907 Brownie #2 isn't half bad as cheap cameras go, though I doubt if it would compete with your new device. I shall have to take it on certain expeditions—though most of the old towns I visit have postcards which virtually cover the whole ground. In Charleston, indeed, there's an old man named Johnson in Hassell St. who sells large prints—real photographs of more than postcard size—for a nickel apiece (less than the Brownie pictures would cost me), & has a range of subjects as wide as I could ever think up myself. One thing I ought to do is to catch some old Providence landmarks before they perish. I wish I had taken pictures of that intensely colonial region (a nigger slum) at the foot of Olney St., now swept away to make room for the boulevarding of N. Main St. The old S. Water St. warehouses were pretty well celebrated by camera, brush, & graver before they went.

Concerning punctuation—I never bother about its fine points, because editors usually hash things up to suit themselves. There are, of course, a few basic essentials which have to be managed carefully, but the minuter details are largely trivial, custom-governed, & subject to diverse usage. No two people punctuate alike, but I don't begin to kick until I come across some text with the ultra-modern affectation of underpunctuation. Then I see red—for many of these almost commaless texts are actually difficult to follow.

Now about the specific cases you cite. In the appositional matter I'd say that the exact context ought to determine the insertion or absence of commas. Hard & fast blanket rules are never applicable to matters like this. The crucial thing, I judge, is whether the given phrase is *really appositional in spirit*, or is virtually a single composite title like *Jones the Grocer, Richard the Lion-Hearted, Bildad the Shubite*, & so on. You don't say "Alexander, the Great, conquered Persia." In the cited case of Jones, everything depends upon the circumstances. If the statement deals with one of several Joneses known to the persons conversing, & wishes to point out that it was the grocer Jones instead of the stockbroker Jones who was present, it ought to read "Jones, the grocer, was there." On the other hand, if it is known to have reference to a definite individual always thought of in connexion with his business—as John the Shoeman, George the Waiter, Peter the Barber, &c.—then the commas may well be dropped. Whenever the *indefinite article* is used, commas are of course compulsory under all circumstances. It is *always* "Jones, a grocer, was present"—though I've seen ultra-modern texts which defy this sensible rule. As for the insertion of a comma betwixt month & year—I don't think there's any real preference. All one need to do is to try to be uniform—& I don't even try that! When the *day* is included, there *must* be a comma—as *November 15, 1932*. Perhaps the conclusiveness of this usage gives a shade of preference to *November, 1932*. Regarding the comma before the last of a series, I always include it, though aware that some academic usage would dispense with its presence. My reason is rhetorical rather than logical—to preserve the equal vocal time-interval in utterance. Lacking the final comma, one is apt to read "one,—two,—threeandfour." I believe that punctuation ought to mark vocal or rhetorical pauses as well as purely logical divisions, & govern my own usage accordingly. In the other sentence you cite, I would probably say "Reconstruction was necessary, & during its completion an accident happened." This is more like your first than your second version, but it has one comma less than either. Punctuation of this sort is rhetorical . . . . & there is no need for it to be otherwise when the meaning is clear. It is a mistake to regard punctuation as anything but a surface adjunct to language. In ancient times (except for paragraph divisions) it did not exist, & its mutations have been numberless ever since its beginning in the Middle Ages. It has nothing to do with grammar, but is merely a convenient device for clarifying the meaning of written language and making instantly obvious certain relationships whose correct perception would otherwise require considerable attention. About the use of "Esq."—until the close of the 18th Century in both Old & New England it was confined to the members of armigerous families or to persons whose standing in the community was virtually equivalent to armigerousness. Thus the owner of the first globe, telescope, & coach in Providence was *John Merritt, Esq.,* whilst one bought (or rather, *ordered*) shoes of *Mr. Robert Perrigo,* the cordwainer, at the sign of the Boot in Cheapside near the Great Bridge. With the growth of a democratical society it became increasingly difficult to draw the nice distinctions involved in the use of "Esq." & "Mr.", hence several alternative usages grew up. One—the earliest, & still surviving in Great Britain—was to extend the use of "Esq." (especially in addressing envelopes) to virtually anybody above the grade of bootblack or coachman. The other was to give a corresponding extension upward to the term *Mr.* (an extension *downward* had occurred long before, wiping out the "Goodman" of the 17th century), applying it to everyone, & reserving the "Esq." for attorneys & men of notable & exceptional substance or influence. For this latter usage there is really no excuse at all, since there is absolutely nothing in the legal profession to correspond to the idea of quality originally residing in the word "esquire". If lawyers represent quality, than so do professors & artists & scientists & men of education generally. If the term is to survive at all, it must be to represent men of a degree of taste & education which corresponds to that of landed gentry in earlier times. This is logical—even more logical in its deep cultural significance than the pedantic & snobbish attempts of certain purists to restrict "esquire" still to technically armigerous persons. Landholding & armigerousness no longer form the line of distinction betwixt those men of developed personality whom we recognise as "gentlemen", & those less developed individuals whom we cannot so recognise; & if we would perpetrate the use of "esquire" as a quality term, we must apply it in consonance with existing realities rather than in a vacantly archaic or etymological way. I see no reason for departing from the usage customary at the centre of our civilisation—London—hence shall continue to use "Esq." in addressing gentlemen. Nor shall I be too snobbish in borderline cases—for anyone whom we encounter on anything like a plane of equality ought to receive the courtesies due an equal. Thus although I wouldn't address my tailor as Harry Steiner, Esq., or the Waldorf counter man as Constantine Pappadoppoulous, Esq. (if that's his monicker), I certainly would give the designation to anybody (however moderately crude or ignorant) with whom I hold correspondence on literary or amateur journalistic subjects. Good old Tryout (81 last week) may be a quaint child of nature, but he's C. W. Smith, Esq. to me! In recent years I have (I think) noticed a slight increase in the use of "Esq." in the United States, especially by publishing firms & the booksellers who send out catalogues. It is rarely that I get a catalogue addressed without "Esq."

Harking back to date usage—another thing I notice of late is the spread of the form *15 November, 1932* as distinguished from the honest old *Nov. 15* form. This started in Great Britain during the 19th century, (a few cases in the

18th) & has made vast headway there—being perhaps the dominant form to-day. In America it was first used by somewhat affected persons, but it certainly seems to be spreading. I don't & shan't use it—what was good enough for an English gentleman of the 18th century is good enough for me—but if you watch closely you'll notice it oftener & oftener in your morning's mail.

Hope your Texas trip won't be eliminated altogether. Actually, it's all the better to have it in midwinter when the weather up here is utterly intolerable. I, myself, wouldn't take a southern trip unless I could make it last till at least the middle of May—for it's hell to get all accustomed to a civilised temperature & then be shot back into the horrors of the Arctic. It's bad enough in mid-May—I'll never forget how I suffered in 1930 when I hit the chill of Philadelphia after the mildness of Charleston, Richmond, & Fredericksburg.

I'll surely be grateful later on (though there's no hurry) if you can return that epistle with all the data about Nieuw-Amsterdam dialects & Jersey Dutch. It forms a valuable item in any library of Americana, & was surely appreciated during its brief sojourn on my archaic shelves.

Yes—I hope the Bloomingdale visit will pan out. It depends largely on the recovery of Little Belknap's mamma from a recent attack of food-poisoning. If all is well, it might occur within two or three weeks. I'll keep you posted, & hope that we can have some sort of a gang meeting if the thing does materialise. My aunt's improvement makes it quite feasible at this end. The other day she took quite a ride in the street-cars, & seems to be gaining ground constantly despite the continued use of a single cane.

Returning to proofreading—I've just spotted another slip in our article. In the first column there's a redundant parenthesis mark after *Rhode Island* in the place where Block's *rodtlich eylandken* is spoken of. Ought to be a plain comma. The more one reads an average text, the more of these damn things one can spot! By the way—it's too bad some of your doughnut note had to go.[3]

Yesterday was gratifyingly warm—so much so that I took my work out on Prospect Terrace in the afternoon. Today not bad—but one can't depend on anything now.

Blessings & good wishes—Grandpa von Kasje.

Notes

1. "Band of elegant [or well-dressed] cats."
2. "The Dreams in the Witch House."
3. WBT's footnote to HPL's article read as follows when published: "EDITOR'S NOTE: There are some who believe that the Pilgrims brought their doughnut recipe directly from Holland—that the housewives of Leyden obligingly imparted the secret of their cruller recipes to the residents-to-be of New England. The names of cruller, doughnut, and olykoek have become as hopelessly intwined as the dough of the

doughnut itself, which took its name from 'dough-knot'—a long strip of dough twist-ed like a section of rope. The cruller was so called from the Dutch *krullen,* to curl; olykoek, or 'oil cake,' was its popular New Netherland name. Older generations in New England called crullers 'fried cakes' to distinguish them" (p. [4]).

[97]　[ALS, JHL]

March 13, 1934

Jonckheer:—

Your highly interesting communication of the 11th appears to have crossed my card acknowledging the delightful Williamsburg booklet—which I now return with the utmost gratitude & appreciation. I hope to Pegāna I can get to Williamsburg when next I proceed southward. As I may have mentioned, I am invited to Florida May 1st—tho' there is still much fi-nancial uncertainty about my ability to accept. I shan't go unless I can arrange to stop at least briefly in CHARLESTON & St. Augustine. Abundant thanks for the retainable cuttings. My aunt—whose recovery is steady even if at the moment less than gazelle-like in results—is taking an extension course in cen-tury-old Manning Hall. New Orleans street names are surely quaint enough—a Gallic characteristic not without certain analogies (cf. Rue Sault au Matelot) in ancient Quebec.

No—James Ferdinand had not mentioned the bookplate incident. Glad the slip involved no extra expense. Slip me a copy of the finished product when you get a supply—I admired your tentative design immensely, & am anxious to see how it came out in print. If it's anything like your earlier triumphs, the Sage cannot fail to be radiantly satisfied! Incidentally—I guess I spoke on my card about our learned colleague's plunge into the matrimonial abyss—at the Unitar-ian parsonage at Ridgewood, N.J., on March 2, with the worthy Pearl K. Merritt of Brooklyn as a gaoler. I never thought he'd get that far—but I dare say years weaken resistance. Well—I hope he bears up well, & that the new alliance will prove both endurable & reasonably permanent. It ought to be a success if pre-vious consideration & mature reflection count for anything. His new bookplate comes just at the right time to start the new household right!

Congratulations on your *Printer's Ink* article![1] I've noticed scores of quasi-heraldic advertising & trade-mark devices, & dare say very few of them fail to violate a dozen or so basic principles of the armourer's science. Some day I might try my luck with a versified parallel betwixt the ancient & modern form of stage coach, although my confidence in the aptness & merit of my metrical performances has waned as my critical discrimination has gained the perspec-tive & objectivity of old age. Thanks for the suggestion. "The Cloven Hoof of Simeon Slater" sounds highly alluring, & I hope that Wright will be less insensitive to its merits than he was in the case of an earlier Slater or Slaader![2] Perhaps you are wise in giving Simeon a more exotic & impressive setting than the Catskills.

Thanks immensely for the loan of the photographs, all of which I have examined with the keenest interest & admiration. That camera is certainly a gem—marvellously clear in catching detail. Good old Kleiner looks as graceful as usual, & you & David Frederic shew up to splendid advantage. The scenic views are immensely appealing—even the niveous ones, as viewed from a congenial indoor temperature of 82°. That window thermometer reading, however, gives me a chill in spite of the friendly radiator! You seem to have had as bad a minimum as we did—ours being 17° below, which shattered all records since the establishment of the local weather bureau. I was glad to see the views of your domicile, inside & out. Some of those aestival landscapes are ineffably haunting—especially the hilltop with worn-down stone wall, & that mysterious, apocalyptic sunset. Some day I must try to get some views of the westward vista from my windows—the twin towers of Memorial Hall, the downtown skyscrapers, & the distant rural horizon with the spire of St. John's popish church on Federal Hill silhouetted against it.[3] Incidentally—your office-window view is surely a study in futurism! The trick pictures are delightful, & would surely have had Grandpa puzzled but for the thoughtfully enclosed keys. That octopus-rooted tree is a choice item in itself—& in general, you are surely to be congratulated on having such a splendid diversity of landscape effects at your command. Of enormous interest is the quaint set of necropolitan views, perpetuating the deeds, attainments, aphoristic wisdom, & historic solicitude of your spire-surmounting progenitor. Those inscribed stones are certainly rare bits of family heritage—heirlooms of a sort which not many lines can hand down. David Frederic is lucky to be growing up amidst such tangible reminders of the modelling influences which extend behind him! That document concerning a just-averted Russian invasion seems to open up striking & unfamiliar channels of historic & diplomatic anecdote. Why don't you try to resurrect the entire tale & present it in *De Halve Maen*? Mijnheer Douwe[4] surely was a consistent Franklin fan, & his architecturally adapted farm of the celebrated epitaph is delightful. As per request, I return this absorbing gallery—with renewed expressions of gratitude & appreciation. Added thanks for the offer to send certain select prints permanently. I'll try not to be porcine in the extent of my requests—let's see—I'd like that one of yourself, the one of Mijnheer Douwe's gravestone & epitaph, & perhaps any one of the field stone inscriptions. If I were hoggish I'd grab at that hilltop landscape—but I'll try to restrain myself. You Dutchmen always were strong on landscapes—as I am, in the lesser field of mere appreciation. I don't know any pictures that move me more than the rural vistas of Ruisdael, Hobbema, Cuyp,[5] & others whose names I can't recall. There are quite a number of these Dutch landscapes in the Pendleton house at the School of Design . . . . as you doubtless know.

Unusual is surely having a hard time, as the enclosed card will confirm. As you see, Crawford is trying to print it himself. Do you see *The Fantasy Fan*? If not, I can let you have a copy of the latest issue. March W T is an average number. I find C A S's drawing very haunting—though you don't share my admiration for his art.[6] Price has moved from New Orleans to Pawhuska, Okla.—in the oil country among the Osages—where a partnership in a garage has lessened the pressure of hack writing for him. He gives all sorts of descriptions of the oil industry—so that I wonder if he wouldn't make a good potential contributor to the Texaco Star? If you're interested, drop him a line—E. Hoffmann Price, 10 Whiting Apts., Pawhuska, Okla. Thanks for the climatic note—I read Dr. Huntington's dictum when it appeared, though (despite Rhodinsular pride) I can't help personally preferring Key West to Newport temperatures.

Lots of good temporary exhibits at the School of Design Museum—Etruscan & Egyptian tomb paintings, Shaffordshire china, & now (vide enc. cat.) a rather notable group of Hispanic paintings. Beastly weather despite the warm Monday I spoke of on my card. Last Sunday the hill was so slippery that crowds of collegians were lined up on the sidewalk to watch & spoof the grotesquely skidding motorists. Some of the cars got completely turned around. At last my aunt—with admirable civic spirit—telephoned to the police station to have barriers placed at the head of the street till it could be sanded. I myself slipped down three times—lucky some old men are tough! ¶ Recent reading—Dunsany's "Curse of the Wise Woman", the celebrated "Anthony Adverse", Merritt's "Metal Monster", & Count de Prorock's [*sic*] account of his Carthaginian excavations. Also the White Pine monographs on Colonial architecture.[7] Marvellous stuff—you ought to look 'em up. I find that in one place New England architecture has encroached on N.Y. State.

Well—my aunt & I both send regards to all. Why don't you & Sonny get together & try to call a gang meeting? ¶ Yr obt Servt—Grandpa van Kasje

Notes

1. Not located.
2. HPL appears to be referring to Farnsworth Wright's rejection of HPL's "Beyond the Wall of Sleep" (1919), which features a character from the Catskill Mountains whose name is alternately spelled Slater or Slaader.
3. St. John's Catholic Church (1871), 352 Atwells Avenue, the edifice that became the Free-Will Church of the Starry Wisdom sect in "The Haunter of the Dark." The steeple fell in 1935, and the church was razed in 1992.
4. See HPL to Lillian D. Clark [27 May 1928]: "Talman's own lineal ancestor, Douwe Talman, was murdered in his home by the band of Claudius Smith, a leader of the 'skinners', whilst guarding his hoarded gold at the advanced age of 90. He was seated on the chest holding his treasure when run through with a bayonet—& it is interesting to note that Talman has just bought this chest from a distant relative at a cost of $50.00" (*LFF* 672).

5. The Dutch painters Salomon van Ruysdael (1602–1670), Meindert Hobbema (1638–1709), and Aelbert Cuyp (1620–1691).

6. Clark Ashton Smith illustrated his own tale, "The Charnel God," in *WT* (March 1934).

7. Between 1915 and 1940, the White Pine Bureau produced a series of architectural monographs, titled *The Monograph Series: Records of Early American Architecture,* under the editorship of Russell F. Whitehead (1884–1954). HPL probably refers to Vols. XIII and XIV, on "the architecture of the American colonies and the early republic."

[98]   [ALS, JHL]

Thor's-Daeg
[29 March 1934]

Jonckheer:—

Well—you certainly have done noble by Iacobus Ferdinandus! The portrait resemblance is remarkable! Lux et Fortitudo—superstition & error shall be trampled under foot & trumpeted to scorn! Your design is as delightful in its way as the classic door of 1929—though the latter hits my particular taste a bit closer. I'll surely ask the Sage for a copy of the finished product when he gets his supply.[1]

Thanks also for the articles. You surely make the bar-bend-bendlet-baton question clear enough, & ought to save many an advertiser vast embarrassment. At the same time, there's a lot of advertised products which ought to draw a baton sinister & then some! I return this article herewith as per request. The account of divining-rod superstition in the oil business is very diverting—I must ask Price if he comes across much of that. I believe some rustics still look for hidden water with a hazel twig, & that the metal mining industry is by no means exempt. Seems to me I've seen divining-rods advertised in W.T. & similar cheap rags.

I've just read Machen's new weird book—"The Green Round"—lent me by Klarkash-Ton. Really extremely interesting—with some very potent reflections of that persistent sense of unreal worlds impinging on the real world (cf. "Doom around the Corner") which many imaginative people possess. In the casualness & unexplainedness of the phenomena it recalls some of Machen's queer prefaces—such as that to "The Three Impostors". Its faults are—mainly—a certain rambling diffuseness, tameness, & over-use of typical stylistic mannerisms. Also—the hackneyed run of poltergeist manifestations are dragged in. Hardly one of Machen's greatest—but typically Machenian for all that. I'm vastly glad to have read it, & may buy a copy when I'm less broke.

Well—spring is technically here, & I'm hoping for the best. My aunt & I were treated to a motor ride toward Worcester last Sunday. Quite a lecture—illustrated & with appropriate phonograph selections—on Spanish art at the School of Design last night, by Dudley Crafts Watson[2] of the Chicago Art Institute.

Blessings—
> Grandpa Van Kasje.

P.S. Young Brobst (in town for a tonsil operation) dragged me to a cinema the other day—"The Ghoul".[3] Some of the atmospheric effects weren't bad.

Notes

1. WBT designed a bookplate for James Ferdinand Morton. See Appendix.
2. Dudley Crafts Watson (1885–1972), artist known for floral and marine landscapes and also an art teacher at the School of the Art Institute of Chicago.
3. *The Ghoul* (Gaumont British Picture Corp., 1933), directed by T. Hayes Hunter; starring Boris Karloff, Cedric Hardwicke, and Ernest Thesiger.

[99]   [ALS JHL]

Aug. 3[, 1934]

Jonckheer:—
> Thanks! That P.O. ruling is interesting! Am very grateful for the spelling article. So Dutch has suffered from spelling reformers, eh? Hope they won't go too far! I return the highly absorbing article upon request. Thanks enormously for the genealogical cutting, which goes into my permanent files. Morton—who is now *here* for 3 days—has made a sensational addition to the *Perkins* line we hold in common. We thought John P. who came to Boston in the *Lion* 1630 was the earliest discoverable figure in this branch's, but his ancestry in England back to the *1300's* is now known. Also, it is found that he did *not* come from Newent, Gloucestershire, but from Hillmorton, Warwickshire. The line, from the earliest known ancestor, follows:

1. Perkin (or Peter) Morelley of Shropshire, circa 1380
2. Henry Perkins
3. John Perkins—seneschal of Tho. De Spencer 1400—bad grant of estate
4. William Perkins of Afton Court
5. Thomas Perkins of Afton Court
6. William Perkins of Warwickshire (1495)
7. Thomas Perkins of Hillmorton d. 1528
8. Henry Perkins (d. 1547)
9. Thomas Perkins d. 1592
10. Henry Perkins d. 1608
11. JOHN PERKINS b. 1583—Boston 1630 d. Ipswich 1654
12. John Perkins, Jun. b. 1609
13. Samuel Perkins (in K. Philip's War) settled in Conn.
14. Ebenezer Perkins (came to R.I.)
15. Newman Perkins b. 1711
16. Martha Perkins (m. Stephen Place)

17. Stephen Place Jun.
18. Rhoby Place
19. Sarah Phillips
20. HPL

So Grandpa O'Casey is the 20th generation from old Pete of Shropshire, the contemporary of Chaucer! Franklin D. Roosevelt, author of the preface to your Dutch house book, is also a descendant of this line! We go in for quality! Ask J. Ferd for further details when you see him in N.Y. Now I've got to copy 2 closely typed pages of this dope from Morton's MS. Curse the luck! Would that I were a foundling!

Thanks for the Early Am. Industries chronicle—highly interesting. A museum has just been opened down in Wickford which displays such primitive industrial devices. This will go into my files.

And I immensely enjoyed the new *Halve Maen*—especially the Van Wyck article. The idea that the Dutch curved roof with overhanging eaves is of *Chinese* suggestion is a new one on me! But it really does sound damned plausible in view of Holland's eastern trade.

Well—I surely had a great trip. In St. Augustine a week, Charleston again 2 days, Richmond 1 day, Washington 2 days, Philadelphia 1 day. Saw recently opened Poe cottage in Philada (530 N. 7th St.)—a very impressive small edifice of brick, furnished just as in Poe's time. When I hit NY (broke) Sonny & his parents were starting for Asbury Park over the week end, & at their invitation I went along with them. No cash to stay in NY & look anybody up, though. Home July 10, & I surely was glad to see the rolling hills, stone walls, giant elms, & white village steeples of my native realm. But what a chaos of piled up work awaiting me!!! Aunt well—goes everywhere without a cane. And there is the most fascinating coal-black kitten imaginable at the boarding-house across the back garden. I borrow him constantly.

Morton arrived yesterday morning—we lunched at Maxfield's ice cream place in Warren, & dined at *Jake's*. The old joint is just the same. We were going to the South County today, but I fear the falling of rain will prevent us.

I enjoyed your story in *Marvel Tales*.[1] New W T ought to be out now, but I haven't seen it. Didn't think much of the last issue.

Enclosed are some bookplates which Barlow asked me to give you when he learned of your interest in such things. Probably not of much use to you—but I follow instructions.

Trust all is flourishing at Knollwood.

Blessings—

Grandpa van Kasje

Notes

1. "A Horror in Profile."

[100] [ALS, JHL]

Dec. 5[, 1934]

Jonkheer:—

Bless my soul, but you certainly did well in nine minutes! That's ahead of Grandpa—with or without such inventions of the devil as the writing machine!

You certainly have about everything there is in the camera line! Those little fellows must have marvellous lenses to permit of such vast enlargements! Thanks enormously for the two striking specimens. With a good reading glass I can decipher the marriage license & lottery ticket (not dissimilar items, it would seem!) as clearly as if the originals were before me, whilst the Child—lip-fuzz & all—stands out in all the devilish & decadent sophisticatedness he would like to achieve! Sonny will certainly crow with glee when he beholds this vivid counterfeit presentment! Now he won't have to go to the Brooklyn Museum & stare at the Boldoni drawing of some Dago count who looks like him![1] You certainly know how to handle your subjects—& without any little birdie for them to smile at! I hope to see pictures of the other youngster in course of time. Your idea of having a photographic record of important family antiques & documents is a damned good one, & I believe I'll attempt something of the sort some day—so far as my lesser instrumental facilities permit. Photographs can survive even when time has taken its toll of the originals.

Thanks abundantly for the current *Halve Maen,* whose misprints can easily be forgiven . . . at least, by one not the author of the affected text. Your new member Mr. Sebring seems to be quite a find, & I hope he will continue to enlighten the readers in the finer points of Netherlandish genealogy & etymology. That *van 't* construction has puzzled me for over a quarter of a century—ever since I encountered it in the name of the eminent chemist & physicist *van 't Hoff.*[2] We live & l'arn! Glad to see the note from my Celtic cousin, which I herewith return as per request. Sure there's no kapin' us down!

And shpakin' av us ould Noo-England discindints—thank yez manny a toime fer the tip on that Fall River Loine publication! 'Tis this minute I'm afther wroitin' to Brother O'Christman, & hopin' he'll be sendin' a copy of the paaper by returrn mail. Sure, if 'tis history they're wantin', 'tis I that can give it to em in anny dose they loike!

That "Time Machine" spoof surely was amusing in a mild way—especially the conjectures as to authorship.[3] Belknap told me about it when I passed through Nieuw Nederland on my way north, & I found a copy upon reaching #66. I fancy it must have been perpetrated by someone closely in touch with the correspondence of the group—though it would be unbecoming to make too many guesses. As to *why* it was perpetrated—I'm sure I don't know, being a total stranger to the sportive juvenile psychology which delights in such things ... or could conceive the notion of originating them. As a whole, the thing is undeniably a bit flat—since only a very few persons could understand more than a small fraction of the esoteric allusions. It appears to be generally without malice—the only over-rough touch being the rather pointed exposure of Two-Gun's misuse of the word *gonfalon*.[4]

Speaking of the weird circle—here's something that may amuse you . . . a number of the F F dedicated to the Old Gent. You needn't bother to return this, since Y^e E^d most plentifully supplied me with copies. The next issue was similarly dedicated to your artistic idol Klarkash-Ton.[5]

Well—I trust all has been prospering in Rockland County & among the Dunsanian pinnacles. Doubtless you received my message from antient Nantucket last August. What a place! What a place! See it & die happy! The utterly living past! Since then local events have been few. In October I visited Edward H. Cole in Wollaston & was taken on a trip to a marvellous scenic region in North Central Massachusetts—the autumn foliage being then at its height. Later Cole drove me home in his car, picked up my aunt, & conveyed the expedition to the historic spots of Rhode Island's south county—including Gilbert Stuart's birthplace. My one later trip was to Boston to see W. Paul Cook, who was down from the arctic for a week. We had dinner with Cole, visited the antient Royall house (1737) in Medford, &c.—but it was too cold to do much. Cook had some interesting old documents with him—letters from a soldier at the front in the War of 1812, letters from 49-ers in California, Civil War letters, &c. They were from the family of the late Mrs. Miniter—for whom a memorial brochure is being edited.[6]

Well—Pax vobiscum—Grandpa van Kasje

P.S. Am watching an interesting tiger kitten in the garden outside the window. Judging from his size, he must be a stubbletje!

Notes

1. Giovanni Boldini (1842–1931), Italian painter, painted a portrait of James McNeill Whistler (1897) that is at the Brooklyn Museum. The drawing HPL refers to is unidentified.
2. Jacobus Henricus van 't Hoff, Jr. (1852–1911), the first winner of the Nobel Prize in chemistry.
3. The unsigned story "The Battle That Ended the Century" (whose subtitle was "MS. Found in a Time Machine") actually was by R. H. Barlow and HPL.
4. "The gonfalons sounded a fanfare of triumph for the victor, while the technically vanquished was committed to the care of the official mortician, Mr. Teaberry Quince" (*CF* 4 472–73). A *gonfalon* is a banner or pennant, especially one with streamers, hung from a crossbar, not a musical instrument. Howard misused the word in his drafts of the story "The Scarlet Citadel" (*WT*, January 1933). In the published story, Howard's text reads "The oliphants sounded a fanfare of triumph all over the plain." But in un-

published drafts, he had written "Now the gonfalons sounded a fanfare of arrogant pride, and the victors swept across the plain, their horses' hoofs crunching in the breasts of the vanquished" and "The gonfalons sounded a fanfare of triumph, all over the plain, where the hoofs of the victors crunched in the breasts of the vanquished." The second reading occurs in a typescript that Howard had given to R. H. Barlow in March 1933. Barlow must have shown the typescript to HPL when HPL visited Barlow in Florida in May–June 1934, and so HPL twitted Howard in "The Battle That Ended the Century," written at about that time.

5. The October issue of the *Fantasy Fan* was dedicated to HPL, the November issue to Clark Ashton Smith.

6. The brochure never appeared, but some of the material gathered for it was published in a special memorial supplement to Hyman Bradofsky's *Californian* (Spring 1938).

[101] [ALS, JHL]

☉ 's entry into ♓ [19 February 1935][1]

Hail, Jonkheer!

Thanks effusively for the interesting shipment! That ghost picture is the first I've seen since inspecting the ectoplasmic photographs in the works of A. Conan Doyle, & MM. Flammarion & Chevreuil.[2] Its rough & ready setting surely adds to its effectiveness. In order to beat it, one would have to turn to the cloud drawings of that lady nut on Long Island whom you interviewed in the old *Times* days! Doubtless you still have those specimens in your files. Cutting returned as requested. The New Orleans article is very attractive, & makes me wish I were back there. And the *Charleston* cutting gets me positively homesick! Boy, those ancient churchyards! The Huguenot one is really the very *least* picturesque of them! To get the best effect, try that of the old Unitarian church (built in 1772), which extends through from Archdale to King St. Imagine a picturesquely grass-grown expanse of crumbling 18th century slabs threaded by moss-carpeted walks & immersed in a perpetual green twilight of huge overarching live-oaks festooned with long, trailing crepe-bands of grey, sepulchral Spanish moss! That, ef ya ast me, is what I call a *churchyard!* Good old Charleston!

News! On the festival of St. Valentinus there were born at the boarding-house across the back garden *4 coal-black* brothers or half-brothers (or/and sisters or half-sisters) of my late little friend Samuel Perkins (June–September 1934).[3] Their eyes ought to be open this Saturday. None will be consigned to a premature grave, but I don't yet know whether all will be given away or whether one will be retained. The latter, I devoutly hope! On their behalf the Kappa Alpha Tau sends its warmest greetings to Stubbletje's succession.

The other day I had a letter from Loring & Mussey—young Derleth's publishers, with offices in the same building with Dauber & Pine—asking to see some of my MSS. with a view to possible book publication. Derleth, of course, put 'em up to it. Since this is the 5th time such a request has been made (WT '26, Putnam '31, Vanguard '32, Knopf '33) without tangible results to date, I'm not as naively het up about the matter as I might otherwise be. The stuff will undoubtedly be back soon—so don't believe young Lenin[4] if he tells you that a book of mine is scheduled to appear for the spring trade! I wouldn't even have bothered to send anything if it weren't that I hate to leave any possible stone unturned. I wouldn't like to think that I *might* have a book *if* I had responded to the request. Incidentally—Derleth's 3d detective novel[5] will be out next month, & his first serious book—"Place of Hawks"—will appear in April. The kid certainly is coming along!

Some darned good lectures & exhibitions at one of your two local almae matres—the School of Design. Last week they featured Hokusai—& last night there was an illustrated discourse on Soviet art (in Memorial Hall) which would have had Sonny Belknap jumping up & down & piping!

Did I mention that the elder son of our old amateur colleague Moe has come to Bridgeport, Conn.? He graduated from the U. of Wis. a couple of years ago, & is getting along finely in electrical engineering—having a position with the General Electric Co. He was transferred from Schenectady to Bridgeport this year. I expect him up here the week-end after this, & have also given him the names & addresses of the gang in the N Y zone in case he gets down that way in his wandering Ford. Trust he won't prove a nuisance if he drops in at Room 1830.[6] Name & address: Robert Ellis Moe, 334 Ridgefield Ave., Bridgeport, Conn. I haven't seen the boy since he was a tow-headed little imp of 12 in 1923! How time doth fly!

I read the new Dunsany book—"Jorkens Remembers Africa"—the other day. Not up to the old Dunsany, but none the less very passable in spots. W T continues mediocre—nothing at all of distinction in the Feby. issue. Oh, yes—here's something I've been meaning to send you for a helluva while, just to try to cure you of your chronic unresponsiveness toward Poe. Within its pages you will also find a good article on William Hope Hodgson by our new Kalemite Koenig.[7] Have just been given a copy (in bound magazine-instalment form) of Merritt's "Creep, Shadow",[8] but have had no chance to read it so far. Am on the point of finishing a new novelette (65 pp. script) called "The Shadow Out of Time," but am so damn'd uncertain as to its merit that I won't type it. I think I'll make some amiable critic wade through the original pencil scrawl (if he can!) & judge of whether it's worth expending keyboard work on!

Well—preserve the peace!

—Grandpa van Kasje.

Notes

1. The sun's entry into Pisces.

2. Sir Arthur Conan Doyle (1859–1930), Camille Flammarion (1842–1925), and Léon Chevreuil (1852–1939) were all proponents of spiritualism, "spirit photography," and other pseudo-sciences.

3. See HPL's poem "[Little Sam Perkins]."

4. I.e., Frank Belknap Long, who had embraced communism.

5. I.e., *Sign of Fear*.

6. WBT's address at the time was 135 E. 42nd Street, Room 1830, New York, NY.

7. H. C. Koenig (1893–1959) was a late member of the Kalem Club. HPL refers to his article "William Hope Hodgson," *Fantasy Fan* 2 No. 4 (December 1934): 56.

8. F. Lee Baldwin gave HPL a bound set of *Creep, Shadow!*, which had been serialized *Argosy* (8 September–20 October 1934).

[102] [ALS]

66 College St.,
Providence, R.I.,
July 15, 1936.

Jonkheer:—

Congratulations on the advent—in a thoroughly Talmanic environment—of the diminutive Katrintje Anetje to the household at Knolwent Bouwerie! Commiserations meanwhile on the ills which have been besetting you & the still jonk-er heer! I had chicken-pox at 25, so can realise just how David Vreedrick must have felt. And bum throats are no strange events in my long history.

Just when I dropped my last bulletin I can't be sure, but if it was in February or later you are aware of the strain & chaos prevailing hereabouts for the last half-year. My tasks piled up unmanageably, I had a prostrating touch of grippe, & then my aunt had a worse grippe attack—developing complications & having a long hospital siege.[1] My programme was utterly disorganised—& can never be straightened out except through wholesale neglect & repudiation. My aunt came home April 21, & has since been getting back more & more to her usual condition, but the strain & the cold weather kept me in a state close to utter exhaustion & nervous breakdown—added to which a persistent digestive trouble appeared. Such was my lack of energy that it took me hours to do anything which I could ordinarily do in five minutes. Barlow had invited me south, but I could not arrange to accept—so sat still & shivered. The only thing I accomplished was a file-cleaning around June 1st—a wholesale upheaval which enabled me to keep track of things for the first time since 1932. Meanwhile dozens of letters remained unanswered, tasks were returned unperformed, borrowed books piled up unread, & general hell prevailed. 1936 will surely go down in history as one of my worst years. Relief came only a week ago when the warm weather dawned. Then, at last, my exhaustion, nerve-strain, & indigestion dwindled & disappeared—&

almost over night I was vigorously on my feet again. In the past few *days* I've cleaned up more tasks than in the same number of *weeks* preceding—& am still going strong & praying to Alabad, Ghinu, & Aratza for a continuance of the warm spell! Have begun to take trips—both limited afternoon ones, & an all-day session at Newport last Saturday. Walked to Hunt's Mills[2] yesterday & did a lot of writing on the rocks beside the falls. Next Saturday I expect good old Moe (who is now in N.Y. & will probably look you up) here. I haven't seen him face to face in 13 years, & am rejoicing that the heat & good health reached me in time to let me play the host properly.

Thanks for the new *Halve Maen*—I'll shoot Edkins his copy the next time I write. He, poor chap, is languishing between painful operations for some obscure kidney trouble—& has a rubber tube inside him. I'll be equally grateful when the new issue comes—& meanwhile I hope the second Neiuw Amsterdam play will be as successful as the first. By the way—that *Irish* touch was surely verified by the Tammany of later years. Ye can't kape us O'Caseys down!

Special congratulations are due you for your brilliant performance of chief labours on the second Dutch House book. It sounds like a truly monumental task, & I wonder that you had any time to spare for your regular business! But I'll wager you did the job well—putting even the magnificent preceding volume far in the shade. If I weren't so damned broke I'd order a copy at once—& anyhow I must see your de luxe #1 the very next time I hit the metropolitan zone. The thing fairly makes my mouth water! If you weren't already the Big Shot in the Holland Society, you certainly ought to be now!

Glad both *Dragon-Fly* & *Causerie* reached you—2 issues of each.[3] Barlow was so ashamed of the typography that he almost hesitated to release #2, but I persuaded him that the literary contents was paramount. He certainly has press trouble in plenty—& I wonder whether the fault lies with the old Kelsey or with his scholastic aptitude in this field? Certainly the young rascal *ought* to stick to *writing*—which is his real forte. In the latest issue of *The Californian* he has a long fantasy which utterly surprised me with its fine rhythm, poetic imagery, & cosmic imagination.[4]

Causerie is certainly great stuff, & I'll transmit the complimentary part of your remarks to E A E. I'm sure *I* didn't resent the Florida boosting—every word of which was abundantly *true!* Edkins was wholly disinterested, having not the slightest financial interest in the Sunshine State & its real estate. Regarding the heavy display of the paraphernalia of culture & erudition—we must remember that Ernie is 68 after all, so that the flamboyant impress of the baroque 80's & 90's is upon him for better or worse. That sort of thing went over big in those naive & self-conscious days—& one can't easily outgrow the habits of one's youth. On the whole, & making all allowances both for the topheavy culture & for the esoteric old-time-amateur atmosphere, I thought both issues damn good stuff, & easily the best items to appear in amateurdom in a generation. It is certainly just what is needed as an example by the present crop of young toughs & illiterates who call themselves amateurdom's leaders. Seldom has the scholastic & cultural level been as pitifully low as at present—with most papers mere imitations of the tabloid journalism beloved in kitchen, garage, & factory. The N.A.P.A needs a renaissance, & Ernie is certainly doing his share. So is good old Kleiner—with a series of magnificently lucid & helpful critical articles in the *National Amateur*.[5] As a reviewer, Edkins tries to be fair. I thought him a bit unappreciative of the massed effect of Belknap's poetry—but Sonny quite agrees with the cool estimate now that he's become a sociologist & business man. The Loveman critique—despite the somewhat irrelevant objections to S L's "defeatist" attitude in poetry—is really very acute & sensitively appreciative, & Samuelus is genuinely pleased with it.[6] All told, I'm a decided *Causerie*-fan—& I feel distinctly proud of having reached into the half-fabulous past & brought back to activity a figure as brilliant as its urbane & erudite editor. About the "Psychic Silhouettes"—the only flaw is the attribution of a Latin quotation (which *ought* to begin "certum est" instead of "credo", though the corrupt form is more widely known) from *Tertullian* to *Origen* . . . . who wrote in *Greek*. Well— even the most learned trip up now & then![7]

Glad you've had at least a fleeting glimpse of young Melmoth the Wandrei. His sister-in-law—young Albrecht Dürer's wife[8]—was lately quite seriously injured in a coach accident when returning from St. Paul. Belknap, too, has been under a strain—with devastating overwork, & both patents ill with grippe. His father has been found to suffer from pernicious anaemia, but is now responding very well to the recently-discovered liver diet—which seems to be to anaemia what insulin is to diabetes. I surely hope Dr. Long will soon be in good shape again.

But the worst gang news comes from Texas—where real tragedy has struck. Our good old friend Robert E. Howard—Two-Gun Bob, erstwhile *Texaco Star* contributor—is no more . . . having shot himself through the head on June 11, upon learning that his mother had only 48 hours more to live. Price says he feels "clubbed on the head" by the news—& that goes for the whole crowd. R E H had been worrying about his mother's health for over a year, & toward the last had lost night after night of sleep watching at the patient's bedside; but no one could have expected so drastic an act. Most of us, despite the strongest filial ties, realise that the earlier departure of the elder generation is an inevitable thing, & are prepared to accept the blow with philosophic resignation. Evidently Two-Gun's moody & sensitive streak—as manifest in his bitter hatred of civilisation—ran deeper than we ever suspected. I had thought it as essentially impersonal as Sonny's hatred of the injustices of a capitalistic world—but for once I was wrong. R E H lived 8 hours after the shot, & died without regaining consciousness. 30 hours later his mother died—without knowing of his act. The shock to his father—a pioneer physician—must be overwhelming, but the venerable Texan is bearing up like a true Southwesterner. He has given all of his son's books to the latter's alma mater—Howard Payne College in Brownwood—as the nucleus of a Robert E. Howard Memorial Collection. This is the worst blow weird fiction has had since the passing of good old "Canevin"[9] in 1932. Nobody else in the gang had quite the driving zest & spontaneity of Two-Gun Bob. It is hard to say just what made his yarns stand out so, but the real secret is that *he was in every one of them himself.* Even when he made outward concessions to commercial critics & mammon-guided editors he had an inner force & sincerity which broke through the surface & put the imprint of his personality on everything he wrote. He was really even more gifted than appears from his published work; being (as you are aware) an encyclopaedic student of southwestern & early Celtic history, & having a truly epical power in capturing the colour & repeating the annals of his beloved native region. Had he lived longer—he was 30 last January—he would almost certainly have won distinction in serious literature as a regional author. But even his existing stories are distinctive enough. Never again will the pulp magazines get anything with such force & colour. Of all the other members of the gang, Two-Gun had met only E. Hoffmann Price in person. I'm now telling Price that he ought to write an obituary notice for W T[10]—as I did of Whitehead in 1932. Barlow has prepared an astonishingly fine elegiac sonnet which Wright has accepted.[11] Too bad that little Bobby's professional debut should have so tragic a background. In our long argument of six years, Two-Gun had the last word—for my final 32-page letter must have reached Cross Plains after the fatal June 11th. 1936 has surely taken heavy toll—deaths of weird writers outside the gang including those of M. R. James at 73, & of George Allan England at 59.

Among the phases of my attempted conquest of chaos has been a reading-up of recent issues of W T—as far as the June issue. In looking over the contents I am sadly impressed by the superiority of good old Two-Gun's work over any of the other stuff. How he could surround primal megalithic cities with an aura of aeon-old fear & necromancy! His "Hour of the Dragon" is certainly a great piece of work. "Black Canaan" is likewise magnificent in a more realistic way—reflecting a genuine regional background & giving a clutchingly powerful picture of the horror that stalks through the moss-hung, shadow-cursed, serpent-ridden swamps of the farther south. Other efforts seem pallid by contrast—though Bloch's tales are all excellent according to average standards, while Derleth's "Telephone in the Library" could be a lot worse. Hamilton & Burks are mediocre—though the former escapes his formula fairly well. M. J. Bardine's "Harbour of Ghosts" & Harold G. Shane's "Lethe" both have promise.[12] But the poor old magazine is no galaxy of genius, at that! Young Schwartz has a wild idea of getting some of my stuff reprinted in England, & in connexion with this matter I sent two previously unsubmitted MSS. to W T in order to exhaust all cisatlantic possibilities first. I expected instant rejections—but to my surprise Wright took both.

Recently I corrected the printed copies of "Mts. of Madness" & "Shadow Out of Time" in *Astounding,* & was utterly sickened by the extent to which the former was mangled. To all intents & purposes, the tale is still unpublished! The "Shadow" fared better—though many misprints & a bad style-sheet made the work of correction rather difficult. The job was aggravated by the facts that I was fixing up 3 copies of each tale, & that I had no good MSS. to go by.

The Phantagraph plods along slowly. Before long its publishers will launch a fiction magazine to be called *Fanciful Tales*. Meanwhile two new ventures called *The Planeteer* & *The Science-Fantasy Correspondent* are struggling for a foot-hold. *Fantasy Magazine* carries on in a humble way, & Crawford keeps promising to resume *Marvel Tales*. The book of my "Innsmouth" seems to be stalled midway.[13] Barlow speaks of printing a collection of all my weird verse (i.e., all I'm willing to have printed), but I don't know when he'll ever get around to it.[14] Young Hornig—of the lamented *Fantasy Fan,* & jobless since the transfer of *Wonder Stories* to the Margulies group—is in Los Angeles seeking his fortune.

My pile of unread borrowed books doesn't diminish as fast as it ought. Have just read biographies of Roger Williams by Emily M. Easton & James Ernst—the latter of which emphasises R. W.'s influence on the revolution in England in the 1640's. Am now finishing Santayana's "Last Puritan"—a truly remarkable dissection of the sterile genteel tradition which dominated New England in the 19th century & which is now in its last death throes.

Did I mention the local tercentenary exercises of May 4, during which a mock-session (in full costume) of the rebel legislature of May 4, 1776 was held at the ancient (1761) colony house? I was one of the few spectators fortunate enough to get in. Each old-time deputy was impersonated by a lineal descendant, & the general effect was surprisingly good.

Speaking of historic things—here are a couple of folders which you may find useful for your files. The John Brown (Power St.) & Edward Carrington (Williams St.) mansions are now open to the public as museums, & I visited both the other day. I assume that you know the exteriors of these houses. Both inside & out the John Brown is the finer of the two . . . . indeed, after a close inspection I can say that J. Q. Adams (vide leaflet) was right[15]—& this after having examined 18th century houses all the way from Quebec on the north to St. Augustine & New Orleans on the South. The edifice has an admirably classic symmetry & arrangement, its only possible flaw being a subtle tendency toward rococo over-ornateness on the lower floor. Like most houses in America even as late as the 1800's, it is untouched by the superior classicism of the Adam influence, which became manifest in Great Britain as early as the 1750's or 1760's. I suppose you know the story of the builder—one of the four Brown brothers (John & Joe, Nick & Moe) who became such celebrated merchant princes in the middle 18th century. John's nephew Nick Jr.

was the bird who gave the donation which changed your alma mater's name from Rhode-Island College to Brown University . . . while Nick Jr.'s son was the John Carter Brown of bibliothecal fame. John himself was merely a shrewd grasper who got his art ideas from others. The real thoroughbred was brother Joe—who founded (with Steve Hopkins) the Prov. Library in 1758, & in 1769 imported a telescope to view the transit of Venus with. Joe, a gentleman-architect of distinction, designed the John B. house, as well as houses for himself & brother Nick. You know his own house (1774)—in S. Main St. with the curved pediment. He also designed the Market House (1773) & chose the Gibbs design for the 1st Bapt. steeple (1775). In later life he became a professor of natural philosophy at the college. The John B. house is generally regarded as his architectural masterpiece. He died in 1787, before its completion, but its splendid outlines survive as a memorial to his taste. The numerous French busts stuck around at various places are none of his doing. There is, as you may have heard, a legend that those on the gateposts turn & bow to each other at midnight—a phenomenon I have not personally observed. The Brown house is open only until Oct. 10. Last spring it was bought back into the Brown family, & its ultimate future is not yet settled. The present admission fee is $1.00—a piece of piracy equalled only at the Brewton–Pringle house in Charleston.

The Carrington house—of which I could secure no descriptive or pictorial matter—was erected in 1809 & is the work of the distinguished local architect John Holden Greene—who also did the Handicraft Club, the Unitarian church & steeple, & other early 19th century edifices. This mansion lacks the classic interior symmetry of the Brown house, but is extremely pleasing & homelike. It was recently presented to another alma mater of yours—the R.I. School of Design—with all its original furniture & decorations, to be kept intact for ever. The donor is the last of the family—a Miss Margarethe Dwight, who resides in the ancient Sullivan Dorr mansion at Benefit & Bowen Sts., inherited through another ancestral line.[16] With its stables, coach-houses, cobblestoned courtyard, & extensive grounds & gardens, the Carrington house forms one of the most satisfying domestic units of the early-republic period now on exhibition. In its interior architecture it embodies a rather amusing hybridism seemingly peculiar to late 18th & early 19th century Providence, & also noticeable in the [modern reproduction] Pendleton House—the use of rococo middle-18th-century architecture on the ground floor, & of the newer Adam-period design throughout the upper storeys. Some of the delicate Adam mantels upstairs are among the most exquisite I have ever seen. Admission to the Carrington house is 50¢.

Speaking of old houses—new research connected with the tercentenary seems to have established that the most ancient house still surviving in Rhode Island is the steep-roofed, stone-chimneyed Thomas Clemence house on the farther edge of the village of Manton beyond Olneyville—built in 1656 on land purchased from an Indian named Wissawyamake. Now this is of especial interest to me, as you'll realise if you recall the genealogical exhumations to which you incited me nearly a decade ago—for those mouldering charts record the fact that I am a direct descendant of Tom Clemence in the 8th generation—as follows:

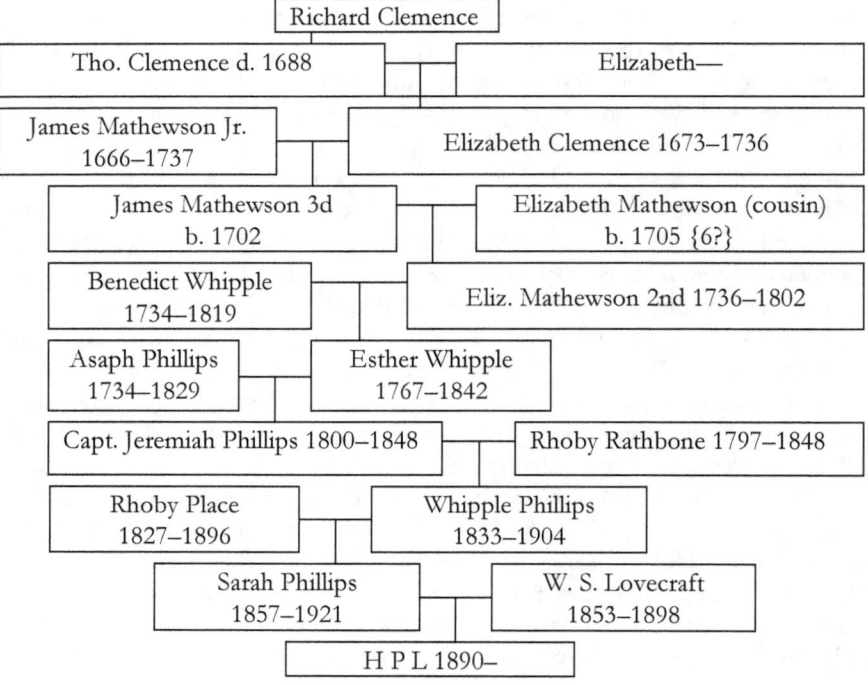

I had seen this venerable place once before, but revisited it last May after learning of its new official dignity as Rhode Island's oldest. It was not at all changed—the present inhabitant & owner being an ancient gentlewoman in destitute circumstances. So far all negotiations for its purchase & restoration by the right kind of an organisation have come to naught. It is today encumbered with added lean-to, easterly extension, dormer windows, & ugly porch—all of which could easily be removed. The foregoing rough sketch shews the place not as it *is*, but as it *was* 275 years ago when Tom Clemence (who was a friend of Roger Williams) lived there. The *well-sweep*, however, is still to be found in active use—one of the relatively few remaining in Rhode Island. Altogether, the house is very typical of middle-17th-century R.I. architecture—

our second period of construction. It is getting quite a bit of publicity this year—more than is any other homestead involving my direct ancestry.

But speaking of *ancestry*—I don't think I've told you of my new discovery . . . . the second full-sized one since our researches of '27 (the first was of various *Perkins* tributaries & extensions, 1932–1934). You may recall how on one September afternoon we dug valiantly at the public library into sundry books of heraldry, raking up coats-of-arms & seeing which would best fit various lines. At that time we were especially captivated by the *Field* arms—three silver sheaves on a black field (no pun!) with a conventional silver chevron stuck up betwixt 'em. The earliest Field ancestor I *then* knew was the Providence settler John (d. 1686), from *three* of whose grandchildren (Mathewsons—children of his daughter Hannah) I am descended. Well—I couldn't swear the handsome arms were his, but I hoped like hell they were! And there the subject rested for *8 years & 8 months*—attesting my lack of enterprise in such matters when unspurred from outside. The sequel occurred just two months ago.

In May of this year I ran into an old lady calling on my then-convalescing aunt—one of three sisters related to us in the Field & Wilcox lines. The listless talk ran to my early interest in astronomy, & pretty soon the ancient gentlewoman remarked 'how appropriate it was that I was descended from *the astronomer John Field or Felde!* '[17] Well, that had me floored! Never heard of the guy! Some joke on Grandpa O'Casey—a star-gazing fan from the age of 12, & never suspected I was the scion of a specialist in that line! Naturally I began asking questions hot & heavy—for I knew damn well that the Prov. settler hitherto forming the frontier of my Field information wasn't any moonstarer. It soon turned out what a behind-the-times dub I am—for I was presently apprised that the whole British ancestry of the Providence Field family has been *a matter of common knowledge* for over a generation—all written up in a 2-volume book by Frederick C. Pierce & published in 1901. What is more, the book had been in the public library all the time, although I had never dug into it deeply enough to find my own branch amidst the bewildering multiplicity of others! To make a long story short, the *grandfather* of the Providence John was the noted Elizabethan astronomer John Field or Felde (b. bet. 1515 & 1525; d. May 1587), whose Ephemeris for 1557 contained the first account of the Copernican theory ever printed in England. Hot dawg! What a bird to catch for one's family tree, & I never knew of the kinship till my old age! This chap was called "The Proto-Copernican of England", & late in life received permission to add to his arms a new crest commemorative of his pursuits—*a dexter arm issuing out of clouds fesseways proper, habited gules, holding in the hand, also proper, an armillary sphere, or.* And I am pleased to add that the hereditary arms to which the college of heralds appended this new crest *was indeed our old black shield & silver garb friend of Sept. '27!* I had wished & guessed right! The Proto-Corpernican was born at East Ardsley in Yorkshire, attended Oxford, & travelled widely abroad, especially in Germany. His wife was Jane Amyas, daughter of John

Amyas of Ardeslowe, of an ancient Yorkshire family. His son William, born in 1570 at Ardsley, married the widow of one George Burdett—born Jane Sotwell, dau. of the Rev. John Sotwell, Vicar of Peniston in Yorkshire. (Damn it—as soon as I find a real *scientist* in an ancestry lousy with clergymen, I have to discover *another* damn divine!) Bill moved to his wife's place near Thurnscoe (Yorks.), & there his children were born. Of these children *two*—John & William—emigrated to New England on the *Lion* in 1630, being shipmates of my other ancestor John Perkins Sr. (also Morton's ancestor) & of my (regrettably!) non-ancestor Roger Williams. Both ultimately followed Roger to Providence, & were given adjacent home lots along the town street—at a point still marked by the line of *Charles Field St.*, named from a descendant. Now (since Brother John is my forbear) this makes the Elizabethan savant my great-great-great-great-great-great-great-great-great-grandfather.

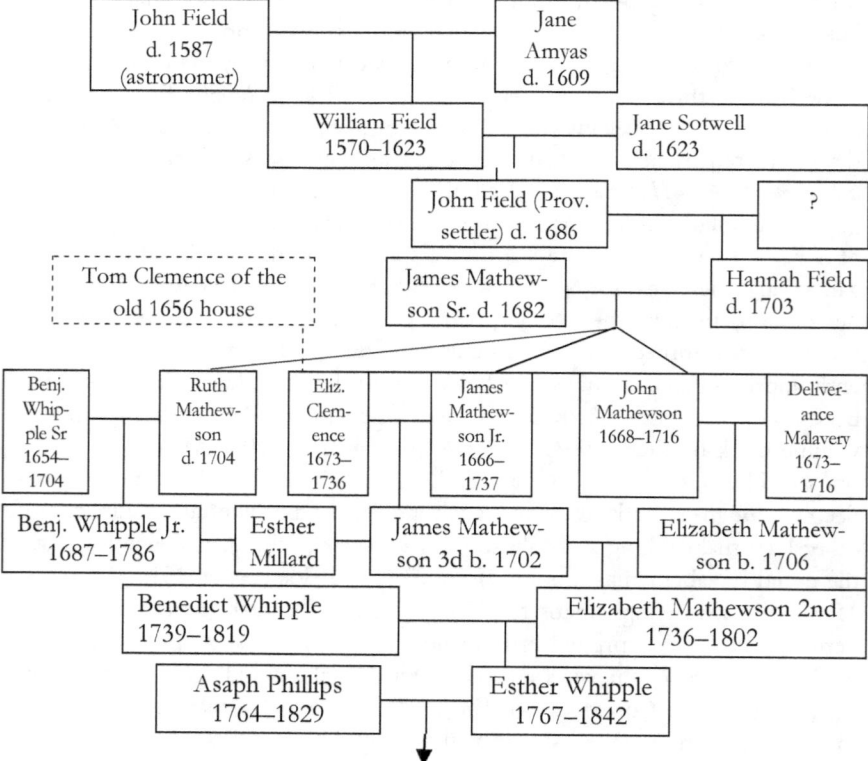

and so on . . . the same as in the Tom Clemence chart two sheets back. It is odd how *three* children of Hannah Field all merged their streams in one great grandchild—Esther Whipple (my great-great-grandmother), Esther's mother, a child of first cousins, herself married a second cousin (Benedict Whipple) from the same source. Well—after my aunt's caller had imparted her lore I did, at last, tackle the 2-volume Field genealogy—which is at both the R.I. Hist. Soc. & the public library. With the Proto-Corpernican as a clue, all was plain sailing—& I easily followed my lineal Field ancestry back for precisely 20 generations—to one Roger del Feld, born in Sowerby, Yorkshire, in 1240. The entire Field line is said to spring from the Alsatian family of the Counts de la Feld, seated at Chateau de la Feld near Colmar & traceable from the 6th century A.D. . . . Gallo-Roman times. Sir Hubertus de la Feld of this house was a follower of William the Conqueror, & was enrolled as an owner of lands in Lancaster & Kent in 1069. The book then leaves a gap—& shews later ancestors (beginning with Roger in 1240) clustering around the West Riding of Yorkshire. Quite a genealogical haul—yet the guy who interests me most, & about whom I am chiefly anxious to learn more, is the astronomer. The Peirce [sic] book says that detailed articles on the Proto-Corpernican can be found in the *Gentleman's Magazine* for May, 1834 & Nov. 1862 . . . I'll have to see if local libraries have files!

Oh, yes—& before leaving the subject of genealogy, let me say that I've lately been passing along a bit of the lore with which you inoculated me so many years ago. Young Barlow, hitherto almost wholly ignorant of his ancestors save in a vaguely traditional way, is slowly getting the genealogical bug, & has sought my help in cooking up a set of charts. I've utilised quite a bit of our '27 lore on his progenitors—among whom, by the way, is certainly one who also adorns my tree. Barlow traces back to one of the many *Valentine Rathbones* of New England—& it is positively known that all these come from a common forbear. When he or I can find that Cooley book (the one where you helped me find my own line in '28 at the N.Y. libe . . . though I later found the whole thing written out among my elder aunt's disordered papers) where old Val (a clergyman of late 18th cent. & father-in-law of Dr. Barzillei Hayward, Brown 1807) hitches on to the original Roxbury Rathbone line, we shall know just what kind of cousins we are! It is curious that of all the gang, only two (Morton & Barlow) have any blood link with me. Bob is of New England stock only on the paternal side. His mother is a Kansan of Virginian ancestry, & a collateral descendant of Pres. James Monroe.

Oh, yes—one more genealogical note! Not long after my "Mts. of Madness" came out, I received a letter from a chap in Cleveland asking where I got the name *Pabodie* for one of the professors therein. He himself was a *Pabody*, & on the alert for all the ancestral data he could annex.[18] He knew about the original William Pabodie of Little Compton, R.I., whose wife was Elizabeth Alden (dau. of John & Priscilla of poetic fame, & the first white woman born in New England), but wanted ampler knowledge all along the line. I told him I had chosen the name almost at random, but mentioned the Providence poet of the 1840's (another William Pabodie—friend of Poe), & suggested that he get in touch with Morton (who himself has a *Peabody* line) for more expert information. Well—he followed my advice, & James Ferdinand has now copped him as a professional client. A lucky event, for Morto-nius was able to supply him with some long-wished links. Meanwhile I had mentioned the survival of old William Pabodie's house in Little Compton (lo-cally called the "Betty Alden House"), & he was mightily interested. He is now getting his father interested, & is full of schemes for trying to buy the place as a museum—either alone, or in connexion with some ancestral or an-tiquarian association. If he does, I hope he'll give me a free pass—though he promises not to charge a dollar like the sharks at the John Brown house! It has also developed that young Pabody is an aspiring fiction-writer. He has sent me several specimens of his work—largely realistic character studies—& I really think it excellent in a quiet way. He may yet be a novelist of note!

During the file-cleaning mentioned earlier in this epistle I upheaved two or three bookplates which I had been saving for you. Are you still desirous of collecting miscellaneous specimens? I'll send these along anyhow. One of them, as you may see, is that of good ol' Ernie Edkins.

Travelling exhibit of Clark Ashton Smith's grotesque sculpture is now at Wandrei's—88 Horatio St. Better not pass it up even though you don't gen-erally appreciate Klarkash-Ton's work; for many who are cold to his drawings think he has found his real plastic metier in sculpture.

New School of Design buildings along lower College St. are going up rapidly. Archway is being reëstablished in its new position, while the old Franklin House at the foot of the hill is reduced to a roofless shell. When re-constructed, the old building will have its upper storeys of ampler height than before. ¶ Site of Jake's still vacant. Eheu fugaces! I haven't yet been down to Wickenden St. to see if Jake's other joint is still running.

I wonder if Belknap or anybody else will call a meeting in honour of Moe's visit? If so, I hope you can attend. His allotted time here is regrettably brief, but he is anxious to spend as many days as possible in Bridgeport with his son.

Well—once more, sincerest congratulations on the arrival of little Trintje, & profoundest hopes that all the family may soon be in the best of health. Hope the reception of the book will be commensurate with its merit. I'll wa-ger it puts it all over Vol. I! Thanks again for *De Halve Maen,* whose articles are always pleasing & illuminating. I had not realised before that the buff & blue uniforms of the rebel army in the American war were of Dutch origin. In your necrology list I note the appearance of an old-time amateur journal-istic name—W. L. Terhune.[19] All the historically-minded amateur journals are mourning his passing. ¶ Seems to be a pleasant day. If it keeps warm, I shall try to get outdoors as soon as a certain amount of writing is cleaned up. // Blessings

    —Grandpa

Notes

1. In fact, Annie E. P. Gamwell had breast cancer and had to go to the hospital for a mastectomy.

2. A resort area in East Providence.

3. The *Dragon-Fly* (ed. R. H. Barlow) and *Causerie* (ed. Ernest A. Edkins) were amateur journals prepared for the National Amateur Press Association.

4. R. H. Barlow, "A Dim-Remembered Story," *Californian* 4, No. 1 (Summer 1936): 72–87.

5. Such as "Bureau of Critics: A Criticism in the Poet's Corner," *National Amateur* 58, No. 2 (December 1935): 12–14; "Bureau of Critics: Poet," *National Amateur* 58, No. 3 (March 1936): 14–16; "Bureau of Critics: The Amateur Parnassus," *National Amateur* 58, No. 4 (June 1936): [1], 15–16.

6. HPL refers to Edkins's reviews of FBL's *The Goblin Tower* and Loveman's *The Hermaphrodite and Other Poems: Causerie* (February 1936): 2–4 and *Causerie* (June 1936): 2–4.

7. Tertullian, *De Carni Christi* (5.4): "certum est, quia impossibile [est]" (it is certain, because it is impossible), referring to the Christian's belief in the resurrection of Jesus Christ.

8. HPL refers to Donald Wandrei, his brother Howard, and Howard's wife Connie (Colestock).

9. I.e., Henry S. Whitehead. Gerald Canevin was a recurring chacater in Whitehead's work.

10. No such article by Price appeared in *WT*, although he later wrote several other articles or letters about Howard for fanzines of the 1940s.

11. R. H. Barlow, "R.E.H.," *WT* 28, No. 3 (October 1936): 353.

12. *WT* 27, No. 5 (May 1936): Arthur Burks, "The Room of Shadows"; Robert Bloch, "The Faceless God"; Edmond Hamilton, "Child of the Winds." *WT* 27, No. 6 (June 1936): Robert E. Howard, "Black Canaan"; Robert Bloch "The Grinning Ghoul"; August W. Derleth, "The Telephone in the Library"; M. J. Bardine, "The Harbor of Ghosts"; Harold G. Shane, "Lethe." Robert E. Howard's "The Hour of the Dragon" was a five-part serial that ran from December 1935 to April 1936.

13. *Phantagraph* and *Fanciful Tales* were published by Donald A. Wollheim (1914–1990) and Wilson Shepherd (1917–1985); *Planeteer* was published by James Blish (1921–1975) and William Miller, Jr. (1921–1979?); *Science-Fantasy Correspondent* was published by Willis Conover 1920–1996) and Corwin Stickney (1921–1998); *Fantasy Magazine* was published by Julius Schwartz (1915–2004) and Conrad Ruppert (1912–1997); *Marvel Tales* and HPL's *The Shadow over Innsmouth* were published by William L. Crawford.

14. HPL did provide to Barlow various typescripts for a book to be called *The Ancient Track,* but as in the case of so many other planned projects, it came to nothing. At the time, Barlow was printing HPL's *Fungi from Yuggoth,* but that, too, was not completed.

15. Adams called the John Brown house "the finest private mansion on this continent." See HVS 25n11.

16. Edward Carrington House (1810; 1812), 66 Williams Street. John Corliss built the original two-story part of the house in 1810. Margarenthe Dwight (1871–1962), a descendant of Carrington, gave the house and many of its furnishings to the Museum of Art, Rhode Island School of Design, as a museum showing the influence of the China

trade in New England. It has been a private residence since 1931. She was also a descendant of Sullivan Dorr, and deeded the Sullivan Dorr House (1809), 109 Benefit Street, to the Providence Preservation Society.

17. But see Kenneth W. Faig, "Quae Amamus Tuemur: Ancestors in Lovecraft's Life and Fiction" 45–46.

18. For HPL's letters to Frederic Jay Pabody (1910–1993), see *Letters to C. L. Moore and Others*.

19. Of Boston, editor of the *Young Sportsman*, the *Boot and Shoe Recorder*, and the *Stamp Collectors Magazine*.

[103] [ALS]

Tuesday
[25 August 1936]

Jonkheer:—

Your note of the 16th arrived only this morning—the 25th—but I hope the delay has not caused you inconvenience. I doubt whether anyone will be much interested in seeing my old stuff, but am none the less sending along a few items. Some of those which I'd like most to send are either lent at present or in magazines & therefore not well adapted to transit—but the accompanying junk is fairly representative. Please be damned careful of it, for my extra copies of things are disappearing & disintegrating with alarming rapidity. Before long I'll have nothing in shape to lend.

As for criticisms of my work—I'm sure I don't know of any worth quoting. Dunsany never saw my stories—the incident you recall being merely his sight of some commendatory verses to him which I wrote in 1919 & which somebody else sent him.[1] Houdini never read any of my stuff so far as I know—except what I ghost-wrote for him. I've never been in touch with any prominent figures, & can't recall any praise ever given me by such. There was some allusion to my junk in a writer's magazine (Am. Author) back in 1932, & in the *N.Y. World* for Jan. 4, 1930 the columnist William Bolitho spoke well of it. I haven't this article of B's in detachable form. Approval of minor columnists (Howard Wolf of Akron—Ted Robinson of Cleveland)[2] a decade or more ago wouldn't mean much—& anyhow, these items are also pasted in my scrap-book. All I can find to send are some old Eyrie sheets with remarks from Wright, Price, & Cummings. I send these along for what they're worth, but guess it won't matter much. Thanks for bothering with this matter—whatever it is—but don't expect any particular results.

I saw the review of the Dutch House book in the *Times*,[3] & will be looking for the one in the same day's *Tribune*. Glad the enterprise is receiving at least a little of the recognition it so amply merits!

I believe I told you of the pleasant visit of Moe & his son July 18–19. Since July 28 Providence's ancient hill has been adorned by the presence of our young friend Robert Hayward Barlow—who is stopping at the boarding-house across the garden on a kind of long-term semi-visit. Property adjustments in De Land may cause a change in his residential arrangements, so that he may head west for Kansas upon leaving here Sept. 1. I've been shewing him the sights [including the empty site of Jakes' . . . whose Wickenden St. establishment (as I ascertained when exploring in that direction with the Moes) is also closed] one by one, & he has simultaneously been raiding the local bookstalls & accumulating genealogical data (reminiscent of our 1927 activities) at the pub libe & hist soc. It turns out that Barlow is my *sixth cousin*—through the following lines of parallel descent:

John Rathbone—b.1658	
John Rathbone—b. 1693	Rev. Joshua Rathbone—born 1696
John Rathbone—b. 1720	Rev. Valentine Rathbone—b. 1724
John Rathbone—b. 1750	Hannah Rathbone
Sarah Rathbone / Rhoby Rathbone	Eliza Jane Hayward
Rhoby Place / Whipple Phillips	Ellen Maria Stowell
Sarah Phillips	E. D. Barlow Jr.
H. P. L.	R. H. B.

Aug. 15 we took a trip to ancient Newport, & on the 20th we went to Salem & Marblehead—pausing at Lynn to pick up young Sterling,[4] who is recovering finely from his operation & will enter Harvard in September. A fortnight ago another guest was here—none other than old Adolphe de Castro, the voluble one-time friend of Ambrose Bierce (later a revision client of mine) whom you may recall from 1928 days. He had been to Boston for the melancholy purpose of scattering his late wife's ashes in the sea in accordance with her ante-mortem request. His stay here totalled 5 days, & we kept him busy with sights. One afternoon he, Barlow, & I sat on a tomb in the hidden hillside churchyard & wrote rhymed acrostics on the name of Edgar Allan Poe, who 90 years ago used to wander through that selfsame necropolis when on visits to Providence.[5]

Well—I trust all flourishes in the metropolitan zone. Any meetings of the gang lately? Kleiner has just shewed me his graceful verses to diminutive Trintje Annetje—of which his cousin surely made a good typographical job![6] ¶ Printed matter goes forward under separate cover. Don't waste too much time about it! ¶ Yr obt grandsire H. Uylipse van Kasje

P.S. Edkins is in the hospital again with a second operation. I surely hope this one will give him some lasting health!

[P.]P.S. I see you've come down in the world —by two storeys!

Notes

1. After HPL and other amateur journalists attended a lecture by Dunsany at the Copley Plaza in Boston on 20 October 1919, Alice M. Hamlet sent Dunsany a copy of the *Tryout* (November 1919) that contained HPL's poem "To Edward John Moreton Drax Plunkett, 18th Baron Dunsany." Dunsany remarked in a letter published in the *Tryout* that the tribute was "magnificent" and that "I am most grateful to the author of that poem for his warm and generous enthusiasm, crystallised in verse" (*Tryout* 5, No. 12 [December 1919]: [12]). Dunsany also read "Supernatural Horror in Literature."

2. J. Randle Luten, "What Makes an Author Click?," *American Author* 4, No. 4 (July 1932): 11–13 (*WW* 56–62). William Bolitho, "Pulp Magazines," *New York World* (4 January 1930): 11 (*WW* 231). Howard Wolf, "Variety," *Akron Beacon Journal* (12 December 1927): 10 (*LR* 403–5). Edwin Meade "Ted" Robinson (1878–1946), "The Philosopher of Folly: A Journalistic Journal," *Cleveland Plain Dealer* (13 March 1923): 10.

3. [Unsigned], Review of *Pre-Revolutionary Dutch Houses and Families* by Rosalie Fellows Bailey, *New York Times Book Review* (23 August 1936): 12. See WBT 78n2.

4. Kenneth Sterling (1920–1995), author, with HPL, of "In the Walls of Eyrx."

5. Adolphe de Castro, "Edgar Allan Poe" (*WT,* May 1937); R. H. Barlow, "St. John's Churchyard," and HPL, "In a Sequester'd Providence Churchyard Where Once Poe Walk'd" (*Science-Fantasy Correspondent,* March–April 1937). HPL's poem was reprinted in *WT* (May 1938) as "Where Poe Once Walked: An Acrostic Sonnet." Maurice W. Moe later wrote a poem of his own and published it, along with HPL's, RHB's, and de Castro's, in a mimeographed booklet, *Four Acrostic Sonnets on Poe* (1936). Henry Kuttner also wrote an acrostic.

6. *To Mistress Katherine Anna Talman, born July 7th, 1936.* [n.p., 1936.]

[104] [ALS, JHL]

The Ancient Hill
—Oct. 6, 1936.

Jonkheer:—

Yours of the 2nd duly blew in, & I learn with interest of the marketing attempts you have in mind.[1] Bless me, yes—go ahead if you have the patience—but don't expect any success. W T, Putnam's, Vanguard, Knopf, & Loring & Mussey all abandoned the idea of a collection after approaching me about the matter, & I have no notion that any other publisher would do otherwise. Just at present young Julius Schwartz (255 E. 188th St., N.Y.C.) has a lot of my MSS. as agent with a view to placing them with some British publisher [in fact, he's had 'em so long that I must enquire about them soon], but I have no expectation that he will succeed. Not long ago that brilliant new W T illustrator—Virgil Finlay, 302 Rand St., Rochester, N.Y.—got in touch with me & offered to illustrate a group of my tales in case the illustrations would increase the chances of their marketability as a book.[2] I told him there was not much prospect that any publisher would care to consider such a volume—pictures or no pictures—& warned him to use his judgment. I suggested that he discuss the proposition with Schwartz if he cared to do so—for certainly, I am done with all direct contact with publishers. However, I'm sure I'd much rather have you act as agent than Schwartz—& rest assured that I shan't begrudge any commission which may be suggested! The only trouble is that the stuff probably won't land anywhere, thus leaving you flat despite my most liberal intentions! I fancy the present activities of Schwartz *in Great Britain* won't interfere with any parallel agenting in this side of the Atlantic. Do you think it would be a good idea to write young Finlay about the illustration angle? Actually, I don't believe he'd need to draw any pictures until after the acceptance of any collection which might be accepted. All he'd need to do would be to show certain specimens of his best work in W T or elsewhere. Anyhow, he couldn't illustrate a collection until after its contents were fully selected. But use your own judgment about all this. I leave the whole damn business entirely in your hands. A full-length novel to order (acceptance not being guaranteed) would be quite a gamble—although I'd enjoy attempting such a thing if I could get the time. Right now I'm trying to reform my programme a bit—thinning out less important correspondence, &c.—though I haven't made very striking headway so far. Certainly, I'll keep the whole transaction confidential—& needless to say I wish you luck, both in connexion with these tales, & in connexion with any tales of Belknap's or Wandrei's or anybody else's which you may handle.

Sorry so many burdens have been besetting you of late, & hope they are now rapidly clearing up. The issues of *De Halve Maen* which I lack are those between April 1, 1935 (Vol. X, No. 3) & Jan. 7, 1936 (Vol. XI, No. 2)—two, I'd venture to guess, unless Vol. X had more than 4 numbers. I'd appreciate the missing numbers if you happen to have any duplicates which you can easily spare—though of course you must not go to any elaborate trouble about the matter.

Meanwhile let me thank you most sincerely for those pages from *Ford News*. The account of the transplanted Cape Cod mill is the best I have seen so far, & both it & the Carolina items will go into my files amidst the most grateful invocations. But the assigned *date* of that mill still puzzles me, as it did when the newspapers published it in connexion with the structure's tragic removal. If it is in truth 1633, then this mill forms the second-oldest edifice of English construction on this continent—only St. Luke's church in Virginia (1632) antedating it. Yet the Fairbanks house in Dedham (1636) has repeatedly been proclaimed the oldest in New England & second-oldest structure English building in America. If the mill really *was* the oldest structure in New England, it seems to me that societies in this section would have fought its sale & removal much more vigorously than they did. It was a crime anyhow to let it go west. Possibly the best authorities do not agree that the present structure contains much of the original mill of 1633. I must make further enquiries.

Glad you got the postcard from Mortonius & me. We had some very pleasant sessions hereabouts.[3] Did Barlow look you up when he passed through N.Y.? He is now settled for the winter with an uncle, & may be addressed % H. M. Langworthy, 810 W. 57th St. Terrace, Kansas City, Mo. Young Robert Moe was here Sept. 19–20—partly to call on someone entering Brown.[4] Autumn weather puts a stop to outdoor reading & writing, but I still get out for occasional rural walks. Of late I have been appreciating Neutaconkanut Hill (the great western ridge at the end of the Plainfield St. car line) as never before—both the magnificent view, & the mystically glamourous woods & meadows & valleys beyond the crest. It is getting to be quite a rival of Quinsnicket with me.

Well—thanks for all the bother with my yarns, & good luck as an agent. But don't hope too much! ¶ Blessings—

Grandpa

Notes

1. Talman was planning to approach the publisher William Morrow about a book of HPL's stories or a novel.
2. Virgil Finlay (1914–1971), one of the great weird artists of his time, illustrated several HPL stories for *Weird Tales* and also the dusk jacket for the posthumously published *The Outsider and Others*.
3. James F. Morton visited HPL in Providence on 11–13 September.
4. Eunice French (1915–1949), an undergraduate studying philosophy.

[105] [ALS, JHL]

The Ancient Hill
—All Soul's Day
[2 November 1936]

Jonkheer:—

Yours of Oct. 27 found me in a hell of a turmoil reading voluminous proofs from two separate sources, but I am now able to snatch a moment in which to acknowledge, with suitable obeisances, the communication in question.

Regarding the stories—I could have told you in advance that your publisher wouldn't want them. The more I look over my junk, the less I like it. It isn't good enough for a book, nor bad enough to be a drawing card in the pulps. It falls between two stools. Of the whole mass of it, only "The Colour Out of Space" & "The Music of Erich Zann" are worth saving. As I have long realised, the cheapening influence of the pulps got insidiously at my style before I was aware of it. Even when consciously repudiating the commercial tradition, I was being more or less insidiously affected by it. And now that I comprehend the fact, & am prepared to be on guard against the tendency, I am less fertile & imaginative than I was. The years have slowed me down. Would that I had had my present practice & perspective in the fictional field when I was in my prime!

Well—these rejections don't surprise me much nowadays. I am now awaiting with patient semi-amusement the inevitable ultimate return of the tales which young Schwartz insisted on sending to some British publisher. But I guess I will call a halt after that; since the postage, & the wear & tear on MSS. & magazine extracts, are hardly to be welcomed!

Which reminds me that I hope you can get my stories back in good shape from the Morrow firm. Alabad, Ghinu, & Aratza grant that those 8 readers were careful! Requests for loans continue to accumulate—from persons getting in touch with me through W T—& I find it increasingly difficult to meet them as my various available MSS. wear out, get lost, or become tied up as those London-submitted stories are. To type new copies is impossible—the effort would complete my reduction to a chaotic congeries of jangling nerves! So please do your best to recover the material in fair condition. Only a year ago those goddam sons-of-beachcombers at Loring & Musseys lost the May '23 *National Amateur* containing my only lendable copy of "Hypnos" & much irreplaceable N.A.P.A. matter to boot!

Now about this nebulous & doubtful book proposition—ten years ago I'd have snapped it up without thinking, but today the old man goes more slowly. While, as I said last month, I have always been vaguely toying with the idea of a full-length book, I have relatively little idea that any publisher would want anything which I could produce at this period. I haven't had time to think of original fiction for a year, & couldn't decide offhand just which of the various ideas in my note-books I'd want to choose for a first novel-length attempt. Moreover—I could never create 15,000 words with any conclusiveness until I had finished the entire story—for I usually change radically as I proceed; often altering the first half of a story unrecognisably in order to reconcile it with elements unexpectedly introduced in the writing of the later sections. What is more, I cannot write to order, & the imposition of a bunch of suggestions & limitations would kill the progress of anything I might get started. When I thought of writing a book-length thing, I had the idea of just going ahead & doing it—without the hampering effect of any suggestions from outside. Then if anyone wished to use it verbatim, well & good. If not, well & good also—for some "fan" magazine would undoubtedly be glad to serialise it, thus getting it before the few who would be most likely to enjoy it. But before beginning anything—even in this manner—I would have to do a lot of choosing among various potential themes; & it is quite possible that I would find myself unequal to the proper development of any of the ideas evolved & jotted down in my younger, more egotistically hopeful, & more ambitious days.[1] I would want to test my ability in private before making any promises—& avoid the ignominious procedure of starting something which I couldn't adequately fin-

ish. The fact is, I believe I ought to get in practice with a few short stories before I try anything more substantial. I am all out of the fictional mood now—
having written nothing original in a year[2]—& really need to work myself back
into it if I expect to evolve anything of any merit. I have indeed been trying to
get some time for fictional experiments during recent weeks, but have been
defeated through the sudden turning-up of unexpected duties & obligations.
Very slowly I am trying to get my correspondence under control without of-
fending anybody—through a policy of slower & briefer replies. Results may
be perceptible before long—& with a lapse in revisory tasks the time for possible story-writing ought to be forthcoming in the reasonably near future.
How soon I would feel justified in tackling a novel remains to be seen.

It appears, then, that I would make a rather exasperating & unsatisfactory
person to deal with just now—but I am none the less grateful to you for having devoted so much time & energy to the discussion of these matters. As to
just what to do or say—it would perhaps be best to avoid the making of any
promises, since my ability to perform is so doubtful. But if the publishers remain permanently in a receptive state, & keep in mind the attitude which they
have formed through their reading of the short tales & through your kindly
propaganda, it is not at all impossible that I might later on send you a rough
plot-synopsis to shew very tentatively to them. If in such a case they indicated
that they might consider a novel of that general nature, I might later—if I
found it practicable to develop the idea—let you shew them the finished
product . . . or part of it. I could not, however, be *bound* to any specific course
at any stage of the proceedings. I never undertake any obligations unless I am
absolutely certain of my ability to fulfil them—& in this case *certainty* on my part
would mean the existence of a completed novel. Of course I have no reason
to assume that the publishers would remain receptive in the absence of any
definite promises—but in that case the only thing to do is to close the incident. Which reminds me that I hope you haven't spent too much time & energy in presenting this matter to the courteous but canny Morrovians. I'd hate
to think of your having gone to an inordinate amount of trouble in a matter
yielding you not the faintest trace of a reward—either material or psychological!

Many thanks for the current *Halve Maen*—in which van Loon's remarks
on the rarity of Dutch were of great interest.[3] That well-advertised banquet of
the 23d sounds highly congenial, & I trust you solid burghers will all have a
genial & festive time with your schnapps, churchwarden pipes, & other echoes of the balmy days of old Nieuw-Amsterdam! Meanwhile I shall appreciate
those missing numbers (all between Vol. X, No. 3 [April, 1935] & Vol. XI,
No. 2 [Jan. 7, 1936]) whenever you happen to come across some duplicates
that can conveniently be spared.

Despite the lateness of the season my outdoor rambles have not entirely
ended—occasional warm days making possible the exploration of the autumnal countryside. It is curious how many attractive rural regions *wholly new to me*

I have discovered within a 3-mile radius since the beginning of October. I believe I previously mentioned my expeditions to Neutaconkanut Hill (west of the town) & to the Squantum Woods (down the E. shore of the bay). Last Wednesday I opened up one more realm of fascinating terra incognita—the region west of Neutaconkanut, & the western slopes of that noble eminence itself. I followed a road which rises gently as it skirts Neutaconkanut's western foot, & which commands an idyllic vista of meadows, groves, stone wells, & cottage roofs. Just before sunset I ascended the hill, & from its dizzy crest obtained an almost stupefying prospect of outspread countryside & orange sky. I then crossed the top of the hill (it is really a sizeable *table-land*) to the eastward parts already known to me—obtaining some fine views from the numerous ridges & hillocks of the lofty plateau. My route was varied— sometimes through the grassy interior, but now & then getting toward the wooded edge where dark valleys slope down to the plain below, & huge balanced boulders on rocky heights impart a spectral, druidic effect. The huge round moon & the glowing lamps of Venus & Jupiter added to the general glamour. Finally I came to more familiar ground—& stood once more on the cityward slope which I have always known. The outspread city was rapidly lighting up, & lay like a constellation in the deepening dusk. Then down the steep hillside to the car line (too cold for enjoyable walking when there's no scenery to compensate for shivers!) & back to the prosaic haunts of man. ¶ Again, profoundest appreciation of your marketing efforts, & regrets that I can't promise anything in the novel line. ¶ Yr oblig'd obt Servt

H P L

Notes

1. HPL refers to the numerous early notes jotted in his commonplace book. Among these is the early note "Witches' Hollow novel?" (*CE* 5.227).

2. HPL's last original story was "The Haunter of the Dark" (5–9 November 1935).

3. Hendrik Willem van Loon, "Lost Language of Holland," *De Halve Maen* 12, No. 1 (16 October 1936): [2].

[106] [ALS, JHL]

Nov. 10[, 1936]

Jonkheer:—

Just a word to let you know how sorry I am that my previous epistle seemed ambiguous. I thought I was quite explicit—but hope I can attain greater definiteness this time. Let me add at the outset that I feel enormously & genuinely pained if I've unwittingly caused you to make elaborate approaches & semi-commitments on my behalf, from which a possible retreat would prove embarrassing. I would not for the world have authorised any definite & immediate discussion of material as yet unwritten; & if my mention of a vague future intention to experiment with a novel (I've forgotten just how I did word my reference in the wish or design which I have cloudily & indefinitely harboured for years) seemed to form such an authorisation, I can do no more than kiss the dust in a thousand obeisances of contrition. What I meant was simply this: that if the Morrow firm was especially well-disposed toward novels (& I did not envisage a time-limit on that state of corporate mind), I would surely take advantage of that disposition, & of your (supposedly permanent) entreé [*sic*] with the firm, to the extent of submitting to them—through you as agent—the very first thing of the kind I ever *might* produce. I possibly added that a knowledge of the conceivable opening (& I fully appreciated the unusual nature of the consideration you are able to secure from the company) would perhaps encourage me to experiment with a novel sooner than I otherwise might—but I did not for an instant conceive of the matter as more than a nebulous, theoretical idea for the rather remote future. I may have mis-read your letter (I can't find it at the moment), but in any case that was the idea I formed; & my reply was based entirely upon it. Nothing could have been farther from my thoughts or wishes than to encourage any definite immediate discussion (of the sort from which it is sometimes so awkward to retreat) of such an enterprise. So pray accept my profoundest apologies if I've caused you to go through any elaborate procedure or expend any persuasive or diplomatic energy in vain! Be at least assured that such a thing was the result of sheer stupidity & misinterpretation on my part, rather than of any inconsiderate negligence or callous & arbitrary capriciousness. I genuflect. I grovel. And my regret is of the most acute & genuine, as distinguished from the formal & perfunctory, sort. Damn it all! But you can at least justify yourself with the firm by telling them—with my cordial permission—that your client is a muddled old fool who doesn't know enough to say what he means the first time! One thing more—don't fancy for a second that I don't appreciate the extreme kindness & thoughtfulness which have animated your intensive efforts to put this matter over! Hell! It would be difficult for me to convey adequately my sense of gratitude! That adds to my contriteness about any troublesome conferences or commitments into which my careless & casual (careless & casual because I thought the matter merely a vague pipe-dream of the theoretical future) phraseology may have led you!

Now as to the "unfathomable" nature of any immediately previous letter—let's see where the trouble lies. The meaning I sought to convey was simply this: that I can't guarantee to produce anything of book length in the immediate future; that the handicap of specifications regarding the "plot" (if any) might make it impossible for me to write a book even if I otherwise could; that I *might* not be able to produce a book *at all*—even in the remotest future & under conditions of the most perfect independence; but that I would certainly be glad (a) to let the Morrow firm see the first tentative novel synopsis I ever did evolve (be that in 1937, 1938, or any damn time[)], or (b) if a novel ever grew up from my pen without a synopsis, to let them see its text in whole or in part. These things were *definite*. True, the matter of the possible submission was left indefinite, but only because it had to be. I tried to be definite about this indefiniteness. At the moment I don't know whether I could write a novel or not. Such things can't be forced. If I agreed to start in trying right now the result could be only dismal flatness & failure. *I* would be placed in the ridiculous position of delivering artificial junk which I could not myself endorse, & *you* would be placed in the equally ridiculous position of having strongly recommended a complete "dud". When I'll ever be ready for such an attempt I don't know—certainly not till I've done a short story or two. And I'm equally ignorant of whether I could go ahead with a story if not allowed an absolutely free hand as to development. The chances are adverse, for external meddling always cuts the ground from under me & removes the motive force which makes the story possible.

So what, under the circumstances, *could* I have said? There was nothing to do but leave the matter *as open & indefinite as the Morrow firm are willing to leave it*. I shall probably be trying some novel of the given kind eventually, whether or not any market exists for it. If the Morrows' [*sic*] attitude of special consideration for matter sent through you (an attitude I greatly appreciate) holds out until the performance of this experiment, well & good. If it does not—that is my misfortune, but an inevitable misfortune! I did not realise, of course, the special pains the firm had taken, or the extent to which they regarded me as committed.

So far, so good. Now as to the best thing to tell them, in view of all considerations. . . . . The course you suggest, so long as it involves only a synopsis as a real obligation, seems to me sensible enough. Indeed, you'll see by my "unfathomable" letter that I suggested a flat termination of discussion *only as one alternative,* in case *the company* did not wish to leave any unsatisfying loose ends dangling. It was for *their* sake, not for *mine,* that I made the tentative suggestion. And of course I still leave that suggestion open as an alternative for you to apply if at any time, for any reason, it seems to become advisable in your opinion. I don't want to ball up the programme of a busy corporation with the uncertainties that hinge on a nerve-racked old man—hence I give you leave to erase everything whenever you choose. If there is any continuation of the state of open unsettledness, it must be through the company's wish, not mine.

Let me repeat for clearness' sake: the course you advise—to give a reasonably strong promise of a synopsis sooner or later, & much less definite suggestions regarding a complete or fractional novel-manuscript in the remote future—will be acceptable to me if you prefer it. But I also give you leave to terminate all discussion if you ever find it advisable for your own sake or the firm's. And in talking with representatives of the firm, feel free to put all blame for difficulties upon me—where indeed it belongs. Do I make myself plain?

As for details & loose ends—I really don't know when I could ever get at the job of tackling a full-length book; since a calm, unhurried programme & an absolute freedom from criticism or directions form a pre-requisite to any major effort requiring concentration—that is, so far as I am concerned. What is more, the thing would have to have a *natural start*—a spontaneous raison d'etre. I've never yet set down deliberately with the idea of "writing some kind of a story". Nothing but hack tripe would ever come of that. What I write is written *because it has to be*—because the idea germinated of itself & demanded expression. At present the things I want to get at are not of novel calibre—& the only way to get around to wanting to write a novel is to get these short-story ideas off my chest first. Indeed, I think my experience shows that the best things I've ever written have been *pendants* to other material—that is, late members of a whole group of things written close together, or at least second members of a pair. In other words, the thing which puts me in the best mood for writing *is writing*. But even so, nothing can be guaranteed. I am feeling wretchedly of late, & the possibility of my having become wholly "written out"—of having lost the zest & imaginative definiteness of younger days—cannot be dismissed. It is entirely conceivable that I shall never complete another work of fiction, long or short—though not for lack of experimental attempts. I have no stomach for charlatanry, & *could* not—even if I *would*—concoct the artificial junk which "successful" commercial hacks pour fourth [*sic*] to such financial advantage. Nor would I, now that I know better, stoop to some of the unconscious cheap tricks which my earlier stuff contained, & on which most of the rabble-popularity of that work was undoubtedly based. However, as I said before, I have for the last few weeks been trying to clear my programme for another of my seasons of fictional experimentation (like the season of 1934–5, when I wrote half a dozen things & destroyed all save "The Shadow Out of Time" . . . . . which was itself the 3d complete version of the same story), & if I do succeed in getting going, it is quite possible that I might arrive at the novel-synopsis stage—or the novel-writing stage. Who can say? It all depends on what occurs between now & then. At any rate, you'll hear from me the moment I *do* have anything in the desired line to shew. Incidentally, it would be less confusing if I had some notion of the kind of thing the Morrow firm prefer—for of all the different novel-ideas jotted down in my note book I might unwittingly choose the very one they want least. Do you know what their tastes are? Do they prefer tenuous things in the best Blackwood vein, or profoundly dark & sinister things in the Machen manner—or what the hell? Surely they must have some idea—if they're so particular about reserving the right to dictate endings—of what they want. Incidentally, if a story of mine were headed toward a certain ending it could never be changed except spontaneously. I would have to finish it in the original way—toward which all the earlier parts would be adjusted—& relinquish the idea of Morrow as a market. You speak of "good plot" as a desideratum—but *plot* has always been a negligible element with me. Plot, in the most conventional sense of the word, has very little place in weird fiction (*atmosphere* being the one crucial element), & I am so little interested or experienced in plot-technique that no series of events of my devising would be likely to satisfy a publisher intent on this artificial device. Thus my synopsis might be ruled out at the start. But time alone will shed more light on these points. I doubt very much if the publishers would accept any novel of mine, no matter how hard I might endeavour to adapt it to their specifications. Probably the entire thing would amount merely to a titanic effort & expenditure of time on my part, followed by a polite rejection. However, that would not make me regret having written the novel if it were really of any merit, since my interest in literature is not connected with publication—momentarily alluring & encouraging though the notion of publication may be. The psychological symbolism inherent in rejections usually cuts me off from *further* writing for a time after each rebuff, but never makes me regret having written anything which I believe to have a grain of merit—which, that is, succeeds to some extent in crystallising the mood I set out to crystallise. The *commercial or financial* side of fiction is of course simply ridiculous to me. I am no garage mechanic or merchant tailor to use the materials of literature in an occupation not only alien but antagonistic to literature—& I have not the happy luck to produce things spontaneously which are likewise marketable. As a source of dependable revenue, original writing is simply *out* with me. I *couldn't* become a successful hack even if I *would*. My growing economic plight is an absolutely *separate* question, on which fiction-writing has no possible bearing. As time passes, I must indeed find some source of the $10.00 to $15.00 per week which I require for subsistence—but this source can never be original fiction. I don't care what it is so long as it's honest—but it *can't* be literary whoredom. The economic status of a man of my age without special training in the clerical or other industrial fields is not pleasant to contemplate (would that I had had the gift of prophecy, & trained myself to some routine industrial or clerical skill independent of literature, in the days when I was young & malleable!)—but the remedy lies in some sort of job-hunting outside writing. I may run an elevator, but I'll never write a hack story!

But I digress. As for Sonny Belknap's remarks on my own classification of my tales—I can only point out with grandpaternal sorrow that the young rascal has completely relinquished his taste in fiction since going commercial. He has forgotten all that goes to make up a sincere piece of narrative self-expression, & nowadays swallows glibly some of the crudest hokum of the pulp tradition. This shews itself not so much in his valuations of *my* work as in his freely expressed opinions of general fiction, both literary & pulp. He solemnly recommends pitiful tripe as good writing, & once tried to justify the cheap stock characters & situations of pulpdom (in an argument with little Sterling) by comparing them to the conventionalisations of the Japanese

Noh-play! In other words, he has stopped looking for the real spirit & essence of a work of fiction, but has begun to appraise fiction according to the popular commercial standard—laying favourable stress on such meretricious tricks as plot-twists, exaggeratedly dramatic tableaux, jack-in-the-box climaxes, snappy dialogue, scene-shifting pageantry, & all the other superficial, artificial devices beloved by his new pantheon of Tremaines, Margulies's, & Weisingers.[1] He doesn't—nowadays—even know what I'm *trying* to do in fiction . . . & wouldn't recognise my success if I ever *did* succeed (which I fear I shall never do), since the result wouldn't have the glossy surface, action, & punch of his latter-day idols. He doesn't realise that I'm constantly on guard *against* doing all the things he now believes *should* be done in a story. Fortunately, his eclipse of fictional taste does not extend to other fields—his judgment of poetry, painting, &c. being unimpaired so far as I can see. And I think he'd get back his fictional taste if he'd get out of the hack-writing field. His lapse is obviously a direct product of a somewhat naive tendency to justify & idealise whatever he does or has to do. Instead of writing pulp tripe & despising it—as he used to despise it before he had to write it—he feels it incumbent upon himself to prove to the world that pulp standards are really sound . . . & that the immortal works of Edmond Hamilton & Otis Adelbert Kline are really profound classics in disguise . . . deep wells of human feeling somewhat conventionalised in the manner of the Japanese Noh-play! With such a new set of criteria, it's no wonder that he thinks his aged grandpa's taste (about what his own used to be or would normally be even now, though somewhat improved since the early 1920 period) is all cockeyed! I wish to gawd somebody would leave him a fortune or give him a fat industrial job, so that he could snap out of pot-boiling & get his fictional perspective back!

Regarding your own opinion of "Erich Zann"—it's hardly a scribbler's place to defend his own efforts, but I wonder how fully you realise just why I wrote the story & what I was trying to do? I seem to remember a promising young man back in '26 or so who couldn't find anything especially potent in Poe! In an argument about fictional taste—or rather, the special field of fantastic-fictional taste—I'd rather turn to a phase not requiring the awkward attitude of self-defence. Let me then say that, so far as I can see, Blackwood's "The Willows" is the greatest weird story ever written, with Machen's "The White People" as a close second, & with things like Shiel's "House of Sounds", Machen's "Black Seal" & "White Powder", Chambers' "Yellow Sign", Poe's "House of Usher", & James's "Count Magnus" as good runners-up. Or if the discussion *must* hinge on my own attempts, let me adopt a negative course & denounce the lousy ones instead of defending the half-passable specimens. Know, then, that "The Hound", "The Horror at Red Hook", "He", "The Moon-Bog", "The White Ship", "From Beyond", "The Tree", & "The Quest of Iranon" might—if typed on good stock—make excellent shelf-paper but little else. The "Cthulhu" thing is rather middling—not as bad as the worst, but full of cheap & cumbrous touches. Indeed, nothing but the "Colour out of Space" really satisfies me as a whole. My regard for "Erich Zann" is negative rather than positive . . . . I place it second merely because it isn't as bad as most of the rest. I like it for what it *hasn't* more than for what it *has*. But I suppose all this sounds very cloudy, unbusinesslike, & obscure.

The secret of a weird tale's power is subtle & elusive—& has nothing to do with the glib formulae of the pulp canaille. Permit me to conclude this phase of discussion with two or three quotations from articles of mine on the subject.

"The true weird tale has something more than secret murder, bloody bones, or a sheeted form clanking chains according to rule. A certain atmosphere of breathless & unexplainable dread of outer, unknown forces must be present; & there must be a hint, expressed with a seriousness & portentousness becoming its subject, of that most terrible conception of the human brain—a malign & particular suspension or defeat of those fixed laws of nature which are our only safeguard against the assaults of chaos & the daemons of unplumbed space."

"The one test of the really weird is simply this—whether or not there be excited in the reader a profound sense of dread, & of contact with unknown spheres & powers; a subtle attitude of awed listening, as if for the beating of black wings or the scratching of outside shapes & entities on the known universe's utmost rim."[2]

"Atmosphere, not action, is the thing to cultivate in the wonder story. We cannot put stress on the bare events, since the unnatural extravagance of those events makes them sound hollow & absurd when thrown into too high relief. Such events, even when theoretically possible or conceivable in the future*, have no counterpart in existing life & human experience, hence can never form the groundwork of an adult tale. All that a marvel story can ever be, in a serious way, is a *vivid picture of a certain type of human mood*. The moment it tries to be anything else it becomes cheap, puerile, & unconvincing. Therefore a fantastic author should see that his prime emphasis goes into subtle suggestion—the imperceptible hints & touches of selective & associative detail which express shadings of moods & build up a vague illusion of the strange reality of the unreal—instead of bald catalogues of incredible happenings which can have no substance nor meaning apart from a sustaining cloud of colour & mood-symbolism. A serious adult story must be true to something in life. Since marvel tales cannot be true to the *events* of life, they must shift their emphasis toward something to which they *can* be true; namely, certain wistful or restless *moods* of the human spirit, where-

---

*as in some science-fiction

in it seeks to weave gossamer ladders of escape from the galling tyranny of time, space, & natural law."[3]

All of which may or may not have some relevance to the topics we have been discussing.

I'm certainly glad to hear of your new arrangements for getting stuff well-considered by various publishers—not merely the Morrow firm. That ought to put you right in the Kline or Lenniger class as a top-notch agent. Indeed you may go so far in this field that you'll either drop the good old *Texaco Star* or relegate it to second place! No doubt you'll reciprocate the publishers' courtesy by never submitting any material which does not obviously *deserve* special consideration. Glad you'll have Quinn & Sonny & the Wandreis on your list of clients. All of these can certainly deliver the kind of goods wanted on schedule time.

About returning the stories—there's no hurry so long as they are safe & likely to return in approximately the same condition as when received. Your remarks on photographic reproduction are highly interesting—especially so in the light of the impressive sample (which I return herewith)—& I shall keep this process in mind for future eventualities. The use of photostats seems greatly on the increase—institutions like the *N.Y. Times,* N.Y. Public Library, & John Carter Brown library offering reproductions of all their treasures at a relatively moderate price. In the case of old MSS., I fancy the question of typing versus photostat would be rather hard to decide. Typed copies with carbons (& I don't begrudge the correction of these—although the photostat's perfect literalness of reproduction is alluring to consider!) would probably form the most desirable duplicates, & I'd probably decide on them if the cost weren't very much in excess of photostats. Now & then I have made arrangements with borrowers to provide me with new copies of badly-worn MSS.—& once a revision-client paid up a bad debt in that way.

By the way—do you still collect bookplates? Here's a specimen sent me by Charles Johnston of De Land—my only link with that idyllic region since Barlow's midwestern move[4]—to whom I once spoke concerning your collection. Pray accept it with the donor's compliments—he vastly admired my bookplate when I shewed it to him, & from that specimen formed a lofty idea of your taste. I admired this Stetson Library bookplate when I encountered it in books there, but didn't have the nerve to ask for a copy. The design shews the main college edifice rather attractively.

Another by the way—has Kleiner (or anyone else) sent you the recent issue of *The Californian* (largest of the N.A.P.A. magazines) with his article & poem on our old gang of a decade ago?[5] You certainly must have a copy, for you are prominently mentioned. If you haven't received one, let me know, & I'll see that you are supplied. Each of the old-timers (especially Kirk, whom R K invests with a particular halo) ought to have this magazine, & an effort will be made to cover them. Have you been in touch with the ever-elusive & migratory Arturo lately? His last known (to me) address was 228 Henry St., Brooklyn . . . . . but that was last January, & 8 months is a long time for our carefree colleague to roost in one place. The rest of the group seem to be fairly reachable . . . . except Orton, who has apparently dropped out of the radius of us all, though his name crops up in print from time to time as a typographical connoisseur. Wandrei—who first became a "regular" in 1928 or 1929—isn't mentioned in the article; rather a regrettable omission, though I presume Kleiner regards the most glamourous period of the Kalem as having ended somewhat before then. Good old Mac receives adequate notice—alas that he isn't still here to read the article!

Edkins' recovery goes on slowly—though I'll wager the climate of Florida (which he has just reached) will speed it up a bit. With all his ills, I envy him the sands of Coral Gables (although I'd prefer the sands of Key West).

Beastly cold tonight. Since tomorrow is an holiday you wouldn't get this epistle any sooner if I mailed it tonight—so I guess I won't brave the frost-daemon. Damn autumn, & triple-damn winter!

Well—as to the main point of the matter under discussion—I guess I've epitomised it with reasonable clearness on page II, 2. If any obscurity remains, let me know, & I'll be glad to elucidate further. The endorsement of your position ought to make things all right with the publishers, & if I find it a psychological impossibility to deliver a novel-synopsis within a reasonable period, it won't be your fault. Blame it on the old gent—crotchety & senile cuss that he is. But I'll surely *try* to cook you up some sort of a synopsis before spring . . . unless you yourself (or the publishers) decide that a "closed account" is preferable. ¶ All good wishes, & renewed apologies for any sort of a mess my vague language may have got you in! ¶ Yr obt Grandsire

    H P L

Notes

1. F. Orlin Tremaine (1899–1956), editor of *Astounding Stories;* Leo Margulies (1900–1975), editor of *Thrilling Wonder Stories;* and Mort Weisinger (1915–1978), editor of *Time Traveller.*

2. These two (nonconsecutive) paragraphs are from "Supernatural Horror in Literature."

3. "Some Notes on Interplanetary Fiction."

4. Johnston was the Barlows' handyman.

5. Rheinhart Kleiner, "After a Decade and the Kalem Club," *Californian* 4, No. 2 (Fall 1936): 45–47, and "After a Decade": 44.

[107] [ALS, JHL]

Feby. 28[, 1937]

Jonkheer:—

Yrs of the 15th found me completely knocked out with an acute intestinal trouble following 2 mos. of dragging grippe. Don't know how long or serious an ordeal I'm in, for but Dr. Dustin plans to call in a stomach specialist Tuesday.[1] Am in constant pain, take only liquid food, & so bloated with gas that I can't lie down. Spend all time in chair propped with pillows, & can read or write only a few minutes at a time. Taking 3 medicines at once.

But I must not delay answering yours of the 15th. Thanks immensely for the antiquarian travel bits, & for the new Texaco Star. No—I didn't get your Steel Number. The last Star I had before this new one was the Texas Centennial issue.

As for that book proposition—I'm devilish sorry to say that it looks rather stalled. I've had no strength since the middle of December & could attend only to immediate things. Now it looks as if all bets were off. I've no idea what lies ahead of me—& any systematic effort seems fantastically remote. You & the firm are unbelievably kind & liberal—but what can a guy do when he hardly has strength enough to walk across the room? If I ever get through this damned mess, & the firm still feels receptive, we may be able to talk more to the point. All my correspondence & affairs are going to hell, though I'm dropping cards—or having my aunt drop them—in important cases.

Hope Belknap's magnum opus will be one of the sensations of 1937. His confidence at least is in his favour.

Good luck with your own pulp experiments. It all depends on what one's basic values & ambitions are. There is certainly vast economic advantage in the pulp field.

Well—I hope all is progressing well with you. Again let me apologise for the apparent letdown, & assure you that the cause is all too adequate. I'll see that you hear of any salient future development.

Blessings & genuflections—

Grandpa van Kasje

Notes

1. Dr. Cecil Calvert Dustin (1894–1976). The specialist was Dr. William Leet.

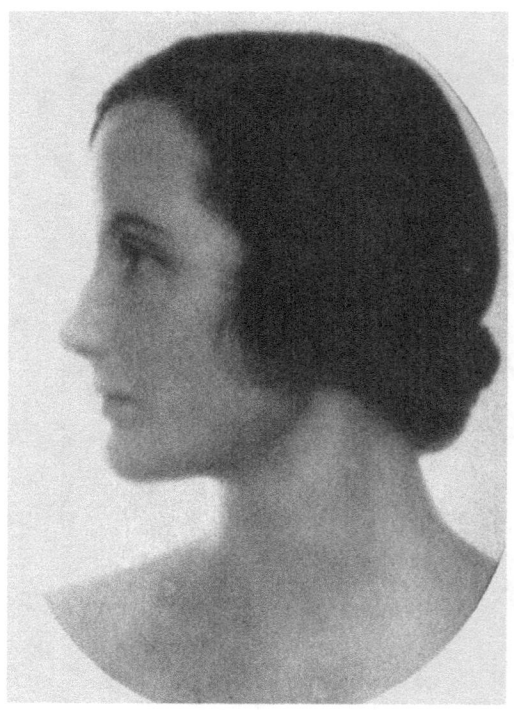

*Above: Helen V. Sully; Below: Helen and Marion Sully,
with Clark Ashton Smith, Spring 1938*

Letters to Helen V. Sully

[1]   [ALS, JHL][1]

66 College St.,
Providence, R.I.,
July 26, 1933

Dear Miss Sully:—

Let me hasten to acknowledge with pleasure the mail from Gloucester, which I found upon my return from Onset—whither I *did* manage to get, owing to the nurse's considerate willingness to stay in Monday & Tuesday afternoons.[2] Thanks enormously for the Sargent–Murray–Gilman booklet,[3] which goes forthwith into my geographic-antiquarian files. I am sorry that historic guidance has been lacking, & wish indeed that I might have been on hand to point out the archaic high spots. However—the guide-book & map ought to be of some avail, so that you probably did not leave the town as an entire stranger. I hope you saw quaint *Rockport* (where the 1812 cannonball is embedded in the church belfry)[4] & the striking sea-cliffs of Magnolia—with the yawning abyss of Rafe's Chasm.[5] The Sargent &c. house must have given you an excellent idea of a typical middle-period Colonial interior—as some houses in Prov. & Newport would have done had it been possible to explore them. The powdering-closets[6] must have seemed odd—though they were quite frequent in Georgian mansions of the better grade. The discovery of some Sully portraits must surely have given you a thrill of pride. Incidentally, you possibly know that Thomas Sully's nephew Robert[7] (himself an artist of no mean attainments) was a favourite boyhood playmate of *Poe's* in Richmond. I have often seen the high wooded bluff at the end of Clay St. (where the "White House of the Confederacy" stands) where Poe & Bob Sully & Tom Bolling used to play in the early 1820's, when Shockoe Creek (now filled in & replaced by a cobblestoned street frequented by motor trucks) used to flow along its base. I hope you explored the old Ellery house at the edge of Gloucester, in order to grasp the atmosphere of the very early—17th century—homes which preceded the Georgian mansions. I likewise hope that you arranged to catch a glimpse of Newburyport & Portsmouth—if only from coach windows. The sea trip was a splendid supplement to any land itinerary—infinitely typical of maritime Gloucester. I've never had such an opportunity.

Too bad your hosts were so merged in the quasi-artistic, heavily disillusioned fabric of self-conscious modernity. This fantastic, irresponsible world of aimless scepticism & "the modern temper"[8] is peculiarly irritating to one with still-valid roots—yet one is compelled to admit that inevitable historic conditions have done much to force such an attitude upon all thinking persons who happen to lack certain emotional anchorages or faculties for exercising a sense of proportion. Assuredly, the increased knowledge of the external world, & of mankind's own nature & motivations, which the science of the past hundred years has brought, has annihilated completely the old set of explanations, assumed *absolute* values, taken-for-granted goals, & conceptions of man's relationship to the infinite cosmos of time & space, on which many of our feelings, interests, standards, & expectations formerly rested. This being so, it is only natural that some bewildered souls should give themselves over utterly to weary, directionless drifting, while others try to find new bases for values & develop capricious, fanatical dogmatisms (like bolshevism & its whole ideology) upon vague postulates which are really quite as unreal as the set just discarded. For my part, I do not believe that any *absolute values* exist; but on the other hand, I cannot help noting that certain types of *attitude*—harmonisation with patterns & backgrounds which long familiarity has raised to the status of a workable (even if fortuitous & illusory) system of reference-points—invariably conduce (even when consciously adopted or preserved without reference to foundation in cosmic truth) toward an adjustment of the individual to his environment which is distinctly less painful (because it preserves to a great extent the illusions of direction, meaning, & interest in life) than any other possible adjustment would seem to be. Thus I am a complete sceptic & a thorough conservative at the same time. My attitude toward a traditional value is to hang on to it (as an aesthetic act) as long as possible, *if it is not positively anti-social as judged by the most* genuine & permanent factors in human happiness & welfare. So far as I can see, the destruction of values leads only to a net impoverishment of life; since new values *of real, subconscious validity* cannot be created over night (& would be no more absolutely well-founded than the old ones if they could be created), while an existence without values is definitely & demonstrably unsatisfying to man's permanent emotions. Pardon philosophical garrulity—but this is the sort of thing Belknap & I continually fight about, & I am still in training from the 2½-days' battle just concluded! (or rather, *suspended*.) Incidentally—among the enclosures is a bit of verse from the "Conning Tower" in Tuesday's *N.Y. Herald-Tribune*[9] which hits the Child's attitude so completely that I fancy I shall in future call him "D'Annunzio Cohen"! "People are not happy"!

I am glad that the rogues' gallery was not left here after all, for I mailed all your non-immediate material to Auburn before going on my trip. By the way—that new Newport booklet is really splendid, & will give you a very well-balanced idea of the town when you get home & read it. As you will note, there are many important sights which had to be missed for lack of time—but which I hope you may include in some future itinerary. Among other things, this booklet establishes the date of the old frigate *Constellation*—1794, or three years earlier than the *Constitution*'s launching. In its treatment of the old stone tower it shews an amusing reluctance to abandon the romantic Norseman theory.[10] Glad to hear that you managed to secure at least a fleeting panoramic view of Boston in the tragically brief time allotted. Was it the Custom-House tower that you looked from? The monument you saw amidst the red brick (presumably of the Charlestown district) was doubtless the famous Bunker Hill Shaft.

I hardly need say how violently I envy you the sight of *Quebec.* Try not to miss anything. Besides the standard sights on the 'rubberneck' coach & trolley trips, you ought to assimilate some of the utterly inimitable vistas which abound so amazingly in the ancient fortress town. Ascend the *citadel* & walk (if current repairs will permit it) around the highest embankment to a point where the spire of Chalmers' Church[11] covers up the one inharmonious skyscraper in the town. You will then have a sweep of urban panorama—from the Parliament Houses on the left to the river on the right—whose sheer, dream-compelling, intoxicating beauty cannot be parallelled (so far as I can judge) in the western hemisphere. Also—explore the narrow byways of St. Famille Hill—Couillard St. & those that cross it. Couillard is what seems to be an eastward prolongation of St. John St. where it bends into Fabrique, while some of the quaint streets lead out to the ramparts. Artists often sketch in this region of fascinating vistas & roof-lines. Likewise—explore St. John St. beyond the walls, & get the quaint hillside vistas up streets like Claire Fontaine & Scott. Don't fail to burrow through Rue Sous-le-Cap in the lower town (if you can olfactorily stand it), or to explore such quaint & narrow ways as Rue Sault-au-Matelot (observe the Gallic tendency toward picturesque names—in Paris there is a *Rue Chat-qui-Peche,* &c.) & Little Champlain St. There is an elevator from Little Champlain up to your lavish hostelry. Furthermore—after getting to the end of Little Champlain, keep on along the stretch betwixt shore & cliff (= Champlain St.) where Montgomery was repulsed & where in 1886 a devastating landslide occurred. The region (with empty, gaping cellars on one or both sides) appears to be wholly deserted, yet if you persist ahead you will come at length upon surviving rows of ancient brick houses—some falling down, some deserted, & some still tenanted by a squalid population. The spectrally sinister air of this hideous backwater—isolated from the healthy world & crowded between the brooding gulfs of the sea & the sullen bedrock of Mother Earth—is of ineffable imaginative fascination. It would enchant Klarkash-Ton, High-Priest of Tsathoggua.[12] I suppose I scarcely need to enumerate the *standard* sights—for the rubberneck outfits see to that. If you persist, you can see the actual skull of Montcalm in the Ursuline Convent.[13] Quebec is one of the most distinctive cities in America, & I feel sure that you will carry away a permanent impression. Notice the unique architectural types—for which you will vainly look anywhere else. Things like French casement windows & half-

blinds are especially typical. Note certain types of roof-line & things like *double* rows of dormer windows. Observe also how tall & narrow the doors are as contrasted with Georgian doorways. Then, too, absorb the charm of the numberless *silver spires & belfries*—results of the local custom of coating such features with tin. It is almost impossible to conceive of any urban vista more provocative of imaginative ecstasy, & of the sense of magical gateways opening on adventurous dream-worlds of exotic wonder, than a chance glimpse of one of these silver spires at the end of an ancient uphill or downhill street; ending with a touch of lunar necromancy a perspective laden with the mystery of years & forgotten secrets. The best examples of such vistas are the steeple of the Men's Congregational Church in the Rue d'Auteuil (cor. Dauphine), seen from St. John St. at St. John's Gate, crowning a breathless uphill prospect of centuried roofs & city walls; that of the Sisters of Charity Church at Richelieu & Glacis Sts, seen downhill from St. John through Glacis or d'Yonville; that of St. Jean Baptiste in Glacis St., seen down Rue Claire Fontaine from any point high above St. John; & that of St. Roch, at Rues St. Joseph & de l'Eglise from many points in the St. John upper-town suburb. The best old mansions are in the lower part of St. Louis St.—near your Chateau Frontenac. A later type of Quebec house or cottage—very typical—has a roof something like this: (cross-section). Note the odd bilingual signs—

NE STATIONNEZ PAS ICI	ARRÊT DE TRAMWAYS
NO PARKING HERE	STOP

&c. &c. I enclose a cutting with comments on Quebec French. One's sense of humour (logically or illogically) is stirred by such shop signs as

BUANDERIE
CHIN LEONG
DU JERE CLASSE

But let me endeavour to restrain my dominant vice of guidebook-writing. The Carrel guidebook & map ought to help—& if you have a caleche[14] the driver ought to know of many choice sights & atmospheric touches outside the recommendations of the Royal Blue Line or the Q. R. L. & P. Co. I cease, lest envy consume me!

As before mentioned, I did get to Onset to see Sonny & his parents[15]—though cold, rainy weather made the pleasure reside more in congenial discussion than in outdoor relaxation. However, we had one good ride through the Cape Cod countryside—seeing villages as quaint as white-steepled & verdure-embowered Sandwich. The spectacle of an immense steamer traversing the canal was also impressive. And what a *kitten* disported on the piazza of our boarding-place! I enclose a pair of Cape Cod cards, & send under separate cover a folder of the region. A very idyllic countryside—though perhaps overrated in comparison to other New England regions. In re-passing through Prov. Belknap stopped off here for a moment before being inexorably dragged on by paternal impatience & anti-Providentianism. By the way—here is a card from Sonny which I can't resist enclosing even through its reference to you may combine with Manhattan's gallantries to tax your ego's powers of expansion! And if you could have heard his *oral* references! ¶ My aunt's plaster cast is reduced, & she may be on crutches in a few days. She sends her warmest & sincerest regards. Kittens now very sportive. ¶ Pardon dulness & verboseness.

> Yr obt Servt
> H P L

P.S. Just as I predicted, the Newport boat prices have begun to fall. Old Sagamore is down to 50¢ for a round trip, & Mount Hope has met Nelseco II's still-maintained 75¢. I await further moves with bated breath . . . if any of the rates get down to a quarter I shall become a virtual commuter!

Notes

1. This first letter to HVS was sent to her ℅ Chateau Frontenac, Quebec.
2. Annie E. P. Gamwell and fallen and broken her ankle c. mid-June.
3. By Levi M. Powers.
4. The First Congregational Church of Rockport at 12 School Street.
5. At Rafe's Chasm Park in Gloucester, MA, where HVS had gone after visiting HPL in Providence.
6. A small room used for powdering hair or wigs.
7. Thomas Sully (1783–1872), British-born American portrait painter. Robert Matthew Sully (1803–1855), an artist in Richmond, VA.
8. HPL alludes to the theme of the book by Joseph Wood Krutch.
9. "The Conning Tower" was a column by Franklin Pierce Adams (1881–1960) in the *New York Tribune* (later the *Herald Tribune*). HPL refers to the appearance therein of D'Annunzio Cohen's (Mortimer Frankel) poem "Ballade of Life, Etc." (25 July 1933, p. 11), which has the epigram "'People are not happy . . . life is passion, conflict, resignation, and, at best, peace.'—From 'The Drama and the Stage.' By Ludwig Lewisohn." The phrase "People are not happy" is repeated in ll. 8, 16, 24, and 28 of Cohen's poem. Cohen published light verse in the *Saturday Evening Post*, the *New Yorker*, and elsewhere.
10. HPL's plot sketch "[The Round Tower]" (*CE* 5.253), used by August Derleth in writing *The Lurker at the Threshold* (1945), is about the stone tower at Newport, RI, which Governor Benedict Arnold (1615–1678) referred to as his "stone built wind mill."
11. The Chalmers-Wesley United Church within the walls of Old Quebec City at 78 rue Sainte-Ursule, Québec G1R 4E8. Designed by John Wells for the Free Presbyterian Church of Canada, and built from 1851–1853.
12. I.e., Clark Ashton Smith, a friend and neighbor of HVS.
13. The skull and a tibia bone of Louis-Joseph de Montcalm-Gozon (1712–1759), commander of the forces in North America during the Seven Years' War, were reinterred in the military graveyard in which his fallen men had been buried.

14. A two-wheeled, one-horse vehicle with a seat for the driver on the splashboard.
15. 24–25 July 1933.

[2]   [ALS, JHL]

66 College St.,
Providence, R.I.,
August 16, 1933

Dear Miss Sully:—

I am surprised to hear that you found Quebec's antiquity submerged by various modern aspects; for notwithstanding the occasional jarring structures (including L'Edifice Price,[1] that skyscraper from which I try to shield myself with a church steeple) & the toll of successive conflagrations, there is enough of the past left to give me a thrill of the most potent & paramount kind. In the first place, the topography is so striking—& so interwoven with history—that the imagination is excited by that alone. Secondly, many of the features which are admittedly neither Gallic nor very ancient are amply exotic & quaint enough to command interest in their own right—& are often reproductions or continuations of vastly older things. Of this type are the *citadel,* the St. Louis & Kent Gates, & some of the picturesque silver-belfried churches. Third—despite fire & "improvement" there actually *is* a vast amount of antiquity left. Seminary—convent—Hôtel Dieu—*city walls* (only specimens in North-America)—grand battery & ramparts—arsenal at Palace Gate (that sheer ascent of wall & cliff as seen from St. Vallier St. on the way to the station is one of the most stupefyingly *mediaeval* effects I have ever glimpsed. It might well be taken bodily from Klarkash-Ton's Averoigne![2])—Notre-Dame des Victoires—the Gen. Wolfe sign—any number of private houses in St. Louis St., or back from Dufferin Terrace around the Governor's Gardens, or in the little network I spoke of on St. Famille Hill—& most of all, the layout of the narrow streets themselves, with their utterly unexpected vistas of ancient roofs, silver spires, lordly river, or green countryside & far-off purple Laurentians. Even the modern or relatively modern houses have quaintness & charm, since they followed traditional French designs till far into the 19th century. And incidentally—some of the worst fires were in the St. Roch or St. Sauveur quarters of the lower town, so that the record of Quebec conflagrations (a formidable one, owing to the intense house-heating required by the subarctic climate) does not imply the devastation of the choicest main district on each occasion. At any rate, I did not find Quebec disappointing; & can agree with Sir Michael Sadler's dictum that it is the most beautiful town in the Western Hemisphere.[3] It is, moreover, the one place (aside from his precious Manhattan) which can get Little Belknap enthusiastic in spite of his ostentatious anti-archaism. Glad to hear the Carrel guide helped you see the sights—you were wise to obtain one for yourself.

I had an idea that Ste. Anne de Beaupre would be disappointing, for the guidebooks admitted that most of the antiquity was gone. That is why I omitted the trip thither (I went on the electric train as far as Montmorency Falls, but returned thence in order to get extra time in Quebec itself) in 1930. The commercialism there is remarked by many. However, the weird chanting in the hillside church must have formed a compensation. As for the omnipresent outstretched palm—it astonishes me to learn that it has reached the dank shadows of Sous le Cap! In 1930, & also last year, I ploughed through the miasmatic air of that sinister burrow without any bids from juvenile models—though perhaps my 1925 grey suit & cameraless hands caused me to be mistaken for a denizen rather than a wealthy American tourist! Where I did encounter the baksheesh-whining[4] horde was in the St. Roch slums—when I took the ride on the observation trolley-car. There, however, the young mendicants were more modest; for it was pen-nees, not neeckels, which formed the object of their clamour. The conductor-lecturer informed his audience that such youthful alms-seekers often suffer injury from vehicles as they dodge about the street to retrieve the coppers flung from the cars—hence at his advice the passengers refrained from heeding the shrill pleas. Glad you secured at least one suitable & unmercenary pose!

It is evident that you have really had a far more representative view of the general Quebec region than I was able to secure on my two regrettably brief trips. The expedition to the Laurentians must have been prodigiously fascinating—as also the glimpses of British life & the royal guidance in the caleche. Glad the driver was so considerate of his Rosie! The photographs of the slide of 1886 (along Champlain St.,[5] which I mentioned as an especially spectral & sinister place with its absolutely barren interval & its broken line of half-ruined houses beyond) must have been harrowing indeed. Did you see the Isle of Orleans? I hope so, for if I am any judge, you could not find that bit of primitive countryside—with its old houses & remarkable church—disappointing. And did you see the Huron village of Lorette? I didn't. I trust you also had a glimpse of Montreal—modern, but not without its quaint & attractive aspects. I wish I could get up to Quebec before the cold sets in, but fear it will be impossible. My aunt's cast came off Aug. 3, but she is not yet able to take to crutches. It looks as if I would be tied closely to the house all the rest of the summer & autumn.

I trust the remainder of your trip will be interesting—the Canadian Rockies ought to form a majestic sight . . . . helping to take away the bad taste of Chicago's grotesque Century of Misdirected Effort.[6] Meanwhile Klarkash-Ton informs me that Auburn has been having temperatures of 108°, & that he killed a rattlesnake not long ago—which was creeping close to him as he sat outdoors writing! My guest Morton (the Paterson curator whom I mentioned to you) came as scheduled, & good weather permitted us to spend most of the time in outdoor antiquarian expeditions. We did not omit ancient

Newport—on whose cliffs we spent an entire afternoon. ¶ Best wishes, & hopes for a pleasant homecoming.

Yr obt hb^{le} Servt—

H P Lovecraft

P.S. The returned guidebooks came safely—& many thanks for the additional Gloucester & Quebec matter sent. Some of the Cape Ann folders will greatly facilitate my next visit thither. From the Quebec matter I judge that sightseeing prices have gone up radically since last year—the Isle of Orleans tour looks very formidable!

Notes

1. Édifice Price (English: Price Building), an 18-floor (originally 16) skyscraper in Quebec City built in 1930–31. It is the tallest building in the Old Quebec historical district, and the official residence of the Premier of Quebec.

2. Smith's imaginary mediaeval land, named after his own Auburn, CA.

3. Sir Michael Ernest Sadler (1861–1943), British educational pioneer and master of University College, Oxford (1923–34). His remark is repeated in *Quebec: How to See It? The Tourist's Guide* . . . (Québec: The Quebec Tourist Guide, [1930?]).

4. In parts of Asia, *baksheesh* is a small sum of money given as alms, a tip, or a bribe.

5. The Quebec rockslide occurred 19 September 1889, after a day of heavy rain. An overhang of slate rock broke off Cap Diamant and slid 300 feet onto the homes of 28 families on Champlain Street, burying roughly 100 people under 80 feet of broken rock. The final death toll exceeded 40 people.

6. I.e., the "Century of Progress" world's fair.

[3]   [ANS postcard][1]

[Postmarked Quebec, Canada,

3 September 1933]

Well—old folks are getting spry, too! My aunt gave me a birthday present of a week's vacation from substitute-nursing (by getting others to come in afternoons while the nurse is out), & I have promptly taken advantage of the opportunity to get up to good old Quebec! I still insist that I'm not disappointed with the place—although Sous le Cap certainly has suddenly blossomed out as a thriving eleemosynary graft! There has been a decided increase in this juvenile mendicancy since last year. Am now on the Ramparts watching twilight steal over the ancient town. Rather too decided twilight for legible writing, I fear. ¶ Hope your trip ended in a suitable blaze of glory. ¶ Best wishes—Yrs most cordially,

H P L

Notes

1. *Front:* Sous Le Cap, Quebec, Canada.

[4]   [ALS, JHL]

66 College St.,
Providence, R.I.,
Septr 14, 1933

Dear Miss Sully:—

I feel quite honoured & flattered by the charitable praise accorded my previous epistolary jottings—jottings which seemed to me far from distinctive or worthy of commendation. I suppose, though, that the 20th century has so far drifted away from the leisurely habits of the 18th century that any vestige of the old order appears uncommon. As you are aware, I am a belated survival of the perwigged Georgian age—hence it is as natural to me to think of letters from the Walpole or Pope or Cowper[1] point of view, as to think of architecture or poetry or rural landscapes from a similar angle. In the inarticulate & overspeeded life of the machine age I have no part. Like the house I now have the good fortune to inhabit, I belong for better or for worse to the ancient colonial tradition. The chief objections against my epistles are commonly (a) excessive length [argumentative letters to Little Belknap, Bob Howard, & others have run as high as sixty (60) pages, $8^{1/2} \times 11$] & (b) illegibility. The former defect I try to remedy when I can, though the latter (in view of the crabbed chirography of old age, plus my unconquerable loathing of the typewriter) is not so amenable to correction. However, I properly appreciate it when any kind soul takes a favourable view of my verbal torrents!

By this time you will have received my card from Quebec, telling of the good luck which enabled me to get there after all. It is certainly unfortunate that your own sojourn coincided with such an era of brewing indisposition. Probably the preceding stages of the trip had been more over-strenuous than you realised—too much continuous activity & too little rest—so that an emphatic protest of nature was in order. That night on the boat must surely have been a gruelling experience, & I hope that a subsequent milder programme forestalled all tendencies toward repetition. It reminds me of times when my record-breaking sick-headaches have occasionally produced painful hiatuses in the delights of travel.

It is also too bad that rain played its discouraging part at Quebec. That was my experience last year—when most of my circuit of the Isle d'Orleans was accomplished amidst pouring floods which thoroughly drenched me even in the brief moments of dodging betwixt the sightseeing coach & the various old houses & churches visited. If I had had more cash this year I would have repeated the Orleans trip in order to see the exquisite, unspoiled 18th century landscape under better lighting conditions. Before many years the delightful primitiveness of the island will probably be a thing of the past, since a bridge is under construction from the Beauport mainland. With free access to Quebec, suburban invasion is sadly certain to come. In seeing the island it pays to take the regular 'rubberneck-wagon' trip, since the coach stops at all the prominent churches & allows the lecturer to explain each in detail—which he really does most intelligently. However—according to a circular which you sent, rates have gone up alarmingly since last year. Sorry your circuit of the city wall was interrupted. Those workmen near St. Louis gate also spoke to me (although on my first trip they were absent—at noonday lunch), but interposed no physical obstacle when I assumed a smile of amiable dignity, said "Pardon" with just enough of the *parr-daw'* sound to make it potentially bi-lingual, & kept right on the way I was headed. These men are the unemployed of Quebec & vicinity—put to work on a huge government project of repairing the crumbling citadel & wall, & housed & fed by the province in the citadel barracks. I saw last year that the citadel masonry was in very bad shape, & read later in the press of some further damage by storms. It is curious how inferior this masonry is to the earlier masonry of the arsenal (1750) at Palace Gate. The citadel dates from the 1820's. Was the churchyard you wished to find that of St. Matthew's Anglican Church—where Sir Walter Scott's brother is buried?[2] That is about the only one I seem to recall—that is, the only one answering to the traditional idea of a churchyard. Too bad you missed it in your pedestrian search—it lies on the main street, St. John, at a considerable distance outside the city wall; on the left-hand side as one leaves the town, at the farther corner of Rue St. Augustin. The church is a modern Gothic affair, but the interments go back to the late 18th century. It is very picturesque, & I never fail to visit it. One thing which may have disappointed you is the absence of the numberless "silver spires" which I had raved about. I saw to my sorrow this month that most of them have been allowed to tarnish since my early impressions were acquired. That glistening coating of tin needs frequent renewal—& I presume the depression has been felt even by the dominant ecclesiastical hierarchy. Last year some of the belfries lacked the magical sheen of 1930, yet the general effect remained. This year, however, the dimming is complete—so that my descriptions must sound overstrained. I noted with humiliation that my favourite old belfry in Rue d'Auteuil—the one so impressive when seen uphill from St. John's gate or from the wall-top near Kent Gate—is now almost black. Yet how elflike & supernally it glistened in 1930! Some of the village churches in the country have kept up their silvering better than those in Quebec City—or perhaps the absence of urban smoke has left an earlier silvering more untarnished. I noticed the "Golden Dog" restaurant, but slender finances caused me to seek humbler fare. The small restaurants along St. John St. offer full dinners as low as 30¢, & one microscopic lunch room kept by a Chinaman broke all records with 5¢ sandwiches! I think I spent less on food than on postcards. I stopped at the neat but lowly place which I patronised before—the St. Paul Hotel near the station. I was the only guest from the U.S. on the register when I signed—shewing that I was surely off the beaten track of tourists! Too bad you had more ticket trouble—but I don't wonder at a mistake or two in complex, long-distance trips of that sort. It is a wonder they are as nearly correct as they are! Anyhow, it is lucky your interpolation proved effective. I hope that your brief Montreal circuit included a view of the city from either Mt. Royal or Westmount, a glimpse of the ancient section with Chateau de Ramezay (1785) & quaint Notre-Dame de Bonsecoeurs (1771), & a general orientation tour of the whole urban area. I was in Montreal only one day—from 9 a.m. to midnight—but I certainly crowded every available second with sightseeing—postponing my inevitable postcard-writing till after dark, when I settled on a bench in Dominion Square prior to entraining for Quebec.

Klarkash-Ton says that Chicago's Century of Mechanical Gadgetry did not impress you very profoundly—which I can well appreciate! I am surely glad that the latter part of your Odyssey atoned for this pallid interval. The trip through Canada's Rockies sounds most delectable, & you were surely fortunate in securing such congenial guidance from time to time. While the storm episode was doubtless terrifying while it lasted, it probably adds to the dramatic variety of the tour in retrospect. I envy you the sight—even though smoke-obscured—of Vancouver; a locality I read of long ago in the boys' books of Kirk Munroe.[3] Ever since those days the idea of the Puget Sound region & of Alaska has had a curious sort of fascination for me—though no doubt the actual territory falls far short of the bygone & romanticised descriptions. Altogether, it was a very delightful thing that you were able to secure this respite from monotony, with its occasional glimpses of characters other than commonplace; & I surely hope that you can repeat—or rather, duplicate—it during future summers. Wish Klarkash-Ton could do likewise. For another trip I would strongly recommend a *southern* route including New Mexico (Santa Fé is said to be intensely interesting, whilst the Carlsbad Caverns are one of the most impressive sights which this planet affords), Texas (especially San Antonio), New Orleans, Natchez, Florida, (St. Augustine above all) Charleston, as much of Old Virginia as possible, (& Chattanooga, Tenn. if it can be worked in) Washington D.C., & historic Philadelphia. In addition, there is much of New York State & of New England which you have not seen, & which would surely repay your inspection. A position in New Jersey or a free year would surely give you an abundance of opportunities to accumulate congenial impressions—though meanwhile, if accounts & pictures from Klarkash-Ton be an indication, your present surroundings are far from unattractive. The hills of California must have a peculiar charm of their own—especially Crater Ridge, whence came that portentous pre-human eidolon which I use as a book-end. I shall be very glad to see the photographs you mention—& hope the camera was not injured in attempting to snap the ancient hillside ogre in the doorway of his cave.

My own trip to Quebec was quite unexpected—& all the pleasanter on that account. While on the outbound journey I paused to look up an ancient house in a Boston suburb that I had never seen before—the Deane Winthrop farmhouse, built in 1637 & having a secret room in the foundations of the massive brick chimney. The rail trip to Quebec was pleasanter than in former years, since the return of King Gambrinus to the States[4] has eliminated the noisy herds of alcohol-seekers which formerly encumbered all Canadian excursion-trains, & whose swinish antics made a nightmare of the return journey. I had 4 days in Quebec—Saturday, Sunday, Monday, & Tuesday till 4 p.m., & all were providentially hot & sunny. Besides revisiting all my accustomed urban sights I walked to Sillery & back, & took a trolley trip to the upper level of Montmorency Falls—seeing Kent House, where Queen Victoria's father once lived. Many hours were spent reading & writing in my favourite spots—Ramparts, Citadel, Montmorency Park, Governor's Gardens, city Wall, Parc aux Braves, Battlefields Park—while on other occasions I merely circulated about absorbing vistas & archaic impressions. In that fascinating tangle of old streets on Ste. Famille hill I decided that St. Flavien is the quaintest of all. One odd thing—at the foot of Mountain Hill, where I had passed a dozen times before, I noticed *for the first time* the ancient tavern sign of Neptune over the Neptune Inn—a worthy counterpart of the Wolfe sign at St. John St & Palace Hill. As my card said, I certainly found Sous-le-Cap alive with little beggars—& at the same time rather less malodorous than formerly. It is possible that some enterprising Gallic Babbit[t][5] has organised the denizens & taught them to exploit the tourist element by cleaning up the street a bit & teaching their young the technique so ably exemplified by the juveniles of St. Roch & Little Champlain St! In Champlain St.—that sinister, ruinous shore strip under Cape Diamond—I found several more houses deserted & torn down. On the same walk I finally succeeded in locating the exact scene of Wolfe's ascent of the cliff—a rather difficult thing to do because of the lack of markers. The local Gauls are not eager to perpetuate their conqueror's fame—indeed, the first Wolfe monument, created in 1832, was destroyed by the natives.

And so the four days passed all too quickly—a kaleidoscopic synthesis of ancient walls & fortifications, dizzying heights, winding, hill-climbing streets of centuried facades, fantastic belfries, dreamlike architectural vistas, & glamourous sunlit expanses of river, countryside, & distant mountains. A feature of constant interest was the *sky*—with grotesque & mystical cloud effects of a sort peculiar to the far north. On Labour Day—at sunset—I watched from the citadel a phenomenon such as I never saw elsewhere. The day was fair, yet something in the air gave the declining sun a singular blood-red lustre—while there ran from the zenith to the southeastern horizon a colossal seething funnel of black rain-cloud whose small end met the earth somewhere beyond Lévis. From the midst of this tenebrous mass forked darts of lightning often shot groundward—followed by faint rolls of distant thunder. Then—as the river & cliffs & steeples still glowed redly in the supernal evening light—a pale bit of rainbow flickered into view over the Isle d'Orleans, with its upper part lost in the titanic cloud-funnel. I doubt if such a spectacle could occur as far south as Providence. I also noticed the eternal mists that hang about the hills & vales near the international boundary—the Lake Memphramagog region. It is certainly true that northern skies have strange & fantastic phenomena unknown in the sun-drenched south—which, as I lately wrote Klarkash-Ton, indubitably plays a part in the mystical temperament of northern as distinguished from southern races. The Teutonic Æsir, the mysteries of Celtic Druidism, & the imaginative legends of North Europe's forests & mountains, are all products of a climate whose mists & vapours, & capricious gradations of light & shade, conduce to feelings of cosmic uncertainty, vague expectancy, & the immanence of unseen marvels. On the other hand, the clear-cut certainties of blazing southern skies have produced the logical, realistic, matter-of-fact Latin. The returning train trip gave some magnificent landscape effects—with the golden light of late afternoon enveloping leagues of outspread countryside & distant, tall-steepled villages in a magical glamour which took them out of North-America & implanted them in Klarkash-Ton's fabulous Averoigne! Then at night, when the full moon rose over ancient forests & hills & sweeps of marshland, there sprang to view still another world of indeterminate phantasy & elusive, half-mnemonic charm. The dawn—which took place in New-Hampshire—revealed some splendid vistas of hill & lake, though swirling mists now & then blurred the landscape. Boston was reached at 9 a.m.

On that final day—a day of mists, showers, & finally a rain which soaked me through in Boston at 8 p.m.—I made a side-trip to my favourite old towns of Salem & Marblehead, some postcard echoes of which I enclose herewith. Salem is much like Newport—& even more fascinating in many ways. One thing there was wholly new to me—a perfect reproduction of the original Salem of 1626 et seq., with log huts, primitive industries, (saw-pit, brick-plant, fish-drying outfit, salt-works, blacksmith shop, &c.) gardens, & all accessories constructed in fac-simile with the utmost antiquarian accuracy & in an ideal landscape setting. I regret that I have no postcards of this exhibit left. The thing itself is the most graphic revelation of pioneer New England life that I have ever seen. Of course, no *original* pioneer huts have anywhere survived—our oldest existing edifice being a full-fledged farmhouse of 1636 in Dedham, between Boston & Providence. Marblehead—a fishing village of infinitely picturesque aspect—is worth a volume of description .... which I will in mercy withhold. Not even occasional showers could dampen my enjoyment of it. Then—in Boston—came the drenching, a call at a friend's[6] when I got partly dry, & finally a midnight coach to Providence. All told, a great trip—even though a brief one.

My aunt [Mrs. Annie Emmeline Phillips Gamwell]—who acknowledges your regards with utmost appreciation & reciprocates with most cordial regards of her own—has made great progress of late, & is now all around the house on crutches or cane .... though we are installing an electrical device enabling her to open the front door from upstairs. The nurse went yesterday—& for the rest of the autumn I may not be as tied down as I have been.

[Possibly I can accompany Loveman to Boston & adjacent antique regions if he gets here next month as he hopes to do.] My aunt adds—seconded by myself—that she hopes you can get here next year, when she will be able to discharge more suitably the functions of a hostess.

As for that copy of "The Star-Treader"[7]—I fancy there are two ways of looking at its presence among the barbarian young. Obviously, it is wasted on 99%—& yet might not its presence some day be the means of kindling stupendous vistas in the mind of one of those sensitive exceptions which even the dullest milieux cannot help occasionally producing? In a way, I like to see a good book diffused as widely as it possibly can be. For long decades a given copy may do no good—& yet there is always a possibility that it may eventually establish some contact favourable alike to author & reader. The more irons in the fire, the better—hence I think a volume hardly can be in too many libraries. By the way—isn't the S.T. still procurable? I think Kirk has a few remaining copies, & I had an idea that C A S himself did.[8] However—I can clearly see & sympathise with your point of view! As to mankind in general—I'm glad that my diffusive maunderings in a former letter sounded sensible. This is a trying age, but I still think that the best way to get something out of the meaningless experience of living is to correlate oneself as well as possible with some continuous stream of thought & feeling & folkways. Only in that way can one preserve a sense of relative significance & direction—without which existence is a pretty flat affair. I certainly prefer even the naivest clods to the disorganised products of modern sophistication. ¶ Autumn is in the offing, hence my outdoor reading & writing sessions are now markedly curtailed. An oil heater is very welcome today! ¶ With apologies for boresome length, I have ye Honour to subscribe myself

Yr most o^bt h^ble Servt

H P Lovecraft

P.S. The brighter & stronger of the kittens you saw here is now a vigorous, playful little rascal whose antics with his mother in the garden form a favourite spectacle of my aunt's as she sits by the window. I frequently borrow him to enliven the household programme.

P.P.S. Providence now has a sightseeing service—circular enclosed. You will recall many of the listed items.

[Enclosures:]

[Postcard][9]

Here is a bit of R.I. rusticity that Morton & I saw—at least, we saw the *buildings*. Good old Greenville retains the atmosphere of about 1820 at the latest—salient objects being the white-steepled Georgian church & the old

Resolved Waterman Tavern (1730). On our way thither—during a cross-country hike—we came across a fine old-fashioned *well-sweep* in native use. ¶ We also took in Warren & Bristol—down the east shore of the bay—& had six flavours apiece of Maxfield's ice-cream (which I mentioned to you). I likewise conducted Morton down the west shore to Pawtuxet & watched him surround 1½ or 2 shore dinners. ¶ On our Newport trip we took the old Sagamore—cheapest of all at this stage of the rate war. Nelseco has come down to a straight half-dollar, & even Mt. Hope quotes half a dollar on weekdays—but Sagamore now offers *2* round trips for 75¢! On the day we went, though, Sagamore was 50¢ & Nelseco 75. Had some rain on the return trip, but it suddenly cleared & gave us a magnificent marine sunset with the western shore outlined against a sea of mystical & beckoning flame.

[Postcard][10]

Marblehead is a perfectly preserved fishing village of the colonial period. Founded 1639, & still looks about as it did in 1760. It consists of sidewalkless streets of small houses (plus a few mansions) built over a craggy, irregular terrain culminating in a pair of headlands. There is no quainter sight in America. On account of its isolation, & because of the somewhat unusual character of the settlers, (Channel Islanders rather than the East Anglian stock dominant amongst the Puritans) Marblehead has always been very distinctive in speech & folkways. At present the fishing industry has declined almost to zero except for lobstering, hence Marblehead depends largely on summer visitors & appreciative artists for its sustenance. This has the unfortunate effect of making it a trifle artificial & self-conscious in summer, but in winter one may see it in all its native conservatism & placidity. There is no quainter spot in the United States.

[Postcard][11]

This is the kind of house with which all our New England towns were built up prior to 1700. Most of those early Newport houses with the bulky pilastered chimneys originally looked like this, though the gables were removed during the early 18th century. More unaltered specimens are left in Salem than in any other American town. This especial edifice was inhabited by relatives of Hawthorne, & he probably had it in mind when he wrote "The House of the Seven Gables". In his youth (he was born in 1804) there were many more of these gabled houses than there are today. Inside, most of the rooms of this house were modernised in the middle 1700's, so that they look newer than the exterior. This house has a secret stairway beside the chimney which leads to a secret room in the attic. Probably a smugglers' storage-place—since the place abuts directly on the harbour. Smuggling was universal in the colonial period—the much-lauded revolution being largely a revenge-gesture of smugglers smarting under proper law-enforcement.

[Postcard][12]

This is a mansion of the 3d Georgian style—the severe, classical style prevailing after 1780. It is rather like some of the mansions (John Brown 1786—Thomas Poynton Ives 1806) which you saw in Providence. Salem is aboundingly full of these early-1800 mansions, since her prosperous sea-trade was at its height betwixt the revolution & the war of 1812. No other city can present quite such a sight as Salem, with block after block of these splendid Georgian mansions in addition to the smaller gambrel-roofers of the 18th century (much like the bulk of old Newport houses) & the spectral gabled reliques of the 17th century. These late-Georgian houses are seen at their best along the north side of Salem Common, or throughout the broad, shady length of sumptuous Chestnut St.

[Postcard][13]

This house was built about 1650, & was originally gabled like the old house on another enclosed card. The gambrel roof was substituted about 1780. This photograph was taken in 1852. You can see the second-story overhang so typical of 17th century houses. (We have none left in R.I.) At present, this house is defaced by a jutting wing on the eastern half of the front facade, housing a drugstore. The house proper is an antique shop—accessible to visitors. In 1692 it was the home of the magistrate Jonathan Corwin, who conducted several examinations of suspected witches in the second-story room at the extreme left of the picture—hence the popular name of "Old Witch House."[14] ¶ Claims that this house is as old as 1635, & that Roger Williams once inhabited it, have been thoroughly exploded by the iconoclastic experts of the Essex Institute—an influential organisation which studies & preserves Salem antiquities, & which operates one of the greatest antiquarian museums in the country.[15]

[Postcard][16]

Here is the view of the Salem pioneer village which I regretted not being able to enclose in preceding letter. Found it after considerable rummaging among disordered effects. Note the *thatched roof* exactly following old English models. These proved to be such a fire hazard that they were prohibited by law, hence no original specimens remain in New England. The *wooden chimneys* (the nearer one of *boards*, the farther one of small logs or saplings laid horizontally & sealed with clay) were also very unsafe, & soon became prohibited. In front of the houses you will see very primitive *mortars* for grinding corn—simply the stumps of large trees with the top hollowed out. Smooth, rounded logs—or sometimes round rocks—served as pestles. The house with the non-thatched roof is a reproduction of Gov. Winthrop's—with its frame brought from England. This edifice—1630—was the first real house of European finish in Salem.

[Postcard]^17

The Ramparts form one of my favourite reading-writing-loafing places in Quebec—others being Montmorency Park, the Citadel, the Governor's Gardens, the city wall near St. John's Gate, & the Parc aux Braves off the Ste. Foy road. You will note the steep roof of your quondam abode in the background.

Notes

1. Horatio Walpole (1717–1797), known as Horace Walpole, British art historian, man of letters, and antiquarian; Alexander Pope (1688–1744), an 18th-century British poet; William Cowper (1731–1800), British poet known for the elegance of his letters.

2. Major Thomas Scott (d. 1823) is buried in the churchyard at St. Matthew's Church, Quebec.

3. Kirk Munroe (1850–1930) was an American writer and conservationist, the first editor of Harper's *Young People* magazine, and author of numerous adventure novels for boys. *Rick Dale: A Story of the Northwest Coast* (1896) features Vancouver.

4. HPL refers to the repeal of the Volstead Act (1920), which enforced the 18th Amendment prohibiting the manufacture and sale of almost all alcoholic beverages in the US. On 22 March 1933, President Franklin D. Roosevelt signed an amendment to the Act that allowed the manufacture and sale of 3.2% alcohol (by weight) in beer and light wines. The 18th Amendment was not fully repealed until the passage of the 21st Amendment on 5 December 1933. King Gambrinus is a legendary culture hero in Europe and a kind of patron saint of beer.

5. George F. Babbitt is the central character in Sinclair Lewis's best-selling novel *Babbitt* (1922), about a go-getting businessman.

6. W. Paul Cook.

7. By Clark Ashton Smith.

8. HPL may have been thinking of Smith's *Ebony and Crystal: Poems in Verse and Prose* (1922). Smith began advertising the book as being for sale at $1.00 (half-price) beginning in the October 1933 issue of the *Fantasy Fan*.

9. *Front:* National Exchange & Smithfield Savings Bank, Greenville, R.I.

10. *Front:* A quaint old street in Marblehead, Mass.

11. *Front:* House of Seven Gables, built 1694 [HPL changed 94 to 60], Salem, Mass.

12. *Front:* A Salem Doorway, Shreve Porch 1818, Salem, Mass.

13. *Front:* Old Witch House, After 1780, Salem, Mass.

14. In WBT 1, HPL mentions contemplating writing a novel about witches. He modified his initial idea to write *The Case of Charles Dexter Ward,* in which Joseph Curwen practices alchemy.

15. HPL praised T. F. Hunt (1841–1898), *Visitor's Guide to Salem* (Salem, MA: Essex Institute, 1916).

16. *Front:* Dwellings of Settlers of 1630 Reproduced Pioneers' Village, Forest River Park, Salem, Mass.

17. *Front:* Les Vieux Canon sur les Ramparts, Quebec, Canada.

[5]   [ALS, JHL]

> 66 College St.,
> Providence, R.I.,
> Septr 27, 1933

Dear Miss Sully:—

Let me hasten to thank you most profoundly for the highly interesting array of snapshots which arrived yesterday. The Quebec glimpses are surely delightful—& that view of the submissive & unmercenary infant has as its background a type of scene (on the steep extra-mural streets like Scott & Claire Fontaine, which rise picturesquely above St. John) which I have wanted very much, but of which I have never found any postcards. "Rosie" looks very sleek, cultivated, & deserving of his master's regard despite the nasal abbreviation perpetrated by the print-maker. Sous-le-Cap's atmosphere shows up very well despite the imperfect results of the shooing [*sic*] process. No doubt the 'neekle'-grabbers reaped another harvest from the vehicle which appears to be headed toward them from remoter reaches of the shadowy byway. The old Newburyport churchyard is very alluring—& I am glad to learn that you had a chance to explore old "Joppy".* Newburyport is one of the most hauntingly quaint towns in America, & its spectral hush & semi-desertion make a churchyard a very appropriate symbol for it. Oliver Wendell Holmes (for it was declining even in his day) once remarked that Newburyport is the one American city which is *finished.*[1] In Haverhill, 8 miles up the Merrimac, they call N. "The City of the Living Dead". Did you see Whittier's birthplace in E. Haverhill & his home in Amesbury? Glad all three gravestone periods were represented, but sorry no fountain was on top. This design certainly seems to have been less popular on the whole than the contemporary urn & weeping-willow. Hope you saw all the representative features of Newburyport—the old church where George Whitefield is buried, the 1801 Unitarian church, grass-grown waterfront, the stately breadth of High St. with the once-bedizened mansion of "Lord" Timothy Dexter,[2] the central Market Square with its 1815 brick buildings, & the unpaved, sidewalkless pre-Revolutionary streets with rotting, half-deserted houses south of the square. When I first saw Newburyport I mistook the central square for a mere neighbourhood shopping centre, & kept on the car (it *was* a trolley-car then) in the expectation of reaching some real "downtown." Only when the

---

Joppy (early Am. rustic pronunciation of *Joppa*) is a local nickname for Newburyport. It was formerly restricted to the small hamlet of tiny fishing cottages at the extreme south of the town, on the shore—being in turn derived from the Joppa (pron. "Joppy") Wharf & Joppa Bank (sand-bar) in the harbour. Probably the original source is the old Biblical Joppa (modern Jaffa) in Palestine—which had a harbour choked with sand like Newburyport. The old Puritans always had their eyes open for Biblical analogies, & drew freely on Holy Writ for their local & personal nomenclature.

line ended—at the "Joppa" fishing hamlet—did I realise that the half-deserted square I had passed through was actually "downtown"![3] As for the view of the ancient Hill-Daemon in the mouth of his cave—really, it has its points despite the artistic haze, the flexible geometry (reminding one of the elastic & paradoxical dimensions in some of Klarkash-Ton's outré realms), & the shading off—like Rosie's nose—of part of the Georgian doorway. The general effect of a colonial portal certainly is there—fan, sidelights, railed steps, & all—& the merciful non-committalness regarding the Old Squire's clock-stopping & proboscidian visage is truly a marvellous asset! I'll surely send a view whenever I get around to the process of taking one—but meanwhile this exhibits the approximate layout so well that I wouldn't mind having 2 or 3 extra copies to send correspondents as a supplement to my verbal descriptions. I enclose a few stamps to cover the cost of a couple of additional prints if it's perfectly convenient for you to get them made. Not the least hurry about it, though. I shall choose a sunny day for my attempt—yet may not get even as good a result as this.

About the "please return" marks on certain items in your package—let me hasten to assure you (as I meant to do orally at the time I stacked them up) that these are *obsolete* notations surviving from long-past loans & *not* applicable in the present case. I ought to have rubbed or crossed the inscriptions out—but there were so many of them that I let the detail slide. However, be assured that everything in the bundle was designed for permanent filing if you have any use for a geographico-antiquarian "morgue." Which reminds me—I might as well pad out the present envelope with some recent cuttings of kindred interest, plus that description of the cruelly & wantonly destroyed row of old waterfront warehouses which I said I was going to shew but didn't get around to shewing. Attached to the latter item is the bit of doggerel which I perpetrated as a vain protest against the impending vandalism.[4] Oh, yes—& as a further disposing of mnemonic loose ends . . . . let me state that that moss found on the rocks at Newport *was* the kind of Irish moss that my friend Morton used to look for as an ingredient of his favourite blancmange delicacy. I shewed him the sample when he was here in August.

My aunt—who has now been downstairs & out in the garden three times—wishes me to transmit her pleased acknowledgment (pending an acknowledgment of her own) of your recent note to her. She agrees with me that the plan you suggest for next summer—of exploring ancient Rhode Island in a car with your entire household—is a delightful one—& one which we sincerely hope will prove feasible for you & your family when the time comes.[5] I would certainly find it a pleasure to act as guide to any scenic, historic, antiquarian, or otherwise interesting objects within a cruising radius—though I'd try not to impose on you as badly as I did on Price when I had him see-sawing all over the South County in a trial-&-error quest for objects & regions which *I* had never seen before! Wish you could persuade C A S to come along.

I join with my little tiger friend at Landlord Fadden's—& with the solemn & furry clubmen of the Kappa Alpha Tau fraternity[6] which meets daily on the sun-warmed roof of a garden shed outside my west windows—in sending most cordial regards & greetings to the 'beautiful boy' whose much-appreciated paw-print helps to sign your document of the 19–20th. I can imagine him with envy . . . . for I have indeed not only pushed a pen beneath grave feline scrutiny, but have often pushed it under the handicap of playful slaps from sportive & juvenile feline paws, as the owners of such paws have jumped to my desk to chew & rustle amongst their old Grandpa's papers! I am now getting very friendly with the huge black-&-white President of the adjacent Kappa Alpha Tau—so that he rolls on his back & purrs like a kitten when I approach & greet him.

Best wishes from aunt & self, & thanks again for the welcome pictures.

Yr oblig'd & obt Servt

H P L

P.S. I learn with sorrow that one of the silver-steepled village churches—that at Valleyfield—which I have always admired while passing through rural Quebec on the train—has just been burned down. Only 20 days ago I saw it in all its glory—& now a mass of charred walls! It was not, however, really old—simply cast in traditional form. Built in the 1880's, & the architect—a local Frenchman—is still alive to mourn over the ruins. It will be rebuilt.

Notes

1. The Holmes comment has not been located. There is a passage about Newburyport in ch. 2 of the weird novel *Elsie Venner* (1861), which HPL read, but there is no mention there that Newburyport is "finished."

2. Timothy Dexter (1747–1806) was a source for the character Obed Marsh in "The Shadow over Innsmouth" (1931), which resulted from a trip HPL made to Newburyport in 1931. See *Letters to Alfred Galpin* (147–51) for lengthy discussion of Dexter.

3. HPL's first visit to Newburyport occurred in 1923, when he went there in the company of the young amateur Edgar J. Davis. See HPL to Samuel Loveman, 29 April [1923]; in *Letters to Maurice W. Moe and Others* 501–4..

4. HPL refers to the destruction of early 19th-century warehouses on South Water Street in late 1929, inspiring HPL to write his poem "The East India Brick Row."

5. HVS did not fulfill her plan.

6. Leslie B. Fadden (1896–1982) was proprietor of The Arsdale, the boarding house at 55 Waterman Street across the back garden from 66 College Street, where HPL often directed visitors from out of town to stay and where he and Annie Gamwell sometimes took meals. HPL referred to the neighborhood cats as belonging to a "fraternity" that he called Kappa Alpha Tau (see WBT 96). HPL's home at 66 College Street was owned by Brown University, and a nearby fraternity house was visible from his window (referred to in "The Haunter of the Dark" [1935]).

[6]   [ALS, JHL]

66 College St.,
Providence, R.I.,
Octr. 17, 1933.

Dear Miss Sully:—

Abundant thanks for the additional prints—& here, sooner than I expected to have any, are some of my own experiments in a similar direction. Wishing a larger picture than my current vest-pocket kodak affords, I exhumed a #2 Brownie bought in 1907 & decided to take a chance with it. As you see, the results are at least slightly short of a total loss—though the perspective of the large house view is distinctly uncertain. I waited for an unimpeachably sunny day—finally conducting operations on the 8th inst. My next attempt will be to get some *interior* views (a much more difficult matter), at least, of the colonial mantelpieces in my study & my aunt's living-room. That will probably require time exposures.

About the hidden churchyard of St. John's—there must be some unsuspected vampiric horror burrowing down there & emitting vague miasmatic influences, since you are the third person to receive a definite creep of fear from it[1] . . . . the others being Samuel Loveman & H. Warner Munn. I took Loveman there at midnight, & when we got separated among the tombs he couldn't be *quite* sure whether a faint luminosity bobbing above a distant nameless grave was my electric torch or a corpse-light of less describable origin! Munn was there with W. Paul Cook & me, & had an odd, unaccountable dislike of a certain unplaceable, deliberate *scratching* which recurred at intervals around 3 a.m. How superstitious some people are! As for the prosaically historical side—this graveyard belongs to the Anglican church founded (as King's Church) in 1723 by the Huguenot Gabriel Bernon[2] . . . . who had fled from France, & had been deported from loyally popish Quebec. Bernon was *almost* but not quite my ancestor—his daughter Sarah having been the first wife of the Benjamin Whipple from whose *second* wife I am descended. The original church was a steepled Georgian affair, & the churchyard (whose interments go back to the 1720's) was not hidden until the house-building of many decades gradually hid it from the sight of both lower & (subsequently laid out) upper highways. But its hillside location must have made it picturesque from the first. The oldest graves are the lowest—nearest the church. Here may be found the impressive altar-tomb of John Merritt,[3] the London merchant who came to Providence in 1750 & had the first coach, first astronomical telescope, & first globes in town. He built a country-seat over the hill in what is now our best residential district—my birthplace falling within the former limits of his demesne. When the unfortunate revolt of 1775–83 came, the rebels changed the name of the church from King's to St. John's. In 1810 the original steepled fane gave place to the present neo-Gothic edifice—the work of Providence's eminent architect John Holden

Greene, who also designed the Unitarian church which you saw.[4] In 1847–8, when Poe was much in Providence calling upon Mrs. Whitman in the neighbouring Benefit St. house,[5] the churchyard formed one of his favourite rambles—its appearance being essentially the same as now. For many years there have been no burials there except of rectors of the church & bishops of the diocese—of which it was recently made the cathedral edifice. There would certainly be no more appropriate place for a tasteful suicide—I must remember it when I come to the end of my cash—but I don't recall reading of any there. I fear the recent tragic event must have occurred against a less vivid background—for Providence is well supplied with necropolitan expanses.

Your Newburyport itinerary must have included a good many high spots. The square near the Garrison Inn is Brown Park—named from Moses Brown *of Providence,* one of the four brothers I mentioned last July . . . . 18th century merchant princes. Moses (a Quaker) had textile interests in Newburyport in the late 18th & early 19th century, & lived for a time in the old white gambrel-roofed house (Dalton Club) in State St. opposite the Wolfe Tavern. I've never been over the Garrison Inn's interior, so in one way you are ahead of me on Newburyport data.

The Longfellow house (brick) you saw in Portland was the poet's boyhood home (the Wadsworth house, belonging to his maternal line) but not his birthplace. The latter is a large yellow wooden house in a now seedy part of the town, near the harbour & the Grand Trunk Station. The family left it so soon after Henry's birth that he had no memory of living in it—but it is nevertheless a museum of a sort . . . . not so well maintained as the Wadsworth house. By the way, if you did not get postcards of the Wadsworth house I can let you have a complete set—a duplicate envelope having turned up recently among my chaotic files.

You missed something in not seeing Salem & Marblehead (the "Arkham" & "Kingsport", respectively, of my tales—which reminds me that "The Festival" is lamentably crude & overcoloured in spots).[6] I think those primitive wooden chimneys were originally lined with clay; but this protection constantly peeled off, so that fires were very frequent. As soon as the town became well-settled, such chimneys were prohibited by law.

As for French-Canadians—I suppose they still feel a certain constraint toward the Anglo-Saxon, notwithstanding the fact that no overt trouble has occurred for generations. I noticed that the natives were not eager to point out Wolfe's ascending place on the Heights of Abraham. The French in Canada have always felt obliged to guard their language & institutions with fanatical zeal, hence have developed a curiously defensive & absorption-resisting attitude. They bring it with them when they filter down the factory-lined river valleys into New England—so that they are today the least assimilable of our foreigners. In Rhode Island we have villages & towns every inch as French as Quebec or Trois Rivieres—with grotesquely steepled church (one or two even silvered in Quebec style), French or bilingual signs, black-gowned children taught in French parochial schools & knowing no English, shovel-hatted priests, & all the rest. Thus the Quebec milieu was not at all strange to me when I first saw it in 1930. Only the other day my aunt & I were taken for a motor ride including passage through Woonsocket, R.I.—& there we saw the typical "Maison a Vendre", "Salle a Louer", "Avis", "Aux Soldats de la Guerre, 1917–18, Erice par Société Jacques-Cartier", &c. which would have reminded you of Quebec & Montreal. One sometimes wonders whether Wolfe fought & perished in vain. In the 1680's Cotton Mather thundered in Catonian strains against the potential French invader—& behold! Just as he feared, French speech & French steeples now rise from the banks of Rhode Island's rivers![7]

I did not realise how low the general educational level of Quebec province is, although of course I knew that the sectarian limitations must make the culture very one-sided. I fancy that scholastic standards vary locally. Montreal is very proud of its schools, & a municipal law makes it obligatory that French be taught in the English schools, & English in the church-managed French ones. Thus all the population is becoming bi-lingual—every young Anglo-Montrealer knowing some French, & every French youngster knowing some English. The almost unparallelled degree of ecclesiastical domination in French Canada is certainly a retarding influence, & seems to arouse resentment in most visitors despite its picturesqueness .... silver steeples, tonsured, sandalled, brown-robed friars, curiously coiffed nuns, &c. Peasants will have their religion, just as workmen will have their whiskey—but the financial drain & intellectual stultification sometimes seem a disproportionately high price to pay for the emotional soothing & titillation. If simple people must grovel before mythical conceptions, they might at least have a less expensive, retarding, & politically bothersome set of idols than those of an arrogant Catholic orthodoxy. Ordinarily I am not at all hostile to any sort of Santa-Claus belief that anyone may wish to harbour, but of late years I feel that formal religions may cause much trouble in the period of social & economic readjustment which lies ahead. All the powerful orthodoxies represent celestial projections of the now obsolescent political order, hence are pledged to defend it against all change. With a mechanised world of radically altered conditions, great changes will certainly be necessary from now on—yet all the official faiths recognise the extinct fabric as sacred, & blindly oppose any rational readjustment based on current needs. Of the various mythologies dominant in the Anglo-Saxon world one might form a scale based on relative absurdity. The least irrational is undoubtedly the very liberal theism represented by Dr. Fosdick[8] & a few other actual thinkers among theologians. Next comes ordinary Unitarianism. Below this stand the loosely liberalised evangelical sects whose orthodox tenets are quietly dropped one by one— Congregationalists, Presbyterians, & the best grade of Baptists. Next— though much higher as an *aesthetic* proposition—comes the Anglican church with its ingeniously evaded 39 articles, & after that (though higher up *aesthetically*) the ancient Catholic hierarchy with its impossible assumptions & eel-like logic-twisting. Lowest of all are the literal & orthodox evangelical sects—the dense & wilfully brainless Presbyterians, Baptists, & Methodists with their hysterical 'kiver to kiver' hill-billy gospel. And the Mormons, Christian Scientists, Holy Rollers, &c. fit in *intellectually* near the bottom, though social prestige gives some of these freak sects a borrowed impressiveness in certain local areas. All of these systems of blindly inherited tradition mean well, & all have the common usefulness of giving people the illusion of significance, direction, & value in the meaningless welter of conscious biological existence. They are the natural conceptions of a primitive & ignorant race, & embody a vast amount of really useful precept—the massed experience of mankind worked out by trial & error & given a fictitious heavenly authority. Certainly, it would cause chaos & harm to strip the world of their influence before a more rational psychological & ethical regimen, based on aesthetics & the actual mental & physical needs of the group in its existing environment, can be worked out & given effective force. We can see already the somewhat squalid decadence in emotional sensitivity & ethical harmony which prevails amongst those "sophisticates" who have lost their traditional faith without replacing it with a suitable aesthetic & practical substitute. The trouble is that substitutes can't be devised over night. They have to grow by gradual accretion through long centuries of homogeneous & continuous experience before they can dominate the subconscious mind & provide that sense of direction & purpose which alone saves life from becoming a nightmare. Exceptions to this rule of gradual growth are very rare—coming only when some psychological accident raises up a new illusion so potently captivating that it sweeps all before it. Such an accident was the blazing up of Islam in the 7th century, & such, to a lesser & perhaps temporary degree, is the spread of communism (a religion despite its anti-theism) in modern Russia. Yes—I read George Moore[9] in youth, & have always thought the Catholic system weak in its relation to individual character. Ironically, it is the least personally strengthening because it is the most purely *religious*. Theoretically—& as a matter of universal acceptance in pre-Reformation times—the function of religion is primarily to exalt & serve some mystical & intangible entity or group of entities outside mankind. It has relatively little to do with human conduct & character— hence in classical & pre-classical antiquity we find religion largely ritualistic & orgiastic, whilst conduct (based on reason) remained the province of the non-religious philosopher. Christianity—or rather, the Judaism on which it was based—was the first religion to take a primary interest in ethics & assume a responsibility for conduct & character. That was the unique contribution of the Semitic temperament to western civilisation—a very doubtful gift; since it removed ethics so completely from the aesthetic & logical field, transferring it to the jurisdiction of a mythical belief, that order & good taste threaten to vanish upon the ultimate & inevitable decline of the mythology. It would have been far better if we had kept our classical conception of ethics as a matter of beauty, good sense, & taste—the province of the non-supernatural philosopher—for its survival would not then have been so imperilled by the decline of religion. As Aryans, lacking the almost savage ethical sense of the desert-bred Semite, we are vastly better adapted to the conception of character as related to beauty, reason, & pride, than to the notion of "divine moral law". Meanwhile our dominant religion has always been torn betwixt two tendencies—one to return to the Aryan concept & become a system of *mystical adoration* letting morals more or less slide or putting them on a bargaining & excusing basis, & the other to live up to the specifically Christian ideal & mould better & more harmonious characters in the immediate world around us. The first tendency breeds the Catholic psychology, & the second the Protestant. As a result, Catholics are more purely *religious*—since Protestants, being after all Aryans to whom the feverish Semitic religio-moralism is impossible save for brief periods (such as that of intensive & literal Puritanism in England & New-England), tend to lay more & more stress on human character & good deeds as opposed to mystical adoration, & therefore to exercise the functions of the classically conceived philosopher rather than those of the classically conceived priest. Today religion is on the decline as an influence—necessarily so, on account of what we have learned about the workings of the cosmos & of our own minds & emotions. It is, then, our task to save existence from a sense of chaos & futility by rebuilding the purely aesthetic & philosophical concept of character & cosmic pseudo-purpose—reëstablishing a realisation of the necessity of *pattern* in any order of being complex enough to satisfy the mind & emotions of highly evolved human personalities. Obviously, the Protestant mind is the one best fitted to execute this important work—best fitted because it is the most philosophical & least religious. While Protestantism itself—as a supernatural faith—will decline because of the graduation of its thoughtful members to philosophic atheism or agnosticism (& of its thoughtless members to decadent & disorganised drifting), its actual work will continue as a sort of legacy. The framework it has bequeathed will serve a useful purpose—ensuring for the increasingly non-religious ethics of the future that force of *traditional continuity* which realists recognise as so essential to any really working system of action or emotion. The steeple, the Gothic tower, & the chromatic & magical twilight of painted windows can still have an effective psychological & social function long after their supernatural background is disavowed. But, of course, only if decadence, speed-&-quantity worship, anti-traditionalism, physical sense-worship, commercial-mindedness, & other emotionally coarsening & impoverishing influences can be held in check. The issue—survival or decadence—is still in doubt. And meanwhile the Catholic religion, a ceremonial & mystical institution independent of the details of conduct, plugs along in its ancient, deeply-rooted way—hampering good social organisation now & then, yet at least giving a consoling emotional opium to millions incapable of an aesthetic or philosophic attitude. There is always room for a kindly narcotic of this sort—at least, until reason solves the perhaps insoluble problem of bringing decent comfort & contentment of a material kind to the totality of the population.

But pardon senile prolixity on abstractions—Grandpa's favourite pastime! That's the way things get going when the invincible & indivisible triad of Belknap, James Ferdinand Morton, & E'ch-Pi-El sit down for a little light persiflage. Regarding The Modern Young Man & his wandering emotions—a detached observer must simultaneously sympathise with the transitional perplexity which drives him to his ugly, feverish, ruthless, & ultimately futile course, & deplore & oppose the pursuance of that course itself. One must, to twist the sense of a line which Mr. Pope writ in my 18th century, "love th' Offender, yet detest th' Offence."[10] Without doubt, the brutally primitive, experimental, socially irresponsible, animally capricious, aesthetically low-grade, callously anti-traditional, & really personally insulting amative attitudes of modern youth are primarily products of reaction against a system of interpreting human relationships which was fully as ridiculous & unrealistic—even if not so emotionally low-grade, anti-social, & insulting to human nature—as the existing opposite. Family organisation was an artificial fetish, & the nature of the emotional ties betwixt individuals was so wholly falsified & reduced to pompous sentimental fiction that no person of sense could survey the popular pretences—either in literature or in speech & manners—without a surge of hilarity, anger, or disgust, according to his temperament. Any "serious" romance of 50 years ago makes comic reading today—values, assigned motivations, human reactions, & so on. Hypocrisy was loathsomely encouraged & exercised, & people in practice had to keep two sets of data in their heads—life & motives as outwardly represented, & life & motives as actually existing. Since the latter phase was not officially recognised, there was no unanimity of knowledge or attitude regarding it. Under religion & the self-deluding psychology it bred, such a mental muddle might well remain permanent. The ethical code enjoined by religion was near enough to the optimum of common sense to prevent acute social friction, & the absurdity of the assigned motivations was suffered to remain unnoticed. When, however, religion began to crack, acute thinkers began to pause & ask themselves how real the commonly assigned values & motives might be; & thence, how much actual validity the existing emotional attitudes & social institutions might possess. That was the age of Ibsen, Wilde, Nietzsche, Shaw, & Wells .... & presently of Freud, Adler, & Jung. After the analysis & shakeup it became pretty clear that the moving impulses of mankind, their relation to the basic structure of the universe, & their manner of operation under various given sets of conditions, are far—infinitely far—from what orthodox religion & conventional sentimentality had assumed. Human instincts were boiled down to about a dozen, the relative strength of these in different individual types & races & under different environmental conditions was estimated, & the multifarious phenomena of human emotional life were traced to the interaction & mutual checking of these instincts, plus the infinite wealth of associational combinations which the memory, the symbolic imagination, & the pattern-sense superimpose upon the primitive substratum. Men's feelings & moods & aspirations were seen to be neither "divine" nor universal, neither eternal nor simple & basic[,] neither consciously ordained nor related to any larger end—but rather to be the net chance results of a complex array of originally mechanical forces peculiar to the organisms bred in this part of the universe; having no larger connexions in time or space, & conditioned by their environment. What the oxidation of iron & the crystallisation of salt & the sensitivity of a sunfish & the anger of a fighting dog are on lower rungs of the organisational ladder, so are the dreams of a poet & the vision of a seer & the devotion of a lover amongst the complex types of organisation called advanced mammal primates, or human beings. Obviously, the flatulent old sentimentalities were pretty thin stuff!

And right here is where the difference between rational balance & hysterical decadence is illustrated. What has been shewn us? Simply that certain phenomena & conditions have *causes* & some *details of operation* other than what was formerly supposed. Has anything suggested that any of the phenomena or conditions ought to be changed or abolished? Obviously not. What we have found out means nothing one way or the other so far as recommending or condemning various courses goes. All it signifies is that supernatural constraint to one arbitrary course does not exist. It sends us back to nature—and any full-witted person realises that this means *our whole complex nature, including the most delicate associational sensitivities* rather than the merely instinctive or simian part of our nature—for guidance, & bids us reconsider our accustomed ways *only so far as is necessary to bring them into harmony with the one reasonable purpose of making the most of our opportunities for symmetrical development & permanent, heightened enjoyment under such environmental conditions as we have or can make.* To assume that the discovery of the mechanical & fortuitous nature of our complex higher emotions at once reduces those emotions to hypocritical ignominiousness, or even to mere equality with the dozen or so primitive dog-&-ape instincts & emotions, is a breach of logic so utterly childish, unjustified, & hilariously ridiculous that I honestly cannot see how any adult person of normal intelligence & grammar-school education can make it. It is to me one of those inscrutable mysteries beyond solution—like the sudden blight which caused the collapse of architectural taste in the Victorian age. I give it up! What is this "young intelligentsia" driving at, anyhow? Don't they realise that the essence of all quality is *fineness of organisation?* What if the *basic substance* of a finely-wrought thing *is* the same as that of other coarsely wrought things. Is a delicate watch or micrometer no better than a horseshoe or flatiron merely because its chemical substance is similar? We know from observation, record, &

analysis how infinitely keener & finer-evolved human life is, than primitive lower-animal life. We can recognise our superior grasp of the universe, & can feel the increased pleasure accruing from the exercise of many emotional & imaginative faculties instead of a pitiful few. This is intrinsic & basic—if we keep our heads clear we don't need any "divine" nonsense to justify the more complex, delicate, & human aspects of life as opposed to the primitive & brutish aspects. The bottom hasn't dropped out of anything merely because we've made a discovery about the mechanism. Nothing of the "dignity & value of human life" has been lost in the change of perspective. And yet what nonsense certain poor devils (both on the theological & on the decadent side, as a matter of fact!) spout! Without a shadow of justification, the decadent "sophisticate" leaps to two *perfectly irrelevant* assumptions—first, that human nature, not being divine & cosmic, must necessarily be bestial; & second, that all highly evolved emotions must necessarily be valueless, non-existent, or reprehensible, *merely because they were formerly mis-explained.* As a complete & puerile violation of all logic, this modernistic philosophy furnishes a classic & immortal example! And yet, as I said at the outset, I can sympathetically understand the feelings of the decadent. He is so exasperated at the outrageous bull & crap of theology-dictated sentimentalism that he feels impelled to fly to the remotest possible extreme. The trouble is that this other extreme is just as silly & even more harmful & violative of richness in life than the first one! He doesn't realise this because he allows his first exasperation to cut off his mind & put blind emotion in the saddle. He feels so much that he doesn't think—hence peters out in futility & brutish degradation.

It is needless to say to persons of good sense & reflectiveness that the one rational object of life is—for all the absence of a deity or of a high-flown cosmic basis of thoughts & feelings—the harmonious utilisation & satisfaction of our existing equipment to the greatest possible extent; a pursuit which, in view of the well-known conflicts between different tendencies & groups of tendencies within us, postulates an intelligent choice of keener, more permanent, & more rewarding faculties over duller, more transient, & less profoundly rewarding faculties for favouring & cultivation. This is not a theological or moral dictum—it is merely materialistic common sense. If it offends the "younger advanced intelligentsia" by sounding excessively like what ancient philosophers used to say, that's just too bad . . . . . . although the youngsters could realise if they'd stop to think that much of ancient philosophy & ethics comes primarily from plain observation & common sense. The trimmings of pomp & poetry are tacked on later. It is true that cosmic "good" & "evil" do not exist—but it is also true that in human conduct & emotional-guiding there are certain courses which (environment being confined within given limits) tend to give profound & lasting satisfaction & expansion to a maximum of our faculties, & certain courses which yield a net return (whatever the momentary effect) of dissatisfaction & frustration. We don't have to call such courses "good" & "evil"—it is never wise to become slaves to nomenclature—but it would be unscientific not to recognise them & differentiate betwixt their properties. So after all, the triumphant & blatant immoralist is in a pretty bad fix philosophically & scientifically. He hasn't much ground to stand on. Unfortunately his voice isn't impaired—so he still makes a great noise.

As for *details*—rational, materialistic ethics will of course have certain points of difference from theistic, traditional ethics; though the hidden rational factor in ancient morals, plus the present psychological value of continuity, will combine to make the future's code much more like the past's than the thoroughgoing modernist will relish. The decent citizen of the machine age will have a disconcerting number of points in common with the decent citizen of the Greek, Roman, mediaeval, & modern Western civilisations. So far as the element of human affection is concerned, there is not nearly enough change to please the young Casanovas who aspire to the carefree refinements of the canine & feline worlds. In spite of their fine talk, & in spite of the mythical nature of that cosmically derived & mysteriously unalterable passion postulated by bygone sentimentalists, it remains a rather obvious fact that of the many perfectly separate elements which enter into any typical human tie (for there is no *one* thing which may be called love or affection; each individual emotion-group classified as such being a complex fusion of various dissimilar factors acting accidentally toward the production of a given resultant expression), those which make for sudden, violent, & transient infatuation are the very lowest in the biological-psychological scale, whilst those which endure over long periods (& it is simply childish—a denial of obvious evidence—to ignore the thousands of well-defined & unmistakable cases of virtually permanent affection on record) belong to that higher, more complex, & more associative order which involve the recognition of finely evolved faculties in their object & afford deeper, maturer, & more poignantly developed psychological satisfactions in their possessor. In other words, when a "young modern" says that a temporary or at least limited affair of intense emotion is the only sort of romance really satisfying to him, he is merely confessing that his emotional development has remained at a rather simian level; that he is not seeking a companion to honour as a fellow human-being, but is looking for a fellow-ape with whom he may amuse his transient & superficial emotions after the casual fashion of the ape species. Without knowing it—for one must give him credit for his naive ignorance if possible—he is giving the momentary object of his doubtful affections the gravest possible insult; that of placing her on a level essentially sub-human, as one who does not possess the qualities which, in really equal & sincerely beloved human beings, elicit so varied & general an array of emotional bonds that the passing of the crude temporary factors is virtually unnoticed in comparison to the tremendous residue of really human affection (recognition of mental kinship, harmony of highly-developed emotions, piling up of tender symbolic & associative factors, &c.) which permanently remains. His is the essentially crippled, cheapened emotional nature which cannot envisage or experience fine shades & subtleties of feeling. He gets on finely with Ovid's Ars Amatoria, but doesn't understand what the tale of Baucis & Philemon in the same author's Metamorphoses is about.[11] In this naive blindness he falls below even the callous gallants of antiquity; insomuch as they recognised standards but did not live up to them, whilst he recognises no standards at all. In defence of his position he points to the certainly large-enough number of persons who find permanent & congenial ties impossible of achievement. Here, again, he is exercising that childish lapse of logic which marks his estimate of human emotion as a whole. Merely because the world is haphazard & imperfect, with certain satisfactory adjustments attainable by only a part of the population, he jumps to the erroneous & irrelevant conclusion that *nobody* can attain such adjustments; that those who say they do merely pretend it, & that it is a waste of time to seek such a type of felicity. In other words, because *some* people can't appreciate music, it is foolish for *anybody* to seek the pleasures of harmony. Because *some* are colour-blind, it is foolish for *anybody* to seek any art other than black & white. What crap! And yet these smart-alec Lotharios call *themselves* acute & sophisticated, & brand the rational conservative as an outmoded fogy! As a matter of fact, the very growth of rationalism from which they draw their silly conclusions does much to emphasise the hollowness of their position—for with the decline of the crazy "one-great-love-in-a-lifetime" hallucination of Victorian days, & the disappearance of the savage anti-divorce prejudices of darker times, the number of permanently unadjustable individuals is bound to be vastly cut down through opportunities for the rectification of mistakes & the formation of new & sounder alliances with better prospects of dignified permanence. There is *less & less* excuse, rather than more & more, for abandoning the quest for that full & permanent union of psychological lives which is obviously the only real fulfilment of human affection on equal human terms.

It seems to me, then, clear that in spite of all his stale, misquoted Freud, his cleverly juggled divorce statistics, & his pompous anthropological extracts from Briffault & Calverton[12] & other flashy conclusion-jumpers, the fickle young modern is holding & defending a false (& if he knew it, insulting) position when he rants in favour of canine romantic ethics. In view of what is known regarding the constituents of human affection, we cannot but conclude that he is upholding cheapness & inferiority against emotional richness & all that we truly respect. Whatever be the possibilities of error, delusion, & disappointment—& in what human venture are they absent?—it seems certain that any person possessing for another the equal & honourable affection which involves respect, congeniality, understanding, & recognition as a fellow human-being of intelligence, as well as the more glamourous temporary factors, will not wish or propose any union other than an open & socially acceptable one intended (whatever melancholy revision the future may perchance dictate) for permanent duration. I may be a crabbed bigot, but any other sort of romantic sighing to a daughter of mine, if I had one, would earn a modernistic gallant an extremely decided momentum down those selfsame stairs which tripped my aunt, transmitted through a hard-soled #8 Regal! In dealing with "advanced & emancipated" youths of this sort, no one need feel impelled to exercise undue tact or harbour undue scruples. Good sense & good taste—proximate principles based on the real fulness of human nature—furnish solidly workable & wholly non-theological standards to which no soberly reflective person will be ashamed to be true. And no excuse is ever needed for acting according to such standards, or upholding them against any of the fly-by-night bolshevisms of fad, fashion, fever, & foolishness! Restoration ethics had their day—but the fame of "unfashionable" Milton has lived longer than that of

> ". . . the sons
> Of Belial, flown with insolence & wine."[13]

But hades, what prolixity! Coming to a specific young modern—Morton & I don't emphasise "Little" Belknap's juvenility so much nowadays except as a kind of spoof to snap him out of certain juvenile attitudes. In fact, during the past year we've rather systematically tried to egg on all the adult stirrings & outreachings which we've noticed in him. There is a tremendous mine of taste, talent, erudition, & general ability in that ki . . . . er—pardon me—middle-aged gentleman, & we old fossils can't help being impatient to bring it out fully as soon as possible. I'm enclosing a page from one of Morton's recent letters (what a pity you didn't meet good old Mortonius!) to illustrate how my fellow-patriarch labours with our triumvirate's junior third. The point of the whole business is that our admiration & liking for Son . . . . er, Belknap . . . are of the vastest & most genuine sort. We simply want to give him a good steering, so that he won't get sidetracked or slowed down. Why, confound it all, I wish I had a quarter of the young rascal's cleverness!

Aunt much improved—has had two long motor rides through autumn scenery—one to that idyllic seaport of *Wickford* which I said you ought to have seen. Another time we descended the hill to the art museum to see the newly dedicated garden in the courtyard—a fascinating spot, as the enclosed cutting illustrates. Getting too cold to sit outdoors & read or write, but I take almost daily scenic walks in the varicoloured woods, or over the spectral country roads north of the town. Frost & desolation will soon be here—tho' C A S tells me of 100° temperatures out your way. Thanks exceedingly for the Mackinac view. I wish that sort of transportation prevailed around here.[14] ¶ And renewed apologies for verboseness—my invariable vice whenever anything like a philosophical argument comes in sight. ¶ Regards from aunt & self—

Yr obt hble Servt
H P Lovecraft

P.S. Kappa Alpha Tau meeting on shed outside the window. Four members present—President (black & white), Vice-President (tiger), Secretary (maltese & white, part Angora), & Novice of the Class of '37. (Maltese) ¶ Surely it's all right to copy my ineffectual Brick Row lines . . . . distribution is what I had it published for! ¶ Just had a W.T. cheque for half of what they owe me. Hope they're likewise loosening up with C A S.

Notes

1. See HVS's "Some Memories of H.P.L.": "After dinner, he took me into a graveyard associated with Poe. . . . [I]t was dark, and he began to tell me strange, weird stories in a sepulchral tone and, despite the fact that I am a very matter-of-fact person, something about his manner, the darkness, and a sort of eerie light that seemed to hover over the gravestones got me so wrought up that I began to run out of the cemetery with him close at my heels, with the one thought that I must get up to the street before he, or whatever it was, grabbed me. I reached a street lamp, trembling, panting, and almost in tears, and he had the strangest look on his face, almost of triumph. Nothing was said" (365–66).

2. Gabriel Bernon (1644–1736), Joseph Whipple (1662–1746), and Nathaniel Brown (1661–1739) established the Anglican Church in Providence in 1721. The original wood building was erected in 1722 and was known as King's Chapel until the Revolution. The Cathedral of St. John that now stands at the site was built in 1810.

3. HPL mentions Merritt (1739–1805) in *The Case of Charles Dexter Ward*.

4. First Unitarian Church (1816), 301 Benefit Street.

5. The John Reynolds House (c. 1785) at 88 Benefit Street.

6. HPL made this comment because the story had just been reprinted in the October 1933 issue of *WT*.

7. HPL to August Derleth, 22 June [1933]: "Woonsocket, R.I. is so solidly French that English is almost a foreign language there. The present mayor is one Felix Toupin, while Dupré, Pothier, Laliberté, Gagnon, Caderette, &c. &c. are the sort of names which predominate both in the city directory & on the rolls of the municipal government. Wherever there are mills, the French-Canadians flock in. Arctic, R.I., Central Falls, R.I., & Fall River, Mass. are other predominantly Gallic towns. Most of the speeches in the Woonsocket City Council are in French. There is a grim irony in the peace-time invasion of New England by the northern foe & whom we fought determinedly from 1689 to 1760!" (*Essential Solitude* 584).

8. Harry Emerson Fosdick (1878–1969), pastor of the Park Avenue Baptist Church (1925–30) and the Riverside Church (1930–46) in New York City, and a central figure in the Fundamentalist-Modernist controversy within American Protestantism in the 1920s and 1930s.

9. George Augustus Moore (1852–1933), Irish novelist, short-story writer, poet, art critic, memoirist, and dramatist.

10. Alexander Pope, "Eloisa to Abelard," l. 192.

11. Ovid's *Ars Amatoria* is a poem in three books instructing men and women how to succeed in the "art of love." Baucis and Philemon were an old married couple, the

only people in their town to welcome Zeus and Hermes who came there in disguise. In gratitude, Zeus turned their cottage into an ornate temple and allowed them to be its guardians. They asked that when one of them was to die, the other would die as well. Upon their death, they were changed into an intertwining pair of trees, one oak and one linden, standing in the deserted boggy terrain. The story appears to have been invented by Ovid in the *Metamorphoses* (8.628–724).

12. HPL refers to the historians and sociologists Robert Briffault (1876–1948) and V. F. Calverton (pseud. of George Goetz, 1900–1948).

13. John Milton, *Paradise Lost* 1.501–02.

14. Mackinac Island is an island and resort area in Lake Huron between the upper and lower peninsulas of Michigan. Nearly all motor vehicles are forbidden there, and horsedrawn vehicles prevail.

[7]   [ALS, JHL]

66 College—

Novr. 24, 1933

Dear Helen:

Certainly, I am no surname-addict! Indeed, so far from pompous ceremoniousness is my quill removed, that my wide range of random salutations includes every sort of informality from "Sultan Malik" (E. Hoffmann Price) to "Young Stalin" (or, before his proletarian evolution, Francis, Lord Belknap); whilst I am habitually addressed in every sort of fashion from "Grandpa" to "Anak"—the latter no Biblical allusion, but a sprightly Chicago gentleman's abbreviation of "anachronism", which he quite correctly applies to an 18th century relique surviving into the 20th.[1]

My aunt, who transmits her sincerest regards, is now vastly better—going everywhere alone, on foot or in street-cars, with only a single cane; & omitting even the latter now & then around the house. Her restoration to active command has gradually given the place an infinitely homelike aspect—with curtains and valances here & there, more pictures hung, more articles of furniture brought from storage, & so on. There is a haunting, elusive resemblance, on a miniature scale, to our old home; and you would certainly never recognise the rear of the house as the disordered barracks or quasi-hospital of last July. Another thing you would never recognise is that small single handful of grey tiger fur which, with its small brother & its black & white spotted mother, you beheld basking in the sunset light of the back garden. That handful is now as lithely graceful & violently playful & purrful a half-grown feline as one could wish to see, though still a constant visitor to our lowly hearth. Day before day before yesterday he paid a brief call of six hours; part of which time he sat precariously in Grandpa's lap, whilst in other moments he explored the scattered papers of my desk or withdrew to curl up drowsily in the neighbouring morris-chair. I am led to understand that he is also a sociable visitor & general favourite among all the inhabitants of his own domicile—your erstwhile lodging-place at 55 Waterman.[2] Only last week I learned that he & his brother (now given away) are merely foster-children of their apparent mother! It seems that last summer she had been despoiled of two very unprepossessing kittens of her own—when lo! one day she appeared in her wonted haunts with a brand new pair—of unknown maternity, kidnapped from some still unfathomed source. Thus my little grey friend may, for all I know, be the missing heir of some kingly house, where his absence is mourned each day with pensive, wistful mewings!

Returning to the consideration of the so-called human race—I would say that the composite phenomenon called "conscience" is very probably shared by other highly-evolved mammals, at least in part. It is based to some extent on fear of the consequences of some infraction of the group's code of folkways, though there is generally a subtler factor involving one's opinion of oneself & dependent on one's acceptance of the group's code as a standard of quality. When one either believes in a mystical system of cosmic obligations, or has an aesthetic respect for a conduct-pattern approved both by antiquity & by a responsible majority today, he tends to regard infractions as symbolic of smallness or inadequacy or inferiority; hence dislikes to connect himself with the idea of such infractions. Defence & expansion of the ego form the chief psychological urge of mankind, & an individual will go to infinite pains to avoid belittlement in his own eyes. When he is absolutely unable to form a self-consoling rationalisation of his conduct, even by the utmost sentimental distortion of the facts, he is brought to face with himself in a position of inferiority—& consequently experiences the painful reaction forming a great part of "conscience." I think there are many persons wholly devoid of this reaction—either because of an insensitivity which obscures the symbolism involved, or because of a genuine lack of respect for the group-code on which the normal idea of inferiority is based. I have seen many persons so widely out of sympathy with the whole conception of patterned behaviour that they flaunt any precept or obligation at will, & without any twinge of embarrassment or psychological pain. This type, in an unsettled age, is becoming more & more numerous. There is of course no such thing as an "innate moral sense". All apparently intuitive ideas of "right" & "wrong" are simply group attitudes (determined by chance, expediency, &c.) subconsciously assimilated. ¶ But stay! Who is this that intrudes upon an old gentleman's philosophic meditations? Speaking of the devil . . . . . & referring back to the preceding page . . . . . . I beg to announce a pleasing caller who has just endeavoured—not too successfully—to sign his name (vide supra) in greeting to you & to the beautiful boy of his own species who furnished so graceful a signature in Harvard crimson last September. He followed my aunt in from lunch (which she takes at the Maison Fadden), & now insists on climbing all over his grandpa—punctuated by sojourns on the desk during which he takes occasional whacks at this provocatively moving pen. With such an handicap to grave thought, I trust you can excuse any lapse in reflective acumen or logical exposition which the ensuing pages may display. This little imp's purr averages more decibels of acoustic energy per cubic inch of his molecular mass than any other feline susurration I've heard in a long while.

¶ Returning to *homo sapiens* (what exquisite irony Linnaeus exhibited in his learned nomenclature!)[3]—whilst, as just observed, the moral sense is a purely accidental product of environment, one must add that it is no less valuable (as some hasty moderns appear to assume) on that account. For one thing, it lends force & effectiveness to the rules which society is obliged to make to ensure its survival. Secondly, it has the aesthetic value of imparting a pattern (connected with the natural emotions & aspirations of the group) to life; from which proceeds all the heartening & stabilising sense of direction, purpose, & interest that makes existence (a distinctly dull & painful process, intrinsically, after the momentary glamour of youth disappears) worth enduring, & that gives it the coherence & comprehensibility necessary to the development of art & the maintenance of a vigorous mental & material civilisation. This sense of direction & purpose is of course an illusion, cosmically speaking; but it is a tremendously convincing & overwhelmingly useful illusion, which no individual, nation, or race can lose without peril to its future. And it quite clearly depends upon the perpetuation of an hereditary group code (in basic essentials—of course, there is always a normal degree of modification resulting from changes in environmental conditions & group technique) rather than on the separate & often conflicting utilitarian individual codes which modern radicals favour; since the latter devices have no opportunity to gain the subconscious imaginative hold & the perfected pattern form so characteristic of widely unanimous ancestral attitudes. It is, of course, not well to delude oneself with the belief that inherited standards & folkways have a *cosmic* basis of obligation. That only weakens their good effect after one discovers that *nothing in existence has a cosmic basis*. But it is well to recognise the practical value of settledness as a social factor, & the aesthetic value of that process of pattern-participation which only ancestral loyalties can effect & perpetuate. One need only survey contemporary society to discover that the most deeply & genuinely miserable people are those with the least amount of traditional anchorage. They have cast off one set of vivifying loyalties, but are (quite naturally) unable to find in life any other permanently & pervasively vivifying influence. The Russian bolsheviki have founded a new set of potentially effective loyalties (*not* individual, as our young radicals wish, but even more rigidly collective than any fanatical orthodoxy of the past!) at a tremendous cost; but even so, the colourless existence they have adopted involves a net loss. What is more, this revolutionary change does not *really* involve a true *transition*, since it is at bottom *less a change than an outright replacement*. The actual members of the real Russian civilisation have by no means gone through a successful metamorphosis & exchanged their old loyalties for new. Such a thing cannot be done. Instead, they are dispersed all over the world—a Grand Duke Cyril in Paris, a Prof. Rostovtzeff at Yale, an Igor Sikorsky in New York, & so on.[4] The people who have founded the new & undeniably effective culture of the Soviets are *under-men who never really belonged to any civilisation.* They were too primitive & close to the bare animal struggle for subsistence to share any but the crudest & simplest attributes of the old culture. It is because they had so little real anchorage in the past that they are now able to devote themselves so wholly to an unknown future. Their case does not apply at all to the people who at present truly share the fruits of Western Civilisation. Literate Anglo-Saxons or Frenchmen or Germans or Spaniards or Italians have absolutely nothing to gain & everything to lose from any wholesale exchange of the past's experience for the uncertain ignes fatui of capricious cultural innovation. (This does not apply to the purely *economic* question—a fiendish problem which must be dealt with separately.) If any of the Western nations should suffer a duplication of the Russian catastrophe, the only real place for the civilised classes would be—as in that tragedy—in exile. Only a sodden & traditionless proletariat could successfully form a new civilisation. For others, it is a case of the old culture (though perhaps not without reasonable modifications involving no breach of continuity) or complete chaos.

What will probably come eventually in Russia is a fresh system of stratification based on natural capacity. The idealists will fight it at first as a violation of the sacred principle of equality, but it will come just the same. Never will superior men submit over long periods to standards & folkways designed for inferior men. The one real service which the bolsheviks have performed for civilisation is their successful attack on laissez-faire capitalism. Old Marx was really right in his prediction that unrestricted plutocracy was drawing toward its finish, & all the mechanised western nations will soon have to face the problem of the artificial redistribution of resources on a more equitable basis. Russia has been a sort of laboratory guinea-pig in furnishing illustrations of de-capitalising technique—& we must be grateful for that even while totally rejecting her equalitarian extremes & her disastrous & cruelly needless attacks on the non-economic phases [unfortunately, the Marxian fallacy of complete economic determinism—which radicals including Belknap swallow so avidly—refuses to recognise any cultural phase as separate from the economic order] of traditional civilisation.

As for an educational policy, & a policy regarding general cultural opportunities, I certainly do not endorse the indiscriminate forcing of unqualified persons to acquire a shallow scholastic-aesthetic veneer—though I differ from you on the point of opportunity-restriction. As I said regarding the specific case of "The Star-Treader" in an unappreciative school library, I see no reason to guard the fruits of culture as esoteric & difficultly accessible arcana for the fortunate or persistent few. There is no danger of beauty's or learning's being harmed through the gaze of the vulgar, & the masses will certainly never absorb enough inappropriate culture to harm themselves or others through mere contact with opportunities. On the other hand, the easy accessibility of avenues of development seems to me an unqualified advantage; insomuch as it opens the way for persons to find their own proper level according to natural capacity *& without reference to the wholly irrelevant element of financial status*. It does not take a bolshevik to realise that intellectual & aesthetic capacity are in no way connected with material earning power or economic good luck—hence I can scarcely regret the excellent (& all too rare) music of certain public radio features, the free museums of art, & the 30¢ (or even the 20¢ & 15¢ second & third run) cinemas with (once in every two or three years) really worthy drama, which offer appropriate mental, emotional, & imaginative nourishment to really high-grade but financially embarrassed people. It seems to me that the richness of a nation's life is definitely increased by the enlargement of its sensitive & appreciative element. For one thing, there is a larger audience & hence more encouragement for genius. For another thing, there is a wider sensitised field out of which exceptional individuals (vastly handicapped & sometimes wholly crushed by enforced ignorance) may develop. So I have no kick coming when—in a stage approximating brokeness—I am able to go to Providence's decrepit Bijou Theatre[5] & see "Anna Christie", "Berkeley Square", or "Henry VIII"[6] for 15¢; or when I am able to browse around New York's Metropolitan Museum for nothing on the free days! But I agree thoroughly that the forcing of education beyond any individual's natural needs is basically wasteful & absurd. Certain rudiments are of course absolutely necessary for social adaptation—so that, in a complex civilisation, the individual unable to acquire them is fit only for custodial segregation. Beyond this point, however, more latitude ought to be observed. Certain types, whose natural abilities & reasonably expected social contacts indicate no need for purely cultural acquirements, should assuredly not be forced to assimilate useless & wearying—& mnemonically short-lived—doses of Virgil, Plato, astronomy, Bach, Botticelli, Baudelaire, & the like. They, & society, will be better served by an education of more purely practical vocational cast. There is, however, an element of naturally inferior persons with superior family & social connexions who require different dealings. One can scarcely bring up the dull son of refined parents to be an illiterate & uncouth elevator-boy, since such a course would result in awkward & painful adjustments. In this type of situation a certain minimum amount of cultural forcing really is necessary in order to give the subject a comfortable basis of companionship & superficial mutual comprehension with those among whom chance has more or less irrevocably set him. The English public schools & universities know how to deal with this kind of thing—often imparting a kindly smattering of civilised manners & catchwords to youths whose intrinsic minds & tastes would suggest far different courses. Amidst the complexities & contradictions of human life the

one supremely fallacious attitude is that of dogmatism & wholesale generalisation. That was the trouble with the old "genteel tradition"—& is today the
trouble with the equally cocksure & indiscriminating bolshevistic tradition of
orthodox Marxio-Leninism. [The overgrown grey handful has now transferred himself quasi-permanently to the circular chair beside me, where he is
curled up in a slumber of abysmal profundity. The abatement of that echoing
purr seems as startling as the hushing of a frozen cataract! . . . . . but pardon
me! I spoke of "abysmal profundity" too soon! The cataract of sound has un-
frozen—for its source was aroused by my turning to view him. But the purr
is sporadic—interrupted by industrious face-washing operations.]

¶ But where was I in my task of settling the world's difficulties? Oh,
yes—bolshevism, decadence, traditions . . . . One of my most animated controversies at present is with a youth of open mind but modern leanings—one
J. Vernon Shea, aet. 21, of Pittsburgh, Pa.—who takes me to task 'for oppos-
ing anything radical or new.' I am endeavouring to demonstrate to him that I
do not oppose everything new, but merely such new things as involve sub-
traction without satisfactory substitution. If I generally oppose radicals, it is
because only about 10 or 20 percent of the changes they suggest seem in any
way desirable when viewed in the light of history. Everything really satisfying
in life is the result of *stability* & *continuity*—since, outside the narrow radius of
crude sensation, virtually nothing has any interest or meaning apart from the
associations twined around it through generations of racial experience. That is
why the machine age tends so greatly to impoverish life—by removing us
from our hereditary adjustment to the landscape, the seasons, the agricultural
cycle, the acts of daily life & industry, & the familiar concepts of distance dependent upon transportational speed. Change sets us down in an alien world
where experiences mean nothing to us because they form no part of any pattern we know. Thus change is, in the long run, intrinsically undesirable despite the transient thrills of pleasant novelty which certain minor
manifestations of it bring. But sometimes wholesale change forces itself on
us, as when blind drift compels us to submit to the intensive mechanisation
of life. [Speaking of *change*—plump! Kittie has just landed in Grandpa's lap in
one violent & unexpected leap! . . . . & now he's sitting on the upper part of
this sheet, critically eyeing my moving pen . . . . . but at last back to the circular chair!] *Then,* indeed, there arises a situation in which we find ourselves in
real need of deliberate readjustment. That is, when an inevitable change inter-
venes to create a new set of conditions at variance with our existing institutions, we *must* modify the institutions to fit the new conditions. This is our
present economic plight—mechanised industry has caused the breakdown of
laissez-faire economics, & possibly even of private property, as working institutions, hence we must evolve a new system of artificially supervised economics & perhaps of collectively owned productive processes in order to
restore the normal circulation of resources. Obviously, there is now a really

legitimate & necessary job for the radical—though at the same time there is also a tremendously important job for the conservative. The radical, given free rein, would attempt to change enormously more than *needs* to be changed; & in so doing would accomplish more harm than good because of the vast number of traditional values destroyed. To work against him & limit change to necessary & desirable points is the normal & indispensable function of the conservative. Of course, the sheer *reactionary* can do more harm than the radical—or at least, just as much—since by insisting on the retention of unworkable elements he precipitates a breakdown or revolt & all of its resultant chaos. What I wish to see is a system which will work—i.e., restore the ability of everyone to get a living in exchange for adequate labour—& which can be evolutionally developed without any ruinous wholesale sacrifice of those hereditary values which alone give the illusion of direction & meaning to life. A couple of days ago a barrage of argument from the *other* side— from a reactionary plutocrat who waxed rich (& is waxing poor again) through the Insull utilities[7]—led me to take stock of my own economic & political views, as modified by the observations of recent years, with unprecedented thoroughness. I wrote that guy almost 20 solid pages of basic discussion which not only dealt with his argument but did much to clarify in my own mind what I actually do believe concerning the nature of property & its manner & proportion of allocation in the community. As a result, I fancy I shall have to call myself a sort of cross betwixt a fascist & an old-time non-bolshevistic socialist. But the socialism is not of the idealistic sort—being rather a wholly materialistic conviction that no feasible apportionment of resources (that is, no apportionment which will not bring tension, starvation, & ultimate destructive revolution) can ever be achieved except through the control of such matters by the forces of government. This harangue[8] was such a complete political credo that I decided to use it intact in the half-dozen or so other controversies with reactionaries now on my hands—hence despite my hatred of typing I copied the thing on the machine & shall circulate the copy among interested correspondents. If your interest in the present transition period is such as to make a random layman's individual, disinterested estimate of the forces at work acceptable reading, I'll send it along later—provided the current recipient doesn't lose it or destroy it in his rage at my irreverent treatment of the Sacred Cow of property & individual initiative. Remind me if you'd like to see it—though of course's it's merely the unprofessional estimate of an onlooker without political, financial, commercial, or economic training. The one amusing & edifying thing about occupying a middle ground like mine is that one can experience simultaneously the abuse of both reactionaries & radicals— thus being able to compare the two psychologies impartially, & achieve an enhanced degree of impersonal detachment. To Hoover Republicans I am as bad a bolshevik as my adopted grandson Belknap; whereas to Belknap & other horny-handed champions of the oppressed I am a dangerous monarchist &

reactionary. Actually, what I advocate is a sort of traditional aristocracy on the social & intellectual side, balanced by enough socialism on the economic side to ensure a stable national structure & eliminate the dangerous envy & restlessness of the less cultivated elements. It probably wouldn't be stretching matters to say that I *am* a monarchist, since I have great respect for the effectiveness of a popular dynasty of dignified, affable, & generous figureheads as a focus for national loyalties. A line of royalty tasteful & sensible enough not to alienate public sympathy through arrogant political meddling & generally outrageous behaviour is a symbol & rallying-point infinitely more powerful than any national flag could be. I can feel the spell myself—it would never occur to me not to think of George the Fifth as *my sovereign*—the logical symbolic head or trade-mark of the race & culture-stream which produced me & of which I am inextricably a part. With breaks in a great racial-cultural fabric—like the unfortunate affair of 1775–83—I have no sympathy. In that case a certain amount of armed assertion to back up parliamentary appeals concerning several points of inept administration under the Crown was perfectly justified—but to carry such assertion to the point of treasonable secession from the Empire was a crime which only greed & personal ambition inspired & effected. In 1775 I might have sympathised on a few points with the rebels in these colonies, but after 1776 I would have been unequivocally on the King's side—as indeed the best inhabitants of America (⅓ of the total population; after 1783 dispersed to Canada, the West Indies, & elsewhere) were. But the old man digresses.

Later

[My guest has withdrawn. Moved by thoughts of nourishment, he began to punctuate his heavy purring with wistful, delicate "-ews" & soulful glances from his seat in the circular chair. A saucer of milk in the kitchen pacified him, but my aunt insisted on my returning him to his home & getting a meal myself at the Waldorf Lunch at the foot of the hill.[9] Having returned from the latter, grossly gorged, I resume the disposition of the problems of mankind.]

Oh, yes—I was speaking of young Shea's attack on my conservative position. He brought up the old gag about the relativity & ambiguity of all ethical systems, though he failed to shew why such a point invalidated a rational & reasonably flexible programme of standards. I pointed out, in my reply, that although the *details* of an ethical code certainly do vary & conflict to some extent, there are certain basic attitudes which quite consistently & quasi-absolutely distinguish the person of evolved & aesthetic life from the callous, haphazard slob. What I would, in general, call the type of superiority manifest in artistic living, is a *sense of pattern* which calls for a certain amount of correlation with wider ranges of action & larger backgrounds of tradition, & which demands the favouring of the more evolved, complex, delicate, & permanently rewarding human sensitivenesses over the cruder, simpler, less correlated,

& less strictly human ones. A superior man has so keen an imagination—so keen & sensitive a consciousness of his location in time, space, & the social fabric—that this comfortable adjustment demands the existence of certain harmonies around him, & the preservation of a certain relationship betwixt his own programme & the activities & aspirations of those whose transmitted ideas & impulses have formed his unconscious standards & reference-points. This makes for a certain natural taste & thoughtfulness in conduct, since coarse carelessness & irresponsibility destroy all suggestion of the pattern-arrangements on which aesthetic adjustment is based. The high-grade individual is delicate, considerate, "unselfish", & non-encroaching because to him such an exercise of respect for the whole social-traditional pattern symbolises the harmony or beauty essential to his personal comfort. Thus the process is *really* no less egocentric & "selfish" than any other human course. It is simply a mature, high-grade, & enlightened selfishness instead of the dull, brutish, disruptive selfishness of the low-grade organism whose comfort does not demand any pattern-adjustment. There is nothing high-flown, mystical, or religious about it. It is simply common sense—a sensitive person's way of getting maximum comfort & pleasure. He could not have so good a time if certain basic forbearances, generosities, delicacies, & rules of non-encroachment were not generally observed in the world; while to advocate their observance by others yet to ignore them himself would involve an element of inconsistency, insincerity, hypocrisy, & falsity so disruptive of the pattern-sense as to be absolutely intolerable. So much for the general principle. As for the details—of course, these are determined largely by the particular pattern-environment into which the individual happens to be born. Harmonious living is not necessarily the same for a Frenchman, an Englishman, & a Persian; nor yet the same for a Greek of the age of Pericles & for a Greek of today. Moreover, there is always a certain amount of dispute regarding the validity or actuality of any given detail as part of the effective, significant tradition-pattern of a certain time & place. But in spite of these variations, it is perfectly easy to differentiate betwixt the evolved living-programme of a high-grade, sensitive person whose nature demands the following of *some* pattern, & the floppy, reckless, uncoördinated plungings & writhings & fumblings of the callous clod (or sophisticated member of the free modern intelligentsia) whose dull (or change-bewildered) nature feels no backgrounds & recognises no harmonic relationships.

Another thing [Gawd help this inexhaustible & polysyllabic garrulity—what a pity the kitten isn't still here to cut off the flow of doddering!] about which I'm fighting with little Shea is the subject of *decadence* & what constitutes it. The boy fancies that Grandpa is using the word in the usual bewildered senile sense . . . . . to express anything new which seems disconcerting & hard to understand from an old-fashioned angle . . . . . . but I am shewing him that my use of the term covers only a specific class of symptoms & phenomena actually connected with that psychology of disintegration which precedes racial & national decline. I don't call everything I dislike or can't understand "decadent". I analyse before I try to classify & name. But like Oswald Spengler (whose monumental "Decline of the West", by the way, Shea *hadn't* read)[10] I recognise certain human characteristics as hostile to the health of the social order, & believe that one may pick them out with considerable precision.

Thus I would say that a *decadent age* is one in which the members of the group concerned are sinking from a civilisation in which many human potentialities are advantageously utilised, to a cultural level which utilises fewer potentialities & imposes a crippled mental-aesthetic life by leaving the finest human sensitivities underdeveloped & wasted. Whenever the traditional patterns of a group begin to break down without the immediate substitution of equally valid patterns, the trend is certainly one which may properly be called *decadence*. A growing lack of sensitive response to accustomed values means a definite decrease in the feeling of direction & meaning in existence, & thus is of course a tremendous emotional impoverishment unless the declining system is at once replaced by some alternative value-system equally practicable to the given group. Such replacement is unfortunately very rare—history tending to shew that the break-up of a race's standards is generally followed by a long period of crude, low-grade, unsatisfying existence before any fresh system of high-grade, satisfying life can be evolved. Decadence is offensively manifest in two ways—in its impoverishment of mental-aesthetic life through the destruction of traditional intangibles; & in its challenge to the material welfare & even to the physical survival of the group as a group through the destruction of clan-pride & the fostering of a supine indifference to the safety & prestige of the governmental fabric. Whether or not decadence masks itself as high-sounding "principle", "enlightenment", "sophistication" & all that, its effect is the same—to impair the harmony & zest of life, & to imperil the welfare & existence of the group. There can be no doubt but that decadence—as manifest in an indifference to traditional perspectives, a relaxation of pattern-rhythms, & a lack of pride & concern for the history, strength, courage, safety, & existence of the national-racial fabrics involved—has been steadily increasing in the western world throughout the 20th century. This decadence, as I think I mentioned in a former epistle, probably springs from various causes—largely the atmosphere of *unsettledness* resulting from our suddenly broadened conception of the universe & from the new conditions created by intensive mechanisation—but its symptoms cannot be mistaken. Careful observation can do much to distinguish its manifestations from those externally similar by-products of restlessness & change which do *not* involve a weary softening & letting-down. Thus Belknap's precious Russian bolsheviks are *not decadent* but merely *alien & primitive*. They are (cf. Sheet II, 1) a new element risen from a mass too primitive to have participated in the old civilisation, & their attitude is the very reverse of the decadent attitude of indifference & scepticism. They did not kill any older culture *of their own*—for the real Russian culture was never theirs in any effective sense. They were like the external barbarians who overwhelmed the weakening (& *truly decadent*) Roman empire & founded a new & different civilisation. On the other hand, many elements in our own western world are unmistakably decadent. Certain "modernistic" tendencies in the arts clearly embody the sort of indifference to backgrounds which means a net impoverishment of mental & aesthetic life; whilst such social trends as historic indifference, general irresponsibility & criminality, unreasoning pacificism, & cloudy internationalism in general, are obviously directly blows against the material welfare & survival of the national fabrics which make possible the continued existence & free play of the various cultural streams. It is quite possible, incidentally, to distinguish betwixt the *primitive, crude evils* of former times, & the essentially *decadent* evils of the present. Against the former the instincts of society were always ranged, so that the crudenesses of life shewed a constant if irregular trend toward abatement. There never was any doubt of the value of an orderly life based on harmonic inheritances, & never any tendency to question the importance of group-survival & group-freedom. It is the decline in these basic imponderables—belief in the value of a continuously-patterned fabric of life, & pride in the strength, integrity, unbrokenness, liberty, & honourable survival of one's own group—which form *true decadence* & establish a steadily downward, instead of upward cultural trend. Unfortunately, the 19th century seems to have formed the turning-point of western culture—the period after which zest & pride & acceptance & loyalty & the will to expand began to be replaced by disillusionment, indifference, scepticism, rejection, & a softening leading to contraction. But of course, it is often hard to classify any given detail of life as decadent or otherwise. It takes thoughtful correlation to decide to what general stream of feeling it belongs. However, we can safely & sadly say that decadence is manifest in one form or another over nearly all the Western World. Certain areas like Italy, Nazi Germany, the Irish Free State, & (perhaps) Spain seem to present a visible resistance to the drift, either through a certain natural youthfulness of outlook & feeling (Ireland, Germany), or through a determined national plan to build up a positive future & pull out of the morass of a former decadence (Italy, Spain). Outside the Western World we can see in Japan a nation still healthy & unbroken, & in Kemalist Turkey a fabric determined to survive even at a woefully high cultural cost. Just what the declining parts of the world will do, remains to be seen. It is not too late to hope that revivals of spirit may yet take place here & there—each in accordance with the particular national temper of the group concerned. I have my eye on Sir Oswald Moseley & the element of British fascists.[11] They may yet help in rearousing a certain vitality in our slackening stream—& corresponding developments on this side of the Atlantic are likewise conceivable. I would not venture to prophesy the future even five years ahead—but at least I make it a settled policy not to discourage any national tendency, however crude, which seems to operate against the prevailing drift toward softness & disintegration. Hence my basic sympathy—despite a deep regret at the capricious, arbitrary, unscientific, anti-cultural, & largely ridiculous extremes to which its visible manifestations have run—with the general attitude behind such desperate remedial measures as German Nazism. I am alive to Herr Hitler's ignorance, neurotic fanaticism, & general absurdity—but (much to the horror of my liberal friends) I am not among those who throw bricks at the poor chap!

Before quitting the subject of decadence, it is well for completeness' sake to mention certain effects which a declining & softening society has upon the *individual* . . . . . . that is, specific effects aside from a general letting-down of traditional restraints & a general indifference to social harmony & inherited pattern-elements. Foremost of all, there is a sharp decline in the hardy virtues which stem from a pride in strength, competence, & independence—virtues like honour, truthfulness, courage, firmness, loyalty, & so on. These decay because their bases—strength, competence, & independence—are no longer highly valued in a fluid & sceptical society. There is also an emphatic growth of childish self-centredness, self-indulgence, & self-pity—a transference of concern from the group & pattern (no longer valued) to the ego. Physically there is a tremendous regression toward sensuousness on the one hand & inertia on the other—that is, a tremendous lapse from any programme which links the physical energies with values & objects & purposes belonging to the imaginative, delicately emotional, or cerebral realms. Earthiness reigns, eroticism (often in grotesquely perverted forms owing to the growing contempt for norms of any kind) usurps a disproportionate place in life, physical & mental softness (dislike of exercise or close, difficult thinking) gains ground, & stamina falls off so spectacularly that the shrinking from all forms of pain, injury, danger, & physical combat becomes a salient feature of the popular psychology. Amusements become passive (spectacles witnessed) instead of active (things participated in). At the same time the typically petty reactions gain force. Men become vain & exhibitionistic, transferring their form of ego-assertion from displays of strength, courage, & skill to flauntings of personal adornments; & the tendency to tickle the ego through the gossiping degradation of others becomes very marked. Of course these are only a few of decadence's stigmata, but they are very typical. One encounters them constantly in individuals, & can likewise trace their effects in the trend of social, political, philosophic, & aesthetic movements. It is perhaps the ego-absorption which most potently influences modern art,—substituting intensive, introspective, & over-subtle analyses of single emotional reactions for well-proportioned & dramatically balanced vistas of collective life. And so it goes. What tedious stuff! But the point is, that when I use the term *"decadence"* I'm not just bandying blanket condemnations of the present & future in the manner of a rheumatic ex-banker or pontifical retired colonel. Right or wrong, I at least have something definite & particular in mind, & don't apply the term beyond its proper limits. As a matter of fact, my long-standing view of Western Civilisation is so close to Spengler's that "The Decline of the West" seemed like a miraculously authoritative corroboration when it was first translated in 1926. I do not, however, agree with Spengler in all details—especially his view (based on a false analogy) of a culture as a quasi-biological organism.

Regarding the question of which sort of life is the more rewarding—a purely cerebral or a purely emotional one—I would say that final advantage probably rests with the former; since it involves a steadier & more dependable set of contacts with the external world, avoids a violent alternation of extremes in which pain invariably predominates, & can exist in rewarding fulness over a vastly longer period in the individual's life than can any regime of sheer emotion. A rational & analytical outlook, by shewing mankind & his phenomena & relationships in their true proportions, does much to banish emotional pain by reducing its cause to visible insignificance. Much pain is caused by the irrational expectation of things which one has no reason to expect, & by an illogical sense of injury or injustice in cases where only the bland, ruthless, impersonal, & inevitable operations of the unconscious & automatic cosmos (as absurd a thing to regard as an *enemy* as the stone wall against which one may hit one's head!) are concerned. A person of sense does not expect much of the universe, hence he is never disappointed. If seldom positively happy, he is at least seldom acutely unhappy. And there is absolutely no question of his infinitely better adaptation to that division of his life-span (30 to his death at 70 or 80 or so) which is by far the longest.

But the average person of sense generally adopts a mixed course, endeavouring to secure the major benefits of cerebralism without forfeiting whatever of value there may be in a temperate & discriminating emotionalism. He learns to accept the agreeable side of emotion in youth, when it becomes him, without allowing it to run to grotesque extremes or tyrannise over him. If he finds no opportunity for its harmonious & dignified exercise, he accepts the circumstance with philosophic resignation; realising that no one has any particular reason to expect happiness, that only a minority ever achieve it anyhow, that it is generally rather brief even with those who do achieve it, & that in a few years the person who has learned to lean on romantic emotion is left desolate, bewildered, & stranded, whilst the resignedly impersonal analyst is always just about the same—at 20, 30, 40, 50, 60, 70, 80, & beyond if his brain holds out. Perspective teaches that emotional pleasure secured at the expense of dignity & harmonic adjustment generally involves so much concomitant pain that it is a net loss instead of a gain. However, one may well be receptive at all times toward any boons which emotion can dignifiedly bring—accepting them for whatever they are worth while they last, but being sensible & analytical enough not to mourn when they fail to fulfil one's imaginative ideals & when they finally disappear. Whatever happiness one has comes wholly by accident; & while we should not despise or reject it whilst it is present, we should refrain from regarding it as a basic "right" or expecting it to be less transient & capricious than it is. Despite the possibility of a few brief spans of emotional & imaginative exaltation, a life founded purely on ecstasy & sentiment is virtually certain to peter out as a tragic & ugly mess.

Concerning Young Melmoth's[12] judgment of Beethoven—one may only remark that youth does love its gestures of iconoclasm! It is a tingling & delectable stimulus to the adolescent ego to shock the community with lofty contempt of the universally admired, & not many articulate beings pass through the teens & early twenties without a display or two of this kind. While it is possible that Melmoth has a personal dislike of the 5th Symphony, I would be inclined to think that his chief objection is the fact that many people like it. Just enough of the old 1927 misanthropic attitude clings around the Dark Odysseus[13] to make him detest anything which bears the suspicion of popularity or usualness. A decade more will see a good many Melmothic dicta amended in the direction of sober moderation. And as for 'horrid words'—remember that to 1908's crop of intellectuals softness is the supreme vice. As judged by the standard of his generation, Young Melmoth is the epitome of urbane tolerance! You ought to see some of the controversial letters I get from other youngsters—*Derleth* for example! In not meeting this enfant terrible, you missed a splendid chance to see the haughty young modern at his haughtiest & modernest! Coming to the "Hill of Dreams"[14]—I must beg that Young Melmoth be excused for any undue ire he may have displayed, since as a doting Machenite I can appreciate his reaction to the idea of this masterpiece's having been forgotten! No non-Machenite can quite comprehend how paralysing such a concept is. Melmoth must feel the same way a Browning fan would feel if he could, by cross-questioning, discover how little I remember of "Sordello", "The Ring & the Book",[15] & all the other rugged Victorianisms which put me to sleep in my youth. But as for the "Hill"—I'll venture a bet that you must have read it very carelessly & in childhood, else you *couldn't help* remembering it. It is really one of the most poignant human documents ever written—an utterly exquisite chronicle of the tragic unfolding of a delicate & sensitive imagination foredoomed to tragedy by its perverse streak of morbidity. The subtlety & power are so omnipresent that even the most prosaic non-fantaisiste generally gets a hint of the magic vividness. The brooding mystery of ancient Wales, with its black Druid woods, wild hills, forgotten Cymric secrets, lonely Roman reliques trickling down the centuries, & underground whispers of frightful Little People & unmentionable midnight Sabbats . . . . . a background to wake a million dormant memories & suggest a myriad formless shadow-pictures of scenes & wonders lost in the gulfs of time & space. And London—the grey labyrinths of its shabby streets, & the old overtaken houses they harbour, & the hints of primal horror they conjure up in the misty dawn & amidst the flickering lamps of evening . . . . . Through all these scenes limps poor hypersensitive Lucian Taylor, an exaggeration of the neurotic artist that lurks in every even half-creative personality. The whole essence of the aesthetic attitude & process in man is summed up in the reactions & tortures & exaltations of this hapless dreamer—what wonders he sees in the wild domed hills & hanging woods; in the ramparts of the Caesars flung against the mystic, beckoning sunset; in the dank forest waters where old roots writhe & twist eternally; in the old, squat cottages crumbled by cycles of sun & wind; in the hieroglyph-like tangles of city streets with their fish-eyed, leering facades; & above all, in the scattered Roman ruins which his fancy reassembles into the splendid fortress town of the Second Augustan Legion! The inexhaustible fertility of imagination which evokes whole cycles of fantastic, pageant-like associative pictures from the sullen, mysterious landscape & the cryptic, unfathomable metropolis is so great as almost to bewilder one. The whole artistic life is epitomised in this quality of having each objective scene or object serve merely as a starting-point for limitless vague overtones, each dizzy with hints of marvels & revelations such as the waking world can never know. In all the woodland reactions & in the Roman dream-life episode I saw a thousandfold-heightened reflection of my own wonder-filled responses to the objective world around me—my old fascinated fear of a certain woodland hollow with gnarled trees & trickling brooks; my seven-year-old glimpses of fauns & dryads in the twilight oak groves; my sense of adventurous expectancy & half-sinister familiarity in the narrow, fanlight-lined streets of Providence's ancient hill; & my haunting—at times almost maddening—sense of misplacement in time . . . . of membership in another century.

But what "got" me was that "Avallaunius" episode where Lucian constructs a vivid & coherent dream-life in the bygone Isca Silurum of seventeen-hundred years before. With uncanny insight into human nature Machen reproduced the very essence of the mystical way I used to throw my fancy back into 18th century Providence . . . . . & no one else has ever—in books or out of them—shewn any real understanding of this relatively rare, though undoubtedly strong & typical, human mood of *time-defying*. Other authors have romantically & artificially played with the idea, but Machen *knows* about it & bodies it forth realistically. That fascination by old streets & bygone ages is a deep & genuine thing . . . . how I used to drag my mother around on the ancient hill when I was 4 or 5! I hardly know what I was after, but the centuried houses with their fanlights & knockers & railed steps & small-paned windows had a strong & significant effect of some sort on me. This world, I felt, was a different one from the Victorian world of French roofs & plate glass & concrete sidewalks & open lawns that I was born into (my old home was a mile east of the ancient hill). It was a magic, secret world, & it had a *realness* beyond that of the home neighbourhood. It had, I knew, been there long before the home neighbourhood existed—& I felt it would still be there after the other had passed away. Then again, it was just like the Hogarth scenes in the big books in the parlour, & just like the pictures in the coloured books about the Revolution which were given me. It was *familiar*—I had *always* known it—I had *seen it before*—it was *part of me* in a sense that no other scene ever was . . . . . & so I dreamed about it by night & visited it by day whenever I could. I used to have (as I still do) favourite *vistas*—looking up such & such a street & wondering *what* lay around the curve at the end. Could I walk into the time of Hogarth & the Revolution if I followed one of those cryptic ways to its unknown end some evening when the twilight was purple & the yellow lamplight flickered up softly behind ancient fanlights & tiny window-panes? On rainy evenings, when the little old gas-lamps cast strange reflections on the glistening cobblestones & brick sidewalks, I could almost *see* the figures of yesterday plodding along . . . . cloaks, three-cornered hats, queues losing their powder in the rain . . . . & I began to dream of myself in those scenes, witnessing tantalising fragments of 18th century daily life that faded too soon into wakefulness. Once I thought I saw a rider galloping madly over the cobbles, whilst all the windows were flung up by staring white-capped housewives & turbaned slaves . . . . . once I saw a troop of the King's men in red coats with muskets & beating drums . . . . were they off to join Wolfe or Amherst against the French?[16] *God Save the King!* But I loved the ancient fields & farmhouses & stone walls & orchards & deep woods & water-mills & village spires of the countryside, too . . . . And the spell of a great round autumn moon over a rocky hillside field with mystical rows of sheaves . . . . . To walk back through time——it occurs to me that in all the cosmos there is nothing truly fascinating as *the idea of time*. It somehow seems as if nothing can be deeply significant except in its relation to the *time-stream;* & indeed, no other factor or situation or drama in the universe can enthrall & interest me half so much as one which involves some miracle or defiance or overleaping or surprise or paradox connected with *time*.

Well—the point is that in "The Hill of Dreams" Machen portrays & illuminates this very psychology with greater mastery than I shall ever achieve—or, for that matter, than anybody else, including the later Machen, is likely to achieve. Carl van Vechten calls it "the most beautiful book in the world".[17] Harry Hansen says, "we shall never walk again in Bloomsbury Square without hearing the trumpets & catching something of the strange, exotic beauty of "The Hill of Dreams['']."[18] Young Belknap, Melmoth the Wandrei, Klarkash-Ton, Bernard Dwyer, Talman—virtually everyone seems to share my enthusiasm. Besides your adverse verdict, the only note of dissent comes from this same Shea whose controversial attacks I have mentioned. He was fascinated on a first reading, but says he found it a trifle unsatisfying on a second reading. With me, however, it holds its charm permanently. I'll wager your reading was early & cursory!

Hades, what a letter! Well—cheer up—Shea's, in the same mail, has *46* pages. Hope you've skimmed through lightly enough to avoid the worst extremes of ennui. Weather getting cold, but October was very mild, & I had any number of rural walks up to & including Nov. 2. Also, day before yesterday was mild, so that I strolled out into a countryside bleak with barren boughs. ¶ Sorry to hear of Klarkash-Ton's mother's accident. My aunt can amply sympathise with her. Belknap's mother is under the weather, too—food poisoning.

With apologies for length

Yr obt Servt

H P L

P.S. Interested to know that you have a violin. I took lessons between the ages of 7 & 9, but my enthusiasm wore off, & the practicing made me so nervous that the matter was dropped on physician's orders. As a reaction, I forgot how to read music in so quick a time as to interest any modern psychologist. This infantile "fed-up-ness" probably accounts for my lack of musical taste in later life.

Notes

1. HPL's correspondent Ernest A. Edkins, who at the time was 66 years old, called HPL Anak. The "children of Anak" are mentioned in Numbers 13:22. See also Joshua 15:13.

2. See HVS 5n6. R. H. Barlow stayed there in 1936, and Marian F. Bonner, a friend of Annie Gamwell, lived there. It is no longer standing.

3. Swedish zoologist Carl Linnaeus (1707–1778) coined the term *Homo sapiens* ("intelligent man") for the human race in the 10th edition of his *Systema Naturae* (1758–59).

4. Kirill (Cyril) Vladimirovich (1876–1938), Grand Duke of Russia. Cyril Mikhail Ivanovich Rostovtzeff (1870–1952), ancient historian. Igor Sikorsky (1889–1972), Russian-American aviation pioneer in both helicopters and fixed-wing aircraft.

5. Originally the Westminster Theatre, an early burlesque house (known as "the sinkhole of depravity," or "the Sink"), at 368 Westminster Street; not to be confused with the Bijou Theater (1908–25; now razed) at 164 Westminster Street.

6. *Anna Christie* (MGM, 1930), directed by Clarence Brown; starring Greta Garbo, Charles Bickford, George F. Marion, and Marie Dressler; a remake of the 1923 film, both based on the play by Eugene O'Neill. *Berkeley Square* (Fox Film Corp., 1933), directed by Frank Lloyd; starring Leslie Howard, Heather Angel, and Valerie Taylor. Based on the play by John L. Balderston. *The Private Life of Henry VIII* (United Artists, 1933), directed by Alexander Korda; starring Charles Laughton, Robert Donat, and Franklin Dyall.

7. Samuel Insull (1859–1938), capitalist and utility magnate who pioneered the concept of utility holding companies and offering publicly traded securities, and his brother Martin were indicted in October 1932 for embezzlement and larceny in connection with a scheme to shore up securities controlled by Martin. Insull's utility empire had been forced into receivership in April 1932, though the companies were fundamentally sound, because New York banks refused to renew notes due. HPL is apparently alluding to his correspondent Ernest A. Edkins, who was head of merchandising for Commonwealth Edison of Chicago, an Insull venture.

8. "A Layman Looks at the Government," dated 22 November 1933. The TMs. does not survive, but it is preserved in AHT.

9. At 205 South Main Street.

10. HPL himself apparently read only Volume 1 of the two-volume set.

11. Sir Oswald Ernald Mosley, 6th Baronet of Ancoats (1896–1980), British politician who rose to fame in the 1920s as a Member of Parliament. In the 1930s he became leader of the British Union of Fascists.

12. I.e., Donald Wandrei (a pun derived from the title of C. R. Maturin's Gothic novel *Melmoth the Wanderer*).

13. Another pun, alluding to the title of Wandrei's second book of poetry, *Dark Odyssey* (1931).

14. The novel by Arthur Machen. Wandrei was an ardent admirer, as evidenced in his essay "Arthur Machen and *The Hill of Dreams*," *Minnesota Quarterly* 3, No. 3 (Spring 1926): 19–24; rpt. *Studies in Weird Fiction* No. 15 (Summer 1994): 27–30.

15. *Sordello* is a narrative poem by Robert Browning, published in 1840, consisting of a fictionalized version of the life of Sordello da Goito, the 13th-century Lombard troubadour depicted in Dante's *Purgatorio*, Canto VI. *The Ring and the Book* (1868–69) is a verse novel of 21,000 lines, published in four volumes.

16. For Wolfe see WBT 80n1. Jeffrey Amherst, 1st Baron Amherst (1717–1797), commander in chief of the British army in North America, also participated in the conquest of Quebec. He subsequently became governor of the province of Quebec (1760–63).

17. Carl Van Vechten (1880–1964), *Peter Whiffle: His Life and Works* (New York: Alfred A. Knopf, 1922), 196. Knopf also published Machen's book and promoted it using Van Vechten's inferred quotation: "I haven't altered my opinion. It [Donatello's "David"] is the most beautiful statue I have ever seen, just as Debussy's l'Après-midi d'un Faune is the most beautiful music I have ever heard, just as The Hill of Dreams is—have you read it?"

18. Harry Hansen (1884–1977), American journalist, editor, literary critic and historian. The quotation from the *Chicago Daily News* has not been located.

[8]   [ALS, JHL]

66 College St.,

Providence, R.I.,

Feby. 6, 1934.

Dear Helen:—

I am surely sorry to hear that your health has been below par, & trust that its recent up-swing may prove emphatic & permanent. Probably that long trip was more exhausting than you realised at the time—with its constant travelling, varied excitements & anxieties, continuous strenuous exertions, & inadequate chances for genuine rest. The really ideal trip is one in which long pauses for leisurely repose & unhurried, gradual sightseeing can be made— allotting not less than a week to every separate "high spot." Still, if one has only limited time & cash, there is much to be said for a swift dash which covers an enormous amount of diverse territory. Probably one accumulates enough unique & vivid impressions to pay amply for any incidental fatigue or debility—

indeed, I don't fancy you regret your Odyssey despite its presumable consequences. I am sorry, too, to hear of Son's indisposition—from which I hope he may soon emerge. To match—or overmatch—this painful bulletin I must record the melancholy *disappearance* of the very young tiger gentleman who sent you his signature & whom you saw in his extreme infancy. Shortly before Yule he was missing from his usual haunts at the Fadden mansion, nor has any word of him since been received. One may only hope that his fate has not been a tragic one. His black-&-white (or rather, in order of preponderance, white-&-black) foster-mother occasionally comes to call on us, but little Alfred himself is only a memory. Eheu! However, the sleek warriors of the Kappa Alpha Tau fraternity are nearly always in sight—so that I do not lack for varied glimpses of my favourite species. The huge tiger Vice-President[1] is a particular friend of mine.

I am indeed grateful for that cedar twig—whose unusually pungent & aromatic odour helps to vivify in my mind the typical Placer County landscape— American River, Donner Lake, Crater Ridge, &c—so familiar to me through the view cards & descriptions now & then furnished by Klarkash-Ton. If reports be correct, you have had a marvellously mild—though mystically grey— winter, which a denizen of New England's subarctic shores may appropriately envy. Which reminds me—before long C A S may have a first-hand emissary from the outside weird-writing world in the person of the breezy & peripatetic E. Hoffmann Price—who has pulled up stakes in New Orleans & is now in Oklahoma en route to his native California. I trust you may have an opportunity to see this genial & gifted wanderer—who, by the way, was in Providence only three weeks before your own passage through that ancient realm.

Thanksgiving I did something I have been wanting to do all my life— consumed the traditional feast on the historic soil of ancient *Plymouth* (less than 40 miles from here), where the whole custom started 312 years ago. The day was miraculously warm—up to *68°* in the afternoon—& I spent it all in the venerable Pilgrim town, going over all the familiar sights & unearthing many new ones. I will enclose a couple of cards illustrating the pilgrimage. Plymouth has an atmosphere all its own, & its extreme age never ceases to arouse reflection. In what a wilderness did it take root in 1620! There was then nothing north of it save the struggling town of Quebec on & under its beetling cliff, the lesser hamlets of Tadoussac on the St. Lawrence & Port Royal in Acadia, & the fortress & trading-post of Pentagoët in what is now Maine. West & south only the mysterious black woods with their unknown savages till the tiny Dutch trading post (not yet the town of New-Amsterdam) on Manhattan Island was reached. Then the wilderness again down to the banks of the James—where lay the nearest settlement of our own people— the dominion of Virginia, only 13 years old. Below that another stretch with only the moss-grown foundation-walls of ruined Huguenot houses along salt inlets till one came to the frowning walls of Spanish San Augustin . . . . . 55 years old, & having many houses which still survive in this year of 1934. A new

& unspoiled world—& look at the mess its later inhabitants have made of it!

As you have indeed heard from Klarkash-Ton, I spent 15 post-Christmas days in the decadent Manhattan vortex as the guest of my gifted grandchild Commissar Belnapovitch, head of the local Soviets. The transition was especially marked in view of the immediately preceding home Yuletide—with gifts & greens around the ancient hearth, a borrowed cat for atmosphere, & a twilight trip half-way down the hill with my aunt (who now gets about everywhere with a single cane) to hear the carol-singing in the yard of the old brick Beckwith mansion.[2] I took the New York coach after midnight—& shared a metropolitan breakfast with the House of Long. During the ensuing days I saw most of the group—especially Young Melmoth the Wandrei—& met several literati or near-literati who were new to me. I saw the old year out at Loveman's—& received from him some unexpected & undeserved gifts (an Egyptian ushabti, a Mayan image, &c) which have vastly enriched my modest museum-shelves. Naturally I did not neglect the museums, & I obtained two or three book bargains of especially satisfying quality.

But I could never like New York. The dull solidity of architecture, the absence of greenery & open spaces, the ugly alternations of garishness & squalor, the verminous hordes of distorted aliens, the ceaseless stridor & seething, the absence of traditional landmarks, impressions, & folkways—the whole wretched mass sickens & exasperates me after about a fortnight. What you say about the special physiognomy & mannerisms of the denizens seems to me essentially true. Likewise their conversational peculiarities—though some of the pseudo-languid diction, artificial "wisecracking", & exaggerated show of "sophistication" or "initiatedness" displayed in Greenwich-Village circles is not so much Manhattanese as Bohemianesque; being more or less typical of self-conscious, would-be-professional aesthetes wherever such beings congregate in mutual-flattery groups of the "Latin Quarter" type. Probably the Manhattan near-literati represent this pose in its most exaggerated form—& no doubt their conversation is more subtly & profoundly esoteric than that of their provincial congeners. I have seldom attempted to de-code the cryptic profundities of these urban philosophers, since their more intelligible utterances give no indication of any great cultural treasures behind the owlish masque. This type always gives me a highly unpalatable mixture of discomfort & boredom—such as one usually feels when faced by a group whose language, interests, moods, thoughts, motivations, & values are both alien & in part wholly incomprehensible. I feel like an explorer amongst a queer African or Polynesian tribe whose policies & recreations are beyond gauging or prediction, & am rather ill at ease unless there are a few more "white men"—regular folk from the real America—present. Some of Loveman's group—persons interested in the theatre & the dance—impress me more in this way than do even Wandrei's literary-artistic coterie. To analyse their points of difference from main-stream people would be difficult, but you are surely right in attributing much to their inactive life amidst a strident & grotesquely artificial environment. Add to this a neurotic egotism nourished on bizarre & occasionally anti-social concepts & manifested in an habitual clannishness & contempt for the normal world, & you have the main outlines of the breed. They have cultivated the habit of despising so strongly that they are no longer interested in anything but the minute analysis of their own feelings, the relation of their own experiences & contacts, & the witty derogation of both outsiders & their own absent colleagues. Of the *details* of their motives, interests, & values I have never been interested enough to make a study—but they certainly live in an odd enough little world of their own. I can't say that I envy them—for they seem to me to have lost vastly more than they have gained. Their utter, drifting rootlessness & inability to derive pleasure from ordinary sources is certainly nothing more than downright callousness—despite their habitual boasts of supernormal sensitivity. However—young people are occasionally fascinated by them for a time, since they seem to represent some important & closely-guarded secret. They'll amuse Wandrei & Belknap for a while—& then the boys will see through them & merely tolerate instead of welcoming them. As I said, it isn't fair to New York to take this species as its typical representative. Within the metropolis are all sorts of scattered groups & strata; some keeping alive the stately traditions of an elder Manhattan almost sunk from sight, & others fully sharing the moods & reactions of the American main stream. The trouble is that it takes months or even years to discover a group of one's own kind in the vast heterogeneous babel—& even then there is no geographical solidarity, since the members are inevitably sprinkled over vast areas of repulsive alienage. The most normal New Yorkers are pushed out more & more toward the suburbs—Flatbush, Riverdale, Flushing, Jamaica, Staten Island, White Plains, New Rochelle, the New Jersey shore, & such places. Yet the parents & grandparents of many of them dwelt in Manhattan & Brooklyn. That is the most melancholy thing about New York. It is not merely a foreign city—one would not mind that so much. It is, on the other hand, an intruding growth which has seized & killed an American city & is now writhing mockingly above the disordered ruins . . . . . amidst which we may see just enough landmarks of the old American order to give us a feeling of sadness & bitter irony. This miserable mess did not exist before 1900—the New York of that day being a distinctive phase of life now forever closed. It had its own weaknesses—such as an undue regard for size, wealth, & display—but it had strong points to compensate for them. It must have been a bracing & interesting place—I never saw it, since poor health forbade my travelling till late in life. But it is gone now—& the present Levantine tumult rages above its scattered stones much as a dirty Turkish village now sprawls above the crumbled towers of vanished Troy.

Merritt, the "Moon-Pool" man, was certainly a long way from being a cadaver. On the contrary, he is an exceedingly vital character & full of plans for new work. He is associate editor of the Hearst Sunday supplement—the "American Weekly", so-called. I can well understand your young friend's enthusiasm for "The Moon Pool", for it is really one of the most distinctive popular (as distinguished from carefully literary) weird novels ever written. Far from being mid-Victorian, its original version first appeared in the All-Story Weekly for June 7, 1918[3] . . . . . & it certainly took all the breath out of me! Never short of Poe had I seen such an aura of unholy magic cast about a scene or a region . . . . . lonely Ponape, in the Pacific . . . . . the unknown Cyclopean ruins lingering from a fearsome primal world . . . . . the horror of the natives . . . . . the happenings when the moon was full . . . . . . the *chanting* . . . . the seven lights floating down the moon-path . . . . "A-va-lo-he!" . . . . Ah, me—but I wish there were something today which could give me the kick that tale did 15 years ago! However—the *book* as later published isn't equal in charm to the original novelette. Merritt wrote a sequel to the novelette in which he was distinctly influenced by the cheap magazine ideal; & the published book not only includes that, but omits some of the touches in the early part which formed the chief imaginative assets. I still have the fast-crumbling sheets of the old novelette—though Merritt himself lacks a copy! As for the other choices of the one-time ten-year-old—they certainly showed a distinctive mind & taste! I don't wonder that he's a Harvard professor at 24!

Your early glimpse of the now famous Ruth Slenzski (however it's spelt)[4] is certainly vastly interesting to look back upon. Such a Spartan regimen as that imposed on her seems barbarous & pathetic even in view of the present brilliant results. Surely, musical genius is not so frail & uncertain a thing that it must needs be forced in infancy at the expense of normal childhood enjoyment & leisure. It seems to me that a slower training, with rational vacational intervals, would have produced just as much in the end, even though such early proficiency might not have been attained. But of course one can't be positive about such matters. I certainly hope I shall have an opportunity to hear her at her present stage, though of course my unmusical ear would be deaf to much of the subtle & unique charm of the rendition. As coincidence would have it, one of my correspondents has lately heard her playing for the first time— over the radio—& writes in the same mood of astonished enthusiasm which seems to have characterised both yourself & the newspaper critics. Unspoiled youth—sincere & free from self-consciousness & acquired mannerisms— certainly has a vast advantage over jaded maturity in the practice of any art; but music is the only form of expression which can be fully mastered while the mind is still thus unspoiled. It would be assuming a good deal gratuitously to say that such examples of childhood beauty-creation argue the existence of a "higher power", but we surely must marvel at the rare cases in which a discriminating sensitiveness to harmonic rhythms & basic human moods develops instinctively in very early life. Of course, all genius is very largely a matter of unusual natural development, whether it occur early or late. Mere talent can indeed be sharpened by hard work; but the poignant & special aptitude which goes beyond mere talent & draws on the subconscious is a biological, innate matter. It can't be governed from outside, & we are unable to formulate any sort of laws to explain or measure it. Its very essence is irregularity.

Abruptly descending in the scale of values—I doubt very much whether music could have been my primary mode of expression. Possibly I would not have reacted so violently against its higher manifestations if my childhood lessons had been less academic, & on a more elementary instrument, yet after all no real musician could ever have been scared off as I was. Moreover—if I had any innate taste I would not enjoy cheap tunes . . . . as I frankly & unashamedly do. I can understand a thwarted musician's caring for *no* melodies at all—but I can hardly picture him with a gang of fellows whistling or howling the tin-pan ditties of the period with overt & genuine gusto, as Grandpa Ec'h-Pi-El must confess to having done in the lost golden days of '06 & thereabouts! It took the bizarre & nondescript tonal & rhythmical hashes of post-war jazz to get me disgusted with popular ballads—& even now I relish the old-time inanities when they are revived on the "raddio" . . . . though this may be merely because they recall the lost illusions & optimisms of the youthful period when I first knew & ululated them.

Regarding "The Hill of Dreams"—I could almost guarantee that your second perusal will reveal subtleties of beauty & pathos which the first juvenile skimming left hidden. Of course any such cerebral & emotional history drags at times—but the whole thing is a tremendously poignant chronicle of aesthetic sensitiveness & the desperate struggle for adequate expression. No one who has reacted strongly to the beauty & mystery of the external world, & then failed utterly to capture his profound, complex, many-nuanced, & mistily-outlined impression in the words or pigments or tones of his chosen medium, can fail to see himself potently mirrored in many aspects of Lucian Taylor's life & character. Early in the novel the crux of the matter is summed up in plain words:

> "He wrote & planned & filled the waste-paper basket with hopeless efforts . . . . There was enough of difficulty to appal; from following the intricate course of little nameless brooks, from hushed twilight woods, from the vision of the mountains, & the breath of the great wind, passion from deep to deep, he would come home filled with thoughts & emotions, mystic fancies which he yearned to translate into the written word. And the result of the effort seemed always to be bathos! Wooden sentences, a portentous, stilted style, obscurity, & awkwardness clogged his pen; it seemed impossible to win the great secret of language; the stars glittered only in the darkness, & vanished away in clearer light. The periods of despair were often long & heavy, the victories very few & trifling; night after night he sat writing after his father had knocked out his last pipe, filling a page with difficulty in an hour, & usually forced to thrust the stuff away in despair, & go unhappily to

bed, conscious that after all his labour he had done nothing. And there were moments when the accustomed vision of the land alarmed him, & the wild domed hills & darkling woods seemed symbols of some terrible secret in the inner life of that stranger—himself."[5]

Ever since reading this book—in 1923—I have longed to see the strange & haunted region—Caerleon-on-Usk, the ancient Isca Silurum of the Second Augustan Legion in Roman days—which it reflects, & which was the boyhood environment of Arthur Machen. Just recently I secured Weigall's "Wanderings in Roman Britain", & therein found all my tantalising impressions confirmed. It appears that within the last decade the long-buried Caerleon amphitheatre has been unearthed—& found to be in almost perfect condition after its long centuries of oblivion. The Second Legion was at Isca from 78 to 368 A.D.—it then being transferred to the East Coast to guard against the ever increasing menace of the Saxons. Weigall's book makes Lucian's Roman dream-life (H. of D. Ch. IV) stand out with doubled vividness.

My aunt conveys her best regards—& joins me in expressions of sympathy regarding the Newport-sprinkled dress. When in Newport I felt rather guilty in holding up the expedition through dread of a half-dollar pressing bill—but now I regret that I did not give caution free play . . . . though, come to think of it, that would have substituted a rather monotonous church-door vista for a number of sights which were perhaps worth the damage they caused. I wore that 1928-Sunday-best apparel to Onset & Quebec in its slovenly unpressed state—& am somewhat glad I did in view of the cataclysmic soaking I got in Boston on the final evening of the latter trip. I had successfully dodged showers all day, but in getting from the North Station to W. Paul Cook's house I was caught in an electrical cloudburst which left me much as if I had emerged from the heaving deep. And I had on the new straw hat which I carefully *didn't* wear to Newport! Results: cravat, total loss; hat, usable as 1934 secondary lid; suit, pressed but oddly out of shape around the lapels. Such are the vicissitudes of existence.

I'm glad my grandson's portrait reached you safely—I was present in an advisory capacity at its mailing, & recommended sundry cardboard reinforcements. No—I don't think it unduly flatters its subject, although it naturally shews a more pleasing visage than the harshly Rembrantesque electric-light snapshots from Young Melmoth's amateur studio.[6] Melmoth apparently likes the realism which leans over backward in its starkness—especially if it chances to be applied to the other guy. He took some of Belknap himself, & me last month—you may have seen them. Young Stalin is very much in shadow, & has an air of jaded cynicism which probably pleases him vastly. Melmoth is his usual jaunty self—though I made him comb back his artistically neglected locks before I snapped him in a solo pose. And poor old Grandpa looks as blank as usual—the old gentleman's mouth having been caught slightly open in the lone seated portrait.

Speaking of pictures, though—the marvellous weird drawings of Melmoth's kid brother nearly took the breath out of both Belknap & me. We had seen minor specimens of his art before—older things like the illustrations for "Dark Odyssey"—but this new material struck us like a thunderbolt. The boy is certainly a genius—at this rate he'll be right in the class with Doré & Beardsley & John Martin & Sime & Segrelles[7] before long. The union of fantastic, diabolic conception & mature technique is astonishing—I wish Klarkash-Ton could see his best stuff. Oh, yes—& as to pictures, it was only *last week* that I found my missing Roerich catalogue.[8] It had fallen behind a pile of brochures (the old Masters of Art series) which I seldom remove as a whole, but which I at last took down for rearrangement. This reminds me—Merritt of the Moon Pool is a close friend of Roerich; a bond of fantastic interest, plus a rather naive joint credulousness regarding various phenomena of an unseen world, conducing toward their congeniality. Merritt tried to tell me of instances of telepathic communication betwixt Roerich & himself—although I couldn't see anything which coincidence & ordinary news diffusion couldn't cover.

I regret profoundly that that sea-serpent cutting was incomplete—& hope that the missing portion was less important than the context would suggest. Such monsters appear to be especially in fashion just now—a whole cycle of comment having grown up around the alleged denizen of Loch Ness. Klarkash-Ton & I have recently been exchanging items regarding this mysterious entity. I wouldn't be at all surprised if some day a giant marine entity were to be tracked down & made visible beyond the possibility of doubt. Still, the present Caledonian specimen may be something far less unusual & exciting.

I saw some interesting Etruscan tomb frescoes (or rather, copies of them) at the local museum this week. They show the surprising maturity of Etruria as early as 500 or 600 B.C.—& arouse fresh speculations as to the origin & race-stock of the strange people who painted them. The major influence, of course, is Greek; but there is a distinctly local touch which was eventually bequeathed to the Roman art tradition.

I presume Comrade Belnapoff has told you all about his new hobby of tropical fish. He sits by the hour gazing at the microscopic denizens of his aquarium, & is climbing new heights of zöological knowledge in his efforts to learn what species won't eat this or that other species. His new proteges share my own ideas anent temperature—requiring about 80° at all times. They have to be so carefully watched & heated & oxygenated that they must form quite a responsibility—but so far their master has deemed them amply worth the trouble. Financially they are rather dangerous—for when Belknap is turned loose in a shop full of tanks he can't resist the lure of new & exotic specimens—being as bad as Loveman in a bookshop or myself in a postcard shop in Quebec or Salem.

Well—I'll cease, lest ennui bring on a relapse of that travel-exhaustion from which you have so lately recovered. If I start to finish this page I'll probably run over on to another, so I'll call an abrupt & merciful halt.

With every good wish, & hoping that Son may soon be quite his old self & able to lick any man in the Kappa Alpha Tau (at this moment the Vice-President is walking the fence below my window despite the cumbering snow),

I remain

Yr most ob^{t.} h^{ble.} Servt
—H P L

P.S. If "The Hill of Dreams" is hard to get in Auburn, I'll be glad to lend my copy. I recall that C A S could not get certain Machen books.

[Enclosures:]

[ANS postcard][9]

This house is not in its original condition, since the gambrel (double pitched) roof did not exist till considerably after 1700. The original roof was undoubtedly a high peaked one—such as can be imagined by prolonging the lines of the lower pitch upward till they meet. The widows must have been outward-swinging casements with small leaded panes of diamond shape. Since this picture was taken, the place has been restored to the condition it probably had about 1750—paint & blinds removed, small-paned windows substituted, &c—but no attempt has been made to restore the original status of 1677. ¶ There has been considerable restoration of ancient Plymouth houses in the last three years, & I fancy the main part of the village will always retain much of its 18th century aspect. Nothing, however of the first Pilgrim generation remains—indeed, everything as old as that was swept away long before the Revolution. The present Town Hall was built about 1720, & many houses of approximately similar date survive.

[ANS postcard][10]

This ancient cemetery—behind the First Church—[is] ineffably fascinating. It covers a picturesque, irregular hill; & the stones go back far into the 1600's. An abundance of skulls & crossbones, winged cherubs, urns, & weeping willows; though I didn't find any fountains. At sunset it is a tremendously impressive sight—with the grotesque, centuried slabs silhouetted against the shadowed outspread countryside beyond the village, & the blazing orange west. Turning eastward one may see the placid, historic harbour stretching away beyond the roofs & church towers of the ancient village—& on the evening I was there, a great round moon turned the water to a sheet of silver flame. ¶ I have no blood from the Plymouth colony, but Belknap is descended from the Doty's—many of whom lie buried on the hill. Wandrei's mother comes from the Howlands—also represented here.

[Postcard, no message]¹¹[11]

Notes

1. A cat HPL referred to as Count Magnus Osterberg. See also HPL to Clark Ashton Smith, 11 February 1934: "Of other local felidae [. . .] one may mention the white & black huntress at the boarding-house across the back garden[. . . .] Last summer [. . .] she adopted two exquisite little tigers [. . . .] One [. . .] (an utterly fascinating & incredibly companionable little rascal) became my most frequent visitor & constant playmate. Because of his sprightly, insolent precocity I called him *Alfred Galpin* after our iconoclastic young friend" (*DS* 533). Galpin (1901–1983) was a composer, French scholar, and longtime friend of HPL.

2. See WBT 14n7.

3. Actually 22 June 1918.

4. Apparently Ruth Slenczynska (b. 1925), American pianist who played her debut in Berlin at age six and made her debut in Paris with a full orchestra at seven.

5. *The Hill of Dreams* (New York: Alfred A. Knopf, 1923), 40–41.

6. See *Arkham Sampler* 2, No. 4 (1985): 13, for "Rembrantesque" photo, which R. Alain Everts dates to 1930. It is probably of the same vintage as the photograph of Wandrei in *SL* 3.406, referred to below, and another in *SL* 2.329.

7. Josep Segrelles Albert (1885–1969), Valencian painter and illustrator, whose work was displayed at the Roerich Museum in 1931.

8. HPL frequently visited the Nicholas Roerich Museum (in his day at 103rd Street and Riverside Drive in Manhattan, now at 319 West 107th Street), devoted to the Russian painter Roerich (1874–1947). Roerich is mentioned six times in *At the Mountains of Madness*, as HPL suggests that the city of the Old Ones is reminiscent of Roerich's paintings of Himalayan monasteries. See Bibliography under Roerich Museum.

9. *Front:* Old Harlow House, Built 1677, from Timber of Old Fort, Plymouth, Mass.

10. *Front:* Governor Bradford's Monument, Burial Hill, Governor of Plymouth Colony, 1621 to 1657, Plymouth, Mass.

11. *Front:* State House, Providence, R.I.

[9]   [ALS, JHL]

YMCA—
Charleston, S.C.,
April 30, 1934.

Dear Helen:—

As you will perceive from the postmark, or as Klarkash-Ton may have mentioned, I am off on another of my irresponsible long-distance jaunts—this time bound to visit a young bibliophile & incipient fantasy-writer named R. H. Barlow in De Land, Florida. I certainly need the thawing-out of a decently civilised climate, for New England has been through the worst winter within the memory of living man—17 below zero on Feby. 9, which shattered all records since the establishment of the weather bureau.

Naturally I paused in decadent Manhattan for a week with my grandchild Belknap—seeing also the two Wandreis, the gallant Mr. Southwick,[1] good old Loveman, young Talman, Kirk, Kleiner, Leeds, Morton, & others of the group. All appeared to be flourishing—& I was impressed anew by the tremendously powerful drawings of the younger Wandrei. Donald has very kindly photographed some of these for Klarkash-Ton & me, & if you are interested I am sure that C A S would be delighted to show you his copies.

On Sunday, April 22, I set out for the South at midnight—spending Monday morning in Washington. As usual, I just missed the prime splendour of the famous cherry blossoms—but was amply content to spend the 4 hours at my disposal in exploring the ancient Georgetown section, which was there (as a Maryland town, founded circa 1750) before the capital was laid out. That afternoon I had an hour in Richmond, & in the evening came an hour in Raleigh, N.C.—which I had never seen before, since my former route south was farther inland. I reached Charleston—my favourite of all towns—at dawn Tuesday amidst sensations curiously like those of homecoming. There is no other place like Charleston—a perfect survival of the 18th century, as you may be aware through some of the folders & booklets I unloaded on you last summer. I am herewith sending along a few more cards—some of which I trust do not duplicate material you have. Charleston is probably the most truly civilised place in the United States; since it blossomed early, maintained close contact with Europe, & drew to itself an exceptionally high-grade type of colonist. It was first settled in 1670, when Charles II granted the colony of Carolina to a small group of Lords Proprietors headed by Anthony Ashley Cooper, Lord Ashley—later Lord Shaftesbury. Not many of the Proprietors came over in person, but they sent out a very select group of settlers under Col. Wm. Sayle to found a "town of trade" on the great harbour where the province's two leading rivers (named Ashley & Cooper in honour of Lᵈ Ashley) meet the sea. The first town was established on the west bank of the Ashley; but, this site proving unfeasible, the colonists moved a decade later to the narrow peninsula between the Ashley & Cooper. This second town, founded in 1680 & called Charles-Town until 1783, is the Charleston of today. At first the new settlement comprised only a small walled space on the bank of the Cooper River; but these limits were soon transcended—giving rise to a thriving city whose topography & street system are curiously like New York's. The ancient walls, reinforced in 1703, are now all demolished except for one of the bastions . . . . which lies at the present Cumberland St. & is known as the "old Powder Magazine." I am sending a view of this. Besides the colonists from Great Britain, Charles-Town drew a large quota of great planters from the West Indies—who took up extensive estates in the lowlands back of the town, but lived largely in the city because of the prevalent fever & malaria of the country. There were also Yankees from Massachusetts, Dutch from New York, a few Virginians, & a vast & tremendously influential influx of Hugue-

nots from France after the revocation of the Edict of Nantes. These Huguenots soon became Anglicised, but they left a distinctive impress on Charleston life. One can trace French elements in the unique local architecture, while
typical Charleston surnames to this day are Manigault, Ravenel, Prioleau, Pon,
Fayssoux, Lesesue, & so on. Charleston today contains the only Huguenot
church in the U.S. Later—in 1792—an additional French element reached
Charleston—the same refugee planter element from St. Domingo (fleeing
from the negro uprising) which contributed so much to New Orleans. The
high percentage of gentry among all the settlers, the aristocratic mode of government established by the Lords Proprietors & not wholly abolished when
Carolina became a Crown Province in 1719 (div. into N. & S. Carolina 1729),
& the growth of a distinctly *urban* life unlike the rural squirearchy of Virginia,
all combined to give Charles-Town a mature, polished, & European way of
life at a very early date—so that the town never had a crude or frontier period. Literature, drama, & the amenities of life appeared at a time when the
more northerly colonies were engrossed in more primitive matters—though
Newport in my own state was not far behind. Indeed—the cultivated plantation & town life of southern Rhode Island, which I mentioned last summer
when exhibiting the waterfront mansions of Newport amidst gathering
raindrops, gave Newport & Charles-Town much in common, & established
ties of considerable closeness betwixt them. The great Newport miniaturist
Malbone moved to Charleston & became the instructor of the scarcely less
famous Fraser, whilst a branch of the Charleston Middletons emigrated to
R.I. & is still represented in our town of Bristol. When the Bostonians were
printing psalm-books & talking through their noses, the Charlestonians were
writing poetry & criticism & priding themselves on their purity of speech.
This un-provincial cultivation was vastly promoted by their isolation (through
leagues of febrile marshland) from the rest of the colonies, & their consequently close relations with England. Gentlemen sent their sons to Oxford &
Cambridge instead of to the provincial colleges, & these youths generally
made the Grand Tour of the Continent & acquired all the poise & breadth of
civilised Englishmen. One result of Charleston's unique culture is the absolute purity of the local speech—which still survives. There is not a trace here
of the familiar negroid drawl commonly known as a "Southern accent" &
picked up by Virginia & Georgia planters from their slaves. (The "Ah reckin
he's gōn dahn to de cote-haouse" kind of thing). On the contrary, the pronunciation of the old Charleston gentry cannot be distinguished from that of
the gentry of Providence. I have twice been mistaken for an old-
Charlestonian by old-Charlestonians who have heard me talk at length, yet my
speech is wholly that of my native town. It is only among the lower-class out-
landers from Georgia or the Piedmont belt—shop clerks, motormen, &c.—
that one hears any "ah reckin" talk in Charleston.

Charleston's prosperity was founded successively on general agriculture, indigo, rice, & cotton—its heyday perhaps being the period of the early re-public—around 1800. There were many obstacles—Spanish, Indian, & pirate wars, fever, hurricane, earthquake, &c.—but the stamina of the people has survived through everything. The closeness of Spanish Florida was a great menace until that province became British in 1763, as part of general treaty following the fall of Quebec. Today there is much stagnation & genteel pov-erty, but the fineness of the culture is not dulled. Something of a literary & artistic renaissance is under way, & many cultivated northerners are settling in Charleston & bringing a certain amount of wealth.

At the time of the unfortunate revolt of 1775–83 Charles-Town was strongly rebel despite its social conservatism. However, His Majesty's fleet un-der Ld Rawdon & Sir Henry Clinton took the town in 1780 & held it till the close of the war. The Civil War was also a calamity to Charleston—especially in conjunction with the great fire of 1861 (not connected with the war). The geat earthquake of 1886 was another blow. On the credit side—Charleston has wholly eradicated yellow fever. The city was the capital of S.C. till about 1790, when the inland town of Columbia was built to house the state government.

Charleston began to assume its present aspect around 1730. The earliest surviving houses date from 1720 or 1722. French & West Indian influences ear-ly gave the local architecture a highly unique stamp, & the subtropical climate brought about certain autochthonous modifications of standard Georgian de-sign. Brick & stucco became the favourite building ma-terial, & *tiled* roofs grew prevalent after 1735. Gables & roof-curves of distinctly French type predominated, while the West Indian pointed roof was practically uni-versal. As a concession to the climate *walled gardens* be-gan to develop in abundance, while the characteristic Charleston porch of several stories on the side of the house, with door opening into the street, (so different form the balconies or "galleries" & patios of New Orle-ans) was fully evolved before 1800.

Typical Charleston roof-line (comp. with Quebec

Delicate wrought iron work—intro-duced by German craftsmen—is another old Charleston fea-ture. Some of the grilles & gateways rival anything in New Orleans. Each house generally had a coach-house & servants' quarters at-tached to it . . . . . many of these still surviving, though converted into dwellings.

Another type of
Charleston gable—
possible French
influence.

The crude sketches on this page endeavour to give some notion of typical
Charleston features. Besides these distinctive houses, there are some more
like the Georgian houses of northern towns—with standard wood or brick
facades having balanced door & windows. In the Charleston type the door is
rarely in the centre. Many houses were built of seasoned cypress wood—
which survives about as well as brick & stone. Early public buildings (cf. Old
Exchange in accompanying cards) followed standard Georgian designs; but
after the Revolution the pillared neo-classic type became universal. (cf. card
of Old Market) Scores of these still survive. With typical conservatism,
Charleston did not discard the Georgian & classic motifs in the 1830's & 40's,
as other cities did; but continued to employ the old patterns (albeit in a subtly
coarsened form) until after the Civil War. Very few houses were built during
the Dark Age of American architecture on account of the financially depressed state of the town—hence Charleston presents to this day a dominant
aspect not unlike that which it possessed when Sir Henry Clinton took up his
headquarters in the Brewton mansion (still in fine condition) near the foot of
King St. Of houses built after 1750 hundreds survive—& there are literally
thousands before 1800 or 1820.

   Such, then, is old Charleston—queer old gables, brick & stucco & cypress facades, tiled pointed roofs, wrought-iron grilles & gateways, many-
storied porches, columned churches & public buildings, high-brick garden
walls, crumbling old coach-houses & servants' quarters, bits of frank ruin &
desertion here & there, grass in cobblestoned lanes, coal-black gullah negroes
with a queer patois, thick Georgian steeples, old granite & cypress hitching-
posts, antiquated artesian wells [despite city water the old families prefer the
wells, & send their servants each day to get drinking water in cans], numberless friendly cats, unexpected grass-grown alleys & courts, great spreading
live-oaks & feathery willows, magnolias & azaleas & flowering vines, vivid
green creepers trimming old brown brick walls like lace, constant music of
ancient belfries & distant roosters' crowing, bright flaming sunsets followed
by the quick violet dusk of the subtropics, with heightened odour of blos-

soms & song of night-birds . . . . . . Ædepol, what an earthly paradise! The *street-cries* of Charleston—uttered by negro hucksters—form a volume in themselves. They are not as numerous as of yore—but to an outlander they form an element of tremendous charm. "Swimpy, raw, raw!" [Shrimp] . . . "She-craib, She-craib"! [Sea-crab] . . . . & kindred vocal selections following tonal patterns which you, as a musician, could classify better than I. The gullah negro speech differs from standard English more than any other authentic native dialect in N. America.

As I mentioned, Charleston is shaped like New York City—long & narrow. At its tip is the Battery—but a very different sort of thing from the Battery which Wandrei shewed you last summer! *This* Battery is still the focus of wealth & fashion—with splendid mansions, a great hotel, & a splendid sea-wall & park of spreading live-oaks. All the finest homes & gardens of Charleston are crowded toward the tip of the peninsula—where they have been for 200 years. The great longitudinal (N. & S.) streets—reading E. to W.—are East Bay, Church, Meeting (Providence & Pawtucket, R.I., have the only *other* Meeting Sts. in the world), King, Legare—Archdale—St. Philip, Rutledge Ave., & Ashley Ave. The great cross streets—reading northward from the Battery— are Tradd, Broad, Market, Wentworth, & Calhoun. Tradd St.—named from Robert Tradd, the first child in the colony—has the most old houses of any American street—being virtually in its 1750 condition today. Broad St. is the financial section; King above Wentworth the shopping section. Calhoun St.— with Marion Sq. extending between King & Meeting—marked the northern boundary of the colonial town. Here is the largest hotel & the 'bus station. The corner of Broad & Meeting is the civic centre—P.O., Court House, City Hall, &c.—with an old park where I sit & write in the shadow of a statue of William Pitt erected in 1769. In lower Church St. is an art & literary colony which I *hope* will not grow into a Greenwich Village. One of Loveman's friends—the artist Prentiss Taylor[2]—now lives there . . . . I was supposed to look him up, but was somewhat relieved to find him out of town. The ancient churchyards of Charleston form a story in themselves. Several of them adjoin one another, & through this concentrated oasis of green shade & curious slabs there runs a right of way open to the public & called the "Gateway Path." I never fail to traverse this several times on each visit to Charleston.

But what's the use? Who could describe old Charleston in anything short of an encyclopaedia-sized book? It stands alone as a survivor of the splendid old civilisation that the rest of America fell away from—& is certainly the place where I shall live if the northern climate ever drives me south. It has the feel of *home* as nothing else outside Providence does. No one ought to miss seeing Charleston . . . . it surpasses New Orleans incomparably, despite the wider celebrity of the latter. If you ever make that once-planned trip East, don't skip old Charleston, & don't spend less than a fortnight there!

On this visit I have met a highly interesting & erudite local antiquarian—

an ancient gentlewoman named Miss Willis, author of the standard history of the 18th century Charleston stage. This venerable scholar, descended from the oldest Charleston stock & still inhabiting her well-preserved hereditary mansion (built 1730–34) in Tradd St., has furnished many side-lights on Charleston tradition with which I was previously unfamiliar. Her book is a genuine masterpiece of its kind, & ought to interest you because of its full account of the famous *Sully* family from which Thomas the artist (& his artist-nephew who was Poe's playmate in Richmond) sprang. As you may be aware, the Sullys were perhaps the leaders of the Charleston stage between 1792 & 1810 or 1820. Matthew Sully, the father of the clan, was the son of a gentleman of ancient family in Long Crandon, England, who moved to London in Matthew's youth. Matthew studied for Holy Orders, but interrupted his career to marry against his father's will. Being disowned, he went on the stage; & quickly attained a measure of success. Of his nine children, most also followed him upon the boards. Mr. Sully & his family emigrated to Charleston in 1792, & almost immediately became influential in the theatre there. His eldest son Lawrence (not on the stage) became a noted miniature painter, & his daughter Julia married a French miniaturist named Zolbins—who later changed his name to Belzons. All the daughters were notably gifted & beautiful, & most—after a brief period on the stage—married into the old Charleston aristocracy. Mrs. Sully taught dancing to young gentlewomen. Thomas, the greatest of the clan, was born in Horncastle, England, before the emigration, & at first went on the stage with his father in child roles. He was the youngest son. Before long he turned to art, & apprenticed himself to his brother-in-law, Monsieur Belzons. Quarrelling with this violent tempered Frenchman, he left & went to Richmond to study under his brother Lawrence, who had established himself there. This was in 1801. In 1803 Lawrence died, & in 1805 Thomas married the widow. In 1808 he removed to Philadelphia, where his greatest fame overtook him. Meanwhile his brother Matthew Jr. had also come to Richmond, marrying & settling there. It was *his* son Robert—Thomas's nephew—who was little Eddie Allan's [the adoptive name under which Poe then went] playmate in Shockoe Creek behind the great new pillared Brockenbrough house which later became the "White House of the Confederacy." [vide enc. card] Later Robert studied under his uncle Thomas & became a painter of great celebrity.

The climate down here is just what I need—though Florida will be even better. I have three times the energy, mental & physical, that I have up north. It is full summer in Charleston—rich green vegetation, gorgeous flowers, many really *hot* days, straw hats, & all. In Washn. & Richmond it is merely springlike—with delicate young foliage. And in N.Y. it is (or was when I left) still wintry, with chill winds & bare boughs. There is to me a never-failing glamour in the process of passing—in the course of a few hours—from virtual winter to virtual summer.

In the grey dawn of tomorrow I move reluctantly on to Savannah, where I shall explore all day & take the Jacksonville coach in the evening. The next day—Wednesday—I shall take the coach for De Land, arriving there at 12:15 noon. I have never met my prospective host in person, but fancy I shall be able to recognise him from his pictures. I have described myself to him—1928 almost-soaked-at-Newport-&-wholly-soaked-in-Boston blue suit (now getting out of press again) & all. My temporary address for the next fortnight or so will be % R. H. Barlow, Box 88, De Land, Fla. I don't know how long the visit will be protracted (or how short it will be cut), but when it is over I mean to spend a week in ancient St. Augustine if it breaks me. I travel very frugally—having whittled my food bill down to $1.75 per week, & keeping my shelter bill down to $3.75 or $4.00 for an equivalent period. I am also invited to visit a friend in Macon, Ga.[3]—but shan't unless my already-paid-for round trip ticket can be routed through there. Another invitation—when I return north—is from Dwyer of West Shokan, N.Y. (a fantastic poet-artist dwelling amidst the wild domed hills of his birth) . . . . which I'd like to accept but will probably be too broke to do. Doubtful if I can make the side-trip from Richmond to ancient Williamsburg—& *Havana* is a chimerical dream unless I receive an unexpected remittance from a delinquent client. (Two are due me . . . but try & get 'em!) However, what I *can* see & do ought to be enough. Hang me if one sight of ancient CHARLESTON oughtn't to be enough for anybody!

Let me most heartily congratulate Grey Boy upon his recent renaissance of skill & spirit in Big Game hunting! Would that all of us old greybeards could be as spry in our sunset years! And what consideration he shewed in depositing his trophy on a clean paper & properly exhibiting it before consumption! A gentleman of true Kappa Alpha Tau caliber, I vow! Your assistance in his toothless struggle was a piece of heroism in itself—for I'll confess that surgery of that sort is not what I would choose for an ideal evening's pastime! In view of this feat of Son's, I scarcely need enquire whether he has recovered from the indisposition mentioned last January. Such Nimrod-like[4] exploits are obviously not the diversions of an 'interesting invalid'!

Your quondam stopping-place across the back garden from 66 College was this year graced by a set of three exquisite children born to Mrs. Spotty—the lady who adopted the little tigers you saw. Or possibly I mentioned this in a preceding epistle. Two grey—just alike—& one white & black like mother. And what playful little divvles! I enjoyed the whole family while it lasted, but now the grey twins are given away to an appreciative family across the city—to be kept together. The white & black scion is retained—& will doubtless be still youthful & sportive when I get back. Meanwhile the sedate Kappa Alpha Tau has resumed its sessions on the shed roof beneath my windows. Venerable black & white Pres. Randall—who remains invisibly indoors during the winter, being like me in his attitude toward cold—began making his annual sorties just before I left.

Your trip to the vivid & novel Feather River country, with its glimpse of the sinister, macabre Funeral Range, sounds like an almost ideal outing. Pictures & descriptions from Klarkash-Ton have given me some idea of this rugged Californian scenery—of which the region in question would appear to furnish some especially dramatic examples. I know that utterly unaccustomed scenes often have a vivifying charm that nothing familiar can possess, & hope to include some such terra incognita in my next itinerary. Ah, me—if I could only push on to Havana right now! Glad that Son was left in good hands. I'd imagine that Klarkash-Ton would be a good guardian for the race of Bast, since he has spoken of the notable representatives of that hierarchy in his menage . . . . . of ancient Simaetha, the nighted survivor of immemorial Sabbats, & of the bluff & boisterous General Tabasco, victor in many a campaign. Indeed, not long ago I was favoured with a very graphic & imaginatively provocative sketch of Simaetha!

Those picnics with Klarkash-Ton must surely have been delightful—I can visualise them from a splendid enlarged photograph which he lately sent, showing himself & your sister on some picturesque high ground overlooking the distant roofs of Auburn. I wish I could have seen the sketches you made—& hope to see the ones of your home which you speak of sending some time. I violently envy anyone who can draw! Artorius Vigalis de Britannia Romana[5] must have made an ideal literary companion, & I trust you enjoyed your subsequent full reading of it. It fascinated me extremely. I have always felt a peculiar kinship to Rome & its civilisation, hence welcomed this proof of Rome's close connexion with my own ancestry. There is magic in the thought that many of my own unknown forbears—however Nordic & provincial in blood—spoke Latin, lived in Roman towns or villas, served in the legions, wore togas, bore names like M. Julius Civilis or P. Valerius Gallus, & gloried in the title of CIVIS ROMANVS. S.P.Q.R. . . . . Alala![6]

The good old monster of the deep surely seems to be gaining publicity in widely different localities . . . . Loch Ness, British Columbia, & now Los Angeles! Enclosed are a few lines anent this phenomenon which I recently clipped.

I was sorry to hear of Weigall's death. He was tremendously versatile, & had a way of popularising the ancient world without distorting either its facts or its spirit. I wish I had his "Saxon Footprints in Britain"—the companion book to the one you saw.[7]

Well—I must apologise for the length & rambling quality of this infliction . . . it is always harder for me to say anything in little space than to wander all over a whole pad of paper saying virtually nothing . . . . . & a subject like Charleston is quite impossible to keep within bounds! I trust your health is now quite satisfactory, & that you will not attempt any aestival programme so strenuous as to bring on a recurrence of last autumn's fatigue. If you travel eastward—which would be delightful—do it in easy stages . . . & don't omit CHARLESTON!

Best regards—& now southward ho! ¶ Yr obt Servt
H P L

[Enclosures:]

[ANS postcard][8]

This building dates only from 1835—its predecessor having been burned down. The parish is the oldest in Charleston. The first St. Philip's stood where St. Michael's is now, but about 1723 it moved to its present site—St. Michael's having being build 29 years later on the old location. The architecture—with typical Charleston conservatism—is of a Georgian type characteristic of an earlier period. Note the stately 3-way portico. In the churchyard John C. Calhoun lies buried.

in old times the towering spire of St. Philip's—this edifice & the one before it—formed the leading Charleston landmark for mariners at sea. Pardon this shopworn card—the only St. P. view obtainable.

Almost as many cherubs, skulls, urns, & weeping willows as in New England churchyards. There is a type of long-necked cherub quite peculiar to Charleston. Some of the stones were carved in New England & shipped south. There is one slab here carved in *Newport*, Rhode Island—because of the patriarchal plantation life of the Narragansett Country (with town houses across the bay in Newport)—had closer relations with the South than did any other part of New England. It is curious to see our old New England slate in a Southern churchyard.

[ANS postcard][9]

Back of this house is a steep shrub-covered declivity leading down to where Shockoe Creek once flowed. Here—around 1820—little Edgar Poe used to go swimming with his friends—one of whom was your possible kinsman Robert Sully—nephew of the painter Thomas Sully & later a somewhat prominent painter himself.

[ANS postcard][10]

This is the George Edwards house—14 Legare St. (pronounced La-free locally) Note initials G & E in ironwork on either side of the doorway. Since this card was made, the ancient rayed tracery has been restored to the transom. I've tried to indicate this.

[ANS postcard][11]

This church has the sweetest chimes I've ever heard.

Notes

1. The Wandreis were friends with Talbot Southwick (d. 1994) and his wife Lloyd.

2. Prentiss Taylor (1907–1991), American illustrator, lithographer, and painter.

3. John Milton Samples (1887–?), publisher of the *Silver Clarion,* which published some of HPL's early work.

4. Referring to E. Hoffmann Price's cat. According to the Book of Genesis and Books of Chronicles, Nimrod was the son of Cush, the great-grandson of Noah. He was "a mighty hunter before the Lord" (Gen. 10:9).

5. I.e., Arthur Weigall and his *Wanderings of Roman Britain.* See Bibliography.

6. *Civis Romanus* = "Roman citizen." S.P.Q.R. = *Senatus populusque Romanus* (the Senate and the people of Rome). "Alala!" is a Roman battle cry.

7. For the correct title of this book, see Bibliography.

8. *Front:* St. Philip's Church, Charleston, S. C.

9. *Front:* "White House of the Confederacy" (Twelfth and Clay Streets), Richmond, Va.

10. *Front:* Old Charleston Steps, Charleston, S. C.

11. *Front:* St. Michael's Church, Charleston, S. C.

[10]   [ALS, JHL]

> ℅ R. H. Barlow,
> Box 88, De Land, Fla.
> May 26, 1934.

Dear Helen:—

It is with vast contrition that I learn of the perilous state in which my Charleston epistle was received . . . . . a state which I hope may not be duplicated in the present document. If I seem to be tempting fate with the enclosed cards,[1] I may reply that the containing envelope (an honest product of my philanthropic stationer-in-chief, Mr. Frank Winfield Woolworth) is infinitely less likely to succumb to disintegration than were the aging reliquiae of the (to my old correspondents) famous George W. Kirk charity stationery which I have been using for 9 years, & which gave out only during my present season of wandering. Back in 1925 Kirk unloaded on me an infinite number of boxes of envelopes bearing obsolete return addresses—which I thought would last till the end of my, or their, lifetime. As it is, I feel quite bewildered without them—for years I shall be instinctively crossing out an imaginary Kirk inscription in the northwest corner of perfectly blank envelopes!

Well—I am glad the luckily salvaged text proved of interest rather than of ennui. Charleston is a theme on which I cannot discourse briefly or temperately. In me, at least, it dictates superlatives. Your cousin is certainly fortunate to have a residence of the classic, reposeful Southern type, even though it is set in a very unreposeful & non-austral metropolis. Yes—Charleston gardens were still at their best when I was there. I saw most of the notable urban specimens, though I could not visit the famous Magnolia & Middleton Gardens—on ancient plantations—sixteen miles from the town. Regarding Charleston's famous iron-work & its non-use in the North, I would say that climatic needs had something to do with its localism. Balconies & grilles are not so often called for in the architecture of a cold climate, while extensive walled gardens (which might employ wrought-iron grates) are the exception rather than the rule. In view of the notably fine proportion of Pennsylvania's Georgian country-seats, & the exquisite craftsmanship found in New England doorways & steeples, I would hesitate to say that the north is inferior to the Carolina low country in its architectural heritage. It is, rather, that different lines of development were followed—the north sticking closer to the parent English designs, while Charleston assimilated exotic elements (French, West Indian, &c) suited to its special needs. It is very curious, though, that this local Charlestonian school did not more considerably affect Savannah—which is only 100 miles away & still more southerly & subtropical. Savannah took from Charleston only the curved double flight of steps & an occasional use of iron grille-work—otherwise it followed totally different lines, even to the nature of its tombs & gravestones—which shew St. Augustine Spanish & New Orleans French influence. Just another proof of Charleston's complete isolation & fertile self-sufficiency from the earliest times to the present. If climatic considerations ever drive me South, Charleston will certainly be my first residential choice—even though it is not as climatically comfortable as Florida. The reason why I have not long ago pulled up stakes in my boreal native realm is that I am strongly attached to the scenes of youth—to the atmosphere & scenery & foliage & architecture I have always known. Could I ever exist without rolling, boulder-strown hills, rambling stone walls, tall elms, low-pitched farmhouses, & slender white steeples? These things are potent imaginative factors, even though the climate containing them be physically intolerable. Temperaments differ in their emphases—mine is preëminently geographical.

I think you are correct in pointing out the element of pompous hyper-criticism in Rachmaninoff's remarks on the infant prodigy. To my mind it is exceedingly foolish to discourage or resent early development in the arts. When such occurs, there is generally a natural & adequate reason for it—nor is any advantage likely to result from its checking. The only thing I would tend to oppose is *forcing* as opposed to reasonable *encouragement*. A child should never be robbed of the period of care-free play & leisure which not only belongs to it by right, but is really important to its subsequent psychological & emotional equilibrium. Nearly all *forced* prodigies tend to develop ill-proportioned personalities which peter out disappointingly—cases in point being the well-known ones of William Sidis & Winifred Sackville Stoner, Jr.[2] But of course there are cases where the child's natural recreative impulse is in the same direction as its serious talents—permitting a rapid & intensive development without undue forcing. I trust that the small & gifted Ruth may be able to triumph over parentage, overtraining, & criticism alike.

Regarding the parallelism—in some cases amounting to actual organic relationship—betwixt poetry & music, I cannot speak with any authority because of my musical ignorance. I would, however, tend to say (or guess) that the two arts each have certain phases or departments which closely approach certain phases or departments of the other. Though the primary bases of the two are widely different, the common elements of rhythm & association create large overlapping zones. Despite my vast ignorance, there are musical compositions which tend to evoke from my imagination certain definitely *visual* concepts which could be expressed (had one the skill) either in poetry or painting. And conversely, there are imaginative phases of poetry which seem to suggest paintings or musical notes—& aspects of painting which suggest music or poetry or both. The fact is, that all the arts would seem to be fundamentally related despite their profound differences in function & method. Each expresses a certain side of a single definite quality of the mind of highly evolved animal life; a quality best expressed as *a demand for the perception of modulated symmetry*. In practice, of course, this purely aesthetic demand is always mixed to an indefinite & inextricable degree with various factors of *association*, emotional & intellectual. Thus I cannot help viewing a familiar landscape both as a loyal native & as an aesthetic appreciator, while historical & antiquarian interests creep into my appreciations of architecture. These associative elements heighten the poignancy of all artistic appeal; & it is both silly & pedantic to try to rule them out absolutely, as many moderns do. I have no use at all for the theoretical abstract art of futurists, functionalists, & kindred spawn of a sterile & disintegrative modernism. Art without tradition is only a crippled & impoverished remnant—& I hope that no freakish social overturn will ever be allowed to wreck Western Europe's main stream. But I digress loquaciously, as usual!

As for travelling economies—dietary & otherwise—bless my soul, but I don't starve on my $1.75 hebdomedal nutritive quota! It is merely a matter of reducing poverty to a science & extracting a maximum return from a minimum expenditure. My arbitrary minimum quota on trips like this is 25¢ per day—& it is astonishing how far this can be made to go. One's procedure varies, of course, according to local purchasing opportunities. When no good cheap lunch rooms exist, one may subsist amply on canned & package goods—for which purpose I always carry a knife, fork, spoon, & can-opener. Breakfast—a nickel package of very palatable cookies or cheese crackers, plus perhaps a nickel cup of coffee somewhere. Total, 10¢. Dinner—a dime can of beans or spaghetti, with the residue of the breakfast package for dessert, & perhaps another nickel cup of coffee. 15¢ . . . diurnal total, 25¢. And there you are. Two meals a day are all I ever eat under any circumstances, & these are perfectly adequate both in quantity & quality. Merely a matter of studying the problem & exercising judicious selection. One varies such a programme as opportunities permit. In Richmond & Savannah, for example, there are *nickel lunchrooms* in which every separate item costs exactly 5¢. A typical day's programme there would run something like this: Breakfast, cheese sandwich & coffee—10¢. Dinner: hamburg steak sandwich, coffee, pie—15¢. Total, 25¢. And there you are! Charleston, on the other hand, offers marvellous course dinners for 25¢ at the Mexican Chili Palace in King St. & elsewhere . . . . . hence in that venerable town I simply cut out breakfast & gorge to the limit in the evening for my quarter. I can always omit a meal without feeling any difference. So there is no need for the children to have any anxiety over Grandpa's health! The old gentleman has grown into a relatively tough bird in his sunset years—& such selective diets as these do not even begin to exercise a strain on his time-weathered constitution! I have to go below this quantity level whenever I want to knock off a few pounds of weight. Just now, amidst the lavish & gratuitous fare provided by my present genial hosts, the peril is all in the opposite direction—if I escape without indigestion & a double chin I shall be fortunate indeed!

Providence & De Land chapters of the Kappa Alpha Tau unite in sending their sympathy to Son regarding his recent malady—a sympathy mixed with congratulations on his recovery, & commendations of the diligent & self-denying care extended by his family. Good old boy! I am certainly relieved to hear that professional skill finally pulled him through, & that he is now enjoying the reposeful luxury of an indulged senescence. He must be a lordly soul—is he not the grey person in the foreground of the picture with which you honoured my grandson Belknap last Yuletide? The De Land chapter of the K.A.T. is headed by a pure-white patriarch named Doodle-Bug, who has accompanied the Barlovii on many a migration. He is a hunter of great reputation, & frequently goes off on expeditions of several days' duration in the subtropical jungle. I enclose his picture, which I would like to have back ultimately—though there is no haste in the matter. The younger members are "High", a dark & dignified tiger who follows his young master & aged guest on long walks like a dog; "Low", a gentlewoman of much sprightliness & yellowish-tiger colouring; & "Jack", a light tiger as playful as his brother is dignified. An honorary member, admitted on sufferance despite a marsupial rather than feline ancestry, is Henry—an infant opossum about the size of a large mouse. He (& five little brothers who failed to survive despite the tenderest care) was orphaned by a passing motor, & has been sedulously fed with milk through a medicine-dropper. Just now he is beginning to lap milk himself, & to nibble at bits of crushed banana proffered him on an outstretched finger. I think he can be successfully raised to maturity—he is an incredibly quaint little divvle!

As for the trip—I had 8½ hrs. in Savannah, & gave the town a much more thorough exploration than I was able to give it in 1931. It is a tremendously attractive place, though not nearly as quaint as Charleston. It dates on-

ly from 1733, when Genl. Oglethorpe founded the Georgia colony as a haven for poor debtors & a buffer betwixt South Carolina & the hostile Spaniards of Florida. Its subtropical climate is much more marked than Charleston's, as attested by the richer vegetation, taller palms, more abundant Spanish moss, & kindred signs. It is full of public parks & squares with trees & benches, & may perhaps be called the most *restful* city on the globe. The bulk of the houses are about a century old, & the grace & reposefulness of some of the mansions are immense. Garden plots abound, though they do not attain the size & walled dignity common in Charleston. The local architecture is very distinctive, & seems curiously influenced by *New Orleans* rather than by Charleston. It is, however, peculiar to Savannah. Balconies & porches are the things suggesting New Orleans influence. As before mentioned, the old graveyards contain some highly odd tombs & graves. In Christ Church Cemetery the east wall is 10 feet thick & pierced by oven-like above-ground graves like those in the ancient cemeteries of New Orleans. Some of the below-ground graves are obviously copied from Spanish prototypes in the old Tolomato
cemetery at St. Augustine. The chief material for markers & tombs is red sandstone. In many cases the traditional winged cherubs, urns, & weeping willows are found—no skulls & crossbones, since Savannah wasn't founded early enough for such.

After an overnight pause in Jacksonville, I reached De Land at noon May 2, & was met by my gifted young host—a great admirer & correspondent of Klarkash-Ton, by the way. De Land is a modern town which owes all its beauty to its fine subtropical setting—live-oaks, moss, magnolias, &c.—& I will avoid tedious descriptions by sending under separate cover an illustrated folder for your gradually growing travel morgue. The Barlow place is 14 miles west of the village, & out of sight of any other human habitation—in a pleasant landscape of blue lakes & tall Australian pines that stand out against the sunset like the trees in a Japanese print. The house—scarcely completed as yet—is of rustic design with log exterior . . . . of two stories, & very attractive & commodious. The grounds are undergoing appropriate landscaping under the direction of the youthful heir. In the rear is a delectable pine-fringed lakelet on which we row almost daily, & across which is a fine oak grove suitable for outdoor reading & writing sessions. A cabin will eventually be built in this grove—& my young host urges Grandpa to move down & permanently inhabit it! The climate is admirable—85° to 90° day after day, & no chill spells at this season. I feel like a new person—as spry as a youth, & without a trace of the nasal trouble which besets me in the north. I go hatless & coatless, & am maintaining an admirable layer of tan. Snakes abound to a picturesque degree; & young Barlow shoots them for their skins—which he uses in amateur bookbinding. The other day I saw him bag a coach-whip snake all of 7 feet long.

As for my host—Robert Hayward Barlow—he is obviously not the Richard you know, nor can he place that person as a distant kinsman. But he surely is a great boy. He always evaded statements regarding his age, but it now turns out that he *only turned sixteen last Friday.* The little imp! Thus he was scarcely 13 when he first corresponded with me. But for the handicap of poor eyesight (which he will try to have corrected on a northern trip next autumn—when he will meet Belknap & the N.Y. gang) he might be a worthy parallel of the unpronounceably surnamed Ruth in his differing lines of endeavour! Never before in the course of a long lifetime have I seen such a versatile child. He is a writer; painter; sculptor; printer; pianist; marionette designer, maker, & exhibitor; landscape gardener; tennis champion; chess expert; bookbinder; crack rifle shot; bibliophile; manuscript collector; & heaven knows what else! You ought to see the bas-relief of one of my fictional monsters (*Cthulhu*) which he made some time ago from common Florida clay— that & the statuette of the elephant god Ganesa (prototype of Belknap's *Chaugnar*) which he is making for an amiable, eccentric old fellow (William Lumley—also a correspondent of Klarkash-Ton's) in Buffalo, N.Y.![3] Bobby is the younger son of a retired army colonel now nervously broken down & visiting relatives in the North. He has a brother a decade older than himself— an army lieutenant at present stationed in Texas. It develops, amusingly enough, that we have a strain of ancestry in common—both being descended from the Rathbones of Block Island, R.I.[4] The present household, in addition to little Ar-E'ch-Bei & the felidae & opossumlet, consists of Mrs. Barlow, an elderly housekeeper, & the latter's really gifted middle-aged son—Charles Blackburn Johnston—whose paintings excite my unaffected envy. The Johnstons are Virginians of rustic origin, & speak a broad Southern dialect.

Among our diversions have been several trips to ancient places of the sort I dote upon . . . . . including a Spanish sugar-mill at De Leon Springs which antedates 1763 (vide enc.), & sundry sites & reliques at New Smyrna on the coast. New Smyrna is celebrated as the seat of Dr. Andrew Turnbull's plantation of 1768, where indigo & other subtropical products were cultivated by labourers (Minorcan Spaniards, Italians, & Greeks) imported from the Mediterranean. It was named in honour of Dr. Turnbull's wife—a Greek gentlewoman from Smyrna. After some success, the enterprise failed through labour troubles resulting from over-strict overseers—the workmen being finally (1774) released from their indentures & settled in St. Augustine (where their descendants still live) by order of His Britannick Majesty's Governor. Turnbull's ruin was completed by the re-cession of Florida to Spain in 1783. He then went to Charleston & became the leading apothecary there—founding a pharmacy at the corner of King & Broad Sts. which yet survives, & at which I have frequently purchased vanilla ice-cream. Of the Turnbull plantation no trace survives save an old irrigation canal, which still runs its course beside New Smyrna's main street. A more picturesque New Smyrna relique is the vine-clad, oak-shaded ruin of a Franciscan mission built in 1696, partly destroyed by South Carolina troops in 1706, later used as a sugar mill, & finally abandoned. Many stately walls & noble arches of coquina stone remain—the effect of the whole, in conjunction with the tropical background & marks of the jungle's reconquest, being picturesque & exotic to the highest degree.

And so it goes. Though I have been here nearly a month, the phenomenal hospitality of my hosts is such that all suggestions of moving along are vetoed. I must, though, get in motion soon. Hopes of Havana have declined to a minimum. What I positively shall do is to spend a week in ancient St. Augustine—of which I believe you have some cards & a folder or two. I may or may not accept an invitation to visit an old amateur literary correspondent in Macon, Ga. My progress northward will be as slow as I can afford to make it—with pauses in Richmond, Fredericksburg, Washington, Philadelphia, & N.Y.—& possibly a sail up the Hudson to visit Bernard Dwyer at West Shokan, N.Y.

Howard Wandrei's art is extremely remarkable, & I have no doubt but that it will be widely recognised in the future. Photographic reproductions can give no idea of its full power—& the more one examines its imaginative scope & technical perfection the more one admires it. It is of course undeniably decadent—but so is the poetry of Baudelaire & the prose of Huysmans & the art of Beardsley & Rops, & oceans of other great stuff. One may wish that the imagination of the artist were less steeped in abnormality & decay— but one cannot deny the mastery with which he has dealt with his material. This kid is wholly above the artistic grade generally represented by the gang— being virtually on a level with Sime, Harry Clarke, Segrelles, & other recognised masters of the grotesque & the fantastic. I could even understand the characteristically enthusiastic overstatement of Little Belknap when he cried out that Howard Wandrei is "greater than Albrecht Dürer & Goya!" My young host Ar-E'ch-Bei almost went into convulsions of admiration when Donald's photographs of the drawings reached him; & his first reaction was to try to start a scheme for publishing the drawings in the form of 11 × 14″ photographic reproductions to be made by an expert professional photographer. This design is, however, opposed by Donald; who has plans for issuing a series of reproductions himself as soon as he has secured a larger camera & learnt the suitable technique. Little Barlow is a shark for fantastic art, & utterly idolises Klarkash-Ton & his products. Possibly C A S has told you of his recent purchase of that exquisitely exotic water-colour "Beyond Cathay" . . . . . . & he plans to buy more Clericashtoniana as soon as the state of his allowance permits.

Glad you hear more frequently from Young Melmoth & Comrade Belnapovitch. I believe you may see the former before the year is over, since he speaks of a Grand Tour in which the Arcadian meads of Averoigne are included. As for Young Stalin—I presume that the best things for his neurotic self-centredness are the sheer passage of time, plus a constant reiteration of the proportioned facts of the universe in a pleasant, half-humorous way which will minimise his hostility toward them & cause them to linger in his memory till such a time as greater age will enable him to accept them. Some trip or other move removing him from parental dependence would be a boon, but is probably beyond possibility. The passing of years will no doubt produce a certain adult rationality & realisation that the limitations of life are inevitable things to be borne with; while all increases in sound philosophic knowledge are valuable assets whose benefits may be sudden rather than gradual in manifesting themselves. It is true, of course, that an introspective & hypochondriac temperament cannot be instantaneously reasoned or jollied out of its morbid self-centredness; since many of the contributing factors are deeply seated in the unconscious emotions. In a subject as brilliant as Belknap, however, one cannot but feel that many of the factors are intellectual; & therefore liable to gradual correction as sounder ideas of things slip imperceptibly past his guard of hostility & resistance. His natural scientific sense will recognise the universality & inevitability of the restrictions & disappointments which he now regards as deliberate personal injuries inflicted by the malice of a malign social order; & he will discover that the external world is a more interesting thing than his own pulse & weight & aspect in the mirror to spend his time watching. But the rectifying information & sounder standards must be instilled into him gradually & unconsciously & lightly—as good old Jim Morton & I try to instil them. The ideal course would be not so much to make him see how insignificant an individual he is in the universe, as to get him *positively* interested in something definite & objective & (if possible) creative . . . . something which will absorb & distribute his attention & energies in such a way as to leave no time for brooding, self-examination, & self-pity. But of course such saving interests cannot be made to order. They have to be hit upon by accident . . . just to happen of themselves. Sterile social criticism—or even literary criticism—can never be positive & definite enough to turn the trick. There must be some really potent pull like intellectual curiosity, aesthetic ardour, constructive zeal, or other equally positive influences. That such will come in time, there is every reason to hope. Belknap has had enough intellectual zeal (as witness his really profound anthropological studies) & artistic creativeness (vide "The Man from Genoa") in the past to warrant the belief that these things will again absorb his attention & give purpose to his now scattered energies when the force of his present belated adolescence is spent. Time is the great factor—plus a constant encouragement to throw off the parental dominance which perpetuates a far-reaching sort of emotional infantilism . . . the trait which makes one want Fate to hand everything to one on a silver platter. That clearer information regarding cosmic values will help to bring about a psychological improvement seems certain to me, despite the dogmas of those who consider temperament purely psychological. I am myself a case in point. In youth I had a violent, capricious, & ungovernable temper which many might have thought organic—yet this virtually disappeared during my 'teens as a result of the philosophical & scientific studies which made clear to me the mechanical impersonality of the cosmos & the helplessness of all life therein. If my blind emotions could be so completely reversed—or virtually extirpated—by an enlargement of rational perspective; so, I feel confident, can Sonny Belknap's as time & chance provide the requisite intellectual impressions. Just give him leeway—a word of encouragement to realistic thought here, a gentle spoof at false values, brooding & self-centredness there; & at all times a constant presentation of definite objective interests (of the general type shewn by past experience & analysis to be suited to his sort of taste) in a spirit so enthusiastic as to be ultimately contagious. Sooner or later the old "Man from Genoa" mood will snap back; & the world will again seem so interesting to the artist that he'll be too busy observing & mirroring it to worry about his digestion, dignity, apparel, finances, & position in the eyes of others. Everybody tends to grow mellow & sensible in middle age—that is one of the compensations which help to reconcile the person of sense to the vast toll of interests & opportunities taken by the years.

By the way—I trust you did not miss a glimpse of the dashing E. Hoffmann Price when he recently rolled up in his well-seasoned tree-climbing Juggernaut to pay his respects to Klarkash-Ton. A fascinating chap—you may recall my mentioning his presence in Providence just prior to your own advent there. He is now settled (as long as he can settle anywhere) at his parental home in Oakland, Cal.—& it is likely that the recent visit to Averoigne will not be his last.

Pray convey my thanks to your mother for the delightful snapshot of the picnickers near the nighted Temple of Tsathoggua. It is really a splendid view—landscape & figures each supplementing the other to advantage. My young host—an adoring devotee of Klarkash-Ton, as I have mentioned—was tremendously impressed by the excellence with which it depicts the Master, & he begs me to ask you if you will have the benign charity to send another print of it to him for his really notable gallery of weird celebrities. I will hereby second his plea—adding that no more appreciative recipient than he could possibly exist. If, then, you can conveniently do so, it would be a most philanthropic act to send a print to R. H. BARLOW, BOX 88, DE LAND, FLORIDA. His blessings will follow you for evermore!

Which reminds me that I am enclosing several prints of the present visiting session which you needn't bother to return. Any that bore you can be turned over to C A S. Note especially the felidae (a magnifying-glass will bring out the graceful pose of "High" & "Jack") & the view of young Bobby with his rifle & newly-slain coach-whip snake. The landscape garden is largely of his designing.

I trust that all flourishes in Averoigne, & that the trying grind of pedagogical labour will soon abate for the summer. Will your second Eastern trip materialise as contemplated? There is still much to see, & it is certain that all your guides of 1933 would be overjoyed to act in a similar capacity in 1934. A more leisurely itinerary might enable you to avoid the aftermath of fatigue which subtracted from the net returns of the earlier Odyssey.

In conclusion, let me again express my sympathy concerning Son's indisposition. Give him my regards, & tell him to be careful about the quality of the rat cutlets he consumes. We old fellows have to guard our digestions! ¶ With every good wish,

Yr obt Svt

H P L

Notes

1. No cards were found with this letter. Either they were lost or the cards enclosed in letter 9 in fact belong to this letter.
2. William James Sidis (1898–1944), American child prodigy with exceptional mathematical abilities and a purported mastery of many languages. Winifred Sackville Stoner Jr. (1902–1983), prolific poet and child prodigy, author of the poem "The History of the U.S," which begins "In fourteen hundred ninety-two, Columbus sailed the ocean blue," and other mnemonic jingles.
3. Lumley (1880–1960) was an eccentric late associate of HPL for whom HPL revised verse and ghostwrote "The Diary of Alonzo Typer" (1935).
4. HPL pointed out that although Barlow and he were both descended from John Rathbone in seven generations, Barlow was young enough to be his son.

[11]   [Postcard][1]

[Postmarked Saint Augustine, Fla.,

23 June 1934]

On the road again after the longest visit—7 wks—I ever made in my life. The Barlows brought me here last Thursday in the car. It is surely a relief to be amongst old houses again . . . & America has none older than those before my eyes. You'll see pictures of some of them in the assorted junk which I sent last year. Dwellings 2 generations old when Providence was founded are a common sight. Am staying a week—at the same old place I stopped at in 1931. Fine tower room—with a magnificent view—at 4.00 per wk. Absorbing antiquities at top speed—more old houses open as museums than in 1931. ¶ A fortnight ago I visited a marvellous place—Silver Springs, 60 m. N.W. of De Land. There's a chain of placid lagoons there, whose floor is riddled with vast pits 30 to 40 ft. deep & covered with strange marine vegetation. In some of the pits are the huge bones of prehistoric monsters—& in one is a weed-crusted ship's boat which tradition associates with the early Spanish explorers. I saw these things from a glass-bottomed boat. Out of the lagoons flows the

Silver River—as typical a tropic stream as the Congo or Amazon. Palms, cypresses, & trailing moss & vines on the banks, & alligators, turtles, & snakes here and there. I took a 10-mile launch trip on it. ¶ Nearly broke, so will have to cut out some of the intended stops on the way north—though I expect to see Grandson Belknap a few days. Trust you will have a pleasant vacation, diversified by as much travel as you can manage.

Regards & best wishes—

E'ch-Pi-El

Notes

1. *Front:* Oldest Frame House in U.S.A. / Located on St. George Street / St. Augustine, Fla.

[12] [ALS, JHL]

St. Augustine, Fla.,
June 28, 1934.

Dear Helen:—

By this time you will have received the postcard telling of the transfer of my vacational activities to ancient St. Augustine for a week. That week, alas, has now reached its final day; since tonight I take the coach for Charleston. I shall not be able to stay in Charleston any length of time, since my entire cash quota for the residue of the trip is precisely $24.68 (for hotels, food, local carfare when necessary, & all incidentals) in addition to coach fare. If I spend it all at the start, I shan't be able to stop in Washington, Philadelphia, & New York . . . . I've already had to cut out the idea of going up the Hudson to see Bernard Dwyer. But I ought to get two full days in Charleston by stopping over night at the Y—I shall get in before dawn tomorrow, have all that day—& all the next if I stop. Then, at 8:45 p.m. of the second day, I shall take the Richmond coach. That will reach Richmond at 8:30 a.m., & I shall have a day amidst the boyhood scenes of Poe. If necessary, I could make Washington in the evening; but I hope I can stop over one night & make the Washington trip the next day—with a pause of a few hours at ancient Fredericksburg. In Washington I shall have to stop one or two nights in order to pay various promised calls—then a night coach to Philadelphia, getting in at dawn. (I shiver to think of the North again!) In old Philadelphia I shall do plenty of exploring during the day, & in the afternoon will reluctantly board the stage-coach for decadent Manhattan. There, if I have any cash left, I shall pause a few days to see Belknap & the gang. If broke, I shall simply continue on to Providence's ancient hill.

In view of the descriptive & pictorial matter inflicted on you last year, it will scarcely be necessary to describe St. Augustine in detail. You can imagine the charm, for a lifelong antiquarian, inherent in a town founded when

Shakespeare was one year old—& still having houses which were 50 years old when the first load of Pilgrims landed on Plymouth Rock. One can visualise the lone Spanish outpost on the tropic wilderness coast which Drake stormed & sacked in 1586, & against which the guns of Moore (of S.C. 1702), Palmer (1725), & Oglethorpe (1740–1742) thundered in vain. Even then it had the same street system that it has now—narrow lanes parallel to the waterfront & leading into a central plaza. The houses were plain & dignified—of coquina stone [formed by action of water on small shells, & quarried on Anastasia Island off the coast] with wooden upper stories & balconies, & having high walled gardens & low circular walls or fountains. Many of them remain just the same today. After 1590 some great mansions were built—with courtyards or patios in the rear, & with heavily pillared arcades & outside stairways on the courtyard side. These greatly recall the houses of New Orleans, which were built under Spanish influence, despite the French population. Of these the Governor's mansion (1591), now the post office; the Treasury building (1690)—later a private residence & now open as a museum; & the house (1755) now serving as a public library are among the most notable survivors. The massive stone fort—successor to many temporary ones—was built in the 17th & 18th centuries, & is today the "show place" of the town. The sunswept terreplain of this vast stronghold—with its splendid seaward vista—is my chief reading, writing, & loafing place in St. Augustine. The venerable city gates are likewise fascinating—& the old graveyards are a study in themselves. No skulls, cherubs, urns, & weeping willows here, but curious crosses & every sort of odd slab & monument & tomb. Oddly enough, the English in Savannah copied many of these bizarre Spanish mortuary paraphernalia, despite the presence of thoroughly normal English tombstones in Charleston (as far N. of Savannah as St. Augustine is S.) The cemeteries of St. Augustine are the most neglected I have ever beheld. In one of them may be seen the tomb of Don Antonio Francisco Sanchez de Mier (d. 1825)—cracked wide open & exposing an empty cypress-wood coffin. But the charm of old San Agustin cannot be captured in any one feature. It is diffusive, intangible, & atmospheric—old lanes & gardens, great spreading live-oaks, sagging balconies, fortress towers, luxuriant palms, & all the other attributes of an ancient subtropical outpost. These last few evenings a great round moon has added to the magic of the spectacle—beckoning me across the Bridge of Lions & the level sands of Anastasia Island to a deserted beach, where the effect of moonlight on the open ocean is positively beyond description. Nothing in sight but silver-lighted sand & sea & sky—plus the stately lighthouse far to the south. Another marvellous effect is that of sunset from any point shewing the pinnacles of St. Augustine in the distance against the west. It is magnificent from the Bridge of Lions, where I often sit & write, but still more so from the base of a long lagoon which stretches south from the main hotel district. From that vantage-point one may see the baroque spires of the gaudy

Hotel Ponce de Leon softened by distance, & vividly companioned by the huge Byzantine dome of Flagler's ostentatious Victorian church. Under these circumstances, the gaudy buildings take on both dignity & enchantment—looming up beyond the lagoon against the flaming northwest like the domes & minarets of a fabulous Arabian city—perhaps that never-found Irem, or City of Pillars,[1] which was builded by the Djinns before the coming of mankind to the earth. One feels a poignant sense of adventurous expectancy, as if this far, ethereal city held unguessed wonders about to be unveiled—& it is with regret that one realises how completely a nearer approach, or even a change of light, will ruin the illusion. Just at this moment I was interrupted by one of the most peculiar characters I ever saw in my life—who marched dignifiedly up to the Plaza bench on which I am writing & opened a conversa tion in the broadest Pennsylvania German dialect. He was about 60 years old, with bushy iron-grey beard & shaven upper lip, & was roughly though not untidily attired. Observing the rapid scratching of my fountain pen, he took his cue therefrom: "Saay, stranger, air yew writin' home? If ye are, yew tell the folks that you've just met a man in the Plaza at St. Augustine who ain't washed his feet in 45 years, & the Board o' Health can't make him!" Somewhat astonished, I very tamely rejoined something like "How extraordinary—quite a record—was it an election bet?" Whereupon the Personage continued: "I come from Lancaster, Pennsylvania. I'm a Dunkard [old Penn-German religious sect like the Baptists—they have an old church (1702) in Germantown which I've seen & will see again when I pass through Phila.]. I used to be a travellin' salesman on the road, & I made good money—enough to retire on. But you tell the folks you've just met a man who ain't washed his feet in 45 years, & the Board o' Health can't make him!" Before I could further interrogate this exponent of piety & resolution he had begun to drift haughtily on—& I did not seek to detain him. Obedient to his command, I shall certainly "tell the folks" when writing my daily diary-postcard to my aunt later this afternoon! St. Augustine is quite a haven for odd characters—that's why I fit in with the atmosphere so well.

But to resume after this interruption—one striking thing here is the Indian burial-ground just unearthed some distance north of the city gates—on the site of the old Indian village of Seloy, later called Nombre de Dios by the Spaniards. The skeletons rest with folded hands, evidently so placed by the Franciscan fathers whose proteges the natives were. They will not be removed, but will lie just as found—staring sightlessly upward row on row, each body & its adjacent earth protected by a cement boundary, & the whole covered with a suitable building. Thus the public will be able for evermore to view exhumed skeletons *in situ*—a macabre privilege not often available in the past. The effect is really quite gruesome. The discovery occurred 6 weeks ago—in the park marking the supposed landing-place of Ponce de Leon in 1513. Savants from the Smithsonian Institution have been down to see the osseous reliques, & seem to regard the find as one of considerable importance.

These various mortuary topics seem to fit in gruesomely well with your recent sombre reflections—though in a sense they ought to subtract from the force of the latter, insomuch as they tend to exhibit death in a sort of large-scale, impersonal perspective—part of the ceaseless kaleidoscope of historic drama & natural change.

It would seem to me that the cure for a feeling of oppression like yours—oppression at the thought of inevitable human losses, & of the often meaningless ceremonials attending the disposal of mortal remains—ought to lie in an increased sense of *objectivity*, & a heightened realisation of the true proportions of the universe & of the insignificance of mankind & all its affairs therein. There is no need of drugging oneself with immortality-myths in order to be tolerably contented during the brief span one lives. If we had never heard of the extravagant promises of the various religions, & of the sentimentalised conception of human ties based upon these promises, we would not be so disturbed by those inevitable results of change which we know must come to all. There is no reason why anyone *should* be sure of retaining all the landmarks—either human or non-human—to which one has grown used & of which one has grown fond; so that the realistic analyst accustoms himself from the very first to the idea of tantalising impermanence in every department of life. Parents & friends die; beloved houses & landscapes become hopelessly altered or destroyed; social milieux & other environmental supports decay & become metamorphosed; & one's self grows old, exiled from the beauty, vividness, & adventurous expectancy of youth, & doomed to be a more or less impatiently tolerated onlooker. These are the basic & inescapable conditions of life—but just *because* they are basic & inescapable we can build certain palliatives or defences against them. Knowing that nothing & nobody is certain of lasting, we can wisely refrain from pinning too much of our hold on life to any one object—human or otherwise—or limited range of objects. We can cultivate the *sense of pageantry & panorama*, & think of the terrestrial scene in terms of historical movements & races instead of in terms of specific individuals. Not that we need to abandon all kindliness & affection toward individuals; but that we ought to remember how transient & infinitesimal all individuals are, & to avoid making our entire sense of equilibrium & contentment dependent upon the life & proximity of a few definite persons. The stream of race & tradition is deeper, stabler, & more important than the atoms which compose it. Memory & objectivity join hands in making existence a little more tolerable. When we bring ourselves to realise that *time* is only one element in an infinitely complex cosmos, we tend to protest less when something that *is* becomes something that *has been*. The difference between "is-ness" & "has been-ness" tends to vanish—we feel that the mere quality of duration does not amount to so much after all. Why should a thing be "immortal" in time, when the basic fact of its *having existed* is virtually equivalent so far as the larger universe is concerned? The difference between a friend who *has lived* & one who *still lives* is not as vast as one might imagine. Both exist as images in the mind, & may be regarded with equal affection. The same is true of a house or scene or other beloved object or condition. Of course, the change is unfortunate; for a past object does not impinge as responsively on our consciousness as a present one; but philosophy teaches us that a certain amount of unfortunateness is absolutely inevitable. When we are all braced to expect, as a matter of course, a certain amount of misfortune, we are infinitely better able to bear it. We know that virtually every pleasant thing must pass—so when one goes, we console ourselves by enjoying the many other pleasant things which are generally left. The greater our philosophic & aesthetic expansion, the more sources of contentment we shall generally be able to find in life. When we lose individual things, the drama of the whole racial pageant is left to us—& so on. And so with the tragedy of personal ageing & of changing milieu. In these matters the great healer is the ability to become predominantly *objective*—to cease to think about oneself—or one's relation to the surrounding pattern—at all, but to cultivate an impersonal *spectator's* interest in the dramatic seething visible on every hand. What if one's familiar landmarks *are* washed away? What if one *is* grey & ugly & stranded in the listless, beauty-bereft deserts of age or middle-age? The sense of deprivation in such cases is infinitely lessened by a sort of psychological self-annihilation—a decision *that one no longer exists at all* except as a spectator, in a darkened auditorium, to an external drama. As soon as one completes this self-annihilation, he can regard the external pageant with a genuine interest but little tinged with regret at his own lack of a pleasant connexion with it. Then, too, there is the tremendous refuge offered by pleasant aesthetic & intellectual activities, either creative or appreciative. This boon really has three separate phases, any one of which can be a substantial aid. First, there is the inestimable benefit of *merely being busy* with something which one is able to consider worth doing. When we are busy at anything at all we generally have no time to brood over our misfortunes. Second, our activities are often intrinsically pleasant & satisfying—sometimes poignantly so. And third—a great deal of art & philosophy is consciously & specifically of a consolatory or escape-opening nature. That is especially true of the weird art of which Klarkash-Ton & I are so fond. The real raison d'etre of that art is to give one a temporary illusion of emancipation from the galling & intolerable tyranny of time, space, change, & natural law. If we can give ourselves for even a brief moment the illusory sensation that some law of the ruthless cosmos has been—or could be—suspended or defeated, we acquire a certain flush of triumphant emancipation comparable in its comforting power to the opiate dreams of religion. Indeed, religion itself is merely a pompous formalisation of fantastic art. Its disadvantage is that it demands an *intellectual* belief in the impossible, while fantastic art does not.

After all—for the average person life is not by any means as bad as it might be. Of course, real *happiness* is only a rare & transient phenomenon; but when we cease to expect this extravagant extreme, we usually find a very tolerable fund of mild contentment at our disposal. True, people & landmarks vanish, & one grows old & out of the more glamourous possibilities & expectancies of life; but over-against these things there remains the fact that the world contains an almost inexhaustible store of objective beauty & potential interest & drama . . . . . all at the disposal of anyone philosophic enough to go through the process of psychological self-annihilation. To divide one's interests & affections rationally; & to get so interested in the drama of what's going on that one forgets one's own part—or lack of part—in the environing turmoil—these are the secrets of sensible living. We would not resent the inevitable greyness & disappointments of life so much, if religion & sentimentality did not so viciously teach us to expect more. This false teaching of orthodox tradition is something which ought to be done away with—though I hope it can be disposed of without destroying other & really valuable parts of our traditional heritage. To sum up—if one can be sensible & realistic, there's no reason why one shouldn't have a decently good time out of life if one can be sure (as I wish to hades I could!) of an income equivalent to $10.00 a week till death.

Regarding funerals & interments—there are two sides to the matter. On the one hand, it is undeniably appropriate that relatives & friends should have a chance to register their esteem for a deceased person; but on the other hand, the existing ceremonies (conducted over a decomposing corpse which has scant meaning after the *person*—the *mode of motion* in the brain cells—has ceased to exist) are frankly barbaric & superstitious . . . . . originating in savage rites designed to make cadavers stay put in their graves instead of stalking stiffly among the living by night. To my mind, *cremation* is the only sane & tasteful way to dispose of a body—& it surely ought to be done without publicity or ostentation. A non-religious *memorial service* might in many cases be highly appropriate—but its nature ought to be determined by circumstances, & it certainly ought not to centre around any material fetish so crude & unimaginative as an urnful of calcined phosphates or a coffin-full of glassy-eyed nitrogenous carbon compounds! However—life is so trivial at best that it doesn't pay anybody to worry about the ultimate disposal of his bones. What does it matter what happens to the cast-off reliquiae of any one atom in the cosmos? The person himself no longer exists—so the business is of no primary concern to him. They can dump my carcass down the sewer for all I care—I'll be out of it! Of course there is an element of aesthetic appropriateness which may justly give each individual certain wishes in the matter of his final rites, & I heartily endorse the idea of leaving instructions regarding such.

I'd advocate cremation, & a non-religious memorial service for family & very close friends only. My point is that the matter isn't really important enough to worry about—especially when one is young & not likely to be a subject of mortuary rites for 60 years or more. I am reminded of an argument with a friend some years ago on the topic of burial—he was only 40 & in good health, but was actually acutely worried about the sort of funeral he would get. Himself a sturdy agnostic, he felt that he could not stop his very proper Methodist wife from giving him an orthodox funeral—& the notion preyed on him. I simply laughed him out of his perplexity with a reiteration of the query "what of it"? Would the irony of such a thing be any greater than any of the numberless ironies & inconsistencies of life? As a rational cynic, conscious that he would not be existing when his wife staged her harmless circus over his reliquiae, he ought to be amused rather than distressed at the prospect. Of course, it would be all right to leave instructions—maybe his wife *would* follow them after all . . . . & maybe he'd outlive her . . . . but surely there was no use in getting excited over trifles . . . . . & anyhow, he might not die for another forty years! Well—he saw the point, & joined me in my smile at the matter. He's six years nearer death now, & his wife is still alive & pious, but he doesn't worry any more![2] He just shrugs his shoulders & leaves the whole thing to Fate—which is, in the last analysis, about all anybody can really do about anything! And so I'd advocate others to do. There are enough worries in life without carrying them over into death. What we don't know won't hurt us!

Little Bobby Barlow, my erstwhile host, certainly is quite a boy—& he will be effusively appreciative of any picture of his idol which you can send him. Just now he is having Klarkash-Ton lend him a representative assortment of his more ambitious pictures—such as C A S circulated amongst the gang in 1926—& before he's through with them he'll undoubtedly buy one or more. Perhaps I told you (or perhaps C A S has) that he has already purchased the gorgeously colourful "Beyond Cathay". Did I also mention that he has named his windowless treasure-closet—where he keeps all his rare books & magazines—"The Vaults of Yoh-Vombis", after Klarkash-Ton's story? He is just now delighting in a genealogy of Tsathoggua sent him by that dark god's distinguished high-priest!

Your coming trip to the Sierra Nevada sounds enviable to the nth degree, & I feel sure the simple living & majestic environment will do much toward banishing all melancholy & mortuary thoughts. There will, of course, be an element of the strenuous; but the sense of adventure & liberation will undoubtedly make all the hardships worth undergoing. From having seen the Presidential Range in New Hampshire I can form some idea of the rugged vistas you will have—& C A S has sent me many cards eloquent of Californian grandeur. Permit me to wish you an uniformly pleasant trip, with many a surprise in the form of gorgeous vistas & fancy-awaking incidents.

Glad to hear that Young Melmoth is actually scheduled to make the California trip, & hope he may rearrange his programme in such a way as to arrive at a convenient season—even if it takes a geological, archaeological, or other expedition to manage it! At present I believe he is home in St. Paul—where he ought to be darned glad to be after his long sojourn amidst the freaks & soaks of Manhattan & Greenwich Village.

What you say of Lord Belknap's—or rather, Comrade Belknap's—possible round-the-world travel debut astonishes me vastly, & I surely hope he can be egged on to a realisation of the dream. I've urged such a thing on the little imp for half a decade—& if you can turn the trick you will certainly qualify as a sorceress worthy of Averoigne or Zothique or Hyperborea or any other region where sorcery flourishes! Most assuredly I shan't mention having heard of the idea—or do anything else to scare him off. Revolutions in ways of living have to come in gradual steps, & be semi-unconscious—while the separate phases usually need to be half impromptu & seemingly spontaneous. One of Sonny's barriers against travel is a nervous fear that his mother will not be safe (from heart disease or getting run over by a motor or being knocked on the head by a robber) unless he is around. He thinks that she ought never to be alone in the house, or to go out on the street alone, & he is afraid his father will not see that she is thus guarded every minute. Whenever he is away for an afternoon or evening he has moments of worry for fear his mother has gone out alone or has been left alone in the house. Of course this is a sheer neurosis, but it will have to be overcome by gradual stages. I am convinced that it hs this, rather than any actual dread of lone travel in itself, which keeps him so closely tied at home. Just now he is certainly shewing signs of an emergence into wider & more independent ways—& everything ought certainly to be done to give the process a gentle & imperceptible encouragement. Yes—I fancy that possession of an independent financial competence would do much to modify his bolshevistic leanings, since he is one to form opinions emotionally & aesthetically—from personal experience & immediate appeal—rather than impersonally & at long range.

The case of your friend who became a communist is certainly pathetic in the extreme—though it must not be thought that all communistic belief is synonymous with deterioration. Actually, there are many persons of the highest character & most impeccable background who honestly think that a general communistic programme forms the only ultimate solution of the present breakdown of capitalism—a belief which they derive from the abstract & impersonal study of national resources & their distribution; & which does not, of course, necessarily involve any endorsement of the sudden social changes & absurd formal "ideologies" advocated by the orthodox Marxians & discontented European riffraff. Such persons do not wish to see all traditions & settled ways of living ripped up indiscriminately, but they do feel that mankind will not be able to continue its civilisation unless its stagnating inequalities of resources & opportunities are eventually diminished through some far-sighted plan of distribution & some adequate way of enforcing that plan. To them, some sort of communism (in each case suited to the history & traditions of the race involved) seems the only way to enforce a civilisation-preserving economic plan—hence they believe it will have to come in the end . . . . . though without any wholesale repudiation of general folkways & preferably without any violent revolution. The number of these honest & analytical communists or semi-communists seems vastly on the increase, & I cannot but fear that they will play into the hands of the wild & unscrupulous bolshevik upheavers. But they must not be confused with the disintegrated personalities who revolt savagely against civilisation & clamour for a totally new order. These philosophic "communists" are not to be found in Greenwich Village or the ghetto, but in some of the choicest & most dignified American homes—I've just encountered one amongst the most ancient & settled stock of St. Augustine! I don't agree with their equalitarianism, but I have to admit that they are honest theorists rather than morbid emotionalists or savagely atavistic "rebels". When a whole economic order is perishing through evolution & changed conditions—as laissez-faire capitalism is now doing under the impact of the machine age—it is no wonder that *every* possible substitute is soberly considered by responsible, intelligent, & personally far-sighted persons. Thus it is erroneous to fancy that there must be something the matter with anybody who believes in communism—that he must be a criminal, a foreigner, a savage throwback, or a psychopathic case. It is true, of course, that criminals, foreigners, throwbacks, nuts, & fools *do* flock to the banners of *any* cause even remotely connected with upheaval & change—since their disorganised & inferiority-conscious minds, so inadequate in *this* civilisation, always have a pitiful feeling that they'd be better off under *some other*—*any* other—regime. But the converse is not true—for there are many sincere advocates of change who are not at all inadequate under the dying order, & who call for modifications not from any personal standpoint, but simply because they perceive that the present system is unable to survive in the long run. They want a new order speedily or gradually installed, so that a general collapse to savage disorganisation & anarchy may be avoided. To sum up the matter, one can't condemn a whole theory or point of view merely because one has encountered some unfortunate or undesirable individuals connected with it. Attitudes & perspectives & race movements are greater than any of the individuals exemplifying them.

For my part, I hope it will not be necessary to resort to communism; since so much of the communistic programme—including its most culturally destructive parts—wastes its energy on the quest for an *absolute equalitarianism* which is *not in the least necessary for the restoration of economic equilibrium*, & which indeed has many intrinsically undesirable features. Some change *must* have come, since in an intensively mechanised world *unsupervised* capitalism leads inevitably to the grotesque cornering of resources, & to an increasingly vast amount of *permanent* unemployment, even in the most "prosperous" times.

Belknap is right *thus far*. But to my mind, the *gradually* modifying influences of a programme of government supervision of wealth & industry—a programme involving *no major social or cultural overturn,* but resembling rather old-time socialism, modern fascism, & the Roosevelt New Deal carried somewhat further—will solve the problem infinitely better . . . . & infinitely less destructively . . . . than any new "ideology" or ruthless "proletarian dictatorship" could even begin to do. In the case of the United States, I believe that the only way to secure a workable economic order is to begin modifying in a small way, & gradually increase the scope of governmental control before either the crazy old-line Republican "individualists" or the equally crazy modern bolshevik malcontents can have a chance to wreck the whole works. Just how far it may be necessary to go, nobody can say at the present moment. I fancy the government will eventually have to take over & operate on a non-profit basis the largest utilities & industries, yet do not see why a small-scale retail capitalism cannot linger on indefinitely. It seems to me that the present administration—despite a few of the errors unavoidable in any programme of experimentation—is moving in exactly the right direction; so that until it exhibits some very contrary tendency, I can be quite accurately set down as a thorough Roosevelt man . . . . . & this despite the fact that my forbears were without exception Federalists, Whigs, & Republicans in the respective days of those parties (or modifications of a party).

But all this does not, of course, make the case of your friend any the less disastrous & pathetic. It seems very clear that she was the victim of an unsettled, ill-adjusted temperament from the start; & that with her, communism was merely an incident in a sort of neurotic revolt against normal surroundings. I doubt if any alien taint in her heredity could be held responsible, since biology does not work in such conveniently explicable channels. It is really more folklore than fact to suppose that all anti-social or anti-cultural tendencies in a person are due to "bad blood" or to a "foreign" or "peasant" heritage. Actually, our social & cultural attitudes are infinitely more environmental than heredity; whilst foreign or peasant blood seldom predisposes one toward any aberration therefrom. If an inferior strain* in one's ancestry exists, it is much more likely to make one merely stupid or vicious—or both—within the accustomed social circle, than to inspire any especial divergence therefrom. In general—& especially in countries where stratification has never been rigid—arbitrary social caste is seldom much of an index to intrinsic superiority or inferiority. Cases of individual deterioration of various kinds (in some purely nervous, in some mental, in some emotional—producing a wide variety of eccentric, aberrant, & occasionally repulsively anti-social types) occur constantly in the best of families—including the very oldest & most unmixed; so that it is

---

*by that I mean *genuinely* or biologically inferior—i.e., with definitely malorganised brain-tissue or definitely coarse or twisted emotions

needless to look for a foreign or socially inferior element in any subject's heredity. Indeed—even if such an element did exist, the chances would be only slight that that was the real cause of the deterioration. I could cite a pitiful number of cases of personal disintegration which have occurred in households of the most unquestionably fine ancestry—indeed, the most pitiful case of all was one in which the heritage involved was the least open to question. Incidentally—when we reflect upon the strong element of ruthlessness, selfishness, arrogance, & self-indulgence which—together with good manners, taste, intelligence, responsibility, & a certain sense of honour—once formed a typical part of the aristocratic character, we need not wonder at the degenerate specimens now produced by the old families . . . . specimens in whom the old instincts of self-gratification & unrestraint are forced by social change to seek new outlets. The wonder is that old-time aristocratic blood does not constitute a definite taint! This is especially true of the very ancient & immemorially ruthless & vicious aristocracies of continental Europe.

In most cases, though, I fancy that personal disintegration is caused by factors far more local—individual physiological accident, especially as affecting the functioning of the obscure endocrine glands on which most of our emotions & personality depend, & unfortunate accidents of environment caused by lack of understanding of the subject's particular nervous type. In the case of your friend, I'd imagine that she had a badly working nerve & gland system to start with, & that it may or may not have suffered through lack of the scientific application of the best psychological treatment. Probably no *known* method of treatment would have been of any use, so that one may refer the trouble altogether to obscure physiological malformation or malfunctioning. Now while of course hereditary accident—the way the genes & chromosomes of thousands of ancestors known & unknown happened to get juggled in her especial case—must have had something to do with this trouble, it would be fallacious to attribute the thing to any *specific* hereditary cause such as foreign blood. That's not the way these things work—as we may see by the vast number of similar cases where hereditary is unquestioned. All we can say is, that when the countless varieties of germ-plasm that form even the best of us get combined in a certain way—a way absolutely impossible to foresee, even by the strictest eugenist, & therefore absolutely impossible to avoid once in a while—the result is an individual with faulty nerve & gland functioning, & therefore with emotions departing from the race's recognised norm. Other causes of this individual aberration are wholly recent—disease acquired & transmitted by parents or immediate ancestors; congenital malformation of the embryonic or infant subject; physiological accidents to subject involving organic lesions or traumata, & so on. The race will always breed its pitiful odds & ends, & these will always be doubly pitiful when their aberrations are linked with lofty heritage or distinguished intellectual or aesthetic capacity. We weep at a tragedy like the late Hart Crane[3]—but find a saving grain of comedy when aberration is linked with stolidity or mediocrity, as in the case of my unwashed Dunkard caller of an hour ago. What a piece of work is man!

The problem presented to your friend's family by her unruly tendencies & parasitic bolshevik spouse is certainly a tough one—& it would take a diplomat, psychologist, attorney, & policeman combined to make any headway with it. Poor old grandfather—I can feel for him! It is conceivable that middle age—if one can wait patiently—will sober up the wayward subject & bring a new perspective in its train. When—or if—that occurs, she might possibly be persuaded to divorce her evil genius & settle down to a life of quiet endeavour in some field or other—music, art, teaching, social service, or things equally within the range of her many talents. But one never can tell. There's no use in harbouring the false optimism which declares all problems solvable. Some troubles simply have no solution, & that's all there is to it. However, intelligence & philosophic detachment can usually help to make anyone's problem just a bit lighter than it would otherwise be.

And right here I must pause—for coach time approaches, & if I don't get my diary-card written home now, it won't get a St. Augustine postmark.[4] My coach leaves at 5:20 p.m. & gets into Charleston at 3 a.m. I'll finish this in the 'bus station at Charleston while waiting for the dawn!

P.S. Did I mention that (despite a rainy period in De Land which washed away the road & caused lakes & rivers to rise alarmingly) *every day* of my sojourn in St. Augustine was hot & sunny? I never saw such a piece of luck!

July [*sic*] 29—
Charleston, in His Majesty's
Province of South-Carolina

God Save the King! Back on soil whose heritage is old England's instead of Spain's! What a trip! I dozed on the 'bus & crushed the edge of the crown of the new 50¢ straw hat I bought in Savannah on the down trip . . . . but I shall continue to wear it. Nor did I finish this epistle in the 'bus station. Thought I'd go to the Y & register for the coming night—incidentally leaving my valise & getting a free shower—when the honest old night clerk bowled me over by offering me the *advance* use of the room which I took for the *next* night . . . without extra charge! A true Southern gentleman, by Gad! The joke is, that while he thought I was getting only the tail end of a night's use of the room, I was actually retiring at about the hour I do anyway! So I hit the hay & arose afresh this morning at eleven—with my room all ready for a second night, & only a dollar off the scanty roll. Present funds—$23.43—half a dollar of which is tied up at the Y for a key deposit. That ought to let me make the major stops scheduled at the outset of this epistle—though it'll be down to about $23 even when I hit the Richmond coach tomorrow night. Got a card from Sonny saying that the maid had left, & that therefore he can't act as my host in N.Y. Hence I may not stop in the metropolis at all . . . . & if I have any cash, may shoot up to West Shokan. Or I may go straight home . . . or I might stop with Loveman a few days if he has space for a lodger. Well—it doesn't matter.

As I come to complete this interminable document, I see that I really covered all the necessary points in St. Augustine. Much as I hated to leave that exotic outpost, I shall hate worse to leave old CHARLESTON. It was like a homecoming to get back to English soil—Georgian doorways & steeples, & skulls, cherubs, & urns in the churchyards . . . . . more northerly flora . . . . no tall palms, & very little Spanish moss. I spent the morning wandering through the ancient streets & churchyards, & got a 10¢ ice cream breakfast at the old pharmacy at King & Broad Sts. which was founded in 1782 by Dr. Andrew Turnbull—the ill-starred planter of New Smyrna, Fla., to whom I referred in my preceding epistle. I must get a postcard of the pharmacy to send to a lineal descendant of Dr. Turnbull's whom I met in St. Augustine. Am now on a bench in the Battery next to the sea—writing letters & trying to augment my coat of St. Augustine tan. Sorry to see that some sort of blight or drought has denuded some of the ancient live-oaks of the park area behind me since last April. By the way—pray tell Son that I met a most exquisite & diminutive representative of his species in the 'bus station this morning—just a purring handful of black & white, & as playful as a little dynamo. Bless my soul! Despite the ungodliness of the hour I had to stop & play with the little rascal for a full fifteen minutes—& I shall be around to see him again! Also tell Son that Jack (the kitten at Barlow's who ate a poison snake & was half-paralysed by it) is virtually his vigorous self again, except that he carries his head a little to one side as if the nerves or muscles of his neck troubled him. I hope Son himself is well.

Good old Charleston! How can I leave it? Anyhow, I have the rest of to-day & all of tomorrow to circulate around its venerable lanes & among its moss-grown tombs. It is curious how, of all places save Providence, this seems most like *home* to me. And yet I never set foot in it till April 27, 1930!

And so it goes. I surely hope you will have a delightful Sierran vacation, & trust that both Vandreian & Belnapian visits may materialise. Regards to C A S when you see him—I wrote him this week from St. Aug.

Best wishes, & apologies for length.

Yr obt h^ble Servt

E'ch-Pi-El.

P.S. Enclosed is a folder describing that picturesque Silver Springs & Silver River region which I mentioned on my postcard.

Notes

1. Entry 47 in HPL's commonplace book concerns Irem. It is mentioned in "The Nameless City," "The Call of Cthulhu," "History of the 'Necronomicon,'" and "The

Last Test" (with Adolphe de Castro).

2. It is unclear to whom HPL is referring. Evidently the person in question was born in 1888.

3. Crane committed suicide in April 1932. HPL had met him several times.

4. Apparently a card to Annie Gamwell. Non-extant.

[13]   [ALS, JHL]

66 College St.,
Providence, R.I.,
July 15, 1934

Dear Helen:—

Home again at last! Meanwhile I trust you duly received my reply to your earlier letter—written largely in St. Augustine & mailed from Charleston. I had two days in old Charleston, both crowded to the limit with congenial sightseeing. Then, having taken the 8:45 p.m. coach for Richmond, I had another day amidst the boyhood scenes of Poe. I not only covered Poe's urban haunts, but went out to my favourite Maymont Park beside the James—an exquisite landscape garden (Italian & Japanese) laid out on the wooded bluffs & ravines, & once forming a private estate. What is more, I found a really excellent cheap hotel only two doors from the site of the old Allan home at Main & 5th St., where Poe grew up! The next day—July 2—I moved on to ancient Fredericksburg—Gen. Washington's home town, which has changed but little since his day. The old brick houses with their transomed doorways still drowse as of yore beside the shallow (but once navigable) Rappahanock; disturbed only once—by the shells & slaughter of the War between the States in 1862. On the edge of the town is the old country-seat of Col. Lewis—Genl. Washington's brother-in-law—while close by is a great oak-shaded rock overlooking a verdant valley, where the general's venerable mother used to sit & read by the hour. Near the spot—Meditation Rock—old Mrs. Washington now lies buried beneath an imposing granite slab. Her house in the village—given her by her distinguished son in 1771—is still in good condition & open as a museum. Meditation Rock is a favourite spot of mine, & there I sat—reading the N Y Times—until it was time to take the Washington coach. I spent two days in Washington, during which I did the following things that I had never done before—(a) explored the interior of the capitol, (b) explored the interior of the impressive Pan-American Union, (c) visited Rock Creek Park, (d) ascended the Washington Monument (stupendous view!), & (e) inspected the furnished interior of Arlington—the old Custis-Lee mansion on the heights across the river in Virginia. This latter place is utterly delightful. I saw it unfurnished in 1925, but it has now been restored just as it was in the early 1800's, & forms a perfect example of an old Virginia plantation house. I dreaded to take the Philadelphia coach & leave this last outpost of the south behind! However, I made the most of my single day in Philadelphia; exploring ancient Germantown with its stone houses, seeing a bit of the awesome Wissahickon Gorge, & taking in the colonial high spots of the city proper—many of which remain, though scores of old landmarks vanish each year. One narrow alley near the Delaware (originally Elfret Alley—now part of Cherry St.) is *entirely* as it was in colonial times—houses, pavements, & all. There is a drainage channel among the old cobblestones in the centre of the street. But the principal Philadelphia sight, beyond a doubt, was the Poe house at N. 7th & Spring Garden Sts., where the bard dwelt from 1842 to 1844. This is a small brick cottage amidst a garden in the rear of a larger house. I had seen it often before; but a few months ago it was restored & opened as a museum, so that I now entered & explored it for the first time. It is certainly fascinating in the extreme—furnished exactly as in Poe's day, though only two or three pieces (notably a chair & a desk) were ever really his. In the adjacent large house an ample collection of Poe reliques—comparing favourably with those in the Poe shrine at Richmond & the Fordham cottage in N.Y.—has been assembled; & here I saw copies of nearly all the magazines containing the first publication of the various tales & poems. The whole thing is really vastly impressive—& in the twilight it would not have been difficult to fancy the dark singer back amidst the scenes he once knew so well.

That same evening I reluctantly took the coach for N.Y., where I found Belknap & his parents about to depart for Asbury Park & Ocean Grove over the week-end. At their invitation I went along with them, & had some interesting arguments with Young Stalin amidst the murmur of waves & sea-winds. I had no cash for a prolonged Manhattan stay, so looked up no one else save Loveman—with whom I spent an interesting evening, & who quite overwhelmed me by giving me a choice object from his private museum—a horn carving of a slim black bird poised for flight, made by a Yankee seaman in the India trade, & shewing the influence of Oriental art traditions. I had long admired this object—which I call "The Bird of Space", & whose flights I insist must reach out into the illimitable cosmos beyond the solar system & the galaxies known to human eyes.

At midnight July 9–10 I took the Providence coach—& was well-nigh paralysed by the first cold weather I had struck since my southern trip. I beheld an exquisite sunrise over western Rhode Island, & finally saw the distant spires & domes of Old Providence blazing in the golden morning light. Home again!

Since then I have been reading up accumulated papers & magazines, & trying to get various neglected matters straightened out. As usual, I do most of my reading & writing in the open air—taking the materials along in a satchel. I am now on a bench in a very pleasant park in the southern part of the town. It is really quite amusing to consider how *strange* my native northern landscape seems to me after my long weeks in tropical Florida. Even Charleston seemed a bit barren after De Land & St. Augustine; while Richmond—with no live-oaks or Spanish moss—struck me as veritably subarctic! It was in Fredericksburg that I first became thoroughly reconciled & reoriented to the northern scene—a scene which is actually more delicately beautiful than any tropic vista, & which has the added advantage of resembling the old-world landscape around which our hereditary traditions are entwined. By the time I reëntered New England I was fully able to appreciate & rejoice in its rolling hills, rock-strown pastures, stone walls, winding roads, low farmhouse gables, & white, elm-embowered village steeples. I found my aunt in extremely good health—going everywhere without either a cane or a perceptible limp. And more—at your stopping-place of a year ago there is an utterly exquisite *new* kitten (born last month, & not to be confused with the February kittens I mentioned) whom I am borrowing on every possible occasion. His name is Samuel Perkins, & he is coal-black except for faint traces of a tiger substratum. Never have I glimpsed a quainter little rascal—he looks like a bear-cub of paperweight size! He is still a bit wobbly on his feet, but is even now beginning to shew signs of playfulness. I hope to have him as a frequent visitor henceforward, & can imagine how fascinating he will be in a fortnight or so, when he is stronger & more active. The black-&-white February kitten has grown so rapidly as to be well-nigh indistinguishable from her similarly marked mamma!

But all these eastern vistas of tame & settled regions will no doubt seem very dull to you amidst your present rugged & majestic environment! I trust that your outing—both in Berkeley & in the Sierras—has so far proved not merely equal to, but far beyond, your expectations; & that the remainder may be not less delightful. I shall be interested to hear of the scenes & impressions you have encountered. And meanwhile I hope that the contemplated southern trip of your mother & sister may materialise without a hitch. Was there much New Orleans material in that bundle I sent last year? If not, & if your mother would like any booklets, folders, maps, or other pointers to help in formulating an itinerary, I'd be glad to lend items from my files. How far east is the voyage planned to extend? It would really be a shame to miss St. Augustine & Charleston—& anyhow, *Natchez* simply *must* be included. Did I send any folders of that? It is near enough New Orleans (200 or 250 m, I think) to be a logical part of any Crescent City trip. Mobile also is fascinating—though perhaps a trifle anticlimactic after Natchez & New Orleans. I suppose the route will also touch Sante F, & the pueblos of the Southwest—fascinating places which I have never seen.

Let me thank you exceedingly for the delightful snapshot in the garb of the 1850's—which has a reposeful grace reminiscent of saner, better-ordered times. The costume really is tremendously becoming, & I can imagine how well it must have been received at the "Gold Show" in "Woods' Dry Diggings". Klarkash-Ton sent me a booklet describing this colourful celebration, & I was extremely interested to learn more of the '48 & '49 background of old

Placer County. It is curious how taste in costume seems—roughly—to parallel taste in architecture. These costumes of the '40's & '50's had an aesthetic harmony which was soon lost amidst the freakish extravagances of the '70's—& in much the same way (although the decadence began sooner) the neo-classic & simple Gothic edifices of the '40's, which possessed an admirable dignity & rhythm of line, gradually gave way to the bauble-encrusted & jigsaw-mangled horrors of the post–Civil-War period. Speaking of pictures—if you'll let me know the De Land specimens which Klarkash-Ton won't hand over, I'll see that you get duplicates—since young Barlow still has the negatives. In fact, all you need to do is to tell which ones I sent you (I've forgotten which I sent to whom)—& I'll then ask Barlow to supply the rest. Meanwhile here is Barlow's first experiment with his *new* camera—a 5 × 7, although this portrait is cut down. It's a wonder the lens survived such a subject![1] You can retain this if you like—or relegate it to the waste-basket—since I have quite an ample supply. Ultimately Barlow wants to go quite deeply into art & trick photography—double exposures, retouching, &c—in order to create weird synthetic monsters & landscapes like those in the drawings of Klarkash-Ton. Yes— you'll certainly hear most gratefully from the kid if you send him that view of Klarkash-Ton with yourself & sister which he wants. He'll probably wear you to death with minute enquiries about his hero—for his worship generally tends to take a biographical form. Possibly I mentioned that he is intensively collecting data about the late Dr. Whitehead, with a view to issuing his collected letters with a biographical preface.[2] A highly remarkable child—only 16 last May, yet incredibly precocious & adultly thorough in many directions.

Regarding the sombre reflections of last month—I trust that your present trip, with its constant sequence of external objects of interest & its vivid variety of impressive, mankind-dwarfing landscapes, has done much to dispel them & to relegate their bases to a suitably insignificant place in the background. There is nothing like a combination of engrossing impressions & awesome natural scenery to restore one's sense of harmony & proportion. I hope, too, that my St. Augustine–Charleston epistle may have contained one or two suggestions calculated to minimise the formidable aspect of things. After all, nothing really matters in the ceaseless round of the limitless cosmos—a cosmos amidst which man & all organic life forms only the most trivial incident—except in the most local way; & this local teleology can hardly go beyond the reasonably harmonic adjustment of the individual to the forces within & behind him . . . . a state best achieved through a realistic facing of the conditions of existence, with all their inevitable frustrations & shortcomings, & a philosophic determination *not to expect more than the mediocre pittance of contentment which the cosmos actually has to offer.* Once we cease to maintain the extravagant & often grotesque demands upon life which ill-founded mythologies & ridiculous conventions of sentimentality have unfortunately taught us to maintain, we achieve a degree of resigned tranquillity amidst which we are free to busy ourselves with the infinite array of interesting things in the external world—the intrinsic beauty of nature & art, the drama of history & change, the stimulating play of intellect & imagination, & so on. And with these things at our disposal, we generally find (except when oppressed by unusual handicaps such as extreme poverty) that the process of being conscious brings enough rewards to repay us for the trouble of maintaining it. Some, indeed, are probably fortunate enough to derive even *more* pleasure from existence than they would from oblivion. Roughly speaking, I'd tend to say that of all the human race about half are just as well off alive as they would be dead. Another quarter would be better off dead, while the remaining quarter are distinctly better off alive than they would be dead. In general, the more interested in things *outside himself* a person is, the better time he is likely to have in the world. When anybody becomes introspective—constantly watching himself & his own emotions, & constantly worrying about the exact emotions of other people toward him—he is almost certain to become utterly miserable . . . . & useless to the community, to boot. That is really one of the best-defined forms of what we may call *decadence*. It is associated with the spineless & lethargic old age of the race or culture, & crops out continually in the literature & arts of a feeble or moribund group. There is altogether too much of this decadent introspectiveness in the art & thought of the present western world to make well-wishers of that world feel comfortable—although it is rather debatable just what, specifically, to do about it. I can sympathise with the basic wish of those dictatorial systems—like German Nazism—which try to discourage the neurotic art & literature of introspection & to foster in its place the healthy, extroverted, objective art which characterised our civilisation in its youth. It may be that such efforts to guide art are futile, since the well-springs of art are so deep & so bound up with historic conditions hard to change. Certainly, some of them are tremendously ridiculous & disastrously anti-cultural. But just the same one can understand why these national regenerators like Mussolini or Hitler or Mustapha Kemal[3] or Stalin try their hardest to promote an aesthetic atmosphere favourable to active objective life, contented social adjustment, & the healthy relative selflessness which encourages group enthusiasm, stamina, & progress toward a given collective end. The greatness of nations, like the happiness of individuals, undoubtedly rests on an *objective* habit of mind & emotions.

Concerning the relative merits of epistolary & personally present acquaintances—I fancy it is all a matter of individual temperament. Some people have a psychology which best fits them for first-hand social contacts; while others find that too much gregariousness brings out more of irritation than of interest, hence prefer to limit their contacts to that impersonal exchange of ideas which long-distance correspondence provides. Actually, human beings differ far more than is commonly assumed; so that many things which we popularly regard as simple & universal are in truth highly complex & infinitely varied. This is especially true of the motives & emotions lying behind human relations & acquaintanceship. Unintelligent tradition postulates some single mystical force called "friendship", & weaves a whole cycle of sentimental myth around it & its supposed properties; whereas in truth there is no such *one* thing—almost every separate case of human acquaintance & liking being due to some separate & individual combination of many dissimilar elements. If one takes any two cases of acquaintance or liking or mutual interest at random, the chances are that the motives & emotions behind each are totally dissimilar if not utterly antipodal. Only the *external* aspect—the fact that *some* sort of congeniality results—is similar, yet from that deceptive similarity any number of absurd folklore generalisations are made. For the most part, friendship is a device to magnify the ego. People seek others to serve as a sort of flattering mirror or sounding-board, so that they may appear enhanced in their own eyes. The average person acquires a sense of inferiority unless he has an audience to encourage & applaud him—hence much of the gregariousness of mankind. Other causes of human acquaintanceship are more primitive—an instinctive fear of solitude inherited from days when race-survival depended upon a massed defence against enemies, or a diffusive extension of such specialised instincts as the parental, filial, or amative. Still other causes are connected with imaginative inadequacy—a person is so lacking in resourcefulness that he does not know what to do except when supplied with the external suggestions & cöoperation of others. Ascending in the scale of intelligence, we find another & wholly distinct source of friendship in the intrinsic pleasure of exchanging ideas & impressions with others capable of understanding & parallelling them. This last is closely connected with the general creative impulse behind art & scholarship, whereby the individual feels a wish to formulate & transmit the impressions & experiences he receives. And so on, & so on—not counting the spurious forms of friendship whose motives are purely mercenary or otherwise concerned with direct material advantage, though these are tremendously prevalent. Well—although every separate instance of personal acquaintance usually involves (at least to some extent) *more than one* of these distinct elements, it is probably a fact that in each case some one element *does* very largely predominate. And it is very natural that some persons should prefer other sorts. The more analytical the individual, the more decided will be his preferences—since the undiscriminating person is flattered when anybody notices him for *any* reason, & weaves his own self-complacent interpretation for his own benefit. The least discriminating persons are the best "mixers"—the likeliest to find congenial friends everywhere in large quantities. Their own motives for acquaintanceship probably centre in imaginative inadequacy—the need for external suggestion—& egotism; joined to a powerful nucleus of instinctive gregariousness & solitude-fear. It is easy to satisfy them. They are not quickly alienated by dulness, overbearingness, or overdemonstrativeness in others, & they emphatically prefer personal acquaintance to correspondence. The latter, indeed, since it involves only the idea-exchanging element, is of little or no interest to most of them. At the opposite pole stands the person whose discrimination is very keen, & whose taste in acquaintanceship is limited to certain kinds. He, obviously, cannot find congenial acquaintances so readily as his gregarious brother. There are only certain sorts of persons to whom he has anything to say, & who can say anything which will interest him. Those who force uncongenial forms of acquaintanceship on him quickly become a nuisance. Just where he will find the right kind of friends—whether in person or in correspondence—depends on just what kind he is looking for. In the case of one whose object is primarily *the exchange of ideas & impressions,* the chances are that he will most readily find kindred spirits in correspondence; since what people put into their correspondence is generally ideas & impressions. Not that he couldn't eventually find such spirits in person—for there *are* many individuals whose chief interest (in conversation as well as correspondence) is the exchange of ideas—but that he can find them *quickest & most numerously* by letter; since a vast lot of people deal principally with ideas *when writing,* yet turn largely to other elements when in face-to-face company. (Thus many are splendid correspondents, yet dull or overbearing as personal companions.) Regarding your own case—I fancy you belong essentially in the category of those who look mainly for idea-exchanging acquaintanceships, & who rather dislike those founded on other elements. This, naturally, makes it harder for you to find suitable friends than as if you were less discriminating; & it also explains why you find & retain epistolary friends more readily than those of the face-to-face sort. The condition is not to be wondered at, & is probably shared by many more persons than you realise. I suppose this discriminating fastidiousness loses one a certain amount of simple gregarious pleasure which more callous persons enjoy, yet I am not at all certain that it is to be wholly regretted. Probably the rewards of intelligent idea-exchange with the few persons whom a discriminating individual *does* care to know, are measurably greater than the rewards which the bluff "mixer" derives from his wide array of heterogeneous & unselective contacts. The thing to do is merely to jog along quietly & self-sufficiently; seizing opportunities for congenial idea-exchange whenever they present themselves—either epistolarily or conversationally—& not worrying if only a few of the contacts thus established prove worthy of permanent retention. A solid, choice circle of a few friends is every inch as good as a crowd. In the course of time the number of really congenial friends acquired is bound to increase. Perhaps a majority of them will be epistolary—especially since letters give one a world-wide radius to select from, whereas face-to-face acquaintanceship is confined to the comparatively small population of a limited geographical area—but a few personal ones will be bound to develop. And you have plenty of time to let nature take its course in the matter—for the very best of friends are those whom one acquires in full maturity, when one's mind & tastes are thoroughly crystallised & conscious of what they want. I myself—with whom idea-exchange is also the only major basis of acquaintanceship—have found this to be very emphatically true. Virtually all my "social" life is that of correspondence, since the local associates of my youth have dropped completely out of my circle of interests & assumed the status of mere nodding acquaintances. Today I don't really *know* anybody in Providence—& of the various people I do know . . . . Belknap, Klarkash-Ton, Young Melmoth, Barlow, Morton, Price, & so on . . . . . . the great majority did not appear on my horizon till I was much older than you are. I never heard of Belknap till I was 29, & never exchanged a word with Klarkash-Ton till I was 32! All these friends have come very slowly & gradually—they are the minority who have stuck in the sieve through which scores of casual acquaintances have passed to unknown realms beyond. And that, I fancy, is the way all really congenial & enduring circles of friends are built up. Not merely a matter of years, but a matter of decades. One of my aunt's best—or likely-to-be-best—friends is a gentlewoman whom she met only last year![4]

June [sic] 16

It grew dark as I reached the above point, so that I am concluding this on the following day. Weather is getting warmer, so that I feel more in my element. I am this time writing in another & more rural open-air spot—the exquisite Quinsnicket or Lincoln woods five miles north of the city. This is perhaps my favourite of all spots, since it represents the rustic colonial Rhode Island of yesterday with a peculiar intensiveness. It is a state park reservation, carefully kept to its primitive 18th century aspect. The wooded parts are weird & striking—with bold hills & ravines, great rocks, & unexpected pools—while the adjacent farmlands are a perfect survival of the past, with ancient stone walls, gnarled orchards, & low-pitched houses extending all the way back to 1670. One old house—the Eleazar Arnold house, built in 1687—has a north gable end entirely of stone, with an incredibly huge chimney & fireplace. My present seat is by the roadside at a point carefully chosen for its scenic vista . . . . for as I look eastward I see an extended prospect scarcely distinguishable from the choicest landscapes of Old England. The ground drops abruptly, revealing a narrow white road curving between green, stone-walled meadows—with steep, mysterious woods on the south, & a sharp acclivity crowned with ancient farmhouses on the north. Here & there great elms & graceful clumps of oak & maple arise, whilst at the very bottom there sparkles the limpid blue of a wide mill-pond. Beyond the pond, on an abrupt green slope, the village of Saylesville arises—its slender church spire piercing dense greenery directly in the line of sight, & quaint ancient gables peeping out of the distant foliage beside it. The effect of the whole is beautiful & impressive beyond description—the veritable soul of old & new England combined, with all those pleasing suggestions of historical continuity which inhere in familiar forms & evidences of long-centuried habitation on the same spot. Only an ancient land, with the memory of still more ancient lands behind it, could yield a scene like this. Whenever I behold this prospect I am driven well-nigh to desperation because I can neither draw nor paint it.

It is well that I have scenes like this at my disposal, lest I perish of envy through the books & pictures of Old England with which my travelling friend Edkins (the chap who read the Weigall book after you) is philanthropically flooding me. He has sent seven books so far—including a volume of Pennell etchings of London, & marvellous pictures of Cornwall, Somerset, & various manor-houses of Southern England;[5] so that I am acquiring a closer visual acquaintance with the Mother Land than I ever had before. And the more pictures I see, the more I long to behold the living, ancient reality. Old England! Yet the resemblance to the New England scene is startling. After all, the landscape I have always known is essentially that which my forbears knew across the sea. If climatic rigours ever drive me south, there is nothing I shall miss more than the traditional elms & oaks & birches & willows of the past— & the architectural lines which go with them. They will always be part of a persistent dream, even though my waking eyes become habituated to palms & moss & live-oaks & sweet-gums & all the typical forms of the subtropics. For the present, I shall hang on amongst them, let the winters torture as they may! But pardon the rambling impelled by the scene before me. Landscape & architecture are the things that most evoke my maudlin loquacity! ¶ Again congratulating you on your present trip, & hoping its conclusion will surpass even its start, I remain

Yr most ob^t Servt

H P L

Notes

1. See frontispiece, *SL* 5.
2. Henry S. Whitehead (1882–1932). Barlow cut stencils for *Caneviniana* but never printed it. Paul Freehafer circulated it through FAPA in the early 1940s.
3. Mustafa Kemal Atatürk (1881–1938), revolutionary statesman, writer, founder of the Republic of Turkey, and the first Turkish President.
4. Perhaps Marian F. Bonner, who roomed at the nearby boarding-house.
5. Joseph Pennell (1857–1928), American graphic artist and illustrator, noted for landscapes and architectural scenes. The volume in question may be *Haunts of Old London* (London: T. N. Foulis, 1914), consisting of 25 of Pennell's etchings. The book on Cornwall is S. P. B. Mais, *The Cornish Riviera* (London: Great Western Railway Co., 1934; *LL* 635). The Somerset book is apparently Maxwell Fraser, *Somerset* (London: Great Western Railway Co., 1934; *LL* 351). The book on manor-houses are unidentified.

[14]   [ALS, JHL]

Ancient Nantucket
—Septr 2, 1934.

Dear Helen:—

As you have doubtless deduced from the folder sent a few days ago (to Auburn, in view of your probable return thither about this season), Grandpa is up to his old travelling antics again![1] It's simply impossible to keep the old gentleman at home when there's any cash to cover 'bus & boat & boardinghouse & beanery expenses, & any warm weather to make outdoor existence tolerable! Incidentally, I trust you duly received my earlier card telling of Morton's visit & the trip to ancient Newport. The present spree started out with a visit to a friend near Boston——which of course included Salem & Marblehead side trips. Pictorial echoes of these are enclosed herewith. Then, after my host had returned me to Providence in his car, came the second & climactic half of the outing—a half not yet quite over, & involving a marvellous repository of antiquity which I had never seen before; nothing less, in truth, than a sojourn upon the ancient island of Nantucket. Nantucket! Observing its stupendous charm, & its incomparable degree of preservation of the past, I could kick myself for not having invaded it long ago . . . . a place only 90 miles—6 hours by coach to New Bedford & steamer on the sound—from my own College St. doorstep!

For be it known that Nantucket holds the supreme championship among old towns.[2] Newport . . . . . Charleston . . . . Quebec . . . . Gloucester . . . . not one is as utterly & basically unchanged since the old days as is this dignified & lovely island port. Here we have a Yankee whaling town of a century or more ago, without anything to indicate that the century or more *has* gone . . . . save the presence of motors & the absence of tall masts & the smell of whale oil along the waterfront. What a place! Cobblestoned streets with nothing but colonial houses on either side—hitching-posts & horse-blocks & silver doorplates—horses & carriages—graveyards with skulls, cherubs, & urns—narrow, garden-bordered lanes—ancient belfries & steeple—old churches with galleries & box pews—picturesque waterfront—*everything* that the most exacting antiquarian could possibly ask!

I'm staying a week, & fancy I've seen about all there is to see. My room—in a colonial hostelry called The Overlook, with small-paned windows, wide floor-boards, 6-panel doors, & all the rest—is on the 3d floor, & commands a splendid view of town, harbour, & sea. In the past few days I've explored old houses & churches, the 1746 windmill, the Hist. Soc. & whaling museums, &c., & have seen Saturn through the 5″ refracting telescope of the Maria Mitchell Observatory. This latter adjoins the birthplace of the celebrated astronomer Miss Mitchell, who was a professor at Vassar College from 1865 to 1888. I've explored every inch of the quaint streets & alleys on foot, & have covered the suburbs on a hired bicycle. This, incidentally, is the first time

I've been on a wheel in 20 years—I thought I might have grown awkward at it, but actually I had forgotten nothing. I merely hopped on & sailed along as though I had dismounted only the day before. It quite brought back my long-vanished youth . . . . so that I feel at this moment as if I had to hurry home for the opening of Hope St. High School! I wish it weren't conspicuous for old gentlemen to ride bikes in Providence! In one place—when the wind was with me—I must have made 25 or 30 miles an hour—anyhow, I passed two cars! Nor was there any fatigue or after-effect. It was just as though the early 1900's had come back . . . or as though I had never ceased to ride. At the beginning of my sojourn I took a motor sightseeing trip around the entire island—viewing ancient Siasconset (locally pronounced "Sconset"—a fishing village with tiny cottages & rambling lanes, now a summer resort) & other notable points. Naturally, I've done some reading on the island's history & antiquities at the venerable Athenaeum (now a public library), & have made copious notes on the local architecture. Nantucket was settled about 1660 by some families from Massachusetts who were disgusted at the bigotry of the narrow-minded Bay Colony . . . . they had been fined for the "crime" of sheltering Quakers during a storm! In 1664 the island became a part of the new Province of New-York, formed from the old Dutch possessions, & in 1692 it was transferred to Massachusetts, to which it has ever since belonged. The settlers were very considerate of the original Indian population, & lawfully purchased all their lands.

Whaling lay at the base of Nantucket's prosperity. At first whales were killed just off shore, but when they became extinct here the islanders fitted out whaling-brigs for long voyages—even to the Pacific. In time Nantucket grew rich & dignified—as the fine old mansions & schools & churches attest to this day. During the tragic revolt of 1775–83 the island was neutral ground, & many of its sons remained loyal to our rightful Sovereign. Admiral Sir Isaac Coffin, Bart., of His Majesty's Navy, who in 1826 endowed a famous school in the town, was a scion of the ancient Nantucket stock. Then came decline—to be checked only by the island's rapidly-growing popularity as a summer-resort. The "summer people" have in general been very appreciative, & have helped to preserve & restore the vestiges of the past. The year-round population has shrunk to not more than 3800—all descendants of the ancient families . . . . Macys, Coffins, Folgers, Starbucks, Gardners, Pickhams, Husseys, &c. Benjamin Franklin's mother—Abiah Folger—was a daughter of Nantucket. Today the natives subsist through an increasingly precarious fishing industry.

The town—called "Sherburne" prior to 1795, & since then "Nantucket" after the island itself—lies in a large harbour on the northern coast—as the map in the folder will show you. It is very beautiful—with fine old trees, though the rest of the island (low, rolling country) has been unwisely deforested. The climate is, like that of all islands, rather equable. I've been beastly cold this week, yet the winters are so mild that many shrubs & creepers unknown to the rest of New England flourish finely. The horrible winter of

1933–4 failed to kill the hedges here, though vast harm was wrought in Providence. Well—this is my last full day on the island. Tomorrow night I hit #66—& the next day my aunt will depart for a fortnight's visit in Ogunquit, Maine. I can't conceive of going *north* at *this* time of year, but she doubtless knows what she wants. The present trip, I fancy, just about closes my 1934 travel season. It's really too late for me to be visiting a northern seaport, for half the time I've been half frozen. There was no heat in the hotel even on cold days, & I had to drape a blanket over my 1928 blue store clothes.

I am surely glad to hear what a delightful & inspiring time you have had—& am pleased that the return to every-day life could be tempered by an intermediate seacoast session at Inverness. Your mountain experience sounds arduous & thrilling indeed—especially to one who is apt to be disconcertingly dizzy in high places. And it was fortunate, too, that you could encounter some sound philosophical discussion calculated to dispel the macabre reflections of recent months.

The Unicorn's horn sounds like a vastly hazardous proposition, & I doubt if I would have followed the party except on a dare. I am a wretched climber & balancer, & had to practice by discouragingly difficult stages before I could hold my own among the young monkeys of my day. Unlike Young Melmoth I have no *urge* to jump off high places—but on the contrary am darned afraid I'll *fall* off! It's just as well, I'm sure, that you adopted a milder programme after that Unicorn feat. Your violin-playing must have placed the camp vastly in your debt! Most doubtless realised the handicaps under which you laboured. Mr. Curtis[3] sounds like a most gifted & interesting artist, & you were surely fortunate in receiving one of his sketches. How I envy anyone who can record & preserve his impressions in effective pictorial form!

Yes—Belknap will really have to depend on time & his own maturing attitude to pull him out of his maternal fixation & kindred neuroses. Others can do no more than help to create a general atmosphere favourable to the development. I think the emergence is slowly taking place. The past two years have seen a growing reaching-out after external contacts & experiences, & a gradual groping toward greater independence, which will gain momentum as further time passes. I think that Mrs. Long formerly aggravated the trouble through over-solicitude—not demands for attention, but a protective care which prompted over-attentiveness as a return. Now, however, I believe that she realises the need of fostering independence, & favours more freedom on Belknap's part. But of course such late changes must be gradual. She will still now & then be oversolicitous, & he will now & then be both over-dependent & over-anxious. Time & increased doses of common-sense are what will turn the trick. So far as Belknap is concerned, active *objective* interests are what he needs.

It is surely unfortunate that the California strike has aroused such bigoted political feeling—but human emotion is the most difficult thing in the world to control.[4] This is surely one of the most uncomfortable ages to live in that the last century or so has produced! I still hope, however, that the Anglo-Saxon nations can become adjusted to the conditions of the future without a violent upheaval. If the extremists on both sides can only be kept in check, the middle-grounders will probably be able to devise a safe course through the one method—trial & error—applicable to so unprecedented a muddle.

Regarding the advantages & disadvantages of a general attitude of detachment—of course one loses considerable pleasure & interest if one feels no kinship whatever to anything human. So extreme an attitude would of course be a mistake. The right idea is to follow a sort of middle course whereby one may take a rational interest in the buzzings of the human hive without being completely dominated by its mechanism. To recognise empirical forms & relationships as *proximately* valid—valid, that is, on the surface & for the moment—& to take from them whatever harmonious pleasure can be taken; but to realise, behind it all, that visible objects & patterns are purely transient & capricious things . . . . . . things whose meaning is not basic or cosmic, & from which too much cannot be expected. Only this *underlying* realisation—a realisation which does not need to be obtruded into all of one's every-day thoughts & moods—can (in the absence of childish soporifics like religion) save one from the extremes of disappointment & painful disillusion. It does not have to be a ponderous or heavily-borne thing—indeed, in many it is purely instinctive, temperamental, & quasi-unconscious. It simply means the extension of one's rational sense of proportion from small objects & issues. In other words, it means a resolution & capability to use one's emotions instead of to be used by them. Thus I do not think it could greatly hamper one's appreciation of the simpler beauties of life, whose appeal is to the most direct forms of sensory perception. Rather would it teach us to accept those simpler beauties as intrinsic ends in themselves—roses to be gathered while we may—uncomplicated by mythical linkages to non-existent eternal things. I have a fairly detached & impersonal perspective myself, but I don't see that it has dulled in any way my appreciation of the drama of history, of the loveliness of the sunset, of the grace of noble architecture, or of the charm of shapely black kittens like little Sam Perkins![5]

I surely wish you could persuade your mother to take that Southern trip. After all, vicarious travelling is pretty pallid beside the real thing . . . . . I'd heard & read a lot about Nantucket, but the sight of the actual place . . . . oh, boy! By the way—I'm enclosing a card which may interest your mother . . . . Providence's nearest parallel to San Francisco's "Portals of the Past",[6] a card of which she so kindly sent me last month. This Benedict Memorial[7] is in the modern or southwestern part of the town which you did not see—though I hope you can cover all the ground on some future trip.

New England certainly has a peculiar charm not found elsewhere in America—the charm of a distinctive landscape bearing the evidences of a continuous, well-adjusted life of many centuries' standing; a life expressing itself in architectural forms perfectly suited to the topography & to the prevailing institutions. This is what Europe has in abundance—but which never became transferred to the New World except in New England . . . . though the New Netherland Dutch & Pennsylvania German regions . . . . & perhaps the unspoiled parts of French Quebec . . . . . vaguely approximate it. In Florida & California & the Southwest the Spaniards created isolated buildings of beauty, but produced no instinctive outgrowth from the peculiar local landscapes involved. In the Anglo-Saxon South, too, there were beautiful plantation-houses & beautiful towns; but no general sprinkling of cottages & villages exactly suited to the countryside. On the contrary, the small farms of the South tend to look rather awkward & squalid. Ditto for French Louisiana. And of course the pioneer regions had not the basic conditions needed to develop such a spontaneous folk growth. Thus New England stands alone as a bit of the Old World transferred bodily to the New—a virtual *extension* of Old England itself. That is really what it is, as we may readily appreciate when we consider the conditions of the great 17th century colonisation. Other parts of the country combined [?] vast land areas with a thin & slowly arriving population. New England, on the contrary, was a region no larger than Old England—into which, between 1630 & 1645, poured shipload after shipload of settlers . . . . . colonists reckoned in tens of thousands. Clearly, the pioneering stage could not last long under such conditions. Among the settlers were representatives of every art, craft, & trade in England—not merely planters & farmers, as elsewhere. Towns grew up thickly from the very first, & in them craftsmen & merchants followed the same pursuits that they had followed in England. Farmers were so numerous that their holdings dotted the whole coastal strip on which they were settled—one farm touching another, till in a single generation the coast was so crowded that some of the young folk had to strike out more deeply into the wilderness—into central Massachusetts, Maine, & the Connecticut Valley. Here was indeed another England on a small scale—& this as early as 1650 or so. Towns with thousands of inhabitants & bristling with mediaeval gables (see enclosed card of John Ward house, Salem), & a countryside as thickly settled as the old world, with European cottage architecture adapted to the local terrain & building materials. And this form of life kept on & on without a break . . . . unbroken even now in many quiet backwaters . . . . . piling up traditions, refining hereditary usages & forms, & building gradually on never-changed foundations . . . . just as in Europe. By the time of the Revolution the country was *old*. The periwigged, knee-breeched men of 1775 could behold all around them houses 100 or 120 or 140 years old—some in long-abandoned styles of architecture, & already falling to decay. And still the pageant rolls on . . . . the cycle of the years, with slow growth on original foundations. Rolling fields—stone walls—giant elms—winding roads—low-roofed cottages—clustering barns & byres—gnarled hillside apple-orchards—white village steeples rising from clouds of verdure & seen in the distance across fertile valleys—blue streams winding amidst grassy plains—rocks in fantastic outcrops & groupings—deep woods from which a magic twilight never departs—towns with steep hill streets & fanlighted doorways & gleaming-columned court-houses—waterfronts with rambling wharves & clustering warehouse gables—brick Georgian mansions glowing redly in the sunset . . . . all the myriad phases of one homogeneous growth; one coherent whole. That is ancient New England! Of course, this applies only to the *old* New England—the parts where the real population still live in the traditional way. There is none of it left along the great urban trunk lines . . . . . Dagoes, Poles, hot-dog stands, factories, bungalows, skyscrapers, garages, & all that . . . . but these are fungous growths peculiar to no one region. An eruption symptomatic of the disease of a mechanised pseudo-civilisation. In Nantucket, thank heaven, the real thing yet survives! I don't think any amount of familiarity could really satiate one with the subtle, lingering charm of New England. Of course the winters are beastly & barbarous—but I shall feel lost indeed if they ever force me to leave this ancient realm for one more physically habitable.

I was greatly interested in what you said of Inverness—& thanks for the sketch map which makes the layout intelligible. I know that California must be exquisitely lovely, & hope to see at least a bit of it some day. I've just met an old Nantucketer who has been to Auburn & likes it.

As for the rival plans for next summer—I'd certainly recommend the Eastern trip as yielding vastly greater results in proportion to the energy put into it. The combination of picturesque Old Southwest, lovely Old South, & haunting New England & Quebec would seem to me to surpass anything else which could be thought of—though of course you know what you'd like best. If you do take the trip, call on me for any desiderate information about any regions I know . . . & of course I'll be delighted to act as guide to any Southern N. England points which may be on your itinerary. ¶ Glad to hear that Son is well. The K.A.T. & Sam Perkins, appreciating your greetings, salute you with cordiality. ¶ My aunt always has a standing order of regards to send. ¶ And with similar regards I have yᵉ Honour to subscribe myself,

Yʳ most obt Hᵇˡᵉ Servᵗ

———E'ch-Pi-El

Notes

1. HPL had sent postcard folders from Nantucket to Clark Ashton Smith and Edward H. Cole.

2. See "The Unknown City in the Ocean."

3. Unidentified, but possibly Leland S. Curtis (1897–1989), American artist, mountaineer, environmentalist, and Antarctic explorer, who lived in California.

4. HPL refers to the West Coast Waterfront Strike of 1934 (9 May–17 July 1934), led by longshoremen and leading to the San Francisco general strike (16–19 July). Even after the strikes were settled by arbitration, longshoremen and other workers continued to wage strikes into October.

5. See HPL's poem "[Little Sam Perkins]."

6. The remains of Alban Nelson Towne's Nob Hill house, at 1101 California Street in San Francisco, stand along Lloyd Lake in Golden Gate Park. After the earthquake of 1906 and fire had devastated the building, Towne's wife presented its portico to the park in 1909. All that remains are the ionic columns of the entrance.

7. The Benedict Memorial (known as the Temple of Music) is a vast stone structure on the shore of Cunliff Lake in Roger Williams Park in Providence, commemorating Benedict Arnold (1615–1678), an early colonial governor of Rhode Island (1663–66, 1669–72, 1677–78).

[15]   [ALS, JHL]

66 College St.,
Providence, R.I.,
Octr 28, 1934.

Dear Helen:—

I am surely glad that the Nantucket views proved of interest. The place itself is more fascinating than any pictures could possibly shew, & I certainly hope I can get there next summer, if only briefly. It ought, too, to form an item in any eastern itinerary which you may arrange. There surely is a curious difference between typical scenes in different parts of the country. New England probably reproduces Old England in atmosphere & topography about as well as does any section of the New World—although scenery of much the same type extends all the way down the Atlantic Coast to North Carolina. It is in New England that the architecture springs most spontaneously from the spirit of the soil, with low, graceful forms shaped by generations of continuous life & subtly harmonised with the natural contours of the landscape. Here, as nowhere else in the Western Hemisphere, is a perfect welding of human & landscape elements such as one finds in the settled regions of Europe. Nor is New England devoid of variety—since there are many different zones of geography & architecture, each equally harmonious within itself. My own zone is the coastal one, with quaint seaport towns & a low, rolling countryside threaded by winding, stone-walled roads & diversified by deep woods of oaks & elms & maples. Altogether different from this is the inland Massachusetts region with villages clustered around triangular greens, huge taverns of distinctive architecture, steep hills clothed with pines & white birches, & narrow glens with rushing brooks & waterfalls. Vermont, with its crowded green peaks, is still another story—& Maine is a whole chapter in itself. And the White Mountains form a separate fragment from another world!

I offer no apologies for my devotion to these scenic survivals of other days, since to my mind "progressiveness" is a thing absolutely meaningless in itself. The whole notion of continuous "progress" toward a presumably "superior" goal is a mere post-Renaissance innovation, & is already losing some of its charm for thoughtful analysts. What most benefits mankind is *not constant change, but satisfactory adjustment.* When a race has achieved a certain settled harmony with itself, its way of life, & its geographical setting, it is not only very foolish but actually criminal to wish it any change. Change is the enemy of everything really worth cherishing. It is the remover of landmarks, the destroyer of all which is homelike & comforting, & the constant symbol & reminder of decay & death. It is change which makes one old before his time by snatching away everything he has known, & substituting a new environment to which he can never become adjusted. Happy is the man who can grow up & flourish & grow old & die in the same ancient house in the midst of an unchanging countryside. For him half the terror & tragedy of aging does not exist, for he never loses the visible world of his youth. Never does he face the hideous alienage of one whose eyes wander vainly for the sight of some familiar thing. And so I deplore all needless change, & feel no shame in my love for all that is old & stable. The only sort of opposition to change which is culpable, is that which insists on the retention of such old forms & institutions as have become really harmful through their conflict with a new (& inevitable) environment utterly different from that which evolved them. Even in this case the culpability does not imply that the environmental change is necessarily desirable. Such changes are generally mere matters of sheer, uncontrollable drift, which we have to face whether we will or no. But when they *do* occur it is of course needful to bring practical institutions into harmony with them, in order to restore the same degree of approximate equilibrium which we had before they occurred. Thus the inevitable growth of the machine age has rendered our system of laissez-faire economics obsolete & unworkable, so that we can never have peace till we replace it with some fresh system fitted to the new conditions & restoring to average men the power to earn a living. Yet a preaching of this need of replacement does not argue the desirability of change in itself. Rather is it an attempt to recapture a harmony which is lost. And side by side with this recognition of *necessary* change, there can exist an equally strong mood of protest against *unnecessary* change. Indeed, the more landmarks we *have* to lose, the more tenaciously do we need to cling to those which we *don't* have to lose. Thus the same thinker who urges a change of property-allocation or industrial regulation to fit an inevitably changed economic trend, may simultaneously—& with perfect logic— give zealous battle to any proposed change in folkways, art forms, or philosophic assumptions, which he may feel to be unjustified, or essentially unrelated to any genuine environmental mutation. We must save *all that we can,* lest we find ourselves adrift in an alien world with no memories or guideposts or points of reference to give us the priceless illusions of direction, interest, & significance amidst the cosmic chaos. Hence the natural function & social value of the antiquarian & cherisher of elder things. To them we owe much of our sense of comfortable continuity & appropriate placement. It is surely a tragedy that so many things *needlessly* change. The east as well as the west suffers from the desecration of the tourist—the wide, straight cement roads, the garages & filling stations, & all that. But at least there are a few mercifully unspoiled backwaters left, where one may see the visible forms known to his forefathers, & absorb a trace of that sense of place & permanence without which all life above the primitive level would form a meaningless & maddening vortex. I can certainly sympathise regarding the burning of your home & the loss of all your familiar possessions. I was altogether disorganised when I lost my original home in 1904, but I have at least managed to hang on to the books, furniture, pictures, & other objects most vital to me. When *those* have to go, it will be about time for the old man to follow them into nothingness! Still—with a fair amount of cash, anyone can even now find havens remote from the visible evidences of change & decay. Some of the old coast towns & mountain villages of New England linger to this day as the[y] were when the republic was young. And even in the larger places there are oases where a good deal of the cherished & the accustomed can yet be found. The same is true of the South. He who dwells in Charleston—say in Legare or Tradd or Lamboll or Gibbes St.—has little immediate reason to think that the world has changed since 1800 or 1820. In such a place even the Civil War & the machine age & the depression have produced only minor dents. Yes—& I think parts of Quebec would afford the same sense of continuity to anyone able to derive it through French cultural symbols. This is especially true of the Isle d'Orleans.

This autumn I have had some very refreshing glimpses of traditional scenes, notwithstanding the general inclemency of the present month. On warm days I have taken many pedestrian jaunts to rustic realms north of Providence—while on Oct. 19–21 I paid a brief visit to my host of last August in the Boston region—Edward H. Cole—& was taken on some magnificent scenic rides in his well-heated Chevrolet. Oct. 20 we visited north central Massachusetts & enjoyed some superlatively fine vistas of autumn foliage, distant hills, steepled villages, rocky glens & waterfalls, & everything that goes with inland New England at its best. We lunched in the ancient & unspoiled village of West Townsend—of which the enclosed card gives only the very faintest suggestion—in a rambling tavern built in 1774. Here, also, we found a quaint "general store" precisely like those of a century ago. On the 21st Cole & his wife took me back to Providence, picked up my aunt, & continued onward into Rhode Island's famous Narragansett Country—the region where E. Hoffmann Price & I did so much exploration just before your passage through Providence. This is the most distinctive region in New England— where the social order departed furthest from the pattern of Puritan yeoman-ry. Here, as in the South, there were large plantations with many slaves before the Revolution—with an agricultural & patriarchal life in full swing. Dairying & horse-breeding predominated—Narragansett cheeses & Narragansett pacers being known over half the world in the 1750's & 1760's. The Church of England predominated (with Quakerism as its main rival); & houses of worship were situate in lonely woodland regions, as in Virginia, whither congregated the planters each Sunday in their coaches or on horseback. Life was predominantly rural, despite such attractive villages as Updike's Landing (now Wickford) on the coast, & Little Rest (now Kingston) somewhat inland. The great plantation-houses had gambrel roofs, & were usually vastly enlarged specimens of the New England farmhouse model. Only one or two of these can be found today—so tragically complete was the passing of the old life after the revolution. The scenery is of especial loveliness—in places closer to Old England than anywhere else in America. Well—on this occasion we explored ancient Wickford with its crumbling wharves, great elms, & centuried white houses, & continued southeast to the sprawling old snuff-mill on the Narrow River where the great painter Gilbert Stuart was born in 1755. The mill—built in 1750—has lately been restored in every detail, & the obliging caretaker set the great wheel going for our benefit. The adjacent river & meadow & woods & stone-walled road held an autumnal beauty altogether too poignant for adequate expression except by a poet—& twilight brought a violet magic parallelled only by the glimmering vistas of dream. I could scarcely bear to think of leaving—though a return to the city had to be made in the end. Cole, however, was so captivated by the region (which he had never before seen) that he attempted some pioneering which got us momentarily lost! Since that day I have had one pedestrian outing, but the season is getting late for such things now. The leaves are beginning to fall, & desolation & chill will soon be upon the land. Then the long hibernation, relieved only by hopes of returning spring!

And now let me congratulate you most sincerely on the resumption of your musical career, & on the bright prospects held out by your distinguished instructor! The fact that a specimen of your playing wholly reversed the attitude of the august maestro would seem to indicate talent vastly beyond the common order, so that diligent study & practice will be eminently worth your while. It is surely the greatest of all satisfactions to find that one can really achieve progress in one's chosen art—& I imagine that music *is* your particular art, notwithstanding your accomplishments in other fields. I don't think there is anything extravagant in your teacher's prophecy of success—& it would certainly be rash to set limits to your development. You can't tell, any more than anyone else, what reservoirs of genius may or may not be tapped in the course of your advanced musical education. It's just as well not to be conceited or over-expectant—for it is to *music itself*, & not the personal ambition attached to music, that your primary attention should be devoted. But at the same time it would not be surprising if some day you discovered yourself to be a first-rate artist—having grown to be such without knowing it! I'm sure that the harbouring of musical ambition need not make your teaching any the less effective. The fact is, another friend of mine whose ambitions are wholly musical (in the line of *composition* rather than performance) is at present an instructor of French—& no less competent in that capacity because of his larger aspirations. This chap—Alfred Galpin[1] of Appleton, Wis.—has studied in Paris under the late Vincent d'Indy[2] & others, & has had compositions of his played by the Chicago Symphony Orchestra. But the main thing is to have a medium of aesthetic expression for its own sake—whether or not this lead to any dizzy heights or widespread fame; hence I can congratulate you on your present course without waiting to see the size of the type in which your name will appear on concert programmes of the future!

Speaking of music—I enclose an account of a highly interesting lecture which my aunt & I heard the other night. You doubtless know all about the lecturer & his work. I enjoyed it immensely—even though to me the historical side may have appealed more strongly than the purely musical. The selections were rendered with what I would call supreme skill—& just to make the cast an all-star one, the music-turning was accomplished by Prof. S. Foster Damon, eminent poet & authority on Thomas Holley Chivers. With Mr. Howard's[3] thesis I found myself in as much agreement as is possible for a layman with no real right to an opinion. He deplored the laboured, conscious efforts to create a purely autochthonous American music, when as a matter of fact no really authentic, spontaneous body of melody could exist apart from the continuous stream of European heritage. How naive to fancy that our European stock could express itself (as some moderns believe it can) in the musical traditions of the Indians or of the plantation negroes! And more—it is equally absurd to fancy that conscious, cold-blooded striving can ever create a true type of aesthetic expression. That is not the way art grows. What is authentic must be unconscious & spontaneous—something produced not to fulfil certain formal technical requirements or to prove certain abstract theories, but simply because the producer naturally feels like doing things that way. This is of course just as true in other arts as in music—& ought to be remembered by the architectural modernists who so painfully strive "to express our current machine civilisation" by means of aberrantly ugly concoctions of rootless steel & glass construction. These fellows *think* they are representing the present as Ictinus[4] represented classic Greece & as Wren[5] represented Queen Anne's England—but if they would stop to think, they would realise that Ictinus & Wren achieved their effects not by grimly resolving to "express their periods", but merely by creating such forms as appealed to them, without any thought of time or place. Moreover—Ictinus & Wren did not exclude all elements from the past. Instead, they built upon & modified the main streams of art which they inherited. Hence to my mind all these

396 ❀ *Letters to Helen V. Sully*

anti-traditional radicals are up a blind alley. Their products are not art, because they come from theory instead of from feeling. And they do not represent this age, because they do not embody those attributes of the European main stream which this age has inherited. But I digress.

Your argument regarding the modesty or egotism of genius must have been interesting indeed—& I presume you were right, in the long run, in maintaining that great aesthetic creators tend to have an overdeveloped ego, while persons eminent for pure intellect preserve a realistic sense of proportion & are more interested in their work than in themselves. At first—so absurd is the egotistic attitude—one feels tempted to say that *no* truly great person can be self-centred; but after examining concrete cases one has to change one's opinion. The secret is, I suppose, that art is almost wholly non-intellectual—& in many cases anti-intellectual. The supreme artist usually has no chance to cultivate a sense of proportion or scale of philosophic values; & is so wrapped up in the process of emotional expression that he cannot take a clear objective glance at himself, the whole human race, & the universe. Retaining much of the narcissism of infancy, he continues to think of his own moods & caprices as the central facts of existence & the most important things in the world. It is unfortunate that such a defect has to accompany the greatest creative skill—but if the skill be truly great, we can afford to excuse its concomitant drawbacks. The most exasperating spectacle is that of the inferior pretender who, without any of the skill or substance of greatness, possesses the coxcomb vanity & coddled neurotic egotism commonly associated with artistic eminence. These pathetic clowns fancy that they are great because they have the weakness which great persons sometimes have—as if all club-footed persons were as great as Byron because Byron had a club-foot! Actually, egotism is simply a result of the absence of thought. It is not absolutely universal among the foremost artists—Virgil, Milton, Wren, Copley, Wordsworth, Galsworthy, & scores of other front-rank creators have been thoroughly normal & modest—because the moment one starts to *think,* he cannot help dropping it at once . . . . & there is nothing about great art which utterly forbids its practitioners to use the frontal lobes of their brains. Scientific thinkers, of course, are modest; since the primary requirement of a sincere observer & interpreter is a clear perspective & sense of coördination. The really analytical brain perceives from the start that the mysteries of the external world are a million times more dramatic & interesting than the limited round of its own local phenomena, or the totally irrelevant question of how it is regarded by the meaningless crowd of other brains around it.

I trust that pleasant days have not wholly departed from Woods' Dry Diggings—the autumns there being distinctly milder than those hereabouts. No doubt many opportunities for outdoor activities still exist—which is true only in a very limited sense in New England. Your long trips to the music lessons must be very pleasant when the weather is favourable—& even when it isn't, the stimulus of artistic progress must help to dispel the monotony of travel.

With every good wish, both for immediate matters & for the long-term musical course—& with the best regards of my aunt & myself,

I remain

Yrs most sincerely—

H P L

Notes

1. Alfred Galpin (1901–1983), amateur journalist, French scholar, composer, and protégé, then longtime friend, of HPL. When he lived in Appleton, he was MWM's high school student.

2. Paul Marie Théodore Vincent d'Indy (1851–1931), French composer and teacher.

3. John Tasker Howard (1890–1964), early American music historian, radio host, writer, lecturer, and composer. His *Our American Music* (1931) was an early general history of music in the U.S.

4. Ictinus was an architect active in the mid-fifth century B.C.E., a co-architect of the Parthenon.

5. Sir Christopher Wren (1632–1723), one of the most highly acclaimed English architects in history.

[16]   [ALS, JHL]

66 College St.,

Providence, R.I.,

Jany. 14, 1935.

Dear Helen:—

I was very glad to hear the news from Averoigne last month— news which takes on an added interest from my having since seen the youthful wanderer around whom it centres.[1] You certainly had a strenuous season—with so many local activities competing with the guest of honour for your time & attention. I appreciated the postal bulletins I received, & could well imagine the congeniality of the sessions. Too bad they had to be interrupted by the wearisome collegiate event—though the musical interruption doubtless had its compensations. Regarding your good work after a spell of relaxation—I think that in many cases a respite from arduous continuous application is a great asset in every kind of scholastic, artistic, or intellectual pursuit. With too much practice & concentration spontaneity departs, & a kind of confusion springs up to paralyse effort. On the other hand, a vacation gives the unconscious part of the mind an opportunity to digest & correlate the wealth of material presented to it—so that the latter can imperceptibly become a usable part of the individual personality. After such a seemingly fallow but actually assimilative period, results are often vastly better than before. The exotic meal with your teacher & fellow-pupils must have been exceedingly pleasant.

The various Melmothic events were surely well selected—& seem to have been as delightful to the voyager as to yourself. Those hydraulic diggings[2] sound picturesque in the extreme—& the subsequent emergence on the brink of the river cañon must have formed a very appropriate climax. The American would seem to be a notable & impressive stream throughout its length—I have many views of it on photographic postcards sent me by Klarkash-Ton over a period of years. Sunset must have lent the striking landscape many added charms—& the petrified trees were a feature in themselves. At the old home we used to have some specimens of petrified wood obtained by my grandfather in the west; but these have somehow vanished amidst the vicissitudes of many movings. The San Francisco events doubtless had other charms of a more urban kind. Though not ancient as compared with the cities of the east, San Francisco seems to possess a curious mellowness & attractiveness arising partly from its topography, partly from its history, & partly from its present moods & folkways. I've always hoped I might see it some time, though I wouldn't spend even a nickel's 'bus fare to visit its synthetic southerly rival Los Angeles. Too bad you didn't look in on E. Hoffmann Price in Oakland—though in a way he deserved neglect, since he didn't call on Young Melmoth when he was in New York in '33. Melmoth seemed to have enjoyed his hours with Klarkash-Ton as well as the more glamourous ones elsewhere. I can well picture the sense of bereavement which must have attended his departure, & hope that he can repeat the visit at greater length on some other occasion. His trip certainly seems to have done him good—it is a wholesome thing to be away from the hectic dumps of Greenwich Village!

I trust that your Christmas season in southern California was not an anticlimax. Let me thank you especially, by the way, for the Yuletide card with its clever sketch of the Russian church at Fort Ross. As I have said, I envy anyone who can do anything in the pictorial line. This specimen of exotic colonial architecture interested me vastly when your mother described it last autumn, since I had not known that any Russian buildings survived on this continent south of Alaska. It is curious how many different nationalities left their architectural impress—great or slight—on the soil of early America. Besides England, there was France to the north & Spain to the south—& Holland, Germany, Wales, & Sweden in more or less minute spots . . . . . to say nothing of Russia, as represented in Alaska & California. In modern times immigrant populations have imported still other schools—as, for instance, the Italian ecclesiastical architecture so abundant in Providence's Italian colony.

Christmas hereabouts was very pleasant—forming a sort of culmination to a series of art events . . . . lectures & exhibits . . . . scattered throughout December. Some of the latter were highly interesting—especially a demonstration of painting by two local artists, a portraitist & a landscapist, during which each executed a specimen of his art in full view of the audience. Of the exhibits, the enclosed catalogues (which need not be returned) give a typical idea. The fact that all of these events take place within a block or two of 66 College makes them doubly pleasant for us. At Christmas we had a tree—the first time since my boyhood. All of our old decorations had long been lost in the gulf of time; but I obtained a new array of baubles, tinsel, & lights at Mr. Frank Winfield Woolworth's, & in the end achieved a spectacle of festive splendour which quite rolled away the years! Our feast—as on Thanksgiving Day—was at the hospitable Maison Fadden across the back garden.

On Dec. 30 I took the midnight coach for Manhattan to pay my grand-son Belknap a brief visit. Since Young Melmoth had but lately landed from his voyage—to be joined shortly afterward by his artist-brother in a Green-wich Village flat—& since my youthful Florida host of last spring . . . little Bobby Barlow . . . was also in town, the event had about it much of the aspect of a convention. Barlow—who has been spending the winter in Washington getting ocular treatment & taking art lessons at the Corcoran Gallery—arrived in the metropolis on Christmas morning, & was steered by Belknap to a quiet hotel a few blocks north of the Villa Longa. Belknap took him in tow & introduced him to the various museums, bookstalls, & art galleries—so that he was quite a Manhattanite by the time I was on the scene. He had never been in N.Y. before—except once in infancy. My week in N.Y. was extremely pleasant—involving glimpses of all the gang, old & new. At our principal meeting—Jany 2nd at Belknap's—15 were present—Morton, Loveman, Kirk, Kleiner, Leeds, Talman, Barlow, Belknap, the two Wandreis, Koenig, &c. &c.[3] On another occasion we assembled at Loveman's—our host getting out his marvellous collection of Klarkash-Tonic drawings for our inspection. There must be between 300 & 400 in all—& some of them are astonishingly powerful. I had seen them in Cleveland in 1922, but this second glimpse had all the thrill of a first inspection. They were absolutely new to Long, Barlow, & the Wandreis—for it is only recently that Loveman brought them to N.Y. During these two meetings we all composed a joint letter to Klarkash-Ton, which Loveman later sent along with a missive of his own. I trust all this safely reached the High-Priest of Tsathoggua.

I called at the new Wandrei place—a very pleasant apartment at 155 W. 10th St., above a restaurant called "Julius's",[4] which Belknap tells me is very famous amongst the 'bohemian' villagers. There were many new things at the museums, & I regret that I did not have time to make a wider round of them. Barlow rather concentrated on the Metropolitan—plus the art rooms at the public library. Art is his specialty, & he is a particular devotee of Howard Wandrei, whose masterfully sinister drawings he wants to reproduce photographical-ly for circulation. We encountered several book bargains—Barlow finding an excellent old copy of George W. M. Reynolds' "Wagner the Wehr-Wolf" for 15¢, while Grandpa picked up a good modern edition of Lewis's "The Monk" for a dollar. The weather was, on the whole, quite favourable; only 2 days be-ing so cold as to give me acute trouble. Even on those occasions the all-extensive subway system permitted me to get about with a minimum of damage. Barlow returned to Washington on a morning coach Jany. 7th, & I embarked for Providence the following midnight. My final session was at the Wandrei place. Belknap—rather exhausted by a strenuous fortnight—went home at 11 p.m., whilst Young Melmoth & Young Albrecht Dürer saw the old gentleman off on the New England coach. Had a smooth & drowsy trip home—when I struck the suburbs of Providence I thought I was still in Danielson, Conn.! There was a picturesque fog—which hung on several days before giving place to colder weather. At 7 a.m. Jany. 8 I ascended the steps of #66 & passed through the fan-carved doorway of my hilltop lair.

I trust that all continues to flourish in Averoigne, & hope that the Abbot of Vyones[5] is finding some way to curtain the onerousness of his daily round. Price may be around before long—probably bringing with him a young Berkeleian admirer of Klarkash-Ton . . . one Fred Anger. Price, by the way, is investigating real estate at San Carlos & Redwood City & may be settling down soon as a landed squire.

Regards to yourself, your mother, C A S, & Son.

Yr most obt hble Servt—

E'ch-Pi-El

[Enclosure: Brochure of a Japanese print exhibition with brief annotations by HPL.]

Notes

1. HPL refers to a visit to Clark Ashton Smith made by Donald Wandrei in late 1934. HPL then saw Wandrei on his own visit to New York City in 31 December 1934–7 January 1935.

2. Clark Ashton Smith wrote four haiku under the title "Old Hydraulic Diggings."

3. Also present were Dean P. Phillips (a friend of Loveman) and his unnamed friend, and a fifteenth unidentified person.

4. In Greenwich Village. Now recognized as the oldest continuously operating gay bar in New York City.

5. Vyônes, the principal town of Averoigne, from Smith's story "The End of the Story."

[17]   [ALS, JHL]

66 College St.,
Providence, R.I.,
March 5, 1935.

Dear Helen:—

I am surely envious enough at hearing of the vernal weather which Averoigne has been enjoying! Ædepol! blossoms in February in N. Lat. 39°! Thanks for the tantalising specimens—I can visualise the whole exquisite spectacle from your vivid description. Most assuredly do I hope that this early terrene awakening has not been followed by any anticlimactic cold snap. There seems to have been a phenomenally fine spell all the way up the Pacific coast—friends in the southern part of Washington write of the beginning of agricultural operations there. As for Providence—if I had a vocabulary as large as Klarkash-Ton's, with every word a blistering oath, I couldn't begin to convey any opinion of our recent meteorological conditions. The enclosed picture will tell the tale more urbanely than I could. *This* is what we had all through late January & the greater part of February! Naturally my own excursions from these steam-heated precincts were neither numerous nor extensive. Now, however, the worst of the season is obviously past—& on the 21st, at 8:18 a.m., the sun crosses the vernal equinox on its northward course!

Glad that Son is duly enjoying the season, & hope his current streak of exemplary conduct may continue indefinitely. I was glad to see a picture of him in a group a couple of months ago—he's certainly the handsomest & stateliest gentleman I've glimpsed in a long while! Which reminds me that on Feby. 14 there were born at your erstwhile caravanserai across the garden here 4 coal-black little imps—brothers of the late Samuel Perkins (June '34–Sept. '34) of cherished memory. There has been much frantic telephoning in an effort to find good homes for all—but I devoutly hope that at least one will be retained. A few of the dignified members of the Kappa Alpha Tau have appeared on the clubhouse roof, drawn forth by the milder weather—& before long I hope to see a sizeable representation of them. I trust that Mother Simaetha duly flourishes on Indian Hill, & wish that through some miracle Genl. Tabasco might wander back to his accustomed haunts. Farther southwest in your state E. Hoffmann Price (in his new hilltop home near Redwood City) has been honoured with the companionship of a highly remarkable snow-white personage who voluntarily strayed in from nowhere & proceeded to settle down after consuming (I transcribe literally) 3 saucers of milk & 2 large bowls of spaghetti & diced meat. The newcomer has received the name of Nimrod because of his prowess in the chase as well as on the field of battle. Not long ago he clawed a gopher out of its hole & brought it for his master to admire before devouring it. Still more recently he nearly terminated the career of a huge dog who looked too interestedly at his bowl of beans. Price intervened for the canine's sake. Nimrod also enjoys riding in the Price juggernaut (Ford 1928) whilst his master crawls along at 90 miles per hour. Possibly Price will bring him along on his next trip to Averoigne. If so, I trust that he may regard Simaetha & Son as friends rather than as potential adversaries!

I learn with extreme interest of your musical progress, & congratulate you sincerely on the tremendously promising developments of recent weeks. It seems to me that the new teacher was wise in urging you not to transfer your primary allegiance from the instrument with which you have already done so much—although on the other hand I fancy a mastery of the piano is vastly useful to any musician, no matter what his own special instrument is. From the few musicians I know well, I gather that piano-skill is almost universal among them—be they vocalists, violinists, composers, or bass-drum players. Therefore your latest arrangement is probably the most sensible possible one—to continue dominantly as a violinist, but to supplement this major pursuit with a good working knowledge of pianoforte procedure. Your trial duet surely must have been a highly remarkable performance—& one attesting great & unusual natural talent. It certainly seems to me, from all the evidence, that you possess every qualification for really serious & distinguished work in music; & I trust you will not cease to develop this rare & fortunate aptitude. Glad you can arrange for more frequent minor lessons to supplement the major lessons—the latter ought surely to be the more profitable because of the former. The need of continued teaching surely is an exasperating handicap, & I hope you can ultimately arrange to eliminate it—if only for a time. My musical friend in Wisconsin—Alfred Galpin, who has studied under the late Vincent d'Indy & wishes to be a serious composer—has been handicapped in the same way, being a French instructor in Lawrence College. Just now he has ambitions of escaping pedagogy for a year because of a timely legacy. As for nervousness—I don't suppose there is any way of extirpating such a thing, since virtually all creative artists seem to have something of the kind saddled on them. But the unpleasant effects of nervousness will certainly diminish vastly after you have learned to harness up your hypersensitiveness exclusively—or at last mainly—in the service of a definite & adequate phase of art. It is my opinion, from long observation, that the major trouble of most nervous persons is that they haven't any especial thing which they want overwhelmingly to do, & which is sufficiently within their powers to make a reasonable degree of success possible. Once they discover such a thing, a large share of their sensitive energy is detached from random considerations & put to work in a really fruitful & satisfying field. And of course, no one has as good a chance as a sincere artist to discover & profit by an ardent interest of this kind.

Extremely glad you had a chance to hear & meet Hoffmann[1] [*sic*]—who is surely a renowned & influential figure these days, though I can recall when he was hailed as a boy prodigy. His consideration for his audiences surely stamps him as a generous & magnanimous character all apart from his art—although on the other hand it is hard to blame a person like Kreisler,[2] whose fund of energy may be so much less, that he simply could not carry on if he had to attend to any responsibilities other than performing. I was amused, by the way, to read the other day a confession by Kreisler that in his early days he 'put over' many compositions of his own by attributing them to forgotten masters of bygone centuries.

The new San Francisco Opera House surely sounds like a bit of the ancient world's sumptuousness transferred to the present! How astonishing that so gorgeous an affair could appear in the midst of the present economic turmoil! I trust its acoustic qualities may be on a par with the rest of its magnificence—& am sure you will find the performances there prodigiously impressive. It will be interesting to contrast the work of the company in that dazzling setting with its work in Sacramento's more ordinary environment.

Sorry that dealings with members of the so-called human race prove perplexing at times—but it appears to be a fact that perplexity & disappointment are inevitable whenever one depends much on the reactions, opinions, & actions of the species, or allows himself to be concerned about the various shades of emotion, attitude, & procedure in individuals. I always feel sorry for those strongly emotional, gregarious, & sensitive persons who are continually worried about the opinions & sentiments of others toward themselves. It seems to me that they fail to form a perfect picture of the blind, indifferent cosmos, & the fortuitous, deterministically-motivated automata who form a sort of momentary insect pest on the surface of one of the least important of its temporary grains of dust. What people are, & what they think & feel & do, are pure accidents of cosmic mutation. We can't expect them to be other than they are—each separate individual moulded by a trillion inevitable conditions of heritage & surroundings. All one can do is to observe these cosmos-driven automata, study their general & individual instincts in the objective manner of natural history, & entertain no expectation that any can be much other than it is. When this or that automaton represents some quality or furnishes some influence which interests or pleases one, then the sensible thing is to expect of it only such things as are connected with that quality or influence. We might wish that various qualities of interest & agreeableness could be concentrated in the same person, but this occurs only by accident at rare intervals. In practice, no member of one's circle of acquaintances is likely to represent more than one or two of the human qualities which one relishes & admires. When one does, it is imply a fortunate accident. However—there is nothing truly tragic in the existing condition *if one expects nothing more*. From the material at hand, taken as it is, one may often make up a very interesting circle. Now & then a particularly congenial individual turns up—but there's no way of finding such an one except through constant observation of the miscellaneous passing stream. At other times an individual with some interesting qualities will prove so ultimately unadjustable that elimination, total or partial, is necessary—but whatever annoyance or regret attaches to such a condition may be softened by reflection on its naturalness & inevitability. And as one grows older—if a philosophic perspective be constantly maintained—the importance of human beings steadily decreases in one's sight, so that absorption in some adequate aesthetic, intellectual, constructive, or administrative activity (an activity which emphasises the individual ego directly, instead of secondarily, in relation to other egos) becomes a paramount & satisfactory emotional life . . . . supplemented, of course, in many cases, by such rational attachments to human interests as favourable accident may happen to allot to one. It is certainly not necessary to be a misanthrope. One may enjoy friends without taking them too seriously or expecting too much of them—& may even happen to encounter a few who seem to deserve serious consideration. The great point is not to expect too much. Ideal human adjustments are not a natural "right" to which everyone is "entitled". They are, on the contrary, mere lucky accidents of none too great commonness. When they can occur, one may well congratulate himself on having stumbled on to a good break. But when they don't occur, there is no sense in feeling cheated, melancholy, or dissatisfied. Such an indifferent deal is about what the average person gets. The most sensible course in life is not to expect much, but to make the most of the scattered & fragmentary material at hand. A lot of people are interesting & valuable in specific ways—so the thing to do is to enjoy each for his own specialty & expect no more. By adding all one's acquaintances together one may usually—with the use of good sense, skill, & imagination—patch up a hand-picked human environment of very tolerable interest, stimulation, & satisfyingness . . . . . . an environment distinctly worth living in when supplemented by non-human objects of beauty, significance, & favourable symbolism. But the tranquillity & value of such an environment depend on one's ability to be content with the material as it is—to let each individual play his own part, & expect no more of him. It doesn't do to become too concerned about any of the individual human atoms—or groups of atoms—or to worry excessively about one's own adjustment to any or some or all. The people on Mars will never know that any human race exists—the people on Neptune can never know that the earth exists—the people on the planets of Alpha Centauri can never know that the solar planets exist—the people of trans-galactic systems can never know that the sun exists—the people of the remotest nebulae can never know that our immediate stellar universe exists. A few trillion years hence there will be no consciousness in existence that can know of the former existence of such a thing as a human race. The universe will be just as it would have been had no earth existed. With which typical flourish Grandpa concludes an equally characteristic ream of sententious senile maundering.

Local news—except for the neighbouring kittens—undistinguished. Heard a couple of good poetry readings at the college—one by Susanna Valentine Mitchell[3] [Gammell] of this city, the other by the celebrated Archibald MacLeish, author of "Conquistador." Of lectures there may be noted a highly interesting address on Japanese prints in general & good old Hokusai (1760–1849) in particular, held at the local museum in connexion with an exhibition of the prints. Great stuff—I have always been exceedingly fond of the delicacy, tranquillity, & exquisite harmony of Sino-Japanese art. Enclosed are some cuttings illustrative of this event—which ably supplements similar events of last December.

A more recent lecture which my young friend Belknap would have raptly absorbed was also at the museum & illustrated with lantern-slides—contemporary Russian soviet art. I was really quite astonished by the amount & quality of some of the work, for I had not thought so much of the aesthetic impulse & the old Byzantine tradition had survived. Despite the silly Marxian effort to deny the existence of any art without social motivation, there is much skill & vitality among some of the soviet painters. They amount to more than their theories would permit if literally enforced—& as the soviet culture mellows & lets down its extreme revolutionary propaganda I presume they will get still better. Amusingly enough, their art does not tend to be even nearly as radical as the insane "abstract" junk of the decadent so-called artists of the western world's "modernistic" schools. But on the other hand, there is a vast amount of commonplace crudity of mere poster grade—the direct fruit of the Marxian ideal. Whatever upturn may come, the cataclysm of 1917 was a tragic setback which can scarcely be neutralised in a century's time. The only advantage gained by artists in the upheaval is a sense of the *future* in civilisation. That's what the bolsheviks have which we haven't. They are at the beginning of an era—however poor & lopsided an one,—whereas we are at the obvious end of an era ... or at least of a distinct phase of an era. We don't know what's coming, hence cannot appraise the real significance of anything new in western life. Their art is barbaric & nascent; our modern art is decadent, senescent, & hesitant. But that's not saying that soviet art is anything for other nations to copy. Each to its own—the Slav is saying something that we couldn't say even if we adopted his political system. My own opinion is that an obviously sterile age like the present ought not to try to create anything new. Conditions are not favourable for the expression of the momentary environment—the environment has nothing crystallised enough or certain enough to be expressible. A far more sensible course at present is to emphasise such elements in the age-long main stream as are equally valid in all ages—to devote energies to the expression of the universal rather than the transient. A kind of neo-classicism, it seems to me, is the least absurd ideal to follow amidst an age of turmoil & uncertainty. Such deliberate & intelligent archaism has been practiced before with successful results—as when the Egyptians of the 18th Dynasty (age of Tut-Ankh-Amen) thoughtfully worked in the classic forms of the departed 11th Dynasty .... or when the markedly decadent 26th Dynasty (6th Cent. B.C.—time of Persian conquest) attempted a general restoration of ancient Memphian art. It is obvious, especially in the latter case, that the classic revival furnished infinitely more beauty than any attempt to "express the contemporary age" could have done. But again Grandpa maunders into ponderous abstractions!

A fortnight ago I had a letter from Loring & Mussey of N.Y.—young Derleth's publishers, egged on by him—asking to see some of my tales with a view to possible book publication. Since this is the 5th time in a decade that such a request has been made (W T 1927, Putnam 1931, Vanguard 1932,

Knopf 1933)—without tangible results so far—I am not as naively excited over the matter as I might once have been. Nevertheless I've sent along some junk—just on the general principle of leaving no stone unturned. I expect to see it back before long.

Well—again let me congratulate you on your musical progress, & on the solid & unmistakable genius of which it seems to me a definite index. Likewise on the springlike weather which makes such an encouraging development appropriate! ¶ Regards to Son—& may his angelic period continue long upon the earth! ¶ All best wishes—

  Yr obt h^ble Servt
    E'ch-Pi-El

Notes

1. Josef Casimir Hofmann (1876–1957), Polish-American pianist, composer, and music teacher. He gave his first recital at the age of five.
2. Friedrich "Fritz" Kreisler (1875–1962), Austrian-born violinist and composer, regarded as one of the greatest violin virtuosos of all time.
3. Susanna Valentine Mitchell Gammell (1896–1979), author of the poetry volumes *Journey Taken by a Woman* (1935), *In the Bright April Weather* (1952), and *Make New Banners* (1954). Her *Collected Poems* appeared in 1966. Born in Philadelphia, she was at this time residing in Providence, where she edited *Smoke* (1931–37), a poetry magazine.

[18] [ALS, JHL]

        66 College St.,
         Providence, R.I.,
           April 24, 1935.

Dear Helen:—
     I am glad to hear of the exquisite spring which is following the season of storm & flood—a spring vastly to be envied in this sub-arctic region, where even now a few flowers, a slight budding of certain shrubs, & a slowly growing greenness of the turf are the only conspicuous vernal signs. Each spring I curse the asperities of this detestable climate more & more loudly—for the wasting of the greater part of the year in bleak barrenness & shivers seems doubly criminal as one grows old. Even now the gardens of Charleston & St. Augustine are in full glory, while Richmond & Washington are lovely with delicate new foliage. Only a close attachment to my native soil has prevented me from migrating long ago to the genial shores of South Carolina, Georgia, or Florida. However—in less than a month more, New England will be radiant with a beauty scarcely to be paralleled elsewhere. The floral splendours of Averoigne's meads are surely a compensating reward for the tempests lately endured—& I can visualise the ordered quaintness of your class's succulent garden, with its exotic suggestions of ancient Nueva Mejico.

Landscape gardening always appealed to me to a tremendous extent, & in youth I used to pore over the tattered family copy of Downing's celebrated treatise (1849) on that subject.[1] My grandfather was a most enthusiastic amateur gardener, & I occasionally sought to duplicate his experiments on a very small scale. I, however, (since my tastes have always been primarily architectural) spent more time on the laying out of paths & flagstones, & the allocation of urns, sun-dials, & termini, than to the actual cultivation of flowers. To me, the supreme pleasure was the creation of *whole scenes*—& I was rather reprehensibly careless regarding the details. I trust you duly warn your youthful charges against this error—impressing it upon them that good total effects are to be obtained only through a close & conscientious attention to details.

However—judging from reports, you have certainly earned the season of mildness you are now enjoying! The gales & freshets of this month seem strangely unlike what an outsider usually expects of California—though from your mention of Sacramento levees, & as I judge that floods are not uncommon. Indeed, I recall a story of Ambrose Bierce's in which something of the kind figures rather prominently & gruesomely (the aqueous exhumation & transposition of coffins being involved).[2] The flooding of Auburn Ravine must have been an impressive & disconcerting spectacle—doubly so from its accompaniment by all the sights & sounds of the storm-king's wrath. Once in a while New England has troublesome floods—though these are more generally connected with long rains (as in the case of the historic inundations of Nov. 1927), or with the melting of ice in the spring, than with any sudden or violent tempests. Such, I judge, is usually the case in the Sacramento Valley. I hope that the present damage may not prove too disastrous—either as regards crops or as regards buildings & public works in & around the capital.

Rhode Island, during the first half of March, had a deceptive promise of an early spring; so that for a time my hibernation was temporarily broken. I took several trips out to the apparently awakening countryside at temperatures as high as 65° & 71°—on one occasion indulging in a 12-mile walk. As soon as spring officially arrived, however, winter unofficially returned—April being distinguished by rain, gales, & even a flurry or two of snow. I regretted my inability to get south this year. Early in May I shall spend a few days in the Boston zone—with side-trips to ancient & picturesque places—but it will be just my luck if the weather is polar & generally abominable. In June there is a bare possibility that a friend & I may take a trip around Vermont in his car— exploring regions farther north in that picturesque commonwealth than I have ever been except on trains at night bound to & from Quebec.

Glad to hear that the new lessons are progressing smoothly & enjoyably—but sorry the cervical trouble brought an interruption. I surely hope that all traces of the latter may soon be gone. These unheralded & inexplicable visitations are always exasperating, but fortunately most of them are not of long duration. It is paradoxical that the mending is more painful than the original affliction!

I trust that the burdens of Education Week were at least partly atoned for by brilliant performances on the students' part. It seems unfair that you should so repeatedly be saddled with the duties of others—yet of course there is a compensating satisfaction in the tacit proof of your superior abilities thus afforded. The old idea of noblesse oblige—the responsibilities of the governing class, &c. Your septuagenary chorus must make an impressive showing—or sounding—& I hope all the participants rose to the occasion on the 12th. The two 8th grade classes are fortunate in ending the season with a level of musical instruction undoubtedly higher than that which they have been getting! But all this—plus the garden work & the drawing instruction (which I think you once mentioned as forming part of your tasks)—must make a devastatingly exhausting programme! With my vastly more limited nervous energies, I always envy & admire those who—like yourself, young Derleth, my friend Morton, & other capable souls—can sustain crowded schedules of arduous, exacting, & complicated activities.

Heard a number of interesting lectures recently—including (vide enc.) a particularly good series on the late Dr. Franklin, whose setting took me pleasantly back to that 18th century of which I form, psychologically, so inextricable a part. I was glad to see the lecturer (a really notable authority on Am. history)[3] emphasise a point I have always realised from Dr. F's own writings—namely, that despite his insistence on thrift & individual caution, the philosopher did *not* sponsor any such programme of laissez-faire capitalism as some of the modern defenders of that system are seeking to justify with his authority. He expressly proclaimed the need of governmental supervision of commerce & industry under certain conditions, & in general uttered sentiments which would indicate his position as a New Dealer were he alive today. Prof. Crane further demonstrated that Franklin's casual utterances, addressed to the simple masses as in Poor Richard's Almanack, greatly bely his actual convictions when they imply his worship of purely material success. This series so impressed me, that on the night following the second one I had a most picturesque dream involving Dr. Franklin & myself, & centreing in a curious distortion of time (such as Klarkash-Ton might devise for one of his tales) whereby an area of 1785 merged imperceptibly into an area of 1935. Franklin & I were riding horseback from Philadelphia to New York through the world of 1785—he being just returned from France. I knew that something terrible & inexplicable had happened to *time*, & that there lay somewhere ahead of us a hideous nightmare of machinery & decadence called *1935*. Franklin would not believe me—but some rumour had reached New-Brunswick, for as we rode through that place we found frightened crowds in the streets & heard bells tolling in all the steeples. Around Metuchen we encountered a curious fog—& in Rahway we could see the spectral shapes of 1935 (new buildings, motors, modernly dressed persons) impinging on the cobblestones, gambrel roofs, Georgian facades, & knee-breeched inhabitants of 1785. Even then, however, Dr. Franklin insisted that we were merely subject to some bizarre delusion. Half way down the Elizabethtown road the fog vanished, & we were in the full world of 1935—with our horses rearing at the bewildering streams of motors. At last Franklin realised that something was gravely wrong—for he saw passers-by staring amazedly at our costume. Once he put his mind to the problem, he seemed to have no difficulty in grasping what had happened; & so ample was his scientific training, that he could appreciate the modern uses of the electrical fire which he had so spectacularly snatched from the heavens in 1752. In (modern) Elizabeth I stopped to purchase some clothing of 1935, donning it in the shop. Dr. Franklin, however, refused to alter his semi-Quaker attire, & continued to receive curious stares. In Newark we left our horses at a livery stable & took the Hudson Tubes for New York, emerging at 33d St. Here no one noticed Franklin's costume, & we walked about freely—I pointing out to the philosopher various marvels & horrors (like the Empire State Bldg., the foreign populace, the strange conveyances, & so on) of 1935, whilst he attempted to adjust them to his previous knowledge. During this rambling ciceronage, & without the attainment of any dramatic denouement or the approximation of any logical story-plot, I began slowly to drift into wakefulness. Thus the vision ended—aimless & pointless, but a striking testimonial to the substance of Prof. Crane's historical discourse!

I am surely sorry to hear that so many congenial correspondents have developed umbrageous, jaundiced, & generally intractable tendencies; & hope that a period of reflection may cause at least some of them to acquire— perhaps gradually—a broader, sounder, & mellower perspective, so that a resumption of epistolary exchanges will prove feasible. I don't think you need fear that any shortcomings in your own temperament are responsible for such facile asperities. Rather would I tend to lay the matter to various qualities of human nature in general, as bewilderingly acted upon by the conflicting philosophical & social-aesthetic currents of a decadent, unsettled age & milieu. I would not be surprised if the degree of egocentric arrogance & invidious pique in each of the various delinquents were found to be proportionate with his degree of sympathy toward the infantilistic & hedonistic folkways & doctrines of 'bohemianism' or Greenwich-Village modernism. This psychology of quasi-exhibitionistic vanity & anti-traditional subjectivism seems to me peculiarly adapted to the bringing out of certain annoying & unpleasant traits always latent in the non-analytical human mind & emotions—traits connected with an exaggeration of the ego, an emphasis on the element of *monopoly* in nearly all activities, & a curious & disastrous tendency to personalise & sentimentalise all sorts of human contacts & exchanges of ideas; so that the subject makes of every type of acquaintanceship or friendship something which cannot logically be made of any save the most exceptional family or prospectively family relationships . . . . . a kind of mirror for his own image of him-self, to be valued only so far as it reflects him in impressive & gratifying pro-portions. This type of attitude is constantly exemplified in the moody, egotistical person who is never content to exchange ideas & impressions for their own sake, but who invariably pauses to invent & dissect some mystical, imaginary link betwixt himself & every person with whom he effects such ex-changes. Hence the mawkish, sophomoric essays on "true friendship" so of-ten perpetrated by persons of high-school age—or at least, high-school psychology. Hence, too, the boresome, puerile, & often impertinent custom of minutely studying the personal emotions of all one's acquaintances toward oneself; & the attendant cycle of callow exaltations & depressions based on the fancied fluctuations of reciprocal regard observed or assumed in this or that individual. It is a very pathetic spectacle—this transference or extension, as it were, of the conditions of serious romance to domains where such con-ditions are basically & manifestly inapplicable. For the general tendency, of course, modern egocentricity is not wholly responsible—indeed, the simper-ingly sentimental Victorian age was a great offender in this direction. But one cannot deny that radical modernity has vastly aggravated the fallacy, & sub-stantially increased the virulence of many of its effects. Having repudiated the rational aesthetic pattern laid down by human experience, whereby the field of intense & monopolistic regard is reduced within well-defined & recognisa-ble limits, the emotional modern appears to seek a position in which he can enjoy the undivided homage of as many other persons as possible; rather un-reasonably complaining if any of these fails to exalt him with that singleness which he himself does not accord to anyone! Not, of course, that every mod-ern consciously subscribes to this extreme. It is merely the *tendency* toward which the over-emotionalised 'bohemian' is impelled by the influences domi-nant around him. Some display it more than others—according to their de-gree of susceptibility to popular fashion & mass-suggestion. As for a panacea for such a state—alas! Could we so easily mould the blind, irrational philo-sophic currents which sweep certain generations along with them, the whole problem of social, political, & economic adjustment were a simple one! Actu-ally, there is very little to do save to preserve one's own clearness of perspec-tive & impersonality of attitude—endeavouring to spread a rational philosophy whenever an opportunity occurs, & always discouraging the growth of out-of-place attitudes, customs, & points of view. In the course of time it is very possible that psychologically sounder modes of aesthetic-ethical education, & a riper cultural experience which recognises the inevitable futili-ty & unpleasant results of egocentric sentimentalism, will naturally & sponta-neously correct some of the extravagances of the present chaotic period. The trouble with these emotional egotists is that they expect too confoundedly much of existence. They represent a typical modern neurosis whose first great exponent (as someone pointed out last summer in the *Atlantic*) was the

French author of a century ago—Stendhal.[4] They want to cut a great swath in the world—to do what they please, receive the undivided homage of everyone they encounter, & enjoy on every hand those delicate & specialised emotions of regard which (if they but knew it) are actually of exceeding rarity, & are dependent for their existence on the very sort of life-patterns & limitations which the modern radicals refuse to recognise! Sooner or later they will learn that they can't have their cake & eat it . . . . that they can't expect to retain varied & interesting contacts with other minds if they insist on mixing with those mental contacts the incongruous fumes of romantic sentimentality, & the silly & exasperating practice of measuring reciprocal esteem & classifying friendships on a minutely graduated quantitative scale. The two kinds of thing are simply irreconcilable. In some cases, of course, *sheer egotism* predominates—stark grasping after empty precedence & monopoly, without any admixture of boarding-school sentimentality. Thus a person acquainted with a certain person of prominence will sometimes take pitiful & puerile pains to prevent any of his other friends from meeting that person. He feels that knowing a celebrity confers a kind of reflected distinction, & is unwilling to share that distinction with any more people than he is obliged to share it with. But of course this type of pettiness is more or less allied to the other. It has the same egotism at its base, & it acts on the same fallacious conception of friendship as some mystical attribute of enormous personal importance. Thus when a young friend of mine boasted of corresponding with H. G. Wells,[5] he could not comprehend why I refused to regard that circumstance as of vast importance. Of course it was pleasant to be in touch with a great man—but the only thing that would have been of *importance* would have been my friend's ability to *think & write as powerfully* as Wells. And so it goes. I have said that there is no direct remedy for the trouble—& that is true so far as the offenders themselves are concerned. Those, however, who are bothered by the exacting caprices of those offenders may certainly escape much annoyance by adopting a position of increased impersonality & widened perspective, & realising how trivial after all are the issues involved. Of course there is no sure preventive against the loss of certain highly stubborn acquaintances of imperious & unreasoning temper; yet the rate of loss may be very substantially cut down by the adoption of a fixed position of rationality whereby all exacting & presumptuous expectations are met with lightness, ridicule, & non-notice, & all communications confined to such matters as are relevant to the alert interests on which the acquaintanceship is based. When, for example, some writer is confronted by a request from some egocentric & monopolistic acquaintance that he give him *all* his original MSS. for a collection, the sensible thing for the writer to do is to laugh at the vain sap, tell him pleasantly to go to the devil, & continue discussion as amicably as before. In 9 cases out of 10 it will work—& the acquaintance will not be alienated. Indeed, in perhaps 1 case out of these 9 the vain panhandler may be made to see the absurdity of his ways & led to adopt a more sensible attitude. And so on . . . & so on . . . Of course, all this does not mean that friends of truly sympathetic attitude & genuinely profound devotion ought lightly to be dismissed. To them is due a serious consideration in proportion with the intensity & undividedness of their own esteem. The real point is to preserve that principle of proportion by refusing to let varied ego-feeders claim such a degree of consideration as *only* the profoundly & particularly devoted merit. As for the attitude of those few genuinely devoted ones themselves—it is one of the marks of a *genuinely* profound esteem, that it involves no such monopolistic attitude as that of the ego-caterer. With actually thorough friends, these problems of tact & discrimination *do not exist.* Monopoly & jealousy become truly justified only in matters of domestic relationship wholly removed from any of these cases. The fact is, that matters of personal adjustment & friendship really demand just that laissez-faire policy which is becoming unworkable in the economic field. The secret of harmony is to refuse to take the institution of friendship too formally & seriously. Let the various types of acquaintance flounder about as they will, until each finds its own natural niche or drifts out of the picture. And don't attach too much importance or regret to their ego-impelled flounderings. The process of natural selection makes for the best ultimate results. Nor is this course a really cynical or misanthropic one—for just as it disfavours the arrogant & the insincere, so does it favour the profound & the sincere by singling them out & assigning them merited positions of consideration.

But holy Tsathoggua, what ponderous didacticism! Thus speaks the oracle, heavy with the infallible wisdom of the ages . . . . . reviving among mankind those lost principles of perfect equity & sound harmony which perished amidst the civil wars of bygone & millennial Poseidonis! A cheap way to sound important—but anyhow, I don't try to burst into print with such flatulent tripe as a lot of half-baked Pythagori & peanut Platos do! So far as actual cases go,—as I said before, I trust that time & reflection will before long banish the sulks & cognate anfractuosities into which the fads & perspectives of the moment have temporarily led a group of actually admirable & brilliant minds. Give 'em plenty of leeway, & the best of them will be back on the list in the end!

I am sorry to learn, from recent bulletins, that Klarkash-Ton has been having so hard a time. It appears that both his parents are ill, & that their care devolves solely upon him—a situation of course complicated by the remoteness of the locale & the generally poor facilities prevailing. I surely hope that vernal warmth & its concomitant fresh-air possibilities may help the elder Smiths toward an early recovery & relieve the Abbot of Vyones from his aggravated responsibilities. On the credit side of the ledger I note with pleasure that Wright has accepted four more offerings from the Citadel of Zothique.[6]

I believe I mentioned the arrival, on Feby. 14, of four little niggers at your quondam pausing-place across the garden. Of these, there has been retained on the premises one exquisite little rascal bearing the name of John Perkins. He is now strong & wiry, & just beginning to purr—& his eyes still have the wide violet quality of infancy. He is in almost every respect a duplicate of his late & sincerely lamented elder brother Samuel (June–Sept. 1934), save that his small inky expanse is broken by one tiny white shirt-stud. A more playful & pugnacious young devil never skipped on four feet—& if he guards his health well, I am sure he will develop into an ideal member for the Kappa Alpha Tau. Naturally he is a frequent & welcome guest at #66, & I have made several attempts to get a snap-shot of him .... a difficult job in view of his elusive & kinetic qualities! The only even rudimentarily successful snap is one which I got when my guest was on the desk before me, dividing his interest betwixt some of Grandpa's papers & the westward view. I then obtained a sort of blurred close-up with a portrait-lens—though in Mr. Perkins' brief interval of relative stability I did not have time to gauge my distance correctly, & consequently secured a sort of bob-tailed & crop-eared effect. I'll enclose the print for Son to see—in fact, he can retain it if he wishes. This was the last of a roll of 8 which I started in August, & whose *first* subject was my late little friend *Sam* Perkins—held by my aunt. I think I'll also enclose that print. What an exquisite little electron of night he was! Oh, yes—& while I'm in the enclosing business I'll also slip in one of the intermediate views—a glimpse of the ancient Warren waterfront taken March 3 when (as I believe I've previously mentioned) I guided a pleasant young visitor among the antiquities of my native state. Said visitor appears in the foreground. You will note the boat in drydock, the venerable marine warehouse whose gable appears on the right, & in the background (best observed with a magnifying-glass) a group of colonial dwellings in Water St. I rather like this view—for to me its jumble of component elements is distinctly typical of New England's ancient seaports. Warren—originally known as Brooks' Pasture—was the ancient Sowanus, royal seat of the Wampanoags & home of Massasoit, the Pilgrims' early friend. It was on Plymouth-Colony soil (Mass. after 1691), & taken into R.I. in 1747 upon the adjudication of a boundary-dispute by George II. The village began to arise shortly before King Philip's War—about 1670—& upon joining R.I. received its present name from Admiral Sir Peter Warren, leader of His Maj^{ty's} victorious naval forces at Louisburg in 1745. It was a great whaling & privateering centre, & during the unfortunate revolt of 1775–83 was bombarded by the regulars. Later the sea-trade declined, & factories & foreigners crept in—but it still holds much of the charm & atmosphere of old. I believe I pointed out its white Georgian steeple to you from the Newport boat. None of the accompanying prints need be returned.

Local news—to the 2 walnut filing cabinets obtained Jan. 21, I added on March 23 no less than *6* small 4-drawer papier-maché-&-wood-frame cabinets (probably meant to be shoe-boxes!) obtained at a dollar each at a bargain sale. Their size ($22 \times 13 \times 9\frac{1}{2}''$) enables me to tuck them in out-of-the-way

places without disturbing the general furnishing scheme. Thanks to them—&
the 2 others—my odd pamphlets & papers are in better order than they've
been before for a quarter of a century . . . yet even so, a lot remain in cardboard boxes or on open shelves. ¶ Regards from my aunt & myself—& I join
with Mr. Perkins in sending particular regards to Son. ¶ Yr obt Servt—

H P L

P.S. Besides the other prints, I'm enclosing a second blurred close-up of Mr.
John Perkins—examining something on Grandpa's desk. Also a shot of my
aunt. None need be returned.

Notes

1. Andrew Jackson Downing (1815–1852), an American landscape designer, horticul-
turalist, writer, editor of the *Horticulturist* (1846–52), and prominent advocate of the
Gothic Revival in the U.S. For his book, see the Bibliography.
2. HPL refers to "The Famous Gilson Bequest" in *Can Such Things Be?*
3. Verner W. Crane (1889–1974), professor of history at Brown (1920–30) and the
University of Michigan (1930–59) and author of *Benjamin Franklin, Englishman and
American* (1936) and other works.
4. Eugene Bagger, "The First of the Moderns," *Atlantic Monthly* 154, No. 4 (October
1934): 495–508.
5. See HPL to Marian F. Bonner (22 March 1936): "Certain young friends of ours [i.e.,
R. H. Barlow] have written to dignitaries like H. G. Wells, Machen, Dunsany, etc., and
have spent good postage mailing copies of their first books (usually printed at their own
expense) to Santayana, the late Mr. Kipling, the late George Sterling, H. L. Mencken,
and other high lights—including the book departments of all the leading newspapers
and magazines" (*LFF* 1037).
6. Smith had sold "The Chain of Aforgomon," "The Treader of the Dust," "The
Black Abbot," and "Necromancy in Naat."

[19]   [ALS, JHL]

% R. H. Barlow,
Box 88, De Land, Florida.
July 11, 1935.

Dear Helen:—

As you see—& as you may have previously learned through a
card acknowledging a Yosemite card from your mother—I am emulating
your household in sporting a temporary aestival address. In other words, I am
repeating my last year's visit to that gifted young writer-artist-printer-book-
collector who is such an admirer of Klarkash-Ton's . . . . the amiable & super-
hospitable Master Robert Hayward Barlow. I left Providence on June 5th, &
shot straight down to ancient Fredericksburg, Va. without any pause. After

7 hours amidst the colonial houses & scenic attractiveness of Genl. Washington's home town I resumed the southward pilgrimage, stopping only at good old *Charleston*—America's most fascinating city. Here I spent a day & a half—then proceeding to Jacksonville for a night's rest & reaching De Land June 9 at noon. The moment I struck the Carolina low country I grew stronger & more active—indeed, this southern trip has caused me to feel really *well* & comfortable for the first time in 1935. Sleep actually *rests* me, which it has not been doing in the north. Sooner or later I'll have to move down here permanently. I'm now repeating my 1934 visit with minor variations. Barlow's father—a retired army colonel—is now at home. An elder brother—Wayne—a 2nd Lt. at Ft. Sam Houston, Texas—has been here on a furlough & has formed a delightful companion; but recently his leave expired & he had to depart for the west. Of the felidae described last year Doodlebug (snow-white patriarch) vanished last autumn, but there are rumours of his being alive as an atavistical roamer of the jungle. High has seceded from the Barlow fold & joined a neighbouring menage, but is still as friendly as ever. Low has been given to a grocery store in Eustis—while Jack, his neck still a trifle stiff from his snake-bite experience of '34—is the dean of the outdoor clan. Henry Clay (yellow) & Alfred A. Knopf (grey semi-tiger) are fall '34 kittens of Low's, & permanent additions to the extra-mural establishment. Within the house are two lordly & pedigreed Persians (yellow—full brothers & precisely alike in aspect) brought down from Washington (where Barlow studied art from Sept. to June) by my youthful host. Of these one—Cyrus—is extremely playful & affectionate, whilst the other—Darius—is as yet haughty & aloof, though he exhibits subtle signs of mellowing. All of these furry gentry send their regards to Son—who we hear has been receiving the competent & sympathetic oversight of Klarkash-Ton during the absence of his "folks". Meanwhile we read, write letters, classify books, set type on sundry printing projects, explore the country, do revisory work when necessary, & in general follow the programme of last year's visit. My host has built a cabin across the lake (I helped him), to which—for the sake of seclusion—he has transferred his press, desk, & other vital accessories. On June 17—as mentioned on the card to your mother—we visited a fascinating place . . . . Black Water Creek, a tropical river flowing in sinuous curves through a lush jungle of tall, moss-draped cypresses, leaning palms, twisted roots, pallid flowers & leprous fungi, black earth, sunken logs, vines & creepers, serpents & alligators . . . . . & everything else suggesting the Congo or the Amazon. It was like the river at Silver Springs which I described last year—even more enjoyable because we (Bob, Wayne & I) explored it in a slow rowboat instead of being hurried along in a launch. Just how long the present visit will last I really don't know. I expected to be returning north by this time—to meet an old friend [M. W. Moe, father of the brilliant young fellow who explored N.E. under my guidance this spring] who will be visiting N.Y. from the west—but my almost fanatically

hospitable hosts refuse to let me set any date for moving along. So insistent & evidently sincere are their importunities, that I may be lingering hereabouts as late as August. The (to me) bracing quality of the climate makes me highly amenable to persuasion. Palmettoes, live-oaks, Spanish moss, temperatures between 80° & 88° . . . . all these things are insidious attractions which help to give Florida a sort of Lotophagan or Calypsonian quality. Summer or winter, it surely is the climate for Grandpa E'ch-Pi-El! I enclose some cards reminiscent of this & other austral scenes.

Only this idyllic tropical setting enables me to contemplate without acute envy the grandeur-filled itinerary you have been pursuing . . . & even so, my wish that I might behold such western wonders is undiminished. Certainly, you could not have chosen a more impressive & imagination-stirring scene for a vacation—& your vivid description brings out its charm & majesty to the full. Vernal Falls must be a tremendous sight—whether giving an impression of terrifying might, as at first, or presenting a milder aspect, as later in your story. That trail beaten by the spray is surely unique. Glad you have had so ample a sojourn, & that your mother & sister were able to share part of the experience. It must have been soothing & invigorating after your trying & exhausting school session & other worries—both the scenery & the exercise doubtless playing their part. In my opinion there is no tonic & relaxation like travel of the right kind—& this surely seems to have been of the right kind. I am sorry, though, that any tonic was so badly needed; & hope that next year will prove an easier & less troubled one.

The camping trip up the Little Yosemite must have been memorable indeed—I can picture those distant, dawn-gold cliffs at Washington Lake! The bear-scratched aspen grove is surely a quaint sight—I, for one, had never heard of the sportive ursine custom responsible for the markings. If the Thompson-Seton[1] [*sic*] theory be true, the competitive & gaming instinct must certainly lie deep in the psychological makeup of all the mammal kingdom! Your new trout-cleaning erudition will undoubtedly prove of use on later expeditions. Hope the rattlesnake didn't cause any acute peril before you slew him. Snakes are numerous down here—but I haven't seen any so far except from a boat. Glad congenial companionship has not been lacking—& trust that the problem of premature departure versus the possible musical engagement managed to adjust itself. It is really a pity to have to leave a pleasant place before the potentialities are exhausted—as I reflect now, while postponing my own departure northward.

As a whole, the Yosemite certainly is a place which must be seen sooner or later. I first became impressed by it years ago, when revising the poems of a delightful old gentleman who had travelled there & written much about its glories in his own quaint way.[2] This year I have had further sidelights from my friend E. Hoffmann Price—now of Redwood City, Cal.—who has made a trip to the Yosemite & sent several views thereof. (Thanks in advance, by the way, for the pictures you are about to send.) Price, incidentally, will probably be visiting C A S before long—in company with a young weird tale enthusiast from Berkeley named Fred Anger.[3]

As for Grandpa's bad boys—alas, I knew that all too many of them subscribe to theories of value & codes of procedure which sound sadly strange & defective to old gentlemen! I don't palliate crude expressions or ideals—& when I say that I hope maturer thought & added years will rectify certain rashnesses, coarsenesses, & asperities, I do so with no ignorance of present conditions. Bless my soul, but I've scolded more than one of the little rascals with true patriarchal severity for ultra-modern perspectives & aspirations expressed, & not-very-traditional dealings boasted of. If I were their actual father I'd tan some of their young hides for them—though even then realising that their foibles come from the overpowering (to all but those of very deeply-seated traditionalism) impact of the times rather than from any dark, innate diabolism. It is a difference in *zeitgeist*—in subtle environmental suggestion—which causes the great-grandsons of the grave, scrupulous, fastidious youths of the Poe period (the age of Hawthorne's & Longfellow's & Lowell's & Holmes's & Emerson's youth) to resemble their forbears so little in ethical theories & practices. An unsettled age fosters unsettled characters—& I hope that the gradual attainment of a new social-intellectual equilibrium in the years ahead may give the infants of today a better "break" than that received by the "lost generation" born in the century's earlier decades. So don't fancy that you have, as an individual, any tendency to bring out the cruder side of various personalities. It is not you—nor any other one person—but the whole wretched age & the chaos of emotional theory it has bred. I could cite instances wholly unconnected with yourself in which some of my young friends have made me wish I had the paternal right to give them just the least admonitory taste of a good leather strap. Nowadays the most *deeply* agreeable characters are those reared under special conditions in which traditionalism bulks large. West Point is a salutary influence—as the naive, straightforward, un-subtle character of Barlow's brother Wayne seems to attest. A darned fine chap! It's a pity that formative schools like that aren't open to the whole community.

Reverting to earlier travel chronicles—I guess I mentioned my antiquarian trips of early March with young Moe—son of my old friend in Milwaukee. This bright & pleasing young scientist visited me again April 27–8—coming as before in his faithful Ford & once more employing my guidance on scenic & antiquarian rounds . . . . a two-day programme.

Saturday the 27th we tackled a region not wholly unfamiliar to yourself—none other than ancient *Newport*. Going by land, however, we saw the various sights in a different order—& took in a few you did not have a chance to see. We avoided the Mt. Hope toll bridge & used the public "Stone Bridge" from Tiverton below Fall River—going down the island of Aquidneck by the east road & coming back by the west road. The day was warm & sunny—ideal in every way. On the down trip we saw a splendid rustic scene—an ancient windmill (*not* the one your sharp gaze discerned when the old man couldn't pick it out) on a knoll, with old farm buildings & a flock of sheep around it. The *perfect* pastoral antiquity of the scene led us to photograph it. Later we proceeded to "Whitehall" (about which I told you, but which there wasn't time to see during your brief sojourn), 1729–31 home of the eminent Dean Berkeley, after whom ("westward the course of empire takes its way") your own native town was named. This edifice is still kept in good condition by the Colonial Dames. We also saw the neighbouring rocks on which the good Dean sat whilst writing his famous "Alciphron". Our next step was that strange & impressive cleft in the seaward cliffs called "Purgatory" (like the Churn in Marblehead & Rafe's Chasm near Gloucester), where the ocean pounds thunderously in. Thence to the regular cliffs—& down the 40 steps—which you descended in 1933. While down on the rocks there—where you saw the fisherman—I slipped up & got rather soaked in looking for a sea-cave. After that the town proper—which you managed to cover pretty thoroughly. 1698 Quaker Meeting-House, 1726 Anglican Church, 1739 Colony-House, 1749 library, 1760 Market House, 1763 Jews' Synagogue (where you saw the Italian caretaker & heard his rambling harangue), & private dwellings as old as 1675. We left the car & made the rounds on foot—but were spared the annoying rain of '33. After doing the city we returned northward via the west road—where we saw the Overing farmhouse . . . scene of Genl. Prescott's capture by a small boat party of rebels in 1777. Just beyond that—in the deep twilight—we came upon the windmill which you *did* see from the boat. Then the Stone Bridge, Fall River, & home.

Sunday the 28th we went to ancient *New Bedford*—Nantucket's successor as the world's great whaling centre, whose last lone exemplar of the industry put to sea only 11 or 12 years ago. The marine museum was closed—but after a tour of Johnnycake Hill (cf. Melville's "Moby Dick")[4] & the centuried waterfront we set off southward to sample something still better. This was the Round Hills estate of Col. E. H. R. Green (son of the old miser & financier Hetty Green) in South Dartmouth, where the old whaling barque *Charles W. Morgan* (built 1841) is preserved at a lifelike wharf—but solidly embedded in concrete as a permanent exhibit. We went all over the vessel—which is tre-

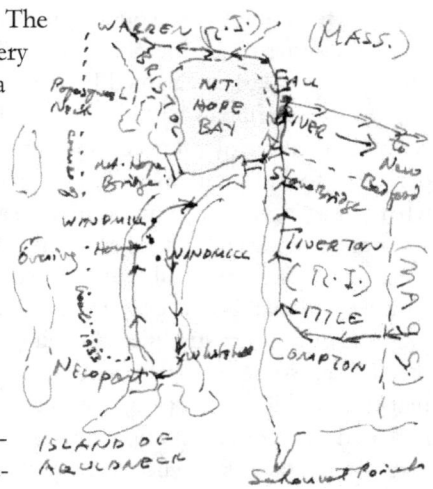

mendously interesting—& snapped some pictures of it. On the Green estate is also an ancient windmill moved from Rhode Island . . . making a total of *3* seen during our 2-day rounds. We then explored a region—where southern Mass. adjoins southeastern R.I.—which I had never seen before in my life. Splendid unspoiled countryside with rambling stone walks & idyllic white-steepled villages of the old New England type. Of the latter the 2 best specimens—Adamsville & Little Compton Commons—are both in R.I. Adamsville contains the world's only known monument to a *hen*—perpetuating the fame of the *Rhode Island Red,* a breed developed in that village from East Indian & Chinese gallinaceous forbears. At Little Compton Commons can be found the home & grave of Elizabeth Alden Pabodie—daughter of the famed John Alden & Priscilla Mullins of Plymouth, & first white woman to be born in New-England. This region was once the seat of the Sakonnet Indians—whose squaw-sachen Awashonks was persuaded by the noted old warrior Capt. Benjamin Church not to join King Philip's conspiracy of 1675. It was settled from Plymouth about 1673, & (like Barrington, Warren, & Bristol) came into the Province of the Massachusetts-Bay in 1691, & into Rhode-Island (when a boundary dispute was settled by George II) in 1747. Capt. Church lies buried not far from Little Compton Commons. Well—at last we turned north through Tiverton, where on our left we had some marvellous views of low-lying fields & blue water. At one point we could see the Gothic tower of St. Paul's School's chapel (the work of Ralph Adams Cram)[5] near Newport—which I pointed out to you in the distance from another direction. Whilst in Tiverton we passed the home of the navigator Capt. Robert Gray, who in 1792 discovered the Columbia River in the far-off Oregon Country on your own Pacific Coast—naming it after his stout Rhode Island barque. Then back home via Fall River (an ugly mill city across the line in Massachusetts) & ancient Warren . . . which latter I described in an earlier epistle.

The following week-end (May 3–4–5) I visited my friend E. H. Cole in the Boston zone, but cold weather seriously hampered our sightseeing. We covered ancient Marblehead, however—which is fascinating under any conceivable set of conditions. I forget whether or not you saw Marblehead while in Massachusetts. If not, you surely missed something! A perfect survi[vi]ng seaport of the 18th century with huddled gambrel roofs. Undoubtedly you have postcards of it.

Speaking of antiquities—& getting back to Providence—I have lately learned with sorrow that *another* row of ancient buildings in my vicinity is about to feel the vandal's hand. You may possibly recall my speaking of my rage at the destruction of the waterfront warehouses (1816) at the foot of the great hill in 1929–30.[6] This time the scene of devastation is *College St. itself*—the doomed row being that huddle of quaint houses & archways reaching from Benefit St. downward to the foot of the hill—on the same (N.) side as the court leading to #66, but beginning ¾ of a block lower down. I shewed them to you in 1933 . . . . you may recall the friendly kitten hovering around them. Included in the cataclysm are the house of Brown's first president (built 1771),[7] that typical 1750 specimen (with a characteristically Providentian double flight of steps) on the corner of Benefit St.,[8] & one of those rare old archways leading under parts of a building to inner courtyards[9] (I pointed these out to you)—of which the only perfect survivors in America are those on Providence's ancient hill. (There is a bricked-up specimen in Richmond, & a boarded-up one in Philadelphia.) On this site will ascend the new main building of the R.I. School of Design. Two palliating & consoling features exist: (a) the preservation, restoration, & incorporation into the new edifice of the bottom (& only brick) house of the ancient row—the old Franklin House,[10] with its quaint inn-yard archway. Thus the survival of *one* of the archways is assured. And (b) the choice of a splendid Providence-Georgian design for the new structure. The building's lower units will harmonise with the surviving Franklin House, while the upper parts will blend in pattern with the residential edifices higher up on the hill. One part will even have a "monitor roof" like #66—a form especially typical of Providence in the 1790–1820 period. The change is regrettable, yet it is fortunate that the character of the new building  will be the same as that of the old ones.[11] Obviously, Providence is remaining dominantly true to its traditional Georgian heritage, & avoiding the 'modernistic' epidemic from which even Boston is not quite immune. Only a few parvenu business firms down town have adopted the meaningless absurdities of modernism. The same, I may add, is true of ancient Charleston & Quebec.

I'll transmit your regards to my aunt—& you may consider hers as transmitted to you. My young black friend John Perkins is getting to be a burly fighting man according to latest advices . . . . he even threatens the peace of the elders of the Kappa Alpha Tau on their shed roof. There is another kitten (black & white like his mother) at the boarding-house, but he has been promised to another family & will probably be gone before I get home. Mr. Perkins & the K.A.T. beg to extend, through me, their sincerest regards to Son.

Advices from Indian Hill indicate that Klarkash-Ton's parents are better—though still feeble, & creating a problem with which only a capable & determined personality could cope. Price expects to visit C A S soon. Incidentally, have you seen the results of C A S's new hobby—sculptural carving? He tells me he has made several statuettes in talc, rhyolite, & dinosaur bone (you doubtless know of the local deposits of the latter)—& specimens sent to R H B & me are impressive indeed. This *carving* involves, of course, a technique very different from Ar-Ech-Bei's *modelling*.

Again congratulating you on your trip, & extending sincerest regards to yourself, your mother, & Son, I remain

Yr obt hble Servt

E'ch-Pi-El.

P.S. Enclosed are some snapshots illustrating the New England explorations chronicled on Sheet III. These may be retained for your collection if they are of any permanent interest. The one of the windmill & sheep is my own favourite.

Notes

1. Ernest Thompson Seton (born Ernest Evan Thompson, 1860–1946), American author, wildlife artist, and a founding pioneer of the Boy Scouts of America in 1910.

2. Probably Eugene B. Kuntz (1865–1944), a clergyman and amateur poet whose slim book, *Thoughts and Pictures* (1932), HPL edited and co-published. Kuntz lived in Clovis, N.M.

3. William Frederick Anger (1921–1982), weird fiction fan and late correspondent of HPL (1934–36). For HPL's letters to him, see *Letters to Robert Bloch and Others*.

4. Johnnycake Hill is a narrow lane in New Bedford where the Seaman's Bethel (a chapel serving sailors) was located. Melville used the locale as a setting in *Moby-Dick* (1851).

5. Ralph Adams Cram (1863–1942), a noted architect and author of *Black Spirits and White: A Book of Ghost Stories* (1895).

6. See HVS 5n4.

7. James Manning (1738–1791), American Baptist minister, first president of Brown University. His house no longer stands.

8. HPL refers to the Samuel Westcott House (1824) at the corner of 240 Benefit Street and 36–38 College Street.

9. The "rare old archway" to which HPL refers was at 20 College Street.

10. The College Building of the Rhode Island School of Design (1936) incorporates the facade of John Holden Greene's Franklin House Hotel (1823); it also has a large archway midway up the hill that reiterates the former carriageway between the previous buildings at the site.

11. Ironically, HPL's house at 66 College Street was moved in 1959 to 65 Prospect Street to make room for construction of the List Art Building.

[20]   [ALS, JHL]

                              % Barlow, Box 88,
                                 De Land, Florida
                                    August 15, 1935.

Dear Helen:—

    The doubling of the bulletins from the Palatium Sullianum was, let me assure you, a pleasure & not a burthen at this end![1] In my reply to the maternal instalment—whose vivid pictorial & descriptive echoes of the Yosemite trip aroused my joint gratitude & envy—I gave most of the details of recent Floridian days. It remains only to add that I expect to break away at last within a week or so, & begin my reluctant (so far as climate is concerned) progress toward the frozen north & the ancient gables of College St. Bro-keness will probably prevent many pauses by the way—but I shall see some-thing of venerable *Charleston* if it kills me. No—the trans-lacustrine cabin here was not designed for Grandpa's residence—although young Bob continually urges that the old man totter down for good & inhabit another & more spa-cious cottage (on the main road, where the family first "homesteaded" in 1925) on the Barlow property. Whether he'd be so insistent if I actually started to move down, is another matter! Some day I'll have to seek a less rigorous clime than my native one—but I'd hate to be as far as this from ancient roofs & spires & gardens. Charleston or St. Augustine would be much more in my line. However—financial arguments are all-powerful, & in the end I may not find it possible to live *anywhere* on a planet so exacting in its economic de-mands! One never can tell—it's all a matter of opportunity. But this surely is the *climate* for me—my energy & activity have been trebled or quadrupled since last spring, & I dread the plunge back north into hibernation & lassi-tude. Ædepol, but I wish the planters of the New England colonies had de-cided to kick out the Spaniards & settle in Florida, so that Providence might have been situate on the banks of the St. John's instead of on the banks of the Seekonk! Why anybody wants to live north of Lat. 30° is beyond me!

However—from all accounts, the paradisal qualities of Florida seem to be pretty well echoed on the Pacific slope! Your Yosemite trip must have been a marvellous experience—while the Carmel sequel surely added the ul-timate finishing touch. I can visualise these regions quite clearly of late, since my friend E. Hoffmann Price (whom you will probably meet when he next visits Klarkash-Ton) has taken to sending me detailed travelogues of his Ter-raplane jaunts, elucidated with large-scale maps obtained from various petrol stations. Not long ago I received quite a liberal education regarding the Mon-terey peninsula—including Carmel. This is a region once familiar, I believe, to both Ambrose Bierce & George Sterling.[2] The pure white beach must be unique & striking indeed—while the deep blue sky & ocean, the roseal flora, the graceful dunes, & the twisted & exotic cypresses, would seem to complete a scene of unsurpassable glamour. That pseudo-sunset effect connected with the gnarled, wind-flattened cypresses & their attendant lichens is something of which I had never heard before. I can well imagine the varied impressive-ness which these trees must have under different conditions of lighting & at-mosphere—& your sketch helps greatly in giving an idea of their massed aspect atop the dizzying cliffs. Some day I surely hope I can assimilate all this bizarre splendour at first-hand!

In the present case the hyper-congenial conditions of your sojourn must have heightened a glamour already great. I am surely glad that your return from the first trip was sufficiently early to permit of your going on the second & unexpected outing—an outing in which art, nature, & society seemed to join in a peculiarly felicitous synthesis! Events & conditions surely did make a very close approach to the ideal—the pleasant housing, the visiting celebrities, the constant musical background, the impromptu quartette, & best of all, the participation & promises of the Philadelphia maestro. I most surely hope that the plan of the latter to include you in his own quartette may materialise when the time comes. The honour & opportunity would certainly be great— especially for one so well fitted to "make good" artistically. In any case, you have reason to feel vast satisfaction in the very broaching of the idea . . . . which is an obvious testimonial (& by no means the first one) to the impression produced on artist-teachers of the first rank by your performances. It is assuredly clear—beyond the need of further demonstration—that you do indeed possess musical endowments of a very genuine & solid nature— endowments auguring brilliantly for your future progress.

With all these distinctions & favourable prospects, it is singularly unfortunate that your rejoicing has to be tempered by reactions of a dismal & destructive nature; & I feel sure that you will shake free of the latter when you give the future—& the values of existence in general—a wider, more cöordinated, & more philosophic consideration. No one ought to feel *less* 'hopeless, useless, incompetent, & generally miserable' than one with your ample, diverse, & undoubted gifts, proved competence & responsibility, resilient youth, graces of aspect & personality, & rich & varied capacity for aesthetic & intellectual experience. To an unbiassed observer, no person could seem a *less* logical candidate for self-belittlement & futilitarian despair—indeed, it seems clear that a sober & analytical survey of your own qualities on the one hand, & of general cosmic & terrestrial values on the other hand, must inevitably act as a banisher of gloomy & depreciating thoughts, & a fosterer of a favourable estimate which, even if it does not breed positive egotism, will at least produce a rational sense of adequacy leading to contentment. Don't permit yourself to be depressed or sidetracked by mere moods (which in themselves are often simply glandular reactions without meaning) or by hasty symbolisms built up from events which are in themselves essentially trivial. Keep a firm grip on facts—fixed realities & stable values—& at all times exercise a judicious sense of proportion. Let the sheer spirit of scientific enquiry dissolve what seem on the surface to be depressing considerations. If you feel 'hopeless' or 'useless', ask yourself what logical standard of situation or expectancy, or what level of adequacy & performance, you actually fall short of. In nine cases out of ten you will discover that your dismal estimates were unjustified. Yea—in ten cases out of ten, so far as I can judge in the present instance. Of course, it is advisable to remove any concrete & active irritants or depressants which your environment may contain . . . . but after you have eliminated all you can, you may well adopt a policy of maximum ignoring toward those which remain. The knowledge that you are doing the best you can, & that your course is indeed an adequate & sensible one, ought to fortify you to a vast extent against obstacles, uncongeniality, under-appreciation, criticism, & all the other exasperating daily drawbacks of ordinary life.

That your mother is likewise affected by this feeling of futility I am equally sorry to hear—& I hope that she can share with you the exercise of a more positive & scientific philosophy. But if the atmosphere of Auburn is really as uncongenial & oppressive as it seems, I surely hope that your household can arrange to migrate en masse to a more bracing, encouraging, & sympathetic milieu! Certainly, Klarkash-Ton has found the place cramping & repellent—although during recent years he refers to it & its denizens far less bitterly than in the early 1920's, when I first knew him. Some places do indeed appear to have a natural hostility in relation to certain types of temperament—& when this is the case, the only logical procedure would seem to be separation. I can understand the repugnance & hesitancy with which you contemplate the quest for another position—but hope that you will encounter some good opening if indeed you feel a move to be necessary. There will, of course, be disadvantages in leaving a region as lovely as picturesque Averoigne would seem to be—& Klarkash-Ton would naturally feel himself tremendously a loser. This increasing cantankerousness which you notice in him may perhaps be an effect of his tragically heavy responsibilities rather than of anything else. From all reports, his present situation is little short of unendurable—yet no immediate avenue of escape would seem to exist. Even the projected visit of E. Hoffmann Price had to be postponed because of a relapse on C A S's father's part. However—in determining a place of permanent residence it is the needs of your own family which must first be consulted. Let it be hoped that you can eventually find a way to return to a less culturally & socially barren region—where frequent congenial contacts & varied activities will keep you all too pleasantly busy to permit of the growth of dismal & needless introspections. Isolation—especially the isolation which savours of hostility—is certainly a bad thing in excess, & one is surely right in taking steps to curtail or banish it.

As for the Old Gentleman's rascally little grandsons—I certainly shall have to do some stern disowning or birch-rod chastising if the more "Bohemian" of them persist in carrying their modernistic ethics to extremes! Some of these young cubs ought to be brought up short & taught in a forcible fashion those now-neglected branches of aesthetics which deal with conduct & human relationships. Blast the brats! However—when they venture their opinions or launch their less creditable reminiscences in their Grandpa's direction, they meet with a cool & stony discouragement which is probably more effective than the printed dissertations or posterior paddlings one might be tempted to administer. They have been given to understand that the old man does not consider their feats or perspectives in the least commendable— hence I have not been made a co-recipient of the gabbling proffered by the arch-offender to Klarkash-Ton. So far as your angle of the matter is concerned—it is doubtless of some consolation to reflect that such mis-bestowals of confidence & emotion are the rule rather than the exception in these days of disordered standards & "liberalised" manners. In the absence of generally acknowledged & properly practiced codes of address & behaviour, there is no way in which cheapness can well be distinguished from worth except after long acquaintance & elaborate tests based on reactions to various situations under all possible conditions. The only guide to peace & security amidst such a mess is a policy of reticence, self-sufficiency, & slowness in acknowledging or bestowing marked evidences of emotion toward others. In other words, a thorough appraisal & analysis—more minute than may have been necessary in the days of greater taste & higher codes—should precede any progress of a friendship to such a stage as involves free personalities in conversation or correspondence, or manifestations of personal interest & emotion which might be subject to indiscriminating misinterpretation or crude exploitation by characters inwardly of the wrong sort. Since such open-eyed discrimination in no way involves a lack of wholesome cordiality, or of unreserved openness in the discussion of any ordinary subjects, it can scarcely be resented—or regarded as arrogance or stiltedness—by any person worthy of subsequent admission to a more confidential & unguarded sort of acquaintance. Indeed, it would be almost a test of a worthy person that he would applaud such rational caution. Thus no one need fear that a suitably discriminating & keenly analytical policy in matters of acquaintanceship would tend to alienate or offend those who after all are deserving of confidence & esteem. If all this sound exasperatingly like mere archaism or Victorian narrowness, it must be remembered that—despite various grotesque extravagances of surface display—the older codes did indeed possess a very sound foundation of good sense, based on an age-long knowledge of human nature & unchangeable emotional reactions. The proof of the pudding is in the eating. Can it be said that the "liberal" manners & easy, flexible codelessness of our "enlightened" young moderns have produced a greater amount of happiness & contentment, & a better adjustment of the individual & his emotions to the external world, than were produced by the more thoughtful manners & more artistically observed standards of the conservative past? Is it not rather true that "modern" attitudes have vastly increased, rather than decreased, the net sum of human restlessness, discontent, misery, & tragedy? Decidedly, no one need feel ashamed or embarrassed at the application of the epithet "old-fashioned" in matters of social conduct. The use of this term in an unfavourable sense is, indeed, strong evidence that the user is one whose opinion has no claim to intelligent regard. Not, of course, that even the most tasteful & logical adherence to time-tried policies is any automatic guarantee of absolute happiness & contentment. It is the bitter lesson of life that all extremes of felicity are largely *accidental,* & that one cannot expect to parallel the good fortune of certain others by following an identical course. "Justice" & "rewards" are romantic conceptions without foundation in reality, & vast harm is done—through disappointment, disillusion, & bitterness—by the popular promulgation of the false notion that they exist. Those mortals are unhappiest, who have expected more than they can be reasonably guaranteed to receive (though others may have received as much through *sheer chance*). Perfectionism & namby-pamby optimism, then, are out of the adult picture. What rational analysis & traditionalism *will* do is to *cut down* the amount of misery which is commonly encountered through aimless & standardless blundering; to *lessen* the probability of mistakes & their resultant woes, & to increase the individual's opportunities for evolving a tolerably satisfactory compromise with the environment & forces around him. But could anything on earth do more?

As to the normality—or the reverse—of one of your age having no real friendships save in letters: it may be admitted at the outset that such a restriction is not to be desired. Certainly it is preferable, if possible, to possess a circle of first-hand, accessible acquaintances whose conversation & imaginative responses may help to give one that sense of importance & adjustment so necessary to extreme contentment. Companionship of a lighter sort—involving sharers of the commoner diversions & emotions, & objects around whom the romantic imagination & sense of adventurous expectancy may be woven—is likewise very much to be wished for . . . . especially in youth, when it may be looked for without inappropriateness. However—granting these premises—we must nevertheless realise that the possession of such types of direct companionship depends to a great extent upon uncontrollable chance. We can, it is true, cultivate such qualities as are most likely to attract friends—but (such is the absolute uniqueness & aloneness of each individual mind) we cannot be sure that chance will bring us into contact with any substantial number of persons capable of congenial friendship with us. The more complex, individual, & distinctive we are, the more emphatically true this is. All commonplace people have vast hordes of friends, since they possess no individuality to hamper the action or sheer instinctive gregariousness. But those of highly specialised tastes are forced to wait until chance & coincidence bring within the same geographical area & social circle others possessing the same relatively rare qualities. Naturally, this causes the distinctive person to have fewer friends than the average person—since they have to be collected one by one from a class vastly restricted in the first place, & certainly unlikely to be widely represented in any single physical locality. The reason why one sometimes has so many more congenial correspondents than face-to-face friends, is that correspondence allows one to draw upon a wider geographical area than does conversational friendship. It is easier to find congenial people when one has the whole extent of one's civilisation to draw upon, than when one has to limit oneself to a radius of 50 miles or so. There is, however, no distinction other than quantitative involved. Since one can collect a certain number of congenial *correspondents* in a given time, there is no reason (in any ordinary case) why he cannot collect at least a few equally congenial *direct friends* if he allows a much longer time for the careful scouring of the vastly smaller area with which he is in first-hand personal touch. Thus it seems to me that your present absence of congenial personal associates is nothing to worry deeply about. It is admittedly unpleasant—but it is clearly a matter of mere chance & of no necessary permanence. You may have no personal friends at the moment (neither have I in Providence), but that is no reason why you may not have dozens when chance rearranges things a bit by sending you to other localities or by sending suitable persons to your locality. These shifts of base are frequent among the generality of mankind; & the rearrangements of the population which they produce often give rise to new & unexpected personal friendships of the greatest possible congeniality. Auburn may indeed be barren—but a future move to Berkeley or Oakland or Sacramento or San Francisco or Monterey or somewhere else may suddenly plunge you into the midst of some social milieu fairly teeming with congenial characters. We have to take what comes—but good fortune is surely no more unlikely to ensue than is bad fortune. It's all a matter of chance. Anyhow, the point is that you have no reason at all to feel any marked discouragement or melancholy. In basic reality, you have more reasons for a sense of adequacy & reasonable contentment than millions of others. Granted that the *present period* is a low spot in which even tolerable contentment is impossible, it is surely evident that your endowments & prospects are such as to make an end of that period certain. It is largely a question of time & incidents. Whereas many others are not fitted to take advantage of the various shifts of fortune which befall mankind, you *are*. These little rearrangements of environment—opportunities & new deals—are constantly occurring; & the very next of them may so alter your circumstances as to make life very tolerable. Remember that *this is not irresponsible & platitudinous optimism.* Only a few persons ever attain acute & ecstatic happiness, & only a minority are even moderately happy. These degrees of felicity are simply chance boons which may or may not happen to befall any one person. If one stumbles upon happiness, well & good. That's just a piece of luck. But if one doesn't, there's nothing which can be done about it. Most never do—so it is well not to *expect* any great good of existence. What most persons *can* rationally expect is a kind of *working adjustment* or *resignation* in which *active pain* is cut down to a minimum. It is likely that a *majority of persons* could attain such a state of *tolerable equilibrium* as this through the exercise of the intelligence & a disciplining of the emotions. This, therefore, *should be the only norm* in matters of expectation & endeavour. Half of our misery—perhaps more—comes from our mistaken notion that we *ought to be happy* . . . that we somehow, for some mysterious reason, "deserve" or "have a right to" acute happiness. The utter fallacy of this notion is something which should be widely inculcated—for just as long as people *think* they ought to be happy, they will extract an added unhappiness & bitterness from the fact that they are not . . . . & most are not & never can be. What they must learn is that *the highest consistent & practicable goal of mankind is simply an absence of acute & unendurable suffering*—a sensible compromise with an indifferent cosmos which was never built for mankind, & in which mankind is only a microscopic, negligible, & temporary accident. That is the most which the average person will ever get out of life, & he might as well trim his sails accordingly. Anything more is purely *accidental*—& while one may be at liberty to dream idly of such happy accidents, or to enjoy them in the rare event of their actually befalling one, it is certainly foolish to expect such things, or to feel sullen or envious when (as is usual) they fail to come. All in all, mankind's supreme folly lies in the general striving after excessively high & usually unattainable goals. Really good things *may* happen to one—but they don't very often. The sensible thing is not to expect them, but to consider them as mere "velvet" when through some rare chance they *do* happen along . . . . if they ever do. In the meanwhile we *can* ameliorate our condition, & eliminate certain active phases of pain, restlessness, & discontentedness, by adopting a philosophic & scientific attitude & making the most of our intellectual & aesthetic endowments. Through the cultivation of congenial interests, & the active exercise of one's mind & imagination in creative work & appreciative observation of the external world & the general field of human knowledge, we may gradually build up a fabric of resigned contentment amidst which we shall find it distinctly (even if not very markedly) better to be alive than dead. The *degree* of this advantage of living over non-living depends of course upon the individual, & his natural capacity for intellectual or aesthetic accomplishment, & for interested enjoyment of an objective survey of the external world. But even when the degree is slight, the state of resignation & contentment is none the less to be welcomed. There is no active discomfort in a life which is barely better than oblivion—& that is the kind of life most have. When we realise that we're damned lucky to escape acute pain, we more truly appreciate the condition of not-very-pleasant quasi-painlessness which falls to the lot of most. That is what life is—so why ask for more? Of the cases of *apparent* happiness which we see around us, about a quarter are accidental realities, & three quarters are false facades. Taking mankind as a whole, in relation to its state of happiness, I fancy one could say that half the people living are just about as well off alive as dead. Of the remaining half, about half (a quarter of all people) are *better off* alive than dead, while the rest would be better off dead than alive. Probably about 3 to 5% of the human race are actively happy—& 0.5 or 1% keenly & ecstatically happy. The real art of living is to become resigned to a mediocre muddling along, & to find enough things to do along the road to keep endurably contented. Once we realise that actual happiness is probably out of reach, we are better able to enjoy the little things & objective interests which make the average life tolerable. It helps us to realise that most people are just as miserable—or as lacking in acute happiness—as we ourselves are. That's what life is—& most of those who pretend to be happy are merely bluffing.

And so on . . . & so on . . . . . the ancient phonograph grinding out its mummified wise saws . . . . Delphi, Dodona, & the Academe spouting their stuff . . . . . blah, blah, blah, dah, dah, dah . . . . when, in the course of human events, four score & so & so years ago . . . . friends, Romans, countrymen . . . . to be or not to be . . . . oh, that this too, too, solid flesh would melt . . . in the beginning Tsathoggua created the earth . . . . m m m . . m m m . . . z z z . . . z z z . . . z z z . . . Well, anyhow, the earth can't be quite devoid of pleasures, while there still remains the relief of having Grandpa stop talking pompous philosophy! Which reminds me that I trust you weren't exercising *conscious* irony in expressing the hope that the Old Gentleman is not a "beautifully balanced, contented person". Ædepol! Mehercule! Yuggoth! Yoh-Vombis! Grandpa *beautifully balanced & contented* . . . . gordamighty . . . this way out!

In actual fact, there are few total losses & never-was's which discourage & exasperate me more than the venerable E'ch-Pi-El. I know of few persons whose attainments fall more consistently short of their aspirations, or who in general have less to live for. Every aptitude which I wish I had, I lack. Everything which I wish I could formulate & express, I have failed to formulate & express. Everything which I value, I have either lost or am likely to lose. Within a decade, unless I can find some job paying at least $10.00 per week, I shall have to take the cyanide route through inability to keep around me the books, pictures, furniture, & other familiar objects which constitute my only remaining reason for keeping alive. And so far as *solitude* is concerned, I probably capture all medals. In Providence I have never seen a congenial mind with which I could exchange ideas, & even among my correspondents there are fewer & fewer who coincide with me on enough points to make discourse enjoyable except on a few specialised points. The newer generation has grown away from me, whilst the older is so fossilised as to form very meagre material for argument or conversation. In everything—philosophy, politics, aesthetics, & interpretation of the sciences—I find myself more & more alone on an island, with an atmosphere almost of hostility gathering around me. With youth, all the possibilities of glamour & adventurous expectancy departed— leaving me stranded on a shelf with nothing to look forward to. Most distinctly, the picture is not an idyllic one—& I'd scarcely wish my worst enemy the fate of being no better off than I am. It might be said that I am just about two inches from the suicide level—among that vast majority for whom existence is the *barest shade* preferable to non-existence. But of course that bare shade makes a vast amount of difference. What keeps me alive is the ability to look back to the past & imagine I am still in 1902 or 1903. Of all my dreams, about 0.8 are of that period—with myself in short trousers & at the old home, with my mother, grandfather, black cat Nigger-Man, &c. still alive. Thus the world of the early 1900's still exists for me in about a third of the hours of my daily life. As long as I can retain the books & pictures & furniture & accessories of those days, as I still do, I have something to live for. When I no longer can, I shall move to that lot in Swan Point Cemetery which is reserved for me. Meanwhile, of course, I certainly *do* get a lot of pleasure from books, travel (when I *can* travel), philosophy, the arts, history, antiquarianism, scenery, the sciences, & so on . . . . & from such poor attempts in the way of aesthtic creation (= fantastic fiction) as I can kid myself into thinking I can sometimes achieve. The reason I have been more "melancholy" than usual in the last few years is that I am coming to distrust more & more the value of the material I produce. Adverse criticism has of late vastly undermined my confidence in my literary powers. And so it goes. Decidedly, Grandpa is not one of those beaming old gentlemen who radiate cheer wherever they go! However—I *do* escape the pits of genuine & extreme melancholy through a rational analysis of my situation—whereby I realise that my lot is no worse than the average, that there is no reason to think that it could have been better, & that there is nothing in particular to be done about it. My absence of acute happiness is in the main a direct result of my own limitations. My natural temperament, & lack of special intellectual & aesthetic abilities & personal graces—not the "evil" or "injustice" of the world around me—is largely responsible for the impasse in which my declining years find me. Other elements were contributed by *sheer chance*—but nowhere does human or cosmic malignancy figure. To be *bitter* or *resentful* over something for which only nature & chance are responsible, would be the apex of folly & irrationality. Who can be *angry* when there is no guiding consciousness to be "angry" at? Everything is just as blind & uncontrollable cosmic chance determines it. Therefore I simply say "Oh, what the hell" . . . . & let things muddle along as they will . . . . meanwhile trying to make the most of what meagre endowments, environmental advantages, & intellectual, aesthetic, & antiquarian interests I happen to have at my disposal. I couldn't help matters by brooding on the fact that some others are more happily situated. What's that to me? The happiness of *others* needn't make *me* any the more miserable! So I forego the masochistic luxury of mourning, & simply have as good a time as I can with the existing set-up. And at that, it isn't so bad. I'm no pining & picturesque victim of melancholy's romantic ravages. I merely shrug my shoulders, recognise the inevitable, let the world march past, & vegetate along as painlessly as possible. I suppose I'm a damned sight better off than millions. There are dozens of things I can actually enjoy.

But the point is, that I'm probably *a thousand times worse off than you are* . . . so that in preaching resignation & contentment I'm not in the false position of a fortunate prophet lecturing a real victim of misfortune. The gist of my "sermon" is that if analysis & philosophy can make *me* tolerably resigned, it *certainly* ought to produce even better results with one not nearly so gravely handicapped. You have youth, genuine artistic genius, attractiveness, competence, adaptability, versatility, & solid prospects in general. I have none of these. So if *I* am able to tell the world to go to hell & eke along in endurable mediocrity, you surely—with so many more advantages—ought to be able to work out a tolerable corresponding adjustment. Of course all forms of resignation are more difficult in youth than in unhoping age—but with a truly philosophic attitude a *beginning* can be made at almost any stage of life. When I was young I was of course more restless than I am now. I had more to hope for, & was constantly reaching out & getting disappointed. But even then I realised the element of blind drift in life, & the rarity of human happiness— so that I always placed as little stress as possible on transitory ambitions, & sought to lay the foundations of life in objective contemplation & the enjoyment of the visible external world. A deeply-seated determination to attain resignation & tolerable contentment with little is a vast aid in bringing about such attainment. Take things as they come—remember that happiness is a rare accident attained by few—expect little—learn to enjoy the small & usual things encountered along the way . . . those are the best rules for gaining whatever of contentment the average person can gain.

Before concluding, however, I must not fail to point out that no young person ever need exclude the vague *hope* (not to be confounded with positive *expectation*) of a fortune beyond the average in felicity. In your case—with so much talent, grace, & competence—the foundations for such a hope would seem to be distinctly less insubstantial than in the majority of cases. A transfer of environment—or some new element in the environment of Averoigne— might easily alter matters to such an extent that you would encounter degrees of happiness at present virtually unimaginable. So—as a final homiletic word from garrulous & sententious old age—for Tsathoggua's sake cheer up! Things aren't as bad as they seem—& even if your highest ambitions are never fulfilled, you will undoubtedly find enough cheering things along the road to make existence worth enduring. Sometimes hopes (as of my shutting up, as I promised to, halfway down sheet VI, 1!) prove delusive—but even allowing for these false alarms, the residue of life is not often so bad as to warrant despondency & melancholy. In my own case, it would take the loss of my books & household possessions to make me bump myself off. You, with so much more to live for, certainly ought to be a vastly longer way from the gas-jet or laudanum phial! That is, assuming you are still alive after these 14 solid pages of concentrated bull & high-tension hot air! Yuggoth . . . but how does the old man hold out after such a paralysing fusilade! If the last epistle was held 2 weeks before perusal, this one will probably take an equally long fortnight to wade through—assuming that my increasingly vile cacography makes such wading at all possible.

¶ Since the commencement of this endless document I have set a date for my northward plunge. I shall leave Sunday, August 18—being taken as far as Daytona (where the Barlows intend to spend a fortnight) in the Barlovian family chariot. At Daytona I shall take the coach for St. Augustine, where I hope to linger at least a few days despite increasing brokeness. Then ancient CHARLESTON—home of my soul—where I hope I can hammer out a full week at the Y. Then the long trek to Richmond—where I probably can't stop at all. Ditto Washington. I shall probably have a single day in ancient Philadelphia—exploring the ancient lanes of Germantown & the titanic aisles of the shadowy Wissahickon gorge. At N.Y. I shall collect mail & see whether I have any remittance enabling me to stay there a week. If so, I shall probably linger to that extent, for I have promised to look up dozens of people around the metropolitan zone. It will, alas, be autumn ere I behold the ancient bricks of College St. . . . I dread the chill, but shall have become accustomed to it gradually. The worst thing will be the row of ancient houses demolished during my absence (of which I wrote in my preceding epistle) . . . & the absence of the tiger Vice-President of the Kappa Alpha Tau, who (valiant soul!) has succumbed to the savage fury of an intruding canine. I shall be glad to see little black Johnny Perkins (now a huge & intrepid mass of militant & aggressive fur) & the tiny spotted feline born last spring . . . . to say nothing of my books, pictures, aunt, furniture, & similar household accessories. Three months away from home—& what a devastating stack of accumulated newspapers to read up! I've had the N.Y. Sunday Times's sent down here—so that all until Aug. 4 are already out of the way.

Now for packing—for I have a vast lot of junk, acquired from Bob & elsewhere, to send home by express. My young host has been accumulating an immense amount of printing & binding material, & will soon be able to produce books complete in every detail. I've helped him a bit on his first experimental job,[3] & before long he'll be able to handle more ambitious projects. The first serious job he hopes to tackle is a collection of Klarkash-Ton's poems—entitled, according to a long-existing wish of C A S's—"Incantations".[4] C A S has had no collection published in a decade, & one is certainly due before long. Ar-Ech-Bei expects to get in touch with him on the subject presently.

I shall hate to leave the local felidae of Florida . . . Cyrus & Darius, Henry Clay, & Little Mr. Knopf. Mr. Knopf is purring on the bench beside me as I indite these concluding* lines in the landscape garden.

Last night I beheld—for the first time in a life of nearly 45 years—a phenomenon of great rarity, but which I had always known from books . . . a *lunar rainbow,* pale but clear, spanning the northwestern sky opposite the rising full moon. Several who saw it claimed they could detect prismatic colours, though to my eyes it was merely grey. No one present—& persons up to 66 years were there—had ever observed such a spectacle before. Having seen two total solar eclipses (1925, 1932) & a lunar rainbow, I feel myself quite an experiencer of rare sights! The moon is a great spectacle hereabouts—yielding a white, burning light & forming a magnificent object as it rises above the tall,

---

*"Thank heaven", say you!

grotesquely twisted pines beyond the glassily reflecting lake. It is a veritable picture postcard—indeed, the pine-&-live-oak scenery of Florida make about the best setting for a lunar display that I've yet seen. The effect is now at its maximum because of the moon's fulness.

Well—here endeth the present monument of pseudo-philosophic garrulousness. As I once said before—start Grandpa off on an abstract discussion, & all is lost! ¶ Anyhow, cheer up—for the rest of the world is just as miserable as you are! ¶ Sincerest regards to your mother, & to good old grey Son . . & to C A S when you see him. ¶ Yr obt Servt

E'ch-Pi-El

Notes

1. HPL refers to letters received both from HVS and from her mother, Genevieve Sully. (HPL's reply to Genevieve is apparently nonexstant.) "Palatium Sullianum" is HPL's Latin coinage ("the palace [i.e., home] of the Sullys").

2. George Sterling (1869–1926) was one of the early residents of Carmel, having lived there from 1905 to 1913. At the time, real estate developers were attempting to establish it as an artists' colony. Bierce (1842–1914?) did not spend any significant amount of time in the Carmel–Monterey area.

3. Apparently *The Goblin Tower* by Frank Belknap Long, for which HPL helped set type.

4. Barlow never published *Incantations,* a book Smith conceived in 1925. A section of Smith's *Selected Poems* (1971) contains a section entitled "Incantations," although some of the poems therein date to the 1940s.

[21]   [Postcard][1]

[Postmarked Saint Augustine, Fla.,
21 August 1935]

On my way at last! Went with the Barlows to Daytona & helped them settle for their fortnight's stay there—then by coach to ancient San Augustin. After 2 months & 9 days of rustic modernity, it is balm to my soul to wander among centuried houses & gardens, see quaint balconies & battlements of other ages, & listen to the tinkle of fountains at twilight & the music of cathedral bells cast in 1682! Here is a city in existence 42 years before the landing of the first Virginia settlers, & 55 years before the Pilgrims sought New-England! ¶ Here for a week at the old Rio Vista—on the bay front. Got a complete basement (but above ground) apartment for only *$3.50.* Food down to 20 or 25¢ per day, with canned beans [large cans 5¢ at some groceries] as heavy staple. Having a great time, & in even better shape than in De Land. The seacoast is a great bracer. Moving north Aug. 25—& will get a few hours in Savannah before striking ancient Charleston. Too broke to plan any stay north of Charleston, & don't even know how long I can linger there. But anyhow, it surely has been a splendid trip! ¶ Hope all goes well in Averoigne,

& that you can manage to take some cheerful & bracing trips before autumn & the season of heavy labour sets in. ¶ Regards to everyone—not forgetting good old Son.

Yr ob^t. h^ble. Servt—

E'ch-Pi-El

Notes

1. *Front:* Old City Gates, St. Augustine, Florida.

[22]   [ALS, JHL]

Septr. 23, 1935

Dear Helen:—

I am really tremendously sorry to learn of the death of Klarkash-Ton's mother[1]—for no matter how long-expected it was, & how much it may lessen the complications of his position, it must necessarily be a blow of disorganising magnitude. Whenever such a link with early days is broken—such a focus of childhood memories & tender associations removed—a certain amount of irreparable loss occurs. Having sustained a similar bereavement in 1921—& one nearly like it in 1932 when my elder aunt died[2]—I can sympathise very acutely with C A S . . . & have dropped him a line to that effect. The blow must be hard on the elder Smith,[3] also—especially since his own health is so infirm. But of course in the long run—considering the misery of a feeble & shock-impaired existence—I presume that the event is a merciful one. No doubt the change will to some extent lessen the prevailing strain on Indian Hill—though the care of his father alone will probably keep C A S busy enough. The entire situation is a profoundly melancholy one, though no remedy save time & fate seems to suggest itself. One wonders what plans Klarkash-Ton will make when he is wholly alone—whether he will continue as a hermit of the hills, or whether he will seek urban quarters & acquire a greater gregariousness & mobility. Perhaps the pattern of isolation is so firmly fixed in his psychology that—in view of his settled age—he will not care for any expansion of life & activities. But in any case he will probably have more leisure & quiet for his literary career. His productivity—even now amazingly great in view of obstacles—may be expected to reach tremendous proportions—in prose, poetry, painting, & sculpture alike. I can only hope that finances may not prove an acute problem with him, & that his health may hold out reasonably well. I am passing word of the bereavement on to E. Hoffmann Price in case he has not been directly notified—as I was not.

Turning to ills of a more transient sort—let me commiserate you upon the entomological venom which has so uncivilly interrupted your activities! I can imagine how painful the sting must be—& am glad that a liberal attitude on your principal's part keeps the hardship limited to the purely direct side. By this time, I trust, the effects of the disaster are duly banished.

Regarding matters philosophical—I hope that my preceding epistle did not sound too unrelievedly pessimistic. I am not a *pessimist*, but merely a realistic *indifferentist*. It is just as childishly romantic to postulate an actively hostile & malignant cosmos, as Thomas Hardy did, as to postulate a friendly, "just", & beneficent one. The truth is that the cosmos is blind & unconscious—not giving a hang about any of its denizens, nor even knowing that they exist. It doesn't try to pain them any more than it tries to help or please them—& if any of them can manage to have a good time somehow, in spite of the chaotic jumble of conditions & emotions around & within them, that's quite all right with the universal powers that be. I tried to make it clear in my harangue that the *blind chance* of a happy adjustment to nature—a chance sometimes able to be slightly augmented by good judgment—is never wholly lacking for one who is young, brilliant, & of pleasing personality. Anyone so blessed by fortune *may* through some rare chance attain moments of felicity at least roughly comparable to those depicted in romantic folklore—but such moments are not to be counted on or expected in any average existence. It is not, however, necessary to banish the theoretical hope of such things. When one is young, it is still possible to retain this hope as a sort of piquant stimulus. One *may* have good luck in life, just as one *may* fall heir to a fortune or back the right horse in a race. Not that any happiness is actually as keen as what romanticists depict & expect—but that there is, in a moderate way & in very rare quantity, such a thing. As long as the belief in this tenuous chance continues to be a help, it is to be encouraged. This optimism becomes harmful & undesirable only when carried to illogic & romantic extremes, & made the basis of delusive & extravagant expectations productive of error, maladjustment, & nerve-wrecking disillusionment. It would seem to be the part of good sense to harbour great hopes in a sort of light, indefinite way—extracting from them whatever bracing power their imaginative associations may possess, but keeping also in mind the ineluctable natural laws & probabilities which actually prevail. Naturally such a course is for many difficult; but almost anyone can probably—with suitable efforts & the exercise of coherent logic—approach it in a degree sufficient to remove at least some of the pains & shocks of unrestrained romanticism. In any case it is worth trying.

As to the part played by individual bias—opinions arising from specific personal experiences & difficulties—in the tenure & exposition of a philosophical, social, political, aesthetic, or scientific attitude, one must admit that it always tends to be considerable. The distorting effects of this tendency are escaped only in cases where the individual's chief personal emotion happens to be an enormous zeal for the intrinsic, abstract principles of order, truth, rhythm, & correlation, or else a paramount interest in the aesthetics of racial or general intellectual adjustment as expressed in the constant drama of collective

human aspiration & frustration—or, of course, a special interest in some particular field whose strength drowns out the usual tug of egocentric emotions
so far as that field is concerned. Since such cases of generalised personal
emotion—or of drowned-out egocentric emotions—are so relatively uncommon, it follows that most of our policy & scholarship are indeed an ironic mixture of feeble truth-groping & unconscious personal bias. I would not
make even a slight exception of *politics;* for when we behold the irrational rav-
ings of smug capitalists & vindictive communists alike, we cannot but see that
a blind, mindless clutching at immediate personal advantage—or an equally
blind & mindless reflection of personal experience & background—lies behind
the infantile views & fanatical zeal of both. Most lofty catchwords such as
"human equality", "liberty", "defence of the constitution", "ideals of the fathers", "rights of mankind", &c. &c. &c. spring merely from the apelike greed
or fear or caprice or prejudice of ignorant, self-deluded, & clumsily rationalis-
ing egoists. So far as my own opinions are concerned—I have & can have no
idea of how much part personal bias plays in them. There are, however, a few
circumstances which can be cited in favour of their at least partial impersonal-
ism. For one thing—I have held the same opinions in many cases despite
great changes of actual situation in fields connected with them, whilst in other
cases I have radically changed my opinions without any corresponding
change in situation. Furthermore—to cite a specific case—from the earliest
times, & under the most widely differing conditions, I have always had a strong
abstract interest in the situation & interactions of man as a whole, & in the
question of human values & standards . . . their basis, strength, validity, fixity
or variability, & psychological nature. Thus my attention to the subject of values & philosophic adjustment contains a strong element of active, personality-
free, scientific curiosity which tends to stand apart from personal escape-
psychology & rationalisation.

As to specific advice on a personal problem involving an irrational emotional attachment to one whose influence is uniformly harmful & disorganising—it is of course impossible for any layman to give any recommendation
which would have real value. That job could be handled only by a trained
psychologist—& after a most extensive study of the individual case, & of every possible factor bearing on it. Offhand—& from comparison with the only
analogous case of which I have any first-hand knowledge—I would say that
of the two alternative evils of seeing the disturbing person & being disturbed,
& of not seeing him & thus acquiring a sense of vacancy & discontent, the
latter would be likely to prove lesser in the long run—especially after time
might have a chance to temper the capricious force of the feeling of attachment. But of course such an opinion is largely a matter of mere rough assumption. Unsuspected factors & hidden possibilities of adjustment may be
present, which would dictate an alternative policy. One would have to know,
for example, how much of the disturbing effect proceeded from the basic

personality of either individual concerned, as distinguished from qualities susceptible of change or from conditions imposed by the existing environment. The best way, perhaps, to begin attacking such a problem is to have the affected individual do his own analysing & prescribing—stepping outside himself, looking at the whole thing in an objective, panoramic way, & remembering that all human emotions are no more than the symbol-bedecked results of the functioning of obscure endocrine glands. The less one thinks about his own irrational emotions—the more he can come to recognise them as minor factors & seek absorbing interests outside their narrow radius—the better off he is . . . . . the closer he is to the possibility of a tolerable adjustment to the blind, indifferent forces of the external world.

Your trip to Los Angeles sounds like a highly entertaining event, even though the climate & psychological atmosphere proved uncongenial. I have always fancied that I would dislike southern California, since it is such a backgroundless, traditionless jumble of heterogeneous elements with no roots in the soil. It seems to be a sort of catch-all for odds & ends of the bourgeoisie & for every type of cheap philosophical & aesthetic extravagance—a region of omnipresent & incurable mediocrity & immaturity. And I doubt whether the climate has anything approaching the steady, dependable mildness of Florida. Architecture—judging from photographs & descriptions—tends to be garish & decadent . . . pseudo-Hispanic stuff which would make the Conquistadores turn in their graves . . . . while the scenery would seem to lack the mellowness & richness characteristic of northern California. If I ever were to reach the Pacific coast I doubt whether I would bother to include the Los Angeles region in my itinerary—unless as an incidental in reaching the Southwest . . . New Mexico & Texas . . . which I do want to see. However—like New York—such places generally have a few compensating features. I am glad you had as pleasing & competent a guide as your elder-world cousin-in-law to show you the redeeming side of the region, & that so many major musical advantages were present to relieve the otherwise devastating dulness. Any important art is an universal language & bulwark—making one in a measure at home no matter what the material environment may be. That *second* chance meeting with your old acquaintance was certainly a coincidence of the most remarkable kind—& may, I think, promote a very congenial friendship. The glimpse of San Diego & the Mexican border—& of the tropical shores of La Jolla—must have formed an agreeable supplement to the vacation. I would like to see Mexico—though I would prefer regions far from the U.S. border, where the native life & architecture might be studied in their least mongrelised form.

The Berkeleian conclusion of your outing must have been as enjoyable in its way as the rest—with the added zest of taking your mother & sister by surprise. It is fortunate for the latter that she has such an hospitable family circle in which to sojourn during her collegiate years, & that your mother was able to remain & aid in her acclimatisation—also, that friends are so well represented on the pedagogical staff. The musical privileges offered by your gifted tenant are surely enviable enough—& I can imagine how keenly you appreciated the special complete performance. Taste in music must be a fortunate endowment indeed—admitting one to a field of enjoyment whose opportunities are manifold.

Which reminds me that your own musical progress ought to be a source of the greatest satisfaction & encouragement to you. Congratulations on the acquisition of a new & more eminent instructor—& upon the high hopes he holds forth! The long hours of practice must be arduous; but when one is truly absorbed in an art, such practice is scarcely to be regarded as an unrelieved burden. Nor do I think you need take your preceptor's idea of "wasted years" too seriously. He is naturally critical of lesser men's methods, but despite all this there can be no doubt of the value of much which you have learned. Everything considered, it would appear that you are justified in looking forward to a very substantial musical future.

Glad that the St. Augustine & Charleston cards duly reached you. I had 4 days in ancient Charleston, & dreaded to move onward. In Richmond—the next pause—I had hard work getting used to the non-subtropical landscape again, & was nearly frozen before I made my full round of Poe sites & picturesque gardens. I enclose some Richmond cards which I don't think I sent before. Then came Washington—a day spent largely in the exploration of ancient Georgetown . . . the hilly district across Rock Creek which was a Maryland town long before any D.C. or Federal City existed. Fine colonial doorways abound here. After that, Philadelphia—where I visited (for the first time in 11 years) the suburban estate of the eminent naturalist Bartram,[4] who in 1763 made the first scientific study of Florida plants. This place is now a public park—with the extensive botanic garden & ancient stone house (1731) preserved in excellent condition as an oasis amidst a region now engulfed by factories & rows of shabby houses. I also visited the art museum, where an especially fine temporary exhibit of Japanese prints (including the entire Fujiyama, bridge, waterfall, & poem series of my favourite Hokusai) was on display. Went through the early American wing as usual . . . you'd be interested in one room of early 19th century paintings, where fully eight tenths of the specimens are by Thomas Sully. After that came a brief N.Y. period during which I saw most of the gang—visiting Morton in his museum at Paterson. It took me a long time to get re-acclimated to the chill of the north, but I learned by degrees to bear it. Home Sept. 14—& confronted by a terrifying mountain of accumulated tasks. Absent 3 months & 9 days—& had all the periodicals of that interval to read up! Packages & papers scattered over everything, & the prospect of an especially troublesome verse-revision job in the near future.[5] It's a great life!

And yet—despite a crowded programme which won't get back to normal in weeks—I'm off once again on a brief jaunt! This time visiting my friend

E. H. Cole in the Boston zone, & making sundry side-trips with him in his car. Ancient Marblehead & rocky Nahant Friday. Saturday we made a long pilgrimage to the picturesque, vista-abounding hills of the Connecticut Valley to discharge a melancholy duty—restoring the ashes of a deceased old lady, in accordance with her lifelong wish, to her native soil in ancient & brooding Wilbraham (Mass.). The region looks much as it did when I visited it in 1928—though all who then guided me about are now dead.[6] Some of the mountain scenery—with endless outspread miles of purple hills beyond hills, & glimpses of distant villages with white steeples piercing the autumn-touched greenery—is ineffably fascinating & imagination-stirring. Up in the inland region—near Springfield—the foliage is perceptibly turning to red & gold, whereas in Rhode Island it is still largely untouched. On Sunday I accompanied Cole & his family on a picnic to Cape Cod—where we saw a type of gentle, low-lying, willow-treed, sea-bordering landscape oddly opposite to the rugged, striking inland mountain scenery of the day before. Our route lay through historic Plymouth, which I probably described on the occasion of a previous visit. The foliage around Cape Cod & the Massachusetts South Shore in general is less autumnally touched than that of the Wilbraham country—being more or less like that in Rhode Island. This particular day was magnificently hot, & we certainly had a great time. Lunch in a pine grove near South Yarmouth, & a long loafing & gazing period on the sands of Chatham—with only the blue Atlantic between us & Spain. The dual glimpse of typical New England scenery afforded by this & the preceding day was surely a treat to one lately absent from this ancient realm for nearly 3½ months! Today Cole & I are in Lynn & Swampscott—cruising around on some business of his. I'm getting my correspondence done (as usual on trips, I brought it along) during the intervals when he is commercially occupied. Lynn is a modern manufacturing city, but Swampscott (between it & Marblehead) is a picturesque seashore & residence district lying between Lynn & ancient Marblehead. It consists of picturesquely winding streets which ascend precipitous slopes much in the Marblehead manner—though the houses are not ancient. The foliage & lawns are especially fine—indeed, all vegetation seems to thrive particularly on these New England peninsulas or islands where the sea exercises its equable influence. It is the same in Newport & Gloucester, which you have seen. Shall be home tonight—& this time I trust I shall stay put . . . . despite some talk on my host's part of another trip (with overcoats & heated Chevrolet) later on— over the Mohawk Trail & perhaps up a bit over the Vermont border. Brrr . . fancy Grandpa in *Vermont* in *autumn!* But this may not materialise.

And so it goes. Again let me say how sorry I am to hear of Klarkash-Ton's bereavement. But I hope that some at least slightly easier arrangement for him can eventually be worked out. Dozens of my correspondents have expressed their sympathy concerning the difficult position in which their fictional idol has been placed. ¶ Congratulations on your trip & on your musical prospects—& I trust your yellow-jacket sting is now only a painful memory. ¶ All good wishes—& regards from my aunt.

Yr obt h^{ble} Servt

H P L

Notes

1. Fanny Gaylord Smith died on 9 September at the age of 85.

2. Sarah Susan Lovecraft (b. 1857), HPL's mother, died on 24 May 1921; Lillian Clark (b. 1847), his aunt, on 3 July 1932.

3. Timeus Smith died on 26 December 1937 at the age of 82.

4. John Bartram (1699–1777), early American botanist, horticulturist, and explorer. His house is at 54th Street and Eastwick Avenue in Philadelphia.

5. For David Van Bush, a client for whom HPL had not worked for more than a decade.

6. The deceased woman was Jennie E. T. Dowe (1845–1919), mother of Edith Miniter (1867–1934). HPL wrote about the region in "The Dunwich Horror" (1928). HPL's hosts at the time were Miniter and Evanore O. Beebe (1858–1935).

[23] [ALS, JHL]

66 College St.,

Providence, R.I.,

Dec. 4, 1935.

Dear Helen:—

Your recent programme surely has reached great extremes of strenuousness, & I trust you can find a way to cut down activities a trifle without impairing any major interest. There is always a temptation not to pass up any possible opportunity for entertainment or edification; but beyond certain limits one finds this ceaseless stirring subject to the so-called law of diminishing returns. However, each person knows best what he in particular can stand—& what begins to be a bore & burden rather than a pleasure. There is an art in the judicious *selection* of activities from among the general welter of possible ones. Some temperaments demand more tangible activities than others, but even the most naturally active can overdo matters. Then again, there are different *kinds* of activities. Sometimes the constant physical activity of travel, conversation, & wide public contacts is highly exhausting to an extent which an equal amount of secluded & sedentary activity—reading, study, &c.—would not be. Each individual must choose that type best adapted to his nature—which would seem to refer the subject back to that basic philosophic maxim of old Socrates—"γνῶθι σεαυτόν . . . . know thyself". It is, I think, the mistake of the present generation to crowd its time & spend its energies too much in the pursuit of *objective* activities. In its endeavour to make the most of a brief lifetime, it really defeats its own ends; since when too many things are crowded together in quick succession, none of them retains any value. A far greater net return from life can be obtained through a repudiation of the overspeeded modern ideal, & a return to the sane classic principles of old which recognise the superiority of *being* over *doing*, & emphasise the necessity of *civilised leisure* & of an easy-going reflective & savouring process if one is to extract any solid or enduring satisfaction from the events of existence. The 18th century had the right idea, as the lives & letters of epicures like Walpole & Gray & Cowper attest, & as one can deduce from things like "The Natural History of Selborne", & the thoughtful, scholarly letters & enquiries in the *Gentleman's Magazine*.[1] Naturally it requires an effort to break loose from the example, precept, & unconscious thought-patterns of one's own generation, but I believe the effort will be found profitable by all who persist in it. And it will be easier to one who takes a "long view" of the present age—correlating it with the whole historic stream & perceiving that it marks the definitely decadent end of an era. This is an uneasy & fallacy-ridden period of transition; with most of the comfortable illusions & objects of yesterday's life exploded, yet without any wide, profound, or instinctive acceptance of that newer set of perspectives & goals which must replace the old if any real sort of civilisation is to survive. It ought, therefore, to be *relatively* easy for the philosophic mind to detach itself from immediate values & folkways, & to look about for more universal & better-founded points of reference in the shifting though not wholly incoherent pattern of terrestrial life.

However—I imagine that, in view of the unusual opportunities & honours involved, the recent crowded weeks have not been devoid of compensations. The same *kind* of events, a little more sparsely distributed, would probably form a very rational programme for one whose chief interest is music. And the tributes paid to your ability by competent judges ought surely to give you the keenest kind of incentive.

The autumn in New England has been phenomenally warm, so that my season of hibernation was long postponed. I believe that I last wrote from the midst of a series of Massachusetts outings with my friend Cole—the climax of which was a trip around Cape Cod. All this, only a week after my return from the long summer jaunt, was surely a delightful reintroduction to New England scenery.

On Oct. 8 my aunt & I had a trip to New Haven in a friend's car—which gave me 7½ hours for exploration (I had never been off a moving vehicle in the town before) while my aunt did some visiting. The day was ideally sunny (though I could have wished it warmer), & the ride through autumnal Connecticut scenery (100 m = 2½ hr) delightful. New Haven is not as rich in colonial antiquities as Providence, but has a peculiar charm of its own. Streets are broad & well-kept, & in the residential sections (some of which involve hills & fine views) there are endless stately mansions a century old, with generous grounds & gardens, & an almost continuous overarching canopy of great elms.

I visited ancient Connecticut Hall (1752—the oldest Yale College building, where Nathan Hale of the class of 1773 roomed), old Centre Church (1812—with an interesting crypt containing the grave of Benedict Arnold's first wife), the Pierpont house (1767—now Yale Faculty Club), the historical, art, & natural history museums, the Farnam & Marsh botanic gardens, & various other points of interest—crowding as much as possible (despite my devotion to a leisurely ideal!) into the limited time available.

Most impressive of all the sights, perhaps, were the great *new* quadrangles of Yale University—each an absolutely faithful reproduction of old-time architecture & atmosphere, & forming a self-contained little world in itself. The Gothic courtyards transport one in fancy to mediaeval Oxford or Cambridge—spires, oriels, pointed arches, mullioned windows, arcades with groined roofs, climbing ivy, sundials, lawns, gardens, vine-clad walls & flagstoned walks—everything to give the young occupants that massed impression of their accumulated cultural heritage which they ought to obtain in Old England itself. To stroll through these quadrangles in the golden light of late afternoon; at dusk, when the candles behind the diamond-paned casements flicker up one by one; or in the beams of a mellow Hunter's Moon; is to walk bodily into an enchanted region of dream. It is the past & the ancient Mother Land brought magically to the present time & place. The choicest of these Gothic quadrangles is Calhoun College—named for the great Carolinian (whose grave in St. Philip's Churchyard, Charleston, I had visited less than 2 months before), who was a graduate of Yale. Nor are the Georgian quadrangles less glamourous—each being a magical summoning-up of the world of two centuries ago. Many distinct styles of Georgian architecture are represented, & the buildings & landscaping alike reflect the finest taste which European civilisation has yet evolved or is ever likely to evolve. Lucky is the youth whose formative years are spent amid such scenes! I wandered for hours through this limitless labyrinth of unexpected elder microcosms, & mourned the lack of further time. Certainly, I must visit New Haven again, since many of its treasures would require weeks for proper inspection & appreciation.

But even this trip did not end my 1935 travels. On Oct. 16 at 6 a.m. Samuel Loveman arrived in town on the N.Y. boat, & after a session at #66 we both started for Boston to absorb bookstalls, museums, & general antiquities. We stayed 2 nights—at Technology Chambers in Irvington St.—& managed to take in quite a round of sights. Most of our time was spent in the Egyptian & Greek sections of the Museum of Fine Arts. Back to Providence on the 18th—& that evening Loveman left for N.Y. on the boat. This really ended the travel season—though besides these ample trips I often went out to the local woods & fields until November—taking along my work in the inevitable black bag as I do in summer. There is a peculiar fascination about the New England autumnal landscape when the thermometer stays high enough to let one enjoy it.

Since the advent of the cold my aunt & I have attended several lectures on art & allied subjects at Brown University. One of them—on "Art, Economics, & the American Future"—was by Prof. H. A. Overstreet of N.Y., author of several interesting works on philosophy & psychology;[2] & during the question period the speaker got into an argument with the Governor of Rhode Island, Theodore Francis Green, who was in the seat directly behind mine. Theodore argued that the highest art must be international & non-racial (he is himself a famous collector of Sino-Japanese prints & ceramic art); but Overstreet shewed clearly that every artist, in order to rise to truly universal & international stature, must work through the medium of his own cultural inheritance. A later lecture by Prof. W. B. Savery[3] of the U. of Wash. gave me a keener appreciation of John Dewey—whom I have had a constant tendency to underestimate because of his connexion with the pragmatism of William James.

Regarding shocks & emotional disturbances—the trouble with 'sage advice' is that it has to begin so *far back*—in the very roots of philosophy & ideology—that it seems almost irrelevant until a long process of fallacy-shedding & re-education has been undergone. Of course the basic facts are relatively few & simple, centreing around two major points—(a) that the elaborate system of concepts, values, & emotional attitudes traditionally grouped around human conduct, human relationships, & human affections & esteem is wholly artificial, misleading, & based on a thoroughly false notion of the nature & mechanics of thought, feeling, & behaviour among mammal primates including man; & (b) that in consequence of the foregoing, we must cease to expect certain traditionally predetermined acts, thoughts, feelings, & tastes in persons as a matter of course; must realise that these things are mere accidents of neural & glandular physiology, wholly dependent upon changing aspects of environment, & never stable except in the relatively few cases where philosophic harmony happens to be some individual's dominant interest. Such is the factual foundation—but the average person, when when rationally convinced, is necessarily slow in correlating the truth practically with the varied & hitherto unanalysed events of his emotional life. He must learn by degrees (a) not to attach any great importance to the emotional attitudes of others, particularly their attitudes toward himself; & therefore (b) not to be shocked or grieved when various individuals sharply contravene the patterns one would like to have them follow, or those which ignorant tradition says that all superior persons invariably follow. Be amused by the attitudes of people when such amusement does not involve your own interests or security; but do not give them any advantage over yourself, or feel profoundly grieved or shocked when these attitudes change or are revealed to have been fictitious in the first place. For no temperament or character is anything more than the fortuitous result of several parallel biological processes determined by heredity & environment—the conformation of tissue-cells; the relative development & chemical composition of various filaments; the functioning of pineal, thyroid, pituitary, & other hormone-producing glands; the composition of the blood;

the rate of oxidation & details of metabolism, & so on. Those who know biology know all these things, & the feelings, consciousness, & conduct which they determine, are built up from unicellular protoplasm through the various organic phyla of the planet—built up by a series of accidents & inherent protoplasmic characteristics until in one case the automatic economy of the ant & bee is attained; whilst in another case the variable impulses & stimulus-responses of gorillas, human beings, chimpanzees, orang-outangs, the extinct Neanderthaloids, & other highly-developed primates are produced. The lesson of all this is that there are no basic or absolute "oughts" in the field of conduct & emotion, & that, consequently, we cannot expect these things to correspond to the conventional ideas & expectations preached by tradition-systems whose source is mere mythology & ignorance. When anyone tends to take seriously the high-flown sentimentalities commonly accepted regarding life, character, emotion, & human relationships, the best antidote to such slush that he could obtain is that splendid new outline of biology prepared by H. G. Wells & Prof. Julian Huxley—"The Science of Life." I'm about half-way through a borrowed copy of it, & am quite lit up with enthusiasm & admiration. Never before have I seen the sources of organic form, life, thought, & feeling so clearly & significantly displayed in a manner adapted to the layman.

The only criteria of conduct, thought, & feeling which we can logically envisage are purely *relative* & *proximate* ones, utilitarian & aesthetic in their nature. Human impulses & behaviour are simply *what they are*—wholly outside any *absolute* realm of approval or disapproval. Only when a group begins to have some fixed way of life, as determined by its composition & environment, can we consider any such thing as a *set of preferences* in the matter. *Then,* as a local practical reality, the given group commences to realise that of the wide range of human acts & feelings some are less favourable to collective harmony than others. The group will get on better if certain areas of human instinct & behaviour can be subordinated or discouraged by persuasion, force, or selection (i.e., selection for privilege of individuals in which the inharmonious biological traits are least strong naturally), whilst other areas are emphasised & encouraged through praise, privilege, honour, & tangible reward. Hence the dawn of ethics or morals. At first a wholly utilitarian device, it later becomes aesthetic as the *principle of harmony* & *habit of symbolism* grow in the racial consciousness. Some human acts & impulses (& the persons in whom they seem to predominate) are identified with superiority, whilst others are identified with inferiority . . . . these values, of course, being different in every different group because of a diversity of conditions & needs. But the rational moralist does not expect any alterations in the nature of the species. He knows what especial acts & emotions to encourage, but he does not expect them to reign unalloyed. He knows that dozens of others—some directly anti-social—will always coexist, & therefore seeks merely to make conditions as favourable as possible for the preferred group & as unfavourable as possible for the non-preferred. He devises ways in which one set of natural impulses in society checks some other set—but he does not expect the other set to be abolished. He knows that he has only an unchanging jumble of primate instincts to work with, & learns *what they are like* instead of merely wishing they were something which they aren't. Among other things he knows that there is no such *single* thing as "good character" or "bad character". True, some individuals have favourable social emotions strongly developed (by accident), & when to such a development there is added (also by accident) an aesthetic disposition strongly inclined toward social harmony, we have that extremely rare being, a naturally "good" man. But we must not expect many of him, nor expect even the "best" of his kind to be devoid of various anti-social instincts, as chance may determine. It is quite all right to honour him as a pattern, but we would be idiots *to expect that the majority can share his emotional processes*. That's the big point—*not to be misled by extravagant expectations concerning the inner emotional life of mankind*. We must be satisfied with the psychology of the average law-abiding citizen—who has a vague, cloudy, hypocritical respect for the favourable social emotions, but whose reasonable approximation to social conduct is secured through group pressure (law, force, mass opinion as expressed in grants of praise & privilege) rather than through any inward urge. We must not expect his "inner life" to be anything but what it is—how could it be? Remember that the "really good" man's inner emotional life is only a biological accident. We may have an aesthetic preference for one type over the other, but we must not let this preference affect us too profoundly. Each is what nature has fortuitously produced—& neither is in the least responsible for what he is. Thus in our every-day dealings with the world we must always realise that people are not what they pretend to be. We must not be too critical so long as anybody refrains from overtly anti-social acts, & in all our calculations we must remember that the average person will behave "well" or "decently" only so long as the right sort of social & legal pressure is applied. Never put yourself in such a position that you *could* be harmed by anyone if he *were* anti-social, even though you think he *is* social. You never can tell from exteriors whether a person is really "good" or merely well-restrained by law, convention, egotism, & public opinion. Of course there are sometimes *probable indications* of such distinctions in status, recognisable after long & close observation of the subject in a wide variety of aspects & reactions—but even so, we often guess wrong. It never does to bank on a person's natural qualities too far—or, conversely, to be too shocked or sorrowful when one finds that a seeming paragon of "virtue" is a hypocrite, coward, & criminal. What of it? Æsthetically unpleasant, of course, but it means no more than that a few nerve-fibres & endocrine glands worked a bit differently from the way you thought they worked. It would give me only a mild shock if I were to find that Bobby Barlow is planning my murder, or that Klarkash-Ton has poisoned the wells of Auburn, or that my aunt had murdered my grandfather

30 years ago. All these things are *improbable,* but I know that every human being has latent within him the instincts which produce such acts. Therefore if I
found I had been inaccurate in my previous analyses of the individuals concerned, I would be merely aesthetically & instinctively sorry. I would not be
totally blasted, or feel that the foundations had fallen out of the cosmos. No
chemical, physical, or biological principle which I did not know before would
be involved. And the same way with that unfortunate bugbear of the naive—
excessive concern over *what other people think of one.* It is, of course, very nice to
be highly regarded by as many persons as possible. It is comfortably stimulating to the ego. But we know from our own attitude toward others that a great
deal of the apparent regard we receive is very slight, hypocritical, & perfunctory. Why should it be otherwise? What is one person to any other person
beyond the narrow range in which domestic, parental, & erotic instincts
(themselves capricious, variable, & largely transient) operate? In general, there
are only a few casual reasons why any person should entertain any particular
sentiments of like or dislike for any other person. The "sounding-board"
principle is the widest—i.e., the fact that certain persons react to one's own
conversation in such a way as to make one feel important & wise. Perhaps,
though, the "landmark" principle is equally frequent & potent—i.e., the circumstance that some people are associated with scenes & events which have
enhanced our ego & brought us gratification or agreeable expectancy. Then
there is the *symbolic* principle, whereby some individuals come to represent to
us certain qualities which we like, & which we see (or think we see) in them.
A variant is the *mirror* principle, whereby we fancy we can see & admire our
own traits in others. Another vast segment of human regard is purely *acquisi-
tive*—i.e., based on hope of intellectual or material gain from the persons
"liked". Regard of this sort pleases us because it makes us feel powerful &
important—like monarchs with largesse to dispense. Then there is sheer *admiration* for qualities which we may or may not really possess . . . . though oddly
enough, admiration is often associated with dislike & envy. At any rate the
point is that human liking is a diverse & casual matter *which does not necessarily
compliment its object.* It is pleasant, but it is something whose presence or absence needn't get us all steamed up. I am suitably pleased because old Jim
Morton & W. Paul Cook seem to like arguing with me—but it wouldn't kill
me if they got sick of it & began to regard me as a nuisance. I'd simply let 'em
alone & let everybody be happy. Nor do I lose any sleep right now because
various opponents hate me like hell & disparage my work in & out of print.
I'm neither better nor worse, intrinsically, for the opinions on either side. Of
course, there is a *primitive urge* to crave praise & liking & resent slander & dislike—the old ego doing its stuff—but this urge (like the old primitive emotions regarding human character) diminishes prodigiously when the actual
psychological background of the subject—with its trivial elements of cause &
effect—is sincerely & properly analysed. Most of the heartburns in these mat-

ters come from the powerful & persistent delusions implanted by supernatu-
ralism. In primitive times, when the phenomena of the cosmos were "explained" through religious magic, it was useful & popular to drag in
mythology as an ethical enforcing agent. In its day it worked—but the barbaric process gave rise to crazy delusions about *cosmic* "right & wrong", "sin",
"human character", "inner life", "nobility", "love", "friendship", "virtue", &
so on—sentimentalising & codifying chance biological phenomena, & perpetuating errors of perspective—which will continue to confuse, mislead, &
disappoint us until the discipline of years of sound materialistic thought has
worked it out of our systems. These errors are *still* taught by conventional education & "genteel" literature—a circumstance which gives me considerable
sympathy with *some* of the educational & anti-theological campaigns of the
modern bolsheviks. In no field is this tragic delusion more absurd than in that
of the erotically based compound emotions commonly lumped together as
"romantic affection", "love", & so on. Whole cycles of literature & folklore,
dominated by basic error & childish myth, unite to create entirely false ideas
of the nature, origin, classification, extent, degree, permanence, & characteristic action of these tenuous, capricious, & evanescent phenomena—so that
millions of average persons encounter anguish, deception, disappointment &
bitterness because their deluded & extravagant expectations fail to materialise.
It was bad enough in former times, when the sheer *universality* of the delusion
made everyone more uniform in *action & sense of obligation* (as distinguished
from genuine inward emotion) through sheer mass pressure. Today the situation is infinitely worse, with *variability of myth-acceptance* destroying all uniformi-
ty of standards, understanding as to common goals & meaning of terms, &
equality of sentiment or accepted obligations in such matters. What the
moderns call "emancipation from Victorianism" is merely a plunge into chaos
with some (the backward-looking but insufficiently stable romanticists) at the
mercy of others (the insensitive & unscrupulous realists). The only rational
solution, of course, is to put aside mythological expectation & realise that a
truly glamourous "romantic" adjustment is only a rare & felicitous accident—
much less likely under modern codes (or lack of codes) than under the older
order. It will never be frequent, but will become less uncommon (perhaps
even less so than in former times) if ever a new code (based on the foundations of the old but harmonised with the facts of human psychology, anthropology, & biology) is evolved & stabilised. Under the so-called "new
freedom" it cannot possibly exist, even fragmentarily. But even postulating
the creation & popularisation of a code of maximum effectiveness, romantic
ecstasy of a genuine & permanent sort will remain extremely rare. Indeed, it is
never permanent—success or apparent permanence involving its *gradual replacement* by other no less (or scarcely less) satisfying domestic & family emotions.
For most it must always remain an unattained myth—& the happiest average
person is he who can philosophically let it remain so; knowing that most

people are no happier than he, & resting content with whatever milder & more prosaic forms of sentiment or domestic alliance he can manage to negotiate . . . . or doing without, in case the years get the better of him. He will probably have to rest content with these tag ends—or nothing—anyhow, so he might as well realise that such a state is absolutely natural & inevitable. When he realises that only a few lucky beneficiaries of chance ever have anything better, he will be the more disposed to accept the common lot with a shrug of the shoulders & turn his attention to the other interests at his disposal. After all—the sphere of consciousness is full of varied material for reasonably pleasant activity & contemplation—scenery, history, art, the sciences, philosophy, music, literature, & so on . . . . . And all romance is transient at best—& in many cases some prosaic modus vivendi breeds a greater & more enduring contentment & domestic felicity than the wildest of romances could have done. So the sensible individual never expects very much, never pays any attention to ill-founded & evanescent prospects, is thankful for whatever chance crumbs come his way (& *no one* gets more than capricious chance allots), never feels bitter because he didn't happen to get as much as some luckier devil, is not astonished at a meagreness of happiness which he knows to be the natural order of things & the common lot of most, & keeps himself busy with the various life-interests—aesthetic, intellectual, administrative, &c.—on which he would have had to fall back in any case all too soon. At the same time, if he enjoys the sensation of mystical expectancy, he can for many years nourish the idea that he *may* suddenly find himself one of the few persons to whom some measure of "romantic" fulfilment comes— momentarily or otherwise. The idea is certainly as likely to be true in his case as in anybody else's case. Actually, one's degree of success in arriving at some tolerably adequate & congenial domestic adjustment is a compound matter consisting—in about equal parts—of luck, disillusioned intelligence, & persistence. If the two latter qualities were less rare, the number of fairly well-adjusted & contented persons in the world would be greater. But this is merely one phase of the whole question of emotional equilibrium—the general answer to all of which is that *nothing in the cosmos is really worth worrying, grieving, or getting excited about.* All these things—human character & behaviour, the opinions of others regarding oneself, one's own acts, opinions, & emotions, one's luck or absence of it in romantic adjustment, &c. &c.—are simply natural conditions depending on the fixed laws of biology, psychology, & anthropology; so that it is useless to complain because they are as they are, & not like the myths of that fantastic dream-world invented by mental children wherein "virtue" & "courage" are rewarded, "evil" punished, the "good man" always adored & respected, & each little boy & girl rewarded by the lifelong (or *eternity-long,* since these poor simps believe in immortality also!) "love" & devotion of that "true mate" for whom he or she was "destined" by "fate" from "the beginning of time"—whatever that is. All our wistful protests are wasted on an indifferent universe—so that if we wish to get anywhere toward adjustment & contentment we had better dismiss vain aspiration & set to work studying & comprehending the biological, psychological, & sociological principles underlying emotion & behaviour & conduct *as these things really are*. When we understand the true principles as best we can, we are able to avoid many mistakes & false expectations, to dismiss many irrelevant censures & bitternesses & regrets, & to utilise the existing forces in a thoughtful way productive of the greatest possible contentment & the wisest general course in life. These are goals eminently worth striving for—even at the cost of hard study & of rigid mental discipline in the realm of systematic disillusionment. And there are other goals, too—especially the banishment of that sense of dissatisfaction with one's own work which besets all genuine artists . . . or rather, the banishment of that sense's acutest pangs. Common sense teaches that one can do no more than his best, that the supreme titans in each art are very few, & that there is no reason why everyone should expect to be a titan. What reward do the titans get except a little extra titillation of the ego? Often a very modest degree of aesthetic or intellectual accomplishment—the perfect attainment of some moderate objective—gives an artist virtually the same sense of creation & attainment that the painting of a Mona Lisa or the writing of an Æneid or the composition of a Ninth Symphony or the building of a Parthenon gave the artists who did those things. To discover clearly a very *little* truth; to say or paint perfectly some very limited mood or fragmentary scene—do not these lesser victories perhaps give us just as much of pleasure & of ecstasy as any human personality is able to assimilate? Who can say that the emotions of Shakespeare upon completing "King Lear" were actually as much greater than (for example) Klarkash-Ton's upon completing one of his sonnets or carven heads, as the relative aesthetic stature of the results would imply? Perhaps the "unsuccessful plodders" are not really as badly off as they imagine!

How to start straightening things out? Well—I suppose different methods work best with different people. I myself find it best to begin at the basic & universal end—the scientific & analytical end. Ask of the universe, *"what is anything?"*—& by the time the evidence is all accumulated & interpreted many mundane things which formerly bulked large will sink to insignificance all of themselves for lack of any rationale to buoy them up. I recall in my case what a hell of a temper I used to have—& how that temper gradually evaporated when I realised the automatic & inevitable nature of all the organic reactions determining impulse, thought, & act. I used to fret about people's opinions & all that—but when I fully envisaged the mechanical automatism & essential triviality of all such phenomena I could no longer regard them seriously. Thus powerful emotions about natural conditions often evaporate as soon as the blind, impersonal mechanical-chemical-biological jumble of inevitable causes behind those conditions becomes plainly manifest & explicitly analysed. And our daily judgments & conduct likewise alter as we perceive the true mechanical bases of "character", & the prosaic psychological factors underlying personal relationships & the surface-emotions pertaining thereto. We avoid excessive enthusiasms & injudicious placements of confidence, realising that we can expect of the average person only such environmental reactions as the norm of primate zöology indicates as probable. We become more self-sufficient, & confine our social dealings to the exchange of general ideas & impressions (a world in themselves, & overwhelmingly richer & more profitable as conversational pabulum than anything else could be) as distinguished from displays of personal emotion & estimates of personal regard. We realise that the romantic element cannot successfully tincture any contacts apart from those of serious domestic aim. We learn the meaningless futility of excessive praise or blame, & of violent grief or perturbation at disclosures regarding human "character". We grow independent of others' opinions, & let the public go to hades in its own way. And we perceive the folly & uselessness of wrought-up self-examination & self-criticism—realising that the man of sense never cries over spilt milk, but merely checks error in himself when he finds it—coolly & philosophically—for the purpose of avoiding repetitions in future. Self-criticism should concern only the present & future. No one ever did anybody—least of all himself—any good by brooding over the delusions & blunders of bygone years. All that is worth bothering about is getting a firm grasp on sense & reality & steering as sane a course as possible through the period which *is* controllable—the years ahead. And *straightforward realistic science* is the only guide worth following today. It is the only thread of reality in a labyrinth of exploded falsities. It may be objected that awkward & painful situations often *force* themselves from outside upon even the most philosophic of persons. Well—so they do—but the more philosophic & disillusioned a person is, the less hold they will get upon him, & the sooner he can extricate himself from their toils. Besides—these awkward situations somehow seem to keep clear of persons with a positive materialistic philosophy manifest in all their words & acts & mannerisms & gestures. When people see that anybody is asking little or nothing of the world, avoiding enthusiasms & easy personalities, putting all energies & interests into definite impersonal channels, living largely in an objective world of general knowledge & planet-wide concerns, reserving every trace of the romantic element for one serious domestic prospect (or at least one at a time) or if necessary abolishing it altogether, refraining from sharp criticisms of himself or others, & sinking all egotisms & prejudices into an impartial outlook on man & the universe, they generally cease to pester him with the tangles & feuds & misjudgments which are constantly inflicted upon the naive or emotional or gregarious or myth-deluded person. They know that he knows what he's about, & that they have nothing to gain from slopping around & playing on his emotions & using him as a pawn in their own emotional titillation. Not that they ostracise him—far from it! Rather do they merely decide to adopt a more dignified attitude toward him—to put their best instead of their worst feet forward, & to make him a sharer of their serious ambitious & activities instead of a victim of their caprices, fatuities, & irresponsible treacheries. But the way to attain this state of easy & impersonal adjustment is *not* to think *directly* about it! The very opposite. Let all such considerations go to the devil—ignore the crowd & its sentiments—think only of the universe, its real foundations, & your sensible adjustment to its basic laws & its aesthetic & intellectual rewards. Heed people only far enough to build a bulwark against their encroachments. Lose self-consciousness altogether. And by the time you've forgotten the existence of the social world, you will find its members ready to hail you on a basis of increased sense & superior dignity.

So the voice of sound reason would seem to say, "cheer up!" There aren't any phenomena in the cosmos worth being mournful or depressed about. What the hell do the antics or intentions or emotions of other people matter? Positive happiness may or may not come (seeking never helps), but meanwhile there are a lot of tolerably pleasant things to do—whether or not one can do them just as easily or just as magnificently as some world master. In any case you're probably having no worse a time than anybody else. To hades with dismal brooding! What in thunder is of any real use or significance except planning for a sensible future? And how can anybody plan sensibly except by ditching all myth-born sentimentalities; studying the scientific mechanics of human thought, feeling, & behaviour; & steering a realistic course based on phenomena as they are rather than as one would like them to be—or as the old myths represent them as being? To begin with, don't fail to read—in a thorough, leisurely way—that magnificent Wells–Huxley opus "The Science of Life". Actually, it is more than mere biology—for although it begins with the amoeba & includes the vegetable world, it also leads up to human psychology & even sociology. It is just about as complete a survey of terrestrial life—as a general proposition, & in relation to the specialised phenomena of the more advanced forms—as has ever before been assembled between two covers. It shows all the mechanical & sub-human sources of human feelings & conduct, & explodes sentimental concepts merely by plainly presenting the biological facts. The reader comes to know *why* people feel & do what they do—& as he gains this knowledge he ceases to get excited about the matter. [No—this ain't no advertisement . . . . the Providence Bureau of Lofty Omniscience is unconnected with Doubleday, Doran, & Co. or the Literary Guild!] Since the volume is a 1500-pager, you ought to get hold of some copy you won't have to return soon. I'm reading one lent by young J. Vernon Shea (formerly of Pittsburgh, now 502 Second Ave., Suffolk, Va.)—a bright boy whom I believe I mentioned once before in connexion with some matter or other. Now I feel certain that Shea would be glad to add your name to the lending list—so let him know if you'd like it shot out to Averoigne. Just tell him you're a friend of Klarkash-Ton, of whom he is a vast admirer. I feel sure that the book won't disappoint you—& that it will help to give an aspect of effective reality to the inept & bombastic hot air with which the preceding 13 pages (Yuggoth, what a blast!) have been inflated. . . . . . And so the old coot, continuing to mumble incoherently into the depths of his rusty grey whiskers, nodded vacuously & joined that abyss of slumber into which all his auditors had long been plunged!

Glad to hear that your sister is doing so well at the university—which surely is remarkable in view of the long post-high-school pause. I'd hate to think of the amount of high-school lore which slipped out of my mind during the five years following '08. My health did not permit me to go to the university—indeed, the steady application to high-school gave me a sort of breakdown. I couldn't have stood the pace of college attendance till 1920 or so—when I was around 30—& at that age I would have felt a bit self-conscious among the undergraduates. And what I forgot betwixt 1908 & 1920 must have been plenty! 12 years—& where were the botany & German & Greek & half a dozen different things? The few things I did remember—English, Latin, physics, chemistry, & so on—stuck largely by accident or preference or private brushing-up during the intervening years. But so far as balanced education goes, I'm certainly a total loss till this very day! Just a humly cracker-bar'l philosopher a-settin' raound the stove at the gin'ral store & argyfyin' abaout what I seen in last week's Caounty Argus!

I'm certainly glad that Klarkash-Ton has found such a congenial energy-outlet in his carving, & hope that his nervous condition (which he admits to be a strained & fagged-out one) may steadily improve during the ensuing months—though Yuggoth knows his burdens continue to be great enough. He is certainly one of the most kindly, thoughtful, & appreciative of beings. One wonders what course he will adopt when entirely alone—whether he will continue as a hermit atop Indian Hill, or seek quarters in some more urban environment. Some of his new carven images are certainly powerful in the extreme—he recently gave me a vividly horrible corpse-head called "The Outsider" (after a story of mine), & let me see a curious, archaic-looking thing called "The Hyperborean Snake-Eater" which is designed for young Barlow. He has also sent sketches of other sculptural triumphs, & promises to send photographs—& to lend a fair assortment of the eidola—later on. One rather amusing idea of his is to prepare a hoax for our good old friend Morton—who, as I believe you know, is curator of the Paterson (N.J.) Museum. The plan is to send Morton one of the most archaic-looking eikons—preferably one with a surface suggesting vast age & long inhumation, & with several broken fragments restored with cement—& suggest that it was found in some cryptic & mysterious place . . . such as the Cahokia mounds in Illinois (near which Cook now lives) or the Indian shell heaps near New Smyrna, Fla.—near Bobby Barlow. With the cöoperation of one or the other of these hypothetical archaeologists, one of the Averoigne images might easily give James Ferdinand a highly puzzling half-hour—both as an antiquarian & as a mineralogist. If he asked my opinion I would tell him that the workmanship strongly suggests Hyperborean technique to me—of the pre-human school antedating the founding of the human city of Commoriom, & probably associated with the original furry worshippers of Tsathoggua. That it probably filtered across the Arctic Ocean to Olathoë, in Lomar (circa 100,000 B.C.), & thence southward (across that sea which shrank into the Great Lakes) to the great but now-forgotten kingdoms of Ihli-Nwā & Msû—Rhi, whose tall towers the glaciers wiped out in B.C. 30,000. All of which the mighty curator might or might not recognise as solemn archaeological & historical truth as taught at the University of Vyones & at Miskatonic University in Arkham. If any of the other images look as millennially palaeogaean as the Barlow-bound "Snake Eater" now tarrying at 66, Mortonius certainly is in for a session of perplexed head-scratching!

Hope the Institute didn't prove too great a bore, & that you had no trouble in making vital musico-pedagogical problems seem snappy. Being 'on a panel' suggests forming part of a painting or bas-relief carving, but I presume the actual condition was one of grave discussion of such points as "The Relation of Jazz Bands to Retarded Mentality; a Problem of Cause & Effect", or "Should Whistling in the Classroom be Compulsory, or merely Strongly Encouraged?" I remember Teachers' Institutes, & how we all looked forward to them as periods of liberation. Our ideas of what occurred in them were very nebulous indeed—our primary concern being what *didn't* occur in school! Those were the days when a friend named Chester Pierce Munroe & I claimed the proud joint distinction of being the worst boys in Slater Ave. School—our only rival being a huge youth from a distant & seedy region who boasted 17 years as opposed to our 11 or 12, & whose voice had changed. We were not so actively destructive as merely antinomian in an arrogant & sardonic way—the protest of individuality against capricious, arbitrary, & excessively detailed authority. I can still see "Monk" McCurdy (the 17-year-old) as he lorded it over his chronological inferiors (but scholastic equals) & overawed them with his gorilla-like physiognomy. I haven't met "Monk" in person in 32 years, but believe I'd know him still. About a decade ago I used to see a sign "John McCurdy, Practical Plumbing" on one of the basement shops in the now-demolished *College St.* row toward the bottom of the hill (the place with the ancient colonial archways), & wondered if the proprietor were good old Monk. It's a pity I didn't enquire—for if it was, then College St. has known at least 3 of the old Slater Ave. rough guys . . . the third being Chester Munroe's brother Harold,[4] who was once a deputy sheriff in the Court House. Ah, me—the old times! Censorious colleagues predicted that we'd all be kicked out of high school when we got there—& yet in actual fact it sobered us down. At good old Hope St. they treated us like men, & didn't have any of the omnipresent arbitrary *don'ts* in trivial matters which challenged our individuality at Slater. Thus were our youthful spirits sapped away by an effete civilisation—leaving us the tame, commonplace old dodderers that we are today. I'll bet even Monk McCurdy doesn't swear the resounding oaths he used to affect!

Lecture on the excavations in the Athenian agora tonight at the School of Design. My aunt & I will probably go. Grandpa is always to be found where the dead past is dug up! We had a very pleasant Thanksgiving—dining with friends at your quondam stopping-place across the garden. My aunt sends her sincerest regards.

As I write, an especial friend of mine in the depths of the neighbouring semicircular chair stirs in his slumbers & emits a few drowsy purrs. He is a huge black person, yet has never seen any year but 1935—having been born on the Ides of last February. Possibly I described him to you last spring as a tiny handful of black fur—but bless me, how the young rascal has grown! Little Johnny Perkins! He belongs at the boarding-house, & is the son of white-&-black Mrs. Spotty, whom you met. Much of his leisure is spent over here. He knows who gives him catnip to chew & roll in, so he's a great friend of Grandpa's. He remembered the old man perfectly after my 3-month absence! We send our regards to Son, & hope the entire household at Averoigne may enjoy a pleasant Yule. ¶ Best wishes for better times—

     Yr obt hble Servt—
       E'ch-Pi-El

P.S. I enclose some assorted junk on my usual antiquarian-travel theme which you can either add to your collection or chuck into the waste-basket. You have seen the old house described inside the art week folder—Shakespeare's Head.[5] The postcard fails to do justice to that Yale quadrangle.

Notes

1. For *The Natural History of Selborne,* see Bibliography under Gilbert White. HPL owned at least one volume of the long-running *Gentleman's Magazine* (1731–1907; *LL* 371), as well as Volume 2 of the 4-volume set of *A Selection of Curious Articles from* The Gentleman's Magazine (London: Longmans, Hurst, Rees & Orme, 1809–11; *LL* 372).

2. H[arry] A[llen] Overstreet (1875–1970), chairman of the department of philosophy and psychology at City College of New York (1911–36) and author of *Influencing Human Behavior* (1925), *The Enduring Quest: A Search for a Philosophy of Life* (1931), and *The Mature Mind* (1949).

3. William Briggs Savery (1875–1945) was a professor of philosophy at the University of Washington (1902–45) and a follower of George Santayana, William James, and John Dewey.

4. Chester Pierce Munroe (1889–1943) and Harold Bateman Munroe (1891–1966) were boyhood friends of HPL. John McCurdy, Jr. (1884–1935) worked for a plumbing company as a bookkeeper.

5. The John Carter House (1772), 21 Meeting Street. *The Providence Gazette and Country*

Gentleman (est. 1762) was published by William Goddard in a shop marked by the sign of Shakespeare's Head on North Main Street. John Carter joined the paper in 1767 and by 1768 was sole proprietor. He and his wife moved the business into the house they built on Meeting Street.

[24] [ALS, JHL]

66 College St.,
Providence, R.I.,
May 12, 1936.

Dear Helen:—

Well—I thought it was quite a while since the Averoigne post-rider brought a bulletin from the Chateau de Sully, & I'm surely sorry to hear that so depressing an indisposition was the cause of the hiatus. Lurking obstructions like tonsils surely do form a distracting & enervating handicap, & I fancy you find the relief of their removal well worth any pain which the ordeal itself may have caused. *This* time I trust they will stay amputated, leaving you in good 1933 health & permitting the present state of relative exhilaration to remain paramount. I can imagine how spectral the ether experience must have been, for many report the most macabre & curious impressions in connexion with this process. Very recently some of the best hospitals have been experimenting with new methods of administering ether—prefacing it with the more instantaneous but less permanent nitrous oxide (the "laughing gas" of dental use), & allowing the N_2O anaesthesia to pass gradually into etherisation. But I doubt if any form of anaesthesia (save perhaps the alcoholism which seems so increasingly fashionable) is quite pleasant enough to cultivate as a pastime!

That trouble & illness have haunted the Atlantic as well as the Pacific coast, you may already be aware through reports from Klarkash-Ton. The fact is, that 1936 forms a large black blot so far as this household is concerned—leading me to think of such passages as

". . . whom merciful disaster
Followed fast & followed faster."[1]

and

". . . ruin upon ruin, rout on rout,
Confusion worse confounded."[2]

The year started with a mixture of flagging energies & piled-up tasks which threw my programme into utter chaos—& late in January I suffered a grippe attack which had me flat for a week & increased the hopelessness of my schedule. Then—before I was able to do much more than stagger around—the *real* trouble began!

My aunt came down with a grippe attack infinitely worse than mine,[3] & in March developed complications with necessitated her removal to the hospital . . . . a recurrence of 1933's less pleasant side! Meanwhile I was perforce saddled with the composite duties of nurse, doorkeeper, purchasing agent, secretary, & what-not—which destroyed every vestige of opportunity for the reclamation of my own affairs. Letters piled up unanswered, stacks of unread borrowed books towered toward the ceiling, revision jobs had to be returned unperformed—& black calamity in general reigned. I did not, however, forget for a moment that all this siege was a darned sight harder on the patient than on myself! Happily, my aunt improved very steadily after mid-March, & on April 7 was transferred to a convalescent home. She returned here April 21st, & has since been gaining very well—though she still requires some coöperation in the details of domestic administration. She takes walks on every sunny day—usually accompanied by me—& on April 30 was treated to a pleasant motor ride through the awakening countryside to Westport Point, Mass. However—just to continue 1936's tradition of disaster—she is at present threatened with a dental siege! The general strain, the congestion of tasks, & the beastly cold weather have combined to keep me in an exhausted state little short of nervous breakdown—& I have so little power of concentration left that it takes me about an hour to do anything I could ordinarily do in five minutes. My general programme is in such a hopeless tangle that neglect & repudiation will have to be practiced in order to clear it up. When I think of the amount of creative work Klarkash-Ton is managing to accomplish even now—despite incessant handicaps vastly heavier than mine at their worst—I realise what a comparatively poor fish I am. At any rate, my hat is off to him!

However, I shall feel better when steady hot weather gets here. That's what puts the pep into Grandpa! As if to increase the general misery, this has been one of the most beastly cold springs I can recall—following one of the worst winters. March gave a little deceptive warmth—plus the memorable floods of which you doubtless read in the press [Providence, like most seaports, escaped; but streets were under water 4 miles away, while Hartford—only 60 or 65 m. to the west—suffered a major calamity. Late California performances were quite eclipsed!]—but April was raw & chilly until the very last. The first really genial day of '36 was April 29—& since then there have been a sufficient number of mild days (over 70°) to produce a decided upturn in my health. I take my work out in the open air each sunny afternoon—enjoying the really transcendent beauty of fresh blossoms & delicate verdure which the local landscape has at this time of year. Young Barlow has invited me down to De Land again, but I greatly doubt my ability to go. I certainly wish I could, for a few weeks in the land of palmettos & live-oaks would do wonders for aged bones!

But the general desert of misery has not been without its oases. I have been able to attend lectures (at the college or at the School of Design—in either case only a block from #66) on subjects as diverse as Plato's "Republic", modern art, archaic Greek civilisation, Gilbert Stuart, Rhode Island colonial silversmiths, Chinese contributions to European culture, 5th century (B.C.) Greek sculpture, Philosophy & Poetry (vide encl.), Mayan ruins, & the Michelson–Morley experiment (regarding the velocity of light as affected—or unaffected—by the motion of the observer), on one interpretation of which the Einstein theory is founded. One is never too old to pick up an idea or so!

On May 4th the Rhode Island Tercentenary exercises opened with a parade in colonial costumes which started at the college gate (only a stone's throw from #66, as you may recall) & proceeded down the hill to the ancient market house, where it was joined by Gov. Green in a coach actually surviving from the 18th century. The detachment then proceeded to the 175-year-old colony house in North Main St.,[4] where was held a mock-session of that rebel legislature of May 4, 1776, at which the seditious delegates treasonably disavowed the rightful authority of King & Parliament. In this session—conducted in perfect costume, & in the actual room where the real deputies sat 160 years before—the part of each rebel legislator was taken by some lineal descendant; Gov. Green representing his ancestor Col. Arnold, who presented the original draught of the treasonable resolution. The limited dimensions of the colony-house (which you may or may not recall—at the end of a long uphill parade) excluded all but a moderate number of spectators, but I was lucky enough to get in & secure a really excellent vantage-point. The enclosed rotogravure cutting gives a fragmentary idea of the event. The costuming was so good, & the addresses (text preserved in full in minutes of original 1776 meeting) so well delivered, that one might well imagine (in that absolutely identical setting) the years to have dissolved away, leaving 1776 as a living reality. It was all I could do to keep from crying down the rebel proposers of treason, or from applauding those loyal deputies who urged the reasonable arbitration of existing troubles without recourse to illegal secession. At the end of the session the deputies chanted the newly-adopted formula "God Save the United Colonies"—but I, loyal to the past & to my hereditary Sovereign, murmured without change the familiar rightful syllables—GOD SAVE THE KING!

Various other ceremonies & exhibitions will prolong the tercentenary observations till well into the autumn. Historic mansions will be opened to the public (one, indeed, having been presented to the School of Design as a permanent museum), & displays of colonial furniture & other antiquities will be featured in many places. Last week my aunt & I visited the ancient Stephen Hopkins house (1742) on the hill only two blocks from here—which is now filled with a loan-exhibit of Rhode Island furniture & household objects of the 17th & 18th centuries.

Your Quebec stationery surely aroused a pleasing chain of associations—I haven't seen the ancient northern fortress since Sept. '33, & wish like the dickens I could get there again this year! Nothing I have ever seen quite equals it in beauty & quaintness—the silver belfries, the steep, winding streets, the dizzying ramparts, the centuried grey facades, the beetling cliffs, & the lordly slopes of the citadel, whence can be obtained what is perhaps the finest urban & scenic panorama in North America. Its one rival in general charm is ancient Charleston.

Thanks very much for the Symphony programme, which I studied with much interest—noting your position among other distinguished artists from near & far. Congratulations on your inclusion in this assemblage, & on the splendid & well-received performance given under the direction of the eminent visitor. Dr. Hertz surely set a high standard & aroused a high pitch of inspiration—& I trust that he has left a permanent impress upon the methods & spirits of the orchestra.[5] The programme strikes me—an ignorant layman—as an especially delightful one; indeed, if eminent orchestras would stick to selections as traditional as these, I would be less barbarically indifferent than I am to contemporary musical opportunities! Membership in an organisation as important as this ought to help greatly in furthering your musical career—both as regards artistic experience, & as regards recognition in the right circles.

I am sorry to hear that Klarkash-Ton gets around so seldom these days—& his general predicament really worries me. In my last letter to him I asked whether he could not find some dependable unemployed person who would be willing to stay at Indian Hill & help with the heavier chores in exchange for his food & lodging. I am assuming that the house has enough rooms to lodge a "hired man" if such could be secured. The task of running the whole establishment, caring for an ailing father, attending to 40 hens, & bringing all the water from a distant well, sounds so fantastically impossible that I wonder how any mortal can perform it—& have, besides, sufficient energy to carve monstrous eidola, paint nightmare forms, & plan out a whole new series of tales! The more one admires Klarkash-Ton's stamina in doing what he does, the more one reflects on the marvels he could accomplish if free from environmental handicaps. There is acute tragedy in such a case of genius held in leash. However, as you say, he can have the satisfaction of knowing that he has been all that a son could be. I hope the senior Ashton-Smith appreciates such unfailing devotion. About the travelling exhibit of eikons—I am consumed with eagerness to see it. By this time I hope Loveman has written to acknowledge its receipt. When C A S spoke of not hearing from him I dropped him an admonitory postcard. This has brought *me* no reply, but I trust it has started a message Averoignewards. I can't understand the negligence which many persons habitually show in matters such as this!

I presume the spring in Averoigne is much farther advanced than in arctic New-England, & trust you have been able to enjoy the open air considerably. No better aid to convalescence can be found—as my aunt can testify at the present moment. I hope old grey Son still flourishes—following the laudable example of black Simaetha on Indian Hill. Hereabouts the sprightly Mr. John Perkins & his younger brother Minto (named—by an old lady at the boarding-house[6] who spends her summers in New-Brunswick—for Gilbert John Murray Kynymond Elliot, 4th Earl of Minto, who was Governor-General of Canada around the turn of the century) disport daily in the sunny garden, now & then calling on their old Grandpa Ech-Pi-El to nibble catnip & drowse & purr in the old gentleman's chairs. Lord Minto is black on top & white on the bottom, whilst Mr. Perkins is black in both hemispheres save for a tiny white cravat. Both are sons of Mrs. Spotty, whom you saw in 1933 with her two little adopted tigers.

The new building in lower College St.—to replace the demolished colonial row with the archways which you may remember—is now advanced to the steel-frame stage. It will reproduce Providence colonial architecture in every detail, & will indeed contain the lower of the two old archways—reërected brick by brick, & with the original wooden lintel. The ancient brick building at the foot of the hill has been retained for incorporation into the new edifice, but is reduced to the veriest shell in order to provide for a new fireproof interior. It will be some consolation to have the familiar old gable still in place as one starts upward from Market Square. As I may have mentioned before, the future structure (which will be divided into separate Georgian units to convey the idea of a *row* of old buildings) will belong to the Rhode Island School of Design, housing the library & administrative offices. This neighbourhood—with the college at the top of the hill & the School of Design at the bottom—surely goes in heavily for pedagogy! I ought to acquire at least an elementary education through sheer involuntary absorption!

With every good wish, & renewed sympathy anent your recent ordeal,
I remain
Yr most obt hble Servt
Ech-Pi-El

My aunt sends best regards.

Notes

1. ". . . whom unmerciful Disaster / Followed fast and followed faster . . ." Poe, "The Raven," ll. 63–64.
2. John Milton, *Paradise Lost* 2.995–96.
3. Actually, Annie Gamwell was hospitalized for breast cancer and underwent a mastectomy.
4. The Old State House (Colony House) at 150 Benefit Street (1762).
5. Alfred Hertz (1872–1942), German conductor, music director of the San Francisco Symphony (1915–30), and a guest conductor of the orchestra thereafter.
6. Evelyn M. Staples (1860–1938).

[25]   [ALS, JHL]

66 College St.,
Providence, R.I.
July 26, 1936.

Dear Helen:—

Thanks exceedingly for the fantastic cave-scape which arrived the other day. That grotesque 'elephant's head' might well be an enlargement of some proboscidian entity carved by Klarkash-Ton! I did not know that Washington boasted such subterrene marvels, & must mention this nighted grotto to my young correspondent in Asotin—Duane W. Rimel, a great admirer of C A S. The only caves I've ever been in are the Endless Caverns in Virginia & the system inside Lookout Mountain in Tennessee. This latter contains an underground waterfall 150 feet high—which has never known the light of the sun, & which until 5 or 6 years ago had never been glimpsed by any human eye. Did you explore the Gardner Cave? I envy you if you did! I am interested to hear of your passage through Idaho, for I used to hear much of that state when I was young. My grandfather organised a corporation—the Owyhee Land & Irrigation Co.—to dam the Snake River somewhere near its confluence with the Bruneau & construct a suitable irrigation system, but met with failure through two successive burstings of the uncompleted dam. Having thus been wiped out financially, he damned the Snake River in quite another way! During my childhood he was frequently in Idaho, & I can recall his letters with a Grand View or Mountain Home postmark. I now learn from Rimel that the difficult irrigation project has finally been carried through successfully—thanks to the better engineering methods of another generation. Incidentally—if your homeward route lies anywhere near Asotin, you ought to drop in on Rimel (P.O. Box 100), whose appreciation of Klarkash-Ton's work is profound & sincere. He has recently made his own first placement in *Weird Tales* with a picturesquely ghoulish yarn.[1]

I trust that your stay in Seattle is proving uniformly pleasant,[2] & that you will not miss the absence of a real vacation if you decide to take the longer university course. I can imagine the mystical impressiveness of Mt. Rainier with its shifting mantle of clouds—indeed, I was years ago fascinated by descriptions of it in the (now doubtless forgotten) juvenile books of Kirk Munroe. My own first-hand glimpses of mountains have been few & relatively tame—the maximum being New Hampshire's Mt. Washington . . . a mere 6293 feet as scaled against Rainier's 14,526.

1936 has surely been a bad year for the eastern members of the weird group. Young Melmoth the Wandrei was indeed indisposed during the spring—with a combination of influenza & dysentery—but was fully recovered at last reports. Less fortunate was his sister-in-law, injured in a motorcoach accident & in the hospital with something like spinal & cerebral concussion.[3] Belknap's parents have both had grippe, & Dr. Long is now under treatment for pernicious anaemia. Bobby Barlow's throat & nerves have given infinite trouble—& at #66 my aunt's severe illness (now, fortunately, very largely an unpleasant memory) & my own nervous exhaustion & indigestion rounded out the widespread area of woe.

However—it is the southwest which leads in the tragic news, for the suicide of Robert E. Howard[4] is a supremely stunning blow. When I relayed the bad tidings to Klarkash-Ton I had no particulars, & possibly it was this mere outline which he quoted to you. I have since had a letter from Howard's father—a pioneer physician—& perhaps C A S has also received details. Poor old Two-Gun Bob! His desperate act sprang from a marked excess of filial emotion—for he sent a bullet through his brain upon learning that his mother (about whose pleural illness he had been worried for a year, & at whose bedside he had been losing sleep for weeks) could not live more than 48 hours more. He died 8 hours later without regaining consciousness—& the day after that his mother died without knowing of his deed. The shock to old Dr. Howard must be appalling—wife & splendid only child gone at one stroke—but he is carrying on like a true Texan of the old breed. He has presented Robert's library to Howard Payne College in Brownwood (R E H's alma mater) as the nucleus of a Robert E. Howard Memorial Collection, & is urging E. Hoffmann Price to come to Cross Plains to arrange posthumous MSS. & act as literary executor. Price was the only one of our gang ever to see Two-Gun Bob in person. He would like to comply with Dr. Howard's request, but is not sure he can do so. Poor Two-Gun! Tough & eat-'em-alive as he seemed to be, he must have been highly emotional & neurotic at bottom. Most of us, despite the strongest filial affection, recognise the grim inevitability of the elder generation's passing & accept such bereavements philosophically. To the weird group this event surely is a staggering blow. Price says he feels "clubbed on the head", & I can comprehend his sensation. The "fan" magazines will be full of obituaries[5]—& Barlow has written a really touching elegiac sonnet which *Weird Tales* accepted at once.[6] This sonnet forms Ar-E'ch-Bei's first professional acceptance—& it is surely sad that his debut should have so tragic a background. The suddenness of the event makes it all the more devastating. Price had a cheerful card from R E H dated June 3 (death June 11)—& I had a long normal letter written May 13. My answer to that letter—a 32-page argumentative missive—undoubtedly reached Cross Plains too late to be read. Without question Two-Gun Bob had the last word in our 6-year-long debate (he upheld barbarism, & denounced all civilisation as decadence)—an advantage I won't begrudge him, poor chap, under the circumstances! The blow to weird magazine fiction is the greatest since 1932, when Henry S. Whitehead died. R E H had a peculiar zest & spontaneity which gave his work vitality even when he ostensibly made concessions to cheap editorial standards. But he was greater than his published work—a natural scholar & historian whose love of his native southwest made all his letters alternate epics & lyrics. Had he lived longer—he was 30 last January—he would have made his mark in serious literature. R E H lived in or near Texas all his life. He was of old Southern planter stock, largely Scotch-Irish. He first contributed to the magazines at the age of 18, & was an assured professional success when he died. He was, Price says, a rugged & impressive figure—nearly 6 feet tall, & with the build of a prize-fighter. Very dark except for Celtic blue eyes. He was, all in all, a perfect embodiment of that virile southwest out of which he never went.

Real trips being out of the question this year, local annals are exceedingly tame. My health remained miserable until the hot spell of July 8 arrived, but thereafter I felt quite revivified & rejuvenated. The major local disaster—which caused mighty mourning in the Kappa Alpha Tau fraternity, & which will doubtless elicit the profoundest sympathy of old grey Son when you inform him—was the loss of my two best friends last month. For indeed, Mr. John Perkins (black—b. Feb. 1935) & his brother the Earl of Minto (black & white, b. Oct. '35) are no more. They succumbed simultaneously to some obscure feline epidemic, & lie sadly interred in the garden about which they loved to gambol in life. If any evil poisoner is in any way responsible, I hope the soft-footed warriors of the K.A.T. will spy him out & claw him to sanguineous filaments with savagely sharpened talons. For a while we feared there would be no more kittens at the home across the garden, since the white-&-black matriarch (whom you met in '33 with her adopted tiger children) was given away in May to the psychological laboratory of the college—to be used in teaching successive generations of human youth how astute the furry species can be. But since the dual bereavement old Mrs. Spotty has been recalled from her academic career, & once more roams her accustomed garden oasis, serenaded by all the gallant swains of the K.A.T.

Less dismal news pertains—as might be expected of a tottering fossil—to ancient houses & assorted vestigia of the past. Late in May I visited the extreme western rim of the city to view the ancient Clemence house (1654),[7] now recognised as the oldest edifice in this Colony. Since its builder—Thomas Clemence, a friend of Roger Williams—is a lineal ancestor of mine in the 8th generation, I have more than a superficial interest in it. Tom bought

the land—8 acres—from an Indian named Wissawgawaka, & proceeded to construct a typical stone-chimneyed dwelling of the period. It is much changed today—but the accompanying rough sketch shews it as it originally was. The changes are all of the nature of *excrescences*—dormers, lean-to, porch, &c.—so that it could easily be restored if purchased by an historical or antiquarian society as I hope it may be some day. The present owner & occupant is an ancient gentlewoman in destitute circumstances. In the yard the old well-sweep still remains—one of the relatively few left in R.I.

Incidentally—I learned a week ago of the fortunate restoration of that old Place homestead (where my mother & grandmother were born) whose crayon drawing (by my mother) I may have pointed out to you on the walls of 66. It had been out of our family since 1870, & had begun to shew decided signs of wear. Now it has been purchased by an interior decorator & will be carefully restored to its pristine condition. This venerable farmhouse is in Foster, R.I., about 25 miles west of Providence. I last visited it a decade ago.[8]

But my recent old-house explorations have not been confined to personally ancestral places. Last month two of the Georgian mansions on Providence's ancient hill (considerably south of College St.—you saw them in '33) were thrown open as public museums, & among my few current activities was a thorough exploration of both of them. The enclosed pair of leaflets describes the finer of the two. After a close inspection I can say that J. Q. Adams (vide leaflet) was right[9]—& this after having examined 18th century houses all the way from Quebec on the north to St. Augustine (Key West hasn't any) & New Orleans on the south. The edifice has an admirably classic symmetry & arrangement, its only possible flaw being a subtle tendency toward rococo over-ornateness on the lower floor. Like most houses in America even as late as the early 1800's, it is untouched by the superior classicism of the Adam influence, which became manifest in Great Britain as early as the 1750's or 1760's. John Brown, the builder of the house, was one of four quite celebrated brothers belonging to a local sea-trading family descended from the early settler Rev. Chad Brown. His nephew Nicholas Jr. is the one whose donations changed the name of Rhode-Island College to Brown University in 1804. His younger brother Moses was a well-known Quaker & philanthropist, whilst his grand-nephew John Carter Brown founded the world-famous library of Americana which bears his name. John himself was merely a shrewd grasper dependent upon other people's taste. The really civilised member of the family was his elder brother Joseph, who in the 1750's, 1760's, & 1770's played a great part in bringing Providence up to the cultural level of Newport. Joseph was a scholar & man of taste, & the greatest architect in the town prior to the rise of John Holden Greene. With Stephen Hopkins (whose small house—1742—you saw near 66)[10] he helped to found the Providence Library in 1753, & in 1769 he imported a telescope (now at the Ladd Observatory— I've seen it) to observe the transit of Venus in that year. He designed the John Brown house,[11] as well as houses for himself & brother Nicholas—his own edifice being that brick mansion with the cyma-curved pediment in S. Main St. which you saw;[12] this pediment forming an original idea destined to influence the local architectural tradition very strongly. To Joe Brown are likewise due the plan of the 1773 market house[13] (which you saw—in Market Sq. at the foot of the hill) & the selection of the Gibbs design for the First Baptist steeple. In later life he became Professor of Natural Philosophy at the college. The house so well depicted in one of the leaflets may perhaps be regarded as his architectural masterpiece. He died in 1787, before its completion, but its splendid outlines survive as a memorial to his taste. The numerous French busts stuck around at various places are none of his doing. There is a legend that those on the gateposts turn & bow to each other at midnight—a phenomenon I have not personally witnessed!

The other house—of which I could secure no descriptive or pictorial matter—is the Edward Carrington mansion, erected in 1809 & the work of John Holden Greene. This lacks the classic interior symmetry of the Brown house, but is extremely pleasing & homelike. It was recently presented to the R.I. School of Design—with all its original furniture & decorations to be kept intact for ever—by the last of the family, who resides in another colonial mansion inherited through another line.[14] With its stables, coach-houses, cobblestoned courtyard, & extensive grounds & gardens, the Carrington house forms one of the most satisfying domestic units of the early republic period now on exhibition. In its interior architecture it embodies a rather amusing hybridism seemingly peculiar to late 18th & early 19th century Providence—the use of rococo middle-18th-century architecture on the ground floor, & of the newer Adam-period design throughout the upper storeys. Some of the delicate Adam mantels upstairs are among the most exquisite I have ever seen.

During the warm spell I paid ancient Newport a visit—having an enjoyable sail & threading the centuried streets which you may recall from your brief glimpse. Also sat on the cliffs & did considerable writing. The heat improves my power of concentration, so that I accomplish ten times as much during a hot spell than during an equivalent period of cold weather.

July 18–19 I had an enjoyable visit from my old friend M. W. Moe of Milwaukee (poet-teacher) & his gifted son Robert—the latter (now of Bridgeport, Conn.) the youth who was here with his car in the spring of '35. [Moe's other son Donald is a fellow-student of yours at the U. of Wash. & has some kind of a position in the college library.] It was my first sight of Old Mocrates in 13 years, & I fancy he found Grandpa more changed in aspect than I found him. Bob brought him in the car, & we covered quite a bit of scenic & historic ground in the all-too-brief span of 2 days. We went to the quaint quondam fishing village of Pawtuxet (on a picturesque cove 6 m. S. of Providence's civic centre—now overtaken by the expanding network of city streets), ascended old Fort Independence (on the W. shore of the bay, with a magnificent view of the city skyline on the N. & of the blue water & green shores of the bay on the S.), wound through the foliage-shaded driveways of Roger Williams Park, traversed the deep woods & colonial farmlands north of the city, & as a climax repeated the Warren-Bristol drive which young Bob & I took in March of last year. This was much more enjoyable in July than in

March, & the ancient seaport villages (E. shore of the bay) displayed their colonial doorways & giant elms to maximum advantage. We also took the seaside drive on Popesquash Neck—a sub-peninsula attached to the main Bristol peninsula. In Warren we had an all-ice-cream dinner at Maxfield's (that famous Mecca of all our gang)—mine consisting of grape, pineapple, peach, raspberry, banana, & chocolate chip. Father Mocrates fell by the wayside after 2½ pints, but Son Bob downed 3 pints—with difficulty. As for the Old Gentleman—I surrounded 3 pints with ease & avidity, & would have been good for three more! Weather favoured us greatly, for we had warmth & sun throughout—whereas the very next day was cold & rainy, with Grandpa E'ch-Pi-El heavily blanketed & crouched shivering over an oil heater! Later in the season Bobby Barlow may get north & pay Grandpa a visit—& in September I expect to greet the genial & erudite James Ferdinand Morton. If I get anywhere myself it will be on some brief excursion in or near New England late in the summer. I'd like to see Halifax, Nova Scotia—& I'd also like to get another look at Nantucket. Quebec, too, is waiting to be seen again . . . alas for the limitations of finance!

On July 22 I had a good view of Peltier's comet through the 12″ refractor of the Ladd Observatory (of Brown Univ.—about a mile northeast of 66 on high ground)—an institution which I used to haunt in youth, thanks to the indulgence of the now-dead-&-gone authorities then in charge. The object shewed a small disc with a hazy, fan-like tail. I could have seen it through my own small (3″) glass, but for the roof-&-foliage-obstructed nature of the northern sky in the neighbourhood of 66.

My ceiling-high pile of unread borrowed books doesn't diminish as fast as it ought. Have just read biographies of Roger Williams by Emily M. Easton & James Ernst—the latter of which emphasises R W's profound influence on the course of the civil wars in England in the 1640's. Also finished George Santayana's much-advertised "Last Puritan"—a truly remarkable dissection of the sterile genteel culture which dominated New England in the 19th century.

My library had quite a windfall the other day, when the old lady downstairs in 66 (a teacher—now retiring & going to Germany for 3 years, after which she will settle in Newport for her remaining days) discarded a vast number of books & dumped them in the cellar.[15] Some I did not want—but Ædepol, what a lot I *did* salvage! A 10-volume Chambers' Encyclopaedia (1871—coming to pieces), a biblical commentary (printed in Brattleboro, Vt. in 1835) in 5 huge folio volumes,[16] a Liddell & Scott Greek–English lexicon in fine shape (to replace my own disintegrating copy), any number of history text-books, & a goodly stock of duplicates (Webster's Unabridged 1853—Andrews' Latin–English Lexicon, &c. &c.) to pass on to worthy friends & correspondents. I had work accomodating all the new material, but finally managed it. Also salvaged a fine 11″ × 9½″ cast of that famous (Naples Museum) Orpheus–Eurydice–Mercury bas-relief (Greek—5th Cent. B.C.). Who says one can't get something for nothing now & then?

All good wishes, regards to your mother, & hoping your course will prove unbrokenly pleasant—

Yrs most sincerely—

H P L

Notes

1. "The Disinterment" (*WT*, January 1937).

2. HPL's letter, sent to Seattle, was forwarded to HVS in Auburn.

3. See WBT 102n8.

4. Robert E. Howard committed suicide on 11 June 1936.

5. HPL's "Robert Ervin Howard: 1906–1936" appeared in the *Phantagraph*, expanded as "In Memoriam: Robert Ervin Howard."

6. "R. E. H." (*WT*, October 1936).

7. See HPL to Richard F. Searight (27 August 1936): "It lies just beyond the village of Manton, on the western fringe of Providence's suburbs." *Letters to Richard F. Searight* (West Warwick, RI: Necronomicon Press, 1992), 79.

8. See Kenneth W. Faig, Jr., "Lovecraft's Travelogues of Foster, Rhode Island," *Lovecraft Annual* No. 7 (2013): 75–135.

9. The leaflet HPL refers to stated that John Quincy Adams noted in his diary following a trip to Providence in 1791 that he considered the John Brown House (52 Power Street; 1786, Joseph Brown, architect) "the most magnificent and elegant private mansion that I have ever seen on this continent." It is now the home of the Rhode Island Historical Society.

10. Shephen Hopkins House (1743; original cottage built 1707 by John Field), 15 Hopkins Street. It formerly stood at the foot of Hopkins Street on South Main Street and was moved halfway up the hill in 1804.

11. John Brown House (1786–88), 52 Power Street; now the home of the Rhode Island Historical Society.

12. Joseph Brown House (1774), 50 South Main Street. The feature HPL describes, also known as the "ogee gable," is copied in many of the 19th- and 20th-century buildings in Rhode Island.

13. On Market Square.

14. Margarethe Lyman Dwight was also a descendant of Sullivan Dorr, and deeded the Sullivan Dorr House (1809), 109 Benefit Street, to the Providence Preservation Society.

15. After Alice Sheppard (1870–1961) left for Germany, the lower apartment at 66 College was sublet to Mary Spink, who made a rough catalogue of HPL's library after his death. Sheppard was again listed in the city directory as a resident there in 1942.

16. See Bibliography under William Jenks.

Genevieve Sully, with Clark Ashton Smith, 11 November 1941

Letters to Genevieve Sully

[1]   [ALS]

Out on Prospect Terrace near
66 College St.,
Providence, R. I.,
Septr 20, 1934

Dear Mrs. Sully:—

      I am more indebted to you than I can express for the extremely interesting card of the old Russian chapel,[1] enclosed in your welcome letter of the 1st. While I knew that the Russians had long sought to colonise the American Pacific coast—that, indeed, San Francisco's site was first settled by the Spanish in order to forestall an 18th century expedition from Russia—I had no idea that any structure of Russian origin still existed within the boundaries of the United States' main fabric. Only in Sitka, Alaska, did I think that any Russian edifice remained. Imagine, then, my delighted astonishment in receiving your card & reading the descriptions you so kindly added! Truly, the structure is of tremendous interest—certain architectural peculiarities marking it off from early buildings of other national origins despite its pioneer crudity. The effect of the whole enclosure, with well-preserved walls & other surviving buildings, must be still more fascinating—& I envy Helen her ability to capture some of this quaintness in an artistic medium. The landscape, I judge, must add a great deal to the general effect; while the officers' quarters would seem to merit study as well. I wonder how the rooms looked—though perhaps they were too primitive to bear the marks of any especial decorative school. The mantel—if that fireplace had any adjunct so civilised—would tend to represent some Muscovite equivalent of the Adam–Bulfinch–McIntire period. I dare say the extra-mural houses of the old village have long since perished—but it would be interesting to know what they were like. How few American even suspect the existence of this forgotten chapter of life within the nation's present boundaries! One would like to visualise the scene in its heyday, & know more of the origin & life & subsequent fortunes of the settlers. It is curious how little close knowledge of western history is possessed by the average cultivated easterner. Whole dramas & countless episodes of colonisation have run their course in the west & southwest, all unknown to the nation at large. It is also curious how many different nationalities of Europe besides our own have left their architectural impress on this continent. In Quebec & in Louisiana the buildings of the French still flourish. New York has houses of the Netherlands, & Pennsylvania of the Germans. In certain parts of Pennsylvania, too, one finds distinctive *Welsh* as distinguished from purely English influences . . . . such as the carrying of a heavy car[touche?] round the gable end of a house. In Delaware & adjacent parts of Pennsylvania the houses of the 17th century Swedes are not all gone—this influence being manifest also in Gloria Dei Church (Old Swedes—1699) in Philadelphia. Then in St. Augustine, Florida, the belt of Spanish architecture begins—again accentuated in New Orleans, which was largely rebuilt under the Spanish occupation (1763–1803). New Orleans houses, though French in roof & window treatment, are Spanish in ground plan & details—with patio, arcade, fountain, outside staircase, & vertical iron bars in lunettes above doors & windows. Up in Natchez Spanish & French tendencies are still discernible despite the classic Anglo-American superimposition. Farther west (where I have never been) it would appear that Spanish architecture is mixed with aboriginal designs taken from the pueblo Indians—though in the missions of California this influence is not so apparent. I do not know whether any Spanish edifice aside from missions & ranch-houses exist in California. In Mexico, of course, every sort of Spanish-Indian hybridisation occurs. And lastly comes the faintest & least-known element of all—the Russian—represented by the houses & cathedral of Sitka, & (as I now realise) by the old fort which you have so fortunately seen.

Your whole trip sounds vastly delightful to me—& the indefiniteness of the programme, plyus the untrodden nature of some of the territory, must have greatly multiplied the pleasure. The fishing villages, hilly inland scenes, fog billows, dizzy bluffs, & finally the climactic Russian outpost, all sound like the ingredients of an ideal jaunt—& Inverness is surely no mean base from which to make it. I am surely glad that you have been able to indulge in so imagination-filling a circuit. The unique charm of absolutely new discoveries is something I can poignantly appreciate. By this time you will be aware—through my letter to Helen from Nantucket Island—that I have just made such a discovery myself—& only 90 miles from home! To my mind no appreciative person can travel too much—hence I hope you can take not only the more ambitious transcontinental trip next summer, but the lesser southern one as well. No matter how pleasant the mere *contemplation* of such things may be, I have generally found that the realisation far surpasses it. And so far as forming a correct & balanced idea of a distant region is concerned, there is no question but that a first-hand inspection is necessary. While it is a specialty of mine to learn all about a place before I see it—studying maps, pictures, guide-books, & time-tables in order to save time for actual sightseeing after I get there—I have never known a place to correspond closely to my advance idea of it. There is always a vital element which description, cartography, & iconography cannot touch. What the books & pictures emphasise is seldom the thing which stands out dominantly upon personal confrontation. This has been borne in upon me with renewed force through my Nantucket trip. If you do take the Southern trip I would be delighted to furnish notes & lend maps & pictures covering any part (presumably New Orleans & Natchez) which may coincide with previous vagrancies of my own. And this serves also for the family venture of next year. I do not think that any other sort of pleasure & experience pays me such genuine dividends as does travel—travel to certain historic or scenic spots where every visible object evokes memories & associations. Trips of that type leave a permanent imaginative residue which crops out again & again in dreams, waking thoughts, & literary attempts. I only wish that I might include the Old World—England at least—in my itinerary before I enter oblivion! I certainly hope I can get out to California some time—& appreciate most heartily & gratefully your invitation to that effect. Assuredly, the region is one in which a brief stay would be merely a tantalisation. I have formed some idea of its aspect from cards thoughtfully chosen & kindly sent by Klarkash-Ton, High-Priest of Tsathoggua; & all that I learn makes me the more eager to behold this person. I hope, too, to see you all—a hope which in the case of the Atlantean High-Priest is of 12 years' standing!

I am surely glad that you have as pleasant a place as 'Woods' Dry Diggings' to return to after your recent peregrinations. From what I know of it, it can scarcely be an anticlimax. Your autumns, it would appear, are far milder & lovelier than ours—& the grace of the hills, the atmosphere, & the distant mountains gives this genial lenity the most appropriate of settings. It was certainly neighbourly of C A S to keep your garden in a state of flourishing moistness—& I trust he also attended to the comfort of good old "Son", of whom I have heard a good deal, & in whom I take the fraternal interest of a lifelong ailurophile. I've just had a welcome epistle from Klarkash-Ton, which I shall answer very soon.

Harking back to my favourite species—I read with mixed pleasure & tantalisation of the tiny Russian family of mother & five which you encountered near the ancient stockade. Too bad you could not secure a photograph of them! The efforts of Mme. Alexandra Sergievna Thomashevska to to shew off little Nikolai Ilyitch Thomasevsky, Boris Ilyitch, Marya Ilyevna, Sophia Ilyevna, & Grigor Ilyitch were surely captivating in the extreme—& not precisely parallelled by any case I recall hearing of. It reminds me of a kitten in Florida last spring who was badly poisoned by a snake he killed. As soon as he could use his little legs he proudly led the household down to the lake to view the slain monster! Had I been at the stockade—& in a position to harbour a pet at home—I fear I should have slipped little Nikolai into a sidepocket before departing! I hope they may all find good homes.

Incidentally, I must record a mournful local event which will have its own sombre interest if (as I think it did) I mentioned it in my last 2 epistles to Helen—my closest friend & favourite neighbour since my return from Florida . . . . . the little black kitten at the boarding-house across the back garden, born last June: Little Sam Perkins! He spent a good deal of time over at Grandpa's, climbing over the Old Gentleman & rustling the papers on the desk—& then stretching out like a little ebony wand in the plush seat of a big, semicircular chair, sound asleep! What a tiny dynamo of sportive energy & purring friendliness! As recently as Sept. 7 he was on hand, keeping Grandpa's mind off his work . . . . & now, alas, he is no more! He was found lifeless in the garden on the 10th, with no sign of injury or hint as to the possible malady. In August he had a brief touch of illness, but had long since recovered from that. Poor little Piece of the Night! He lived but from June to September, & will never know what the rigours of winter are. The old Toms on the shed roof—into whose august fraternity he had but lately been initiated—move about with saddened mien & chant in elegiac numbers:

> The ancient garden seems tonight
>   A deeper gloom to bear,
> As if some subtle shadow's blight
>   Were hov'ring in the air.
>
> With hidden griefs the grasses sway,
>   Unable quite to word them—
> Remembering from yesterday
>   The little paws that stirr'd them.

Glad the card safely reached you through forwarding. In my letter to Helen I enclosed another for you—shewing Providence's closest classic analogue to "The Portals of the Past." I trust you also saw the Nantucket folder & pictures. Enclosed are 2 or 3 more of the latter. I reached home Sept. 3—& on the 4th my aunt left for a pleasant fortnight in Ogunquit, Maine, whence she has just returned. I meanwhile wrestled with as many tasks as could be handled amidst a most inopportune & programme-disrupting siege of indigestion, from which I am just emerging. I trust that the massed outings of your own family ended as pleasantly as anything pleasant can *end.*

With regards to you, Helen, & all the household, & renewed thanks for the notable addition to my architectural files,
            I remain
                  Yrs most cordially,
                  H P Lovecraft

P.S. The scene of my present sunset composition is a little park on the brow of Providence's ancient hill about ⅛ mile N. of College St.[2] Outspread before me in westward panorama are the spires & domes of the lower town, & even a bit of the purple rural hills beyond. This is a favourite haunt of mine—I read & write here often. Unfortunately there was not time for H V S to see the spot during her regrettably brief pause in Providence.

Notes

1. Fort Ross, former Russian establishment in what is now Sonoma County, CA (near Healdsburg). The chapel there collapsed in the 1906 San Francisco earthquake but was reerected in 1916 using much of the original structural woodwork. It was destroyed by fire in 1970, and restored a few years later.

2. Prospect Terrace, on Congdon Street in the College Hill neighborhood.

[2]   [ALS]

66 College St.,
Providence, R. I.,
Dec. 2, 1934

Dear Mrs. Sully:—

It gave me great pleasure to receive yours of Nov. 15th, as well as the slightly subsequent postcard from members of the rising generation, resident & visiting. And I must likewise thank you most sincerely for the box of interesting specimens—the elongated, acorn-like object which somewhat baffles my botanical ignorance, & the mute petraean witnesses of bygone igneous forces—forces not so long bygone, I judge from your description. The dark, fire-seared rock has a curious lightness in weight, while the porous lava evokes vivid suggestions of

". . . the scoriac rivers that roll . . . .
Their sulphurous currents down Yaanek
In the ultimate climes of the pole—
That groan as they roll down Mount Yaanek
In the realms of the boreal pole."[1]

The entire array forms a most welcome addition to my permanent collection, & will doubtless excite the envy of such mineralogically inclined visitors as may behold them.

I was surely glad to hear that Young Melmoth's long-wished visit to Averoigne actually came to pass,[2] & can imagine how pleasant it was—or is, if its second instalment be still in force—for all concerned. Besides the card from your household I likewise received one from Indian Hill, attesting the congenial confabulations of Tsathoggua's High-Priest with his devoted acolyte from afar.

It would indeed be providential if such interludes could come oftener in the arduous routine of Commoriom's cryptic fane. It grieves & exasperates one to reflect that a mind like Klarkash-Ton's should be hampered by a ceaseless pressure of heavy & only partly necessary burdens. Very few could do any creative work at all under such handicaps—& it is tantalising to think of what such an imagination might accomplish if given even a moderately favourable environment. Undoubtedly an exaggerated sense of duty makes things harder than they need to be, & I wish that C A S might be persuaded to revolt just far enough to banish the most unreasonable obstacles. Of course, the aged are notably stubborn; but it does seem as if sustained insistence might reconcile the senior Smiths to such 'new-fangled inventions of the devil' as oil heaters & electric power. If they depend on their heir for the daily performance of household tasks, they certainly have no right to impose needless restrictions on his way of performing those tasks. And one wonders just how far the advanced years of Ashtonius Pater really prevent him from sharing—at least to a slight extent—the water-bearing responsibilities of Ashtonius Filius. That whole condition regarding the water-supply seems like a veritable nightmare—& makes one enquire whether, for anything like a reasonable financial outlay, there could not be some arrangement of pipes & gasoline engine to eliminate the barbarous programme of hand transportation. I assume that the climate of Woods' Dry Diggings would prevent any danger of freezing, whilst the merely *occasional* need of pumping water would make the consumption of gasoline merely nominal. In De Land, where I visited last spring, my hosts had a gasoline pumping station which supplied their entire plumbing system with water from a distant—or at least rather distant—artesian well. The system included faucets scattered over a considerable area of ground destined for a future orange grove. But even if any basic changes at the Commorian citadel be impossible, it would seem as if the high-priest might well arrange a few more vacations. Certainly, the effect of unbroken monotony & gruelling labour over long periods cannot be other than deleterious. It will, however, be very difficult to convince the sufferer of this fact—or at least, to induce him to act upon it. One could name any number of instances of persons with whom duty & routine have become an obsession, so that any decided move toward independence—or even toward sheer self-preservation—is well-nigh beyond their power to inaugurate. In the case of Klarkash-Ton, I hardly know what could be done except to reiterate to him in every possible way—gently but insistently—the need for more vacations & for an increase in general self-protective assertiveness. Such ideas, I suppose, would be most effective if inculcated indirectly & half-unconsciously, with a suggestion of casualness—& whenever possible, with an apparent application to other parallel cases rather than to his own. This to be supplemented—when possible—by actual invitations to events & trips of the sort best calculated to freshen the imagination & interrupt the strain of monotony & exaggerated responsibility. Sometimes—& to some people—an invitation can be given with a kind of subtle insistence (which professes to take acceptance for granted as a matter of plain sense & inevitable procedure, & which disposes of objections with easy confidence) that almost takes the subject by surprise & irresistibly batters down his opposition before he knows it. This effect is occasionally intensified by making it appear as if acceptance were a *favour*—the subject being appealed to to *help* in making such & such an event or outing a success, so that his exaggerated sense of duty becomes a weapon against itself. But whether it would work in the specific case of Klarkash-Ton, only repeated experiments could determine. The recent visit of Young Melmoth has undoubtedly been a tonic influence—& so, too, I fancy, were the visits of the breezy & invigorating E. Hoffmann Price earlier in the year. I hope that Price will make future raids on Averoigne—perhaps sweeping or magnetising the reluctant Sieur de Vyones into sharing a few trips in his meteoric & much-doctored Ford 1928 Juggernaut. I may try to suggest as much to the peripatetic Peacock Sultan of Oakland—though of course in so indirect a way as to eliminate all notions of meddling or of impertinently relayed comment. Naturally I shall take every precaution against any mention of these matters in quarters likely to view them indifferently, or to transmit echoes of them to C A S himself.

I certainly agree that the confining, monotonous life on Indian Hill is a handicap rather than an aid to genius. The only beneficial element is the seclusion, & absence of those false standards & misleading influences so common in centres of "sophistication"—but these boons could easily be obtained in a hermitage of a less oppressive, continuous, or compulsory sort. While the absence of Greenwich-Village insincerity, cheapness, shallowness, artificiality, decadence, & overspeeded confusion is an asset, the concomitant absence of rational diversions, vacations, new impressions, & congenially varied literary & artistic contacts is certainly a liability of the gravest sort. It would be ideal if frequent trips to San Francisco & more distant points—including occasional visits to the East—could be added to the round of creative retirement. Incidentally, I believe you may congratulate yourself that our own household has proved a marvellously saving & inspiring influence in the life & art of Klarkash-Ton. Such a congenial oasis in the desert of oppidan[3] incomprehension can scarcely be overestimated, & in various letters to Samuel Loveman & myself he has amply testified to its benign power. Indeed—those who have corresponded with him over a period of years are unanimous in noting the growth of a certain mellowness, which today vastly tempers the unrelieved bitterness & cynicism of his references to mankind & the world a decade ago. That the change is even *physiognomical* is suggested by the reaction of E. Hoffmann Price (last year, when in Providence) to an old picture taken in 1927 & shewing a sad, grave expression. "Hell!" exclaimed Sultan Malik with his characteristic verve, "that isn't the good fellow I've been corresponding with for months! That sober, bitter man could never have written the letters I've been getting!" Such being the trend of the past few years, I surely hope that it will be intensified by further congenial contacts, rather than slowed up or reversed by the cumulative pressure of overwork & monotony. I shall certainly urge the Hierophant of Tsathoggua to guard his health in every possible way—indeed, I am already doing so, since he spoke last month of being run-down, & of having lost ten pounds during the summer. With care, he ought to pull out of any present indisposition, just as I believe he pulled out of a much graver state of pulmonary trouble some 15 or 20 years ago.

One thing I am extremely glad of, is the ever-growing circle of admirers in all parts of the country which Klarkash-Ton has built up through his tales of the last five years. This appreciative group, geographically scattered though it be, must really be a tremendous bulwark against the feeling of despair & neglect which would otherwise engulf a wholly isolated artist. There is nothing superficial or insincere about the admiration—in some cases rising almost to idolatry—which these lovers of fantasy so spontaneously accord to their natural chieftain & divinity. Young Melmoth is a typical disciple—his enthusiasm being easily matched by that of a score or more whom I could cite. Half a dozen youths I know are industriously imitating his drawing technique, while a much greater number indulge in the awestruck emulation of his haunting verse & inexhaustibly dream-provoking fiction. Nor is the older generation less ardent & outspoken in its tributes to the Hyperborean Master. Happily, a good part of this admiration is no secret from its gifted object— indeed, I judge that he has received a heartening number of spontaneous tributes in his mail.* Aspiring fantaisistes turn to him for advice & criticism, & many are infinitely in his debt for freely offered revision & constructive suggestions. The act of *The Fantasy Fan* in dedicating its latest number to him[4] is symbolic of a sentiment well-nigh universal among the lovers of the bizarre & the fanciful. My own devotee-ship goes back to 1922, when—through the kindness of Samuel Loveman—I first saw the nightmare spawn of the Tsathogguan crayon & first drank in the stupendous images of "The Hashish-Eater" & the poems in "The Star-Treader" & "Odes and Sonnets." To this day I can recall the potent spell woven around me by such things as "The Medusa of the Skies", "Ode to the Abyss", "Memnon at Midnight"—& any number of other glimpses down obscure & forbidden cosmic vistas. Single lines & passages cling ineffaceably in my memory—

> "And music still'd to monumental stone"

> "[All days and hours of gladness,] girt around
> With sense of near, unswervable eclipse."

> "Trembling before some nameless Imminence,
> And fellow-guestship with the glutless Worm."

> "The tongueless dooms that dog the travelling suns."[5]

---

*Requests for his autograph are numerous, & his original MSS. are widely sought by collectors of fantastic material. Barlow—my young host of last spring—treasures every scrap of material connected with C A S, & is compiling a bibliography of all his published work.

Nor need anyone apologise for enthusiasm about a genius whose power & authenticity the late George Sterling was eager to acknowledge & acclaim! One may only hope that the future will bring events & opportunities fostering a still deeper development, & giving to the bard a general literary fame at least reasonably commensurate with his tremendous natural endowments.

I am indeed glad to hear that the Nantucket material proved of interest, & regret that you did not act on the momentary impulse to pay ancient New England an autumnal visit. Let us hope that in the spring or summer the trans-Coloradoan leagues may seem less formidable! It seems to me that the best way to avoid monotony on a cross-continent jaunt would be to follow a southerly route through Arizona, New Mexico, & Texas. There would, of course, be stretches of desert—but according to most accounts the southwestern deserts have a certain charm of their own; with curious chromatic & atmospheric effects, occasional vistas of picturesque mountains & mesas, & not a few striking interruptions in the shape of Indian pueblos either inhabited or abandoned. With stopovers at important scenic points like Santa Fé, El Paso, & San Antonio, & with New Orleans as an immediate major goal, I am sure that the journey to the Mississippi could be made far more of a pleasure than a hardship. And of course, after New Orleans there is a veritable *embarras de richesse*—Natchez, Vicksburg, Mobile, St. Augustine, Charleston, Savannah, Richmond, Williamsburg, Yorktown, Fredericksburg (farther west, Charlottesville & the wonders of Tennessee), Washington, Annapolis, Philadelphia, & the closely-packed beauties of New England . . . . the whole culminating atop the dizzy citadel of ancient Quebec. Some of this you have doubtless seen on former occasions, but even so, the number of unrevealed marvels must vastly overbalance the revealed. Nantucket alone—& I speak not as a "realtor" or hotel agent—is worth the price of the trip!

However, it is evident from your recent chronicle that one does not have to cross the continent to find trips of the most thrilling & magnificent sort! Certainly, your mid-November expedition involved as impressive a sequence of glimpses & experiences as one could well ask for—& must altogether have formed one of the most fascinating & delightful vacations on record. Your description is graphic & tantalising, & I shall be grateful for a glance at the photographs if they turned out well., Meanwhile, as previously indicated, I am tremendously indebted to you for the choice array of mineral &c. specimens . . . . & I must likewise thank you for the appealing postcards enclosed. Mt. Lassen[6]—with its sundry plutonic accessories—is surely a thing to admire, shudder at, & remember . . . . & the close call experienced by your friends during the latest eruption must have enhanced in your mind the cosmic horror & ruthless, daemoniac majesty of

> ". . . the scoriac rivers that roll;
> . . . the lavas that restlessly roll . . ."

Looking at the picture, one shivers to think of a swath of cindery dissolution replacing those inviting piny slopes!

Your itinerary seems to have been quite ideal, & it is surely a monumental pity that Klarkash-Ton could not have broken his fetters & accompanied the party. Every type of scenery apparently contributed to the grand total—the placid loveliness of the Sacramento Valley, with its reminiscences of old-world mellowness; the giant oak with its brooding overtones of Druidic mystery (I have repeatedly dreamed of vast, night-black forests of gnarled, great-boled oaks, such as one sees in pictures of Old England); the glimpses of snowy peak, flashing waterfall, crystal lake, & flaming sunset; & above all, the sombre, sinister majesty of the charred, half-desolate Kingdom of Fire surrounding Mt. Lassen.

I had known of Mt. Lassen for years—ever since its return to activity brought it to public notice—yet never, until reading your absorbingly interesting account, had I realised what a marvellous inferno if igneous symptoms stretches around it. Your drive up 9000 feet, environed by slopes hissing with fumaroles, with paths bubbling & steaming underfoot, yet with snow-girt, glassy lakes & green-pointed hemlocks likewise in the panorama, must surely have been like some fantastic, imagined plunge into a grotesquely-painted picture—or a vertiginous whirling through the illusory vortices of some eery, half-febrile dream. What would I not give to have witnessed such a sight! I am sure that I would have been reduced to inarticulateness through sheer inability to express so much through the meagre medium of words. Has Klarkash-Ton ever beheld such sights? I recall his delight in the quasi-scoriac formations of Crater Ridge—one of whose grotesque fragments . . . . . a perfect suggestion of some eldritch pre-human eidolon . . . . . now reposes (through his generous thoughtfulness) as a book-end on a shelf not far from where I sit.

The curiously dramatic or climatic quality of your trip is emphasised by the twilight vista of floating swans. It is really had to imagine any sight more lovely & impressive than this! It must have evoked all the lore woven by the ages around these mysterious, exquisite creatures . . . the Nixies & the Hindoo Apsaras, the mourning Cygnus on Eridanus' crystal tide, & that enchanted daughter of Lir of whom Tom Moore sings in his "Song of Fionnuala"! I surely hope that some degree of success may attend the pictures which you took upon your second & daylight glimpse of the nine snowy gliders!

Altogether, the trip seems to have been singularly packed with adventures & events. The vacant barn would have formed an interesting refuge, though I can well believe that the cabin by the torrent was—considering the temperature—a wiser choice! The devastated area around Hot Lake must be a nightmare country indeed—fit scene for some daemoniac fantasy! And to think it was once a sightly realm of woodland & meadow! I can vaguely visualise it from the scoriac specimens before me. How fortunate that your friends escaped the Pompeio-Herculanean cataclysm in time! That tunnel in the lava sounds like the ultimate word in natural weirdness, & I scarcely wonder that you did not care to share in the exploration. I never before heard of a formation like this, & wonder that it has not been more widely exploited. It was fortunate for you, however, that the region is not more popular—for as you remark, the prevailing solitude undoubtedly enhanced the spectral effect a thousand-fold. The Hot Creek lodging—with its oddly diversified fauna—sounds notably pleasant . . . . . & I am certain that its feline family of mother & five would have engrossed much of my attention. Too bad the conditions precluded pictures of this congenial & widely heterogenous menagerie! Glad that the final day—with its glimpse of Donner Lake & its desert sunset—formed no anticlimax. Surely this must have been a distinguished & memorable trip, even in a region where vivid scenery & fantastic impressions are by no means rare. I wish indeed that both C A S & I might have been participants!

My own limited autumnal peregrinations—the trips to West Townsend, Mass., & to the Gilbert Stuart country in Rhode Island last October—are doubtless known to you through advices reaching Averoigne a month since. They have been followed by only one more excursion—a very meagre trip to Boston & vicinity to see a few friends & absorb a few local antiquities. Cold weather largely ruined this trip, though I did succeed in taking one friend (W. Paul Cook—a great admirer of C A S, who has published some of the latter's work in *The Recluse*) to see a famous old mansion he had never seen before.

[7]The house in question was the old Royall place in Medford—a northerly suburb of Boston lying on the Mystic River. This edifice—erected in 1732–7 around a smaller & much more ancient dwelling—is perhaps the finest specimen of *early* Georgian architecture in New England, & was the home of Col. Isaac Royall, a prosperous planter & merchant born in Maine & later residing for 40 years in Antigua, in the West Indies. It is a large rectangular wooden building of three stories & attic, with double-chimneyed brick ends & adjacent slave quarters. Originally a country-seat, it still lies in a rather thinly settled residential district, with a liberal plot of ground before & behind it. Late in the 19th century it sank to great depths of squalor, from which it was been [*sic*] most providentially rescued & restored through the joint efforts of the D. A. R. & Colonial Dames. It is amply furnished in the antique fashion of its heyday, & contains, besides, a vastly interesting collection of miscellaneous colonial reliques. Col. Royall died two years after completing this northern home, leaving it to his son Isaac Jun.—whose portrait, by Robert Feke of Newport, R. I., still hangs within its walls. This second Col. Royall was prominent in every phase of Massachusetts political & military life, & remained true to our rightful King & Parliament during the tragedy of 1775–83. Returning to the ancestral soil of Old England in 1777, he died it [*sic*] Kingston in 1781. His love of New England was unabated despite its treasonable rebellion against the Crown, & in his will he left to Harvard College a tract of land to be sold for the financing of a chair of law. From this bequest, in 1815, sprang the Royall

Professorship of Law—precursor of the present Harvard Law School. The rebels having confiscated the estate, it was used as an headquarters by Genl. John Stark, & at a later date became private property. Though used mostly as a residence, it served as a boarding & day school for a considerable period in the 1790's. After 1860 it began to go down hill—till leased by the D. A. R. in 1896. Today it is restored to the pink of condition, with its splendid interior panelling, pilasters, cornices, & archways intact & immaculate. All the original wall-paper has been carefully reproduced. One of the patterns, indeed, has been *reprinted from the original blocks*—which were, with miraculous luck, found in an ancient Paris wall-paper manufactory . . . . . whence they had reposed for two hundred years unharmed & undisturbed. I regret that I could find no post-cards of the house upon this visit. Enclosed, however, are 2 or 3 views shewing other (&, I fear, more hackneyed) Boston antiquities.

I trust that Young Melmoth's second sojourn proved longer than his first. I had hoped to see him in Providence this autumn—a postcard from Montreal promising such an advent—but the next thing I heard, he was home again in St. Paul—& after that came the news of his Averoignian advent. Cook & I dropped a joint card to him & to C A S from Boston. If he is still at the Dry Diggings, pray transmit to him my regards—which goes like-wise for everybody else, not excluding Son, who I trust is now enjoying the best of health. I was grieved to learn last month of the vanishment of Genl. Tabasco from the Temple of Tsathoggua. The local Kappa Alpha Tau fraternity—whose tiger vice-president I even now espy on the adjacent shed roof—joins me in extending all the compliments of the season. ¶ Again thanking you for specimens, views, &c.—Yrs most sincerely—H P Lovecraft

Notes

1. Poe, "Ulalume," ll. 14–18. HPL quotes these lines (and more) in *At the Mountains of Madness*.

2. See *Mysteries of Time and Spirit* for a postcard by Wandrei and HVS to HPL dated 21 November 1934.

3. A townsman.

4. The November 1934 issue of the *Fantasy Fan* was dedicated to Smith. The previous month's issue was dedicated to HPL.

5. [a] "Memnon at Midnight," l. 14; [b] "Shadow of Nightmare," ll. 7–8; [c] "The Ref-uge of Beauty," ll. 13–14; [d] "Nero," l. 57.

6. Lassen Peak, commonly referred to as Mount Lassen, is the southernmost active volcano in the Cascade Range of the western U.S. It is located in the Shasta Cascade region of Northern California, and one of the largest lava domes on Earth.

7. Robert Feke (1705/7–1752?), American portrait painter born in Oyster Bay, NY. From 1741 until 1750, he worked in Boston, Newport, RI, and Philadelphia, painting wealthy merchants and landowners.

[3]   [ALS]

66 College St.,
Providence, R. I.
Jany. 27, 1935.

Dear Mrs. Sully:—

I was indeed glad to receive further sidelights on the recent Melmothian visit—whose high spots were chronicled in a letter from Helen last month. As you know by this time through my reply to that letter, I have since had the pleasure of some extended conversations with the young voyager—who reached New York only a week before my own visit to Frank Belknap Long, Jun. in that same chaotic metropolis. All those conversations echoed the delight which the Wanderer took in his Averoignian sojourn, & I can well imagine how universally pleasant the event must have been. The two Wandreis how have a very comfortable joint apartment in Greenwich Village, & hope to keep afloat through fictional labours for the firm of Street & Smith. I can picture, from other specimens I have seen, the charm of the batik which has found its way to Averoigne. Howard W. is certainly a marvellous artist who will some day achieve recognition . . . . & such is his versatile cleverness that he has not only produced splendid batik work, but has invented & constructed with his own hands an improved metal device for executing this kind of design. Still, I think it remains a fact that his actual forte is pen drawing. It is in his drawings that the most typical aspects of his genius appear most fully.

Yes—I do indeed envy you the sight of the impressive Klarkash-Ton pictures which you so tantalisingly describe. I have an uncomfortably keen realisation that—despite the magnificent specimens I *have* seen—the real masterpieces are still unknown to me because of the difficulties of transportation. The finest lot I ever saw at once was an assortment sent to me by express in a wooden crate in 1926 & subsequently sent to New York for the inspection of the gang there. In that batch were some polychromatic Saturnian vistas & resplendently fantastic nightmares which I shall never forget. There were, too, some more tranquil & terrestrial themes—& a set of magnificent paintings in satin in something like the Japanese manner . . . . . conceptions of ineffable delicacy. My elder aunt, herself an amateur painter of no mean attainments, was then living, & was tremendously impressed by C A S's instinctive mastery of colour. Thus I can clearly appreciate what "Exotic Perfume" & its companion—& the haunting "Uranus", too—must be like. All of these things are surely windows out of which one may gaze upon resplendent & inaccessible worlds! By the way—while I was in New York Samuel Loveman once more shewed me the collection of some 300 or 400 drawings which first introduced me to the Sorcerer of Averoigne some thirteen years ago. It was only recently that he brought them from Cleveland, & I had not seen them in all the intervening years. Once more they struck me with all the original force of 1922. They were, of course, altogether new to Belknap, Barlow, & the Wandreis. Barlow became almost delirious over them, & means to photograph as many of them as possible. This blessed little enthusiast may yet be a major means of getting for Klarkash-Ton's art the recognition it deserves!

And now let me thank you most exceedingly for the graphic & interesting snapshots—which admirably supplement the glamourous travelogue of last November. I can see at once the relationship between the picture of desolation & the richly verdant postcard previously sent—a truly tragic case of 'before & after'. The abridged foreground of the photograph does not prevent it from conveying a powerful impression of strange blight & brooding devastation. The other view shews more of the grandeur & beauty of the region—& I am glad that one of the expedition is included. Certainly, that entire mountain realm must be full of an elusive other-worldliness manifest in countless half-perceptible details & atmospheric shadings. I am indeed pleased that my comment of last month seemed to indicate some degree of comprehension of that quality—a comprehension which I could scarcely have attained but for the very adequate chronicle at my disposal.

I reserve special thanks for the recent snap of the conclave at Vyones Priory. No more pleasant group could well be imagined—& I most emphatically include the plump plush cushion in my appraisal! Regarding the reason why this cushion is allowed a constant preëmption of the best seating facilities—I can only say that it lies deep in the psychology of mankind! For some such reason the mighty temple pylons of Bubastis were flung to the sky, whilst sleek-furred denizens, sacred to the patron goddess, lived their luxurious lives & were tenderly mummied & interred before her whiskered image. Nor did a different spirit animate Mohammed himself; who on one occasion, when a beloved feline fell asleep on the loose sleeve of his robe as it lay across a wide chair-arm, cut off the sleeve upon being summoned away rather than disturb the repose of his furry friend. Thus too was it one night in 1927 when the chronicler of these lines was visiting a friend in Massachusetts & doing some writing in the small hours of the morning. An exquisite little puff-ball of jet-black fur had been cavorting among the papers on the desk in the earlier evening, & had finally leapt into the chronicler's lap & coiled up into an infinitesimal globule of tenebrous somnolence. The hours wore on— & still the chronicler could not bear to disturb that dreaming black atom . . . . till finally he decided to keep on writing & make a night of it. Thus he did— his host finding the twain in unaltered positions in the dawn's early light. Ever since then, the said host has cited this anecdote as the one definitive & classic instance of modern ailurophily[1]—a citation by no means unpleasing to one who is proud to stand beside the Prophet as a true appreciator of our planet's most mystical & fascinating species! So pray convey my best regards to the Gray Pillow—who may long, I trust, continue in his wholly unjustified usurpations! Tell him that I invariably resign my best chairs to visiting members of the Kappa Alpha Tau fraternity (which meets on the shed roof across the garden) whenever they deign to honour me with their presence. It's several days now, by the way, since I've seen a Kappa Alpha Tau man—the present weather causing them to emulate me in my hibernation!

I have read of the singular severity of Pacific Coast weather this winter—apparently a reversal of the conditions last year, when it was the Atlantic coast that suffered. I can certainly sympathise—for I can't manage my muscles well enough to write legibly under 73° or 74°, & am generally miserable in every way under 60°. 20° is my absolute deadline of safety—if I'm out in weather colder than that, all sorts of symptoms—especially cardiac—develop. 40° is the sort of temperature I *can* go out in, but don't unless I want very much to get somewhere. I never go outdoors for pleasure under 60°, & am at my best at 80° or 90°. I ought to live in the South—but am tremendously attached to the scenery & architecture of the ancient region I have always known. This winter has so far been fairly decent—as winters go. The cold often keeps me in for 3 or 4 days at a time, but then an interlude of rain or fog occurs, & I am liberated long enough to get necessary errands done. But I don't pretend to do anything but hibernate in winter. In this climate I feel really alive only from about June 15 to August 15! We had quite a traffic-paralysing snowstorm hereabouts Jany. 23–4 . . . deliveries of everything tied up.

Just now I am instituting a long-needed innovation in my study—an addition to my filing system consisting of two dark walnut sets of drawers which I picked up yesterday at a department-store fire sale. I haven't yet decided on their arrangement—perhaps I shall superimpose one on the other, making a single tall cabinet. I've needed something like this for a couple of years, since my loose papers were getting utterly unmanageable. My young friend Long got one for Christmas from his mother—& the sight of that was the final incentive to the intensive bargain-hunt which terminated this week. Now I shall know where a few things are for at least a few months to come!

Again thanking you for the pictures, & extending every good wish for the coming twelvemonth,

    I remain
        Yrs most sincerely
          H P Lovecraft

Notes

1. W. Paul Cook of Athol, MA, recounted this as the opening anecdote in his booklet, *In Memoriam: Howard Phillips Lovecraft: Recollections, Appreciations, Estimates.*

[4]   [ALS]

66 College St.,
Providence, R. I.,
Feby 7, 1937.

Dear Mrs. Sully:—

I was very much pleased to receive your Yuletide bulletin, supplementing moderately recent news from the Indian Hill end of Averoigne. Some time I must try that experiment of omitting cards, for in recent years my list[1] has insidiously grown to quite unmanageable proportions!

The casting experiments had just begin at the time of the last Clericashtonic chronicle, & I am glad that things seem to be going successfully at the atelier. It always seems tragic to me that a painter's or sculptor's work is limited to one "copy"—the fate of which generally passes out of his hands—hence I welcome any process which permits of duplicate or multiple creation. Since I last wrote, the travelling loan exhibit of grotesque figurines has come & gone—& I can assure you that each item was abundantly appreciated during its stay; not only by myself, but by various guests including young Barlow, old Adolphe de Castro (a one-time associate of Ambrose Bierce in San Francisco), & others. The genius & determination which can produce such work under every imaginable handicap deserve more appreciation than prose can convey. I lately tried to convey it in verse—but am aware that this, too, is inadequate in my unskilled hands. The attempt was as follows:

To Klarkash-Ton, Wizard of Averoigne[2]

A time-black tower against dim banks of cloud;
Around its base the pathless, pressing wood;
Shadow & silence, moss & mould, enshroud
Grey, age-fell'd slabs that once as cromlechs stood.
No fall of foot, no song of bird awakes
The lethal aisles of sempiternal night,
Tho' oft with stir of wings the dense air shakes,
As in the tower there glows a pallid light.

For here, apart, dwells one whose hands have wrought
Strange eidola that chill the world with fear;
Whose graven runes in tones of dread have taught
What things beyond the star-gulfs lurk & leer.
Dark Lord of Averoigne—whose windows stare
On pits of dream no other gaze could bear!

Incidentally—I cannot resist enclosing a tribute paid the artist by E. Hoffmann Price of Redwood City, to whom went one of the recent carven entities. The appreciation is so keen & analytical that one can almost see the eidolon from the description. You might let C A S see this tribute sometime—which reminds me that he spoke of being marvellously heartened & encouraged by a recent lecture or series of admonitions from you! I hope, by the way, that the proposed exhibition of grotesque figures in Sacramento this month is duly materialised.

Concerning the Providence Chapter of the Kappa Alpha Tau—I regret to say that the membership is not increasing as rapidly as one might wish after the tragic loss of Mr. Perkins & the Earl of Minto last June. However, it holds its own under the stern leadership of a coal-black, broad-beamed warrior from some neighbouring northward byway. That good old grey Son continues to prosper is surely cause for rejoicing, & I trust he may long remain immune to the current of disaster which has elsewhere decimated the K. A. T. ranks! I can well credit that acuteness of comprehension which you mention, for my old Nigger-Man of more than 30 years ago possessed something very similar. The phenomenon of the cream-bottle lid reminds me of Nigger-Man's instant responsiveness to the phrase "roast chestnuts", which typified his ideal of epicurean delight. No, indeed, Son's place of honour at the family feast does not shock me in the least—for to my mind no mark of distinction is too great for a truly worthy representative of the Kappa Alpha Tau! And I'm sure his rare depredations from the plates of human fellow-banqueters must have a charm & grace sufficient to excuse them completely! Would that it were practicable for my aunt & me to harbour such a gentle depredator at #66! Which reminds me that my young friend Barlow has just sent me a delightful little figure of a sleeping black cat—a product of his recent sculptural activities at the Kansas City Art Institute.

The reappearance of your friend from the memoried mists of the century's turn must surely have formed a pleasing & impressive experience, the more so because of the distant lands which she has meanwhile inhabited. It is curious what a sense of unbroken continuity can sometimes exist on such occasions—though of course an even annual correspondence helps to bridge the gap. The existence of a congenial younger generation in both cases must have helped to make the occasion festive, & it is truly unfortunate that the visit could not have been prolonged. Meeting—or even writing—a really congenial friend of other years does often have a singular power to turn the clock backward; minimising the intervening span & restoring all the issues & incidents of the earlier age to a fresh vividness & distinctiveness. Something of the same effect is likewise achieved when any especially typical or symbolic link with a bygone period turns up.

This reminds me of very roughly parallel episode in my recent annals. Back in the early years of the century, when I was a Shakespearian enthusiast & more of a theatregoer than I am now, I used to enjoy the local visits of Robert Mantell's[3] repertory company—in which the very fine work of the "second man" (Fritz Leiber,[4] who took such parts as Iago, Edgar, Bassanio, Faulconbridge,

Richmond, Horatio, Macduff, Antony &c.) impressed me as being even better in some cases than Mantell's[5] own. Especially did I admire his Faulconbridge, & the way he recited those stirring final lines of "King John"—

> "This ENGLAND never did, nor never shall,
> Lie at the proud foot of a conqueror,
> But when it first did help to wound itself.
> Now these her princes are come home again,
> Come the three corners of the world in arms,
> And we shall shock them. Nought shall make us rue,
> If ENGLAND to itself do rest but true."[6]

Well—I lately had occasion to revive those memories of a quarter-century ago, when I received (through *Astounding Stories*) a letter from Mr. Leiber's *son & namesake*—a fanatical devotee of weird fiction & of the aesthetic, psychological, & philosophical background behind it. Young Fritz (25, a U. of Chi. graduate, & entering his father's profession) has one of the keenest minds I have ever encountered, & in a couple of months' time has become one of my star correspondents. His dark tales, in a style reminiscent of James Branch Cabell & Dunsany, shew a profound understanding of the vague emotions behind the eternal human groping for cosmic concepts; while his art work (in a macabre vein not untouched by futurism) invites a certain amount of comparison with Klarkash-Ton's. The paternal genius certainly reached the second generation in this case—for whether or not young Fritz equals his sire on the boards, he'll certainly get somewhere in other fields if he keeps on at his present rate. He has had classic thespian experience—having played in his father's companies (which have never visited Prov.) in recent years those self-same roles which in my day Fritz I played in Mantell's companies. A photograph of him as Edgar in "Lear" shews a strong paternal resemblance which certainly flings my memory back to 1910 or so in the most spectacular way!

I trust that your Seattle interlude ended as pleasantly as it began, & that the return trip included a suitable variety of novel landscape effects. The visit from young Barlow of which I spoke in July lasted a month—during which the versatile author-artist became quite acclimated to the Providence scene. Midway in that period the picturesque old-timer de Castro (known as Dr. Danziger in the Bierce & San Francisco days) shewed up for a week, & on one occasion the three of us sat on a tomb in a hidden hillside churchyard just north of #66 & composed rhymed acrostics on the name of *Edgar Allan Poe*, who 90 years ago used to wander in that selfsame necropolis while on visits to Providence.[7] The autumn was not as early & severe as I had feared it would be, & I was able to prolong my woodland walks until well over the line into November. One feature of my recent rambles was the discovery of two exquisite rural regions within a three-mile radius of this house which I had never seen before. The winter, too, has not been very severe as yet, so that I can still get out of the house when I have to.

I trust that your Yuletude was uniformly pleasant. We had a decorated tree, & the weather was gratifyingly mild. Of gifts one of the most distinctive was perhaps that which came quite unexpectedly from one of the youthful weird-fan-magazine editors (one Conover of the Maryland Eastern Shore[8])—for lo! when I opened it I beheld before me the yellowed & crumbling fragments of *a long-interred human skull!* It came from an Indian mound near the sender's home. Reflective fancy strives to evoke the image of him to whom it once belonged ... a sanguinary chief ... a crafty medicine-man ... who knows? ¶ Best 1937 wishes for all the household.—Yrs most sincerely—H. P. Lovecraft

[Enclosure: TNS postcard from E. Hoffmann Price to HPL, postmarked Redwood City, Cal., Dec. 22, 1936.]

Notes

1. Kenneth W. Faig, Jr. suggests that the list of addresses that R. H. Barlow copied for August Derleth following HPL's death ("Lovecraft's 1937 Diary," *Lovecraft Annual* No. 6 [2012]: 153–78) was his list of Christmas card recipients.

2. HPL used this title only here and in a letter to Elizabeth Toldridge. More commonly the poem is titled "To Clark Ashton Smith, Esq., upon His Fantastic Tales, Verses, Pictures, and Sculptures."

3. Robert B. Mantell (1854–1928), a heralded Shakespearean stage actor who made several silent films.

4. Fritz Reuter Leiber, Sr. (1882–1949), American Shakespearean stage actor who also had a successful career in film.

5. Fritz Reuter Leiber Jr. (1910–1992), American writer of fantasy, horror, and science fiction, poet, actor, and chess expert. He corresponded briefly, but extensively, with HPL. For HPL's letters to him and to his wife Jonquil, see *Letters to C. L. Moore and Others*. Leiber's father (1882–1949) was a Shakespearean actor on stage who also had a successful career in film.

6. Shakespeare, *King John* 5.7.118–24.

7. See WBT 103n5.

8. Willis Conover. See WBT 102n13.

Appendix

H. P. Lovecraft

[Some Backgrounds of Fairyland]

The term *fairy* has in modern times been applied to so wide a variety of imaginary entities, that its original meaning is almost lost in favour of a more inclusive significance. The true fairy, as developed by early Celtic folklore, was undoubtedly a female nature-spirit equivalent to the dryads, naiads, and other local nymphs of classical antiquity. Such a spirit is in essence a personification of some aspect of the natural world, and every branch of Aryan Mythology teems with examples. Dawn-maidens, cloud-maidens, fountain-maidens, tree-maidens and the like exist abundantly, under various names, in the legends of all Aryan peoples; and it is not remarkable that the highly imaginative Celts should have evolved one of the most notable of all systems of such beings.

Evidence seems to indicate that the pre-classical Gauls—and, by inference, other Celts—possessed an active belief in beings corresponding to what we recognise as true fairies. After the coming of Roman influences many classical features were undoubtedly woven into this belief, though not so many as to destroy its distinctiveness.

The true Celtic fairy was originally a female of graceful human aspect and average size, dwelling in some specific environment and possessing such supernatural attributes as the power to change form, control the sea and the wind, heal sickness, and divine future events. From these powers the name of *fay, fée,* or fairy was derived in mediaeval times from the Low Latin *fatare,* to enchant; itself derived from the standard Latin *fatum,* fate.

True fairies were generally benignant rather than malignant, though when wronged their revenges were ample and certain. They were frequently loved and married by mortal men, and always exacted heavy penalties when such favoured mortals broke faith with them. Fairies often took it upon themselves to preside at the birth of individuals, over whom they would retain a protective guardianship throughout life. This linkage of the beings with human destiny or *fate* may have been instrumental in the choice of their final name—derived indirectly from *fatum.*

Such are the original fairies commonly met with its pre-Elizabethan tradition and literature. Parallel to them, however, had always existed a wholly separate line of mythological creation whose attributes were eventually to become mixed with those of the fairy world—just as the attributes of both were likewise to become mixed with a third element derived from actual experience.

489

This separate line of myth was also one of natural personification, albeit of a far different and darker cast; having to do with those *night-daemons* or personifications of *darkness* which appear in all Aryan mythologies as thieves or mischief-working entities more or less inimical to man. The element of thievery or mischief-making symbolises the theft of daylight by darkness.

Typical examples of the Aryan night-daemon are the *Panis* of the Hindoos; the characters Cacus, Polyphemus, Cerberus, and Orthos (Geryon's dog) in classical mythology; the Genii and Afrits (to cite a Semitic borrowing) of the Arabians, and the elves, daergar, or trolls of the Teutonic north. As time progresses, and antiquity fades into mediaevalism, we see many of the traits of these night-daemons transferred to the fairy species—causing the latter to become mischievous, predatory, nocturnal, and sometimes hostile to mankind. Discrepancies in fairy nature increase with the years, so that eventually different groups and orders of fairies—good and bad, large and small, male and female—came to be recognised. Finally we reach a point where all sorts of dissimilar beings of air, earth, sea, and nether caves are lumped together in the popular mind under the single and erroneously collective term of "fairies". There are sylphs of the air, gnomes of the earth, undines of the sea, and salamanders of the fire. Each element and region has its especial sort of fairy, till the list includes such things as nixies, leprechauns, kobolds, brownies, goblins, mermaids, banshees, little people, and countless other variants. In many of these beings the attributes of different lines of myth are blended complexly and inextricably, creating extreme types of mongrelism.

So much for the purely mythical side. It is now time to consider an antipodally diverse side of the fairy's ancestry which has no connexion with the primal legends of our Aryan heritage—a side which from the earliest ages had tended to mix itself with the lore of night-daemons, and which consequently became adopted into fairyland along with the contact of Aryan races with some alien stock of darker colouring and diminutive physique encountered during the struggle for the settlement of Europe. That such a contact occurred, can for many reasons scarcely be doubted; and we see reflections of it in all the traditional descriptions of such "fairies" as embody chiefly the attributes of night-daemons.

Such earthy or underground spirits have, in European folklore, a peculiar set of fixed, special qualities in no way to be traced to the general night-daemon myth. They are conspicuously small, conspicuously repulsive, consistently subterranean in habit, generally primitive in their arts and crafts, usually hostile or fearful toward human beings, and given to certain definite practices such as the theft of human infants accompanied by the substitution of their own. They have a profound lore connected with nature, and indulge in secret communal rites varying from the merely grotesque to the unutterably repulsive. Their weapons are generally bows with primitive stone-headed arrows.

Viewing all the evidence, anthropologists have for many generations felt certain that these persistent elfin or fairy characteristics are due to historic memory rather than to mythological imagination. That is, the traditional elf, troll, gnome, kobold, leprechaun, brownie, or imp is not purely an Aryan night-daemon, but a synthesis of the night-daemon with a very genuine dwarf or pigmy race of men whom the Aryans at one time or another displaced and drove into underground hiding, and who afterward kept up a furtive and vindictive course of reprisals against their conquerors.

Driven underground, decimated in numbers, and hunted down whenever seen, the vanquished dwarfs became sly creatures of the night—sallying forth by stealth to waylay lone travellers, steal infants for nameless sacrifices, despoil lonely farm houses, shoot from ambush, and otherwise vent their hatred of their Aryan conquerors. In time it is certain that many Aryan renegades went over to them and joined their number—as men in savage places "go native" today—and that they succeeded in inculcating their repulsive system of fertility-worship amongst a decadent stratum of the Aryans, thus giving rise to the furtive *Witch-Cult* with its sinister organisation and ceremonies, and its obscene and orgiastic Sabbat.

Memories of these waspish, uncouth, and miniature enemies could not but be extremely vivid among the conquerors of Europe; and it is not remarkable that the creatures—so unlike men as the tall, blond Aryans conceived humanity—became blended with the ancient hereditary lore of night-daemons which antedated our ancestors' entrance to the region. Had the Aryans not encountered this squat, dark race, it is probable that their night-daemon myths would have continued to remain in a more or less ambiguous and plastic form. To the conquered little people we undoubtedly owe the existence of elves, duergars, trolls, gnomes, and kobolds as our forefathers conceived them.

It now remains to enquire who those conquered dwarfs really were, where they lived, and when and where our invading forefathers encountered them. Also, whether the whole body of Aryans found such beings in their path, or whether the conflict was limited to a part of the Aryan people and merely reported by hearsay to the rest. We must remember that the presence of a certain legend among a certain people in a certain region by no means proves that the events of the legend really happened to that people in that particular place. The legend may have been borrowed outright from some other people—either of that region or of another region—or it may concern something which happened to the given people in another place—perhaps a very distant place—which the people occupied at some earlier stage of its racial history.

In the opinion of the older mythologies, and of many modern ones, the little people of elfin lore represent none other than the squat Mongoloid stocks of northern Europe—Lapps and Finns—whom the Aryans found upon their entrance to that region. The size, colour, accomplishments, and manners of these stocks in their purest forms lend much plausibility to the hypothesis; and it is highly probable that they covered a much larger area of the European continent than is now the case. Another argument is the fact that most of the legends of small underground beings seem to come primarily from the North—from those Teutons who most directly encountered the squat Mongols in the battle for the continent.

A more modern and much bolder theory identifies our dwarfish foes of prehistoric times with the Neanderthaloid sub-men which shambled over Europe about 30,000 B.C., and which were exterminated by the successive waves of true human beings who swept into the region after that date. This theory, while vastly interesting, has much less standing than the one previously mentioned.

A third theory—taking into account the existence of evil-dwarf legends in regions remote from the Lapp-Finn belt—(for example, the Little People of the British Isles, and the Kalli Kanzari of modern Greece, which are not wholly traceable to nature—spirits of the faun-satyr order) postulates some hitherto unknown race of dwarfs (either Mongoloid or otherwise) which populated wide areas of Europe at a very remote though not palaeolithic period. This theory has considerable vogue at the present time, and is upheld by the existence of certain prehistoric excavations in Southern Austria which seem to have been made by men of less than normal stature. At the same time it would not do to make too much of the idea, since an originally wider diffusion of the Lapp-Finn (or easterly Hunnish) stocks might easily account for dwarf architecture and artifacts in areas remote from their historic habitat. Most conservative anthropologists think it unlikely that—despite the vivid legends of diminutive Picts and elfin brownies in Scotland, tiny fairies and subterrene leprechauns in Ireland, sinister underground "little people" in Wales, and Robin Goodfellow's merry crew in England—any miniature race has ever actually inhabited the British Isles. We derive such tales entirely from the experience of our ancestors at a former stage of migration on the European continent.

A fourth theory—the least probable of all—holds that the small, dark opponents of the Aryans were merely members of those less blond Caucasian stocks which disputed the possession of Europe at the dawn of history—Mediterranean and Iberian races whose stature and pigmentation would naturally seem aberrant to a pure Nordic. This view would of course provide for an actual meeting of Celts and "little people" in the British Isles. However, it is easy to detect the weakness of such a theory. To begin with, Mediterraneans are not small enough to be called dwarfish—certainly not small enough to inhabit the subterranean *Erdstalle* of Southern Austria. Secondly, they are not enough unlike Nordics to give rise to the tremendous sense of alienage and repulsion evident in most legends. It is ridiculous to imagine normal, regular-featured Iberians as the models for trolls and kobolds. The most that can be said is that possibly some episodes of conflict betwixt Nordics and Mediterraneans may have been confused in Nordic folklore with other tales dealing with encounters with the older dwarf race. Such complexities must always be reckoned with in anthropology—indeed, we cannot swear that two, three, or four wholly different dwarf races, encountered at different times, did not play a part in forming the traditional picture of the elf, kobold, or mischievous fairy. Lapp-Finns of the north, Hunnish stocks of the southeast, unknown stocks of varied habitats, and even dark Iberians of later times may all have figured in the composite legend-building—later encounters being interpreted in terms of earlier ones, and battles on one terrain being twisted into connexion with bygone battles in far different regions. Nor should it be forgotten that the purely mythical element of the night-daemon, with which the early Aryans confused their strange opponents, must always be looked for.

Recent discoveries of large numbers of *Erdstalle* in Austria make it likely that the Danube region was at least a leading seat of the prehistoric dwarf-Aryan conflict. These artificial caverns, plainly constructed by a race not over five feet tall, and holding artifacts indicating a late stone, copper, and early bronze-age date, are occasionally of great elaborateness; some apparently being temples, while others are clearly refuges (like the burrows of small animals) from enemies of larger physique. About 700 of them are known, many of which have been used for centuries as cellars by the inhabitants of the region. The artifacts betray considerable skill—as indeed does the engineering of the caves. Occasional skeletons found nearby reveal a race of about the size of the degenerate Ainos of Japan, the Veddahs of Ceylon (whom Haeckel placed lowest in the human scale), or certain pigmy races of Africa. Ethnologists hesitate to name racial affiliations, but there is nothing to prove that these *Erdstallerbauer* (as the Austrians call them) were not of the same Mongoloid stock as the Lapp-Finn and Hunnish races. Much research remains to be performed in both the archaeological and ethnological field.

Meanwhile, however, there is no dispute concerning the part played by some small, dark race in shaping the hostile, mischievous, diminutive, and subterranean side of the later traditional fairy. Added to the myth of the night-daemon, this element has thoroughly mongrelised the earlier genuine fairy of Celtic nature-myth.

That many other elements, mythical, legendary, and historical, have gone into the making of many types of elf or fairy, it would be absurd to deny. All natural legend-building is infinitely mixed and complex, involving numerous borrowings from every conceivable source; so that we may justly regard the three main fairy origins—nature-spirit, night-daemon, and earthly dwarf—as merely the essential or dominant backgrounds in a field of limitless variety and compositeness.

Fairyland as a whole—the differing superstitions of different nations, and the various streams of myth or memory entering into the weird folk of various regions—is a profound study in itself, and one which has received much attention from scholars such as the Grimms, Keightley, and Lang. The

Celt has no monopoly—even of the true fairy which he created. Needless to say, each race and country adds to its traditional elves and fairies an abundance of local and family traits all apart from the more generalised heritage of the elusive creatures. Racial and national temperament, too, plays a large part in any country's selection of a favourite fairy type. Thus some countries may lay emphasis on a mythic being close to the pure-fairy of Celtic antiquity, whilst others may specialise in beings derived mostly from the dwarf and night-daemon elements. Early English fairy-lore includes some examples of the pure type—as in the legend of Thomas of Erceldoune and his seven years in the domain of the fairy queen—though a larger number of legends depict a miniature, good-natured, prankish race of pleasing aspect. Welsh, Scottish, and Irish fairies are less genial on the whole—the complimentary terms "good folk" or "gentry" being euphemisms designed to placate a somewhat feared element. Continental fairies vary widely, those of Germany being perhaps the best-developed. Germanic legend includes magnificent examples both of the pure fairy and of the impish troll and gnome. In the more southerly nations, the importance of the grotesque elf seems to diminish. Many nations assign to the fairies a definite social and political organisation, with King, Queen, and other dignitaries—thus the Mab, Titania, and Oberon of popular legend. Fairy lore in the East, as developed by the Islamic nations, is an extensive separate study; as is the elaborate world of classified elemental spirits described by Paracelsus and the Comte de Gabalis.

Another separate topic for research is the manner in which each nation correlates its fairy lore with its more formal and serious religious beliefs. Thus in rural England a fairy is held to be the wandering spirit of a dead person, too earth-bound for heaven, yet not lost enough for assignment to the realm of Lucifer.

Belief in fairyland is today largely a matter of history in most parts of the world, though in Ireland many surprisingly literate persons still profess to retain faith in the "good folk". To such devout disciples, our present survey will no doubt appear equally blasphemous and unnecessary.

The Pool

Recommendations for Revision—Synopsis.

N.B. For a new suggestion as to a different *beginning* for the tale, see top of sheet IV. This mode of beginning can be used no matter what plot-variant you decide to follow.

The pool in this story had better be one of the few remaining vents betwixt the upper world of life & the fabled under world of the dead (others elsewhere on the globe can be hinted at). Use the Graeco-Roman conception of the world of shades—cf. Æneas's descent into Hades in the 6th bk. of the Æneid, & Ulysses' in the 11th book of the Odyssey. It must *always have existed*—hence it would be well to carry back the legendry & whispers to the very earliest times—Roman & Gallo-Druidical pre-Roman, with hints of primordial Cro-Magnon & Neanderthal ages behind even these. Let it be known that buildings on this site have been destroyed horribly & inexplicably *whenever persons living in them or issuing from them* have actually sought to descend into the pool & plumb its mysteries.* This is the legend. In order to keep the tale well motivated, do not fail to connect all destructions of buildings, & all kindred disasters, with especially determined attempts to enter the pool. Let the carved lintel be from a Gallo-Roman villa of (say) 100 A.D.—its inscription might well be:

STVLTI. VNICI. STAGNVM. ADEVNT.

NAM. IN. IMO. INTERITVM. PESTEMQUE. LATITANT.

Anglice—

FOOLS. ALONE. THE POOL. APPROACH.

FOR. IN. ITS ABYSM. ANNIHILATION. AND A CURSE. LURK.

In all the old legendry there must be numerous accounts of strange persons & shapes who have sought to enter the pool—*especially* strange beings, as distinguished from the local inhabitants who were moved by mere curiosity. These strangers must have displayed a desperate determination, purpose, & secret knowledge wholly alien to those of the natives. Now as to what those beings are—it will not do to have them merely the unburied dead; for if all unburied dead lingered above ground in a kind of half-life, there would be legions of them wandering about, so that they would be no rarity. Indeed— there would be, by this time, (considering the vast hordes killed & left on battlefields) more of these "undead" in the world than there are living persons! Let us, then, seek to narrow the field & find a *special class* of person who, upon dying, is forbidden to enter the nether world. At once it occurs to us to use the celebrated *witch-cult* as a basis of selection. But how? First, though, let us account for the extraordinary precautions taken to guard the pool—precautions not likely to have been taken against any *small* class of beings. Here we come back to your idea of the unburied dead. Let it be, then, that *all* unburied dead are forced to remain above ground *in the form of spectres or wraiths*—not in actual bodily form—& that the pool is guarded in order to exclude *these shades* from the nether world of the dead. You can suggest this

---

*You might hint that these destructions coincided with attempts so determined as to have been *successful* for one or two participants, though most perished in the catastrophe.

in hinting of the old legendry—speaking of rumours of vast armies of ghosts (battlefield dead) congregating about the pool at certain times (especially Walpurgis & All-Hallows), but always dispersing in disappointment. Living beings who from curiosity attempt to penetrate the pool are always found hideously & inexplicably mangled. *They never disappear.* Make this plain, since at the last you will want to use the *disappearance* of the boy & stranger as an indication *that they have successfully passed through.** The peculiar strangers— "undead"—who storm the pool are always beaten off with horrible suffering,† (cries heard, &c) but are not killed or mangled because they are not living bodies in the strictest sense. Thus we have three classes of would-be entrants to the pool:

(a) shades of the unburied dead. always* beaten off

(b) living beings—killed & mangled* (though their shades later go through. after burial)

(c) the "undead"—beaten off* with suffering but without bodily harm.

> *i.e., if you decide to adhere to your original intention of having one or *both* pass safely through.

And now—who are these "undead"? Well—here's a suggestion. It is an *actual* legend—indeed, probably a ceremonial fact—that a member of the loathsome mediaeval witch-cult was always buried *face downward* for certain occult reasons,‡ whenever anyone knowing of his membership could arrange to be on hand & see that the provision was carried out without exciting the suspicions of survivors. Now would it not be a good idea to have your half-dead people witch-cult members *who had not been buried face downward?* Of course, you can vary all this as you wish—but you can easily see why an unusual & restricted class is needed. This class would naturally tend to be of just about the size you assume when you include certain seers, magicians, &c. in it. All members would necessarily have strange powers & properties—not only because of their anomalous position betwixt life & death, but because of their membership in the witch cult. It may be assumed that they still cooperate with the cult, & take part in its infamous Sabbats. You can find out all about this cult in "The Witch-Cult in Western Europe", by Margaret A. Murray, which is in the main reference department (not circulation) of the 42nd St. library. Of the various "undead" of Central France, most know of the pool's properties, & refrain from making attempts upon it. From time to time,

---

*except in half-hinted cases of *success,* which always involve widespread destruction for those who assist—& the destruction of neighbouring buildings.

†largely a *psychological* suffering from the sheer sight of the Guardian Thing

‡Cf. entry 142 in HPL's commonplace book: "Members of witch-cult were buried face downward. . . ."—ED.

however, bold exceptions occur; giving rise to many picturesque legends. These exceptions may be noted with especial frequency after the battle of Poitiers—when among the slain & unburied soldiers were, presumably, many members of the witch-cult. Occasionally the wandering "half-dead" seek the aid of actual living beings in forcing an entrance to the nether world, whilst at other times they marshal the unbodied shades in the region. The present tale concerns an attempt of the former kind. In my opinion the tale had better be rewritten from the start, intensifying the *abysmal antiquity* of the pool legends, & embodying scraps of hinted legendry in accordance with the plot finally decided upon. The strange archer, who intends to use the boy as a decoy in his attempt to enter the nether world, ought to be a more definitely sinister & evil figure than in the existing version. Atmospheric touches suggesting this abnormal age & ambiguous state should be added, & the boy should fear him at the same time that he is fascinated by him. The stranger should play upon the boy's plainly visible curiosity regarding the pool. Incidentally, it ought to be made clear just why the "undead" are so anxious to get down below when they seem to be well off enough up here. You might have their upper-world, post-mortem existence a *painful* one—at least at times. Possibly they have to exist half of each year as werewolves or something like that. Or on the other hand, it may be that their new half-dead state gives them information of marvellous pleasures they are missing in the nether world. Perhaps their upper-world life is one of utter boredom, owing to the loss of some essential life-property corresponding to the traditional "soul". At any rate, they want to get down very badly, & the old archer thinks he can use the boy as a means. If I were writing this tale, I'd have the boy hideously killed (as the inn is destroyed) by the nameless Guardian of the Pool (or as a sacrifice to lure the thing forth) (whose nature, as manifested by previous killings, reported glimpses, building-destructions, trails & prints in the vegetation, &c. &c., may be hinted at in the early legends) whilst the 'half-dead' archer slips into the abyss. It would, though, be quite permissible to employ some subtler decoy-stratagem & have the boy safely accompany the stranger into the nether world. At any rate, make it clear that the *total disappearance* of any being near the pool is a possible indication of safe & miraculous passage to the nether regions. Not positive, tho', in case you wish to introduce the ironic touch of having the archer fail. One thing—you must use more subtlety in describing what the boy glimpses when he climbs out over the pool & looks down. This is a superlative high spot, & needs the greatest possible care in development—emphasis & detail as well as subtlety. Remember that what the boy sees is part of an age-old nether world, through which move the forms of those who have entered it *ever since the beginning of life on this planet.* Clearly, it is superficial & unconvincing to confine a first glimpse to a group of mediaeval horsemen. What is seen under this aperture is merely a small area of the nether world, & the figures crossing this area must be *curiously mixed* & derived from *all preceding ages*—ape-man, Neander-thalers, Cro-Magnons, other primitive men, animals recent & extinct, Mongoloids, Gauls, Romans, Franks, Frenchmen, armies of every kind. Naturally, only a chance fraction of this subterraneous population will cross the limited field of vision during any given short period, but this fraction must be *varied enough* in race & period to be representative of the whole population. On account of recent large battles, of course, mediaeval soldiers will be quite numerous—but there have been other, older battles, & of them vast evidences must remain. Your series of successive heavens might eliminate some warriors, but I am skeptical about the effectiveness of this idea. Would you have this merely the first of a series of worlds like a set of Chinese boxes, with everyone finally dying into other inner realms? That, of course, would eliminate older denizens—but the idea looks a bit cumbrous to me. Assuming a steadily cumulative population, local civilians would probably outnumber warriors despite the great battles occurring in the region. But at any rate, what the boy sees in his first, random-timed glimpse must not be any specially appropriate pageant. It must be simply a cross-section of the ordinary life of this part of the nether world. The sight had better be described slowly & impressively—for the various objects will unfold themselves to the watcher very gradually. The whole visible area is vague, distant, & half-veiled in obscurity. It is a kind of queerly exotic landscape, like nothing ever seen in the upper world of the living. Finally one or two figures move across it—figures so strange that the boy gasps in surprise. Perhaps they are Roman legionaries—perhaps a family of ancient Gauls—perhaps a knot of Aurignacian or Mousterian primitives—perhaps Gallo-Roman civilians—perhaps Teutonic Franks—perhaps monks, soldiers, or other mediaeval personages. A goodly variety of different types *belonging to widely different ages* ought to float silently across the field—unless, of course, you use the multiple-heaven idea. The boy, naturally, is half-stupefied with wonder—an emotion you must bring out clearly. Finally you can have him see a knot of Poitiers warriors—or whatever type of sight is most significant in the light of the ensuing narrative. Don't fail to emphasise the unusual *conditions of vision*—the vertical perspective whereby the watcher is looking down on the heads of the nether-world denizens. If you like, you can have this slightly modified by some queer refractive property of the waters—for of course they are no ordinary waters, since they remain thus suspended betwixt two realms. You might barely suggest the disquieting presence of yawning black gulfs extending laterally into the earth from the submerged walls of the pool—the presumable abode of the Guardian of the Gate. Pile on plenty of colour & wonder, & let the astonishing nature of the spectacle be reflected in the boy's reaction to it. This brings us to the point where your MS. leaves off. Now let us see if we can form a good synopsis of events to follow.

Obviously, the boy's curiosity is whetted to a supreme degree, & he

overwhelms the stranger with questions. The stranger, answering these, (&
here you have a chance to tell more about the nether world & the conditions
of entering it) sees in the boy a good means of effecting an entrance; hence
leads him on to the greatest possible extent. The story he tells is something
which was barely hinted at in the ancient legendry. (you can insert some
glancing allusion to it earlier in the tale, when first discussing the legends, if
you wish) & which concerns the *very, very few persons or shades or "undead" who
actually did penetrate successfully to the nether world.* These cases of success were
invariably accompanied by the destruction of all living human beings who
aided, & of all buildings—& even trees & other vegetation—near the pool;
but the stranger does not tell the boy of these drawbacks. You can *hint* them, though,
so that the reader can understand the final climactic catastrophe without subsequent explanations. It is well to end a tale on a high note, without the
dragged-out piecing-together of threads which always suggests anticlimax. In
general outline, the stranger's plan can well be just as you proposed—i.e., to
have the Nameless Thing lured out of the pool so that one or more beings
can enter the nether world unscathed before It returns to Its guardianship.
And your idea of having a sacrifice the lure is likewise a good one. Now what
about details—the exact nature of the sacrificial lure, &c? Well—let us see
what would naturally appeal most to a hideous & titanic Elemental bound to
a stern guardianship under the earth. This being may be presumed to be of
the sort habitually frequenting the awful Sabbats on the lonely hills at Walpurgis & Hallowmass. Yet It is perpetually denied the privilege of participat-
ing in these Sabbats, because of the necessity of guarding the gate during
such events. Indeed, the guarding has to be *all the more rigorous* at Sabbat-time
as compared with other times, for there are then stirring the greatest possible
numbers of uncanny beings who would jump at the chance of entering the
nether world in the absence of a sentry. All the old legends speak of the increased presence of monstrous shades around the pool at Walpurgis & Hallowmass. The Nameless Thing, then, is avid for unmentionable Sabbat-rites
which It is habitually denied . . . . . a circumstance which the strange archer
fully realises, & of which—with the boy's help—he is determined to take advantage. In developing a plan he is cautious in what he tells the boy. A *human
sacrifice* is really needed, but he tells the boy a *goat* is what must be offered.
This seems simple, since there are many fine goats among the varied live-
stock around the inn. Roughly summarised, the stranger's plan is to assemble
the ghosts & "undead" of all the neighbouring countryside at some time *other
than Hallowmass or Walpurgis,* when the Thing will be off its guard & free from
the inhibitions which keep its half-brain alert at such seasons. Its attention is
to be aroused by a celebration of the most shocking & hideous pseudo-
Sabbat ever held in France . . . . a pseudo-Sabbat in which there will not be
one living participant except the boy destined for the sacrifice. The way to
tell all this—since there will be no principal survivors left above ground—

may be difficult, but there are methods of circumventing the obstacle. For one thing, you might boldly break the "classical" rule of transmission & let the reader share the literary omniscience of the author, as Poe does in the "Masque of the Red Death"—of which there are no survivors. Better, though, to leave a human link. Of course the stranger has told the boy to reveal the plan to no one, but you might have the command broken in the case of a particularly discreet playmate—who, in addition to his discretion, is too frightened to repeat the tale until after the catastrophe. If you use this device, you can speak of his fright—how he shunned his little friend of the inn after hearing the monstrous tale, & how his fright (having been noticed & connected with the catastrophe) led to his being later questioned forced to divulge what he knew.* But there is a third alternative, also. Of course the ghosts & undead summoned to this hellish pseudo-Sabbat (you can call it an "Estbat", which was the actual name applied to irregular convocations of the witch-cult. *Sabbats,* in the true sense, occurred only at Walpurgis & Hallowmass. *Estbats* were largely business meetings, but there were also rites—so you can safely use the name) would naturally expect to share the archer's entrance to the nether world—this being indeed the inducement which brought most of them. [The reason they had not tried this very method oftener was that it had seldom occurred to them. Also, the human sacrifice had to be *voluntary,* or at least *not resistant.* It would not do to sacrifice a *captured* mortal. Victims, to be effective, must be voluntary—or else, as in the present case, secured by trickery.† However, it would be natural for the deceived Monster to see through the trick & get back to Its post before *all* of so vast a throng of ghosts and undead could pass into the pool. Thus we may assume a certain number of Estbat-participants to have been left disconsolate in the upper world—shut out at the last moment—& to have told their tale later on to certain mortals whom they met by night in lonely taverns. If you use this third method, or indeed in any case—you might have the tale *begin* rather differently—letting the whole subject be brought up in a conversation between a mysterious stranger & yourself in some lonely French inn *at the present time.* The stranger is one of the old undead participants in that bygone Estbat—perhaps—ironically—*the archer himself*—who has not yet succeeded in getting into the nether world. You might begin the tale by having yourself seated as a traveller, in the very inn concerned—that is, one of the later inns built on its site. You notice the old lintel from the ancient Gallo-Roman villa, which seems, somehow to be miraculously preserved through all calamities, wonder

---

*It would be a fine & supremely ironic touch to have *the old archer himself*—instigator of the whole business—among the "undead" ones left out.
†Still more—perhaps the method *is* sometimes tried, but frustrated because of the Thing's wariness. It has not much brain or memory, but just enough to retain a few impressions occasionally.

whether it is really a Roman survival, idly translate the inscription, & feel curious about the pool described. You ask the landlord, but he crosses himself & says little. Then you try to go through the door—having gathered that the pool lies beyond. At this the landlord stops you, & tells you a jumble of hideous legends dating from the earliest times to the present. He does not go into details, nor need you set down anything save the general hints suggested at the beginning of this outline. [However—if you use the playmate method of telling the boy's story, you can have this case come up very impressively. The landlord selects this to tell in full, because the boy dwelt in this very place, & was one of his collateral ancestors. You can easily devise a start for this sub-narrative. The landlord can say, "Yes, Monsieur, & more—there was, in the old time, one from this very inn . . . . or the inn that was here . . . . who tried to go into the pool, but men never saw him again. There were rumours—& people shivered at what he had told one of his little playmates. In the end there came a night when the inn was full of strange guests from unknown places—& the next morning there was no inn, nor any who had slept there, nor any of the trees & growing things that had stood nearby—only a heap & tangle of crushed things without life." With this start, the landlord tells the tale as far as the revelation of the archer's plan to sacrifice a goat & slip with the boy into the nether world—as far, that is, as the boy had told his playmate. The landlord adds the common report—of the destruction, & how the playmate was questioned; supplying certain conclusions of his own. Don't try to use his own words, for pseudo-mediaevalism is hard work. Say "The tale told by the landlord was a strange one indeed, & I listened raptly as the dim candles of that ancient tap-room guttered in disquieting blasts of night-wind. The way to the pool, he said, led from the back door of the inn out into the humid greenery of the forest—&c. &c. &c." When the landlord is through, & goes a way to attend to various tasks, a mysterious stranger sidles up to you & says he has overheard the tale. He can tell you more. He is a man of bizarre & disquieting aspect—so much so that you had noticed him before in the dimly lighted inn. He seems to know an abnormal amount about bygone times. He begins abruptly—"There was more than most people know. It was no goat that was sacrificed. Do you think a goat would have drawn the Thing forth, or that all the wraiths of the countryside would have come for the mere killing of a goat? I have heard things repeated from very strange sources—listen, Monsieur!" He supplies what the landlord has been unable to tell, & only at the very end (cf. Dunsany's "Poor Old Bill" in "A Dreamer's Tales") do you suspect, by elimination, that he must be one of the "undead" Estbat-participants himself. All this digressive material within these brackets implies your use of the *second* or playmate device of narration, supplemented by the Estbat-survivor device. Forget it if you intend to use the third device alone.] If you *do* intend to use the third device alone, have the landlord's information stop with frightened & whispered generalities.

There is no more for him to tell unless he has heard from some special source of the boy's wish to enter the pool, & of the real significance of the archer. Lacking such information. this particular calamity would not seem greatly different, in public retrospect, from others. Of course, undead survivors of the hellish Estbat might have told others long ago, & thus divulged the inside tale to general knowledge, but I think it would be more effective & dramatic to have it otherwise. In this case, let the stranger overhear your colloquy with the landlord, & approach you after the latter departs. He strikes up a conversation displaying uncanny acquaintance with the remote past. "Why," he says, "there was a boy from this very inn—or the inn that was here—who tried to go into the pool, but men never saw him again. There were rumours—but I can tell you more! I've never told anyone before—but I know. You are very interested in these old things are you not? Then listen." As in the case of the landlord—if you had him tell the tale—don't try to use the stranger's own words. Use the same device you would use with the landlord—saying: "The tale told by the queer stranger was a bizarre & frightful one indeed, & I listened raptly as the dim candles guttered, &c. &c. &c." Have the ending climactic, & (as in the bracketed alternative) do not have the nature of the unwholesome narrator divulged except by elimination at the very end. Of course, you don't *have* to use this device of having the tale told to you by landlord or stranger or both—but I think it greatly increases the effectiveness of the whole business. Likewise, you don't *have* to have the boy sacrificed. You could manage to let the goat do, or use some drugged human being other than the boy. But all the same I think the boy is the logical victim, & I think it would be a neat bit of cosmic irony if his sacrifice—the old plotting archer himself, were among the left-behind—& the final narrator of the story. Your idea, of course, has hitherto been to have the archer a less malign character than I envisage him—but you must remember Montague Rhodes James's warning (& Blackwood's occasional pathetic examples) as to the feebleness of *benignly* supernatural stories. If this is a horror-story, make it so! If not, you'll have to follow the Barrie tradition & abide by the results. Some—like E. M. Forster in "The Celestial Omnibus" can get away with such wild whimsicality without being too utterly namby-pamby, but all that stuff is outside any province of mine.

Well, let's see where we are now. We have discussed the main probable trend of the plot, & the best ways of getting this to the reader. Now let us see how we can develop the final climactic episode—the hideous Estbat & the entrance of the monstrous celebrants to the nether world; preferably with the old archer ironically left behind to tell the tale in later centuries.

The archer has asked the boy to help—under the impression that a goat is to be sacrificed. On the day preceding the appointed night the inn fills up with mysterious strangers who impress the local people as oddly as the archer himself did, & who are long afterward talked about. Never before has the inn been so full—but some of the strangers tell a tale of a great religious pil-grimage. However, the alien, unholy, & unearthly aspect of the pseudo-pilgrims is not lost upon the local people, & is remembered by them in their gossip after the inn & all its tenants have disappeared. That evening, at the direction of the archer, the boy drugs (harmlessly, he is assured) the food of his parents & indeed of all the *living* human tenants of the inn, so that the night may be free for the celebrants of the awful pseudo-Sabbat or Estbat rites. The rites themselves are held in the woods betwixt the pool & the inn, & are begun at midnight after all the people are drugged & asleep. A huge rock has been rolled to the top of a woodland knoll to serve as an altar, & the fattest he-goat from the inn's farmyard has been brought as a sacrifice. The aspect of the strange "undead" as they issue from the inn's rear door or troop from other parts of the forest is monstrous & panic-breeding in the extreme—& still more hellish are the shapes of unbodied ghosts & nameless Sabbat-elementals that answer the occult summons of the archer & material-ise out of the circumambient air. It is all the archer can do to keep the boy from screaming aloud, but he finally succeeds. In describing the nameless beings & rites of the Sabbat you can use your own imagination—pieced out by descriptions in the previously mentioned Murray book, or by the descrip-tions & illustrations in Lewis Spence's "Encyclopaedia of Occultism"—which you can find on the open shelves of the South Hall (western wall) at the 42nd St. library. Go the limit—do in prose what Clark Ashton Smith does in water-colours. Probably you know as well as anybody else how to suggest half-amorphous, tentacled *things* with rugose heads, semi-proboscises, miscellaneous bulging eyes at various anatomical points, & other choice nightmare characteristics. You might include our old friends Alabad, Ghinu, & Aratza. Let Spence or Murray suggest the Estbat or pseudo-Sabbat ritual, & be sure to include a chant designed to tempt the Pool Thing forth. Let the goat be sacrificed with much ceremony—the odour of fresh blood evoking hordes of bat-winged elementals from the black woods. At this point the boy expects to see the Pool-Thing—but the archer knows that the *right kind* of blood-smell has not yet appeared. Use your judgment about the sacrifice of the boy—about the most effective amount of horror-increasing reticence to use. When that is over, the actual climactic moment comes. A sickening bubbling in the pool which makes even the ghosts & ghouls & undead & obscene morbidi-ties stop aghast in their chanting, & huddle behind the trees as far as possible from the altar & the dripping things upon it . . . . . . a wheezy snorting . . . . . . a pushing upward of the earth as the present silt-coated banks meet the pas-sage of a Shape too vast for their compass . . . . . and *then* . . . . & **then** . . . . great Sathanas! Samaël have mercy! . . . . IT . . . IT . . . **what is it?** . . . . .

Some of the monstrous celebrants flee insanely into the haunted night at the very sight of IT . . . . .. throwing away their chances of nether-world en-trance rather than risk the madness which another look would bring. Dark

Abaddon, what an Entity! Not quite matter, not quite gas, not quite fire, not quite aether . . . . jellyfish, worm, octopus, lizard, bat . . . . . brother of Great Cthulhu, Cousin of Chaugnar Faugn . . . . Elephant or Cyclops? Gorgon or Hydra? And vaster than St. Peter's Cathedral in Poitiers . . . Iä! Shub-Niggurath! The Goat with a Thousand Young! The Black Goat of the Woods With a Thousand Young! N'ghaa . . g'hahh! Yrrr . . hha . . . H'na . . . gggll . . . . . [The next day, appalled by that scene of devastation, people told of the hideous sounds which had disturbed their dreams, notwithstanding the remoteness of the spot.] There was a rending & crashing of great trees, & a floundering as nameless nostrils sought blasphemous blood. But It never spoke, for It had no voice. Hideous & unmentionable urges seemed to fight with implanted destructive commands within Its hazy half-brain. It floundered betwixt the altar & the near-by inn, & wiped out the latter & all its occupants with a blow from one of Its gelatinous brown tentacles. Then the great descent began—& all the ghouls & ghosts & undead & abnormalities which had not fled in fright began to crowd into the pool in a turbulent stream. They would leap in, & seemingly plunge downward through the water for an infinite space, finally floating out into the air of the nether world & landing safely on the mystic soil. All the entities fought desperately for a place in the mad exodus, but at last they saw The Thing turn about & flounder back toward the pool with a new air of determination. The chance was gone. Only a few more reached the beckoning water before the sniffing & wheezing & floundering drew perilously near. The rest, disappointed, fled precipitately into the depths of the black oak forest (including, if you adopt a new ironic touch, the old archer who had planned the whole thing. But do not reveal this until the final climactic moment. He was so busy directing his scheme that he was left behind[)]. That was all. The next day local people found the inn & all its inhabitants gone, & all the neighbouring vegetation monstrously mangled and devastated. It was not merely *crushed,* but seemed to be eaten, burnt, or dissolved to a semi-pulp by some unknown & inexplicable corrosive agent. No one who had slept in the inn was ever seen again. Landlord, boy, archer, guests, pilgrims—all vanished. Though (the strange narrator hinted as the candles flickered near their sockets) among the "undead" there are rumours of those who, in later centuries, climbed out over the pool on the branches of new trees that had grown to antiquity there, & saw within its depths an alluring nether world. [whose denizens including one strangely like the bygone archer they had known, unless (as I hope) you adopt the ironic touch of having the archer himself left out—making him the present stranger-narrator]

Well—that'll do for one session! I suppose the foregoing is rather confusing, but I don't see how it can be otherwise when we've not yet decided on just which plot-variant to use. You can regard all this as mere conversation touching on the general theme & turning up fresh ideas at random, from among which you are at liberty to select a quota to suit yourself—arranging & developing them as you choose. Personally, I favour the most horrible version—with the sacrifice of the boy, & telling or the whole tale to yourself by the undead stranger (if not the old archer himself, a friend of the old archer, to whom the latter had given all particulars when inviting him to the Estbat) in the uncanny, candle-lighted Inn where the ominous blackened lintel towers with its ancient Roman warning. When the tale is over you can have the stranger glide out through the forbidden rear door under the ominous lintel. As he glides, you add a bewildered query as to how he knows all this—to which he replies in some subtle climactic way which clearly shows him to be the old archer himself. To atone for the chaos of the foregoing, I will prepare a synopsis of the version I prefer. You can substitute & modify it at will, & if you like, I'll discuss the matter further. In case of such discussion, please return this comment in order to refresh my memory.

N.B. It may be assumed that the archer did not return to the region of the pool for long centuries. Perhaps he is just back—& about to make another attempt to enter!

THE POOL

¶ Author travelling near old Poitiers puts up at strange old rural inn which takes his fancy. Notices ancient Latin lintel inscription & asks landlord about it. Landlord is frightened & evasive—hints old legends—horrible fate of the curious, &c—(here tell as many as possible & prepare the background) tells of successive destructions of many inns, & stops author when he attempts to go through door. Author returns to his table. For some lime he has noticed a stranger of peculiar & disquieting aspect, whose talk of old times with various guests holds an element of abnormal familiarity. Stranger, having overheard colloquy with landlord, approaches & begins to tell story of boy & inn & archer & pool to author.

¶ The story of the boy, inn, archer, & pool, told (as begun in original MS.) by stranger, with uncanny evidences of "inside" knowledge [due to fact that he is really the old archer himself] Boy, long ago, longs to plumb secrets of the pool, which is entrance to nether world. [Give details of guardianship & describe 'undead'.] Archer, longing to reach nether world. plans to use boy's curiosity as a tool. Arranges hellish Estbat or pseudo-Sabbat to lure Guardian Monster forth, summoning ghosts & undead, & telling boy to drug everyone in inn on the appointed night. Intends to sacrifice boy, but tells latter a goat is the victim. Undead arrive as pilgrims, living humans are drugged. Sabbat-rites are started betwixt inn & pool. Goat sacrificed. Boy sacrificed. IT flounders forth & wreaks devastation. Many of the hellish celebrants succeed in entering pool, but some are left behind & flee into forest. Among these, it appears impossible to deny, is the stranger now telling the tale, but he does not at this moment admit that he is the old archer who planned it all & sacrificed the boy. Indeed, he only darkly implies (& that as late as possible) that he is an "undead" witch-cult member at all.*

¶ Aftermath remarks by stranger-narrator, perhaps elicited by puzzled questions of author. What the local people found the morning after the horror—inn gone—forest &c crushed—all persons connected with the inn missing. Also—remarks about possible later glimpses (by undead or others) into nether world. Author still bewildered by curiously "inside" nature of tale, as stranger rises & glides to the ominous door under the lintel. (Landlord & others busy elsewhere & not looking. Anyway, taproom is virtually deserted because of late hour.) Stranger unlatches (or *unbars*—evidences of fear & precaution on part of inn-builders desirable) rear door & stands on threshold as author, following him across the room, presses final & insistent questions as to *how he knows so much*. Then—as a climax—stranger gives hints unmistakably implying that he is the archer† . . . . . . & glides out into the haunted night, shutting & latching the door after him. Author does not follow. Use your judgment about suggesting possible future attempts of archer to enter nether world.

NOTE: Be very adroit in describing witch-cult phenomena—do not refer to cult like modern anthropologist for remember that the stranger who tells the secret is a member anxious to conceal as much as possible. Have facts contained in elliptical half-hints—"They who gather on the hills"—"They who sacrifice to the Goat"—"They who follow the Black Man". Use "they", because the stranger in speaking tries not to admit that he is one of them.

Wilfred Blanch Talman

Cloisonné and Other Verses

Acknowledgement is made to *Leslie's, Casements, The Brown Jug,* and to various magazines of the United Amateur Press Association for permission to reprint a number of the poems contained herein.

TO MY MOTHER

Cloisonné

One day I saw a dainty vase
 Of sky-blue cloisonné,
Filled, in its pawnshop resting-place,
 With dreams of old Cathay.

---

*He has tried all along to convey the idea that he *heard* the story from some undead person.
†use great care & cleverness devising ways to hint or imply this. It is a vital point.

I bought it, set it on a shelf,
    Bright-polished till it shone,
And all its dreams on my poor self
    Poured downward from that throne.

As time went on, I own with shame,
    It gave me Jess of joy,
Until at last my vase became
    Like any common toy.

With cob-webbed dreams of yesterday,
    Now old and dead with rust,
My little vase of cloisonné
    Lies covered thick with dust.

Home-coming

Kanaka, the gloomy-winged storm clouds have scattered
    Along the horizon far out to the lee;
The glowing red sun with its halo of rainbows
    Has dipped in the clouds at the edge of the sea.

Kanaka, the breakers roar loud on the atoll;
    The surf crowns the coral with showers of foam;
The breeze blows the spray with a sparkle of silver
    From your outrigger's bow, as you paddle toward home.

Kanaka, the gold-pebbled beach stretches nearer—
    The little thatched hut that the palms beckon o'er;
There's a thrill in your heart as you top the last comber
    And Maloa waits for her love at the door.

The Lane of Loveliness

On the Lane of Loveliness, trod every day,
White, wide blossoms strewn along the way
Sunlit patches on the shaded trail
And liquid bird-notes through a leafy veil.

Sunlight, sunlight, bright upon each bend,
Making every step a song, every mile a friend,
Warm the path my footsteps tread, pipe a tune the while;
Along the Lane of Loveliness lead me with a smile.

On the Lane of Loveliness, trod every day,
Hillsides lost amid a haze of gray,
Wind-tossed branches and storm-swept sky,
And swirl of rain where tangled meadows lie.

Raindrops, raindrops, tinkling overhead,
On the green and mossy roof just above my bed,
Lull me with your slumber song-adventurous it seems,
Along the Lane of Loveliness , to wrap one's self in dreams.

Barque of Dreams

I make my mind a barque of dreams, and reach the joy to me denied,
Of floating 'round the world without a care for wind or tide.
I dock at sunny Zanzibar, and watch the dhows drift down the bay
Where ships are laden low with gold and pearls from far away.

I glide past verdant Celebes, with coral reefs and beaches fair;
My wander-loving heart is lured to Java's scented air;
I scud before the trade-wind's breath, and race the clouds for countless miles
Past green lagoons festooned by palms in sunlit atoll isles.

From Hong Kong, where the seas are gold and junks sail by on motley wings,
To Honolulu, breaker-kissed, the God of Beauty sings.
Within a thousand ports of call on storm-lashed seas or tranquil streams
Adventure waits expectant for my barque of silvery dreams.

Gypsy Trails

Gypsy lad, gypsy lad,
    Break your camp when the sun is new;
Patterans mark trails of gold
        Over the hillsides wet with dew—
        Hills of mist through a haze of blue .

Gypsy lad, gypsy lad,
    Trails are long when the sun is high,
Dusty white on the upland roads;
        Valleys below where rivers lie—
        Lakes blue-hued from a turquoise sky.

Gypsy lad, gypsy lad,
    Twilight falls when the sun is low;
Spread your bed where the crickets sing,
        Lie and dream in the campfire's glow
        Lulled by boughs that the night-winds blow.

Fantasy

You lead me by the sacred altars where
    The incense of old dreams is burning faintly,
Distilling subtle fragrance to the air,
    Through cloisters beautifully arched and quaintly;
And all the fragments of my dreams are there
Before those shrines whose arabesques are fair.

And, dreaming in the dusk, I wander to
    That one lone candle, slim and white, and burning
Slowly, the while I kneel, with ardor true,
    Clasping your heart in mine with tender yearning.
Dear Priestess, when the light flames high anew
You know my heart is making dreams for you.

At Sunset

A clinging wish, as vague as some dim, misty dream—
    A vision, silver-lined, with haunting hold-
A little cottage underneath the maple shade,
    And sunset tinting windows red and gold.

A bed of roses, just beyond a picket fence
    That sifts the level sunlight shining through;
A gravel path, a twining honey-suckle vine,
    And, waiting for me in the doorway, you.

Mignonette

A scent that floats enchanting in my mind
    Like light around the nimbus of the moon,
And lingers on the sweetness of the wind—
    Soft echoes dying slowly, all in tune.

A perfume wafted gently through the dusk—
    A vision of your face, so white and fair—
A little dream of mignonette and musk,
    When you sang to me in the garden there.

Songs

Could you but know the songs my heart is singing—
    Old songs, with plaintive notes of long ago,
Soft tunes, sweet cadences with beauty ringing,
Quaint melodies of rippling laughter, bringing
    Wild anthems lover's hearts must always know.

Each melody an echo of the yearning
    In some fond breast in days when earth was new,
And sung in awe before an altar burning-
Songs full of love, whose echoes keep returning
Dear one, my heart sings all these songs to you!

Jeanette

Though I dislike your modern ways,
    Your too-familiar air;
The charm your supple form displays;
    Your manner debonair ;
The way your evening gown is cut;
    Your cigarette,
You still remain, through all your faults,
    My sweet Jeanette!

You lure me with feigned innocence,
    Much bolder than you ought;
With daring, calm irreverence
    And charm your creed has taught;
O'er ankles slim you roll your hose;
    You swear, and yet
I can't resist the things I hate, My sweet Jeanette!

Height

Some souls soar, singing, to the sun,
    Whose blinding heat their vision mars,
But others live whose visions run
    Beyond the sun, among the stars.

Dream Ships

My argosies with their golden sails
    Filled with dream-winds light and true,
        I send away
        At dawn each day,
    Laden with lots of love for you.

Will my argosies with golden sails
    Return on the dreaming breeze so true,
        With the last red ray
        Of the fading day,
    Laden with lots of love from you?

Death

A stately ship stands in the offing now,
    Out past the reef where broken waves are drumming,
Her sails lit up with sun, bright gilded prow,
    And rigging taut through which the breeze is humming.
    Some day another· ship is coming;
No breath of wind shall whisper through her spars,
    And I, through phantom sails, shall view the stars.

Haunted Island

On a low, black isle in the Spanish Main
      Strange things occur, 'tis said,
And night by night the moon gloats white
    On the conclave of the dead.

In the dead of night when the wind s low
There are grim, white shapes that come and go—
Ghostly galleons drifting by
On the rolling sea where moon-tints lie;
Mist-hung shadows of masts and spars,
Hazy hulks under haloed stars;
The creak of block and the flap of sail
And ghastly shapes on the after rail.

Raucous song in the forest dim;
Splash of oars at the beach's bim,
Boats beached high at the water's edge
And the gleam of sword on a shelving ledge;
Click of cutlass and rasp of spade,
Whispering voices in palm-fringed glade
Where ghostly forms in the dusk convene
With a chest full of treasure borne between.

A sharp command and a rush of feet;
A clas of arms in the dim retreat;
Muffled oaths and a musket's roar
And pale-hued lights on the moonlit short;
Crimson sands 'neath the green lagoon
And a formless shape that swings high and free
From a moldy rope on a gnarlèd tree.

In the dead of night when the wind is low
There are grim, white shapes that come and go
Hazy barques on the pounding surf;

Rattle of spade in the sandy turf;
The tread of feet and voices low
And the gleam of gold in the lantern's glow
Till rising dawn's first cold, gray strand
Strikes flame from a shore of barren sand.

On a low, black isle in the Spanish Main
   Strange things occur, 'tis said,
And night by night the moon gloats white
  On the conclave of the dead.

Ballade of Creatures Abroad by Night

These are the creatures abroad by day:
  Fauns and satyrs and elves and gnomes;
Naiads and dryads and centaurs play
  As Great Pan pipes in their forest homes,
But soon after sundown the werewolf roams,
  His eyes agleam in the witch-fire's light;
The old crones' brew in their cauldron foams—
  These are the creatures abroad by night!

Drunken old Dutchmen Van Winkle knew
  Play at bowls with a thunder cloud;
Jovial phantoms by day, these few,
  Till dusk brings ghouls with an earth-stained shroud
And demons of dreadfulness, bloody-browed.
  When doors and casements are fastened tight
To keep out the spell of the ghostly crowd—
  These are the creatures abroad by night!

High on the peak of a Kaatskill crag
  The Old Squaw drowses till evenglow;
Darkness awakens the fiendish hag
  And spirits marshalled by Manitou.
Pallid-tongued specters that whimper low,
  Astride the winds on a vampire-flight,
With slavering priests to the sabbar go—
  These are the creatures abroad by night!

Crown Prince of Darkness, Satanus, pray
  Pierce our eardrums and blind our sight;
Nor haunt us, lest we become as they—
  These are the creatures abroad by night!

Adventure Land

I have found my land of romance—
    I have tasted of its beauty;
I have dwelt among its people
    Whom its lure has made its slaves.
I have watched the crimson sunsets
    And its ruddy sun at morning
Spill a molten stream of color
    On its phosphorescent waves.

I have wandered up its rivers—
    Roamed beside their boiling torrents;
Loved the streams that run forever
    Starting out from God knows where
I've encamped deep in its vallies;
    I have dreamed upon its hilltops
Heard the roaring of its breakers
    Breathed its blossom-laden air.

I have drunk its gin and arrak
    In the purple shade of palm trees,
Where the yellow sands dip downward
    To an emerald lagoon.
I have wooed its dusky maidens—
    Kissed their brimming lips of scarlet—
Listened to their love-shy whispers
    'Neath a lonely silver moon.

I have sought for shells and trepang;
    I have dealt in pearls and copra;
Battled with its sturdy tempests—
    With its fever and its rain.
I can hear the South Seas calling—
    Hear the crooning of the trade-winds.
It's my Paradise of romance,
    And it claims my soul again!

Fragment

Steep walls of mist that bend before the rain—
Dull, leaden clouds that blur the haloed view
Of lights, soft pointing from each crystal pane,
Through shadows looming deeply o'er the lane,

Beneath the hazy oaks the path winds through.
Dear dusks of days whose memories bring sorrow—
Dim, guiding lights that pierce the veil again!
How sweet the thoughts whose ecstasies we borrow—
The streams that echo footsteps through the rain.

Izrim

I was Izrim, who lived in the long ago, dwelt beast-like in the forest. And I, Izrim, looks [*sic*] for beauty where there is no beauty to be found. "Izrim wastes his time looking into the distance when he might be hunting or fishing for the tribe." Thus my abode apart from my fellow-men, and they mocked me, saying, "Izrim is an ass." The neighbors scorned me.

And I, Izrim, built on the top of a hill an image, an idol made from the soft, white clay that I found in the river-bed. And to me the idol was very beautiful, for in it there was more than clay. In it there was the soul of the man who was to come—man as I thought he ought to be—and before my idol I stood in awe.

I knelt before my idol in the morning when I awoke, and at noon, when I was far off, seeking for food to sustain life, I saw my idol on the hill in the blue distance, and I stretched out my arms and worshipped it. And at night when I rekindled my fire from embers left through the day, I watched its flow light up the whiteness of my idol, and again I fell upon my knees and adored that which I had made, though I knew not why.

But my fellow-men laughed at me. they laughed and threw stones and clods of earth at my image—for my fellow-men did not understand beauty. They jeered when I drove them away with clubs and fire-brands, but soon they ceased to bother me and said among themselves, "Let us not ridicule Izrim. He is a fool, but he has something which we have not. Let us watch him worship his idol." And afterward, when I practiced my sacred rites, my tribesmen gathered and looked on, and sometimes I thought that some of them worshiped with me, but I could never be sure, for they were ashamed to confess before their fellows.

And so all my life I, Izrim, lived alone, and through worshipping my idol I learned to dream. And in my dreams I was happy, and though my neighbors sometimes still mocked me and threw stones at my image.

Many rains fell upon the earth, and the winds lashed them against my idol and weakened it, and the warm sunshine dried it out so that great cracks appeared upon the surface. Sometimes the stones which my tribesmen threw chipped off fragments of the brittle clay. These blemishes I filled with more of the soft, white clay from the river bed, and I was sad, for I saw in my image not the white purity which it firs had possessed, but a mass of muddy patches swaying lopsidedly and threating to fall in each gust of wind. I tried to make other idols, but in none of them could I see any of the beauty of my first attempt, so I cast the useless clay away, or used it to repair the damage done to the image I still worshipped, though always with disappointment in my heart.

Then one day there came a tremor of the earth, and I saw my idol sway upon its rude base and fall to the ground, broken in jagged bits. I threw myself prostrate among the pieces of clay and wept, and my fellow-men gathered around me and jeered, saying, "Izrim's idol has fallen! What a fool he is to worship an image of life as it might have been! How much better if he had tried to live like us!" But I thought that not all of them mocked me. Some looked at my fallen idol and were sad.

And there among the ruins I, Izrim, who lived in the long ago, died of a broken heart, and my tribesmen buried me where my image had stood and piled its fragments upon my grave so that the wild bests might not feed upon me. . . . . . .

I am the spirit of Izrim, dreamer of the ape-man,. Come down through the many aeons of time in the form of man, and in these days when men build great towers of steel and masonry that reach into the clouds, and few men build images to worship, I, Izrim, mould my soft, white clay into an image of man, and I bow myself down to that which I think man ought to be. My fellow tribesmen mock me as they look upon my image, and they say among themselves, "this Izrim is an ass. He follows false gods and worships the things which are not. How much better if he would but walk our way!" As I look upon their faces I see nowhere in them the reflection of the soul that I have put into my idol. All that is there is a cunning look of greed and lust and love for worldly things, just as in the faces of the ape-men many eternities ago. But here and there I see one in whose eyes there is a soft glow, as in the eyes of my idol . . . . .

And so I live alone and worship my idol, and when the rain, the wind, and the sun so beautiful to me, I go down to the river-bed for more clay, and with my crude tools I repair my idol with sadness in my heart. My image is yet quite new and white, but the cracks are becoming more numerous, and I, Izrim, am becoming sadder each time I kneel before that which I love.

I am the spirit of Izrim, dreamer of the ape-men, who lived in the long ago. . . . .

The Curse of Alabad and Ghinu and Aratza

The pot simmered as the old woman stirred it with a wooden ladle. Light from the great, open fireplace showed deep wrinkles in her skin as she knelt to sprinkle herbs into the mixture. A parrot squatting on the sand-strewn floor croaked contentedly as it preened its feathers. Smoke filled the dim room.

"*Ach, mijn kleintje,*" said the old woman, turning and speaking to the parrot, "a fine cure it will be for the child. A fine cure"

"A fine cure!" echoed the parrot thickly, spreading its wings.

"But if the child dies, they will blame me. already they say that I have magic. When last year I cured her child the wife of Arie Ver Veelen seemed afraid of me. she seemed afraid of me—dost hear, *mijn kleintje?*"

The parrot waddled away toward a dark corner in unconcern. The old woman went on mumbling to herself.

"And if again I cure the child they will call me a witch. Only yesterday Johannes Kuyper would not meet me when I walked on the Claasland Road to Nayack. He went across a field so that he would not have to come near me. they are all afraid, *Mijn kleintje!*"

The parrot's eyes glared unblinkingly out of the dark corner. Pushing a wisp of hair back under the white cap whose two starched points stood out stiffly over each ear, she turned again to stirring the mixture in the pot.

"*Ach,* and it was well I learned how to mix herbs and roots and juices from my mother's mother in Amsterdam! Many things shew knew! And often have I been *dokter* to these stupid Dutchmen. But they are afraid of me, these good people. They think that I have magic because——"

A door opened, letting a hint of twilight into the little shack, and a young man entered and seated himself beside a table. His eyes glistened in the firelight, but their stare was fixed and vacant.

"Ah, Hendrick, *mijn zoon,* you are come for supper!" said the old woman, without glancing around.

"*Mijn moeder, mijn moeder,* why did we have to Nieuw Nederlandt?" He buried his face in his hands, sobbing. "All day I have tried to find work at the harvest, but they do not want me, even for nothing. They back away from me when I come near them. Even Squire Yaupy De Vries sent me off, and said that I brought evil spirits."

The old woman sighed, and continued to stir the pot over the fire. The parrot, scrambling clumsily upon the table, rubbed its bill against the young man's sleeve.

"I know. They say that I am a witch," muttered the woman, too low for him to hear. "For all that Hes Brummel does for them they say that she is a witch—because she lives with her half-wit son and her parrot; because she can cure children when they are ill. But little I know about magic. Only I know that once, in Amsterdam, when my mother's mother was angry with a neighbor, she cursed him the next day his won was drowned in the canal where he was playing with his little boats, and they said it was because she cursed him: because she called down on him the curse of Alabad and Ghinu and Aratza——"

"The curse of Alabad and Ghinu and Aratza!" screamed the parrot, beating the table with its wings. "The curse of Alabad and Ghinu and——"

The young man raised his head, startled.

"Hold, hold, *mijn kleintje!*" exclaimed the woman, dropping the ladle and reaching quickly for the excited parrot. "No curses here! Should the child die, Hes Brummel would be to blame. No death curses now!"

The joints of her knees cracked sharply as she straightened up. Reaching high up on a shelf, the old woman brought down a bottle and carefully brushed off the dust. Into it she poured a portion of the mixture which she had been stirring, and set the pot by the side of the fireplace to cool.

"I have made a cure for the sick child of Arie Ver Veelen," she said to her son, who had dumbly watched her every move. "I shall take it there before it gets too dark."

He continued to gaze at her vacantly while she pinned a shawl about her narrow shoulders. Picking up the bottle, she held it before the light of the fire, nothing the color of its contents.

"A find cure it will be," she crooned. "A fine cure!"

The young man's gaze follower her to the door, and returned to stare fixedly before him. The parrot hopped down from the table and went to a dark corner to preen its ruffled feathers and croak monotonously.

It lacked but a few minutes of complete darkness when Hes Brummel climbed the slope leading to Arie Ver Veelen's house. The building was much more pretentious than her own shack of unpainted wood. It's walls were of square blocks of red sandstone crowned by the gambrel roof with curved, sweeping eaves characteristic of early Dutch colonial houses. From behind the double oaken door came the sound of a woman singing a lullaby:

"Trip a trop a troontjes!
De varken en de boonjes,
De katjes en——"

Hes Brummel knocked, and the lullaby stopped abruptly. The upper half of the door swung open.

"I have brought some medicine—for the child. Maybe it will do as good as last year. Is he any better?"

"No, no better," answered the woman in the doorway, taking the bottle and noticeably shrinking away. "All the day he has had a fever."

She shut the door without a word of thanks. Hes Brummel trudged down the hill into the darkness of the hollow where she dwelt.

When she pushed open the door of her shack, Hendrick was sitting where she had left him, still gazing blankly at the fire, which had now been reduced to red embers. On a high shelf there was a sound of scratching and cooing, and of something hard and dry trickling down upon the floor. The son's head turned and his eyes dreamily regarded the old woman, who looked upward at the shelf where the parrot had been scratching the contents of several small wooden boxes. Roots and herbs and strange dead things strewed the floor beneath the crouching bird upon the shelf.

With a scream the old woman mounted a chair and dragged the parrot down. holding it by its legs, she slapped it first on one side of the head and then the other. The birds squawked in pain. Green feathers dropped upon the sanded whiteness of the floor.

"Do not hurt the bird, Mother," pleaded Hendrick, turning in his chair.

The old woman ceased, one hand remaining upraised for another blow. She seemed astonished that her son should care what happened. The parrot flapped free and perched itself upon a narrow window-ledge.

"I'll teach that devil-bird to spill my roots and herbs!" she snarled, showing yellow teeth. Hendrick was not listening. He had returned to his occupation of staring blankly at the fire. The parrot glared evilly from the window.

"The curse of Alabad and Ghinu and Aratza be upon the!" shrieked the bird, clicking his bill. "The curse of Alabad and Ghinu and Aratza! The curse of——" The voice trailed off into a series of indistinguishable sounds. Hes Brummel stood regarding the bird for a moment, then shrugged her shoulders and threw some more wood on the fire.

Running footsteps were heard on the road that led past Hes Brummel's shack. They came near, passed, and the sound was lost in the distance. A half-hour later came the crunch made by cart-wheels going in the opposite direction. Low voices were swallowed by the night. Lights gleamed in Auert Polhemus' grist mill a mile down the Hackensack creek.

A dozen Dutch farmers and their wives were gathered in the mill beneath the light of crude lanterns. They looked at each other and nodded their haeads as Arie Ver Veelen spoke.

"There is no doubt that this woman is a witch," he was saying in Dutch. "Only tonight she came to my wife with some medicine for our sick child, and while my wife answered the door, the child died. He was not dead before Hes Brummel knocked. Last year she gave him some medicine that made him well, but tonight she bewitched little Joris so that he died."

The nodding heads became more emphatic. Auert Polhemus slapped his dusty breeches.

"She should be thrown into the mill-pond," he declared. "It is the old water test. If she floats, she is a witch, and must die. If she drowns she is innocent and someone else has bewitched the child."

"*Ja, ja!*" came from the nodding circle. Several men rose without further instructions, took some rope which hung over a beam, and started up the creek toward Hes Brummel's

They were back before long, with Hes Brummel bound hand and foot. The old woman hissed and snarled and spat, clawing at the men's faces with her bound hands. Men and women lined up along one edge of the pond, holding lanterns over the black surface. As Hes Brummel was thrust forward toward the brink, footsteps were heard, and two men scrambled down the opposite bank.

"What's going on here?" inquired one of them, an old man who supported himself by means of a gnarled cane.

One of Hes Brummel's captors]scratched his head.

"Well, Squire Yaupy," he answered respectfully, "Truth is we think old Hes Brummel here is a witch. We're just going to make sure by throwing her into the pond. If she floats she's a witch, and we'll take care of her afterward, but if she sinks she's all right and we won't bother any more about it."

Squire Yaupy De Vries threw back his head and laughed. He slapped his companion on the back.

"That's one good way to decide it—eh, Jake?" he asked. "But I know a better way." He made his way carefully around the edge of the pond while the crowd waited in silence, but some of the women shook their heads ominously, as though they disapproved of any more lenient course of justice. "You, Auert," he continued, "go over to your house and get your family Bible. We shall see whether God outweighs the devil."

Several of the people caught the idea and nodded in approval. Others either shook their heads the other way or looked blank. Auert Polhemus was back in a moment lugging the Bible by an iron chain attached to it. It was an enormous book, iron bound, with wooden covers. Hes Brummel, still struggling, was pushed ahead of the crowd back into the mill, the two pans of the great flour-scales were dusted carefully, and the Bible was laid on one of them.

"If the woman you say is a witch is outweighed by the Bible," said Squire Yaupy, "she is a witch beyond any doubt. On the other hand, if she outweighs the Bible, she shall go free. Auert, will you look to the balance?"

Auert stepped forward, and Hes Brummel's slight form was lowered slowly into the opposite pan of the scales. The balance wavered for a moment, and then the Bible shot upward. The miller was evidently puzzled.

"She's heavier," he at length decided, while a murmur of disapproval came from the farmers.

"Then how can she be a witch?" argued the squire, turning to the assembly. "She outweighs even the word of God."

Heads continued to shake, but the squire took no notice of them. At a nod from him Hes Brummel's captors loosed her bonds. Feeling herself free, the old woman darted to the door and turned to glare at her persecutors.

"The curse of Alabad and Ghinu and Aratza be upon thee!" she spat, as she retreated into the darkness.

"See that? See that, Squire?" asked one excited woman. "Only a witch can curse like that! Some of us'll hear from that curse, we will!"

The life of the scattered community went on peacefully for several days. Arie Ver Veelen's child was buried in the little plot of ground which the settlers had set off for a cemetery. Hes Brummel's half-wit son continued to roam aimlessly around, but the old woman did not show herself. Along the creek Polhemus' grist-mill clattered daily, and the sound of the great wooden hammer beating cloth in Pye's fulling mill could be heard for some distance. Oxen and carts passed on the rutty road.

One drab morning when the sun was overcast, Roelof Pye came running breathlessly up the slope to Arie Ver Veelen's house. Grietje, Ver Veelen's wife, was busy in the kitchen with the midday meal. Roelof clattered through the house and confronted her, his breath coming fast and his face pale.

"Your· little Katrina! he gasped. "She was playing in the mill and she fell under the hammer—under the big, heavy hammer that beats the cloth. She was crushed, and she lies there now, all bloody——"

The woman fell to the floor in a heap, sobbing.

"My little Katrina! *Mijn schoon lammetje!* First was Joris, and now Katrina *Mijn liefste kind!*" She rocked back and forth in agony.

Pye lingered for a moment, then, seeing that he could do nothing further, walked slowly back toward his mill. On the way he met two of his men carrying the little girl's body, crushed beyond recognition, back to her home. The woman's wailing could still be heard.

The news spread quickly over the settlement. Daily tasks were abandoned and men and women gathered in little groups, looking ominously toward Hes Brummel's shack. Today, however, no smoke issued from its chimney. Hendrick had not been seen all morning. They wondered if the old witch had not departed, now, that her work of revenge was done. the murmuring grew louder as the handfuls of settlers merged into one large group moving toward the unpainted wooden building in the hollow.

They gathered around the door, but no one had the courage to be first to enter. Nothing could be heard from within. Suddenly Arie Ver Veelen, a wild look in his eyes, dashed toward the door and shattered the latch. He stood for a moment blinking in the semi-darkness of the hut. Other men followed and looked over his shoulder.

As their eyes became accustomed to the dimly lighted interior they saw, huddled in the ashes of the fireplace, in a pool of blood, the recumbent figure of Hes Brummel with the parrot perched jauntily on her head. An open red would from ear to ear showed where her throat had been cut. On the opposite side of the room, crouched in a corner, Hendrik laughed softly and insanely caressing a gleaming knife.

Ver Veelen turned to run from the horrible scene, and stumbled into the men behind him. He was panting with fright.

"The curse of Alabad and Ghinu and Aratza be upon thee!" shrieked the parrot from the mangled both of its mistress. "The curse of Alabad and Ghinu——"

The bird's chattering sank to a muffled croaking as it preens its feathers. Not one of the crowd had remained within earshot.

A Horror in Profile

Hartman walked down the brilliantly lighted hallway of the museum, pushed open the door of the office, and snapped on the light, shaking glistening beads from his umbrella. The room was unusually warm. Paynter, the curator, no doubt had closed the window when he left for dinner and neglected to turn off the steam heat.

It was one of those late winter nights when a thaw brings sloppy streets, humid mists hang over dirty snow, and unseen water gurgles eerily through flooded gutters. Blood moves slowly beneath oppressive clothing at such times.

Hartman removed his overcoat, glanced at his watch and saw that he was nearly a half-hour early for the trustees' meeting. Though he stumbled with the valve on the radiator, the more he turned it in either direction the more steam hissed. The window refused to be stirred at all. The little trustee shrugged resignedly, gave up the attempt and, extracting a rumpled handkerchief, wiped the thick lenses of his spectacles free of mist and mopped his lean face. With hands clasped behind him, drawing forward his already dropping shoulders, and with the light streaming upon his bald head, Hartman stood and gazed out of the window over the mist-veiled street.

"Tonight," he mused, "I must make them vote that additional appropriation. It's shameful having Smith and Claudel tramp all over Zuniland without knowing where their next meal is coming from or whether their two-man expedition will be recalled as soon as they stop at a town. They must keep searching until they find the tomb of Tantazuxi.

"Tantazuxi! Long before Coronado came he was walled in his tomb and forgotten by all but his own people. He was the true king—the deity—of the Seven Cities of Cibola that even Coronado could not find in his day, so long had they been hidden. I spent most of my life looking for them and failed. Much more is now known of their location. More has been read on the picture rocks of the Southwest. Smith and Claudel took up the search where I left off. If they were successful—"

Engrossed in his thoughts, he turned with a gesture intended to indicate the adjoining room of the museum, which should be filled with gold and pottery treasures of Tantazuxi when its sponsored archaeologists returned from their expedition. But Hartman's hand paused in midair, then fell slowly to his side.

A man stood in the shadow near the office entrance, although Hartman had heard neither the opening nor the closing of the door. The visitor's face was half turned away from the museum trustee.

"Smith!" exclaimed Hartman. "What a start you gave me! I could scarcely believe my eyes at first."

The man uttered a word of greeting, but did not turn his head. He continued to stare at untidy shelves on the opposite wall, piled with books, papers and miscellaneous museum specimens that the curator had not had opportunity to classify.

"You have failed!" Hartman accused, his shoulders drooping even lower and his face expressing keen disappointment. "You must have failed or abandoned the search, or you would not be here. And tonight we were to vote a extra appropriation to continue the expedition! Your last message was so full of hope, too, and only a moment ago I was thinking of the triumph we would all enjoy if you were successful. Why did you return without orders?"

"We did not fail," said Smith in a dry voice that seemed very far away. "We were successful—very successful. We found the tomb of Tantazuxi." He still gazed at the shelves.

Hartman's eyes lighted and his head reeled.

"You found it? Good! Good! And you hurried here to let us know as soon as possible. Tell me about it! Tell me now!"

Smith raised a restraining hand.

"Please do not come near me," he said, "and pardon me for not looking you in the face. I am injured—badly injured." A faint smile—a smile that had no trace of mirth in it—played about the corner of his mouth that was visible to Hartman. His words came as though there was an impediment in his speech.

"My presence here may be a warning," said the explorer. "I came not of my own will, but impelled by some other power. I shall not share in the glory of the discovery, and you shall see why.

"The Seven Cities of Cibola will soon be an open book to you, but in them you won't find what you expect. Claudel will return with maps and sketches, and you may reap what triumph there is. He will conceal all traces of our visit—trust him for that. No other person will find the way until you are fully prepared to gather everything in the cities. I shall remain in Zuniland. That country has my body and soul."

Smith shifted his weight from one foot to the other and cleared his throat. His voice still seemed to reach Hartman from a great distance. The room was still stiflingly close.

"Our last message was from the village at Buchane Mountain," Smith continued. "Not far from there we found the clue that led us straight to the burial place of Tantazuxi in the first of the Seven Cities. The other nearby cities we did not visit.

"It was I who found the pictograph crudely outlined above the sheltered ledge of a cliff, covered with fungi and matter that the years had deposited in corrosive form. We had slept one night on the ledge which jutted out like a gigantic step at the cliff's top.

"A day of feverish work scraping off the accumulation, copying and translating the picture-writing beneath, revealed all to us. Another day brought us to the summit of a mountain in an isolated part of the Southwest, from which we searched the rolling land below with the aid of a field glass.

"From that height every irregularity of the ground below stands out in relief. It was not difficult to discern several horseshoe-shaped mounds and others compact and angular. They were seven in number. I can scarcely describe our joy when we knew we were looking upon the buried cities of Cibola, which from any other point of view would have appeared simply gentle undulations like the other hills around them. Taking note of the highest spots of the mound nearest us, we hurried down the mountainside.

"Claudel, I noticed, had fallen into a gloomy mood after our first exultation had passed. It was not hard to read his thoughts. He was afraid that I, being the nominal leader of the expedition, would receive all the credit for the discovery. Knowing that a man who feels in danger of losing the fruits of his life work may act desperately, I watched him closely that night. The next day, when we commenced tunnelling into what we thought to be one of the most promising ridges, my vigilance relaxed as my excitement was intensified.

"Our digging was a frenzy, without method and with little caution. We knew that we were within but a few feet of the find of a century. The first room into which we found our way was disappointing. It was probably a watch-tower of some sort, and we obtained only a few pieces of pottery. These, however, were far different from any we had previously seen in the Southwest, showing an unusually high type of culture.

"Though our hands were raw and blistered, we made another cut into the sloping side of the mountain, working until the sun had set, and I was almost exhausted.

"At last we struck a wall of crudely-mortared rocks and worked our way to a low doorway, which had been carefully filled with primitive brick. It was Claudel's turn to enter the breach that we soon made, while I stood guard. I heard him shout after he had been gone only a few moments, but there were no words in his joyous cry. For a time, as I stood with nerves on edge in the dusk, I could hear him calling and could now catch such words as 'Bodies . . . god . . . Tantazuxi . . . dead'. I was impatient to follow but still clung to the last shred of caution a long time past when he did not call, but finally I saw the flash of his electric torch.

"'Smith,' he said as he straightened up and took a long breath, 'Tantazuxi's tomb! He was a bird-god, Smith!'

"I could not wait to hear him babble of the bodies within, of Tantazuxi himself seated overlooking an immense burial crypt, and of ancient picture-writing on the walls. I snatched the electric torch and stooped to pass through the entrance.

"'You left everything as it was?' I asked, as I encountered the warmer air.

"'Everything,' he said, but I saw he kept one hand behind his back but didn't notice the look that must have been on his face.

"The room was truly immense, although its ceiling was low. Whether it had been built for a temple or a tomb I do not know, but its appearance was that of both. The skeletons of more than two dozen persons, preserved by ages by their exposure in the close air of the room, lay in two semi-circles with their heads facing a raised throne at the far end. On this stone dais was a figure that raised gooseflesh between my shoulders.

"Seated so that its profile was turned toward me and the skeletons on the floor, was something which at first seemed to be a gigantic bird; but no bird, I realized, could sit upright. Even in its seated position, Tantazuxi—I knew instinctively that it must be he—loomed taller than a man. Skirting the semi-circle of skeletons, I stood squarely in front of the figure. I could see then that only half of it was bird-like. The other half was human, but brutal in the extreme.

"I wondered for a moment what sort of embalming process the ancients of this country used to thus preserve the flesh. Then I caught the gaze of that one piercing bird-eye and was struck by the thought that Tantazuxi might not be dead. Behind the dominating beak-like nose that swerved downward and inward were two close-set eyes, one the eye of a man and the other that of a bird, both enormous, black as onyx, and glowing with life-like intensity. To be in the same room with them was to be gloated over by a monster perhaps partly alive after centuries in the close air of a hidden tomb.

"Turning my electric torch toward Tantazuxi's feet, I saw upon the base of the throne a pictograph—three pictures only, but with a significance in keeping with the aspect of bird-god. '*Tantazuxi izcatl ancatl*—Tantazuxi claims his own' in characters so ancient that I had to ponder a moment to remember the absolute words to express them.

"I had followed Claudel's footsteps in the heavy dust, which covered the bodies on the floor, but not the body of the bird-god. His tracks led around to the human side of the figure, but with Tantazuxi's eyes watching me, I had no desire to follow them. I had seen enough for a time; the air was close and I was tired. All could wait until morning.

"When I emerged, Claudel's attitude had changed. He was no longer breathless with excitement, no longer bubbling over with desire to speak of the strange things within the tomb. We stumbled through the darkness to a boulder near the tomb's entrance, and spread our blankets beneath it.

"'You went behind Tantazuxi,' I said to Claudel. 'What did you see there?'

"'Please do not ask me now,' he implored as he threw himself upon a blanket. 'I'm dog tired. You'll know before morning.'

"I awakened bolt upright, as though in a nightmare. Someone was bending over me in the dim, cold light that comes before dawn. It was Claudel, and he was holding something before my face and muttering. My right side felt paralyzed. What I saw when I glanced down seemed incredible, but with my left hand I touched the right side of my face and found that the horror had indeed come to pass.

"Scarcely any strength was left in my body and I could resist but feebly, making uncouth noises in my throat, as Claudel bound a rope about me and dragged me to the floor of the tomb. He said nothing; his eyes were wide and staring.

"When I recovered my voice it seemed scarcely like my own, but I spoke pleadingly to him. I argued, appealed to his common sense, his loyalty, even his sanity. But he bent his body to pass through the doorway, hauling me after him like a sack of meal, and made no answer.

"Through the heavy dust of the room's floor he pulled me, and into the darkness behind Tantazuxi's seated figure. There, flashing his electric torch, he drew something from beneath his shirt and held it before my eyes. It was brown, withered, wrinkled like a dead fungi.

"In a flash I knew! Grinning like an ogre, Claudel directed the beam of light upon the head of the bird-god and the gaping hole in its skull. Tantazuxi's brain—dry, withered by heat and age, but *living*, like his body! His brain had turned me into a creature half-man, half-bird! He had claimed me for his own! I looked at the talons that protruded from my tattered sock and buried my face in the dust, shuddering.

"I myself once broke the skull of a long-buried member of an older race and drew forth the brain, dessicated and preserved by years of entombment. Claudel had seized the opportunity to take the brain of Tantazuxi for a prize, and the living brain of the bird-god, released from its narrow confines in the half-outworn skull, had found a resting place for its cruel thoughts in his own jealousy-mad senses. That release had transferred in an instant many years' accumulation of unwholesome lore to the mind of my former companion. He, too, had been claimed by Tantazuxi.

"I raised my head again as I heard Claudel climbing upon the throne. He replaced the brown brain in the cavity from which it came and stroked the vulture-like face as one might rub the head of a pet dog. With his lips close to Tantazuxi's human ear, he muttered some words that I barely understood, except that I knew them for an aboriginal invocation to the sacrifice.

"Tantazuxi's shoulders heaved, his limbs moved, his head rose. I saw him rise to his feet and half turn to gloat down upon me with his evil eyes. As Claudel sprang to the floor, Tantazuxi stepped down from his throne and advanced upon me, one emaciated human hand and one wing outstretched. Behind him he left alternating marks of a naked human foot and a hideous triple-taloned claw. Again I turned away my face, and my screams made little hurricanes of dust along the floor. I thought every breath would be my last, for I felt the presence of the thing standing over me. But the pinch of those talons, the piercing pain from that strong beak, did not come.

"I heard a sound of digging overhead—digging that went on and on with the speed and endurance of superhuman strength. One—two—three—four— five—six—I counted the strokes, continuing for what seemed hours. Whether it was my grave that Claudel was digging I did not know, but I did know that standing watch over me was a frightful monstrosity, neither man nor beast.

"There was a rattle of falling earth—a flash of dim light and Claudel's shovel came clattering into a little niche near where I lay. The bird-god was on the other side of me, and I stole a glance at what the light revealed. The shovel had fallen into one of many little niches, like pigeon holes in a desk, in the wall beside me. They were kilns for firing earthenware, used by a people whose deity had been an obscene abnormality from the borderland of human shapes.

"The sound of Claudel's heavy breathing as he climbed out of the chimney-hole came clearly to me. He was soon back inside the tomb, leering, with a bundle of fagots, which he threw into the niche. Then he turned to Tantazuxi and spoke again—"

Smith broke off his narrative suddenly, raising a finger. Hartman heard steps in the hall.

"I must go," said Smith. "They are coming to the meeting. They would not understand as you have. I shall not see them, nor shall I see any man again."

His hand was on the knob of the door as Hartman moved to restrain him, but the step the trustee began was not finished. His foot seemed to plunge downward without finding the floor, as if he were walking off a precipice. He put out a hand to break his fall as Smith faced him with a farewell gesture.

For an instant Hartman saw the explorer's full face—a face shaped like a bird's, yet resembling no bird that Hartman had ever seen. A protruding, steely eye of immeasurable depth glinted opposite a human eye, both above an evil black beak. Purple-brown feathers in tufts, revealed scaly, pink skin beneath, descended from the crown of the head and were lost beneath the collar of the man's gray shirt. Half of the mouth was beak, with no mobile lips fashioned for speech. As a flood of bright light flickered before the trustee's eyes and went out, he felt the closing in of darkness to blot the scene from his vision. His body struck the floor and lay still.

Paynter, curator of the museum, burst in with two other trustees and dropped on one knee beside the fallen man.

"Gad!" he exclaimed. "Hartman's fainted. Help me revive him, will you? I thought I heard something fall."

The others, with their combined strength, managed to raise the window. Paynter brought water, dashed it in Hartman's face, and rubbed his wrists. In a moment the man on the floor opened his eyes, staring wildly at the faces above him. They helped him to a divan in a corner.

"There, old fellow, you'll be all right now," boomed the jovial Paynter. "Deucedly hot in here. Don't blame you for fainting. Just lie still awhile until you're yourself."

Hartman continued to stare at him, uncomprehending, and then gazed in bewilderment about the room, as if in search of someone.

"Listen to this," commanded the curator, turning to the light and excitedly tearing at a yellow envelope. "Here's a telegram handed me just as I left home. Probably from Smith and Claudel—yes, Claudel signed it.

"By George, they found Tantazuxi's tomb!" Paynter's face fell suddenly as he read on. 'Smith dead. Caught in earthslide. Smothered before I could dig him out.'

"Poor Devil! That's certainly bad luck. He's a great loss to science. Hmm. The body won't be sent back. Claudel cremated it with the best means at hand, acting on a wish he'd heard Smith express.

"Say, there must be some mistake here at the end of the message. It can't make it out. Either it's a mistake or another language. *Tantazuxi izcatl ancatl.* Perhaps Hartman—

"My God, he's fainted again!"

Texaco at Home: V—Providence

Roger Williams, who had left the Massachusetts Bay colony after a disagreement with the Puritan fathers, was met by some Indians on the bank of the Seekonk River in Rhode Island one day in 1936, and greeted with the salutation "What cheer, Netop!" The word "netop" was the Indian word for "friend," and "what cheer" was a familiar English greeting of the period.

From that time Providence, Rhode Island, founded by Roger Williams, has been the netopian city of the United States. The phrase "what cheer" appears in the city seal, is used as the name of business organizations and fraternal lodges, and the police of the city of the Providence have "what cheer" on their badges to greet the tourist or stranger. Rhode Islanders established the "What Cheer Restaurant" in San Francisco during the gold rush of '49, and What Cheer, Iowa, received its name from Rhode Island settlers.

Like many another Texaco city, Providence is a city of superlatives, although some of the boasts of its residents are expressed cautiously. Providence has the widest bridge in the world, though some may say that the "Great Bridge" is but nine bridges side by side. A certain museum curator may be correct in saying that Bowen Street, close to traffic since the advent of the automobile, is "the steepest street this side of San Francisco."

Providence is the greatest jewelry manufacturing center in the country; it has the finest collection of Americana in the John Carter Brown Library, Brown University, the most distinctive collection of colonial furniture and the most varied and numerous examples of colonial architecture.

The spire of the First Baptist Meetinghouse is generally acclaimed the most beautiful in America, and the Providence county Court House, recently claimed to be the largest building of Georgian architecture in the world. Court is still called to order by a bailiff who announces that justice is to be sorted out in the name of "the State of Rhode Island and Providence Plantations." Rhode Island and Providence Plantations were separate civil units in earlier days.

The name "Plantations" has been retained in a telephone exchange, along with "Angell," commemorating Thomas Angel, companion of Roger Williams, and "Gaspee," an echo of the first blood of the Revolution, three years before Lexington and Concord. A group of Providence citizens captured the armed British revenue schooner *Gaspee* when stranded on a sand bar, put the crew ashore and burned the vessel. The *Gaspee's* commander was wounded.

In the halcyon days of New England commerce on the sea, Providence stood out sharply the four Brown brothers, "John and Joe, Nick and Moe" were merchant princes whose love of the city helped greatly to lay permanent foundations of culture. John Brown's house is still standing, preserved in its traditional elegance. In 1799 John Quincy Adams called it "the most magnificent elegant private mansion that I have ever seen on this continent." Nicholas Brown gave his name to Brown University, and the Moses Brown preparatory school takes its name from one of the brothers. Joseph Brown was one of the greatest amateur architects and scientists prior to the Revolution. His house still stands on South Main Street, and in 1924 the Providence Gas Company, when erecting an office building, faithfully adhered to every detail of its façade.

Providence cherishes its antiquities. With the exception of a row of picturesque warehouses, reminiscent of seafaring days, that had to be torn down before the march of progress, every effort has been made to preserve landmarks hallowed in New England history. The house of Stephen Hopkins, signer of the Declaration of Independence, has been preserved, and also that of Esek Hopkins, first admiral of the United States Navy. The Golden Ball Inn, where Washington, Lafayette, and other Revolutionary dignitaries were entertained, survives, and so does the home where John Carter, who learned the printing trade from Benjamin Franklin, hung out the "Sign of Shakespear's Head" and was one of the city's first printers.

As late as 1829 Providence was built around part of a core, the headwaters of Narragansett Bay. Across the seaward end of this core was the Weybosset Bridge, connecting part of the old Pequot trail to Connecticut with the hilly side of the village. Other bridges were built from time to time, and in the last years of the nineteenth century the core was finally covered over to allow for the building of the Union Station of the New York, New Haven and Hartford Railroad, a road that is a large user of Texaco products. Some of these bridges that were built were connected to make the "Great Bridge," now covered with Texaco asphalt.

Over the "Great Bridge" pass the street cars and buses of the United Electric Railways system, which in Providence are lubricated by Texaco. In all there are 33 bridges in Providence. The newest of them, the Washington Bridge from Providence to East Providence, was recently dedicated, and Texaco Asphalt Binder was used in its construction, and Texaco Asphalt for the approaches. Both the city of Providence and the State of Rhode Island buy asphalt from The Texas Company.

Many historic spots have been virtually untouched. The Providence Chamber of Commerce occupies the old Market Building in Market Square, built in 1773. South Main Street is still almost as much o fa waterfront street as it was in the heyday of shipping. Wooden buildings stand there that are memories of the era of sailing ships. From a steel hillside a series of streets that tumble from South Main into South Water are named Sovereign, Doubloon, Dollar, Dime, Bullion, Guilder, Cent, Coin, Gold, Silver, Packet, India and Patriot.

The devoutness of the old New Englanders is shown in streets named Hope, benevolent, Benefit and Amity. In the Elmwood section there is a Peace Street and a Plenty Street.

The streets of Providence were not paved until 1761, when the Brown brothers started a battery to pass the Weybosset Bridge and a little of Weybosset Street. Westminster Street, now the chief street of the city, was a causeway paved with shells in 1710. Benefit Street wound and twisted at first to avoid the graveyards that were on the property of every family, but was later straightened when the graves were removed to allow for great traffic.

In the Athenaeum, a library on Benefit Street, Edgar Allan Poe and Sarah Helen Whitman carried out a literary courtship that has since become famous. A block above, up College Hill, is University Hall of Brown University, built in 1770 and used as a barracks for French troops during the American Revolution.

The First Baptist Church, the spire of which is so noted, was first called the meetinghouse, and was built by the same men who founded Brown University with a view to having a place "for holding commencements in." Brown commencements still take place there, and the commencement procession is led by the sheriff of Providence County, resplendent in evening dress silk hat, brilliant sash and sword.

The 26-story Industrial Trust Building, recently erected, though it ranks among the tallest buildings of New England, would not be thought a monster in many cities; but considering the fact that it has its feet firmly embedded in the salt marsh shore of the old core, it is a skilled piece of engineering.

Rode Island's State House, designed with the collaboration of Stanford White, stands on a hill overlooking the part of Providence that was formerly the core and is now the civic center. The building is the most imposing in the state, and with the exception of St. Peter's in Rome, has the largest marble dome in the world.

Providence, on the main highways between New York and Portland and between Albany and Cape Cod, is called the "Southern Gateway of New England," and for The Texas Company is exactly that. With the exception of portions of New England that are supplied from the terminals at Bayonne, New Jersey, and Portland, Maine, New England is supplied with Texaco products from the Texas Company's 65-acre terminal in Providence. Yonkers bring petroleum products to the Providence Terminal, some of which are shipped by barge to Chelsea, Massachusetts, where there is a new sales department terminal: Fall River, Massachusetts; Newport, Rhode Island; Portland and Bangor, Maine, and New Haven and New London, Connecticut. Tank cars from these places supply Texaco Petroleum Products to most of New England.

At the Providence Terminal there is an ethyl plant where Texaco Ethyl Gasoline is blended, and an asphalt compounding plant, from which Texaco Asphalt is supplied to nearby points at the desired temperature. Sometimes asphalt from the Providence Terminal is shied directly to Canada.

A new building to house the sales department has just been completed on the Providence Terminal property. In the last quarter of 1928, a countrywide drive on motor oil sales was won by Boston District, and the zone taking in Providence and Woonsocket led the zones of Boston district in both gasoline and oil sales for that period. During 1928, the same had an increase of 50 percent in sales over the preceding year and in 1929 topped that record by 58.78 percent.

One of the three airports in Providence is serviced by Texaco, equipment has been installed in another for Texaco service, and the third has signified its intention of changing to Texaco in the near future.

A Texaco service station next to the Providence Biltmore Hotel, probably the smallest station in Rhode Island, does the largest volume of business for its size, it is believe, of any service station in the state.

In Providence there is a netopian spirit—a spirit of friendliness—that delights both the tourist and the person who comes for a long period of residence or a short one. Such a feeling goes far to eradicate the belief that New England's residents are cold and austere, as they have been sometimes pictured. Perhaps Roger William's [*sic*] ideals have become so ingrained that they continue centuries after, even though Providence has become a cosmopolitan city, with many nations represented in its population.

The Story Teller

A Tale of Christmas

The old man came out of the dim shadows of the rear of the deserted bookshop. In his hand was a shabby wreath that he had hung on the door just before Christmas for the past two years. he pulled a stepladder up in front of the door, blew some of the accumulated dust from the wreath as he twirled it slowly, and mounted and ladder painfully, a step at a time.

"Christmas again!" he mused. "Seems as though last Christmas was only a couple of weeks ago. Well, it's just the same all the year 'round for me, and when a man gets old the weeks and months don't mean anything."

"*Christmas again!*" *he mused*

He carefully straightened the wreath, which seemed determined to hand askew. Then he reflected that every time the door opened its equilibrium would be disturbed. With a gesture of resignation to the perversity of the wreath, and perhaps to the perversity of all things in the world, he shuffled down the stepladder with the same painful movements he had used in mounting it.

Out in the street people were hurrying past, intent on making the rounds of a certain number of stores on their Christmas shopping lists before the closing hour. They bent their heads into a wind that carried the portent of snow. Down in the corner of the newspapers that a sweater-clad boy in front of his shop was trying to sell was a notice, printed in black type—"Only 10 Shopping Days to Christmas."

Henry McCay leaned against a shelf which displayed the latest books, adorned with splashy covers of the holiday season, and watched those who passed by. He knew only too well that they would not stop to look at his books. Years ago, when there were not so many lending libraries, and when the department stores did not cut prices to a bare margin of profit, many of them used to buy books. But it was different now. One could even get the books of the month by mail, without venturing out into the cold or wasting time while old Henry McKay shuffled around his shop looking for a desired volume.

McKay's landlord was threatening to raise the rent of the bookshop, and McKay had been having a hard time scraping together the few dollars requited up to now. Instead of a good living and ten percent from his business, he was making a poor living and one per cent. All over the city there were bread lines this winter. His bank balance, accumulated dollar by dollar, had melted away during a recent illness. He owed several persons small sums of money. A cheerless Christmas loomed ahead.

Before McKay's hair had become gray and his hands shaky, he had wanted to become an author. He knew that he had an inner talent for it. as a story teller he was superb. During the few years he had been at school the younger children would flock around him and insist, "Tell us a story, Mr. McKay?"

But when he tried to write, he learned that publishers and editors were difficult to approach, especially when they discovered that the material the young man McKay was bringing them was not what they wanted. McKay himself knew that the things he put on paper were not the same things he would tall to a child sitting on his knee. His education was insufficient as a vehicle for the written expression of stories about knights and fairies and privateers and pirates.

Standing by the door of his shop, looking out at a Christmas throng, McKay was startled out of his dream of the past. Someone was about to enter. The man turned down the collar of his overcoat. It was Russell Minton, publisher.

Some of McKay's hopes of authorship had once centered about Russell Minton. The publisher had come to the bookshop a number of years before in search of a rare first edition. McKay had it, safely stowed away in the back of his shop. Minton came several times after that, once with one of his children. McKay had told the little girl a story while the publisher browsed among the books as the child listened with rapt attention, McKay saw out of the corner of his eye that Minton had stopped thumbing pages and was listening. McKay went home that night and painstakingly wrote what he thought was a good story for children. He put it in the mail the next morning, addressed personally to Mr. Minton. It came back with a brief, polite rejection slip. Many more stories came back. McKay, discouraged, stopped writing.

"Good evening, Mr. Minton," said McKay. "I have some good first editions that will make excellent Christmas presents."

"I have no doubt of that," said the publisher, but frankly, I'm not giving first editions this year. I didn't come in to buy anything. Instead I came to invite you out to my country place for a few days before Christmas."

"But I can't leave the whop," protested McKay. "I'd lose all my Christmas business."

"Unless I'm mistaken," rejoined Minton, your Christmas business will be small. It might pay you to take a rest. There's something I'd like to talk over with you. I'll be expecting you the day after tomorrow."

When Minton had left, McKay sat down wearily. In order to make a good appearance at Minton's house he would need a new suit, new shoes, and several dollars for a railroad ticket. Wrapped safely in brown paper and hidden in the back of the shop was a set of the "Commentaries of Curtius Gallus," one of his prized possessions. McKay had hoped to keep this rare work for himself. Only a few days before, an neighboring bookseller had inquired for the set. McKay knew that the bookseller would give about half its value.

Minton had said he had something to talk over with him. McKay took the bull by the horns. Perhaps here was his chance. He took the heavy parcel lovingly from beneath his dingy desk, shut up his shop, and shuffled down the street.

The living room of the publisher's home, with its deep rugs and heavy window drapes, was warm and quiet in the evening. A fire blazed cheerfully beyond the hearth. McKay leaned back in the soft chair and closed his eyes. He wondered how many stories he would have to sell to Minton to buy luxuries such as this—for he was again determined to sell his talent to Minton in some way. That afternoon, shortly after he had arrived, McKay had inquired of the publisher what it was he wanted to talk over.

"Weill, I'd rather not say just now," said Minton. "Perhaps in a day or two. I have a number of things on my mind right now."

McKay wondered, alas, how he could get enough money to buy another set of the "Commentaries," as well as enough to pay his advance in rent.

Shrill laughter came from the other side of the door leading from the living room to the rest of the house. It burst open and the publisher's daughter, now about eight years old, came running in with her little brother.

"Tell us a story, Mr. McKay?" she asked, pulling a cushioned footstool up before the fire. "Tell us a story like you told me once before?"

McKay smiled, "Why, I'm no good at telling stories," he said modestly.

"Oh, yes you are, Daddy says you can tell stories fine."

The publisher's daughter came running in with her little brother

The little boy stood silently with his hands behind his back and coyly refused an invitation to sit on the old man's lap.

"Once upon a time—" began McKay, after the fashion that all story tellers begin, and began a story of fairies and giants and witches and goblins that made the eyes of the little fellow almost pop out of his head.

"Telling stories to the kids again, eh?" asked Minton, coming over to McKay. "By George, but you're a master at that. I only with you wrote them as well as you tell them!"

The next night, and the night following, the children came into the living room as McKay sat before the fire. An older daughter of the publisher was sometimes in the room when the inevitable tale began, but when McKay started to speak she always rose quietly and left.

During the day, McKay lounged about the house, not quite content, though a vacation was an unusual thing with him. For one thing, he wished that he could have a volume of the "Commentaries of Curtius Gallus." The publisher's library was a well-stocked one, but it was possible that he never had had any interest in the contents of the "Commentaries." McKay spent most of his time reading his host's books, but he seemed to feel most keenly the loss of his own rare volumes.

Sometimes the children took walks with him through the fields. The old man made Mother Nature seem to them so much like a real person that they almost expected to meet her coming around a clump of bushes in her wind-blown cloak.

The night before Christmas the weather was even colder than it had been for the past week. the fire was welcomed by McKay that night, and he had begun to look forward to the evening visits of the children. He was dreaming again after they children had goon. Perhaps he dozed, for suddenly he noticed that Minton was standing beside his chair.

"Merry Christmas, McKay," said the publisher, extending a slip of paper. "Your stories have been excellent." The old man took the paper and held it toward the light.

"One thousand dollars!" he exclaimed. "You're certainly not going to pay me for telling stories to your children!" The old man's face clouded. "I can't accept it. I haven't been reduced to charity yet."

"Charity, man? Who said anything about charity? That check is for advance royalties on your book." And the publisher thrust something forward.

McKay's hand trembled as he took from Minton's hand a series of unbound pages covered with printed matter and rough drawings. He felt the publisher's hand on his shoulder.

"*You're certainly not going to pay me for telling stories to your children!*"

"McKay, we needed some new children's tales, and I knew you could do that. My oldest daughter has been just outside the door every night when you have told your stories to the children. She has taken down every word in shorthand. Yesterday I had them set up in type to see how they'd look, and an artist sketched in a few of the illustrations. Just dictate a few more stories in your evenings and you'll be another Hans Christian Andersen."

The old man turned to him. He could say nothing. Words seemed choking him, but he could not express his thanks. The publisher understood, and with a final pat on McKay's shoulder, left the room.

McKay crossed to a window and pulled aside the drapes. A few flakes of snow ere falling, seeking the company of others that had covered the ground lightly a few days before. And then the old man spoke the first childish words that he had uttered to himself in a long time.

"Santa Claus," he said, "if there are some poor children you want to give some stories to next Christmas I know a rich author who's going to write them."

Bookplates

Lovecraft Revisited

According to Frank Belknap Long's mother, I was the most practical of the Kalem Club members. One manifestation of that practicality was that I seldom threw anything away. Recently I dredged from the depths of my files three sheets of newspaper copy paper, untouched for more than thirty years, that may shed some extra light on the personality of Howard Phillips Lovecraft.

The sheets bear the pencilled title "Lovecraft, Long, Talman—image psychoanalysis." Some extraneous material on them places their date in the middle or late 1920's. Lovecraft, Long and I were apparently alone, but I have only the vaguest recollection of the event and don't know where we were. We must have been discussing man's cognitive structure and the effect of his subconscious upon his thought and actions, for eventually we set about psychoanalyzing one another. We did this by the simplest possible method—the "word association" test in which a person replies instantly with the first words that come into his head to a word given him orally.

Only Lovecraft's replies seem important, but to keep the record complete I shall reproduce the results of the entire tests, with abbreviations, capitalizations and punctuation as they were in the original. The handwriting is that of all three of us. I seem to have offered the first set of words, and written my companions' replies to them:

	LONG	LOVECRAFT
archer	Robin Hood	figure of man with bow
tower	Norman tower	stone cylindrical tower
boom	hollow sound—vulgarity	ditto—artillery
lake	dark, silent pool and trees	blue rippling water in sun
tracks	animal in snow	footprints Crusoe
tesselation	tiled floor	tiled floor Roman villa
hide	skin of animal nailed to door	skin of elephant carried by Africans
profile	silhouette	as in a textbook of drawing
Godfrey of Bouillon	vague pagentry of crusades	large boned stubborn man
treasure	Treasure Island	nail studded chest with shiny coins
tides	sea beach fishing nets	text book diagram lapping of Seekonk
mauve	ditto	mauve decade
staircase	actual staircase	Adam Georgian staircase
bailey	name	Old Bailey

Perhaps at this point we felt that the second person to answer was being influenced by the first reply, since the replies were not recorded simultaneously, so Lovecraft was switched to first respondent. Long chose the next set of words and added his own impression.

	LOVECRAFT	TALMAN	LONG
Buddha	tarnished bronze Buddha conv.	abstraction of statue Buddha prop.	golden Buddha (conv.)
Idol	Cthulhu	tall, slim, modernistic, Angular	multibrachiate Thibetan
conquest	eagles of Rome	decorative sword at an angle	Attila, Nap. wars
civilization	anc. city in cultivated fields	Book with word as title	Medit. civil. Anc. & mod.
Europe	marching men (not military) of Aryan cast	map of S. Europe	map of Europe
Viking	beaked ship in N.— Viking ship	Viking head in conv. manner	attack on Saxon castle by armed Viking guilds
medieval	squalor—ignorance	battlemented wall— coat of a.	
witchcraft	black woods	oak grain on stocks	Cotton Mather
Indian	R. I. Indian	crouching N. Amer.	comp. N. Amer.
Einstein	white field with black lines crossing	Germany and genius smoking pipe	Person himself— Jew—
Darwin	the man, with symbolic burst of knowledge irradiating outward	monkey's tail with monkey attached	man himself, with work, in garden setting
revolt	sullen, stubborn ignorance	castle interior with 2 men gazing out at battle	rebel artist

Perhaps this also was not entirely satisfactory. It may be our replies seemed too thoughtful and not sufficiently spontaneous. So at this point we made it one-on-one and, from the looks of the handwriting, also speeded up. Lovecraft chose the next ten words and recorded my replies, and then I did the same for him and for Long, apparently so rapidly that some of the words are almost indecipherable. For some reason, Long's responses to the last four words are in Lovecraft's handwriting; he may have taken over for me at the end.

TALMAN			LOVECRAFT	
ship	boat	smoke	pipe
time	infinite space	sail	ship
portico	port-cochere	white	color
speed	racing car	elevated	height
walk	flagstone walk	robe	gesture of flinging
tree	heraldic tree—Joyce Kilmer	shade	eclipse
fleece	lamb	cat	sinuous motion
scroll	artistic ornament	wheel	revolution
arch	Old Mexican masonry in jungle	glass	interposed —?— vague & indef.
darkness	the transverse passing of an area of blackness	cotton	white—fleecy--diffuse

	LONG
life	living & dead (cells?)
laughter	Rabelais
bubble	soap
shield	med sh
metal	strip
dial	sun dial
red	sq. of color
wave	sea on beach
palate	human palate
capital	letter H

Perhaps some psychologist who is also a fantasy fan may be able to deduce something new in Lovecraft's personality from his responses in this test. To me they mean little more than did two decades of acquaintance-ship—that aside from certain odd physical characteristics and some assumed and inadvertently acquired eccentricities, he was a normal, gifted person.

Letters to *Weird Tales*

Wilfred B. Talman writes from New York: "Permit me to congratulate you on what I think are· the big highest quality shorts you have run in any issue of WEIRD TALES I have seen. My vote goes to *The Thing in the Cellar*, by David H. Keller. *The Devil's Bride* is great, and would get my vote if it weren't for the splendid indirectness of the 'cellar' story. *The Devil's Bride* gathered considerable momentum in the current issue that it didn't have in the first installment."

May 1932

"Congratulations on the latest W. T.," writes W. B. Talman, from Spring Valley, New York. "I'm sure that no other pulp magazine can begin to compare with its typographical appearance and general effectiveness. Your new artist's technique blends very well with the tone of the magazine. and the last few covers are not nearly so stiff and gaudy as those that preceded them. I like Long's story, *The Brain-Eaters,* in the issue before last about as well as anything he's written. Quinn's serial, *The Devil's Bride,* was a knockout. Seem. to me your magazine *is* hitting an unusual standard these days when most publishers are raking the bottom of the 'ice-box' for material they have been holding in uncertainty—or so the rumors have it."

October 1932

W. B. Talman writes from Spring Valley, New York: "I too want to compliment you on the increasingly good appearance of WT. When every other magazine is taking on a cheaper appearance, it is refreshing to see one that looks continually better. The cover on the last was a knockout. Why not continue to make judicious use of black?—it seems to fit the general theme. *Dead Man's Belt* in a recent issue was one of the most remarkable stories I've read for a long time-not so remarkable from a weird standpoint, but from other points of view."

August 1933

Rheinhart Kleiner

To Mistress Katherine Ann Talman

Born, July 7th, 1936

Blithesome lady, nobly born,
Happy is your natal morn!
Sire and dame do both assure
Wit and beauty that endure!
Therefore, bring well endowed,
You must make your parents proud;
You, whose ancient line commands
Honor, since New Netherlands

You shall see a world awry,
Crowns descend, and kingdoms die;
Old and New, defending life,
Closing in relentless strife!
Still untroubled, find your way
Over ruin and decay;
With a spirit free from sham,
Drawn from old Fort Amsterdam!

Take a place among your peers,
Daughter of the pioneers!
Maiden, matron, mother—these
Be your gracious destinies!
May new heroes spring from your;
Presidents and poets, too!
Haply, yours a fame that waits,
Worthy these United States!

Genevieve Sully

Letters to *Weird Tales*

Genevieve K. Sully, of Berkeley, California, writes to the Eyrie: "Several months ago I was much impressed with the story, *The Ninth Skeleton,* by Clark Ashton Smith, which appeared in your magazine. Your last issue printed a poem by the same author, *Nyctalops,* which is certainly one of the most original and haunting things I have read for a long time. A magazine which prints such high-class writing is deserving of praise, for most of the magazine poetry today is pretty poor stuff."

"I would like express my admiration for *The Uncharted Isle* in the November issue," writes Genevieve K. Sully, of Auburn, California. "Clark Ashton Smith's work always has literary distinction and when that quality is coupled with superb weird imagination, one finds a story well worth reading. May I express a belated ward of praise for Frank Belknap Long's story in the September number, "The Man from Egypt"? Mr. Long's writing denotes an acquaintance with the finer things, and I for one should be glad to read more from one with his scholarly attitude of mind. Both of these writers whom I have mentioned have nothing of the commonplace about their work, and you are to be congratulated upon your good taste including their stories in your magazine." [January 1931]

Glossary of Frequently Mentioned Names

Barlow, R[obert] H[ayward] (1918–1951), author and collector. As a teenager he corresponded with HPL and acted as his host during two long visits in the summers of 1934 and 1935. In the 1930s he wrote several works of weird and fantasy fiction, some in collaboration with HPL. HPL appointed him his literary executor. He assisted August Derleth and Donald Wandrei in preparing the early HPL volumes for Arkham House. In the 1940s he went to Mexico and became a distinguished anthropologist. He died by suicide. HPL's letters to Barlow have been published as *O Fortunate Floridian* (Tampa, FL: University of Tampa Press, 2007).

Bates, Harry (1900–1981), editor of *Strange Tales* and *Astounding Stories.*

Blackwood, Algernon (1869–1951), prolific British author of weird and fantasy tales whose work HPL greatly admired when he read it in 1924.

Brobst, Harry K[ern] (1909–2010), late associate of HPL who moved to Providence in 1932 and saw HPL regularly thereafter. He notified some of HPL's correspondents of his final illness and death.

Bullen, John Ravenor (1886–1927), amateur poet from Canada. HPL edited his poems, *White Fire* (1927), for posthumous publication.

Cole, Edward H[arold] (1892–1966), longtime amateur associate of HPL, living in the Boston area; editor of the *Olympian.*

Cook, W. Paul (1881–1948), publisher of the *Monadnock Monthly*, the *Vagrant*, and other amateur journals; a longtime amateur journalist, printer, and lifelong friend of HPL. He first visited HPL in 1917, and it was he who urged HPL to resume writing fiction after a hiatus of nine years. In 1927 Cook published the *Recluse*, containing HPL's "Supernatural Horror in Literature."

de Castro, Adolphe (1859–1959), formerly Gustav Adolphe Danziger, author, co-translator with Ambrose Bierce of Richard Voss's The Monk and the Hangman's Daughter, and correspondent of HPL. HPL revised his stories "The Last Test" and "The Electric Executioner."

Derleth, August W[illiam] (1909–1971), author of weird tales and also a long series of regional and historical works set in his native Wisconsin. After HPL's death, he and Donald Wandrei founded the publishing firm of Arkham House to preserve HPL's work in book form. For the joint correspondence of HPL and Derleth, see *Essential Solitude.*

Dunsany, Lord (Edward John Moreton Drax Plunkett) (1878–1957), Irish writer of fantasy tales whose work notably influenced HPL after HPL read it in 1919.

Dwyer, Bernard Austin (1897–1943), weird fiction fan and would-be writer and artist, living in West Shokan, NY; correspondent of HPL. For HPL's letters to him, see *Letters to Maurice W. Moe and Others* (2018).

Eddy, C[lifford] M[artin] (1896–1967), pulp fiction writer living in the Providence area for whom HPL revised several stories in 1923–24 and who also worked with HPL on ghostwriting work for Harry Houdini in 1926.

Edkins, Ernest A[rthur] (1867–1946), amateur journalist associated with the "halcyon days" of the National Amateur Press Association (1885–95). He came in touch with HPL in 1932.

Gamwell, Annie E[meline] P[hillips] (1866–1941), HPL's younger (maternal) aunt, living with him at 66 College Street (1933–37). She had been married (1897–1936) to Edward F[rancis] Gamwell (1869–1936).

Kirk, George [Willard] (1898–1962), member of the Kalem Club. He published *Twenty-one Letters of Ambrose Bierce* (1922) and ran the Chelsea Bookshop in New York.

Kleiner, Rheinhart (1892–1949), amateur poet and longtime friend of HPL. He visited HPL in Providence in 1918, 1919, and 1920, and met him frequently during the heyday of the Kalem Club (1924–26). For HPL's letters to him, see *Letters to Rheinhart Kleiner* (2005).

Leeds, Arthur (1882–1952?), an associate of HPL in New York and member of the Kalem Club. He was the author (with J. Berg Esenwein) of *Writing the Photoplay* (Springfield, MA: The Home Correspondence School, 1913; rev. ed. 1919).

Long, Frank Belknap (1901–1994), fiction writer and poet and one of HPL's closest friends and correspondents. Late in life he wrote the memoir, *Howard Phillips Lovecraft: Dreamer on the Nightside* (1975).

Loveman, Samuel (1887–1976), poet and longtime friend of HPL and Donald Wandrei as well as of Ambrose Bierce, Hart Crane, George Sterling, and Clark Ashton Smith. He wrote *The Hermaphrodite* (1926) and other works.

McNeil, [Henry] Everett (1862–1929), author of historical and adventure novels for boys; member of the Kalem Club.

Moe, Maurice W[inter] (1882–1940), of Appleton and Milwaukee, WI. Amateur journalist, English teacher, and longtime friend and correspondent of HPL. His son **Robert Ellis Moe** (1912–1992) visited HPL in Providence several times. For HPL's letters to the Moes, see *Letters to Maurice W. Moe and Others* (2018).

Morton, James Ferdinand (1870–1941), amateur journalist, author of many tracts on race prejudice, free thought, and taxation, curator of the Paterson, NJ, museum, and longtime friend of HPL. For HPL's letters to him, see *Letters to James F. Morton* (2011).

Munn, H[arold] Warner (1903–1981), prolific contributor to the pulp magazines, living near W. Paul Cook in Athol, MA.

Orton, Vrest (1897–1986), a correspondent of Lovecraft living in New York. He designed the cover for W. Paul Cook's *Reclude,* wrote *Dreiserana, a Book about His Books* (1929), founded the Stephen Daye Press in Brattleboro, VT, and in 1946 started the Vermont Country Store.

Price, E[dgar] Hoffmann (1898–1988), prolific pulp writer of weird and adventure tales. HPL met him in New Orleans in 1932 and corresponded extensively with him thereafter.

Quinn, Seabury (1889–1969), prolific author of weird and detective tales to the pulps, notably a series of tales involving the psychic detective Jules de Grandin. editor of *Casket and Sunnyside* beginning in 1925.

Shea, J[oseph] Vernon (1912–1981), young cinema and weird fiction fan from Pittsburgh who began corresponding with HPL in 1931. For HPL's letters to him, see *Letters to J. Vernon Shea, Carl F. Strauch, and Lee McBride White* (2016).

Smith, Charles W. ("Tryout") (1852–1948), longtime amateur journalist, editor of the *Tryout,* and friend and correspondent of HPL.

Smith, Clark Ashton (1893–1961), prolific California poet and writer of fantasy tales. He received a "fan" letter from HPL in 1922 and corresponded with him until HPL's death. For the joint correspondence of HPL and Smith, see *Dawnward Spire, Lonely Hill* (2017).

Wandrei, Donald (1908–1987), poet and author of weird fiction, science fiction, and detective tales. He corresponded with HPL from 1926 to 1937, visited HPL in Providence in 1927 and 1932, and met HPL occasionally in New York during the 1930s. He helped HPL get "The Shadow out of Time" published in *Astounding Stories.* He met Helen Sully in 1933 on her trip to the east coast, and again in 1934 when he visited Clark Ashton Smith in Auburn, CA. After HPL's death he and AWD founded the publishing firm Arkham House to preserve HPL's work. For the joint correspondence of HPL and Wandrei, see *Mysteries of Time and Spirit* (2002).

Wandrei, Howard (1909–1956), younger brother of Donald Wandrei, premier weird artist and prolific author of weird fiction, science fiction, and detective stories; correspondent of HPL.

Whitehead, Henry S[t. Clair] (1882–1932), author of weird and adventure tales, many of them set in the Virgin Islands. HPL corresponded with him and visited him in Florida in 1931. HPL wrote a brief eulogy of Whitehead for *WT.*

Bibliography

A. Works by H. P. Lovecraft

Books

The Ancient Track: Complete Poetical Works. 2nd ed. Edited by S. T. Joshi. New York: Hippocampus Press, 2013.

The Annotated Supernatural Horror in Literature. 2nd ed. Edited by S. T. Joshi. New York: Hippocampus Press, 2012.

The Battle That Ended the Century (with R. H. Barlow). [De Land, FL: R. H. Barlow, 1934.] Text in *CF* 4.

Charleston. [New York: H. C. Koenig, 1936.] Text in *CE* 4.

Collected Essays. Edited by S. T. Joshi. New York: Hippocampus Press, 2004– 06. 5 vols. [*CE*]

Collected Fiction: A Variorum Edition. Edited by S. T. Joshi. New York: Hippocampus Press, 2015, 2017. 4 vols. [*CF*]

Dawnward Spire, Lonely Hill: The Letters of H. P. Lovecraft and Clark Ashton Smith, Edited by David E. Schultz and S. T. Joshi. New York: Hippocampus Press, 201.

Essential Solitude: The Letters of H. P. Lovecraft and August Derleth. Edited by David E. Schultz and S. T. Joshi. New York: Hippocampus Press, 2008. 2 vols.

Further Criticism of Poetry. Louisville, KY: George G. Fetter, 1932. [Titled by HPL "Notes on Verse Technique."]

Letters to Alfred Galpin. Edited by S. T. Joshi and David E. Schultz. New York: Hippocampus Press, 2003.

Letters to C. L. Moore and Others. Edited by David E. Schultz and S. T. Joshi. New York: Hippocampus Press, 2017.

Letters to Family and Family Friends. Edited by S. T. Joshi and David E. Schultz. New York: Hippocampus Press, 2019.

Letters to Maurice W. Moe and Others. Edited by David E. Schultz and S. T. Joshi. New York: Hippocampus Press, 2018.

Letters to Robert Bloch and Others. Edited by David E. Schultz and S. T. Joshi. New York: Hippocampus Press, 2015.

Letters with Donald and Howard Wandrei and to Emil Petaja. Edited by S. T. Joshi and David E. Schultz. New York: Hippocampus Press, 2019.

O Fortunate Floridian: H. P. Lovecraft's letters to R. H. Barlow. Edited by S. T. Joshi and David E. Schultz. Tampa, FL: University of Tampa Press, 2007.

The Shadow over Innsmouth. Everett, PA: Visionary Press, 1936. (*LL* 591)

Yr Obt Servt: Some Postcards of Howard Phillips Lovecraft Sent to Wilfred Blanch Talman. [Madison, WI]: Strange Co., 1988.

Fiction

At the Mountains of Madness. Astounding Stories 16, No. 6 (February 1936): 8–32; 17, No. 1 (March 1936): 125–55; 17, No. 2 (April 1936): 132–50. In *CF* 3.

"Beyond the Wall of Sleep." *Pine Cones* 1, No. 6 (October 1919): 2–10. *Fantasy Fan,* 2, No. 2 (October 1934): 25–32. In *CF* 1.

"The Call of Cthulhu." *WT* 11, No. 2 (February 1928): 159–78, 287. In T. Everett Harré, ed. *Beware After Dark! The World's Most Stupendous Tales of Mystery, Horror, Thrills and Terror.* New York: Macaulay, 1929. 223–59. In *CF* 2.

The Case of Charles Dexter Ward. In *CF* 2.

"The Cats of Ulthar." *Tryout* 6, No. 11 (November 1920): [6–11]. *WT* 7, No. 2 (February 1926): 252–54. In *CE* 1.

"Celephaïs." *Rainbow* No. 2 (May 1922): 10–12. *Marvel Tales* 1, No. 1 (May 1934): 26, 28–32. In *CF* 1.

"The Colour out of Space." *Amazing Stories* 2, No. 6 (September 1927): 557–67. In *CF* 2.

"Cool Air." *Tales of Magic and Mystery* 1, No. 4 (March 1928): 29–34. In *CF* 2.

"Dagon." *Vagrant* No. 11 (November 1919): 23–29. *WT* 2, No. 3 (October 1923): 23–25. In *CF* 1.

"The Doom That Came to Sarnath." *Scot* No. 44 (June 1920): 90–98. *Marvel Tales of Science and Fantasy* 1, No. 4 (March–April 1935): 157–63. In *CE* 1.

The Dream-Quest of Unknown Kadath. In *CF* 2.

"The Dreams in the Witch House." *WT* 22, No. 1 (July 1933): 86–111. In *CF* 3.

"The Dunwich Horror." *WT* 13, No. 4 (April 1929): 481–508. In *CF* 2.

"Facts concerning the Late Arthur Jermyn and His Family." *Wolverine* No. 9 (March 1921): 3–11; No. 10 (June 1921): 6–11. *WT* 3, No. 4 (April 1924): 15–18 (as "The White Ape"). *WT* 25, No. 5 (May 1935): 642–48 (as "Arthur Jermyn"). In *CF* 1.

"The Festival." *WT* 5, No. 1 (January 1925): 169–74. *WT* 22, No. 4 (October 1933): 519–20, 522–28. In *CF* 1.

"From Beyond." *FF* 1, No. 10 (June 1934): 147–51, 160. In *CF* 1.

"The Haunter of the Dark." *WT* 28, No. 5 (December 1936): 538–53. In *CF* 3.

"He." *WT* 8, No. 3 (September 1926): 373–80. In *CF* 1.

"Herbert West—Reanimator" (as "Grewsome Tales"). *Home Brew* 1, No. 1 (February 1922): 84–88 ("From the Dark"); 1, No. 2 (March 1922): 45–50 ("The Plague Demon"); 1, No. 3 (April 1922): 21–26 ("Six Shots by Moonlight"); 1, No. 4 (May 1922): 53–58 ("The Scream of the Dead"); 1, No. 5 (June 1922): 45–50 ("The Horror from the Shadows,"); 1, No. 6 (July 1922): 57–62 ("The Tomb-Legions"). In *CF* 1.

"The Horror at Red Hook." *WT* 9, No. 1 (January 1927): 59–73. In Christine Campbell Thomson, ed. *You'll Need a Night Light.* London: Selwyn & Blount, 1927. 228–54. In Herbert Asbury, ed. *Not at Night!* New York: Macy-Masius (The Vanguard Press), 1928. 27–52. In *CF* 1.

"The Hound." *WT* 3, No. 2 (February 1924): 50–52, 78. *WT* 14, No. 3 (September 1929): 421–25, 432. In *CF* 1.

"Hypnos." *National Amateur* 45, No. 5 (May 1923): 1–3. *WT* 4, No. 2 (May–June–July 1924): 33–35. In *CF* 1.

"In the Vault." *Tryout* 10, No. 6 (November 1925): [3–17]. *WT* 19, No. 4 (April 1932): 459–65. In *CF* 1.

"The Lurking Fear." *Home Brew* 2, No. 6 (January 1923): 4–10; 3, No. 1 (February 1923): 18–23; 3, No. 2 (March 1923): 31–37, 44, 48; 3, No. 3 (April 1923): 35–42. *WT* 11, No. 6 (June 1928): 791–804. In *CF* 1.

"The Moon-Bog." *WT* 7, No. 6 (June 1926): 805–10. In *CF* 1.

"The Music of Erich Zann." *National Amateur* 44, No. 4 (March 1922): 38–40. *WT* 5, No. 5 (May 1925): 219–34. In Dashiell Hammett, ed. *Creeps by Night: Chills and Thrills*. New York: John Day Co., 1931. 347–63. In Dashiell Hammett, ed. *Modern Tales of Horror*. London: Victor Gollancz, 1932. 301–17. *Evening Standard* (London) (24 October 1932): 20–21. *WT* 24, No. 5 (November 1934): 644–48, 655–56. In *CF* 1.

"The Nameless City." *Wolverine* No. 11 (November 1921): 3–15. *Fanciful Tales* 1, No. 1 (Fall 1936): 5–18. In *CF* 1.

"The Other Gods." *Fantasy Fan* 1, No. 3 (November 1933): 35–38. *WT* 32, No. 4 (October 1938): 489–92. In *CF* 1.

"The Outsider." *WT* 7, No. 4 (April 1926): 449–53. *WT* 17, No. 4 (June–July 1931): 566–71. In *CE* 1.

"Pickman's Model." *WT* 10, No. 4 (October 1927): 505–14. In Christine Campbell Thomson, ed. *By Daylight Only*. London: Selwyn & Blount, 1929. 37–52. *WT* 28, No. 4 (November 1936): 495–505. In Christine Campbell Thomson, ed. *The "Not at Night" Omnibus*. London: Selwyn & Blount, [1937]. 279–307. In *CF* 2.

"The Picture in the House." *National Amateur* 41, No. 6 (July 1919 [*sic*]): 246–49. *WT* 3, No. 1 (January 1924): 40–42. *WT* 29, No. 3 (March 1937): 370–73. In *CF* 1.

"Polaris." *Philosopher* 1, No. 1 (December 1920): 3–5. *National Amateur* 48, No. 5 (May 1926): 48–49. *FF* 1, No. 6 (February 1934): 83–85. In *CF* 1.

"The Quest of Iranon." *Galleon* 1, No. 5 (July–August 1935): 12–20. In *CF* 1.

"The Rats in the Walls." *WT* 3, No. 3 (March 1924): 25–31. *WT* 15, No. 6 (June 1930): 841–53. In Christine Campbell Thomson, ed. *Switch On the Light*. London: Selwyn & Blount, 1931. 141–65. In *CF* 1.

"The Shadow out of Time." *Astounding Stories* 17, No. 4 (June 1936): 110–54. In *CF* 3.

"The Shadow over Innsmouth." In *CF* 3.

"The Shunned House." In *CF* 1.

"The Silver Key." *WT* 13, No. 1 (January 1929): 41–49, 144. In *CF* 2.

"The Statement of Randolph Carter." *Vagrant* No. 13 (May 1920): 41–48. *WT* 5, No. 2 (February 1925): 149–53. In *CF* 1.

"Strange High House in the Mist." *WT* 18, No. 3 (October 1931): 394–400. In *CE* 1.

"The Temple." *WT* 6, No. 3 (September 1925): 329–36, 429–31. *WT* 27, No. 2 (February 1936): 239–44, 246–49. In *CF* 1.

"The Terrible Old Man." *Tryout* 7, No. 4 (July 1921): [10–14]. *WT* 8, No. 2 (August 1926): 191–92. In *CE* 1.

"The Tomb." *Vagrant* No. 14 (March 1922): 50–64. *WT* 7, No. 1 (January 1926): 117–23. In *CF* 1.

"The Tree." *Tryout* 7, No. 7 (October 1921): [3–10]. In *CF* 1.

"The Unnamable." *WT* 6, No. 1 (July 1925): 78–82. In *CF* 1.

"The Whisperer in Darkness." *WT* 18, No. 1 (August 1931): 32–73. In *CF* 3.

"The White Ship." *United Amateur* 19, No. 2 (November 1919): 30–33. *WT* 9, No. 3 (March 1927): 386–89. In *CF* 1.

Poetry [all poems in *The Ancient Track*]

"The East India Brick Row." *Providence Journal* 102, No. 7 (8 January 1930): 13.

"In a Sequester'd Providence Churchyard Where Once Poe Walk'd." *Science-Fantasy Correspondent* 1, No. 3 (March–April 1937): 16–17. *WT* 31, No. 5 (May 1938): 578 (as "Where Poe Once Walked: An Acrostic Sonnet"). In Maurice W. Moe, ed. *Four Acrostic Sonnets on Poe* (1936).

"Psychopompos: A Tale in Rhyme." *Vagrant* No. 10 (October 1919): 13–23. *WT* 30, No. 3 (September 1937): 341–48.

"To Clark Ashton Smith, Esq., upon His Fantastic Tales, Verses, Pictures, and Sculptures." *WT* 31, No. 4 (April 1938): 392 (as "To Clark Ashton Smith").

Revisions and Collaborations

de Castro, Adolphe. "The Electric Executioner." *WT* 16, No. 2 (August 1930): 223–36.

———. "The Last Test." *WT* 12, No. 5 (November 1928): 625–56.

Nonfiction

"An Account of *Charleston,* in His Maj[ty's] Province of *South-Carolina.*" In *CE* 4.

"An Account of a Trip to the Antient Fairbanks House, in Dedham, and to the Red Horse Tavern in Sudbury, in the Province of the Massachusetts-Bay." In *CE* 4.

"Asks Preservation of Old Buildings." *Providence Sunday Journal* 42, No. 15 (10 October 1926): Sec. A, p. 5.

"[Biographical Notice]." In Edward J. O'Brien, ed. *The Best Short Stories of 1928 and the Yearbook of the American Short Story.* New York: Dodd, Mead, 1928. 324. (*LL* 715) In *CE* 5.

A Description of the Town of Quebeck, in New-France. In *CE* 4.

"In Memoriam: Henry St. Clair Whitehead." *WT* 21, No. 3 (March 1933): 391 (unsigned). In *CE* 5.

"In Memoriam: Robert Ervin Howard." *Fantasy Magazine* No. 38 (September 1936): 29–31. In *CE* 5.

"Robert Ervin Howard: 1906–1936." *Phantagraph* 4, No. 5 (August 1936), 4–5. In *CE* 5.

"A Layman Looks at the Government." In *CE* 5.

"The Poetry of John Ravenor Bullen." *United Amateur* 25, 1 (September 1925): 1–3, 6. In *CE* 2.

"The Pool: Recommendations for Revision—Synopsis." *Crypt of Cthulhu* No. 49 (Lammas 1987): 31–40.

"Science and Charlatanry." In *CE* 3.

"Some Dutch Footprints in New England." 9, No. 1 (18 October 1933): 2, 4. In *CE* 4.

"[Some Backgrounds of Fairyland.]" In *Marginalia*. Sauk City, WI: Arkham House, 1944. 174–83. In *CE* 3.

"Supernatural Horror in Literature." *Recluse* No. 1 (1927): 23–59. Rev. ed. in *Fantasy Fan* (October 1933–February 1935). In *CE* 2.

"The Unknown City in the Ocean." *Perspective Review* (Winter 1934, Fourth Anniversary Number): 7–8. In *CE* 4.

B. Works by Wilfred B. Talman

Burials in an Old Grave Yard Opposite the Fair Ground at Orangeburg, Rockland County, N.Y. (with Louis L. Blauvelt). [Newark, NJ, 1927.] Holland Society of New York church record collection, v. 050.

Cloisonné and Other Verses. [Providence, RI]: Bear Press, Brown University, 1925. *Contains:* Cloisonné; Home-Coming; The Lane of Loveliness; Barque of Dreams; Gypsy Trails; Fantasy; At Sunset; Mignonette; Songs; Jeanette; Height. [C]

The Eternal Spring: An Anniversary History of the American Association of Industrial Editors, 1938–1958. n.p.: [American Association of Industrial Editors], 1958.

How Things Began—in Rockland County and Places Nearby: People, Customs, Language, and Manners of Living During the Early Times in a Border County of New York State. New City, NY: Historical Society of Rockland County, 1977.

Lovecraft Was Psychoanalyzed for Fun. [United States]: [publisher not identified], [not after 1980].

The Normal Lovecraft (with others). Saddle River, NJ: Gerry de la Ree, 1973.

Tappantown Historical Society. Book Committee. Tappan. *300 Years: 1686–1986* (with Firth Haring Fabend). Tappan, NY: The Society, 1989.

"Adventure Land." *Unitred Amateur* 22, No. 4 (March 1923): 63.

"At Sunset." *United Official Quarterly* (January 1923): 6. In *C*.

"Ballade of Creatures Abroad by Night." *WT* 22, No. 3 (September 1933): 381.

"Barque of Dreams." In *C. National Amateur* 50, No. 3 (January 1928): 3.

"The Charnel Den." Nonextant.

"Chetwode Arms." Nonextant.

"Cloisonné. In *C.*

"The Cloven Hoof of Simeon Slater." Nonextant.

"The Curse of Alabad and Ghinu and Aratza." *WT* 11, No. 2 (February 1928): 188–92.

"The Curse Wheel." Nonextant.

"Death." *WT* 19, No. 3 (March 1932): 372.

"Death Customs Among the Colonial Dutch. Unpublished TM, JHL.

"Doom around the Corner." *WT* 18, No. 4 (November 1931): 542–45. *Crypt of Cthulhu* No. 11 (Candlemas 1983): 41–44.

"Dragon-Fly." Nonextant.

"Dream Ships." *Oracle* 3, No. 3 (September 1922): 16.

"Fantasy." *United Amateur* 25, No. 2 (May 1926): 8. In *C.*

"Fragment." *National Amateur* 50, No. 3 (January 1928): 6.

"Ghost Proofing the House." Nonextant.

"Gypsy Trails." *United Official Quarterly* (January 1923): 4. In *C.*

"H.P.L. Addressing The Kalem Club." *Ec'h-Pi-El Speaks: An Autobiographical Sketch.* Saddle River, NJ: Gerry de la Ree, 1972: inside back cover; reprinted on front cover of Kenneth W. Faig, Jr. *The Unknown Lovecraft.* New York: Hippocampus Press, 2009.

"Haunted Island." *WT* 11, No. 1 (January 1928): 8.

"The Heads at Gyrwy." Nonextant.

"Height." *Casements* 3, No. 1 (January 1925): 8. In *C.*

"Home-coming." *Leslie's Weekly* 133, No. 3448 (3 December 1921): 781. *New Member: A Magazine of Credentials* 1, No. 1 (May 1922): 10. In *C.*

"A Horror in Profile." *Marvel Tales* 1, No. 2 (July–August 1934): 51–60.

"Izrim." *United Amateur* 25, No. 2 (May 1926): 3.

"Jeanette." In *C.*

"The Lane of Loveliness." In *C.*

"Lovecraft Psychoanalyzed." *Fantasy Commentator* 7, No. 1, (Fall 1990): 65–67; T.Ms. at JHL as "Lovecraft Was Psychoanalyzed for Fun."

"Lovecraft Revisited." *Fresco* 10, No. 2 (Winter–Spring 1960): 48–50.

"Mignonette." *United Official Quarterly* (January 1923): 4. In *C.*

"The Normal Lovecraft: A Memoir to Restore Balance to the Shade of a Man of Delightful Character." In *The Normal Lovecraft* (q.v.) 5–[17]. In S. T. Joshi and David E. Schultz, ed. *Ave atque Vale: Reminiscences of H. P. Lovecraft.* West Warwick, RI: Necronomicon Press, 2018. 109–18.

"Orangetown's Name." *Song of the Mountains* 20, No. 2 (April–June 1986): 3–4.

"Songs." In *C.*

"Southern Seas." *Oracle* 4, No. 1 (March 1923): 4.

"The Story Teller: A Tale of Christmas." *Texaco Star* 17, No. 11 (December 1930): 6–8.

"Texaco at Home: V—Providence." *Texaco Star* 18, No. 5 (May 1931): 23–26.

"'There She Blows!'" *Texaco Star* 18, No. 1 (January 1931): 13–15, 32.

"Two Black Bottles" (with H. P. Lovecraft). *WT* 10, No. 2 (August 1927): 251–58.

"The Wyvern of St. Morteuil." Nonextant.

In *Cloisonné and Other Verses*, Talman acknowledges the previous appearance of one or more unspecified poems in *The Brown Jug*, the college humor magazine published at Brown University in Providence, Rhode Island. Those appearances have not yet been located.

Letter. *WT* 19, No. 5 (May 1932): 582.

Letter. *WT* 20, No. 4 (October 1932): 572.

Letter. *WT* 22, No. 2 (August 1933): 262.

C. Works by Helen V. Sully

"Some Memories of H.P.L." In S. T. Joshi and David E. Schultz, ed. *Ave atque Vale: Reminiscences of H. P. Lovecraft*. West Warwick, RI: Necronomicon Press, 2018. 364–66.

D. Works by Genevieve K. Sully

Letter. In Donald Sidney-Fryer. *Emperor of Dreams: A Clark Ashton Smith Bibliography*. West Kingston, RI: Donald M. Grant, 1978. 190.

Letter. *WT* 15, No. 1 (January 1930): 8.

Letter. *WT* 17, No. 1 (January 1931): 6.

E. Works by Others

Allen, Hervey (1889–1949). *Anthony Adverse*. New York: Farrar & Rinehart, 1933.

————. *Israfel: The Life and Times of Edgar Allan Poe*. <1926> New York: George H. Doran Co., 1927. 2 vols. (*LL* 27)

Andrews, Ethan Allan *A Copious and Critical Latin-English Lexicon, Founded on the Larger Latin-German Lexicon of Dr. W. Freund*. New York: Harper & Brothers, 1854. (*LL* 39)

Appleton, John Howard (1844–1930). *The Young Chemist: A Book of Laboratory Work for Beginners*. Providence, RI: J. A. & R. A. Reid, 1876. (*LL* 47)

Austin, John Osborne (1849–1918). *The Genealogical Dictionary of Rhode Island: Comprising Three Generations of Settlers Who Came Before 1690: With Many Families Carried to the Fourth Generation*. Albany, NY: J. Munsell's Sons, 1887.

Balderston, John L. (1889–1954) *Berkeley Square: A Play in Three Acts*. London: Samuel French, 1928.

Balzac, Honoré de (1799–1850). *Histoire intellectuelle de Louis Lambert*. Paris: C. Gosselin, 1832. Tr. Katherine Prescott Wormeley as *Louis Lambert*. Boston: Roberts Brothers, 1889.

———. *Le Peau de chagrin*. Paris: C. Gosselin, 1831 (2 vols.). Tr. George Frederic Parsons as *The Magic Skin*. Boston: Roberts Brothers, 1888. Tr. Ellen Marriage as *The Wild Ass's Skin*. London & New York: Dent/Dutton (Everyman's Library), 1906.

———. *Séraphita*. Paris: Werdet, 1836. Tr. Katherine Prescott Wormeley as *Seraphita*. Boston: Roberts Brothers, 1889. Freeport, NY: Books for Libraries Press, 1970.

Bartlett, John Russell (1805–1886). *Dictionary of Americanisms: A Glossary of Words and Phrases Usually Regarded as Peculiar to the United States*. 4th ed. Boston: Little, Brown, 1877. (*LL* 77)

Beach, Matthew. "Lovecraft's Consolation." *Lovecraft Annual* No. 13 (2019): 71–90.

Beckford, William (1759–1844). *The Episodes of Vathek* <1912> Tr. Sir Frank T. Marzials. Boston: Small, Maynard, [1922?] or [1924?]. (*LL* 83)

———. *The History of the Caliph Vathek*. <1786> Printed Verbatim from the First Edition, with the Original Prefaces and Notes by [Samuel] Henley. New York: W. L. Allinson, [1868?] or [188-?]. (*LL* 84)

Benson, E. F. (1867–1940). "The Man Who Went Too Far." In E. F. Benson and Brander Matthews. *Two Masterly Ghost Stories*. Girard, KS: Haldeman-Julius, n.d. (*LL* 91)

———. *Visible and Invisible*. New York, George H. Doran, 1923 or 1924. (*LL* 90) [Contains "*Negotium Perambulans* . . ."]

Bierce, Ambrose (1842–1914?). *Can Such Things Be?* <1893> New York: Boni & Liveright (Modern Library), 1918. (*LL* 98)

———. *In the Midst of Life: Tales of Soldiers and Civilians*. <1891> Introduction by George Sterling. New York: Modern Library, [1927]. (*LL* 99)

———. *Write It Right: A Little Blacklist of Literary Faults*. New York & Washington, DC: Neale Publishing Co., 1909.

———, and Gustav Adolphe Danziger [de Castro] (1859–1959). *The Monk and the Hangman's Daughter; Fantastic Fables; [etc.]*. New York: A. & C. Boni, 1925. (*LL* 93)

Birch, A. G., et al. *The Moon Terror*. And stories by Anthony M. Rud, Vincent Starrett, and Farnsworth Wright. Indianapolis: Popular Fiction Publishing Co., 1927. (*LL* 104)

Biss, Gerald (1876–1922). *The Door of the Unreal*. New York: G. P. Putnam's Sons, 1920.

Blackwood, Algernon (1869–1951). *Day and Night Stories*. London: Cassell, 1917. New York: E. P. Dutton, 1917.

————. *Incredible Adventures*. London: Macmillan, 1914. New York: Macmillan, 1914. [Contains "A Descent into Egypt."]

————. *John Silence—Physician Extraordinary*. London: Eveleigh Nash, 1908. New York: Vaughan & Gomme, 1914. (*LL* 107) New York, E. P. Dutton, [1920]. (*LL* 108)

————. *The Listener and Other Stories*. London: Eveleigh Nash, 1907. New York: Vaughan & Gomme, 1914. New York: Alfred A. Knopf, 1917.

————. *The Lost Valley and Other Stories*. London: Eveleigh Nagh, 1910. (*LL* 110) [Contains "The Wendigo."]

————. *Ten Minute Stories*. London: John Murray, 1914. New York: E. P. Dutton, 1914.

————, with Wilfred Wilson. *The Wolves of God and Other Fey Stories*. London: Cassell, 1921. New York: E. P. Dutton, 1921.

Brontë, Emily (1818–1848). *Wuthering Heights*. London: Newby, 1847. (*LL* 666)

Brown, Charles Brockden (1771–1810). *Wieland; or, The Transformation*. New York: T. & J. Swords for H. Caritat, 1798.

Buchan, John (1875–1940). *The Runagates Club*. Boston: Houghton Mifflin, 1928. (*LL* 141) [Contains "Skule Skerry."]

————. *Witch Wood*. London: Hodder & Stoughton, 1927.

Bullen, John Ravenor (1886–1927). *White Fire*. Athol, MA: Recluse Press, 1927. (*LL* 143)

Bulwer-Lytton, Edward (1803–1873). *A Strange Story; The Haunted House [sic]; Zanoni*. <1862; 1859; 1842> Boston: Desmond Publishing Co., [18—?]. (*LL* 145). [The second story is "The Haunted and the Haunters; or, The House and the Brain."]

Bush, David Van (1882–1959). *Peace Poems and Sausages*. n.p.: David V. Bush, 1915.

Carrel, Frank (1870–1940). *Guide to the City of Quebec: Descriptive and Illustrated with Map*. Quebec: F. Carrel, 1897.

Chambers's Encyclopædia: A Dictionary of Universal Knowledge. London: W. & R. Chambers, 1860–68. 10 vols. Philadelphia: J. B. Lippincott Co., 1860–69. 10 vols. [Rev. eds. up to 1935.] (*LL* 185)

Chapin, Howard Millar (1887–1940). *Colonial Heraldry: A Roll of the Arms Used in the English Colony of Rhode Island in New England, 1636–1776*. Providence, RI: E. A. Johnson Co., 1929.

Chamisso, Adelbert von (1781–1838), *Peter Schlemihls wundersame Geschichte* (1814). Tr. John Bowring as *The Shadowless Man*. London: Chatto & Windus, 1910.

Cline, Leonard (1893–1929). *The Dark Chamber*. New York: Viking Press, 1927. (*LL* 198)

Cooley, John C. (1819–1903). *Rathbone Genealogy*. Syracuse: Press of the Courier Job Print, 1898.

Crawford, F. Marion (1854–1909). "The Upper Berth." <1886> In Crawford's *Wandering Ghosts*. New York: Macmillan, 1911. London: T. Fisher

Unwin, 1911 (as *Uncanny Tales*).

Crowley, Aleister (1875–1947). *The Diary of a Drug Fiend*. London: Collins, [1922].

Damon, S. Foster (1893-1971). *Thomas Holley Chivers, Friend of Poe, with Selections from His Poems: A Strange Chapter in American Literary History*. New York: Harper & Brothers, 1930.

De Castro, Adolphe (1859–1959). *Portrait of Ambrose Bierce*. New York: Century Co., 1929.

de la Mare, Colin (1906–1983), ed. *They Walk Again: A Collection of Ghost Stories*. New York: E. P. Dutton, 1931. [Contains "Green Tea" by J. Sheridan Le Fanu.]

de la Mare, Walter (1873–1956). *The Connoisseur and Other Stories*. London: Collins, 1926. New York: Alfred A. Knopf, 1926. (*LL* 243)

———. *The Return*. London: Edward Arnold, 1910. Rev. ed. London: Collins, 1922. New York: Alfred A. Knopf, 1922.

———. *The Riddle and Other Stories*. <1923> New York: Alfred A. Knopf, 1930. (*LL* 244)

Delabarre, Edmund Burke (1863–1945). *Dighton Rock: A Study of the Written Rocks of New England*. New York: Walter Neale, 1928.

Derham, William (1637–1735). *Astro-Theology; or, A Demonstration of the Being and Attributes of God, from a Survey of the Heavens*. <1715> 10th ed. London: Robinson & Roberts, 1767. (*LL* 248)

Derleth, August (1909–1971). *Evening in Spring*. New York: Charles Scribner's Sons, 1941.

———. *Place of Hawks*. New York: Loring & Mussey, 1935. (*LL* 250)

———. *Sign of Fear: A Judge Peck Mystery*. New York: Loring & Mussey, 1935. (*LL* 251)

Downing, Andrew Jackson (1815–1852). *Landscape Gardening and Rural Architecture*. New York: G. P. Putnam & Co., 1849. (*LL* 274)

Doyle, Arthur Conan (1859–1930). *The Captain of the Polestar and Other Tales*. London: New York: Longmans, Green, 1890.

———. "The Mystery of Sasassa Valley." *Chambers's Edinburgh Journal* (6 September 1879 [unsigned]. In *The Mystery of Sasassa Valley; A Night among the Nihilists; Our Derby Sweetstakes; Bones*. New York: George Munro's Sons, [1900?]. (*LL* 276)

———. *Round the Fire Stories*. London: Smith, Elder, 1907.

Drake, H. B. (1894–1963). *The Shadowy Thing*. <1925> New York: Macy-Masius, 1928. New York: Hippocampus Press, 2010.

Dunsany, Lord (Edward John Moreton Drax Plunkett, 18th baron, 1878–1957). *The Book of Wonder* <1912> [and *Time and the Gods* <1906>]. New York: Boni & Liveright (Modern Library), [1918]. (*LL* 288)

———. *The Curse of the Wise Woman*. London: William Heinemann, 1933. New York: Longmans, Green, 1933.

————. *A Dreamer's Tales and Other Stories* [*A Dreamer's Tales* <1910> and *The Sword of Welleran* <1908>]. New York: Boni & Liveright (Modern Library), [1917], [1919], or [1921]. (*LL* 290)

————. *Five Plays.* <1914> Boston: Little, Brown, 1923. (*LL* 276)

————. *Mr. Jorkens Remembers Africa.* London: William Heinemann, 1934. New York: Longmans, Green, 1934 (as *Jorkens Remembers Africa*).

————. *Plays of Gods and Men.* Boston: John W. Luce, [1917]. (*LL* 296)

Easton, Emily. *Roger Williams, Prophet and Pioneer.* Boston: Houghton Mifflin, 1930.

Eberlein, Harold Donaldson (1875–1964). *The Architecture of Colonial America.* Boston: Little, Brown, 1915.

————. *The Manors and Historic Homes of the Hudson Valley.* Philadelphia: J. B. Lippincott Co., 1924.

The Encyclopaedia Britannica: A Dictionary of Arts, Sciences, and General Literature . . . With . . . Revisions and Additions by W. H. De Puy. 9th Ed. Chicago: Werner Co., 1896. 24 vols. (*LL* 318)

Erckmann-Chatrian [Émile Erckmann (1822–1899) and Alexandre Chatrian (1826–1890)]. "The Man-Wolf"; "The Invisible Eye"; "The Waters of Death." In Julian Hawthorne, ed., *The Lock and Key Library* (q.v.).

Ernst, James Emanuel (1893–1948). *Roger Williams, New England Firebrand.* New York: Macmillan, 1932.

Faig, Kenneth W., Jr. "Lovecraft's Travelogues of Foster, Rhode Island." *Lovecraft Annual* No. 7 (2013): 75–135.

————. "Quae Amamus Tuemur: Ancestors in Lovecraft's Life and Fiction." In *The Unknown Lovecraft.* New York: Hippocampus Press, 2009. 14–49.

————, and Chris J. Docherty *Devonshire Ancestry of Howard Phillips Lovecraft.* Glenview, ILL Moshassuck Press, 2003.

Field, Edward (1858–1928), ed. *State of Rhode Island and Providence Plantations at the End of the Century.* Boston: Mason Publishing Co., 1902. 3 vols. (*LL* 332)

Field, John (1520/1530–1587). *Ephemeris anni. 1557. Currentis iuxta Copernici et Reinhaldi canones fideliter per Ioannem Feild Anglum, supputata ac examinata ad meredianum Londinensem qui occidentalior esse indicatur a Reinhaldo quam sit Regij Montis, per horam. 1. Scr. 50. Adiecta est etiam breuis quædam epistola Ioannis Dee, qua vulgares istos ephemeridum fictores merito reprehendit. Tabella deni q[ue], pro coelesti themate erigendo iuxta modum vulgariter rationalem dictum, per eundem Ioannem Feild confecta, Londinensis poli altitundini inseruiens exactissime.* Londini: [In ædibus Thomæ Marshe], M.D.LVI. [1556] Septembris. XII.

Flaubert, Gustave (1821–1880). *The Temptation of St. Anthony.* Tr. Lafcadio Hearn <1910>. New York: Boni & Liveright (Modern Library), 1920. (*LL* 322) [Translation of *La Tentation de Saint Antoine* (1874).]

Forbes, Allan (1874–1955), and Paul F. Cadman (1889–1946). *France and New England.* Boston: State Street Trust Co., 1925–29. 3 vols.

Forster, E. M. (1879–1970). *The Celestial Omnibus and Other Stories.* New York: Alfred A. Knopf, 1923.

Freeman, Mary E. Wilkins (1852–1930). *The Wind in the Rose-bush and Other Stories of the Supernatural.* New York: Doubleday, Page, 1903. (*LL* 354)

French, Joseph Lewis (1858–1936), ed. *Masterpieces of Mystery.* Garden City, NY: Doubleday, Page & Co., 1920. 4 vols. (*LL* 356)

Gautier, Théophile (1811–1872). *Clarimonde.* New York: Brentano's, 1899. *or Clarimonde and Other Stories.* London: T. C. & E. C. Jack, 1908. (*LL* 365) [Tr. by Lafcadio Hearn of "Clarimonde" (1836).]

———. "La Morte amoureuse" ("Clarimonde"). In Gautier's *Nouvelles.* Paris: Charpentier, 1845. In Gautier's *One of Cleopatra's Nights and Other Fantastic Romances.* Tr. Lafcadio Hearn. New York: Worthington, 1882. (*LL* 367)

———. "Le Pied de momie." Tr. F. C. de Sumichrast as "The Foot of the Mummy." In Joseph Lewis French, ed., *Masterpieces of Mystery* (q.v.), Vol. 3.

———, and Mérimée, Prosper (1803–1870). *Tales Before Supper.* Told in English by Myndart Verelst [i.e., Edgar Saltus] and Delayed with a Poem by Edgar Saltus. New York: Brentano's, 1887. (*LL* 368) [Contains Gautier's "Avatar" and Mérimée's "The Venus of Ille."]

Gilman, Charlotte Perkins (1860–1935). "The Yellow Wall Paper." *New England Magazine* (January 1892). In William Dean Howells, ed. *The Great Modern American Stories.* New York: Boni & Liveright, 1920.

Gorman, Herbert (1893–1954). *The Place Called Dagon.* New York: George H. Doran, 1927. New York: Hippocampus Press, 2003.

Hawthorne, Julian (1846–1934), ed. *The Lock and Key Library: Classic Mystery and Detective Stories.* New York: Review of Reviews Co., 1909. 10 vols.

Hawthorne, Nathaniel (1804–1864). *Dr. Grimshaw's Secret: A Romance.* Boston: Houghton, Mifflin, 1882.

———. *The House of the Seven Gables, and The Snow-Image and Other Twice-Told Tales.* <1851; 1852> Boston: Houghton Mifflin, 1886. (*LL* 430) [Contains "Ethan Brand."]

———. *Twice-Told Tales.* <1837/1842> Edited for School Use by Robert Herrick and Robert Walter Bruère. Chicago: Scott, Foresman, 1903 or [1919]. (*LL* 436) [Contains "The Ambitious Guest" and "The Minister's Black Veil."]

Hearn, Lafcadio (1850–1904). *Fantastics and Other Fancies.* Ed. Charles Woodward Hutson. Boston: Houghton Mifflin, 1914.

———. *Kwaidan: Stories and Studies of Strange Things.* <1904> Boston: Houghton Mifflin, 1930. (*LL* 440)

Hoffmann, E. T. A. (1776–1822). *The Serapion Brethren.* Tr. Alex. Ewing. London: G. Bell & Sons, 1892–1908. 2 vols.

Holmes, Oliver Wendell (1809–1894). *Elsie Venner: A Romance of Destiny.* Boston: Ticknor & Fields, 1861.

Howey, M. Oldfield. *The Cat in the Mysteries of Religion and Magic.* London: Rider, 1920, 1930.

Hylton, J. Dunbar (1837–1893). *The Bride of Gettysburg: An Episode of 1863.* Palmyra, NJ: [n.p.], 1878.

Irving, Washington (1783–1859). *The Sketch-Book of Geoffrey Crayon, Gent.* <1819–20> Hudson Edition. New York: G. P. Putnam's Sons, 1880–88. (*LL* 494)

———. *Salmagundi; or, The Whim-whams and Opinions of Launcelot Langstaff, Esq., and Others, etc.* [By Washington Irving, assisted by J. K. Paulding and William Irving.] Nos. 1–20 (24 January 1807–25 January 1808).

———. *Tales of a Traveler* [*sic*]. <1824> New York: American Book Co., 1894. (*LL* 495)

James, Henry (1843–1916). *The Two Magics: The Turn of the Screw; Covering End.* <1898> New York: Macmillan, 1911. (*LL* 498)

James, M. R. (1862–1936). *Ghost-Stories of an Antiquary.* London: Edward Arnold, 1904. (*LL* 499)

———. *More Ghost Stories of an Antiquary.* London: Edward Arnold, 1911. (*LL* 500)

———. *A Thin Ghost and Others.* <1919> London: Edward Arnold, 1925. (*LL* 501)

———. *A Warning to the Curious.* London: Edward Arnold, 1925. (*LL* 502)

Jenks, William (1778–1866), ed. *The Comprehensive Commentary on the Holy Bible.* Brattleboro, VT: Fessenden, 1835–39. 5 vols. (*LL* 505)

Joshi, S. T., and David E. Schultz, ed. *Ave atque Vale: Reminiscences of H. P. Lovecraft.* West Warwick, RI: Necronomicon Press, 2018.

Joshi, S. T., with David E. Schultz. *Lovecraft's Library: A Catalogue.* 4th ed. New York: Hippocampus Press, 2017.

Kipling, Rudyard (1865–1936). "'The Finest Story in the World.'" *Contemporary Review* Vol. 60 (July 1891). In *Many Inventions.* London: Macmillan, 1893.

———. *The Mark of the Beast and The Head of the District.* Girard, KS: Haldeman-Julius Co., [19—]. (*LL* 536)

———. *The Phantom 'Rickshaw and Other Tales.* <1888> (*LL* 537)

———. "The Recrudescence of Imray." In *The Recrudescence of Imray [and Other Stories].* Philadelphia: Henry Altemus [190-?].

Khun de Prorok, Byron (1896–1954). *Digging for Lost African Gods: The Record of Five Years Archaeological Excavation in North Africa.* With notes and translations by Edgar Fletcher Allen. New York: London: G. P. Putnam's Sons, 1926.

Kleiner, Rheinhardt (1892–1949). *To Mistress Katherine Anna Talman, born July 7th, 1936.* [n.p., 1936.]

Krutch, Joseph Wood (1893–1970). *The Modern Temper: A Study and a Confession.* New York: Harcourt, Brace, 1929.

Kurath, Hans (1891–1992), ed. *Linguistic Atlas of New England.* Providence, RI:

Brown University, 1939–43. 3 vols. in 6.

La Motte-Fouqué, Friedrich Heinrich Karl, baron de (1777–1843). *Undine and Sintram.* <1811; 1815> Boston: Estes & Lauriat, [18—]. (*LL* 549)

Lewis, Matthew Gregory (1775–1818). *The Monk: A Romance.* <1796> London: Brentano's, [1924]. (*LL* 567)

Liddell, Henry George (1811–1898), and Robert Scott (1811–1887). *A Greek-English Lexicon.* <1843> (*LL* 568)

Long, Frank Belknap (1901–1994). *A Man from Genoa and Other Poems.* Athol, MA: W. Paul Cook, 1926. (*LL* 581)

Machen, Arthur (1863–1947). *The Great Return.* London: Faith Press, 1915.

———. *The Green Round.* London: Ernest Benn, 1933. Sauk City, WI: Arkham House, 1968.

———. *The Hill of Dreams.* London: Grant Richards, 1907. New York: Alfred A. Knopf, 1923. (*LL* 617)

———. *The House of Souls.* <1906> New York: Alfred A. Knopf, 1923. (*LL* 618) [Contains "The White People" and "The Great God Pan."]

———. *The Shining Pyramid.* London: Martin Secker, 1925; New York: Knopf, 1925.

———. *The Terror.* New York: McBride; London: Duckworth, 1917.

———. *The Three Impostors.* <1895> New York: Alfred A. Knopf, 1930. (*LL* 623)

MacLeish, Archibald (1892–1982). *Conquistador.* Boston: Houghton Mifflin, 1932.

Marsh, Richard (1857–1915). *The Beetle.* London: Skeffington, 1897. (*LL* 642)

Matthews, Brander (1852–1929). "The Rival Ghosts." In *Tales of Fantasy and Fact.* New York: Harper & Brothers, 1896. Rpt. in Joseph Lewis French, ed., *Masterpieces of Mystery* (q.v.).

Maturin, Charles Robert (1782–1824). *Melmoth the Wanderer.* <1820> London: Richard Bentley & Son, 1892. 3 vols. (*LL* 646)

Maupassant, Guy de. *A Selection from the Writings of of Guy de Maupassant.* With a Critical Preface by Paul Bourget . . . and an Introduction by Robert Arnot. New York: D. A. McKinlay & Co., 1803. 6 vols. (*LL* 648) [Contains "The Diary of a Madman," "He," "The Spectre," "The White Wolf," and "Who Knows?"]

Meader, Charles A. (1847–1945). *The Casey Family of East Greenwich: An Account of "Some Men Who Lived on Main Street in a Small Town," from an Address Delivered in St. Luke's Church, East Greenwich, Rhode Island.* [East Greenwich, RI: Privately printed,] 1927.

Meinhold, Wilhelm (1797–1851). *Mary Schweidler: The Amber Witch: The Most Interesting Trial for Witchcraft Ever Known.* Tr. Lady Duff Gordon (1821–1869). London: John Murray, 1844.

Merritt, A. (1882–1943). *The Metal Monster. Argosy All-Story Weekly* (7 August–25 September 1920). New York: Hippocampus Press, 2002. Rev. as *The*

Metal Emperor. Science and Invention (October 1927–August 1928).

———. "The Moon Pool." *All-Story Weekly* (22 June 1918) (*LL* 17). Expanded as *The Moon Pool.* New York: G. P. Putnam's Sons, 1919. [Incorporates *The Conquest of the Moon Pool* (*All-Story Weekly*, 15 February–22 March 1919).]

Metcalfe, John (1891–1965). *The Smoking Leg and Other Stories.* London: Jarrolds, 1925. Garden City, NY: Doubleday, Page, 1926.

Melville, Herman (1819–1891). *Moby-Dick; or, The White Whale.* <1851> Boston: Dana Estes & Co., 1892. (*LL* 651)

Miller, William David (1887–?). *The Silversmiths of Little Rest.* Kingston, RI: [D. B. Updike], 1928.

Molyhuysen, Philipp Christiaan (1870–1944), and Petrus Johannes Blok (1855–1929). *Nieuw Nederlandsch Biografisch Woordenboek.* Dl. 1. Leiden: Sijthoff, 1911.

Morgan, Charles Lanbridge (1894–1958). *The Fountain.* New York: Alfred A. Knopf, 1932.

Munro, Wilfred Harold (1849–1934). *Picturesque Rhode Island.* Providence: J. A. & R. A. Reid, 1881. (*LL* 694)

Murray, Margaret A. (1863–1963). *The Witch-Cult in Western Europe.* Oxford: Clarendon Press, 1921.

Nevins, John Williamson (1803–1886). *A Summary of Biblical Antiquities: For the Use of Schools, Bible-Classes and Families.* Philadelphia: American Sunday-School Union, 1849.

Nicholas Roerich Museum. *Roerich Museum Catalogue.* 6th ed. New York: Roerich Museum, 1930. (*LL* 1087)

O'Brien, Edward J. (1890–1941). *The Dance of the Machines: The American Short Story and the Industrial Age.* New York: Macaulay Co., 1929. (*LL* 714)

———, ed. *The Best Short Stories of 1929 and the Yearbook of the American Short Story.* New York: Dodd, Mead, 1929.

O'Brien, Fitz-James (1826–1862). "The Diamond Lens." *Atlantic Monthly* 1 (January 1858): 354–67. In Joseph Lewis French, ed., *Masterpieces of Mystery* (q.v.).

———. "What Was It?" *Harper's* 18 (March 1859): 504–9. In Joseph Lewis French, ed., *Great Ghost Stories.* New York: Dodd, Mead, 1918.

O'Hart, John (1824–1902). *Irish Pedigrees; or, The Origin and Stem of the Irish Nation.* New York: Murphy & McCarthy, 1923.

Orton, Vrest (1897–1986). *Dreiserana: A Book about His Books.* New York: [Printed at the Stratford Press], 1929.

Parkman, Francis (1823–1893). *The Conspiracy of Pontiac and the Indian War after the Conquest of Canada.* <1851> 10th ed., rev., with additions. Boston: Little, Brown, 1886. 2 vols. (*LL* 739)

Partridge, John [pseud.]. *Merlinus Liberatus: An Almanack for the Year of Our Redemption, 1814.* London: Printed for the Company of Stationers by William Thorne, [1814]. (*LL* 1089)

Pendergast, P. J. (1851–1937?). *Selected Gems.* [Jamaica Plain, MA: Angel Guardian Press, 1917.]

Pierce, Frederick Clifton (1855–1904). *Field Genealogy.* Chicago: Hammond Press; W. B. Conkey, 1901.

Powers, Levi M. (1864–1920). *Sketch of the Independent Christian Church and the Sargent Murray Gilman House: Gloucester, Mass.* Boston: Murray Press, [1919].

Radcliffe, Ann (1764–1823). *The Mysteries of Udolpho.* <1794> London: George Routledge & Sons, [1882]–[192-]. (*LL* 787)

Reynolds, George W. M. (1814–1879). *Wagner the Wehr-Wolf.* London: J. Dicks, 1848, 1857, 1872.

Richardson, Leon Burr (1878–1951). *History of Dartmouth College.* Hanover, NH: Stephen Daye Press, 1932. 2 vols.

Richman, Irving Berdine (1861–1938). *Rhode Island: Its Making and Its Meaning: A Survey of the Annals of the Commonwealth from Its Settlement to the Death of Roger Williams, 1636–1683.* New York: G. P. Putnam's Sons, 1902.

Robbins, Archibald (1792–1865). *Robbins' Journal, Comprising an Account of the Loss of the Brig* Commerce *of Hartford (Con.) James Riley, Master, upon the Western Coast of Africa, August 28th, 1815, Also of the Slavery and Sufferings of the Author and the Rest of the Crew upon the Desert of Zahar in the Years 1815, 1816, 1817, with Accounts of the Manners and Customs of the Wandering Arabs.* <1817> Now Illustrated by Earle Winslow. Greenwich, CT: Condé Nast Press, 1931. (*LL* 1091)

Santayana, George (1863–1952). *The Last Puritan: A Memoir in the Form of a Novel.* London: Constable, 1935. New York: Charles Scribner's Sons, 1936.

Sargent, Lucius M. (1786–1867). *Dealings with the Dead.* Boston: Dutton & Wentworth [etc.], 1856. 2 vols.

Seabrook, William B. (1887–1945). *The Magic Island.* New York: Harcourt, Brace, 1929.

Shelley, Mary (1797–1851). *Frankenstein; or, The Modern Prometheus.* <1818> New-York: H. G. Daggers, 1845. (*LL* 864)

Shiel, M. P. (1865–1947). *The Pale Ape and Other Pulses.* London: T. Werner Laurie, 1911.

Singleton, Esther (1865–1930). *The Furniture of Our Forefathers.* With Critical Descriptions of Plates by Russell Sturgis. Garden City, NY: Doubleday, Page, 1922. 8 parts in 1. (*LL* 875)

Skinner, Charles M. (1852–1907). *Myths and Legends of Our Own Land.* Philadelphia: J. B. Lippincott, 1900. (*LL* 877)

Smith, Clark Ashton. *Ebony and Crystal: Poems in Verse and Prose.* [Auburn, CA: Auburn Journal, 1922.] (*LL* 881)

———. *Odes and Sonnets.* San Francisco: Book Club of California, 1918. (*LL* 882)

———. *The Star-Treader and Other Poems.* San Francisco: A. M. Robertson, 1912. (*LL* 816)

Smith, Sir William (1813–1893). *Smith's Bible Dictionary.* Philadelphia: A. J. Holman Co., [1893].

Spence, Lewis (1874–1955). *An Encyclopaedia of Occultism: A Compendium of Information on the Occult Sciences, Occult Personalities, Psychic Science, Magic, Demonology, Spiritism and Mysticism.* New York: Dodd, Mead, 1920. (*LL* 898)

Spengler, Oswald (1880–1936). *The Decline of the West.* Tr. Charles Francis Atkinson. London: George Allen & Unwin, 1922–26. 2 vols. [Translation of *Der Untergang des Abendlandes* (1918–22).]

Steele, Joel Dorman (1836–1886). *A Fourteen Weeks Course in Descriptive Astronomy.* New York: A. S. Barnes; Boston: Woolworth, Ainsworth & Co., 1873. (*LL* 910)

———. *Fourteen Weeks in Chemistry.* <1873> (*LL* 911)

———. *Fourteen Weeks in Human Physiology.* New York: A. S. Barnes, 1873. (*LL* 912)

———. *Fourteen Weeks in Physics.* <1878> (*LL* 913)

———. *Fourteen Weeks in Zoology.* <1872> New York: A. S. Barnes, 1877. (*LL* 914)

———. *The Story of the Rocks: Fourteen Weeks in Popular Geology.* Rev. ed. New York: A. S. Barnes, 1877. (*LL* 915)

———, and Alphonso Wood (1810–1881). *Fourteen Weeks in Botany.* New York: A. S. Barnes, 1879. (*LL* 1085)

———, and Esther Baker Steele (1835–1911). *Barnes' Popular History of the United States of America.* New York, A. S. Barnes, 1904.

———. *A Brief History of France.* New York: American Book Co., [1875] or [1903]. (*LL* 916)

———. *Brief History of Greece: With Readings from Prominent Greek Historians.* New York: American Book Co., 1883.

———. *A Brief History of Mediæval and Modern Peoples: With Some Account for their Institutions, Arts, Manners, and Customs.* New York: American Book Co., 1913.

———. *Brief History of Rome: With Select Readings from Standard Authors.* New York: American Book Co., 1885. (*LL* 917)

Stephensen, Percy Reginald (1901–1965). *The Legend of Aleister Crowley: Being a Study of the Documentary Evidence Relating to a Campaign of Personal Vilification Unparalleled in Literary History.* London: Mandrake Press, 1930.

Stevenson, Robert Louis (1850–1894). *Dr. Jekyll and Mr. Hyde and The Merry Men and Other Tales.* <1886; 1887> (*LL* 922) [Contains "Markheim."]

Stockton, Frank R. (1834–1902). "The Transferred Ghost." In *The Lady or the Tiger? and Other Stories.* New York: Charles Scribner's Sons, 1884. [First published in *Century Magazine* (May 1882).]

Stoker, Bram (1847–1912). *Dracula.* <1897> Garden City, NY: Doubleday, Page, 1925. (*LL* 926)

———. *The Jewel of Seven Stars.* London: Heinemann, 1903.

———. The Lair of the White Worm. London: Rider, 1911.

Todd, Charles Burr (1849–1928). A Brief History of the City of New York. New York: American Book Co., 1899.

van Loon, Hendrik Willem (1882–1944). Life and Times of Pieter Stuyvesant. New York: Henry Holt, 1928.

———. The Story of Mankind. New York: Boni & Liveright, 1921.

Vlekke, Bernard H. M. (1899–1970), and Henry Beets (1869–1947). "Wilfred Blanch Talman." In Hollanders Who Helped Build America. New York: American Biographical Society, 1942. 223.

Waite, Arthur Edward (1857–1942). The Book of Black Magic and of Pacts: Including the Rites and Mysteries of Goëtic Theury, Sorcery, and Infernal Necromancy. London: George Redway, 1898.

Walker, John (1732–1807). A Rhetorical Grammar; or, Course of Lessons in Elocution. <1785> 1st American ed. Boston: J. T. Buckingham, 1814. (LL 1006)

Walpole, Horace (1717–1797). Jeffery's Edition of the Castle of Otranto, a Gothic Story. <1764> London: Printed by W. Backader . . . for the Publisher [Edward Jeffery], 1800. (LL 1007)

Wayland, Frances M. G. (1840–1926). Arnold Green: A Sketch. [Boston:] Privately printed [at the Merrymount Press], 1927.

Weigall, Arthur (1880–1934). Wanderings in Anglo-Saxon Britain. New York: George H. Doran, 1927.

———. Wanderings in Roman Britain. London: Thornton Butterworth, 1926. (LL 1025)

Wells, H. G. (1866–1946). Thirty Strange Stories. New York: Harper & Brothers, 1897.

———; Huxley, Julian (1887–1975); and Wells, G. P. (1901–1985). The Science of Life: A Summary of Contemporary Knowledge about Life and Its Possibilities. London: Amalgamated Press, 1930. 2 vols. New York: Doubleday, 1931. 4 vols.

White, Gilbert (1720–1793). The Natural History of Selborne. <1789> New York: Harper & Brothers, 1842. (LL 1038)

Wilde, Oscar (1854–1900). The Picture of Dorian Gray. <1890> New York: Boni & Liveright (Modern Library), 1918. (LL 1051)

Willis, Eola (1856–1952). The Charleston Stage in the XVIII Century, with Social Settings of the Time. Columbia, SC: State Co., 1924.

Young, Francis Brett (1884–1964). Cold Harbour. London: Collins, 1924. New York: Hippocampus Press, 2008.

Index

www.ingramcontent.com/pod-product-compliance
Lightning Source LLC
Chambersburg PA
CBHW070347030726
47504CB00001B/93